PEOPLE OF THE SPIRIT

GARY B. MCGEE

GPH®

Gospel Publishing House

DEDICATION

I n honor of Robert and Lois Graber, faithful pastors of Bethel Temple Assembly of God, Canton, Ohio (1959–1999), whose stories of Pentecostal power and blessing became my own.

ACKNOWLEDGMENTS

In the past, the General Council has been well served by historians such as Carl Brumback (*Suddenly from Heaven: A History of the Assemblies of God*), Klaude Kendrick (*The Promise Fulfilled: A History of the Modern Pentecostal Movement*), William W. Menzies (*Anointed to Serve: The Story of the Assemblies of God*), Victor De Leon (*The Silent Pentecostals*), and Edith L. Blumhofer (*The Assemblies of God: A Chapter in the Story of American Pentecostalism*). I am grateful for their contributions and the myriad of other writers who have also told some of the story. For the inspiration to write a biographical history, I am indebted to the distinguished historian Ruth A. Tucker of Calvin Theological Seminary, author of the highly acclaimed biographical history of Christian missions, *From Jerusalem to Irian Jaya*.

Wayne E. Warner, another respected historian, who directs the Flower Pentecostal Heritage Center, reviewed the manuscript and gave insightful recommendations. Glenn Gohr of the Center assisted in the selection of pictures, Joyce Lee came to my rescue on many occasions with needed information, and Brett Pavia coordinated digital projects. I also appreciate the permission of Warner and Gohr to allow me to reprint and add to the General Council time line that appeared in the July 20, 1997, issue of the Pentecostal Evangel. In the publications department of Assemblies of God World Missions, Gloria Robinett has been a constant source of help in rounding up information on missionaries. This book also introduces the work of four graduates of the Assemblies of God Theological Seminary, all budding historians. I am proud of the research capabilities and creative talents of Robert C. Phraner, Darrin J. Rodgers, Kenneth A. Worthley, and Annette Newberry, who each wrote sidebar articles.

I express my thanks to Byron D. Klaus, president of the Assemblies of God Theological Seminary, former president Del Tarr, and senior professor Edgar Lee, for their encouragement in this project. Veteran missionaries Warren and Annette Newberry rendered valuable assistance at a crucial time in the book's development. Longtime friend and retired missionary Leota Morar cheered me on in the writing. George O. Wood, general secretary, and James K. Bridges, general treasurer of the Assemblies of God, read the manuscript and offered many helpful suggestions. To the book editors of Gospel Publishing House, I tip my hat once more in gratitude and respect, especially to senior book editor Glen Ellard, who improved on the manuscript and spared me many embarrassments. Also, thanks to Rebekah Clute, Leta Sapp, Martha Stokes, and Alyssa Medlin.

Finally, I thank the Lord for my wife, Alice, who has shared the vision of this book and helped me find time to research and write it. Both of us know the joys of "growing up Pentecostal" and serving the Lord in ministry.

CONTENTS

UNIT 5: 1969-1992

UNIT 6: 1993-2003

FOREWORD

GEORGE O. WOOD

The Assemblies of God celebrated its one hundredth birthday in 2014. From small beginnings in Hot Springs, Arkansas, the Fellowship had grown to encompass 68 million souls worldwide, including 3.1 million in the United States. Were the three hundred ministers who convened the First General Council of the Assemblies of God in 1914 able to see the Movement God had started through them, I'm sure their hearts would be amazed and overflowing with praise to God.

We don't typically think of one hundred-year-olds as living at the peak of their intellectual and physical powers. Past a certain point, increasing age diminishes people's capacities, not enhances them. Older people increasingly rely on developments in medical science to stay healthy.

Might something similar be true of our Fellowship? Might we have passed our peak effectiveness in accomplishing God's mission? Might our best days on earth lie behind us rather than before us?

I don't think so. Or rather, I hope not. But the answers to those questions depend on two factors.

The first factor is divine. Pentecostalism's founders leaned heavily on Hebrews 13:8 in the articulation of their biblical hermeneutic: "Jesus Christ is the same yesterday and today and forever." Since Jesus Christ had not changed over the centuries, they believed that we should expect He operates today in the same way that He operated in the apostolic church.

Consequently, one hears Pentecostalism's founders speaking insistently of "apostolic faith" and "apostolic methods." We should believe what the apostles believed and do what the apostles did. For Pentecostalism's founders, the Gospels and the

Book of Acts were not a biography of Jesus Christ or a history of the first-century church as much as an instruction book for the Church in every century.

As they read the pages of the New Testament, they discerned the "Fourfold Gospel" or "Full Gospel." This is the Assemblies of God's cardinal doctrine to the present day. Jesus Christ is Savior, Healer, Baptizer in the Holy Spirit, and Soon-Coming King. On occasion, one will hear critics of Pentecostalism argue that we are too focused on the person and work of the Holy Spirit, not enough on the person and work of the Son of God. (Isn't the title of this book *People of the Spirit*, after all?) These critics miss the mark, however. Pentecostals are first and foremost—and then thoroughly and consistently—Jesus people. If we emphasize the Holy Spirit, it is because Jesus has poured Him out on all flesh in the last days (Acts 2:33). We are people of the Spirit, then, because we are Jesus people first.

If Jesus Christ is the same, and if He is Savior, Healer, Baptizer in the Holy Spirit, and Soon-Coming King, then we have a powerful reason to believe that our Fellowship—indeed, the Church as a whole—has not passed its prime. The divine factor assures us that God's purposes for humanity, accomplished in Christ and empowered by the Spirit, move forward without change.

And that brings us to the second factor, the human one. If God desires our Fellowship to increase in missional effectiveness—as surely He does!—then why have so many Christian fellowships declined over the centuries? If God moves forward without change, why do churches change? Why do denominations rise and fall?

The answer, it seems to me, must be found in 1 Corinthians 3:6–7: "I planted the seed [of the gospel], Apollos watered it, but God has been making it grow. So neither the one who plants nor the one who waters is anything, but only God, who makes things grow." Notice that Paul highlights the divine factor in these verses. With the apostle, we must say that if the Assemblies of God has grown in the first one hundred years of its existence, it is because of God. "The Lord has done this, and it is marvelous in our eyes" (Matthew 21:42).

And yet, God doing something does not mean we have nothing to do. Paul planted. Apollos watered. The effectiveness of that labor is in God's hand, but whether we do the labor we've been assigned by God is in ours. Missional effectiveness results from our obedient responsiveness to the call of God on our lives, of doing what He asks us to do when He asks us to do it, then giving Him the glory for the results.

The book you hold in your hands is the story of the Assemblies of God told through the lives of people who did what God asked them to do. They were men and women of different races, ethnicities, and socio-ethnic classes. They were plumbers and professors, clergy and laity, pastors and evangelists, missionaries and aid workers. They labored for a gospel harvest, often with little pay, little praise, and little prominence. Of course, they weren't looking for those things in the first place. What they longed for was the benediction of the Master, "Well done, good and faithful servant!" (Matthew 25:23).

As I consider the character of these Assemblies of God saints, I see three character traits that are especially important. (There are others, but these stand out to me.) If these traits are present, God can use our labors to grow His church. They are humility, hunger, and heart.

The first is humility. Scripture teaches, "God opposes the proud but shows favor to the humble" (James 4:6, cf. Proverbs 3:34). In his autobiography, *Under His Wings*, Pentecostal missionary Harold A. Baker wrote: "my hope for being helpful is based on the fact that in the Bible we are told that God uses the 'nobodies' to confound the 'somebodies' and uses the 'foolish' to confound the 'wise.'" Baker was an educated, accomplished man. But he recognized that without humility, our education, accomplishments, and egos simply get in God's way.

The second character trait is hunger. In His Sermon on the Mount, Jesus Christ taught us, "Blessed are those who hunger and thirst for righteousness, for they will be filled" (Matthew 5:6). The stories you read in this book are stories about people who hungered for more. They looked at the state of American Christianity at the beginning of the twentieth century and knew that God intended the Church to be more than the nominal, institutional, cultural form of religion that was so prevalent in their day. They were "radical evangelicals" who were earnest in their desire to do "the greatest work of evangelism the world has ever seen" in their own generation, and who therefore knew they needed a fresh "baptism in the Holy Spirit" to see that happen.

The third character trait is heart. The shortest verse in the Bible is John 11:35, "Jesus wept." The statement comes near the close of Jesus' ministry, at the tomb of Lazarus. After three years of ministry, the "Jesus wept" statement says He never became calloused toward people. Ministry was not something He did mechanically. He didn't have a miracle switch that He just turned on or off. He felt for people. When He saw the spiritually lost, the socially last, and the economically least, He didn't turn away from them. He turned toward them. Like Jesus, Lillian Trasher didn't turn away from the baby a dying Egyptian mother placed in her arms. Mark Buntain didn't turn away from a crippled child crawling through the muddy streets of Calcutta. The Donaldson brothers didn't turn away from the poor in America's neighborhoods who needed their help. As Pentecostals, they turned toward them.

As the Assemblies of God begins—should the Lord tarry—its next one hundred years of ministry, we must keep the divine and human factors in mind. God will make our Fellowship grow when we do the work He has assigned us with the character traits that magnify His gracious love to sinners and power to transform their lives.

Let us humble ourselves before Him! Let us hunger for more of Him! Let us demonstrate His heart through our lives of service to the ones He loves!

━━━━━━━━━━━━━━━━━━

A final word about this Centennial edition of *People of the Spirit*:

Gary B. McGee was a Pentecostal scholar and personal friend. This book reflects not only his scholarly work in the history of our Movement but also his deeply felt commitment to Pentecostal faith, experience, and mission. It has been widely used in college and university classrooms as well as district schools of ministry to familiarize people with Assemblies of God history and train them for ministry in the local church.

Because the story the book tells ends in 2004, and because Gary entered Jesus' presence in 2008, we have asked Charles E. Self, professor of church history at the Assemblies of God Theological Seminary in Springfield, Missouri, to write a substantive afterword outlining developments in Assemblies of God history to 2014. Other changes include reformatting the book with a new typeset and page size, updating biographical information on people who have died since this book was first published, and—with the help of the staff of the Flower Pentecostal Heritage Center—adding more recent studies to the recommended reading lists at the end of each chapter.

George O. Wood is general superintendent of the Assemblies of God (USA) and chairman of the World Assemblies of God Fellowship.

INTRODUCTION: WORD TO THE READER

GARY B. MCGEE

The heritage and vision of any movement cannot be adequately explained without looking at the lives of the people who made it happen. Their sacrifices and faithfulness, joys and sorrows, hopes and disappointments, are all parts of the larger story of Christians called to advance God's kingdom.

Indeed, the records of the Assemblies of God (U.S.A.) turn from one page of testimony to another. One finds dramatic stories of conversion, healings, baptisms in the Spirit, deliverances from chemical addictions, unusual leadings of the Spirit, and harrowing accounts of danger on the mission field. Much of the story, however, has not been written down.

Besides stories of those kinds, the oral tradition includes memories of hot days at church camp and praying at the altar and pranks in Bible school among young people preparing for the ministry. They tell of romance and marriage, amusement at church picnics, college choir tours, and renewed fellowship at Council meetings.

The founders of the Assemblies of God came from the working class. They were hardworking Americans who caught the vision of evangelizing the world in the last days before the second coming of Christ. As "people of the Spirit," they sought to proclaim the good news of Jesus Christ in word and deed, believing Jesus when He said, "When he, the Spirit of truth, comes, he will guide you into all truth. . . . He will bring glory to me" (John 16:13–14). With baptism in the Spirit, they discovered a joyful experience, a powerful experience that transformed them into dynamic Christian witnesses.

When the skeptics dismissed the Pentecostal message, Pentecostals pointed to the Scriptures and gave their testimony of what God had done in their lives. When many Protestants said that miracles had ended with the first century, Pentecostals fasted and prayed for the sick and the demon possessed, then watched as God proved His willingness to step into human lives. Such belief in God's intervention revolutionized evangelism both at home and on the mission field.

For Pentecostals to go into ministry, it required only a call from God, a willingness to pray and launch out on faith in His provision, and a determination to complete what God asked before moving on. This was no less true for professional ministers than devoted laypeople. To outsiders, such "steps of faith" often seemed reckless and foolish, and in some instances they did fail. Still, the successes have been impressive: Ivan Voronaeff risked returning to Russia after the Bolshevik Revolution to preach the gospel. Demetrio Bazán, Sr., worked tirelessly as the first Hispanic superintendent of the Latin American district to help pastors and their families. David Wilkerson left his comfortable rural parish for New York's inner city to help several boys on trial and wound up starting Teen Challenge. Mildred Whitney, a mother of nine, began the Assemblies of God ministry to the blind in her home. C. M. Ward took the gospel outside church walls to the saloons of Victoria, British Columbia.

Some Pentecostal pioneers courageously broke the racial and gender barriers of their times to serve the Lord. These individuals are recognized throughout this volume for the path they created for generations of God's people to follow. William J. Seymour, an African American, led the Azusa Street Revival and his memory has inspired millions of Christians around the world. Lillian Trasher, noted for her resoluteness, established an orphanage in Egypt that still exists today.

In the past, the denomination has been served by institutional and social histories. Institutions (e.g., local churches, districts, national departments, presbyteries, and schools) have made valuable contributions to the growth and stability of the Assemblies of God. In many instances, however, a church agency came after a person had pioneered the ministry, as is the case with Etta Calhoun and the Women's Ministries Department. Church structures grew because changing times required more teamwork and accountability.

In standard denominational histories, one expects to find long lists of names of persons who served in various capacities, dates of events and convocations, and minihistories of church programs. This preserves the line of appointments, the terms of office, and the sequence of events that shaped the organization. A popular history, in this case People of the Spirit, takes a different approach. Besides an emphasis being placed on people rather than events, the historian's jargon, as well as penchant, is set aside (as much as possible). For example, the use of endnotes has been reserved for only the historical overview chapters at the beginning of each unit as well as the last two chapters. Rather, a recommended reading list is provided at the end of each chapter. Professionals divest themselves of their second natures in the hope of serving the laity as well as their peers and protégés, in my case, the person in the pew as well as in the classroom.

Yet the role of institutions should not be overstated. Grassroots growth came from believers—both clergy and laity—witnessing to their neighbors, teaching Sunday School classes, distributing tracts, planting churches, feeding the hungry, praying for the sick, and carrying the gospel overseas. These represent some of the ways the rank and file of the Assemblies of God have glorified Christ as people of the Spirit.

If you are older, you may find People of the Spirit to be a walk down memory lane. That's good. At the same time, I hope to inspire the younger generation with a past that is theirs too, even if it's not in their memory. That's why I have chosen to relate the history of the Assemblies of God in story; it is, after all, another sense of the word history.

The younger generation needs to hear the stories of ministry and Pentecostal blessing if Pentecostalism itself is to survive in a denominational form. They should also recognize that the Assemblies of God has emphasized the individual's being led of the Spirit within the boundaries of biblical teaching.

Since there are thousands of stories, I have tried to choose those that are representative of the people who have made up the Assemblies of God. Some are well known, but I hope others are entirely new to you. Certain persons have also been included who, though influencing the General Council, chose to remain outside of it for various reasons. All, however, are woven into the tapestry labeled the Assemblies of God.

People of the Spirit contains six units. The first chapter in each of the first five units provides a historical overview of the events in the period of study. The chapters that follow contain stories from the lives of preachers, missionaries, writers, laypersons, and others in that time frame. The two chapters in the sixth unit contain both historical overview and biography.

The first unit traces the development of the Pentecostal movement to the founding of the General Council in 1914. The second takes the reader from that event to the General Council meeting in 1927, at which the delegates adopted a constitution. The third stretches across the Great Depression and World War II to 1947. The fourth begins in 1948 with the emergence of the New Order of the Latter Rain and the healing movement and ends in 1968 with the Council on Evangelism. The fifth traces events between 1969 and 1992. The sixth begins with 1993 and examines important developments to 2003.

Join me now as I tell the stories of many ordinary people who did extraordinary things for God. Through the power of the Holy Spirit, mixed with grit and determination, they and many more people like them made the General Council of the Assemblies of God what it is today.

UNIT ONE
1792-1913

TIME LINE 1792-1913

1792—William Carey calls for the evangelization of the world in his book, *An Enquiry into the Obligations of Christians to Use Means for the Conversion of the Heathen*.

1830—A charismatic movement emerges in Scotland and England inspired by the ministry and teachings of Edward Irving.

1830s—John Nelson Darby and the Brethren movement in England teach a premillennial eschatology with a "secret rapture" that will remove the saints before the seven-year tribulation period.

1835—Phoebe Worrall Palmer, perhaps the most influential female theologian in American history, becomes active in the "Tuesday Meeting for the Promotion of Holiness" in New York City. Through her many publications and preaching tours, she contributed to the rise of the Wesleyan-Holiness Movement.

1857—Great prayer revival occurs in the Northern states; spreads to Northern Ireland, India, Jamaica and beyond.

1867—National Campmeeting Association for the Promotion of Christian Holiness is founded at Vineland, New Jersey, to promote the holiness doctrine of "entire sanctification."

1870—Boston physician Charles C. Cullis begins to pray for the sick according to the promise of James 5:13–15.

1875—A summer Bible conference at the English village of Keswick inaugurates annual conferences to nurture the "higher Christian life."

1882—A. B. Simpson, founder of the Christian and Missionary Alliance, establishes the first Bible institute in America in New York City. Later moved up the Hudson River to Nyack, it became known as the Missionary Training Institute (now Nyack College).

1893—John Alexander Dowie begins to conduct meetings near the Chicago World's Fair.

1897—Charles H. Mason and Charles P. Jones found the Church of God in Christ with headquarters in Memphis, Tennessee.

1901—First Pentecostal revival of the twentieth century occurs at Charles F. Parham's Bethel Bible School in Topeka.

1903–1904—Pentecostal revival occurs in Moorhead, Minnesota, and Fargo, North Dakota; first Pentecostal missionary of the century and a product of the revival, Mary Johnson, travels to KwaZulu Natal, South Africa.

1904—Welsh revival begins, encourages similar revival movements around the world.

1906—Azusa Street revival begins in Los Angeles, one of the most significant revivals of the century in terms of global impact. Pentecostal revival begins in India through the ministry of Minnie F. Abrams.

1907—Pentecostal revival in Dunn, North Carolina, known as the "Azusa of the South," brings several existing holiness organizations into the Pentecostal movement. Revival under the leadership of Thomas B. Barratt in Oslo, Norway, leads to the development of Pentecostalism in Scandinavia, England, and the European continent.

1909—Pentecostal Missionary Union, the first successful Pentecostal mission agency, is founded in England by Cecil H. Polhill.

1910—World Missionary Conference at Edinburgh, Scotland, is the high watermark of the 19th-century Protestant missions movement. Pentecostal movement begins in Brazil through the ministry of Scandinavian-American missionaries Daniel Berg and Adolf Gunnar Vingren and the Italian-American Luigi Francescon. Pentecostals divide over sanctification.

1913—At a camp meeting at Arroyo Seco in the Los Angeles area some believers are rebaptized in the name of Jesus. The "New Issue" begins another division among Pentecostals. *Word and Witness* calls for a "General Convention of Pentecostal Saints and Churches of God in Christ" to meet at Hot Springs, Arkansas.

CHAPTER 1

POWER FROM ON HIGH

In the history of Christianity, there have always been believers who have sought the gifts and power of the Holy Spirit. The Book of Acts records that "signs and wonders" followed the preaching of the gospel (Acts 5:12). Christian congregations also experienced the gifts of the Holy Spirit in their services (1 Corinthians 12 and 14). During the first eight centuries, the reception of the Spirit and His gifts formed an integral, but waning, part of becoming a full-fledged Christian. One church father compared the outpouring of the Holy Spirit to a river (John 4:14), exulting that "we are inundated with the gifts of the Spirit. That fountain of life, which is the river of God, spills over in us."[1]

By the fourth century, however, believers seemed to be expressing less interest in the gifts of the Spirit. The knotty problems facing the Church centered on disagreements about the nature of Christ and the Trinity. And some who explored the ministry of the Spirit clashed with church authorities because their views and experiences did not easily fit into the mold of established doctrine and practice. Such followers of the Spirit soon found themselves condemned and persecuted by the Church.

Occasionally, someone, usually from the ranks of the monks and nuns, testified to ecstatic experiences in the Spirit. For example, Symeon the New Theologian (949–1022), an Orthodox monk who lived in Constantinople (present-day Istanbul), taught that baptism in the Holy Spirit brought greater spiritual awareness of Jesus Christ. He also received what he called the "gift of tears" and may even have prayed in tongues.[2]

The creeds of the Lutheran and Reformed churches in the sixteenth century did not keep people from seeking the restoration of the Spirit's gifts and power.[3] The "prophets" from the German city of Zwickau were the most controversial. The Reformers—Martin Luther, Ulrich Zwingli, and John Calvin—denounced such radicals, for they claimed to receive visions, revelations, and the gift of prophecy. The Reformers believed the Holy Spirit limited His activities primarily to preparing one to receive Christ, as well as the reception of God's grace through water baptism, the Lord's Supper, and the preaching of God's Word. They also believed that miracles had vanished with the Apostolic Church of the first century.[4]

Seventeenth- and eighteenth-century revivalism in Europe and North America influenced later spiritual awakenings. Students of revivals must pay close attention to the doctrine of Christian perfection taught by John Wesley, the father of Methodism. Publishing A Plain Account of Christian Perfection, he urged his Methodist followers to seek a new spiritual dimension in their lives. He described an experience, a sanctifying work of grace after conversion, that promised believers freedom from the defect in their moral natures that prompted sinful behavior. Wesley's associate John Fletcher concluded that Christians were living in an era of the Holy Spirit—a time when they would be purified from their sinful natures and should eagerly expect the return of Christ.[5]

POWER FOR HOLINESS

Inspired by the hope of a truly Christian America, the "holiness crusade" of the Methodists, beginning in the l830s, gained a wide following. A distinctive movement also emerged, teaching a Wesleyan doctrine of perfection ("entire sanctification," the "second blessing," and also known as the "double cure")—an instantaneous purification after conversion. The connection of the Spirit's empowerment with individual

Christian Perfection

John Wesley, the father of Methodism, encouraged believers to seek for Christian perfection, a sanctifying experience of grace subsequent to conversion.

We . . . believe, that there is no such perfection in this life, as implies an entire deliverance, either from ignorance, or mistake, in things not essential to salvation, or from manifold temptations, or from numberless infirmities, wherewith the corruptible body more or less presses down the soul. We cannot find any ground in Scripture to suppose, that any inhabitant of a house of clay is wholly exempt either from bodily infirmities, or from ignorance of many things; or to imagine any is incapable of mistake, or falling into divers temptations.

But whom then do you mean by "one that is perfect?" We mean one in whom is "the mind which was in Christ," and who so "walketh as Christ also walked;" a man "that hath clean hands and a pure heart," or that is "cleansed from all filthiness of flesh and spirit;" one in whom is "no occasion of stumbling," and who, accordingly, "does not commit sin." To declare this a little more particularly: We understand by that scriptural expression, "a perfect man," one in whom God hath fulfilled his faithful word, "From all your filthiness and from all your idols I will cleanse you: I will also save you from all your uncleannesses." We understand hereby . . . one who "walketh in the light as He is in the light, in whom is no darkness at all; the blood of Jesus Christ his Son having cleansed him from all sin."

—John Wesley, "A Plain Account of Christian Perfection,"
The Works of John Wesley (1872): 383–384.

A Mighty Baptism

As I went in and shut the door after me, it seemed as if I met the Lord Jesus Christ face to face. It seemed to me that I saw him as I would see any other man. He said nothing, but looked at me in such a manner as to break me right down at his feet. I returned to the front office . . . as I turned and was about to take a seat by the fire, I received a mighty baptism of the Holy Ghost. Without any expectation of it, without ever having the thought in my mind that there was any such thing for me, without any recollection that I had ever heard the thing mentioned by any person in the world, the Holy Spirit descended upon me in a manner that seemed to go through me body and soul. I could feel the impression, like a wave of electricity, going through and through me. Indeed it seemed to come in waves of liquid love: for I could not express it in any other way. It seemed like the very breath of God.

Evangelist Charles G. Finney (1792–1875) became famous for his theology, methods, and successes in revivalism, as well as his radical social action.

—Charles G. Finney, Memoirs of Reverend Charles G. Finney (1876), 19–20.

transformation and reform in society (e.g., slavery, prohibition) harmonized with popular optimism about human progress.

Over time, the use of Pentecostal imagery (e.g., "baptism in the Holy Spirit," "the tongue of fire") became a characteristic of holiness literature and hymnody. Those who sought to receive Spirit baptism were instructed to "tarry" (Luke 24:49, KJV) for the promised gift to break the power of the sinful nature and usher the believer into the Spirit-filled life. This plateau of triumphant living represented the Christian walk at its best: marked by victorious living over sin, the fruit of the Spirit (Galatians 5:22–25), and outward forms of behavior and dress. For many, the camp meeting provided an ideal place for seeking sanctification: in the company of fellow seekers amid the surroundings of natural beauty far from the evils of the city.

While historic Reformed (Calvinistic) theologians continued to equate Spirit baptism with conversion, revivalists within that tradition maintained that Spirit baptism, as a second work, provided power for Christian witness. Among others, the famous evangelist Charles G. Finney taught that baptism in the Holy Spirit not only enhanced holiness but invigorated Christians for ministry. In England, annual conventions beginning in 1875 at the resort town of Keswick left another Reformed imprint on American holiness thinking. The speakers there rejected the "sinless perfection" of the Wesleyans, talking instead about "full consecration" and the "fullness of the Spirit" that empowered consistent Christian living. This "higher life" in Christ brought with it victory over temptation and sin.

Revivalists such as Dwight L. Moody, Reuben A. Torrey, A. B. Simpson, and A. J. Gordon accentuated the need for divine empowerment. Torrey wrote, "The Baptism with the Spirit is not intended to make us happy . . . not even primarily for the purpose of cleansing from sin, but for the purpose of empowering for service."[6] For an increasing number of people, however, the higher life conveyed physical as well as spiritual blessings.

THE HEALING MOVEMENT

Medical science advanced slowly in the nineteenth century and offered limited help for serious illnesses. Growing interest in the "prayer offered in faith" (James 5:15) led many believers to trust God for physical healing. In 1835 the British philanthropist and Christian Brethren churchman George Müller founded an orphanage in Bristol, England. According to his "faith work" principle, God had committed himself to supply the needs of believers; public announcements of financial problems could only imply unbelief. Stories of miraculous provisions became associated worldwide with

Müller, who was considered a champion of the idealized "faith life."

Even so, the connection between faith and physical healing came with the ministries of others—people like Johann Christoph Blumhardt in Germany and Dorothea Trüdel and Otto Stockmayer in Switzerland. Each one set up a hospice for healing, popularly known in America as a "faith home," where the sick could stay. There they were instructed on biblical promises of healing, encouraged in their faith, and prayed for that they might be healed.[7]

George Müller

In Boston, Charles C. Cullis, an Episcopalian layman and homeopathic physician, concluded in the early 1870s that through faith one could enter the higher Christian life and claim physical healing. Influenced by Cullis, A. B. Simpson, a former Presbyterian pastor and founder of the Christian and Missionary Alliance, testified to his own healing in 1881. Significantly, he dismissed the notion of praying "if it be His will." Since the "Lord Jesus has purchased [healing] for us in His redemption, it must be God's will for us to have it, for Christ's whole redeeming work was simply the executing of the Father's will."[8] Once believers had been sanctified and entered the "higher life," they could, through the exercise of faith, promptly receive healing from every disease (Exodus 15:26).

Although many in the holiness movement did not accept the more radical tenets of the healing movement, it became a haven for those who did. The doctrine of instantaneous purification from sin fit well with the concept of immediate healing by faith. Christ was both the "sin-bearer" and "sickness-bearer." His atoning work at Calvary made possible spiritual reconciliation between God and humankind; through faith it could then reverse the physical impairments caused by the Fall into sin (Genesis 3).[9]

Leading advocates saw the Atonement (Isaiah 53:4–5) as an important biblical basis for divine healing, but opinion varied about the extent to which this could be taken. In Boston, A. J. Gordon suggested that God remains sovereign with regard to suffering and healing. In this way, he distanced himself from the idea that God guaranteed immediate deliverance for everyone who offered the prayer of faith.[10] Others who prayed for the sick, but without Gordon's hesitation, included John Alexander Dowie (1847–1907), founder of Zion City (later Zion), Illinois. Holding tent campaigns in the Midwest and West, Maria B. Woodworth-Etter became famous for miracles of healing in her services. By the end of the century, divine healing, jeered by critics as the "faith-cure," had drawn adherents far and wide.

POWER FOR EVANGELISM

In general, the nineteenth century witnessed remarkable progress in science and technology. Unbridled hope in human achievement, seemingly unlimited potential for discovery and inventions, and aspirations to eliminate human misery marked the confidence of the age.[11]

In spite of this rosy outlook, the moral climate after the Civil War (1861–1865) eroded the positive outlook of many Christians. Under the veneer of popular piety, corruption in government and greed in industry became common. Alcoholism increased, and African Americans, as well as Asian, European, and Latin American immigrants, often existed under conditions bordering on slavery.

Pessimism about the future before the return of Christ began to flourish among evangelicals. This view forecast a bleak future: Instead of a coming period of blessings and tranquillity, a garish nightmare of "wars and rumors of wars" along with famines and earthquakes (Matthew 24:6) would precede the return of Christ for His church (the Rapture). Following seven years of tribulation, a thousand years of peace on earth would come, to be followed by Christ's judgment of the nations. Looking at the contemporary scene, Dwight L. Moody said, "I look upon this world as a wrecked vessel, . . . God has given me a lifeboat and said to me, 'Moody, save all you can.' "[12]

The prophetic clock, however, already beginning to strike midnight, left Christians little time to evangelize. Matthew 24:14 tolled: "This gospel of the kingdom will be preached in the whole world as a testimony to all nations, and then the end will come." When missionaries had trekked to the "ends of the earth" and presented the gospel to the last tribe, Christ would return (Acts 1:8).

Critics of holiness evangelist Maria B. Woodworth-Etter called her "the trance evangelist" because many fell "under the power" during her services. This sketch appeared in the St. Louis Post-Dispatch in summer 1890 to portray people who had fallen on the platform; the woman standing is probably Woodworth-Etter.

Connecting the themes of salvation, holiness, healing, and the soon coming of Christ, many holiness believers referred to these teachings as the "fourfold gospel": Jesus as Savior, Sanctifier (that is, "Baptizer" in the

Holy Spirit), Healer, and coming King. Every Christian who sought for this "second blessing" could then receive "full salvation" in body and soul: cleansed from sin and healed from sickness, empowered for service, and ready for the Lord's return in the "last days" (Acts 2:17–21).

MISSIONS AND MIRACLES

As a rule, nineteenth-century missionaries doubted that miracles or the gifts of the Spirit (e.g., healing, speaking in tongues) were available to them in their work. Instead, they shared the blessings of Western "Christian" civilization to further the gospel. They expected that after a lengthy period of preaching the gospel and "Christianizing" society, Christ would return. As a result, mission schools "civilized" and educated "heathen" students so they would see the superiority of Christianity and embrace the faith. Nevertheless, the number of converts was disappointing— only 3.6 million Protestant communicants and adherents in the mission lands by the turn of the twentieth century.[13]

Some Christians became disheartened when they compared the mission methods of their day to the simplicity of New Testament evangelism. Could a return to the apostolic practices bring greater success? As early as 1824, the question sparked controversy in England at the conference of the London Missionary Society. Presbyterian pastor Edward Irving preached that missionaries should follow Jesus' commands to His disciples in Matthew 10:9,10: "'Do not take along any gold or silver or copper in your belts; take no bag for the journey, or extra tunic, or sandals or a staff; for the worker is worth his keep.'"

In view of the slow pace of conversions on the mission fields, Irving radically proposed that missionaries should depend on faith in God for resources rather than on just the benevolence of mission agencies. The "nobleness of the missionary character" requires dependence on "the Spirit of God, for sustenance, for patronage, for reward, and for a rule of procedure." Although God would bless missionaries dependent on human means, they would fare better if "brought over from resting upon the visible to rest upon the invisible helps, then . . . the full measure of the Lord's blessing [would be] poured out upon His handiwork."[14]

Many saw large-scale revivals as the key to encouraging evangelism and empowering believers for witness. After news of the American prayer revival of 1857 reached Northern Ireland, startled Presbyterians noted unusual happenings. In revival services, hundreds of people fell to the ground, stricken or prostrated by God's power under intense conviction of sin. When word reached the southernmost part of India, believers there spoke in tongues, prophesied, and recounted visions. They too fell prostrate, prayed for the sick, helped the poor, and evangelized non-Christians. One missionary suggested that this marked the first effort by Indian Christians to evangelize on their own initiative.[15]

In another part of the world, missionary Johannes Warneck recorded that from about the 1860s, after the appearance of similar Pentecostal phenomena, the

Fully Surrendered

On Sunday, June 25th, 1865, unable to bear the sight of a congregation of a thousand or more Christian people rejoicing in their own security, while millions were perishing for lack of knowledge, I wandered out on the sands [of Brighton beach in England] alone, in great spiritual agony; and there the Lord conquered my unbelief, and I surrendered myself to God for this service. I told him that all the responsibility as to issues and consequences must rest with Him; that as His servant, it was mine to obey and follow Him—His, to direct, to care for, and to guide me and those who might labour with me. Need I say that peace at once flowed into my burdened heart? There and then I asked Him for twenty-four fellow-workers, two for each of eleven inland provinces which were without a missionary, and two for Mongolia. . . . I returned home with a heart enjoying rest such as it had been a stranger to for months. . . . I had previously prayed, and asked in prayer, that workers might be raised up for the eleven then unoccupied provinces, and thrust forth and provided for, but had not surrendered myself to be their leader.

J. Hudson Taylor, founder of the China Inland Mission

—J. Hudson Taylor, A Retrospect (1954), 108.

Indonesian Christian community increased. In this revival, believers had dreams and visions, signs appeared in the heavens, and in several instances missionaries remained unharmed after unwittingly consuming poison in food given by their enemies (Mark 16:18).[16] Convinced that they had "fulfilled their purpose of pointing the stupefied heathen to the gift of the Gospel," Warneck saw "the power of working signs and wonders" (Acts 5:12) as simply temporary, just as they had been in early Christianity.[17]

German theologian Theodore Christlieb took a different view. Aware of the happenings in Indonesia, he said that "in the last epoch of the consummation of the Church . . . she will again require for her final decisive struggle with the powers of darkness, the miraculous interference of her risen Lord, and hence the Scriptures lead us to expect miracles once more for this period." Christlieb then noted that "in the history of modern missions we find many wonderful occurrences which unmistakably remind us of the apostolic age."[18]

Those who believed that supernatural signs should accompany the preaching of the gospel looked not only to Matthew 10 (verse 8 refers to miracles) but increasingly to Mark 16:17,18: "These signs will accompany those who believe: In my name they will drive out demons; they will speak in new tongues; they will pick up snakes with their hands; and when they drink deadly poison, it will not hurt them at all; they will place their hands on sick people, and they will get well." This interest set the stage for the "radical strategy": an end-times scenario of divine intervention in signs and wonders to ensure that every tribe and nation would hear the gospel before the close of human history.

EXPECTING THE SUPERNATURAL

After midcentury, A. B. Simpson and A. J. Gordon and others put theory into practice by encouraging missionaries to trust God for miracles. Simpson announced, "The plan of the Lord [is] to pour out His Spirit not only in the ordinary, but also in the extraordinary gifts and operations of His power . . . as His people press forward to claim the evangelization of the entire world."[19]

Others shared this expectancy and sometimes it led to unusual testimonies. In South India in 1881, Miss C. M. Reade of the Highways and Hedges Mission prayed to receive the gift of speaking Hindustani to communicate effectively with her hearers. As a result, "'the power came to her as a gift from God.' One month she was unable to do more than put two or three sentences together; while the next month, she was able to preach and pray without waiting for a word. Those who heard her could only say with herself, 'It was a gift from above.'"[20] In 1885, seven British athletes went to China as missionaries. They were known as the Cambridge Seven. Several of them expected God to give them the Mandarin language.[21] Three years later, China missionary Jonathan Goforth, a Canadian Presbyterian, claimed that he gained mastery of Mandarin only after receiving supernatural enablement.[22]

A. J. Gordon contended that "the rigid logic which is supposed to fence out miracles from modern Christendom, does not seem to have been careful to include heathendom in its prohibition. For when it is said that 'miracles belong to the planting of Christianity, not to its progress and development,' it will at once strike us that missions are practically the planting of Christianity."[23] Opponents, however, scorned these ideas as absurd and irresponsible, not foreseeing the impact that healings and "power encounters" (exorcisms, etc.) would have in capturing the attention of non-Christians on the mission fields.

THE CREST OF REVIVAL

As the twentieth century approached, believers on every continent were praying for revival and the outpouring of the Holy Spirit. Prophecy conferences in America warned the faithful that the time for evangelism had nearly expired, judgment knocked at the door, and only a heaven-sent revival could stop the hell-bent destructive course of humanity. Surrounded by millions of non-Christians and the growing resistance of non-Christian religions, mission leaders issued urgent calls to pray for a "special manifestation of the life and power of God the Holy Spirit."[24]

In 1898 at the Third International Convention of the Student Volunteer Movement for Foreign Missions in Cleveland, Ohio, a well-known promoter of missions, Robert P. Wilder, put the feelings of many into words: "Thank God, we are living to-day in the dispensation of the Holy Ghost, and it is possible for you and for me simply to reach out and take this gift of all gifts by faith. . . . God grant that . . . we may be filled with the Holy Ghost and then we will see such results as we have never thought of before."[25]

After the turn of the century, awakenings followed in many countries, the most notable occurring in Australia (1902) and Wales (1904), with the latter prompting revivals in South Africa (1904), India (1905), the United States (1906), Korea (1906), and Manchuria (1908). In the Welsh revival, approximately one hundred thousand people were converted in a matter of months.[26] For many Christians, it looked like their prayers had been answered—the beginning of the great end-times outpouring of the Holy Spirit had begun. The events in Wales that fired the imagination of radical evangelicals also influenced the beginning of the Pentecostal movement.

MISSIONARY TONGUES

Before the turn of the twentieth century, several small but influential Pentecostal revivals occurred in St. Louis, Missouri; Cherokee County, North Carolina; and Beniah, Tennessee, among others. In 1895 in St. Louis, a congregation heard Walter S. Black, a Canadian Baptist minister, and his wife, Frances, speak in tongues. At the same revival, a young woman, Jennie Glassey, reportedly spoke in several dialects of West Africa.

The notion that speaking in tongues functioned as evidence of Spirit baptism held center stage during the revival that swept Charles F. Parham's Bethel Bible School in Topeka, Kansas. There in January 1901 a revival occurred with most of the students and Parham himself claiming to speak the languages of the world. Thinking that months or years of language study were no longer necessary, he foresaw Spirit-baptized missionaries proceeding on faith directly to herald the gospel news.[27] (Unknown to Parham, a Pentecostal revival also broke out among Swedish Americans in Moorhead, Minnesota, in 1903.)

Parham's ministry extended from Topeka to Galena, Kansas; Houston, Texas; and Zion, Illinois. A student at his Houston Bible School, William J. Seymour, an African American, accepted Parham's view of tongues and traveled to Los Angeles to share the news of the Spirit's outpouring. In a setting primed for revival by news of the Welsh revival, Seymour's message ignited a fire that began in April 1906 at the Apostolic Faith Mission on Azusa Street—the Azusa Street revival. Word of these meetings spread through the accounts of eyewitnesses and the pages of the *Apostolic Faith* (Los Angeles), a newspaper published by the Apostolic Faith Mission. Thousands of copies were sent around the world to announce that Pentecostal power had at last been restored in its fullness.

Three months after the revival began in Los Angeles, and unrelated to it, Pentecostalism broke forth in India, for holiness believers had been praying for the outpouring of the Spirit there as well. Stories of believers in India receiving tongues and other gifts of the Spirit convinced the faithful in Los Angeles of the worldwide scope of the Spirit's outpouring. When issues of the *Apostolic Faith* reached India in the fall of 1906, it greatly encouraged missionaries and Indian Christians to keep seeking the fullness of the Holy Spirit and speaking in tongues.

The outpouring of the Spirit prompted other Pentecostal revivals across North America: in Nyack and Rochester, New York; Chicago; Indianapolis; San Antonio; Dunn, North Carolina; and Memphis and Cleveland, Tennessee. News that the "latter rain" had come, fulfilling Joel's prophecy (2:23,28,29), also inspired Canadian revivals, notably in Winnipeg, Toronto, and St. John's, Newfoundland. Revivals in Oslo, Norway; Stockholm, Sweden; and Sunderland, England, inspired similar awakenings in the Netherlands, Germany, and Switzerland. From these revivals, missionaries soon traveled to the mission fields.[28] Although the *Apostolic Faith* published in Los Angeles (there were other newspapers of the same name published in other places) played a unique international role in carrying revival reports, no single model of a Pentecostal revival dominated. Each one shared certain characteristics (especially speaking in tongues), but differed in the makeup of participants, physical manifestations, as well as other features.

Early Pentecostals varied in their backgrounds more than historians have sometimes believed. Although many were poor, the majority came from the working class and, in a few quarters, from the wealthy class. Though most Pentecostal preachers lacked formal ministerial training, a small scattering of college and seminary graduates could be found in the ranks.

Your Daughters Will Prophesy

Did the tongue of fire descend alike upon God's daughters as upon his sons, and was the effect similar in each? And did all these waiting disciples, who thus, with one accord, continued in prayer, receive the grace for which they supplicated? It was, as we observe, the gift of the Holy Ghost that had been promised. And was this promise of the Father as truly made to the daughters of the Lord Almighty as to his sons? See Joel ii. 28, 29. "And it shall come to pass afterward, that I will pour out my Spirit upon all flesh; and your sons and your daughters shall prophesy, your old men shall dream dreams, your young men shall see visions. And also upon the servants and upon the handmaids in those days will I pour out my Spirit." When the Spirit was poured out in answer to the united prayers of God's sons and daughters, did the tongue of fire descend alike upon the women as upon the men? How emphatic is the answer to this question? "And there appeared unto them cloven tongues, like as of fire, and it sat upon each of them." Was the effect similar upon God's daughters as upon his sons? Mark it, O ye who have restrained the workings of this gift of power in the church. "And they were all filled with the Holy Ghost, and began to speak as the Spirit gave utterance." Doubtless it was a well nigh impelling power, which was thus poured out upon these sons and daughters of the Lord Almighty, moving their lips to most earnest, persuasive, convincing utterances. Not alone only did Peter proclaim a crucified risen Saviour, but each one, as crucified risen Saviour, but each one, as the Spirit gave

DIFFERENCES AMONG PENTECOSTALS

Pentecostals differed in certain areas of doctrine as well. For example, early Pentecostals disagreed on tongues as required evidence of Spirit baptism. They also quarreled over the nature of sanctification, their opinions becoming better known as existing organizations accepted Pentecost or new ones were founded. Organizations strongly identifying with Wesleyan-holiness views had been formed before the Pentecostal revival but then joined it (e.g., Church of God in Christ, Church of God [Cleveland, Tennessee], and Pentecostal Holiness Church). Several new organizations adopted Reformed revivalist\ Keswick views (e.g., Assemblies of God). Finally, Pentecostals parted over an understanding of the Godhead: the historic orthodox Christian view of God in three Persons versus a conception of God as one Person, Jesus Christ (Oneness).

Preferences also varied on what form of church government to adopt. The European Pentecostals, along with many Americans, maintained that the New Testament teaches a congregational model. Some appealed to modified Presbyterian structures while preserving the sovereignty of the local church (e.g., Assemblies of God). Others saw the value of hierarchical patterns (e.g., Church of God [Cleveland, Tennessee]). As time passed and more problems surfaced in the Pentecostal movement, organizations were formed to provide accountability, cooperation, doctrinal standards, and

utterance, assisted in spreading the good news; and the result of these united ministrations of the Spirit, through human agency, was, that three thousand were, in one day, pricked to the heart.

And now, in the name of the Head of the church, let us ask, Was it designed that these demonstrations of power should cease with the day of Pentecost? If the Spirit of prophecy fell upon God's daughters, alike as upon his sons in that day, and they spake in the midst of that assembled multitude, as the Spirit gave utterance, on what authority do the angels of the churches restrain the use of that gift now? Has the minister of Christ, now reading these lines, never encouraged open female testimony, in the charge which he represents? Let us ask, What account will you render to the Head of the church, for restricting the use of

Phoebe Palmer, an influential proponent of holiness theology, found equal rights for female preachers in the *"Promise of the Father"* (Acts 1:4, KJV).

this endowment of power? Who can tell how wonderful the achievements of the cross might have been, if this gift of prophecy, in woman, had continued in use, as in apostolic days? Who can tell but long since the gospel might have been preached to every creature?

fellowship. Names went from the grand-sounding National and International Pentecostal Missionary Union to the Pentecostal Assemblies of the World to the International Church of the Foursquare Gospel to the Pentecostal Assemblies of Canada to the Pentecostal Free Will Baptist Church to the General Council of the Assemblies of God. Nevertheless, significant numbers of Pentecostals refused to join any organization; they feared that human directives would override the individual leading of the Spirit.

Early Pentecostals kept in touch through scores of periodicals, informing readers of camp meetings, revival services, and happenings on the mission fields. Such periodicals also included Bible studies and doctrinal articles. Preachers and missionaries traveled widely at home or abroad and kept the saints informed of events. But this fellowship of Spirit-filled Christians struggled with issues that taxed their effectiveness: Missionaries sometimes found they couldn't purchase property because they were not representatives of mission agencies with legal standing; Pentecostals occasionally were persecuted by opponents and ostracized from other Christians; pastors and evangelists were frequently not accountable to anyone for their actions; and doctrinal deviations confused the faithful.

Pentecostals remained evangelical in doctrine and made long-term contributions to evangelism and missions. Their remarkable growth can be attributed in large part to mature leaders—both men and women, pastors and editors, missionaries and laypersons—who provided crucial direction for the young Movement.

RECOMMENDED READING

Burgess, Stanley M. *The Holy Spirit: Ancient Christian Traditions*. Peabody, Mass.: Hendrickson Publishers, 1984.

———. *The Holy Spirit: Eastern Christian Traditions*. Peabody, Mass.: Hendrickson Publishers, 1989.

———. *The Holy Spirit: Medieval Roman Catholic and Reformation Traditions*. Peabody, Mass.: Hendrickson Publishers, 1997.

———, ed. *New International Dictionary of Pentecostal and Charismatic Movements*. Grand Rapids: Zondervan, 2002.

Curtis, Heather D. *Faith in the Great Physician: Suffering and Divine Healing in American Culture, 1860-1900*. Baltimore: Johns Hopkins University Press, 2007.

Dayton, Donald W. *Theological Roots of Pentecostalism*. Peabody, Mass.: Hendrickson Publishers, 1987.

Dieter, Melvin Easterday. *The Holiness Revival in the Nineteenth Century*. 2d ed. Metuchen, N.J.: Scarecrow Press, 1996.

Jones, Charles Edwin. *Perfectionist Persuasion: The Holiness Movement and American Methodism, 1867–1936*. Metuchen, N.J.: Scarecrow Press, 1974.

Kydd, Ronald A. N. *Healing through the Centuries: Models for Understanding*. Peabody, Mass.: Hendrickson Publishers, 1998.

McDonnell, Kilian, and George T. Montague. *Christian Initiation and Baptism in the Holy Spirit: Evidence from the First Eight Centuries*. Collegeville, Minn.: Liturgical Press, 1991.

McGee, Gary B. "Miracles and Missions Revisited." International Bulletin of Missionary Research 25 (October 2001): 146–56.

———. *Miracles, Missions, and American Pentecostalism*. Maryknoll, NY: Orbis Books, 2010.

Weber, Timothy P. *Living in the Shadow of the Second Coming: American Premillennialism: 1875–1925*. Rev. ed. Chicago: University of Chicago Press, 1987.

ENDNOTES

[1] Kilian McDonnell and George T. Montague, *Christian Initiation and Baptism in the Holy Spirit: Evidence from the First Eight Centuries* (Collegeville, Minn.: Liturgical Press, 1991), 149.

[2] Stanley M. Burgess, *The Holy Spirit: Eastern Christian Traditions* (Peabody, Mass.: Hendrickson Publishers, 1989), 53–62.

[3] Stanley M. Burgess, *The Holy Spirit: Medieval Roman Catholic and Reformation Traditions* (Peabody, Mass.: Hendrickson Publishers, 1997), 201–209.

[4] Gary B. McGee, "Miracles and Missions Revisited," *International Bulletin of Missionary Research* 25 (October 2001): 147.

[5] Donald W. Dayton, *Theological Roots of Pentecostalism* (Metuchen, N.J.: Scarecrow Press, 1987), 35–60.

[6] R. A. Torrey, *The Baptism with the Holy Spirit* (New York: Fleming H. Revell Co., 1897), 15.

[7] Ronald A. N. Kydd, *Healing through the Centuries: Models for Understanding* (Peabody, Mass.: Hendrickson Publishers, 1998), 34–45, 142–148.

[8] A. B. Simpson, *The Gospel of Healing*, rev. ed. (Harrisburg, Pa.: Christian Publications, 1915), 76–77.

[9] Ibid., e.g., 24–25, 28–29, 32.

[10] A. J. Gordon, *Ministry of Healing* (New York: Christian Alliance Publishing Co., 1882), 193–223.

[11] John Louis O'Sullivan, "Manifest Destiny," in *Darwin*, ed. Philip Appleman (New York: W. W. Norton & Co., 1970), 511–512.

[12] William G. McLoughlin, *Revivals, Awakenings, and Reform* (Chicago: University of Chicago Press, 1978), 144.

[13] Harlan P. Beach, A *Geography and Atlas of Protestant Missions*, vol. 1, *Statistics and Atlas* (New York: Student Volunteer Movement for Foreign Missions, 1906), 19.

[14] Edward Irving, *Missionaries after the Apostolical School* (Tienstin, China: Tienstin Printing Co., 1887), 97, 100.

[15] Ashton Dibb, "The Revival in North Tinnevelly," *Church Missionary Record*, n.s., 5 (August 1860): 178.

[16] Johannes Warneck, *The Living Christ and Dying Heathenism*, 3rd ed. (New York: Fleming H. Revell Co., n.d.), 175–182.

[17] Ibid., 182, 165.

[18] Theodore Christlieb, *Modern Doubt and Christian Belief* (New York: Scribner, Armstrong & Co., 1874), 332, 334.

[19] A. B. Simpson, "Connection Between Supernatural Gifts and the World's Evangelization," *Christian Alliance and Missionary Weekly* (7 & 14 October 1892): 226.

[20] "A Gift of Tongues," *New Zealand Christian Record* 14 (April 1881): 11.

[21] B. Broomhall, *The Evangelisation of the World: A Missionary Band: A Record of Consecration, and an Appeal*, 3rd ed. (London: Morgan & Scott, 1889), 53.

[22] Rosalind Goforth, *Goforth of China* (1937 reprint, New York: B. Y. Jove, 1990), 134–156.

[23] Gordon, *Ministry of Healing*, 116.

[24] T. Walker, "Present Religious Awakenings in the Church in India," *Church Missionary Review* 58 (May 1907): 280.

[25] Robert P. Wilder, "Our Equipment of Power," in *The Student Missionary Appeal: Addresses at the Third International Convention of the Student Volunteer Movement for Foreign Missions* (New York: Student Volunteer Movement for Foreign Missions, 1898), 263–265.

[26] J. Edwin Orr, *The Flaming Tongue: Evangelical Awakenings 1990–*, 2d ed. (Chicago: Moody Press, 1975), 15–28.

[27] "Parham's New Religion Practiced at 'Stone's Folly,'" *Kansas City Times*, 27 January 1901, 55.

[28] Gary B. McGee, "To the Regions Beyond: The Global Expansion of Pentecostalism," in *The Century of the Holy Spirit: 100 Years of Pentecostal and Charismatic Renewal*, ed. Vinson Synan (Nashville: Thomas Nelson Publishers, 2001), 69–95.

CHAPTER 2

RADICAL EVANGELICALS

Early Pentecostal missionaries quickly stirred interest because of their unusual claims. Veteran missionaries who had spent years struggling to master native languages were stunned by the claims of Pentecostals that God had conferred native languages on them as gifts. Not only that, signs and wonders would supposedly follow their preaching of the gospel.

On the radical fringe of evangelicalism, expectancy of supernatural manifestations had been growing for some time. After Spirit baptism and the prayer of faith, the believer could expect the signs to follow. They could witness the seemingly impossible: healing the sick, raising the dead, casting out demons, and even the divine bestowal of unlearned languages (Mark 16:17–18). Those seeking the restoration of apostolic power, as described in the Book of Acts, included A. B. Simpson; John Alexander Dowie; Maria B. Woodworth-Etter; young missionaries from the Topeka, Kansas, Y.M.C.A.; Frank W. Sandford; Walter and Frances Black; and Jennie Glassey. Identifying themselves with the early Christians, they saw their ministries as simply continuing the work of the Holy Spirit—the "Twenty-Ninth" chapter of the Book of Acts.

A. B. SIMPSON
(1843-1919)

In the study of Christian movements, scholars attempt to identify key leaders, especially a founder, a father (or mother) figure whose commanding presence shaped the movement. Lutherans trace their origins to Martin Luther, Reformed to John Calvin, and Methodists to John Wesley. But in the case of the Pentecostal movement, as in the later Charismatic movement, no commanding figure of their stature appears. Early Pentecostals hesitated to honor anyone as founder except the Holy Spirit. Of course, leaders have been nominated, the best known being Charles F. Parham and William J. Seymour. Yet for various reasons, others could be added to this list, including Gaston B. Cashwell, Ivey Campbell, Thomas B. Barratt, and Minnie F. Abrams. Indeed, Pentecostalism arose as a popular Movement that had as many leaders as it had centers of revival.

Nonetheless, few wielded as much influence on the Pentecostal movement as A. B. Simpson, the founder of the Christian and Missionary Alliance. His influence has endured, particularly in the Assemblies of God. Pastor, promoter of interdenominational evangelism, mission executive and strategist, prolific writer, hymn writer, and spiritual mentor—he wore many hats. Simpson challenged his followers to seek a closer relationship with Christ and evangelize the world in the power of the Spirit. As a result, many of them later became Pentecostals.

Born into a devout Presbyterian home on Prince Edward Island, Canada, in 1843, Albert Benjamin Simpson was converted as a teenager in 1858 and afterward felt called to the ministry. Pursuing the call took him to Knox College in Toronto. After graduating in 1865, he was ordained and became pastor of Knox Presbyterian Church in Hamilton, Ontario, the second largest Presbyterian congregation in Canada, where he served until 1873.

Before Simpson entered his second pastorate, in Louisville, Kentucky, in 1874, he was already longing for a deeper experience of Christ. His reading of *The Higher Christian Life* (1858) by William E. Boardman led to his spiritual transformation, an experience he considered to be the baptism in the Holy Spirit, bringing him personal holiness and empowerment for Christian ministry. Boardman's classic introduced

Gold-for-Iron for Jesus

Around the turn of the century, Mary Alice Reynolds heard of an irresistible deal: she could give up her gold and get iron in its place!

Crazy? Maybe. But to her it made good sense, because giving up her gold would help advance the cause of foreign missions . . . and that was something she wanted to do.

In the early days of the Pentecostal revival over 80 years ago, Mary Alice and her husband, Charles Reynolds—my grandparents—were members of the Christian and Missionary Alliance. From the C&MA an appeal went out: "Gold-for-iron for Jesus!" Those who brought their gold possessions would be given iron and the proceeds from the sale of the gold would be donated to missions.

So Mary Alice Reynolds brought her gold watch and, much to her husband's consternation, her gold wedding ring—her two most prized possessions. A jeweler replaced the gold case with gunmetal, and the watch was returned to Mrs. Reynolds.

The memory of the gift presents a challenge to us as Christians today. What are we doing for missions? Have we sacrificed? Is our love for Jesus so full and sincere that we would obediently give up our dearest possessions at His request? He may not be asking for gold jewelry, but He does ask for our lives.

—*Adele Flower Dalton, "Gold-for-Iron for Jesus,"*
Mountain Movers (1985): 6–7.

Signs and Wonders in Missions

Since the church has lost her faith in a great measure in the supernatural signs and workings of the Holy Ghost, she has lost the signs also, and the result is that she is compelled to produce conviction upon the minds of the heathen very largely by purely rational and moral considerations and influences, and the direct appeal to the supernatural power of God, which the apostles ever made, is rarely witnessed.

A. B. Simpson

The need, however, for these supernatural evidences among the heathen is as great as ever. The Brahmins of India can reason as wide as we. The intellects of China are as profound as ours; the literature of heathen nations is full of subtlety and sophistry that can match all our arguments; but in the touch of God there is something that man cannot answer nor explain away. God has been pleased to give these signs in the work at home in these last days.

—*A. B. Simpson, "The New Testament Standpoint of Missions,"* Christian and Missionary Alliance Weekly *(December 16, 1892): 389.*

him to the Reformed wing of the holiness movement. Leaving Louisville five years later, Simpson; his wife, Margaret; and their children traveled to New York City where he began pastoring the Thirteenth Street Presbyterian Church.

Because of his interest in interdenominational evangelism, Simpson grew uncomfortable with the restrictions of Presbyterian ministry. His search climaxed in 1881, drastically changing the direction of his life: He testified to the healing of a serious heart ailment at the Old Orchard Beach campground in Maine. He also asked to be baptized by immersion in a Baptist church, resigned his pastorate and the Presbyterian ministry, and began evangelizing the poor and unchurched in New York City. In 1882, he organized an independent congregation, the Gospel Tabernacle.

Simpson believed that beginning with the sixteenth-century Protestant Reformation, the restoration of the New Testament church in its original purity and vitality had evolved in some areas. He pointed to, among other things, Wesley's teaching on the sanctified life, the rediscovery of divine healing by faith, and now at the close of human history, the widespread anticipation of the outpouring of the Holy Spirit. Just as first-century Christians had received the "early rain," so nineteen centuries later miracles and the gifts of the Spirit had once again appeared.

In response to a flurry of interest in "missionary tongues" (c. 1890–1892), yet aware of and wishing to avoid the "danger of Irvingism" (controversial teachings of early nineteenth-century Scottish preacher Edward Irving on the gifts of the Spirit), the Alliance convention in October 1892 issued an urgent call: They asked the faithful to pray for the outpouring of the Spirit to help missionaries acquire foreign languages and to enable missionaries to withstand the climates in Africa, India, and China. Although the resolution left a measure of ambiguity about how this could be accomplished, Simpson believed that supernatural manifestations and miracles could still happen, rejecting the assumption held by many that miracles had ended with the apostles.

Like others in the holiness movement, he believed that doctrinal truth—particularly the belief that baptism in the Spirit was an experience separate from conversion (according to the pattern found in Acts 2, 10, and 19)—could be found in the historical parts of the Book of Acts as well as its instructional parts. This restorationist approach to biblical interpretation laid the basis for the Pentecostal doctrine that would stipulate that speaking in tongues indicated being baptized in the Spirit.

Simpson also identified with the evangelical healing movement, stemming from his own physical healing as well as from contact with Charles C. Cullis, a homeopathic physician in Boston and believer in divine healing. Linking healing to evangelism, Simpson believed that such testimonies would gain the attention of nonbelievers at home and abroad by allowing them to see the power of God in action.

Teaching that the second coming of Christ was fast approaching, leaving little time, he ardently supported foreign missions. Simpson uniquely argued that the Great Commission had to be completed before Christ could return. In part he based this on the words of Jesus in Matthew 24:14, "'This gospel . . . will be preached in the whole world . . . and then the end will come,'" and Peter's admonition to believers in 2 Peter 3:11–12, "What kind of people ought you to be? You ought to live holy and godly lives as you look forward to the day of God and speed its coming."

To hurry the goal of proclaiming the fourfold gospel in North America and overseas, Simpson founded several institutions, among them the Evangelical Missionary Alliance and the Christian Alliance (which merged in 1897 to become the Christian

The Missionary Training Institute, Nyack, New York (c.1900)

and Missionary Alliance) and the Missionary Training Institute—the first Bible institute of its kind in America. Offering a shortcut to ministry—students would come to call it "Simpson's matchbox," reflecting his passion for their being set on fire for the Lord's work—its course of study took far less time than that of the usual college and seminary preparation of the mainline clergy. In its early years, the Alliance served not as a denomination but as an association of members from many denominations.

Simpson's Zionist sympathies and confidence in the nearness of the Lord's return led him to lobby the United States government on behalf of Jewish immigration to Palestine. Living for the moment when the fulfillment of Bible prophecies would begin, and already in poor health, he suffered a paralyzing stroke in 1918 after hearing that General Edmund Allenby, British commander in Palestine, had captured Jerusalem from the Ottoman Turks. History had taken an unexpected and dramatic turn. He died a year later.

JOHN ALEXANDER DOWIE
(1847-1907)

Opposite the reserved posture of A. B. Simpson stood the flamboyant and outspoken John Alexander Dowie, nationally known for faith healing and founder of a utopian community north of Chicago: Zion City. Born in Scotland in 1847, his family immigrated to Adelaide, Australia, when he was a teenager. At twenty he announced that God had called him to the ministry and a year later left for the Free Church College at the University of Edinburgh in Scotland to begin his studies.

John Alexander Dowie

Arriving back in Adelaide in 1872, he was ordained as a Congregational minister. But unsatisfied with what he considered the spiritual coldness and worldliness of the mainline churches, he left the Congregational Union to minister independently. Success, however, remained elusive until he moved to Melbourne and erected a revival tabernacle in the heart of the city to preach on divine healing. Four years later he founded the International Divine Healing Association, which eventually had branches around the world.

In a vision in 1888, the Lord told him to carry "the leaves of healing from the tree of life to every nation." Afterward, with his wife, Jane, and their children, Dowie moved to the United States, first to California and then to Illinois. The opening of the Chicago World's Fair in 1893 provided an opportunity that he readily seized. He built a tabernacle and held meetings across the street from Buffalo Bill's Wild West Show and other popular attractions. As stories of healings circulated, newspaper coverage increased. A gifted orator, Dowie not only preached divine healing but loudly attacked politicians, Masons, Catholics, denominational clergy, journalists, and especially medical doctors. He pointedly said, "Divine healing has no association with doctors and drugs, or surgeons and their knives."

He then opened his personal residence as Divine Healing Home Number One, following the pattern of faith homes already established in Europe and the United States, and began publication of Leaves of Healing. Dowie was soon harassed by the Chicago Board of Health and the medical profession for practicing medicine without a license. Although he was arrested many times, the authorities always dropped the charges. Despite such opposition, broad newspaper coverage pushed him to the forefront of the American healing movement.

Independent and difficult to work with, Dowie remained aloof from other healing leaders (e.g., A. B. Simpson), criticizing them and even breaking with his own International Divine Healing Association. In 1896 he organized the Christian Catholic Church, later renamed the Christian Catholic Apostolic Church in Zion. During the next several years, his meetings moved to ever-larger facilities. He opened more healing homes

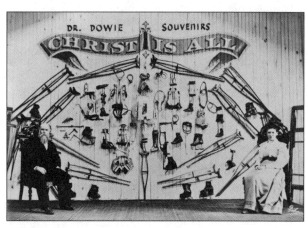

John Alexander Dowie and his wife, Jane, sitting at their booth at the 1893 Chicago World's Fair and surrounded by "souvenirs" from his healing services

and founded other institutions, including a bank, a printing plant, an orphanage, a home for working girls, a home for wayward women, and a day school.

Dowie's ministry, however, took a new turn on New Year's Eve in 1899; he announced the purchase of sixty-six hundred acres of farmland on the shores of Lake Michigan in Illinois about halfway between Chicago and Milwaukee. "Zion City" would be a model Christian community fashioned according to Dowie's plan. Well-designed for future growth, the new community took a motto fitting for a theocracy: "Where God Rules, Man Prospers." He gave streets and landmarks Old Testament names (e.g., Beulah, Shiloh). Economically, socially, and spiritually, the community's regulations reflected a blending of biblical, utopian, and modern concepts. The first residents settled in 1901; four years later, the population had grown to approximately seven thousand people, with many other followers in Australia, New Zealand, Canada, Europe, and South Africa.

In his last years Dowie became unstable and made increasingly eccentric claims. For example, in 1901 he declared himself to be the final manifestation of Elijah (Malachi 4:5–6). Three years later, as "Elijah the Restorer," he declared that he would lead in the full restoration of New Testament Christianity. Indeed, God had commissioned him in the end times as the "First Apostle of the Lord Jesus" to bring about the restored Church.

Dowie's demise, however, came in 1905. While planning to establish Zions in other places, he had a stroke. Unfortunately, the city's economy had faltered and many residents lost their life savings. This undermined Dowie's authority over the community. A year later, he lost the leadership of Zion City. Almost friendless, he died in disgrace at his home in 1907. Apart from the bizarre claims of his later years, his emphasis on the return of apostolic Christianity, divine healing, and the end times helped prepare the way for the Pentecostal movement.

Interestingly, he had identified himself with Edward Irving, calling him "one of my predecessors." Furthermore, he said, "A greater and mightier man of God never stood upon this earth," one who "saw the whole truth as to the Restoration of the Apostolic Church." Many of Dowie's followers subsequently became Pentecostals and key leaders in the Movement.

MARIA B. WOODWORTH-ETTER
(1844-1924)

In searching for others whose holiness beliefs and ministries contributed to the coming of the Pentecostal movement, several names readily appear: Charles G. Finney, Asa Mahan, R. A. Torrey, Charles C. Cullis, and Maria B. Woodworth-Etter. This last name demonstrates the significant role that women played in the holiness movement. After all, the promised outpouring of the Holy Spirit had fallen not only on the "sons" and male "servants," but on the "daughters" and female "servants" as well (Acts 2:17–18), and that without qualification.

Maria B. Woodworth-Etter

From a holiness background, Woodworth-Etter began her itinerant evangelistic ministry about 1880. Traveling through the Midwest, Churches of God in North America, Methodist, United Brethren, and other favorable churches sponsored her meetings. In her preaching, she highlighted the need for conversion. But her fame spread in 1883 when people in her services began to fall prostrate and went into what appeared to be trances. She considered this phenomenon to be evidence of Spirit baptism. Though critics labeled her the "trance evangelist," falling "under the power" was hardly new in revival circles. During early revivals on the American

Handbill announcing meeting with evangelist Maria B. Woodworth-Etter in Ottumwa, Iowa frontier (as well as the revival of 1858–1859 among Northern Ireland Presbyterians), believers rose to tell of being intensely convicted of sins and of their repentance.

By 1885, Woodworth-Etter's beliefs closely resembled the fourfold gospel of A. B. Simpson. She had also begun to travel across the nation holding campaigns, and in many communities significant church growth took place. Yet despite the many conversions and healings in her services, controversy swirled around her. Local authorities sometimes charged her for practicing medicine without a license. And while she was holding services in Oakland, California, she announced that God had revealed to her that divine judgment would fall on the cities of San Francisco, Oakland, and Alameda in eighty days—April 14, 1890. Frightened by this, people sold their possessions and fled to the hills around the Bay Area to await the judgment. When it did not happen, critics were severe and believers were disillusioned.

Nevertheless, she was not deterred. Thousands continued to attend her services and ask for prayer. To publicize the miracles and her ministry, she wrote several books, including *The Life and Experiences of Maria B. Woodworth-Etter* (1888), *Acts of the Holy Ghost* (1912), and *Signs and Wonders* (1916), which provided fascinating reading for those longing to see the restoration of apostolic power.

Woodworth-Etter was the best-known nineteenth-century holiness leader to join and play a major part in the Pentecostal movement, which she entered in 1912. Because the power and demonstration of the Spirit in her meetings modeled the potential of the "radical strategy," her ministry helped form the framework for later Pentecostal evangelism.

THE KANSAS-SUDAN MISSIONARIES (1889-1891)

With the end of the century approaching and Christians wondering how the nations would hear the gospel message before Christ's return, young men at the Topeka, Kansas, branch of the Y.M.C.A. listened intently to the preaching of H. Grattan

Mischievous Doctrines

The healings wrought by Christ and His apostles were then simply portions of a group of miraculous "signs" by which Christianity was ushered into the world eighteen hundred years ago. We have no more reason to expect them to continue than any of the other signs which accompanied them—the opening [of] the eyes of the blind or the ears of the deaf, the cleansing of lepers with a touch, the walking on the water, or feeding the multitude, or even the raising of the dead. Dr. [A.B.] Simpson thinks we need these "signs," and asks, "What right have we to go to the unbelieving world and demand their acceptance of our message without these signs?" We have surely said enough to show that [Simpson] teaches foolish, false and very mischievous doctrines.
—*Fanny (Mrs. H. Grattan) Guinness, "Faith-Healing and Missions,"*
The Regions Beyond (January 1891): 30–32.

Guinness. Several then responded by obeying the divine call to missions. A well-known promoter of foreign missions, Guinness directed the Livingstone Inland Mission in the Congo and a missionary training school in England—the East London Institute. From the meetings in Topeka came the Kansas-Sudan movement.

While waiting for their ship to leave New York City for England and ultimately Sierra Leone, West Africa, the small company of missionaries visited the Gospel Tabernacle and school of A. B. Simpson. Their belief that God would provide for their needs and their confidence in His power to heal immediately created a bond with Simpson and his Alliance. Whether or not they had come to believe in divine healing before they met Simpson, their party headed for Africa believing that God would heal them when necessary and would heal others as they prayed for them. Their expectation that God would miraculously provide them with the needed languages for preaching the gospel is also noteworthy (Mark 16:17–18), for it was being discussed among Alliance members as well. And it was about to be put to the test: They took neither medicine nor foreign language grammars or dictionaries with them.

After arriving in Sierra Leone, they quickly discovered their need to study the native languages. However, they steadfastly refused medicines. Before long, several died from malaria, having declined to take the prescribed quinine. When this story began circulating among mission groups and in newspapers, critics quickly condemned faith healing as well as the belief that miracles could be commonplace in evangelism. Yet several in the party continued in missions work, some joining the Alliance. Although failing to achieve their goals, the attempt by these young missionaries illustrates the desperate concern of radical evangelicals to intensify missionary evangelism.

FRANK W. SANDFORD
(1862-1948)

Although not as well known as Simpson or Dowie, Frank W. Sandford also contributed to the coming of the Pentecostal movement. Born in Bowdoinham, Maine, Sandford was converted in 1880 and later attended Bates College and then Cobb Divinity School. Leaving Cobb because it didn't meet his spiritual needs, he became pastor of the Free Baptist Church in Topsham. Years of ministry there and later in New Hampshire proved to be formative in his spiritual development, beginning with his reading of Hannah Whitall Smith's holiness classic *The Christian's Secret of a Happy Life* (1883). While living in New Hampshire, he attended camp meetings at Old Orchard Beach in nearby Maine, where he embraced holiness teachings on sanctification.

Through contact with A. B. Simpson and the Alliance, he came to believe in divine healing. Sandford also attended Dwight L. Moody's summer conferences in Northfield, Massachusetts, and Reuben A. Torrey's conventions for Christian workers. As a result of his friendship with Torrey, Sandford preached several times at Moody Bible Institute in Chicago. With a friend, he traveled extensively overseas to assess the current effectiveness of Christian missions. Disappointed at what he saw, he concluded

The View from Shiloh

Frank W. Sandford

Following [a pastorate in Topsham, Maine] . . . I made a tour of the world. I visited the missionary fields of Japan, China, and India, touched Singapore, Egypt, and Palestine, and crossed the continent to England.

Perceiving the utter hopelessness of ever evangelizing this world by any method of Christian work then in existence, I determined to turn to apostolic methods.

Accordingly I resigned my pastorate January 1, 1893, and stepped out of denominational labors into a life of utter abandonment to God's Spirit and providences.

Eight years to a day have since passed. During the first three years of this time I have done evangelistic work in tents, groves, schoolhouses, in well-nigh deserted church buildings, etc., working almost exclusively . . . among the neglected portions of my fellow beings.

For several years, however, I have been led by God to erect large [buildings at Shiloh, Maine] in the interests of preparing evangelists for the earth's vast harvest field. . . .

—*Frank W. Sandford, "An Introduction of the Editor to His Readers,"*
The Everlasting Gospel *(January 1, 1901): 2.*

that world evangelization could be achieved only through sending out an elite band of end-time missionaries specially empowered by the Holy Spirit.

Between 1893 and 1899, he founded Shiloh, a utopian community near Durham, Maine; started the Holy Ghost and Us Bible School; published a periodical entitled *Tongues of Fire*; and held evangelistic campaigns. Sandford's authoritarian control of the community, his claims as a prophet, and his independent attitude alienated him from other radical evangelicals. In 1901, he organized the Church of the Living God, considering it a restoration of the New Testament church where the "whole truth" could be heard. On October 1 and 2, he baptized several hundred followers, including Ambrose J. Tomlinson, an early prominent leader in the Church of God (Cleveland, Tennessee). Three years later, the community had grown to nearly six hundred people. Like Dowie at Zion, Sandford dominated the leadership at Shiloh, triggering an avalanche of criticism from opponents.

On the hilltop at Shiloh, he built a large Victorian structure with flags, a prayer tower, turrets, meeting rooms, and accommodations for the residents. Sandford envisioned missionaries traveling from there to the ends of the earth. Discussion also arose over the possibility of God's bestowing known human languages. Students were sent out two by two to evangelize the United States, traveling by faith and believing that God would provide for their needs as they went. Several traveled to Kansas City, Missouri, in 1900 where they met Charles F. Parham (who later joined their group with several of his own followers).

Bible School, Home of the Holy Ghosts and Us Society, Shiloh, Maine.

A postcard from Shiloh, Maine

Sandford's mission strategy led him in 1905 to purchase two ships, a schooner and a barkentine, to expedite world evangelization. In the course of their travels around the world, Sandford and his followers sailed along the coast of many countries. Passing by each one, they prayed that God's power would be released over each country to bring about its conversion. Disaster struck, however, in 1911 when the barkentine was wrecked off the coast of Africa, and several passengers later died from starvation as they made their way back to the States aboard the schooner. Charged with manslaughter, Sandford was sentenced to ten years at the federal prison in Atlanta, Georgia.

Frank Sandford's influence on Pentecostals came from his attempts to bring about the restoration of apostolic Christianity, emphasis on the baptism and gifts of the Spirit, and priority of evangelization. Shiloh and its Holy Ghost and Us Bible School served as the model for Parham's Bible school in Topeka, Kansas.

WALTER (1864–1929) AND FRANCES BLACK (?), AND JENNIE GLASSEY (C. 1877–?)

As the end of the century grew closer, more and more radical evangelicals wondered if God would again bestow the gift of tongues as He had on the Day of Pentecost. Not only did tongues interest members of the Christian and Missionary Alliance and the community at Shiloh (an idea later repudiated by Sandford), but others prayed for this Pentecostal manifestation as well.

Although the events leading to their interest in tongues are unknown, Walter and Frances Black first spoke in tongues at a revival meeting in St. Louis, Missouri, in

1895. Black, a Canadian Baptist minister and graduate of Acadia University and Newton Theological Institution (present-day Andover Newton Theological School), and his wife were engaged in home missionary work in St. Louis. A year earlier, holding services in a rural area of Missouri, they had met Jennie Glassey, a youth of seventeen with a Scottish Presbyterian background. She told the Blacks that when she was Spirit-baptized on March 23, 1894, she had a vision in which God called her to Africa as a missionary. Upon telling God of her inability to speak the native language, she was promised that she would receive it. A few months later, Glassey moved to St. Louis, where she found a welcome in the home of the Blacks.

The promised bestowal of language occurred on July 8 and 9, 1895. On that occasion she had another vision in which the Lord taught her to read Kru (Croo) and other dialects of West Africa. At a later date, she received the "Chinese language." Appealing to Mark 16:17, the Blacks asked fellow believers to lay hands on them and pray that they too might receive. As a result, they began speaking in tongues and felt called to Africa. Together with Glassey, they went home to Nova Scotia to make arrangements for travel to Sierra Leone, West Africa.

Frank Sandford received news clippings about their testimonies given at a public meeting at the Y.M.C.A. in Amherst, Nova Scotia, but only after they had arrived in Liverpool, England, to await passage to Africa. He accepted the credibility of these

The Story of Jennie Glassey

On July 8 and 9, 1895, Jennie Glassey received a wonderful language lesson, the knowledge that had been promised her in her first vision.

The Spirit, she says, came in a vision and unrolled before her eyes a long scroll covered with strange characters. These were in the Croo language. The Spirit read them most rapidly, and she read them after Him. First the Psalms, for she was reared a Psalm singer, a Scotch Presbyterian; and then the Bible. So rapid was the reading that she feared that she would not remember all, but has done so; and speaks the Croo language with great fluency.

She can write the Khoominar language, too, and translation from the Bible in the strange characters is now in possession of the Daily News.

"Our main reason," said Mr. [Walter] Black, "for believing this to be the language of Khoominar is because the Lord has said it was."

The language has been confirmed, first by a sailor who had been at the port of Sierra Leone a dozen times, who was able to exchange a number of sentences with Miss Glassey, and he also described the place and people, which harmonized exactly with the revelation she had received. And again, by a native African, who had traveled extensively in Sierra Leone, and had a partial knowledge of the people, and recognized the strange looking writing of Khoominar, being able to translate the alphabet and understand many of the words.

Mr. and Mrs. Black are perfectly confident that they will also have the power of interpretation in due time.

— "Mission Work," Amherst (Nova Scotia) Daily News (December 9, 1895).

Letter from Shanghai

Mr. [J. Hudson Taylor] talked with us very pointedly for some ten or fifteen minutes, about the work in general, and our own intensions in regard to Thibet (sic). . . .

Then, he said, before going across the border, we must have a thorough knowledge of the Chinese language and customs, and, perhaps more important than that, a familiarity with the Mandarin system of government, and knowledge of how to deal with all grades and characters of officials, besides a good command of Thibetan. The Thibetans are quite numerous in Western China, and very easily reached. We could study the language conveniently at Wuhu, but it would take at least four years to fully equip ourselves for such a tremendous enterprise. Then he told us that in addition to the great amount of labor required, we had to meet at every step an enemy who reigned supreme in this heathen land, and who showed his terrible power here in a way we had never known in America. . . .

All this sounded rather discouraging on the surface, but as I stood there in the presence of that noble man of God, and gazed into his steady, blue eyes, while the hovering of the Holy Ghost brought us into contact with the pulse beats of God's great, loving heart, I knew, and he knew, that Jesus Christ saw no difficulties in opening Thibet to His message, save the unbelief of His so-called servants. He pointed out the overwhelming obstacles in our way, so that we might never attempt to press on in our own strength, seeing it was of no avail; but he knew as well as any one that if our Lord was leading us to Thibet, no words of his could keep us from entering it. . . .

And now I want to ask you a very serious question. Has not our Lord provided for every one of the numbered difficulties just enumerated? Does not Mark xvi: 17 cover the first, Mark xiii: 9–11 the second and third, and Luke x: 19 the fourth? While on the voyage I studied my Bible with reference to these very things, and it seems in me that I must expect these things to be literally fulfilled, or doubt God's Word . . . .

And now, dear ones, I want to say that while I am willing to shut myself up in my study, and stay there until I have thoroughly mastered both languages, if the Lord says so: still I am gladly willing to start tomorrow for Thibet, should He so direct. I am determined to stand with my Lord though every earthly friend desert me and men and devils unite in opposition. What care I for the tornadoes of opposition when I have His smile of approval.

—*William W. Simpson, "Letter from Shanghai, China,"*
Christian and Missionary Alliance Weekly
(July 1, 1892): 13–14.

reports because George B. Peck, a Boston physician and respected member of the Alliance, confirmed them to him in a letter. Sandford favorably published the reports in his *Tongues of Fire*. Later, when visiting Liverpool, he invited them to accompany him to Palestine. (The reasons for their decision to proceed to Palestine instead of Sierra Leone remain unclear.) While the Blacks began pastoring Baptist churches in North America again in 1904, virtually nothing is known about the whereabouts of Glassey.

Nevertheless, the story of the Blacks and Glassey indicate that speaking in tongues had become a hot topic among radical evangelicals. The story of Glassey in particular had a profound impact on Charles F. Parham before the January 1901 revival in Topeka, Kansas.

RECOMMENDED READING

Chappell, Paul Gale. "The Divine Healing Movement in America." PhD diss., Drew University, 1983.

Lindsay, Gordon. *John Alexander Dowie*. Dallas: Christ for the Nations, 1980.

Goff, James R., Jr., and Grant Wacker., eds. *Portraits of a Generation: Early Pentecostal Leaders*. Fayetteville: University of Arkansas Press, 2002.

Hardesty, Nancy. *Faith Cure: Divine Healing in the Holiness and Pentecostal Movements*. Peabody, MA: Hendrickson Publishers, 2003.

McGee, Gary B. "Shortcut to Language Preparation? Radical Evangelicals, Missions, and the Gift of Tongues." *International Bulletin of Missionary Research* 25 (July 2001): 118–23.

Nelson, Shirley. *Fair, Clear and Terrible: The Story of Shiloh, Maine*. Latham, N.Y.: British American, 1989.

Nienkirchen, Charles. A. B. *Simpson and the Pentecostal Movement*. Peabody, Mass.: Hendrickson Publishers, 1992.

Robert, Dana L. *Occupy Until I Come: A. T. Pierson and the Evangelization of the World*. Grand Rapids: William B. Eerdmans Publishing Co., 2003.

J. Hudson Taylor, founder of the China Inland Mission, encouraged missionaries to eat Chinese food, practice Chinese etiquette, and wear Chinese clothing. The picture below of early Alliance missionaries with their musical instruments shows some in Western garb and others in Chinese dress: William W. Simpson (l) and William Christie (r).

Sandford, Frank W. *Seven Years with God*. Mont Vernon, N.H.: Kingdom Press, 1957.

Simpson, A. B. *The Gospel of Healing*, rev. ed. Harrisburg, Pa.: Christian Publications, 1915.

Thompson, A. E. *A. B. Simpson: His Life and Work*, rev. ed. Harrisburg, Pa.: Christian Publications, 1960.

Wacker, Grant, Chris R. Armstrong, and Jay S. F. Blossom. "John Alexander Dowie: Harbinger of Pentecostal Power." In *Portraits of a Generation: Early Pentecostal Leaders*, eds. James R. Goff, Jr., and Grant Wacker, 3–19. Fayetteville, Ark.: University of Arkansas Press, 2002.

Warner, Wayne E. *Maria Woodworth-Etter: For Such a Time as This*. Gainesville, FL: Bridge-Logos, 2004.

———. *The Woman Evangelist: The Life and Times of Charismatic Evangelist Maria B. Woodworth-Etter*. Metuchen, N.J.: Scarecrow Press, 1986.

CHAPTER 3

HERALDS OF
APOSTOLIC FAITH

T he first Pentecostal revival in the twentieth century occurred in January 1901 at Bethel Bible School in Topeka, Kansas, and was led by Charles F. Parham. The Pentecostal movement (also called the "apostolic faith" or "latter rain" movement) grew slowly, remaining a small midwestern movement until 1906. In that year the revival expanded westward to Los Angeles, California, and north to Zion City, Illinois. News of events in Los Angeles and subsequent revivals prompted other revivals across the United States and Canada, Europe, and on several mission fields. Among missionaries in India, however, well versed in holiness teachings and inspired by accounts from Wales, the rise of Pentecostalism occurred three months after the beginning of the Azusa Street revival.

Periodicals such as the *Apostolic Faith* (Los Angeles), *Bridegroom's Messenger* (Atlanta, Georgia), *Evening Light and Church of God Evangel* (Cleveland, Tennessee), *Confidence* (Sunderland, England), *Cloud of Witnesses to Pentecost in India* (Bombay, India), and scores of other publications carried the news of the outpouring of the "latter rain" (Joel 2:28–29) around the world. Pentecostal revivals, led by an assortment of personalities with different cultural backgrounds, shared certain characteristics, with each revival having its own uniqueness.

Where Is the Power of the Holy Ghost?

W hy is it that in the last decade of this nineteenth century the Church of Jesus Christ exhibits such deplorable weakness that our daily papers are crowded with advertisements of what is to be done and carried on in our churches week after week to draw the people in? Have we forgotten that there is a Holy Ghost, that we must insist upon walking upon crutches when we might fly?

—*A. J. Gordon*, Student Mission Power: Report of the First International Convention of the Student Volunteer Movement for Foreign Missions, 1891 (1979), 19.

CHARLES F. PARHAM
(1873-1929)

Charles Parham considered himself to be the founder of the Apostolic Faith movement. In l905 he assumed the title "Projector of the Apostolic Faith Movement." More likely, he was the first to teach that speaking in tongues provides the initial "Bible evidence" of baptism in the Holy Spirit (later known as the "initial evidence"). Thus, his doctrinal views and the revival in Topeka are crucial for understanding the course of the Pentecostal movement.

Handbill announcing locations of services to be conducted by Charles F. Parham

Born in Muscatine, Iowa, Parham faced lifelong struggles with various physical ailments. Amid the uncertainties of life and his own precarious health (a newspaper account would later describe him as "a slight, spare man extremely delicate looking"), the young Parham sought refuge in the Christian faith with its promise of hope for a better day. In l890, he enrolled at Southwest Kansas College in Winfield to prepare for Methodist ministry. Struck with a severe bout of rheumatic fever a year later, he concluded that spiritual rebellion had caused his illness. As a result, he earnestly sought God for healing, promising to work toward his original goal if God would spare him. His health restored, Parham left college after three years of study and at nineteen launched into active ministry in the Methodist Church.

Influenced by Wesleyan-holiness theology and teachings on divine healing, and dogged by disagreements with church officials, Parham left Methodism in l895. After his marriage to Sarah Thistlethwaite, they moved to Topeka in 1898 and opened the Beth-El Healing Home. Twice a month he issued a holiness periodical entitled the *Apostolic Faith*.

Parham's doctrinal beliefs took a new turn in l899 after he learned about the story of Jennie Glassey. Deeply impressed by this and hearing of the apostolic orientation of Frank Sandford's ministry, his interest grew. Glassey's testimony helped him distinguish between the second experience of sanctification and the third for empowerment. The "third blessing" ("fire baptism" for power in Christian witness) had been proposed by the radical holiness preacher Benjamin H. Irwin and may have influenced Parham. In Parham's mind, the Holy Spirit would baptize believers and bequeath the gift of tongues (understood to be unlearned human languages) for world evangelization. This also resolved the problem of evidence for the third work, which had not been effectively settled in Irwin's teaching.

In April 1900 Parham enthusiastically announced that a Brother and Sister Hamaker had taken residence at Beth-El. When God gave them a "heathen" language, they intended to proceed to the mission field. By this time, he had begun to envision sending out missionaries endowed with the ability to preach in foreign languages and equipped with apostolic power.

In late June, Parham decided to tour several well-known holiness and healing centers, with Shiloh, Maine, as his final destination. Initial stops took him to Chicago, where he saw firsthand the activities of John Alexander Dowie, then to Cleveland, Ohio, to visit the work of J. Walter Malone, followed by time spent in Nyack, New York, at the school and faith home of A. B. Simpson. Nonetheless, the weeks in residence at Shiloh and participation in Sandford's one-month campaign in Winnipeg, Manitoba, crowned the trip. And during his stay in Shiloh, Parham said he heard speaking in tongues for the first time when several students came down from the prayer tower after their prayer vigil.

Parham's preaching now resonated with belief in divine healing, radical "fire-baptized" teaching, and expectancy of the Lord's return. And notably, through his own study of Scripture and the influence of Sandford and others, he had come to believe that God would raise up and "seal" the "bride of Christ" (Ephesians 1:13), an elite band of end-time missionaries entrusted to carry out the Great Commission. At the rapture of the Church (1 Thessalonians 4:14–17), Christ would take them with Him to heaven, thereby exempting them from the seven years of Tribulation on the earth to follow. Ordinary Christians, however, would be left to endure this harrowing time.

THE TOPEKA REVIVAL

Returning to Topeka, the twenty-seven-year-old Parham opened Bethel Bible School in October 1900, a new venture modeled after Sandford's school and housed in an elaborate, unfinished mansion known locally as "Stone's Folly." There he shared with the students that when seekers were baptized in the Holy Spirit, they would speak in (unlearned) human languages for the purpose of missionary preaching. Leaving for Kansas City to hold meetings in December, he challenged them to study the Book of Acts for themselves. Arriving back on the morning of December 31, 1900, Parham found they had come to agreement with him, namely, that according to the Book of Acts, believers spoke in tongues when baptized in the Spirit. The pattern of Spirit baptisms in Acts 2, 10, and 19, therefore, established tongues as the biblical evidence of the experience, along with Mark 16:17–18: "They will speak in new tongues."

Parham and his students then prayed to receive the full Pentecostal blessing. Although

Agnes N. Ozman's writing in Chinese
Photo courtesy of Kansas State
Historical Society

Stone's Folly, Topeka, Kansas, site of Bethel Bible School

Agnes N. Ozman [LaBerge]

having previously spoken a few words in tongues, Agnes N. Ozman [LaBerge] became the first to speak in tongues on that occasion, January 1, 1901. In a short time, Parham himself spoke in tongues and reported that the newly equipped "apostles" had spoken in French, German, Swedish, Bohemian, Chinese, Japanese, Hungarian, Bulgarian, Russian, Italian, Spanish, and Norwegian, among other languages. He wrote, "How much better would it be for our modern missionaries to obey the injunction of Jesus to tarry for the same power instead of wasting thousands of dollars, and often their lives, in the vain attempt to become conversant in almost impossible

Healing of Mary A. Arthur

After receiving prayer for her healing from Charles F. Parham at El Dorado Springs, Missouri, Mary A. Arthur of Galena, Kansas, removed her glasses and left to return to the room where she was staying.

Mary A. Arthur

Upon stepping out into the sunlight, she wondered how she would get home. In a letter she describes what followed: "I folded my handkerchief and held it over my eyes, took the hand of my little four-year-old daughter who led me to the spring. We went two blocks to get some cookies for her . . . Soon I spoke to her, but got no answer. I spoke again, but still no answer. Alarmed for her, I lifted the handkerchief off one eye; she was half a block behind me.

Seeing that she was in no danger, I started to replace the handkerchief, when I realized that my eye was open to the light and yet no pain! I looked on a white awning, at a white cloud, then, at the noonday sun. All of this brightness had formerly made me sick with pain, but now I was healed! And not only my eyes! His mighty healing power surged through my body from my head to my feet, making me feel like a new person."

[languages] which the Holy Ghost could so freely speak. Knowing all languages, He could as easily speak through us one language as another were our tongues and vocal chords fully surrendered to His domination." Public reaction followed swiftly. Newspapers in Topeka, Kansas City, and St. Louis featured the revival in a number of articles, at first curious and then negative.

Stung by criticism and disappointed that his message had not garnered more support, Parham hoped to spread the news of the latter rain across the nation. Campaigns in nearby Lawrence, Kansas, and Kansas City, Missouri, however, received only negative publicity. And while not easily disheartened (he had dreamed of expanding his operations in Topeka), the unexpected death of their baby boy on March 16 wounded him deeply. To compound the gloom, Stone's Folly was sold out from under him in July, forcing the evacuation of the property. Though the school continued briefly at another location in the city, the Parhams moved to Kansas City in the fall of 1901. Agnes Ozman returned to city mission work and did not identify with the Pentecostal movement again until 1906. After the move, Parham authored A *Voice Crying in the Wilderness* (1902), the first defense of the Pentecostal movement.

MEETINGS IN KANSAS AND MISSOURI

After attempting another Bible school in Kansas City, Parham left for Lawrence, Kansas, only to be disappointed again. In 1903 the Parhams traveled to the popular resort of El Dorado Springs, Missouri, a community known as a health spa because of the therapeutic quality of its water supply. There he prayed for the healing of Mary A. Arthur from Galena, Kansas. Her dramatic healing in one eye and other ailments drew immediate attention to his ministry. Invited to preach in Galena in October 1903, he arrived and began holding meetings. The astonishing response resulted in over eight hundred converts, a thousand reputed healings, and several hundred baptized in the Holy Spirit with speaking in other tongues. The Apostolic Faith movement had risen to new life.

Parham's camp meeting at Brunner Tabernacle in Houston, Texas. He is standing in the second row to the right near the post. Howard Goss is standing at the right end of the front row.

REVIVAL IN TEXAS

Parham then ventured to other towns in the tristate region of Kansas, Oklahoma, and Missouri. In the summer of 1905, he made Houston, Texas, his headquarters and with his growing band of workers evangelized the communities within a wide radius of the city. To instruct the growing number of workers, he opened a Bible school in December. Parham spent considerable time training his students on how to conduct street meetings and evangelistic campaigns. On occasion, he would have them wear Palestinian costumes that he had purchased to draw a crowd. Howard Goss remembered, "Our leader was a most versatile and entertaining speaker, and while explaining the [biblical significance of the] garments, he could get in enough Gospel to impress any man. It was rare indeed for anyone ever to leave while he was speaking."

For reasons unknown, no one from either Topeka or Houston immediately ventured overseas to try their newfound languages. The local extension of the Pentecostal message may have consumed all their energies and resources. Nonetheless, they found encouragement from testimonies of people fluent in foreign languages who attended the services and recognized the languages being spoken.

By April 1906, the Apostolic Faith movement had attracted as high as eight to ten thousand followers. A chain of events would link the Topeka revival with the widely heralded Azusa Street revival in Los Angeles, California, the revival in Zion, Illinois, and awakenings worldwide.

WILLIAM J. SEYMOUR
(1870-1922)

Expectancy of revival intensified in Los Angeles, California, when believers there read about the remarkable revival in Wales (1904–1905). The pastor of First Baptist Church, Joseph Smale, had traveled there to see the revival firsthand. After returning, he started regular prayer meetings for revival and began preaching on the need to seek the Holy Spirit and His gifts. After a fifteen-week diet of this preaching, the church board complained and Smale left to found First New Testament Church. Another congregation, Second Baptist Church, also experienced division when Julia W. Hutchins, an African American, and several other members embraced the holiness belief of a second work of grace. These new groups of believers continued to pray for the outpouring of the Spirit.

William J. Seymour, an African American, was born in Centerville, Louisiana, to former slaves who raised him as a Baptist. Later, while living in Cincinnati, Ohio, he came into contact with holiness teachings through Martin Wells Knapp's "God's Revivalist" movement and Daniel S. Warner's Church of God Reformation movement, otherwise known as the "Evening Light Saints." Both taught that the outpouring of the Spirit would precede the rapture of the Church.

After moving to Houston, Seymour attended a local African-American holiness congregation pastored by Lucy F. Farrow, a former governess in the Parham

One Accord

Jesus gave the church at Pentecost the great lesson of how to carry on a revival, and it would be well for every church to follow Jesus' standard of the baptism of the Holy Ghost and fire.

"And when the day of Pentecost was fully come, they were all with one accord in one place." Apostolic Faith doctrine means one accord, one soul, one heart. May God help every child of His to live in Jesus' prayer: "That they all may be one, as Thou, Father, art in Me and I in Thee; that they all may be one in us; that the world may believe that Thou hast sent Me."

William J. Seymour

—*William J. Seymour, "The Baptism of the Holy Ghost," Apostolic Faith (May 1908): 3.*

household. Farrow arranged for him to attend Parham's Bible school. There he came into contact with Charles Parham but had to listen to his lectures sitting apart from the other students outside the classroom in the hall, a situation resulting from the racial attitudes of the day. Seymour accepted Parham's view of baptism in the Holy Spirit and God's bestowal of tongues for missionary evangelism.

Neeley Terry, an African American and member of the new congregation led by Hutchins in Los Angeles, visited Houston in 1905 and heard Seymour preach. Returning home, she recommended him to Hutchins since the church was seeking a pastor. As a result, Seymour accepted the invitation to shepherd the small flock. Taking a train westward, he arrived in February 1906.

THE APOSTOLIC FAITH MISSION

Preaching to the congregation on baptism in the Spirit according to Acts 2:4 just two days after his arrival, Seymour immediately encountered resistance. On the following Sunday, March 4, he returned to the church only to find the door locked.

Demons and Tongues

Bishop Alma White of the radical holiness sect, the Pillar of Fire, and one of the most vocal opponents of the Pentecostal movement visited the Apostolic Faith Mission on Azusa Street in Los Angeles to view the events there firsthand. In her book Demons and Tongues, she offered the following assessment: "There is a way which seemeth right unto a man, but the end thereof are the ways of death" (Prov. 14:12)

The above scripture came to my mind as I thought of those who have been caught in the satanic Tongues delusion, which, for a few years after it was started in the old Azusa Street Mission in Los Angeles, swept like a cylone around the world . . . deceiving almost the very elect.

I know that through disobedience or refusal to consecrate themselves to God many have lost their spiritual bearings and ever since have been wandering in the darkness of this world.

Many of the Tongues adherents are persons of this character."

Apostolic Faith Mission, site of the Azusa Street Revival in Los Angeles

Condemnation also came from the Holiness Church Association with which the congregation had affiliation.

Undaunted, Seymour, staying at the home of Edward S. Lee, accepted the latter's invitation to hold Bible studies and prayer meetings there. After this, he went to the home of Richard and Ruth Asberry at 214 North Bonnie Brae Street. Five weeks later, Lee became the first to speak in tongues. Seymour then shared Lee's testimony at a gathering on North Bonnie Brae and soon many began to speak in tongues.

Word of these events traveled quickly in both the African-American and Caucasian communities. For several nights, speakers preached on the porch to the crowds on the street below. Believers from Hutchins's mission, First New Testament Church, and various holiness congregations prayed for the Pentecostal baptism. Finally, after the front porch collapsed, the group rented the former Stevens African Methodist Episcopal (AME) Church at 312 Azusa Street in early April. A Los Angeles newspaper referred to it as a "tumbledown shack." This old, two-story frame structure in the industrial section of the city had more recently served as a livery stable and tenement house. Discarded lumber and plaster littered the large, barnlike room on the ground floor.

The meetings at the "Apostolic Faith Mission" quickly caught the attention of the newspapers due to the unusual nature of the services. Between 300 and 350 people could get into the building, with many others occasionally forced to stand outside. The revival advanced slowly during the summer months, with only 150 people receiving "the gift of the Holy Ghost and the Bible evidence."

Enthusiastic worship marked the services with singing (a cappella at first); testimonies; prayer for the sick; shouting the praises of God; altar calls for those seeking salvation, sanctification, and Spirit baptism; singing in tongues; preaching; times of silence; and persons falling down "under the power." Some received visions and calls to the mission field, with all expecting the imminent return of Christ.

Accounts of the revival spread quickly across North America to Europe and other parts of the world as participants traveled, testified, and published articles in sympathetic holiness publications. Particularly influential was the Apostolic Faith (Los Angeles), issued occasionally between September 1906 and May 1908 by Seymour and Clara Lum. Distributed without charge, thousands of ministers and laypeople received copies at home and overseas. Five thousand copies of the first edition (September 1906) were printed, and by l907 the pressrun reached forty thousand.

Most who visited the mission came to receive the empowerment of Spirit baptism and be equipped with new languages. The Apostolic Faith reported: "God is solving the missionary problem, sending out new-tongued missionaries on the apostolic faith line, without purse or scrip [Matthew 10:9–10, KJV], and the Lord is going before them preparing the way." One missionary, Bernt Bernsten, traveled all the way from North China to investigate the happenings after reading the Apostolic Faith and hearing that the latter rain was falling. Missionaries home on furloughs also attended and spoke in tongues, sometimes identifying the languages spoken by the recipients.

For a short time, African Americans, Hispanics, Caucasians, and others prayed and sang together, creating a dimension of equality that allowed men, women, and children to have fellowship collectively and participate in the worship as led by the Spirit. An eyewitness, Frank Bartleman said, "The 'color line' was washed away in the blood." Although several people could be considered leaders, the best known was the unassuming William J. Seymour. Before long, other Pentecostal congregations grew in the city.

Missionaries who went abroad from the Apostolic Faith Mission included G. W. and Daisy Batman, Lucy Farrow, and Julia W. Hutchins (who joined the revival) to

Leaders at Asuza Street—first row seated (L-R): ? Evans, Hiram Smith, William Seymour, Clara Lum. Standing (L-R): Unidentified, ? Evans, (credited as first recipient of Holy Spirit baptism at Azusa), Jennie Moore (Mrs. William Seymour), Glenn A. Cook, Florence Crawford, Unidentified, ? Prince, Crawford's daughter seated in H. Smith's lap. Inset: Rachael Sizelove.

Liberia; George and Mary Berg, A. G. and Lillian Garr, and Lizzie Frazer to India; Louise Condit, Lucy M. Leatherman, and Andrew Johnson to Jerusalem; Samuel and Ardella Mead to Angola; and Ansel H. and Etta Post to Egypt.

REVIVAL IN ZION CITY

Having watched the growth of the Apostolic Faith movement, Parham recognized the need for more direction and appointed several individuals, including Seymour (West Coast field director), to assist in the oversight. Despite his harsh criticisms of church organizations, the Apostolic Faith movement began to issue credentials to evangelists and others; Seymour received his in July 1906.

While Parham had planned to visit Los Angeles in September, he canceled his plans and went instead to Zion City, Illinois. He certainly could not have foreseen that the Azusa Street revival would have a far greater global impact than any other revival of the twentieth century. Parham's strategy focused on gaining the leadership of Zion City now that John Alexander Dowie had lost control. With international connections (e.g., South Africa and Australia) and an international following of over twenty-five thousand, Dowie's abandoned sheep offered Parham the potential of seeing the Apostolic Faith movement encircle the world at long last. In the meantime, Dowie's former assistant, Wilbur Glenn Voliva, had made important strides toward succeeding him, even though his support fell short of unanimity.

Parham's meetings attracted a following of over three hundred people and made him a contender for Dowie's mantle. The revival that began in September significantly influenced the future of Pentecostalism. The list of those baptized in the Spirit included future leaders and pastors who joined the Assemblies of God, among them, F. F. Bosworth, F. A. Graves, Marie Burgess, D. C. O. Opperman, E. N. Richey, and Fred Vogler. The missionaries who left Zion for the "regions beyond" included John G. Lake (South Africa) and Edith Baugh (India). The revival proved to be among the

The Heavenly Anthem

One of the most remarkable features of the Apostolic Faith movement is what is rightly termed the heavenly anthem. No one but those who are baptized with the Holy Ghost are able to join in.

On Sunday night, Dec. 9, a sister sang in the Gujerathi language of India, the first four verses of the 8th chapter of Solomon's Songs. It was a song such as a bride might sing of the bridegroom. "Awake not my beloved." It was most blessed and beautiful to notice as the Holy Spirit sang through the dear sister; it brought a great wave of heavenly fire and blessing to those present.

It is the harmony of heaven and the Holy Ghost that puts music in the voices that are untrained.

—*"The Heavenly Anthem,"* The Apostolic Faith
(January 1907): 3.

Holy Ghost Meetings

Brother Seymour generally sat behind two empty shoe boxes, one on top of the other. He usually kept his head inside the top one during the meeting, in prayer. There was no pride there. The services ran almost continuously. Seeking souls could be found under the power almost any hour, night and day. The place was never closed nor empty. The people came to meet God. He was always there. Hence a continuous meeting. The meeting did not depend on the human leader. God's presence became more and more wonderful. In that old building, with its low rafters and bare floors, God took strong men and women to pieces, and put them together again, for His glory. It was a tremendous overhauling process: Pride and self-assertion, self importance and self-esteem, could not survive there. The religious ego preached its own funeral sermon quickly.

No subjects or sermons were announced ahead of time, and no special speakers for such an hour. No one knew what might be coming, what God would do. All was spontaneous, ordered of the Spirit. We wanted to hear from God, through whoever He might speak. We had no "respect of persons." The rich and educated were the same as the poor and ignorant, and found a much harder death to die. We only recognized God: All were equal. No flesh might glory in His presence. He could not use the self-opinionated. Those were Holy Ghost meetings, led of the Lord. It had to start in poor surroundings, to keep out the selfish, human element. All came down in humility together, at His feet. They all looked alike, and had all things in common in that sense at least. The rafters were low, the tall must come down. By the time they got to "Azusa" they were humbled, ready for the blessing. The fodder was thus placed for the lambs, not for giraffes. All could reach it.

We were delivered right there from ecclesiastical hierarchism and abuse. We wanted God. When we first reached the meeting we avoided as much as possible human contact and greeting. We wanted to meet God first. We got our head under some bench in the corner in prayer, and met men only in the Spirit, knowing them "after the flesh" no more. The meetings started themselves, spontaneously, in testimony, praise and worship. The testimonies were never hurried by a call for "pop corn." We had no prearranged programme to be jammed through on time. Our time was the Lord's. We had real testimonies, from fresh heart-experience. Otherwise, the shorter the testimonies, the better. A dozen might be on their feet at one time, trembling under the mighty power of God. We did not have to get our cue from some leader. And we were free from lawlessness. We were shut up to God in prayer in the meetings, our minds on Him. All obeyed God, in meekness and humility. In honor we "preferred one another." The Lord was liable to burst through anyone. We prayed for this continually. Someone would finally get up anointed for the message. All seemed to recognize this and gave way. It might be a child, a woman, or a man. It might be from the back seat, or from the front. It made no difference.

—*Frank Bartleman*, How Pentecost Came to Los Angeles *(1925), 58–60.*

Taken from *Azusa Street* by Frank Bartleman, ©1982 by Whitaker House (www. whitakerhouse.com), used by permission, p. 56–58.

most successful and far-reaching events in Parham's ministry. Before long, however, his theory about tongues came under sharp attack from Voliva and the newspapers.

PARHAM'S BREACH WITH SEYMOUR

After the revival had begun in Zion City, Parham left for California in October, an absence that proved to be a tactical mistake. His visit with Seymour and the congregation at Azusa Street had a twofold agenda: first, to consolidate the faithful there within the wider network of Apostolic Faith believers, and second, to correct abuses that had been reported. As it happened, the emotional worship and particularly the mingling of whites and blacks together deeply offended Parham. He laid the blame at Seymour's feet. Like most white Americans at the turn of the century, he firmly believed in the racial and cultural superiority of his race.

Although paternally concerned for the spiritual needs of African Americans, he did not believe in racial equality and feared the mixing of the races. Thus, upon entering the Apostolic Faith Mission, he was appalled by the emotionalism. Making his way to Seymour and greeting him, he turned to the audience and said, "God is sick at His stomach!" In his opinion, God could hardly be "a self-respecting God if He could stand for any such animalism as was in progress there."

He also questioned the authenticity of the tongues spoken because they sounded more like babbling than known languages. The majority of the Azusa faithful remained loyal to Seymour after Parham left with some of the people to establish a rival mission. Within a few years of its beginning, the congregation of the Apostolic Faith Mission became predominantly black with Seymour remaining as pastor.

In later years, Seymour abandoned the doctrine of tongues as initial evidence of Spirit baptism. The differences which arose between Seymour and the white brethren and their eventual break may well have contributed to his decision to reject tongues as initial evidence as well as to exclude white leadership from the Azusa mission. Seymour interpreted their behavior as contradictory. His change in doctrine is set forth in a 1907 issue of Apostolic Faith: "Tongues are one of the signs that go with every baptized person, but it is not the real evidence of the baptism in the every day life. Your life must measure with the fruits of the Spirit. If you get angry, or speak evil, or backbite, I care not how many tongues you may have, you have not the baptism

Azusa Street in Later Years

Having left its mark on the development of worldwide Pentecostalism, the Apostolic Faith Mission in Los Angeles went into decline. By 1915, when William Seymour wrote The Doctrines and Discipline of the Azusa Street Apostolic Faith Mission, the congregation had dwindled to a handful of African Americans. To avoid further racial conflict, the document notably excludes whites from serving as "directors" or trustees of the mission. Neither does it mention the doctrine of initial evidence. After Seymour's death in 1922, his wife, Jennie, served as pastor until her health failed (d. 1936). The building was torn down in 1931.

with the Holy Spirit." This accent on personal holiness—a reflection of Wesley's credo that "perfect love" should characterize Christian behavior—represented a widely held conviction across the Pentecostal movement, both by those who believed in initial evidence and those who did not.

Parham's importance in the Movement fell drastically after he and another man were charged with sodomy in the summer of 1907 in San Antonio, Texas. The details are sketchy and the debate continues over what really happened. The Texas authorities finally dropped the charges and the newspaper announcement—the only remaining source of information on the action—gave no explanation. Parham declared his innocence and said his opponents, particularly Wilbur Glenn Voliva, framed him. In the months that followed, innuendo and rumor, and in particular Voliva's negative press coverage against him, destroyed his reputation. Nevertheless, those closest to him—his wife, children, and a loyal cadre of supporters—unflinchingly maintained his innocence, an affirmation of his personal integrity by those who knew him best that merits consideration.

Ironically, the "Projector of the Apostolic Faith Movement" spent the last two decades of his life in obscurity with a few thousand loyal followers. While soon forgotten, his legacy—particularly his theological connection of tongues as initial evidence of Spirit baptism—increased as time passed.

Through the testimonies of individuals, letters, and publications, Pentecostalism expanded rapidly. In addition to Houston, Los Angeles, and Zion City, centers of revival sprang up across North America and overseas. Belief in the soon coming of Christ and the bestowal of languages intertwined as themes in each of them. Many emerging leaders, both clergy and laity, stirred the faithful to seek for Spirit baptism in order to more effectively witness for Christ.

IVEY G. CAMPBELL
(1874-1918)

As in the holiness movement, Pentecostal women played significant roles. Whether as missionaries, evangelists, pastors, or founders of Bible institutes, their footprints can be found across Pentecostalism. One of the earliest evangelists to leave the Azusa Street revival to spread the news of the outpouring of the Spirit was Ivey Campbell, originally from East Liverpool, Ohio, a town on the Ohio River across from West Virginia.

Campbell became a seamstress by profession. When a holiness evangelist visited East Liverpool in 1901, she attended the services and testified to being sanctified. Leaving the Presbyterian church she had been raised in, she helped in the founding of the Broadway Mission. While in Los Angeles in 1906 to visit relatives, she attended meetings at the Apostolic Faith Mission where she was baptized in the Spirit.

Campbell returned to Ohio in the late fall and began holding services in December at the Christian and Missionary Alliance Church in Akron (later First Assembly of God). From there she preached in East Liverpool, Cleveland, and western Pennsylvania. Since

Converts Claim Strange Powers

Sect with Gift of Tongues Performing Alleged Miracles and Attracting Wide Attention. East Liverpool Girl As Its Leader

In the principal cities of Ohio are being held meetings of a new sect, which although not entirely new, is introducing some very queer beliefs and powers. The spread of the Pentecostal wave is wonderful, and Cleveland, Alliance, Akron and other cities have been thoroughly aroused. The first person, it is believed, to have received the power, the so-called "gift of tongues," was a woman—of course a woman—Miss Iva [sic] Campbell, of this city.

Ivey G. Campbell

Miss Campbell went to Los Angeles to the home of relatives a year ago. It was while there attending the mission services she began using the strange languages fluently. . . . . She says when she first received the Pentecost, or Holy Ghost, God entered her body and heart, and she felt her head and sides widening, as it were. "I felt myself giving over to the new faith," said she, "and then God began speaking to me in a strange language. I did not remember what was said, but I could understand and afterward I found it was the Chinese and African languages I was speaking."

— *"Converts Claim Strange Powers,"* The Evening Review *(January 7, 1907)*: 1.

she was the first to bring the Pentecostal message to East Liverpool, some observers thought that Campbell had started the Movement. She was also a featured speaker at the 1907 camp meeting at the "Missionary Home" in Alliance, Ohio, a Bible school and campgrounds directed by Levi R. Lupton, a holiness Quaker turned Pentecostal. This revival, attended by more than seven hundred people, had a marked influence on the spread of Pentecostalism in the midwestern part of the United States.

Little is known of her later activities, except that she eventually returned to Los Angeles and that her health had declined by 1912. Ivey Campbell represents many lesser-known people—in her case a layperson—who carried the news of the latter rain across the continent.

ELIZABETH V. BAKER
(C. 1849-1915)

Hearing of the revival in Los Angeles, believers at the Elim Tabernacle and Rochester Bible Training School in Rochester, New York, pondered for a year the meaning of the Pentecostal baptism with tongues. Through study and prayer, they became convinced of its validity and sought for it themselves in the summer of 1907. The Elim Faith Home, Elim Publishing House, Elim Tabernacle, and Rochester Bible Training School were founded by the five daughters of Methodist pastor James Duncan: Elizabeth V. Baker, the eldest sister; Mary E. Work; Nellie A. Fell; Susan A. Duncan; and Harriet "Hattie" M. Duncan.

Elizabeth Baker experienced considerable grief in her early years, first from an abusive husband and second from a severe throat condition, from which she was healed sometime around 1881. Her second marriage to a medical doctor led to separation because of his opposition to her participation in the healing movement. Baker's doctrinal beliefs were nurtured by A. B. Simpson, A. J. Gordon, and the faith teachings of George Müller, the famous Christian philanthropist of Bristol, England.

Elizabeth V. Baker

Baker's ministry in Rochester began with the founding of the Elim Faith Home in 1895. Foreign missions also held a prominent place in their work. Following the Pentecostal revival in 1907, the Bible training school produced a number of Pentecostal leaders and missionaries, some of whom later held leadership positions in the Assemblies of God.

GASTON B. CASHWELL
(1862-1916)

Word of the outpouring of the Spirit in Los Angeles quickly reached the South where several preexisting denominations turned Pentecostal. Although there were many contacts between participants at Azusa Street and friends in the South, Gaston B. Cashwell became the "apostle of Pentecost" to that region.

Early Scandinavian Pentecostals

A spiritual awakening among Scandinavian settlers in Minnesota and the Dakotas in the 1890s and 1900s spawned a number of congregations that practiced speaking in tongues and healing. These early revivals originated in Scandinavian pietism. In Scandinavia, believers attended the state church on Sunday and held their own home prayer meetings during the week. In America, immigrants established their own churches without the supervision of the church hierarchy, bringing the fervency of the prayer meetings into the regular services. Leaders in these plains revivals—some of which predated the Topeka and Azusa Street revivals—soon identified with the emerging Pentecostal movement. Scandinavian free mission evangelist Carl M. "Daddy" Hanson first observed tongues-speech during services in Grafton, North Dakota, in 1895 and received the gift himself four years later.

Hanson, ordained in 1909 by Chicago pastor William Durham, was elected in 1922 to serve as the first Chairman of the North Central district (AG). The earliest-known Pentecostal missionary from North America, Mary Johnson, was the product of a Pentecostal revival among Swedish-Americans in Fargo, North Dakota, and Moorhead, Minnesota. Johnson, along with Ida Andersson, who spoke in tongues several years later, departed for Durban, South Africa, in late 1904. While the Azusa Street revival became the focal point of early Pentecostalism, prior revivals, including those in Minnesota and the Dakotas, provided precedents and leaders for the emerging movement.

—Darrin J. Rodgers

Born in North Carolina, he became a Methodist minister in his youth. In 1903 he left the church to join Ambrose B. Crumpler's Pentecostal Holiness Church, a small denomination in which he quickly became well known as an evangelist. Hearing of the happenings in Los Angeles in 1906, he borrowed money for the train fare. Above all else, Cashwell wanted to receive the baptism in the Holy Spirit with speaking in tongues. After arriving, his ingrained racial prejudice against African Americans made

Gaston B. Cashwell
Photo courtesy of International Pentecostal Holiness Church Archives and Research Center

sitting under Seymour's preaching and the notion of asking blacks to lay hands on him to receive Spirit baptism especially difficult. However, after a "self-crucifixion" of dying to old prejudices, he asked Seymour and several African-American youths to lay hands on him in prayer.

Soon after, while listening to Clara Lum read reports of the outpouring of the Spirit in other places, Cashwell began to speak in tongues. He returned home in December 1906 and in January began holding services in Dunn, North Carolina. The month-long revival, held in a former tobacco warehouse, became the "Azusa Street" of the South. Most of the holiness ministers in the area spoke in tongues. As a result, the Pentecostal Holiness Church, the Fire-Baptized Holiness Church, and the Cape Fear Conference of the Free Will Baptist Church became Pentecostal, the latter taking the name Pentecostal Free Will Baptist Church. Cashwell led several prominent leaders into the experience, including Joseph H. King, Nickels J. Holmes, as well as Mack M. Pinson and Henry G. Rodgers, who later contributed to the founding of the Assemblies of God. In January 1908, he traveled to Cleveland, Tennessee, at the invitation of Ambrose J. Tomlinson, to preach the Pentecostal message. Tomlinson and other ministers in the Church of God then became Pentecostals and added their organization to the ranks of the new Movement.

RECOMMENDED READING

The Azusa Street Papers. Foley, Ala.: Harvest Publications, 1997. (Includes a reprint of the issues of the Los Angeles *Apostolic Faith*, 1906–1908.)

Baker, Elizabeth V., et al. *Chronicles of a Faith Life*. 2d ed. Rochester, N.Y.: Elim Publishing Co., c. 1926.

Bartleman, Frank. *Azusa Street: The Roots of Modern-Day Pentecost*. South Plainfield, N.J.: Bridge Publishing, 1980.

Beacham, Doug. *Azusa East: The Life and Times of G. B. Cashwell*. Franklin Springs, GA: LSR Publications, 2006.

Creech, Joe. "Visions of Glory: The Place of the Azusa Street Revival in Pentecostal History." *Church History* 68 (September 1996): 405–424.

Goff, James R., Jr. *Fields White Unto Harvest: Charles F. Parham and the Missionary Origins of Pentecostalism*. Fayetteville: University of Arkansas Press, 1988.

Martin, Larry. *The Life and Ministry of William J. Seymour*. Joplin, Mo.: Christian Life Books, 1999.

Parham, Charles F. *A Voice Crying in the Wilderness*. 2d ed. Baxter Springs, Kans.: Apostolic Faith Bible College, 1910.

Robeck, Cecil M., Jr. "Florence Crawford: Apostolic Faith Pioneer." In *Portraits of a Generation: Early Pentecostal Leaders*, edited by James R. Goff, Jr., and Grant Wacker, 219–235. Fayetteville, Ark.: University of Arkansas Press, 2002.

———. "William J. Seymour and the 'Bible Evidence.'" In *Initial Evidence: Historical and Biblical Perspectives on the Pentecostal Doctrine of Spirit Baptism*, ed. Gary B. McGee, 72–95. Peabody, Mass.: Hendrickson Publishers, 1991.

———. *The Azusa Street Mission and Revival: The Birth of the Global Pentecostal Movement*. Nashville: Thomas Nelson, 2006.

Stanley, Susie Cunningham, *Feminist Pillar of Fire: The Life of Alma White*. Cleveland, Oh.: Pilgrim Press, 1993.

Synan, Vinson. *The Holiness-Pentecostal Tradition: Charismatic Movements in the Twentieth Century*. Grand Rapids: William B. Eerdmans Publishing Co., 1997.

Walling, Aaron. "An Evaluation of the Apostolic Faith." *Assemblies of God Heritage* 19 (summer 1999):10–15.

CHAPTER 4

DISAGREEMENTS AMONG THE SAINTS

I n the years from Topeka to Azusa Street (1901–1906), Charles F. Parham's leadership and doctrinal views dominated the young Pentecostal movement. Like
other holiness preachers, he taught salvation by grace alone, sanctification as
a second work of grace distinct from conversion, baptism in the Holy Spirit for
empowerment as a third experience, divine healing, and the return of Christ. Speaking in tongues, however, set Pentecostals apart from other Christians more than
anything else.

As Pentecostal revivals became widespread in the United States in 1906 and
1907, believers naturally came from more diverse backgrounds. Wesleyan-Holiness believers were not the only ones to attend these meetings. Baptists, Presbyterians, and members of the Christian and Missionary Alliance alike were baptized
in the Holy Spirit. The first dispute among them—though generally unrelated to
denominational background—concerned the value of the Book of Acts for building doctrine. How believers felt about this naturally affected their doctrine of
speaking in tongues as initial evidence. Parham and the majority of Pentecostals
believed that the pattern in the Book of Acts laid the scriptural foundation for the
doctrine.

Unlike the matter of tongues, the second dispute, the nature of sanctification, did
stem from differing church backgrounds. Those with backgrounds in the Reformed
tradition believed that sanctification occurred first at conversion, when a believer
was made to be "in Christ" (Ephesians 1:3), and then progressed from there. This
challenged Wesleyan-Holiness thought that sanctification was instantaneous and
complete. Of course, with Pentecostalism now made up of holiness Pentecostals and
"finished work" Pentecostals, debate followed. This debate, known as the "finished
work of Calvary," came to a head in 1910.

In 1913, a third major dispute arose over the nature of the Godhead; this chapter,
however, addresses only the first two. Naturally, prominent leaders became directly
involved, including two missionaries, a Bible school teacher who also served as a
denominational official, and a pastor in Chicago.

MINNIE F. ABRAMS
(1859-1912)

In the last two hundred years, thousands of single women have dedicated themselves to foreign missions. One such individual, Minnie F. Abrams, left Minneapolis in 1887 to go to India as a missionary under appointment of the Woman's Foreign Missionary Society of the Methodist Church. In the large western coastal city of Bombay (now Mumbai) she helped establish and supervise an orphanage and a school for Christian girls.

But Abrams eventually left her position to begin tent meetings in rural districts where Indians had not been reached with the gospel. While staying near Poona (eighty miles southeast of Bombay) in 1899, she felt directed of the Lord to offer her services at the Mukti ("salvation") Mission at nearby Kedgaon. Founded and directed by the world famous Pandita Ramabai, a high-caste Hindu convert to Christianity, the mission housed hundreds of widows and orphans and provided relief to famine victims. Called the "George Müller of India" because of her faith in God and her charitable ministries, Ramabai needed help in administering the operation and quickly accepted Abrams's offer.

Influenced by the higher life teachings of the Keswick conferences in England, Ramabai, along with other Christians, prayed for the outpouring of the Spirit. In this, she was joined by Abrams, whose views on the sanctified life reflected a distinctly Wesleyan orientation. After word reached India in 1904 telling of the revival in Wales, revival broke out the next year at mission stations in the Khassia Hills of northeast India staffed by Welsh Presbyterian missionaries. Believers there began intensely confessing their sins in "prayer storms" (hours spent in fervent and often loud prayer that pushed aside the traditional order of worship). Eventually the revival spread to Alliance, Anglican, Baptist, Lutheran, Methodist, and Presbyterian mission stations across India. Besides confessions of sin and prayer storms (the most striking features), there occurred dancing, visions, dreams, prophecies, repayment of debts, and even miraculous provisions of food.

Pandita Ramabai

In one of the most celebrated events of the revival, the matron of a girls' dormitory at the Mukti Mission rushed to the quarters of Abrams at 3:30 in the morning on June 29. One of the girls had been baptized with the "Holy Ghost and fire." She related how she had seen fire on the girl and ran to the other side of the room for a pail of water. As she was about to pour it on the girl, she realized that the girl was not on fire. When Abrams arrived, the other girls were crying because they too felt the burning sensation—the purifying power of the Holy Spirit. Soon they confessed and repented of their sins. Before long the mission became a center for revival in South India.

The Object of Holy Ghost Baptism

There is a great deal of misunderstanding about the baptism in the Holy Ghost. Some people have seen the outward manifestation and they think that is the baptism. Now God wants to give you and me the baptism in the Holy Ghost, not that we may be able in the Name of Jesus to speak the word and see souls healed, not that we may speak in tongues, not that we may interpret, not that we may do this great work or that great work that will seem a great thing in the eyes of people, but He wants us to have power to witness so that souls will be brought under the power of repentance

Minnie F. Abrams

and turn to God. Perhaps the witnessing will be in the kitchen, perhaps in the shop or on the street, and perhaps it will be where most people will never pay any attention to it, but He wants you to have power to lead souls to Christ. That is the great object.

What are you seeking the baptism in the Holy Ghost for? Is it for your own enjoyment? Is it that you may have this wonderful experience of ecstasy and joy, and live constantly in the joy of the Lord? Ah no, that is not it. We want power to witness to the death and resurrection of our Lord Jesus Christ throughout all the earth, beginning at Jerusalem, so that souls will come under the power of repentance, and believe on the Lord Jesus Christ and be saved. Let us get the object in view first.

—Minnie F. Abrams, "The Object of the Baptism in the Holy Spirit,"
Latter Rain Evangel *(May 1911): 101–102.*

In the midst of this, Abrams traveled extensively across the country, stirring the faithful to seek the baptism of "burning fire." For a time in some places, people believed that the burning sensation represented evidence of Spirit baptism, much like Maria B. Woodworth-Etter viewed the significance of people falling down ("slain in the Spirit") in her tent meetings. In May 1906, Abrams wrote Baptism of the Holy Ghost and Fire, which two Christian newspapers and a Methodist mission periodical serialized.

The Pentecostal movement in India has special significance since its origins closely parallel those in North America. Christians there hoped as well for the restoration of signs and wonders and the gifts of the Spirit so they might see a harvest of souls on the otherwise "stony ground" of India.

Pentecostal phenomena (e.g., visions, dreams, prophecies) were present from the beginning of the revival. The more radical notion of speaking in tongues, however, seems not to have appeared until 1906, following a spring conference sponsored by the Church Missionary Society (Anglican) at Aurangabad in South India. Abrams was the featured speaker, and she brought with her a "prayer band" of young women from the Mukti Mission. Following the conference, several Indian girls returned to their boarding school in Bombay, where their testimonies triggered another revival in July. Three girls, including a nine year old named Sarah, spoke in tongues, one of them praying in the Spirit for the conversion of Libya. Thus the Pentecostal movement in India began independently of the Movement in America.

When a copy of the Los Angeles *Apostolic Faith* reached the Mukti Mission in December 1906, Ramabai and Abrams acknowledged that they had not yet received the Spirit accompanied by the gift of tongues. So they began seeking this work of the Spirit. Both known and unknown tongues followed, some at the mission speaking for the first time in English, Sanscrit, and Kanarese. Significantly, no mention was made of preaching in these languages.

Reflecting on tongues as one of the signs in Mark 16:17–18, Abrams wrote: "We have not received the full Pentecostal baptism of the Holy Ghost until we are able not only to bear the fruit of the Spirit, but to exercise the gifts of the Spirit. . . . It was these gifts of the Spirit attending the preaching of the gospel which enabled the early church to spread the knowledge of the gospel and establish the Christian church so rapidly."

Given the international fame of Ramabai and the widespread respect for Abrams, many observers accepted the tongues at Mukti as genuine or politely restrained their criticisms. These manifestations of the Spirit gained further credibility in America due to sympathetic newspaper coverage. The *Chicago Daily News* carried the story through reporter William T. Ellis, who had visited the mission in July 1907.

Unlike Abrams, Pandita Ramabai never spoke in tongues. At the same time, she warmly endorsed the experience as a gift of the Spirit. Neither woman, however, identified tongues as essential to Spirit baptism, although some of their colaborers at Mukti did. Abrams believed that those baptized in the Spirit normally spoke in tongues; however, she hesitated to declare it indispensable for the Spirit's infilling. Her tentativeness may have been in response to her critics—some held her responsible for those who identified the burning sensation as essential to baptism. But more than likely, any particular manifestation of the Spirit was outweighed by her strong Wesleyan view that perfect love and the fruit of the Spirit constituted infallible proof of the Spirit's work.

Like others in the early years of the Pentecostal movement, Abrams struggled with understanding how the gift of tongues could function without the gift of interpretation. Given the missionary purpose of the languages received, what was the role of interpretation? And what about unknown tongues that no one could identify? This explains why her revised edition of *Baptism of the Holy Ghost and Fire* (issued in December 1906) refers only to the gift of tongues and lacks Parham's ironclad insistence on them.

In any case, shortly after her book first came out, she sent a copy to Willis and Mary Hoover, Methodist missionaries in Valparaiso, Chile. Mary had been Abrams's schoolmate at Lucy Rider Meyer's Chicago Training School for City, Home, and Foreign Missions, a training school for Methodist deaconesses. As a result, it made a vital contribution to the birth of "Pentecostal" Methodism in Chile.

To promote the ministry in India, Abrams itinerated in the U.S. in 1908, visiting important centers of Pentecostal activity, including the Upper Room Mission in Los Angeles and the Stone Church in Chicago. Burdened to evangelize unreached peoples in north India, she gathered seven single women to return as missionaries with her. Two remained at the Mukti Mission, while the others followed her in evangelistic work. Having had a premonition of her death in two years, she left the United States fully aware that her time was short. Two years to the day of her arrival in Bombay, Abrams died from malaria. Leading missionary periodicals praised her selfless labors and contributions to the revival in India in obituary notices, an unusual honor for one who had so closely identified with the Pentecostal movement.

Willis and Mary Hoover and their children

ALFRED G. GARR
(1874-1944)

One of the best-known Pentecostals in the first half of the twentieth century, "A. G." Garr, served at different times as a pastor, missionary, and evangelist. Converted in a Baptist church, he felt called to the ministry. To prepare, he enrolled at Center College in Danville, Kentucky (where he was born), and later at Asbury College in nearby Wilmore, the latter a Wesleyan-holiness school. There he met and married Lillian Anderson, and together they left for California to pastor the Metropolitan Holiness Church in Los Angeles.

Hearing of the Azusa Street revival, Garr attended its services and was baptized in the Spirit on June 16, 1906, the first white pastor of any denomination in that area to have this experience. When the elders in his congregation did not accept the new teaching, he resigned. But while still in the city, Garr practiced his newly acquired "Bengali" and Lillian her "Tibetan" in preparation for missionary service. After hearing of his plans to travel abroad as a missionary, the believers at Azusa Street took an offering and gave him one hundred dollars for expenses.

Garr's confidence that he had received Bengali and should venture to India was the best-known attempt to apply Parham's teaching on tongues. When they arrived in Calcutta in December, they found a conference of missionaries underway. Invited to a prayer meeting of these missionaries and other Christian workers, they readily accepted. On the next day, Susan Easton, head of the Woman's Union Missionary Society (WUMS) work in Calcutta, opened the doors of the Mission House on Dhurmatullah Street for

Exterior view of Carey Baptist Chapel, Calcutta, India

the Garrs to report on "God's visitation in America." At an evening service they again recounted the events of the outpouring of the Spirit in Los Angeles. Afterward, Pastor C. H. Hook of the historic Carey Baptist Chapel (built by the noted Baptist missionary William Carey) at Lal Bazaar in the city asked them to begin preaching "this blessed 'Truth'" at his church. Pentecostal meetings began there on January 13, 1907.

Garr soon discovered, however, that he could not speak Bengali. Despite the disappointment, he continued to teach tongues as the initial evidence of Spirit baptism even though they might be unknown [i.e., "the tongues . . . of angels" (1 Corinthians 13:1)].

For several weeks, the revival continued at Carey Baptist Chapel before moving to a rented house. Garr was severely criticized by others who labeled him a fanatic. The Methodist press took him to task for insisting on tongues as evidence of baptism in the Spirit. Furthermore, when people were engaged in tongues-speech, one observer said it sounded more like "barnyard cackle" than a human language. Since the revival of 1905–1906 had already dramatically affected Methodist missionaries and believers, many wondered how speaking in tongues could add to what the Spirit had previously accomplished.

In Garr's estimation, the outpouring of the Spirit on the Day of Pentecost when all of the disciples spoke in tongues certified the importance of this manifestation for

Baptized in the Spirit at the Azusa Street Mission, A. G. Garr served as a Pentecostal missionary in India and Hong Kong beginning in 1907.

Tongues, the Evidence

Brethren, God is eager to give you the baptism with the Holy Ghost and fire; but the first thing you must do in order to be able to receive it is to find out that you have not got it. Be honest with yourself and God, and ask yourself the question: What evidence have I that I am baptized with the Holy Ghost? Does your evidence consist in blessing that rests upon your preaching and praying, or in power to cast out devils, or in power to heal the sick? Do you not see that these manifestations, precious as they are, are not the evidence of the baptism with the Holy Ghost? We find that all these spiritual gifts were exercised by the saints in the Bible prior to Pentecost. I have been unable to find any record that any one of the Old or New Testament saints had the gift of tongues until after they had received the baptism. Another fact is worthy of note: where it is recorded that men tarried for the promise of the Father, it is not stated that they were seeking tongues, but they were seeking the baptism with the Holy Ghost only. Yet God gave them the gift of speaking in tongues in every case where the baptism was received; and they received it immediately after they were baptized with the Holy Ghost.

—A. G. Garr, "Tongues, the Bible Evidence,"
Cloud of Witnesses to Pentecost in India (September 1907): 43–44.

the entire Church. With the disappointment in tongues for preaching, he might have been tempted to discard the phenomenon altogether, but that did not happen due to the transforming nature of the experience. In the context of Bible study and seeking empowerment for world evangelization, he demonstrated the close relationship between the Pentecostals' intense desire to restore the spiritual dynamics of the New Testament church and pragmatism. Simply put, when the application of tongues for preaching failed, he went back to the New Testament to gain a more accurate understanding but didn't question the fundamental integrity of the doctrine. In this way, he took the lead among Pentecostals in reviewing the function of tongues.

With their preaching value now questioned, praying in tongues provided the source of power in the Spirit-filled life. He remarked, "It is the sweetest joy and the greatest pleasure to the soul when God comes upon one in all one's unworthiness and begins Himself to speak in His language. Oh! the blessedness of His presence when those foreign words flow from the Spirit of God through the soul and then are given back to Him in praise, in prophecy, or in worship."

So tongues in the Book of Acts demonstrated a different function of the Spirit than that described by Paul in 1 Corinthians 14:13. Paul explained tongues as having meaning for the individual in private prayer and also in public worship, where it required the gift of interpretation for everyone present to be encouraged in the faith.

After leaving India in the fall of 1907, the Garrs spent time in Hong Kong, preaching once again on Spirit baptism. While their ministry there prospered, personal tragedy struck when their baby died at birth and their two-year-old daughter and their maid died from the plague. Returning to Hong Kong several years later, Lillian prematurely gave birth to a son who weighed only three pounds. Unable to find milk that Alfred, Jr., could keep on his stomach, the Garrs feared that he too might die. In desperation, Garr cried out to God, "Lord, this is all that I have left. Dear God, please heal my boy, and let him take some kind of nourishment." He heard the Lord tell him to give the baby Eagle Brand condensed milk and he would live. Wondering where he could find Eagle Brand milk in Hong Kong, Garr searched desperately from store to store. Finally, a Chinese merchant told him about receiving a shipment of milk he had not ordered and didn't know what to do with. When Garr examined it, he found it was Eagle Brand milk. Praising God for answered prayer, he took it home to his son, who thereafter became strong and healthy.

Because of antiforeign sentiments in China at the time, the Garrs returned home and began evangelistic work. Later they moved to Charlotte, North Carolina, where he pastored the Garr Auditorium, for many years one of the largest Pentecostal congregations in the country. His son, Al Garr, Jr., lived to become a popular gospel singer, and the testimony of Eagle Brand milk became well known in Pentecostal circles.

The controversy that developed in India over the role of tongues in the life of the believer and in the Church paralleled the same discussion elsewhere, particularly in the United States. But the fact that it occurred on a mission field should not be a surprise since it was a missionary use of tongues that had been assumed. Although Garr stoutly defended tongues' normative nature for Spirit baptism, both in his preaching and in Pentecostal periodicals, others began to write more extensive treatments. One such writer was George F. Taylor, a first-generation Pentecostal in the southeastern United States and prominent leader in the Pentecostal Holiness Church for many years.

GEORGE F. TAYLOR
(1881-1934)

Like many early Pentecostal leaders, George Taylor created new enterprises for strengthening the Movement and remained intimately involved in them until his death in 1934.

He wore many hats in the years he served the Pentecostal Holiness Church, among them author; founder, educator, and administrator of three Bible schools; and general superintendent. Few could have imagined that the little boy born with a palsy-like condition in a home near Magnolia, Duplin County, North Carolina, would make such significant contributions to the self-understanding and maturing of the Movement. Like many others, what he lacked in training he made up in zeal, picking up what he needed to know along the way. Reflecting his restless energy to learn, just a few years before his death he completed a master of arts degree in history at the University of North Carolina at Chapel Hill.

George F. Taylor

After leaving the Methodist Church, he joined the holiness movement, receiving a license to preach in 1903 from the Holiness Church of North Carolina. When Gaston B. Cashwell brought the Pentecostal message to the South, Taylor was one of the first baptized in the Spirit at the revival in Dunn, North Carolina, on January 15, 1907. Later that year, he published a book-length exposition on Pentecostal beliefs entitled *The Spirit and the Bride*.

In his book, written just one year after the beginning of the Azusa Street revival, he defended the Pentecostal movement against the criticisms of holiness leaders. Going on the offensive, Taylor chastised them for having professed the baptism in the Holy Spirit for years without any manifestation of the Spirit. Nevertheless, holiness criticisms of Pentecostals grew more and more strident in the years that followed.

Taylor focused much of his attention on the Book of Acts. He noticed that speaking in tongues was the most important manifestation to accompany Spirit baptism on the Day of Pentecost. [The "rushing mighty wind" and "cloven tongues like as of fire" he viewed as limited to that occasion (Acts 2:1–3, KJV).] What's more, Luke did not specifically mention any of the gifts of the Spirit (e.g., wisdom, knowledge, faith) in Acts 2 like Paul did in 1 Corinthians 12. Finally, he noted, Luke's later reports on Spirit baptism either included tongues or implied their presence (Acts 8:17–18; 9:17–18).

He responded to the widespread charge that Pentecostals exalted the gifts of the Spirit above the Giver of the Spirit; Taylor said this was a complete misrepresentation

Filled with Light and Power

Just like that of other early Pentecostals, Thomas B. Barratt's testimony reflects the close correlation between the baptism in the Holy Spirit and the concern for evangelism. He returned to Norway and became the Pentecostal "Apostle to Scandinavia," his influence extending into Sweden, Finland, Denmark, Switzerland, and Germany.

On November 16, 1906, Barratt received the Pentecostal baptism in New York City when other believers laid hands on him with prayer:

Thomas B. Barratt

"I was filled with light and such a power that I began to shout as loud as I could in a foreign language. I must have spoken seven or eight languages, to judge from the various sounds and forms of speech used.

At times I had seasons of prayer in the Spirit when all New York, the United States, Norway, Scandinavia, and Europe, my loved ones and friends, lay like an intense burden on my soul. Oh, what power was given in prayer!"

— *Thomas B. Barratt quoted in Donald Gee*, The Pentecostal Movement, *(1949)*, 14–15.

of the Pentecostal movement. He noted that Pentecostals were aware that when they sought the Holy Spirit, He would testify of Christ (John 16:13–15). Then one could properly seek the gifts of the Spirit. In the appendix to the book, Taylor gave six points of advice to those seeking Spirit baptism.

1. You must be straight in the Scriptures.
2. You must be right with God.
3. There is a death subsequent to the death of the "old man." (Dying to self should occur before and even after one has been instantaneously sanctified.)
4. You must carefully count the cost.
5. You must look to Jesus alone.
6. You must praise Him.

Indeed, Pentecostals focused strongly on the work of the Holy Spirit in glorifying Christ, who in turn baptized them in the Spirit.

WILLIAM H. DURHAM
(1873-1912)

The second major controversy—differing opinions over the nature of sanctification—reached a peak in 1910. Was it instantaneous, as the Wesleyan-holiness Pentecostals taught, or progressive throughout one's life? More than anyone else, William H. Durham of the North Avenue Mission in Chicago challenged the holiness doctrine of the second work of grace taught by Parham, Seymour, Taylor, and many other Pentecostals. Born in Kentucky and converted at a Baptist church in 1898, he experienced "the crisis" of entire sanctification three years later.

Hearing of the Azusa Street revival in 1906, he was impressed when acquaintances began to speak in tongues. Seeking to experience the Pentecostal baptism himself, he traveled to Los Angeles to visit the Apostolic Faith Mission. There he received the baptism in the Holy Spirit in March 1907 and returned to his pastorate a changed person. He then began to publish *The Pentecostal Testimony*.

William H. Durham with his
first wife Bessie

People traveled great distances to attend the services at North Avenue and hundreds were baptized in the Holy Spirit. Some became notable Pentecostal leaders, such as A. H. Argue of Winnipeg, an early Canadian leader, and Eudorus N. Bell of Fort Worth, Texas, later the first general superintendent of the Assemblies of God. Before their departure as missionaries to Hong Kong, Robert and Aimee Semple (later McPherson) worked at the mission where at one point Aimee testified to the instant healing of a broken foot. In 1910, several students at Moody Bible Institute were baptized in the Spirit, including Andrew Urshan, a Persian-American who went as a missionary to Persia (present-day Iran) in 1914.

The North Avenue Mission contributed to the overseas expansion of Pentecostalism through other ethnic groups in the area that it reached, notably Swedes and Italians. Three of the earliest missionaries to Brazil—Daniel Berg, Adolf Gunnar Vingren, and Luigi Francescon—all had contacts with the mission.

After Durham's Spirit baptism, his ministry in Chicago grew to such an extent that it rivaled Los Angeles as a center of influence in the Movement. He struggled, however, with the holiness doctrine of sanctification, even though he had earlier testified to experiencing it. Through studying the atonement of Christ, he argued that a complete transformation in the heart of the sinner takes place at conversion—the gift of salvation in its complete power. In light of Paul's statement in 1 Corinthians 15:22 about the resurrection of believers, Durham concluded, "The simple truth is that a sinner is identified with Adam. A believer is identified with Jesus Christ. No man is identified with Adam the first and Adam the second at the same time." Grace at conversion, therefore, finds perfection in continued growth.

At the annual Pentecostal convention in 1910 at the Stone Church in Chicago, Durham preached a stirring sermon entitled "The Finished Work of Calvary." One wit described it as a "shot heard around the world." A year later, Durham resigned and moved to Los Angeles to proclaim the true biblical teaching on sanctification at the hub of the Movement. Opposition mounted swiftly. Reflecting their displeasure, Elmer K. Fisher and members of his Upper Room Mission refused to give Durham a hearing. Moving to the Apostolic Faith Mission and speaking there in Seymour's absence (he was traveling in the East at the time), Durham stubbornly and aggressively preached his message. When Seymour returned, he locked Durham out of the building. Finally, with the help of Frank Bartleman, Durham formed a new congregation at another location with approximately six hundred followers.

Durham's North Avenue Mission in Chicago

The controversy grew increasingly bitter. Durham concluded that Satan had blinded his opponents to the truth. Charles Parham entered the debate, denouncing "The Finished Work of Calvary" and stating: "The diabolical end and purpose of his Satanic majesty, in perpetrating Durhamism on the world, in repudiating sanctification as a definite work of grace, has now been clearly revealed." Parham believed that Durham had committed the "sin that leads to death" (1 John 5:16). Finally, Parham publicly prayed, "If this man's doctrine is true, let my life go out to prove it; but if our teaching on a definite grace of sanctification is true, let his life pay the forfeit." After Durham's untimely death on July 7, 1912, Parham crowed, "How signally God has answered." Rarely have the advocates of holiness debated with more rancor and backbiting.

Presbyterian Missionary to China

Alfred E. Street, a graduate of Williams College and Auburn Theological Seminary, wrote in 1907: About a year ago the burden of prayer became greater and greater, increasing night after night. Finally I went to the mission at 328 W. Sixty-third St., Chicago (Englewood) asking only one question, "Why do I not receive the baptism? What is the matter with me?" The good friends prayed with me and said that nothing was wrong; I only needed to wait.

Praise the Lord they were right, for the first time I knelt at the altar on Sunday afternoon, March 17, the power began to seize me and I laughed all through the following communion service. In the evening at about 11 p.m. I knelt. After some little waiting I began to laugh, or rather my body was used to laugh with increasing power until I was flat on my back laughing at the top of my voice for over half an hour. On arising I found that I was drunk on the "New Wine" (Eph. 5:18), acting just like a drunken man in many ways and full of joy.

On kneeling to meet the Lord again I was suddenly seized with an irresistible power of beseeching with groanings that could not be uttered, asking the Lord to have mercy on me a sinner and telling Him that I wanted to "go all the way" with Him. . . . Then coming to and kneeling I felt my jaws and mouth being worked by a strange force. In a few seconds some baby gibberish was uttered, then a few words in Chinese that I understood and then several sentences in a strange tongue. Oh the unspeakable glory of being able to actually praise the Great God and Savior of men in the Spirit.

—A.E. Street, "Pentecostal Experience of Reverend A.E. Street," *Intercessory Missionary* (June 1907): 34–35.

At the time of Durham's death, the "finished work" sector of Pentecostalism had grown to considerable proportions. Durham's *Pentecostal Testimony* and tracts had been sent out in the hundreds of thousands, extending his teaching far beyond his own personal itinerary. His impact on the Pentecostal movement proved to be profound, drawing a large segment of them closer to Reformed doctrine on this point. Several emerging leaders who shared his theology invited their followers to attend a convention in Hot Springs, Arkansas, in April 1914, the first General Council of the Assemblies of God. Only those holiness Pentecostal bodies in the Southeast and the Apostolic Faith associations of Parham and Florence Crawford preserved the Wesleyan view.

Yet on the grassroots level, differences between the Wesleyan and Reformed views of sanctification often remained rather fuzzy. Believers in both camps stood up in testimony meetings to announce that they had been "saved, sanctified, and baptized in the Holy Ghost." For many years, the article on sanctification in the Assemblies of God's Statement of Fundamental Truths was titled "Entire Sanctification," a distinctly Wesleyan term for instantaneous sanctification.

In the years following the Topeka, Azusa Street, and Indian revivals, the Pentecostal movement circled the globe. Even so, these driving years of restoring apostolic faith and practice did not keep Pentecostals from contemplating questions of biblical interpretation, Spirit baptism, and sanctification. Contrary to the criticisms of opponents, Pentecostals come from a rich background of doctrinal and biblical reflection.

RECOMMENDED READING

Abrams, Minnie F. *The Baptism of the Holy Ghost and Fire.* 2d ed. Kedgaon, India: Mukti Mission Press, 1906.

Blumhofer, Edith L. "William H. Durham: Years of Creativity, Years of Dissent." In *Portraits of a Generation: Early Pentecostal Leaders,* edited by James R. Goff, Jr., and Grant Wacker, 123–142. Fayetteville, Ark.: University of Arkansas Press, 2002.

Durham, William H. "The Finished Work of Calvary." *Pentecostal Testimony* 2:3 (1912): 4–7.

Garr, A. G. "Tongues, the Bible Evidence." *Cloud of Witnesses to Pentecost in India* (September 1907): 40–47.

Hoover, Willis Collins. *History of the Pentecostal Revival in Chile.* Translated by Mario G. Hoover. Lakeland, Fla.: By the translator, 2000.

Jacobsen, Douglas. *Thinking in the Spirit: Theologies of the Early Pentecostal Movement.* Bloomington, IN: Indiana University Press, 2003.

McGee, Gary B. "Minnie F. Abrams: Another Context, Another Founder." In *Portraits of a Generation: Early Pentecostal Leaders,* edited by James R. Goff, Jr., and Grant Wacker, 87–104. Fayetteville, Ark.: University of Arkansas Press, 2002.

———. "The Calcutta Revival of 1907 and the Reformulation of Charles F. Parham's 'Bible Evidence' Doctrine." *Asian Journal of Pentecostal Studies* 6 (January 2003): 123–143.

Synan, Vinson. "George Floyd Taylor: Conflicts and Crowns." In *Portraits of a Generation: Early Pentecostal Leaders,* edited by James R. Goff, Jr., and Grant Wacker, 325–345. Fayetteville, Ark.: University of Arkansas Press, 2002.

Wacker, Grant. "Travail of a Broken Family: Radical Evangelical Responses to the Emergence of Pentecostalism in America, 1906–16." In *Pentecostal Currents in American Protestantism*, edited by Edith L. Blumhofer, et al., 23–49. Urbana, Ill.: University of Illinois Press, 1999.

York, H. Stanley. *George Floyd Taylor: The Life of an Early Southern Pentecostal Leader*. Xulon Press, 2013.

CHAPTER 5

"FAITH LIFE" MISSIONARIES

For three years after the Topeka revival in 1901, Pentecostals focused exclusively on evangelizing the home front, given the apparent absence of any traveling overseas as missionaries. Three years later, the first Pentecostal missionary, Mary Johnson, left Moorhead, Minnesota, for South Africa in November 1904, along with her colleague Ida Andersson, who spoke in tongues several years later. Both were products of an early Pentecostal revival in Moorhead among Swedish Americans who were unaware of Charles Parham's Apostolic Faith movement.

Beginning in 1906, however, the Pentecostal movement became worldwide, with missionaries traveling to many parts of the globe. By the end of the decade, two hundred or more ministered abroad, underlining the fact that the history of Pentecostalism cannot be properly understood apart from its missionary vision.

At least four different groups of missionaries served overseas as a result of the Spirit's outpouring: the ill-prepared, the hardy souls who persevered and adjusted to their new contexts of ministry, veteran missionaries, and Bible institute graduates.

The first group represented those who had been called, but due to their feelings about the urgency of the hour and their desire to model the "faith life" in their ministries (that is, without pledged support), took little or no time to gather financial resources. Neither did they study the history, culture, or language of the country they were going to. Their zeal often outweighed their wisdom; although they shared the gospel, their overall impact appears to have been generally short-lived and disappointing. Disillusionment crept in as harsh realities surfaced: the need for language and cultural studies, dependable financial support from the home churches to meet expenses and expand activities, long-term strategies for the discipling of converts, training of ministerial candidates, and the development of indigenous churches. Information is limited about those who failed because Pentecostal editors had little interest in publishing their discouraging stories.

Bright spots, however, can be found across the landscape of early Pentecostal missions. Hardy pioneers who endured believed that faith in God's provision made up for what they lacked. Among them, the successful ministries of four missionaries in particular deserve attention: Charles W. Chawner (South Africa), Martin L. Ryan (Japan and China), and Daniel Berg and Adolf Gunnar Vingren (Brazil).

CHARLES W. CHAWNER
(1861-1949)

Baptized in the Spirit at the East End Mission in Toronto, Canada, in 1907, Charles and Emma Chawner were the first Canadian Pentecostal missionaries to head overseas. The mission, having been founded by James and Ellen Hebden in 1906, became a powerhouse for Pentecostalism in eastern Canada much like the revival in Dunn, North Carolina, had been for the American South.

In a vision early in 1907, Charles said, "I felt a shock go through me that shook me like a leaf. I was made to laugh and cry by turns, to feel myself under a mighty power, shaking different parts of my body, sometimes the whole frame, at the same time feeling such an inexpressible joy that I was dealt with thus; on the third day I saw in a vision numbers of dark faces on the hillsides and I among them, and through my own lips a message was given to me that I should be among them, bidding me not to tarry long in one place, that there was much land to be possessed, and Jesus was returning soon."

Eleventh Annual (1908) Report of the Christian and Missionary Alliance

A. B. Simpson

Another result of the influence of which we have been speaking has been the sending forth of bodies of inexperienced and self-appointed missionaries of foreign lands under the honest impression on their part that God had given them the tongue of the people to whom they were to minister the Gospel.

Without preparation, without proper leadership, and without any reasonable support, several of these parties have gone out to heathen lands only to find themselves stranded upon some foreign shore without the ability to speak any intelligible tongue, without the means of support, or even of returning home.

These unhappy victims of some honest but misleading impression have been thrown upon the charity of strangers, and after the greatest sufferings have in most cases with much difficulty been compelled to return to their homes, disappointed, perplexed and heartbroken.

In some cases our Alliance branches have been seriously disrupted by such outgoing parties and a strain created which it will take years to heal.

The temptation has come to new missionaries to abandon the study of the native language and wait vainly for some supernatural gift of tongues.

—*A. B. Simpson*, Eleventh Annual Report of the Christian and Missionary Alliance *(1908), 11–12.*

Charles W. Chawner in South Africa with native youth

A year later, with less than two hundred dollars in his pocket to purchase their steamship tickets and for expenses once they arrived on the mission field, the Chawners set sail. Between Canada and Liverpool, England, en route to South Africa, the Lord spoke to Chawner. God informed him that upon reaching the train station in London to visit his aging father, he "should find a man between a column and post at the station who would show [him] a quiet place to rest for the night. Praise Him all this came to pass." Upon reaching South Africa, they journeyed to KwaZulu Natal, where they spent the rest of their lives in fruitful missionary evangelism working with the Pentecostal Assemblies of Canada.

Sent by the Board of Boards

Kenneth E. M. Spooner was called as a missionary to Africa in 1906, during a service at A. B. Simpson's Gospel Tabernacle in New York City. Identifying with the Pentecostal movement, he received encouragement from friends at Bethel Pentecostal Assembly in Newark, New Jersey. The Spooners were among the early African-American Pentecostals who dedicated their lives to missionary service. He later wrote: "We arrived in Cape Town January 21, 1915. Let me say right here, it was a miracle that we ever got into the country. I was told by an official five years afterward that it was the fault of the officer at the port that we were permitted to land. There is, said he, a law that the coloured population of South Africa must not be increased from without. This was the reason why no mission board would undertake to send us to South Africa.

What is impossible with man is possible with God.

—*Kenneth E. M. Spooner,*
A Sketch of Native Life in South Africa (1930), 10, 14.

MARTIN L. RYAN
(1869-1910?)

Unfortunately, little is known about the background of Martin L. Ryan, even when and where he died. Yet he significantly contributed to the Pentecostal revival in the Pacific Northwest and missionary evangelism in Japan and China. Receiving a letter telling of the revival in Los Angeles, he wrote, "I fell on my knees and agonized Godward a bursting soul of appreciation; a great . . . conviction seized me, and I rushed out of the office shouting and praising God. The fire had struck my soul." Moving from Salem, Oregon, to Spokane, Washington, he led in the Pentecostal revival in that region. In late summer 1907, Ryan, editor of the *Apostolic Light*, and twenty members of his congregation, including their children, sailed as the first contingent of Pentecostal missionaries from the West Coast to East Asia.

While the earliest strategy centered on testimony, proclamation, and miraculous signs and wonders, Ryan proved an exception. After arriving in Japan, several in his party then traveled on to Hong Kong. However, he remained for a time in Japan, having noticed the large number of students from other parts of Asia attending Japanese universities. He concluded that one of the fastest ways to reach the Orient with the gospel would be through evangelizing students so they would come to Christ and carry the message of salvation to their homelands. Such a farsighted strategy was rare among Pentecostal missionaries.

The first Pentecostal missionaries from the West Coast to the Orient (1907). Center row (adults), Rowena Ryan (second from left), Martin Ryan (third).

DANIEL BERG (1884-1963) AND
ADOLF GUNNAR VINGREN (1879-1933)

By far the highest growth of Pentecostalism anywhere has taken place in Brazil, today numbering in the multiplied millions. Along with the Italian American Luigi Francescon, the origins of the Movement point to the Swedish Americans Daniel Berg and Adolf Gunnar Vingren. Berg had been raised in a Baptist home in Sweden and immigrated to the United States in 1902. On a later visit home he experienced the baptism in the Spirit. Vingren arrived in America in 1903 and, after working as a laborer to raise the necessary funds, he studied in the Swedish Department of the University of Chicago Divinity School. Berg and Vingren met for the first time at a Pentecostal convention sponsored by the First Swedish Baptist Church of Chicago.

A year later, Vingren accepted the pastorate of a Swedish Baptist congregation in South Bend, Indiana, with Berg joining him sometime afterward. At a Saturday night service, a member of the congregation, Adolf Uldine, prophesied to Vingren that he should go to "Pará" and preach the gospel. Uldine later gave the same prophecy to Berg. However, not knowing the location of Pará, they visited the Chicago Public Library, where they discovered that it was a state in Brazil. Sharing the news of their plans to leave for South America, they were dedicated as missionaries by William H. Durham at the North Avenue Mission.

Daniel Berg

With the financial help of a Swedish Pentecostal church in the city, they departed on November 4, 1910, arriving in Belém, a major coastal port and the Pará state capital. Finding a Baptist church, they were welcomed by the pastor, who invited them to stay in his home. However, their warm reception turned cold when they began preaching on the Pentecostal baptism.

Like other Pentecostal missionaries, they prayed for God's provision. Berg worked as a foundry man in a steel mill and with his earnings paid for their lessons in the

News from Brazil

God is wonderfully blessing the work and revivals are breaking out everywhere on this field. I have just returned from a trip along the Amazon, wherein we had a blessed time telling the people of God's love in Christ toward them. Along the rivers of the Amazon we now have eleven missions, and God is blessing the work more and more. I have baptized in water during the year 126 souls, and many have also received the baptism with the Holy Spirit.

—*Daniel Berg quoted in "Missionary Extracts,"*
Pentecostal Evangel (November 3, 1917): 13.

Adolf Gunnar Vingren

Portuguese language, while Vingren took care of pastoral responsibilities. They continued holding services with the eighteen church members who had left with them. When the Movement expanded, it later became officially registered with the government as the "Assembly of God" in 1918.

Inspired by a prophecy and committed to preaching the gospel and Spirit baptism, the humble work of Berg and Vingren grew into the largest Protestant denomination in Brazil, the Assemblies of God. Many Swedish Pentecostal missionaries followed in their wake, and American missionaries arrived later.

Veteran missionaries comprised the third group of missionaries, most of whom served in India, where the Pentecostal revival had also been growing. Apart from India, however, other missionaries could be found in China and a few in Latin America, among them, Alice C. Wood (Argentina) and Harold A. Baker (China).

ALICE C. WOOD
(1870-1961)

When Pentecostals journeyed abroad in the early years, they often thought Jesus would return before they would ever have a chance to go home and see their families again. They would next meet in heaven. Spending little thought on furloughs home, a few remained on the mission fields for most or the rest of their lives. One such missionary was Alice C. Wood, who devoted her life to Latin American missions.

Born the seventh child in a family of ten on a farm near Belleville, Ontario, Canada, Wood's father served as a lay Methodist preacher, and her mother was a member of the Friends Church. While still a teenager, her parents died. Fortunately, her foster parents encouraged her to participate in the local church, which she did with great enthusiasm. She later enrolled at the Friends' College in Pickering, Ontario. During a holiness meeting in 1894, she professed to being "sanctified," not an unusual event among these holiness-oriented Quakers.

Moving to the United States, she studied at Friends' Bible Institute and Training School in Cleveland, Ohio, founded by J. Walter Malone, a holiness leader in the Ohio Yearly Meeting of Friends. There she learned about the imminent return of Jesus

25 Years in Argentina

Praise the Lord for His wonderful faithfulness! To celebrate the anniversary I called together as many members of the assemblies as could come. The power of God fell copiously, bringing forth confessions, burdens of prayer in the Spirit. Everyone enjoyed the fellowship and returned to their assemblies with fresh courage and zeal. My joy-cup was full, for I felt it was one of the happiest days of my life.

—Alice C. Wood, *"Twenty-Five Years in Argentina,"*
Pentecostal Evangel *(April 27, 1935):* 11.

Alice C. Wood

Christ and divine healing. At the conclusion of her stay there, she began pastoring a Friends Church in Beloit, Ohio. After hearing a missionary from Africa speak, however, a call to missions altered her future plans. Resigning the church, Wood sought permission from the Christian and Missionary Alliance to go to Latin America as a missionary. She then spent three months at the Alliance school in Nyack, New York, and then several years of ministry in Venezuela and Puerto Rico.

Back in the United States, she heard about the outpouring of the Spirit in Los Angeles and began to seek Spirit baptism with speaking in tongues. Although present in the Pentecostal revival at Nyack in May 1907 and the large Pentecostal camp meeting in Alliance, Ohio, in June, she did not experience the "full consummation" (tongues) until several years later. With May Kelty, another Alliance missionary, she went to Argentina in 1909 and began working in the city of "25 de Mayo." As a result of their efforts, the "Pentecostal Mission" there became one of the earliest Pentecostal centers in Argentina.

In 1917, Wood affiliated with the Assemblies of God. She remained in Argentina for over fifty years, planting churches, starting Sunday schools, starting a day school, and opening a Bible institute. Late in life she returned to the United States.

HAROLD A. BAKER
(1881-1971)

In the preface to his autobiography, *Under His Wings*, H. A. Baker informs the reader about his motives for writing the book: "My reason for believing that this autobiography will help some readers is not that I am 'somebody,' a person of such natural qualifications as to command attention. On the contrary, my hope for being useful is based on the fact that in the Bible we are told that God uses the 'nobodies' to confound the 'somebodies' and uses the 'foolish' to confound the 'wise.'"

Given this humble sentiment, the reader might be surprised to discover that Baker graduated as a top student from Hiram College in Ohio; served as president of the local chapter of the Student Volunteer Movement for Foreign Missions (SVM), the collegiate Young Men's Christian Association, and the college literary society; debated in speech competitions; and won a highly prized academic scholarship with his grade point average. With this background, he clearly stands out as an exception among most first-generation Pentecostal missionaries.

After graduation in 1909, he married Josephine Witherspoon, a college classmate; both had dedicated themselves to going to Tibet as missionaries. Due to a shortage of funds, however, the mission board of the Disciples of Christ asked them to wait until monies became available. In the interim, Baker moved to Rochester, New York, to pastor a Christian Church. Yet despite his successes, he struggled spiritually, and sermon preparation became a weekly agony. Two years later, they were finally able to become missionaries.

While working on the China-Tibetan border for five years, they met Pentecostal missionaries who told them of divine healing and baptism in the Holy Spirit. This opened new spiritual vistas for them. By the time of their furlough home, they had become convinced of the biblical integrity of these doctrines. Uncomfortable with the growing "modernism" in the Disciples of Christ and now seeking for Spirit baptism, he resigned his ministerial credentials.

After being baptized in the Spirit, the Bakers wondered how they would return to China as independent missionaries. Corresponding with Allan Swift, a missionary with the Pentecostal Missionary Union (England) they had met in China, he invited them to return to China and work with him. Unexpectedly, a Pentecostal congregation sent them a thousand dollars to help them on their way. Thus, two months after their Pentecostal baptism, they headed for the Far East as independent missionaries, free at last from denominational restrictions. Traveling to Yunnan province, they opened an orphanage and evangelized tribal peoples.

Sometime in the 1930s, the orphans received visions of heaven and hell. Baker wrote these down and published them as *Visions Beyond the Veil*, a book that sold tens of thousands of copies and was eventually printed in thirteen languages. Many other publications followed, making him one of the better-read Pentecostal writers. Although he remained an independent missionary, he had strong links with the Assemblies of God. Their long tenure in China continued until one year after the Communist takeover in 1950. True to their calling as missionaries, they ministered to Navajo Native Americans in New Mexico and later among the Hakka people of Taiwan.

Unlike many missionaries at the beginning of the twentieth century, Pentecostals had seldom received training in colleges, universities, or seminaries before they went to their fields of ministry. Like Baker, however, there were notable exceptions. To meet their need for ministerial training and spiritual formation, some attended Bible institutes. The Bible institute offered the student an intensely biblical education—a dynamic spiritual atmosphere through daily chapel services, prayer meetings, and missionary services—and a speedier entry into the ministry.

Among those with a postsecondary education behind them before 1920, the largest number had studied at A. B. Simpson's Missionary Training Institute at Nyack, which in turn became a model for Pentecostal schools. Such schools included Rochester Bible Training School in Rochester, New York; Bethel Bible Training School in Newark, New Jersey; Beulah Heights Bible and Missionary Training Institute in nearby North Bergen, New Jersey and Bible and Missionary Training School in Norwalk, Ohio.

While offering few courses in missions, the spiritual discipline learned in these schools and the willingness of their graduates to adapt to the needs on the mission fields generally produced deeply committed missionaries. Their growing presence on the rosters of the Assemblies of God gradually reduced the high turnover in personnel. Among them were Christian Schoonmaker, who studied at Nyack, and Esther Harvey, who studied at the Bible and Missionary Training School in Ohio.

The Fire of the Holy Spirit in Ka Do Land

Harold A. Baker

There was a very remarkable outpouring of the Holy Spirit upon the Chinese children of the Adullam Mission in Yunnanfu, China. The children, mostly boys, the majority fell below the teen age, had nearly all been rescued out of a beggar life on the streets of the city.

Meetings were held with these children twice a day. Suddenly in one of these services, the heavens opened, and the veil was so drawn aside that the children were allowed to see the things of the unseen worlds as face to face. This continued for a period of eight weeks.

We expected that after those days of preparation the Lord would send the older of the Adullam boys into the surrounding mountains to preach the gospel to the many primitive tribes who occupy these unevangelized regions. But God opened other doors among other mountain tribes twelve days' journey away.

This new door was miraculously opened by God. A young married man of the Ka Do tribe who had never heard the gospel, but who knew a little about the claims of Christianity . . . for material motives more than any other decided to become a Christian. Accordingly he discussed this with the other fifteen families of his village.

This village was soon followed by other villages turning to Christianity in a mass movement until there were soon six hundred families. At this time I was invited to be the first missionary to visit this movement. Everywhere God-prepared hearts were found who heard the gospel for the first time. The mass movement soon spread to 2,500 families of perhaps 10,000 people.

The young man who had first decided to become a Christian returned with us to the Adullam Mission on that first visit into Ka Do Land. He was converted, received the Holy Spirit and after a few weeks returned to his home in the mountains. He was uneducated and knew only the fundamental things of the Lord. But upon his return to his village and upon his telling the people about the working of the Holy Spirit among the Chinese children where he had received the Holy Spirit, the people in the village wanted to seek the Holy Spirit.

This they did, and He fell among them mightily. This fire of God rapidly spread to other villages. Other young men now came with the former one to the Adullam Mission . . . to learn more of the Lord, study the Bible, and seek the Holy Spirit. Their stay was short, but as soon as they arrived the Holy Spirit began to fall among them in power, until nearly all who came received anointings, some speaking with other tongues, some speaking in prophecy. . . .

Upon their return to their mountain tribes they went everywhere among the villages preaching repentance, and the soon coming of the Lord, and the need to receive the power of the Holy Spirit . . . . Within a few months the fire spread all over Ka Do Land and into the other tribes, until the villages where no one received miraculous anointings of the Holy Spirit were very few.

—H. A. Baker, "What Wonders Hath God Wrought?" Pentecostal Evangel (July 15, 1939): 4–5.

CHRISTIAN SCHOONMAKER
(1881-1919)

With the growth of the Pentecostal movement across India, several mission stations of the Christian and Missionary Alliance were deeply impacted, with a number of missionaries speaking in tongues. The Dholka mission and boys' school in Gujarat became an important center of Pentecostal activity. It was the staff of this mission that welcomed Christian Schoonmaker at the turn of 1908.

Schoonmaker had a Methodist background, worked for the Salvation Army, and enrolled at the Missionary Training Institute at Nyack in 1905 to prepare for overseas ministry. When Pentecostal revival broke out there in May 1907, he pondered the importance of speaking in tongues. After taking up residence at Dholka, he finally received Spirit baptism himself during revival services. From there he and two female missionaries traveled to the Alliance girls' school at Kaira where another Pentecostal awakening occurred. In the course of the visit, he met Violet Dunham, an Alliance missionary, who soon became his wife.

Christian Schoonmaker

Obeying God's Call

An excerpt of a sermon by Christian Schoonmaker, a missionary to India, at the General Council in St. Louis in 1916:

When I mention the difficulties on the field, do not get the idea I am questioning whether God is not able to do the exceeding abundant or not, but naturally these things come up, and it is not until you face them in the fear of God that you get to the place where you believe He will undertake for you. God gives us the rest of faith. Beloved, those at home and those of us who go forth possessed with one desire, to hasten the completion of God's visitation to the Gentiles, realize that we have Jesus with us always. Just as surely as God brings you into a place where you, from the bottom of your heart, give all that you have into His hands and keep it there, He will open your vision and make you to realize the crying need of millions. A sister in the meetings in Toronto this last summer was under the power of the Spirit and her face was glorified before our very eyes. She had a vision of lost dying souls and was preaching to them.

I believe . . . that it is in the regions beyond that the mightiest displays of God's power are going to be given in these last days. Do not think of refusing to go because things in the homeland are likely to be more safe than abroad. Do not let any consideration keep you back. If God calls you, the safest place for you is in His will.

—*Christian H. Schoonmaker,*
"God's Estimate of a Heathen Soul. What is Yours?"
Latter Rain Evangel *(November 1917): 17.*

Joining a long list of Alliance members who had become Pentecostals and refused to compromise on the importance of tongues as evidence of Spirit baptism, the Schoonmakers resigned from the organization after their return home in 1914. An invitation to pastor a Pentecostal mission in Toronto facilitated his meeting other young men who would one day play prominent roles in the Pentecostal Assemblies of Canada and the Assemblies of God (U.S.A.). One young man that he mentored spiritually, Noel Perkin, served for thirty-two years as the director of foreign missions for the Assemblies of God.

With German submarines still menacing shipping, the Schoonmakers risked returning to India anyway and arrived in Bombay in 1918. Shortly afterward, Violet gave birth to their sixth child. With the three older children enrolled in boarding school, the rest of the family moved to Lonauli in the hills to the east of Bombay. While Christian traveled several hundred miles to the north to explore where new missions might be established, the flu broke out in the city and endangered Violet and the three small children. Many died in the epidemic, and she became fearful of leaving their house for supplies and water with the little ones staying behind. At this time, while changing trains in the north country and unaware of what was happening in Lonauli, Christian heard a voice saying, "Go home! Your wife needs you." He obeyed immediately and subsequently moved the family to a safer location.

Schoonmaker and other Pentecostal missionaries recognized the value of cooperation among themselves and organized the Indian Assemblies of God in 1918 at a conference in Saharanpur. The delegates elected him as chairman; his leadership, however, lasted only a short time. In the winter of 1918, he became infected with smallpox when an epidemic broke out. Like other Alliance and Pentecostal believers, he had remained true to the doctrine of divine healing and had refused vaccination. To accept the vaccination would have signaled unbelief, a sure sign of compromise for those who wished to live the faith life. After being quarantined, he died an untimely death at thirty-eight years of age early in the following year.

Violet Schoonmaker remained in India as a missionary until her retirement in 1951, a notable example of the commitment of many early female Pentecostal missionaries. Five of their six children followed in their footsteps and became missionaries.

ESTHER B. HARVEY
(1891-1986)

Born in Port Huron, Michigan, Esther Bragg grew up attending Presbyterian and Methodist churches. From her childhood, she had been afflicted with a physical problem that grew worse with age. When believers from a local mission visited her at home, she let them pray for her, after which she was healed. Leaving the Methodist church to attend services at the mission, she heard the call to missions. Bragg then enrolled at Etta Wurmser's Bible and Missionary Training School in Norwalk, Ohio, in 1911, where she was baptized in the Spirit.

A sometime member of the Alliance, Wurmser had established this school for the training of Pentecostal workers.

Two years later, leaders at the school ordained the twenty-year-old Bragg, after which she began preparing to go to India as an independent faith missionary. Acquiring the funds for the trip, however, severely tested her faith because she couldn't rely on help from her parents. In several churches where she preached, no offerings were taken for her. Finally, like Gideon, she put a fleece before the Lord to determine if He had really called her to be a missionary: "I told the Lord I must be very sure that it was His will for me to leave that fall and if it was His will then he should give me one hundred dollars." While preaching again in several rural churches, she received ninety-five dollars.

Esther B. Harvey with
daughter Zaida

Invited by her aunt to speak at the church she attended, Bragg thought she would easily receive the remaining five dollars. Yet when the service ended that night, the people only wished her good luck. The difficult journey to the church and the disappointing response taxed her faith. But just before Bragg left for the train station to return home the next day, an elderly woman in a horse and buggy stopped and handed her the last five dollars. When the woman had heard that no offering had been taken, she couldn't sleep that night, concerned that Bragg might leave before she got there. The testing of Bragg's faith, characteristic of the experience of many other independent missionaries, toughened her resolve to trust God in greater crises still to come.

With the rest of the missionary party she had accompanied, limited financial resources forced them to stay for ten days in a dilapidated and unsanitary Indian hotel after reaching Bombay. Finally, making her way to the Pentecostal Mission at Nawabganj, United Provinces, in North India, she settled in to begin work. There she met James Harvey, a former soldier in the British Indian Army, who now led the mission. After their marriage in 1914, they affiliated with the General Council of the Assemblies of God, which had come into being just months before.

The Harveys renamed the mission Sharannagar Mission ("place of refuge") and concentrated on evangelism. But when famine struck, they quickly responded to the needy who appeared at their doorstep. Esther recalled, "Could we preach the love of God to these and turn them away naked and hungry to die along the wayside? The Lord gave us Isaiah 58:4–14. 'Is not this the fast that I have chosen? To loose the bands of wickedness, to undo the heavy burdens, and to let the oppressed go free, and that ye break every yoke? Is it not to deal thy bread to the hungry, and that thou bring the poor that are cast out to thy house?'" In obedience, they built quarters for widows, former prostitutes, and women rejected

The Day of Miracles

Some people tell us the day of miracles is past but we know it is not. Our God is the same yesterday, today, and forever. I remember once some years ago, we were being severely tested financially and didn't have money to buy grain for our big family.

We used to buy our grain twice a month, on the first and the fifteenth. (We cannot do that now as we don't always have the money. We have to buy for a few days at a time.) At that time we bought for two weeks. The time was up and there was no money. The grain was weighed out every day for cooking and we had purchased just enough for two weeks.

The matron came to tell us there was only enough grain for the next day. We told her there was no money to buy more. They would just have to pray for the Lord to do something. Those women had a prayer meeting that night.

Early in the morning the matron awakened the women to go and weigh out the grain to cook. She did not even go first to see if there was grain there. They had prayed and she expected to find grain in the bins and sure enough there was. When they had weighed it out last there was just a little left over. She got out the scales and began to weigh it out pound after pound. Sure enough there was enough and a little over. She weighed the rice pound after pound the same amount as she had every day. There was enough and a little over, and the same with the dahl.

I don't remember when the money came to buy grain but the Lord multiplied the grain until the money did come. Thank God, the God of Elijah still lives today!

I confess at times when we have been so terribly tested financially, my faith has sometimes failed and my heart has almost failed me for fear. But as I meditate on the many marvelous answers to prayer in the past, my faith is strengthened, and I am encouraged to go on and believe God.

—*Esther B. Harvey, The Faithfulness of God (1949), 33.*

from their homes, and also added a boys' school, the present-day James Harvey Memorial School.

James died in 1922 and Esther carried the work on faithfully until her retirement in 1961. Her ministry focused on administering the institutions they founded and promoting them before the home constituency in the United States. Never claiming to be a preacher or Bible expositor, her gifts centered on administration. Many early Pentecostal periodicals carried letters from Esther Harvey, telling of the tears and triumphs at Nawabganj. While the mission may have run on faith in God's provision, Esther kept the saints in America informed about their responsibilities in supporting missions. Through the years, the Harveys' ministry contributed significantly to the growth of the Assemblies of God in India.

When people approach the study of missions, they usually concentrate all of their attention on the missionaries. Unfortunately, this can obscure the work of those on the home front who pray, sacrifice, raise money, and forward offerings to those sent overseas. A key supporter of Pentecostal missions in the early years was Minnie T. Draper of Ossining, New York.

MINNIE T. DRAPER
(1858-1921)

Minnie T. Draper

Following the death of Minnie T. Draper in 1921, the *Pentecostal Evangel*, the official voice of the Assemblies of God, praised her leadership, though she never joined the General Council. She had long provided for "one of the greatest Pentecostal missionary centres in the country, where every quarter the largest missionary collections of any Pentecostal Assembly are taken up year after year." This remarkable woman born near Waquit, Massachusetts, grew up in Ossining on the Hudson River, north of New York City, not far from Nyack. She faithfully attended the Presbyterian church and supported her mother and herself by teaching.

When overwork took its toll, she became an invalid for four years, with the medical profession unable to offer any relief. Hearing of the doctrine of divine healing, she visited A. B. Simpson's Gospel Tabernacle in New York City and was prayed for and healed. From that time on, she trusted Christ as her Healer and never consulted physicians for the rest of her life.

Joining the Christian and Missionary Alliance, she became an associate to Simpson in the ministry of healing and speaker in Alliance conventions. In 1893, she assisted in the founding of an Alliance branch in her hometown of Ossining, then known as "Sing Sing" and famous for its prison. Out of this venture, Ossining Gospel Assembly came into being.

When news of the Azusa Street revival reached Draper, she responded cautiously as did others in the Alliance. However, longing for a deeper work of the Spirit in her

Newark, New Jersey, was the home of the Bethel Pentecostal Assembly and its training school: (l to r) men's dormitory, the four-story Bethel Bible Training School, and Bethel Pentecostal Assembly.

The Bethel Conventions

For a number of years, the Bethel Conventions, of sacred memory to hundreds of God's people throughout the East, were a source of great blessing. Many who came went home and started prayer meetings from which have grown flourishing churches, while others received the call of God to heathen lands. An outstanding characteristic of these early days was the missionary giving; it was a common thing to receive as much as seven to eight thousand dollars in a single missionary offering.

—Watson Argue, *"The Get Acquainted Page,"* Latter Rain Evangel *(July 1936): 14.*

Edgar and Mabel Pettenger spent many years ministering among the thousands of miners in the mines of South Africa. They are pictured here with Henry B. Garlock (right), the first Assemblies of God field director for Africa.

life, the Lord appeared to her one night in her room and "hours elapsed wherein she saw unutterable things, and when she finally came to herself she heard her tongue talking fluently in a language she had never learned."

Draper identified with other Pentecostals at a time when the new Movement had begun to come under heavy fire from others in the Alliance. Nevertheless, while she continued working with the Alliance (until 1912), she became involved in several new enterprises, which provided Pentecostal members of the Alliance and those who had left with opportunities for evangelism at home and abroad. First, she contributed to the founding of Bethel Pentecostal Assembly in Newark, New Jersey, in 1907. A special supporting relationship developed between the Ossining Gospel Assembly and the Bethel congregation, and they joined together in their efforts in missions, despite their status as independent churches.

Second, this mutual association bore fruit in 1910 with the incorporation of the Executive Council of the Bethel Pentecostal Assembly. Often called the Bethel Board, it directed the activities of the church in Newark and established the Pentecostal Mission in South and Central Africa (PMSCA). This became the first successful Pentecostal mission agency in North America. Draper served as president from its inception till her death in 1921.

The Newark agency established a field council in South Africa, which directed the activities of its missionaries there, as well as in Swaziland and Mozambique. Missionaries also went to Liberia, as well as Mexico and Venezuela. By 1925, PMSCA had a budget of $30,150, second only in financial support and personnel to the Assemblies of God, with which it had close ties. To prepare ministers and missionaries, the Bethel Board launched a third endeavor in 1916, the Bethel Bible Training School.

A returned pioneer missionary from China with the Alliance, William W. Simpson served for a brief time as its first principal before returning to the field. A considerable number of Assemblies of God personnel prepared for ministry at this school, including Edgar and Mabel Pettenger, Ralph and Lillian Riggs, and Anna Richards Scoble, all of whom served with PMSCA and held or later held membership in the Assemblies of God.

Unlike many Pentecostals, the former Alliance members who served on the Bethel Board recognized the importance of organizational structure and Bible institute training. Perhaps the most striking feature of the Bethel Board appears in its roster. Several wealthy Pentecostals served as members for many years. At times when the board faced an important decision and deadlocked, the chair would call in Cora O. Lockwood, an older woman in the Newark congregation who had little money but was viewed as a person with unusual spiritual insight. She would pray and discern the will of God and then cast the deciding vote, although not actually a board member. She also sacrificed for missions by blessing and supporting her daughter Edith and son-in-law Howard Osgood, who served as missionaries in China and Malaysia for many years.

Understanding how to make money work on behalf of missions, the board invested funds on the stock market. Needless to say, it suffered a serious setback in 1929 with the stock market crash, and much of its overseas work was curtailed. Many of its missionaries entered the Assemblies of God and continued at their posts. A lasting legacy of PMSCA can be found in the large Full Gospel Church of God in South Africa.

RECOMMENDED READING

Baker, H. A. *Under His Wings*. Taiwan: By the author, n.d.

Bays, Daniel. "The Protestant Missionary Establishment and the Pentecostal Movement." In *Pentecostal Currents in American Protestantism*, ed. by Edith L. Blumhofer, et al., 50–67. Urbana, Ill.: University of Illinois Press, 1999.

Brubaker, Malcolm R. "Evolving Models of Missions: A Case Study of the Assemblies of God in North India: 1918-1949." PhD diss., Regent University, 2011.

Bundy, David. *Visions of Apostolic Mission: Scandinavian Pentecostal Mission to 1935*. Uppsala, Sweden: Uppsala Universitet, 2009.

Chawner, Charles, and Emma Chawner. *Called to Zululand: A Story of God's Leading*. Toronto: n.p., c. 1923.

Harvey, Esther B. *The Faithfulness of God*. 2d ed. Battle Creek, Mich.: Grounds Gospel Press and Book Store, c. 1949.

Law, E. May. *Pentecostal Mission Work in South China*. Falcon, N.C.: Falcon Publishing Company, c. 1916.

McGee, Gary B. "Three Notable Women in Pentecostal Ministry." *Assemblies of God Heritage* 6 (spring 1986): 3–5, 12, 16.

Miller, Thomas William. *Canadian Pentecostals: A History of the Pentecostal Assemblies of Canada*. Mississauga, Ontario: Full Gospel Publishing House, 1994.

Owen, Michael G. "Preparing Students for the First Harvest." *Assemblies of God Heritage* 9 (winter 1989–1990): 3–5, 16–19.

Rodgers, Darrin J. *Northern Harvest: Pentecostalism in North Dakota.* Bismarck, N.D.: North Dakota District Council of the Assemblies of God, 2003.

Schoonmaker, Violet. *Christian Schoonmaker: A Man Who Loved the Will of God.* Landour, Mussoorie, India: Hyratt Press, c. 1959.

Spittler, Russell P. "Implicit Values in Pentecostal Missions." *Missiology* 26 (October 1988): 409–424.

UNIT TWO
1914-1927

TIME LINE 1914-1927

1914—More than three hundred people meet in Hot Springs, Arkansas, April 2–12 to organize the General Council of the Assemblies of God. E. N. Bell elected first chairman; J. Roswell Flower elected secretary. Office established in Findlay, Ohio. Second council held in Chicago, November 15–29. In Chicago the delegates elect A. P. Collins as chairman and close the council by committing themselves "to Him for the greatest evangelism that the world has ever seen." World War I begins.

1915—Headquarters and printing operation move to St. Louis. J. W. Welch elected chairman at third General Council. (Two councils were held in 1914 and then annually until 1921; biennially from 1923 to present.)

1916—Amid Trinitarian-Oneness debate delegates adopt Statement of Fundamental Truths.

1917—Foreign Missions Committee organized. Missionary offerings for the year: $10,223.98.

1918—Headquarters operation is relocated to Springfield, Missouri, with 6th General Council held there.

Germany and the Central Powers surrender.

1919—Name of *Weekly Evangel* changes to the *Pentecostal Evangel*; Missionary Department established with J. Roswell Flower as the first secretary-treasurer. Stone Church, Chicago, hosts General Council.

1920—E. N. Bell replaces J. W. Welch as chairman. General Council joins the Foreign Missions Conference of North America, an inter-denominational agency providing needed services for mission agencies since 1893.

1921—Council meets in St. Louis. Stanley H. Frodsham named editor of the *Pentecostal Evangel*.

1922—William J. Seymour dies.

Central Bible Institute opens.

1923—Aimee Semple McPherson dedicates Angelus Temple in Los Angeles, one of the first megachurches in America. E. N. Bell dies in office; J. W. Welch succeeds him.

1925—John T. Scopes in Dayton, Tennessee, goes on trial for teaching evolution in a public school. He was found guilty at what was popularly called the "Monkey Trial." The trial denoted fundamentalist efforts to outlaw such teaching in the public schools.

W. T. Gaston elected chairman. Elsewhere, Etta Calhoun organizes the first Women's Missionary Council.

1927—Constitution and bylaws adopted at Springfield council. Efforts fail to change denomination name to Pentecostal Evangelical Church.

CHAPTER 6

THE SAINTS JOIN HANDS

People walking by the Grand Opera House in Hot Springs, Arkansas, in April 1914 must have wondered about the goings-on in the loud, exuberant meetings. Over three hundred Pentecostal believers had gathered to consider moving beyond just spiritual unity to a limited measure of organizational unity, a church organization with legal standing. They hoped this would do a number of things: contribute to a greater unity among their churches, conserve the work at home and abroad, lead to a better system for supporting missionaries, encourage local congregations to charter with a biblical name, and start a new Bible training school.

Everyone attended—pastors, evangelists, missionaries, laypersons. Some had come long distances. Traveling by faith and with little cash, however, could challenge a person's digestive system. Young Willie T. Millsaps from Tennessee suffered a personal martyrdom, having only enough money to eat bananas and peanut butter during the conference.

Although the delegates were Caucasian, at least one featured group was African American. The respected Bishop Charles H. Mason of the Church of God in Christ, formed not quite twenty years earlier, brought his choir from Memphis to sing. Mason preached in an evening service and graciously prayed

Charles H. Mason

God's blessings on the new General Council of the Assemblies of God.

THE ROAD TO HOT SPRINGS

While several existing holiness organizations in the South had become Pentecostal, most independent Pentecostals prized their freedom. Still, they cherished fellowship with other Spirit-filled believers in the many Pentecostal networks of conventions and camp meetings. Such networks provided a measure of unity for the Movement, and Pentecostal periodicals kept the faithful informed about coming events. The representatives of the churches who went to Hot Springs came from various backgrounds: Churches of God in Christ (white) from Alabama, Arkansas, Mississippi, and Texas; believers from Zion City, Illinois; Pentecostal missions in Chicago; Association of Christian Assemblies in Indiana; and former members of the Christian and Missionary Alliance, among others.

Like other early Pentecostals, they came from a cross section of American society, in contrast to the stereotype that has portrayed them as coming primarily from the impoverished and deprived segments of the population. Historian Grant Wacker notes that Pentecostal leaders lived in "modestly comfortable circumstances, generally a notch above the stable working class standing of the Pentecostal rank and file."[1] The believers who gathered at Hot Springs carried with them industriousness and determination that forged the success of their new endeavor.

The Grand Opera House in Hot Springs, Arkansas

The stage and box seats (center) as seen from the balcony of the Grand Opera House

Visitors and delegates at the First General Council of the Assemblies of God, Hot Springs, Arkansas, April 2–12, 1914. Kneeling across the front are the first eight men elected as the Executive Presbytery.

NETWORKING

Pentecostal networking laid the basis for the founding of the Assemblies of God. One influential group came from an association formed in Alabama and Mississippi by Henry G. Rodgers, Mack M. Pinson, and others who were products of the Cashwell revivals in the South. For membership, one simply needed to demonstrate the fruit of the Spirit. However, when they took the name Church of God, people easily confused them with the already existing Church of God that had headquarters in Cleveland, Tennessee.[2]

On another front, Howard Goss, representing a number of Charles F. Parham's former Apostolic Faith followers, gained permission in 1911 from Bishop Mason to ordain white ministers. This arrangement permitted them to issue credentials under the name "Church of God in Christ and in unity with the Apostolic Faith Movement." Rodgers's and Goss's groups later consolidated in 1912 at a convention in Eureka Springs, Arkansas. Three hundred and sixty-one ministers, including eighty-four women, joined in the merger. There the faithful traded opinions about forming an even broader association of Pentecostals.[3]

The vague relationship, however, with Mason's Church of God in Christ and the shakiness of the association led some of the more perceptive leaders to think of a bolder solution to the growing needs of the Pentecostal movement. *Word and Witness*, published by E. N. Bell in Malvern, Arkansas, carried the formal call for a "General Convention of Pentecostal Saints and Churches of God in Christ" in its December 20, 1913, issue. It was signed by Bell, Pinson, Goss, Arch P. Collins, and Daniel C. O. Opperman.

Some wondered if they would be called compromisers for participating in an organizational meeting. Goss, however, remarked, "From the Book of Acts, as well as from our own experiences, I was led to see that even Spirit-filled people needed some restraint. Just as a good horse still needs a harness to produce worthwhile results, the movement needed a legal form of written cooperative fellowship."[4]

PROBLEMS HERE AND THERE

Pastors and editors alike were frustrated with the selection and support of missionaries. Anna C. Reiff, editor of the Chicago-based *Latter Rain Evangel*, began to address the complex "missionary problem" in 1913. Like other editors who distributed monies to missionaries sent in by her readers, she didn't want to support individuals who had defected doctrinally or morally. Some self-appointed missionaries also seemed to do more traveling to and from the States than sowing on the foreign field, creating "a great deal of dissatisfaction among people in the homeland who have the evangelization of the heathen on their hearts."[5] They never stayed on their fields long enough to establish a work. Reiff called for some process of missionary selection. She charged, "While we are strong in our conviction that everyone on the field who has a real call from God should be supported, we do feel that some have been sent out who should never have gone."[6]

Although Pentecostals in England had founded the Pentecostal Missionary Union in 1909, similar attempts in Canada and the United States met stout resistance. Fears that human organizations would curtail the ability of missionaries to be led by the Holy Spirit fueled suspicions.[7] When a group of ministers formed such a union in Ohio, the *Gospel Witness*, an early Pentecostal publication from Los Angeles, chastised them for being blinded by the devil. The writer angrily ordered "these self-constituted Popes and Archbishops, who would 'lord it over God's heritage' under the guise

We Need a Cooperative Fellowship

My work often necessitated that I go wherever there was trouble, help the one in charge to quieten the sheep, arbitrate if necessary, and assist in restoring the congregation's confidence in God and in their leader. This God always helped me to accomplish. But the damage, nevertheless, was becoming great.

Within the congregations it was much the same. A member who had a wrong attitude could go from one church to another, and might even be received by the new pastor with open arms, no matter how much he had misconducted himself in his former church. Some pastors were tempted to harbor and protect troublemakers because the individual's family, his presence, or his offerings made a good showing. And, perhaps he could indulge himself in a small bit of personal gloating that, as an up-and-coming pastor, he had added to his congregation a person intelligent enough to appreciate his superiority, and thus pay it tribute. Such a one really should have been reproved and sent back home to make his wrongs right. But surprisingly few freelance pastors saw the importance, or the necessity, for doing so.

So, I concluded that in church work, as in all else, men of honor naturally flowed together to stand against all forms of wrong, whether from neglect, or through the gamut of self-indulgence, greed, dishonor, and on to outright sin.

—*Howard A. Goss quoted in*
Ethel E. Goss, The Winds of God *(1977), 275–276.*

Daniel C. O. Opperman's short-term Bible school at Joplin, Missouri. Opperman and his wife, Hattie, are standing in the back row to the far right.

of protection, to vacate the offices which they have assumed and to lay aside the authority which they have arrogated to themselves."[8] This was strong language. What appeared to be at stake, however, was the future of the Movement.

False teachings occasionally made their rounds. Leaders recognized the importance of helping believers balance and correct their spiritual experiences with the teachings of Scripture. But ministers found themselves in a catch-22. They felt reason was opposed to a walk in the Spirit (a look at the liberalism in the seminaries and the formalism in the mainline churches of the day only reinforced their position). When their people strayed from doctrine, ministers especially felt their lack of formal training; they saw the need for sound doctrinal teaching.

So despite some Pentecostals scoffing at formal ministerial training, residential Bible institutes continued to be founded. A more unusual educational venture also performed an important service: short-term schools for workers. Conducted principally by Daniel C. O. Opperman, the former principal of John Alexander Dowie's Zion City school system, these schools lasted from four to five weeks and located wherever there was sufficient interest.[9] Between December 1908 and October 1914, he directed at least eight training programs—the first three were each billed as "The School of the Prophets"—in Texas, Mississippi, Missouri, Alabama, Iowa, and Arkansas. In Opperman's schools, "Bible studies were seasoned with prayer, fasting, and practical experience through street meetings, jail services, revival meetings, and other forms of ministry."

Another of Opperman's short-term schools opened in Eureka Springs, Arkansas, in April 1916. An announcement advertising the school in the *Weekly Evangel* (later the *Pentecostal Evangel*) warned, "Loafers, curiosity seekers, strife-making busybodies and such like are not invited and will not be welcome." Instead, "This school is for those who want to diligently seek God's face and study His Word."[10]

At times, Pentecostals' lack of legal standing created obstacles to buying property. One missionary in China purchased property and constructed a building under the legal umbrella of the Presbyterian Board of Missions. Although well intentioned and with the goodwill of the Presbyterians, this course of action could not adequately give permanence to their efforts. Ministers at home also needed recognition of their ordinations for various practical reasons.

THE FIRST GENERAL COUNCIL

Of the three hundred delegates who attended the first General Council on April 2–12, 1914, one hundred and twenty-eight registered as ministers and missionaries.[11] However, before the Council took any formal action, four days were devoted to prayer and fellowship. Walter Higgins remembered a "halo of glory that rested over the sessions from day to day." This came as "God saw fit to bless this meeting with a visitation of His Holy Ghost. The praises rose from those gathered in the service, seemingly, like a mighty sea."[12] This spiritual uplift created a deep sense of unity and allayed the fears of some about creating an authoritarian denomination. Mack Pinson preached the keynote sermon on the "Finished Work of Calvary," clearly identifying the posture of these believers on the issue of sanctification.

The delegates closed ranks and approved the "Preamble and Resolution on Constitution" and incorporated under the name General Council of the Assemblies of God. The preamble explained the doctrinal basis for the new fellowship of churches. It further set forth principles underlying the unity and relationship of believers and the sovereignty of local churches. Until 1927, when a constitution and bylaws gained approval, the preamble provided the basis for cooperation among the growing number of believers, pastors, evangelists, missionaries, and churches in the Council. Delegates also adopted the name "Assemblies of God" (Hebrews 12:23, KJV), a familiar term in the holiness tradition that emphasized Christian unity. Thus, from the beginning, the concept of "voluntary cooperation" among the churches has been a hallmark of the Assemblies of God.

Incorporation had many benefits. Ministers there were particularly interested in qualifying for clergy discounts on the railways. At a time when many could not afford cars or the expenses of long-distance travel, the inexpensive access to passenger trains aided evangelists and other church workers in their travels.

In addition to their other decisions, the delegates elected a twelve-member Executive Presbytery to conduct the business of the Council between meetings— distributing funds to missionaries, overseeing publications, serving as corporate legal custodians, and providing continuity between the annual conferences, as well

Preamble and Resolution on Constitution

WHEREAS God, our Heavenly Father, sent His only begotten Son, the Lord Jesus Christ, into the World, Who purchased and redeemed fallen man with His own precious blood, and called out of the world and saved a people, of whom He built and established His church (Assembly of God. Matt. 16:18), upon the foundation of the Apostles and Prophets, Jesus Christ Himself being the Head and Chief Cornerstone (Eph. 2:20), and organized and baptized it with the Holy Spirit, with its government upon His shoulders (Isaiah 9:6, 7), said "the gates of hell shall not prevail against it" (Matt. 16:18); and

WHEREAS, He gave the holy inspired Scriptures, (both old and new covenants, Heb. 8:6–13) as the all sufficient rule for faith and practice (2 Tim. 3:16), as follows: "All Scripture is given by inspiration of God, and is profitable for doctrine, for reproof, for correction, for instruction in righteousness: That the man of God may be perfect, thoroughly furnished unto all good works," we therefore shall not add to nor take from it (Rev. 22:18); and

WHEREAS, He commanded that there should be no schism (division, sectarianism) in His body, the GENERAL ASSEMBLY (Church) of the firstborn, which are written in heaven (Heb. 12:23); and

WHEREAS, we recognize ourselves as members of said GENERAL ASSEMBLY OF GOD (which is God's organism), and do not believe in identifying ourselves as, or establishing ourselves into, a sect, that is a human organization that legislates or forms laws and articles of faith and has unscriptural jurisdiction over its members and creates unscriptural lines of fellowship and disfellowship and which separates itself from other members of the General Assembly (Church) of the first born, which is contrary to Christ's prayer in St. John 17, and Paul's teaching in Eph. 4:1–16, which we heartily endorse:

THEREFORE, BE IT RESOLVED, FIRST, That we recognize ourselves as a GENERAL COUNCIL of Pentecostal (Spirit Baptized) saints from local Churches of God in Christ, Assemblies of God, and various Apostolic Faith Missions and Churches, and Full Gospel Pentecostal Missions, and Assemblies of like faith in the United States of America, Canada, and Foreign Lands, whose purpose is neither to legislate laws of government, nor usurp authority over said various Assemblies of God, nor deprive them of their Scriptural and local rights and privileges, but to recognize Scriptural methods and order for worship, unity, fellowship, work and business for God, and to disapprove of all unscriptural methods, doctrine and conduct, and approve all Scriptural truth and conduct, endeavoring to keep the unity of the Spirit in the bonds of peace, until we all come into the unity of the faith, and of the knowledge of the Son of God, unto a perfect man, unto the measure of the stature of the fulness of Christ, and to walk accordingly, as recorded in Eph. 4:17–32. ....

RESOLVED, SECOND, That we recognize all the above said Assemblies of various names, and when speaking of them refer to them by the general Scriptural name "Assemblies of God;" and recommend that they all recognize themselves by the same name, that is, "Assembly of God" and adopt it as soon as practicable for the purpose of being more Scriptural and also legal in transacting business, owning property, and executing missionary work in home and foreign lands, and for general convenience, unity and fellowship.

—General Council Minutes (1914), 4–5.

as planning them. They chose E. N. Bell as general chairman and the much younger J. Roswell Flower (he was only twenty-six) as secretary-treasurer. For ministerial training, R. B. Chisolm's Nashoba Holiness School in Nashoba County, Mississippi, and Thomas K. Leonard's Gospel School in Findlay, Ohio, won recommendation. The General Council later set up the short-lived Midwest Bible School in Auburn, Nebraska (1921–1922). More permanent schools would follow.

Curiously, the Council restricted the role of women in ministry to that of "helpers in the gospel."[13] This carried the blessing of Bell and reflected his Southern Baptist upbringing. Even though early Pentecostalism produced many capable and successful women who served as evangelists, missionaries, pastors, and mission or school administrators, the delegates chose to limit their activities. However, they were too late.

Women who had been converted, baptized in the Spirit, and called to the ministry chose to believe that in the outpouring of the Spirit, women would prophesy as stated by Joel (Joel 2:28–29; Acts 2:16–18). With this in mind, they had already become engaged in various kinds of ministry and planted churches across the nation. Ordination of women as missionaries and evangelists was approved in 1914, but ordination as pastors was over two decades away. By the 1930s, women's involvement in professional ministry had begun to decline. Sizable numbers of women, however, continued to serve as evangelists and in foreign missions, but with little access to formal decision-making processes.

In regard to marriage and divorce, the Council recommended that divorced persons remain single. It also refused to give ministerial credentials to people who had

First Executive Presbytery of the Assemblies of God, April 1914. Front (l to r): Thomas K. Leonard, E. N. Bell, Cyrus B. Fockler. Back (l to r): John W. Welch, J. Roswell Flower, D. C. O. Opperman, Howard A. Goss, Mack M. Pinson.

District Councils Established

The Pentecostal Movement has not yet fully realized the tremendous import of the Hot Springs meeting last April. A glorious pattern, as in Acts 15, was there followed, showing how God's people can get together for mutual co-operation and fellowship in the Gospel of the Kingdom. Up to that time, any movement in the direction of co-operation was looked upon with severe criticism and fear, lest the Pentecostal Movement drift into a man-made organization, just like all other movements have done in the past. At the same time it was keenly felt that there should be some way of getting together for counsel and fellowship free from sectarian bondage. The Hot Springs Council . . . is proving to be a pattern for local companies of Pentecostal people all over the United States as they are meeting together in the different conventions and camp meetings this summer.

— *"District Councils Established,"* Christian Evangel *(August 22, 1914): 1.*

remarried while their previous partner was still living.[14] That decision has proven to be controversial especially in present time.

Whether within a few months or several years, ministers and churches began to form district councils that usually spanned several states. Among them, the Tristate district (Texas, New Mexico, Arizona), Northwest district (Washington, Oregon, Idaho, and western Montana), North Central district (Wisconsin, Minnesota, North Dakota, South Dakota, and eastern Montana), Southeastern district (Alabama, Florida, and Georgia), and the Eastern district (New York, New Jersey, Pennsylvania, and Delaware).

The early development of the Iowa and North Missouri District Council reveals the challenges that districts faced. Formed in August 1914 at the annual camp meeting in Davis City, Iowa, it grew steadily, but with many weak and unstable churches.[15] "Most of the ministers were inexperienced and not capable of holding meetings too long in one place," remembered Eugene Hastie. "One who later became a very capable and prominent minister said that when he began to preach he had only 14 sermons; when these were used he would look for another place." This meant that few stayed long enough to mature new congregations; instead, they preferred to move on to another community for their next evangelistic campaign. "Consequently, all too often a good work would be started, and then left alone, or at the best in charge of a novice," he added. "In view of these facts it is no wonder that . . . fanaticism developed in places."[16]

In 1916, the General Council established the General Presbytery to provide a more representative body than the Executive Presbytery to handle the judicial and executive needs of the organization between gatherings of the General Council. With limits placed on its authority, the General Presbytery—comprised of leaders from each district—could not replace the ultimate authority of the General Council, made up of ordained ministers and lay delegates, when in session. Through the years the composition and size of both the Executive and General Presbyteries have changed, while their functions have remained essentially the same.[17]

COUNCIL LEADERS

To some extent, the two leaders of the new organization were a study in contrasts. Bell had studied at Stetson University in Florida; Southern Baptist Theological Seminary in Louisville, Kentucky; and the University of

J. Roswell Flower and E. N. Bell

Chicago Divinity School. Flower had immigrated to the United States with his parents to join John Alexander Dowie's community at Zion City, Illinois. Disillusionment, however, had led the family to move to Indianapolis where they joined a local branch of the Christian and Missionary Alliance. Having had no formal training above public school in Canada, he had begun to read law under the guidance of a local attorney to prepare for a career in law before he was called to the ministry. In contrast to the younger and shorter Flower, Bell stood a head taller and was his senior by twenty-two years. What brought them together? Pentecost and the need for "divine order"—as Bell liked to say—among the churches.

Bell was a forty-five-year-old bachelor when he joined the Pentecostal movement and was one of its best-educated leaders in the early years. While pastoring a Baptist church in Fort Worth, Texas, he heard about the Pentecostal revival at William Durham's North Avenue Mission in Chicago. Taking a leave of absence from his congregation in 1907, he went eagerly seeking for Holy Spirit baptism, which he received eleven months later on July 18, 1908.

Returning to Texas, he found that many in the congregation had received the same experience, and he decided to stay at the church for another year. Before long, he joined with former followers of Charles Parham (Howard Goss, L. C. Hall, D. C. O. Opperman, and A. G. Canada) to save what they could of the Apostolic Faith movement. In the years that followed, he married a widow from Fort Worth, preached in various camp meetings and short-term Bible schools, and edited the Movement's periodical *The Apostolic Faith*, which later merged with Mack Pinson's *Word and Witness*. Settling down to pastor his first Pentecostal congregation in Malvern, Arkansas, he continued editing *Word and Witness* and became increasingly respected as a Pentecostal leader.

After the organizational meeting of the General Council in 1914, Bell served two nonsuccessive terms as general chairman (renamed general superintendent in 1927): 1914 and 1920 until his death in 1923. He influenced the Assemblies of God in many ways, from his perspective on the place of women in ministry, to his advocacy of tongues as initial evidence, to his insightful "Questions and Answers" column in the *Pentecostal Evangel*.

J. Roswell Flower made an even greater impact on the Assemblies of God by cofounding with his wife the *Pentecostal Evangel* and working in several influential denominational posts of leadership—especially as general secretary of the Council.

He also played a major role in the early years in steadfastly upholding the doctrinal teachings of the Assemblies of God.

Called the "saintly peacemaker" by his friends, Arch P. Collins followed Bell as general superintendent (at Bell's request) at the second General Council gathering in Chicago in November 1914. Another former Southern Baptist, Collins had prepared for the ministry at Baylor University. While pastoring in Fort Worth, he and his wife received the baptism in the Holy Spirit. When he left the church to join the Pentecostal movement without any guaranteed salary, his denominational friends asked, "What will become of your family?"

Ida and Arch P. Collins

"Social ostracism was to be [our] lot," Collins recalled. "But I committed all to God. One after another the children would receive the blessed Holy Spirit, until all nine of them, seven girls and two boys, had received. Then we were the happiest family in the land."[18]

During the heat of controversy over the nature of the Godhead that began to fracture the unity of the organization in 1915 (discussed on pp. 110–111), Council delegates chose John W. Welch to serve as general superintendent. A long-time pastor in the Christian and Missionary Alliance, he had received the Pentecostal baptism in 1910 while ministering in Oklahoma. Welch served in many capacities: twice as superintendent (1915–1920 and 1923–1925); as general secretary; as teacher at Glad Tidings Bible Institute in San Francisco; and as president of Central Bible Institute in Springfield, Missouri. Former members of the Alliance, including Welch, Flower, and Daniel W. Kerr, soon replaced those leaders who had come from the Apostolic Faith movement. In one way or another, each one protected and shaped the development of Assemblies of God beliefs.

Flower recalled that in 1923, Bell had been sent to meet with the Southern California district officers on a matter of business. Suffering physically, but without understanding the cause, he cut short his trip and returned home. "Filled with concern," John Welch visited him to inquire about his health. "While they were sitting in conversation, in the front room of Brother Bell's home, suddenly Brother Bell was stricken with a heart attack and slumped to the floor. Brother Welch tenderly gathered him in his arms and there the spirit of Brother Bell slipped away to be with Christ," Flower remembered. "A short time later, I arrived on the scene. I shall never forget the expression on Brother Welch's face and the tone of his breaking voice as he told of Brother Bell breathing his last in his arms."[19] Ministers in the Council had revered him as a model Pentecostal leader and as a "brother beloved."

Not all transitions in leadership passed smoothly. When Welch and Flower proposed a constitution in 1925, the incensed delegates at the General Council meeting in Eureka Springs, Arkansas, voted them out of office. Welch went to pastor a church in Modesto, California, and Flower traveled eastward to pastor in Scranton, Pennsylvania. (Ironically, after tempers calmed down, the 1927 General Council unanimously adopted a constitution.) The Council then elected William T. Gaston to succeed Welch as general superintendent. He served until 1929.[20]

DISAGREEMENTS ON DOCTRINE

The endurance of this new Pentecostal "fellowship," as the Assemblies of God would be known by insiders, was soon tested on vital points of doctrine. In its second year, the General Council faced a potentially disastrous crisis on the biblical understanding of the Trinity. It arose in part from the strong Jesus-centered piety of the fourfold gospel, more popularly known among Pentecostals as the "full gospel": Jesus Christ as Savior, Healer, Baptizer, and coming King.

Interest had been growing since 1913 in restoring what some Pentecostals believed to be another apostolic pattern, one that required water baptism in the name of Jesus Christ *only* (Acts 2:38). But the matter involved much more than just an option from baptizing in the name of the Father, Son, and Holy Spirit as commanded by Jesus in Matthew 28:19. It represented a serious departure from biblical teachings and historic Christian doctrine. Called the "New Issue," it eventually led to a major division in the General Council in 1916. After the adoption of a strongly worded Trinitarian creedal declaration, those members who embraced "Jesus Name" or "Oneness" teachings walked out of the meeting. Ultimately, 25 percent of the ministers withdrew over the doctrine.

Hot Times in Maryland

It is truly wonderful what the Lord is doing in Maryland. After the good meeting we had in Cumberland where they put us in jail, wife and I had an invitation to come to Westernport, Md., to preach in the United Brethren Church.

On Monday night the Lord met us in a cottage prayer meeting. We continued much in prayer and on Tuesday night the Lord met us and mightily baptized four with the Holy Spirit, the minister being the first one to receive.

On Friday night we met at the church where we had a wonderful service.

Then the chief of police came into the church with a bunch of deputies and ordered us to vacate the house, which we all refused to do in the name of Jesus. Then the chief, with rage, grabbed me and said, "I'll take you to the lockup." People in the congregation took hold of me and pulled me one way and the police the other way. I was pulled out of the church where there was a mob of people estimated at about one thousand persons.

I was taken out and the chief became so nervous that he let go his hold of me. His son, who was a saloonkeeper, ran up and struck me twice on the head. Someway the Lord helped and protected and I can say that it did not hurt me. . . . I prayed and praised the Lord and re-entered the church. When the saints saw me enter a shout of praise to God went up for His deliverance to me.

—A. B. Cox, *"Hot Times in Maryland,"* Christian Evangel *(July 25, 1914): 1.*

Earlier debates over tongues as initial evidence and sanctification had divided the broader Pentecostal movement. Now another separation had begun.[21] Although Oneness believers departed from historic Christianity on this one vital point, they have otherwise remained Pentecostal in doctrine.

The *Statement of Fundamental Truths* assured members and outside observers of the soundness of Assemblies of God doctrine. Without belief in historic Trinitarian doctrine, the potential growth and evangelical identification of the organization would likely have been scuttled. But its adoption was not without reluctance and pain. As Pentecostal believers, members of the General Council had prided themselves on seeking revival fire and spiritual unity. To them, the Assemblies of God stood apart from the spiritual deadness of the historic churches. They wanted nothing to do with lifeless creeds and confessions. Thus, the formulation of the *Statement of Fundamental Truths* amounted to the reluctant swallowing of a bitter pill. Nevertheless, concern to protect the faithful from doctrinal error won out.

Two years later in 1918, internal controversy brewed when old questions resurfaced over the necessity of tongues as evidence of Spirit baptism. Church leaders once again had to reflect on the organization's doctrinal and spiritual identity. After much discussion, the Council reaffirmed the doctrine of initial evidence and highlighted it as the "distinctive testimony of the Assemblies of God."[22]

EXPANDING MINISTRIES

Ministers, missionaries, and laypersons concentrated their energies on many different activities in serving God. These included street meetings, revivals, camp meetings, church plantings, missions, and other activities. John Welch, the secretary of the Council in 1920, when referring to home and foreign missions, said: "The General Council of the Assemblies of God was never meant to be an institution; it is just a missionary agency."[23] Despite the implied simplicity, the task of bringing order to the sometimes chaotic problems of missionary finances placed unbearable demands on the time and energies of the Executive Presbytery.

At the third gathering of the General Council in Chicago in 1915, the mission zeal of the organization once more overflowed when it went on record as promoting the evangelization of the heathen according to New Testament methods.[24] While everyone envisioned the evangelistic and church planting practices of the Early Church, not until the 1921 Council would the methods be more carefully defined according to the "Pauline example."

The General Council in Chicago in 1919 marked a milestone in its development when it voted to establish its first department, the Missionary Department. Although the new department held responsibility for pioneer church evangelism, or "home missions" in the United States, it focused primarily on foreign missions. Regardless of the fact that he had never served as a missionary or traveled abroad, J. Roswell Flower received appointment as the first full-time missionary secretary-treasurer (i.e., head of the department), a position that principally had oversight of distributing funds to the missionaries. When he took office in 1919, the Assemblies of God supported 206 independent-minded missionaries with offerings for them that totaled $63,548 for the year.[25] In less than ten years, the missionary list would jump to 277 names and giving would reach $300,000.[26]

Administrative expenses for the office, utilities, and postage were to be covered by offerings from the churches. However, few congregations wanted their missionary dollars spent for the missionary secretary's salary or office equipment. They preferred that it went directly to the missionaries on the cutting edge of evangelism. Because of the Council's policy of sending 100 percent of all designated and undesignated missionary offerings overseas, financing office expenditures plagued the Council for years to come. As an immediate solution, the department received a subsidy from the earnings of Gospel Publishing House. The sale of subscriptions to the *Pentecostal Evangel* was also channeled to meet these costs.

People did not wait to hear from church leaders to become involved in various kinds of ministry. In the minds of the saints, Pentecost and ministry went hand in hand. At the Assembly of God in Houston, Texas, Etta Calhoun called a group of

women to intercessory prayer on behalf of the missionaries. Before long, they added practical assistance to their prayers. Although women's auxiliaries had long existed in the Protestant denominations to support missions, this was a new venture for Pentecostals.

Officially, the Assemblies of God frowned on establishing charitable institutions overseas. In the *Pentecostal Evangel* in 1920, Flower ruled out "building up charitable institutions, hospitals and schools as do the denominational [mission] societies."

Etta Calhoun

Prompted by the nearness of Christ's return, he said, "The Pentecostal commission is to witness, *witness*, WITNESS."[27] But when word reached Calhoun and her cohort five years later that the children at Lillian Trasher's orphanage at Assiout, Egypt, needed clothes, they sent enough for three hundred children. Had Calhoun read Flower's announcement? If she had, it probably wouldn't have stopped her. Human need called for immediate response, and Pentecostals gave generously to such appeals.

Calhoun's activities met with such enthusiasm and success that the Texico district (Texas and New Mexico) invited her to organize the Women's Missionary Council (WMC) in 1925 to assist the district "in the great missionary enterprises of the church as well as carrying forward our own work among the prisons, the sick, and the poor of our own land."[28] National recognition from the General Council swiftly followed, and women founded WMC chapters across the country.

Permission to plant new churches came from the Lord, not from church officers, in the early years. Pioneering pastors believed that obedience to God's call and faith for His provision would supply whatever needs might arise. Churches were started in homes, storefronts, tents, brush arbors, vacant theaters, rented halls, and older church buildings. Indeed, Howard Goss had leased the Grand Opera House itself in Hot Springs several months before the 1914 Council for his growing congregation.[29]

Few church planters across the Pentecostal movement in the early years had the benefit of attending a Bible institute and had to learn on the job. Young Clifford Crabtree, a farm boy Spirit baptized in an Aimee Semple McPherson campaign in Washburn, Maine, in 1917, joined with two friends and traveled to Georgia to evangelize. There they met three evangelists, Carro and Susie Davis and Minnie Scott. The Davis sisters, who had left teaching school to preach the gospel, mentored him in doctrine, grammar, and diction. Like many other early Pentecostals, they preferred to rely on the immediate inspiration of the Spirit for preaching in place of sermon preparation (Luke 12:12). When he preached, they took notes and then critiqued him afterward—an experience he described as a "terrible discipline."[30] The investment paid off. Crabtree returned

Clifford Crabtree

to New England with the Davis sisters to pioneer churches that began in open-air evangelistic meetings, tents, and rented halls. After they parted ways, he and his wife, Helen, continued planting churches in Nova Scotia and Prince Edward Island before returning to Bangor, Maine, for a long pastorate.

In a few places, congregations with sufficient means erected traditional church buildings. For example, the Ossining (New York) Gospel Assembly, constructed in 1914, included custom-made stained glass windows (built, as it was, largely through the generosity of a wealthy heiress and member, Mary S. Stone).[31] Stone also gave seventy-five thousand dollars to endow the operation of a nearby house for furloughed or visiting missionaries. (After ninety years, the endowment, although on a diminished scale, still contributes toward missionaries.)

Starting churches, however, took a toll on preachers and their families. District organizations, still in their infancy, could not offer much help. So established Assemblies sometimes sent offerings or gave "grocery showers" to keep food on the table. Texas church planter W. D. Taylor recalled that God "supplied our needs many times in the early years. We never [asked for] an offering, but somehow the need was met. In 1927 my appendix ruptured. My church stood by in prayer almost two days and nights. God healed me. We raised our family trusting God."[32] Such projects called for stamina as well as faith.

Persecution could also be intense. When Oklahoma sharecropper Rufus Nicholson was converted and called to preach, he and his family evangelized in the boomtowns that sprang up in the oil fields across the state. "We would stretch a line of lights, put up a windbreak around the choir and platform, borrow a piano, and rent heavy boards for seats from a lumber yard," wrote his daughter Jewell Nicholson Cunningham.

Rowdies did their best to disrupt their services. At the Bixby Assembly, "Men would come right into the service and yell curses louder than Papa could preach.

Rocks rained on the roof, and a cat was thrown through the window." Rufus, however, didn't flinch. "Somebody threw a rotten egg at Papa while he was preaching, but with his style of preaching he was a moving target and hard to hit. . . . But it got rougher. Shots were fired over the roof, and one night a big railroad tie was rammed through the front door and came scooting down the aisle. A deacon decided to stop the disturbance. When he went outside he was knocked unconscious by a man wearing brass knuckles. . . . People would tell us on the streets that they wanted to come to the church but were afraid. But we always had a packed church anyway. For those who dared to attend the services, God more than made up for the persecution. Many received the blessed Holy Spirit, and several went into the ministry from the Bixby congregation."[33]

MOVING THE HEADQUARTERS

Today over a thousand people work in multiple ministries at the Assemblies of God headquarters—making it hard to imagine the simplicity of its operation in the early years. After the Hot Springs Council in 1914, Bell and Flower accepted T. K. Leonard's offer of his church and Bible school property in Findlay, Ohio, as a headquarters. He also offered the use of his small printing press for publishing the *Word and Witness* and the *Christian Evangel*. (*Word and Witness* soon merged into the *Christian Evangel*. For a short time, the name was changed to *Weekly Evangel* before becoming the *Pentecostal Evangel* in 1919. The name was changed again in 2002, this time to *Today's Pentecostal Evangel*.)

In Findlay, Bell and Flower got five dollars a week for living expenses. "Beyond this," remembered Alice Reynolds Flower, "God took care of whatever was lacking to meet our simple needs. . . . Those first six months were wonderful days of proving God."[34] A year later, the Council authorized moving the offices and printing equipment to St. Louis, Missouri. On the Mississippi (and being forty times larger than Findlay) it offered a better location for publishing.

T. K. Leonard's Gospel School and publishing house in Findlay, Ohio. It served for a short time as the first headquarters of the General Council of the Assemblies of God.

Gospel Publishing House staff at the second headquarters facility in St. Louis, Missouri (ca. 1916). J. Roswell Flower is in the back, center. The man on the right was a frequent headquarters visitor.

But a bigger city also meant greater expenses. Unable to afford larger quarters in the city, even with someone's personal loan of sixty-five hundred dollars to the Council, Bell scouted several Missouri and Iowa towns for a relocation site. That's when he learned that real estate values in Springfield, Missouri, were depressed and several buildings offering good possibilities for expansion were available. They could also be purchased without the Council going into serious debt.

Flower then visited the city and confirmed Bell's recommendation. Consequently, the headquarters moved to Springfield in 1918 and took over what had been a grocery and meat market, putting the heavy printing equipment on the first floor and the editorial and executive offices on the second. Few if any realized how effectively the new home would shield church leaders from the urban decay and ethnic and social tensions that would later rack the country.

THE GREAT WAR

Four months after the Hot Springs Council, the Great War (World War I) began. Pentecostals believed that events foretold in Daniel, Matthew 24, and the Book of

The Assemblies of God moved its headquarters to this building on West Pacific Street in Springfield, Missouri, in 1918.

Revelation were about to be fulfilled. Several British Pentecostals spent the war in prison or in alternate service because they declared themselves pacifists and refused to support the war effort. In their estimation, Jesus had commanded that people should love their enemies. When the United States entered the war in 1917, the Assemblies of God notified the federal government of its pacifist position on military service and bearing arms. At the same time, it pledged its loyalty to the government.

Those thumbing through the Book of Revelation while reading newspaper headlines carefully watched for the "signs of the times" (Matthew 16:3). Many speculated about the appearance of the Antichrist. One reader of the *Pentecostal Evangel* wrote the editor and asked if the emblem of the International Red Cross was in fact the mark of the beast referred to in Revelation 13:16–17.[35] Others later looked for a possible link between the League of Nations (founded after the war in 1919) with the confederacy of the ten nations mentioned in Revelation 17:10–16.

The founding men and women of the Assemblies of God were caught between the times: their time and the time of Christ's return. They established the General Council as a legal institution to further their goals. However, while affirming loyalty to the American government, they viewed their refusal to endorse the war effort as proclaiming their "citizenship [to be] in heaven" (Philippians 3:20). Then again, when the Council approved a constitution and bylaws in 1927, it moved further down the denominational path (albeit with other Pentecostal groups). When the Second World War appeared on the horizon, most Assemblies of God people thought of it as a just war, particularly after the Japanese attacked Pearl Harbor. Consequently, they largely supported the war effort. Still, Assemblies of God believers saw themselves as "Christ's ambassadors" (2 Corinthians 5:20) in a hostile world within a heartbeat of receiving the divine wrath.

Pentecostal Saints Opposed to War

The Pentecostal people, as a whole, are uncompromisingly opposed to war, having much the same spirit as the early Quakers, who would rather be shot themselves than that they should shed the blood of their fellow-men. Because we have given [in a previous article] this bit of war news is no reason that we are in favor of war, but rather that our readers may have some knowledge of how the war is actually affecting our own people, who through forces of circumstances are compelled to be in the midst of the terrible conflict. Indeed, some have already urged us to arrange for a great peace council among the Pentecostal saints, to put ourselves on record as being opposed to war at home and abroad. We are told that many German brethren, when commanded to take up arms, have refused to do so and have suffered martyrdom as a consequence. Others, because they have been compelled to do so, have gone with the armies, not knowing how to do otherwise, but praying that God will save them from taking the life of any man. . . .

— *"Pentecostal Saints Opposed to War,"* Weekly Evangel (June 19, 1915): 1.

Among the Soldier Boys

Richey

We wish to report victory among our soldier boys.

On Friday night, I believe was one of the sweetest meetings we have had, and over a hundred soldiers came up to the front and knelt down, praying and asking God for Jesus' sake to forgive, save and keep. Then on Saturday night we had an old time testimony meeting, and oh it was touching to hear them tell how they had found Jesus! One Catholic boy got up and told how the night before was the first Protestant meeting he had ever been in and that God had saved his soul.

Dear ones, God is working, do not lose faith, hold on, for eternity will only tell what your prayers mean for thousands of boys in these camps. Keep praying.

—*Raymond T. Richey. "Among the Soldier Boys,"* Pentecostal Evangel
(March 30, 1918): 15.

LIGHTNING IN A BOTTLE

Many observers have wondered what caused the dramatic growth of the Pentecostal movement and Assemblies of God over the twentieth century. Better organization? Superior management skills? More financial resources? Though the value of these factors can never be discounted, the answer lies elsewhere: in the people who made it happen. "Brothers, think of what you were when you were called," Paul reminded the Corinthian believers. "Not many of you were wise by human standards; not many were influential; not many were of noble birth. But God chose the foolish things of the world to shame the wise; God chose the weak things of the world to shame the strong" (1 Corinthians 1:26–27). Pentecostals saw themselves when they read this passage.

Like their holiness predecessors, they published extensively—tracts, booklets, books, and many periodicals. In looking at the history of the Assemblies of God, one readily sees the personal dynamic at work in the pages of the *Pentecostal Evangel.* A letter published in its April 7, 1923, edition shows how the networking of Spirit-filled believers could assist in church planting. Wesley Stowell and his wife reported they had joined the General Council while living in Petoskey, Michigan. In the fall of 1922, with limited resources, they moved to Gulf Port, Florida, to start a church. "We are working among poor people, mostly fisherman," they wrote. And like others with a heaven-sent call on their lives, they readily confessed: "We are willing to sacrifice ourselves. We feel that what is done must be done quickly."

Initially conducting Sunday School and Sunday evening services, they soon needed a building for their growing congregation. A real estate agent had given them property, but they had little money and the price of lumber was high. After asking the *Evangel* readers to pray that God would supply their needs, they wisely added a practical request: "If any of the General Council workers are near us at any time, we will be very glad of some help."[36]

President Samuel A. Jamieson (center) with faculty and students at Midwest Bible School in Auburn, Nebraska (1920–21). This was the first school established by the General Council.

The explanation of the spectacular growth lies in the intense belief among Pentecostals that through Holy Spirit baptism and the restoration of the gifts of the Spirit, the spiritual power of the New Testament church had been restored. Combined with a pragmatic willingness to use virtually any means available to accomplish world evangelization, the Pentecostals set to their task with unusual vigor. Historian Grant Wacker notes: "On one hand Pentecostals' conviction that God's Spirit literally took up residence inside their physical bodies authorized tongues, healings, visions, resurrections, and other miraculous phenomena that had largely disappeared from American Protestant culture, especially mainline groups. On the other hand that same conviction also authorized a kind of swashbuckling entrepreneurialism that left many observers amazed when they were not appalled."[37] In this regard, "Pentecostals' distinctive understanding of the human encounter with the divine . . . enabled them to capture lightning in a bottle and, more important, to keep it, decade after decade, without stilling the fire or cracking the vessel."[38]

This accounts for the Stowells' readiness—without any financial guarantees—to sacrifice themselves to evangelize and build a church in Gulf Port. Confidence that God would provide the necessary finances did not preclude their contacting a sympathetic realtor and recruiting workers from the readership of the Evangel. In looking back they would say, "God did it all!" Through the years, Council members—filled with the fire of the Holy Spirit and a savvy ability to get things done—would find innumerable ways to share the gospel at home and abroad.

The chapters in this unit tell the stories of such Christ's ambassadors who sometimes braved trying circumstances to follow God's call on their lives.

RECOMMENDED READING

Alexander, Paul. *Peace to War: Shifting Allegiances in the Assemlbies of God*. Telford, PA: Cascadia Publishing House, 2009.

Beaman, Jay. *Pentecostal Pacifism: The Origins, Development and Rejection of Pacific Belief Among the Pentecostals*. Hillsboro, Kans.: Center for Mennonite Brethren Studies, 1989.

Blumhofer, Edith L. *The Assemblies of God: A Chapter in the Story of American Pentecostalism*. Vol. 1 and Vol. 2. Springfield, Mo.: Gospel Publishing House, l989.

Brumback, Carl. *God in Three Persons*. Cleveland, Tenn.: Pathway Press, 1959.

————. *Suddenly From Heaven: A History of the Assemblies of God*. Springfield, Mo.: Gospel Publishing House, 1961.

Clemmons, Ithiel C. *Bishop C. H. Mason and the Roots of the Church of God in Christ*. Bakersfield, Calif.: Pneuma Life Publishers, 1996.

Corum, Fred T., and Hazel E. Bakewell. *The Sparkling Fountain*. Windsor, Ohio: Corum & Associates, 1983.

Gohr, Glenn. "The Historical Development of the Statement of Fundamental Truths." *Assemblies of God Heritage* 32 (2012): 60–66.

Goss, Ethel E. *The Winds of God: The Story of the Early Pentecostal Movement (1901–1914) in the Life of Howard A. Goss*. Rev. ed. Hazelwood, Mo.: Word Aflame Press, 1977.

Horn, Ken. "The Centennial of the *Pentecostal Evangel*." *Assemblies of God Heritage* 33 (2013): 4–15.

Hall, J. L. *The United Pentecostal Church and the Evangelical Movement*. Hazelwood, Mo.: Word Aflame Press, 1990.

Manley, Anabel. *WMC History: 1925–1975*. Houston: By the author, 1975.

McElhany, Gary Don. "The South Aflame: A History of the Assemblies of God in the Gulf Region, 1901–1940." PhD diss., Mississippi State University, 1996.

Reed, David A. "Origins and Development of the Theology of Oneness Pentecostalism in the United States." PhD diss., Boston University, 1978.

Wacker, Grant. *Heaven Below: Early Pentecostals and American Culture*. Cambridge, Mass.: Harvard University Press, 2001.

Warner, Wayne. "A Powerful Witness in New England: The Pentecostal Legacy of Clifford and Helen Crabtree." *Assemblies of God Heritage* 14 (summer 1994): 10–13, 27–29.

ENDNOTES

[1] Grant Wacker, *Heaven Below: Early Pentecostals and American Culture* (Cambridge: Harvard University Press, 2001), 205.

[2] J. Roswell Flower, "History of the Assemblies of God" (mimeographed, 1949), 19.

[3] Questions remain about this loose-knit association since there are no existing minutes, and it is unclear when it was organized or even how often it met. The Flower Pentecostal Heritage Center holds nearly one hundred ordination certificates of individuals in this network who joined the Assemblies of God. None of them were signed by Mason or even mention the city of Memphis, the location of the Church of God in Christ headquarters. For information, see Wayne E. Warner, "A Call for Love, Tolerance, and Cooperation," *Assemblies of God Heritage* 14 (fall 1994): 3–4, 31.

[4] Ethel E. Goss, *The Winds of God*, rev. ed. (Hazelwood, Mo.: Word Aflame Press, 1977), 272.

[5] Anna C. Reiff, "Things Missionary," *Latter Rain Evangel* (March 1913): 15.

[6] Anna C. Reiff, "The Missionary Problem Again," *Latter Rain Evangel* (September 1913): 14.

[7] The Pentecostal Mission in South and Central Africa, set up in 1910 by the Bethel Pentecostal Assembly of Newark, New Jersey, was a notable exception; see Gary B. McGee, *New International Dictionary of Pentecostal and Charismatic Movements*, 970.

[8] *The Gospel Witness*, 1, 2, 13. The writer referred to the founding of the Pentecostal Missionary Union (U.S.A.) by Levi R. Lupton and others at the 1909 camp meeting in Alliance, Ohio.

[9] Eugene N. Hastie, *History of the West Central District of the Assemblies of God* (Fort Dodge, Iowa: Walterick Publishing Co., 1948), 31.

[10] Glenn Gohr, "D. C. O. Opperman's Short-Term Bible Schools," *Assemblies of God Heritage* 11 (spring 1991): 6–7.

[11] General Council Minutes, April 1914, 8.

[12] Walter J. Higgins, as told to Dalton E. Webber, *Pioneering in Pentecost: My Experiences of 46 Years in the Ministry* (Bostonia, Calif.: By the author, 1958), 42.

[13] E. N. Bell, "Some Complaints," *Word and Witness* (20 January 1914): 2.

[14] General Council Minutes, April 1914, 8.

[15] Hastie, *History of the West Central District*, 59.

[16] Ibid., 61, 63.

[17] William W. Menzies, *Anointed to Serve: The Story of the Assemblies of God* (Springfield, Mo.: Gospel Publishing House, 1971), 121.

[18] A. P. Collins, "A Baptized Baptist Preacher," *Christian Evangel* (23 January 1915): 1.

[19] J. Roswell Flower quoted in Fred T. Corum and Hazel E. Bakewell, *The Sparkling Fountain* (Windsor, Ohio: Corum and Associates, 1983), 216–217.

[20] Edith L. Blumhofer, *The Assemblies of God: A Chapter in the Story of American Pentecostalism* (Springfield, Mo.: Gospel Publishing House, 1989), 1:258–259.

[21] Ibid., 1:221–239.

[22] General Council Minutes, 1918, 8.

[23] "A Missionary Movement," *Pentecostal Evangel* (13 November 1920): 8.

[24] General Council Minutes (combined minutes), 1914–1917, 9–10.

[25] General Council Minutes, 1920, 36.

[26] General Council Minutes, 1927, 48–49.

[27] J. Roswell Flower, "The Pentecostal Commission," *Pentecostal Evangel* (12 June 1920): 12.

[28] General Council Minutes, 1925, 66.

[29] Goss, *The Winds of God*, 281.

[30] Wayne Warner, "A Powerful Witness in New England: The Pentecostal Legacy of Clifford and Helen Crabtree," *Assemblies of God Heritage* 14 (summer 1994): 13.

[31] Lindsley Schepmoes, "Assembly of God Groups Stress Mission Work," *The Ossining, New York, Citizen Register* (3 November 1960).

[32] W. D. Taylor, "His Grace Is Sufficient," in *Reflections of Faith*, edited by Jeffrey B. Champion (Springfield, Mo.: Assemblies of God Benevolences Department, 1983), 10.

[33] Jewell Nicholson Cunningham, "Evangelizing and Pioneering Throughout the Southwest," *Assemblies of God Heritage* 5 (spring 1985): 4.

[34] Alice Reynolds Flower, *Grace for Grace* (Springfield, Mo.: By the author, 1961), 60–61.

[35] E. N. Bell, "Questions and Answers," *Pentecostal Evangel* (26 January 1918): 9.

[36] Wesley Stowell, "Openings for Workers," *Pentecostal Evangel* (7 April 1923): 15.

[37] Wacker, *Heaven Below*, 15.

[38] Ibid., 10.

CHAPTER 7

WORKING FOR AN AMERICAN HARVEST

At the second General Council in Chicago in November 1914, delegates unanimously declared: "We commit ourselves and the movement . . . for the greatest evangelism that the world has ever seen." Like the first disciples, they took seriously these words of Jesus: "Do you not say, 'Four months more and then the harvest'? I tell you, open your eyes and look at the fields! They are ripe for harvest" (John 4:35).

During congregational worship, prophecy and interpretations of tongues often reminded believers to evangelize because "night is coming, when no one can work" (John 9:4). "Over and over messages were given in the Spirit," said J. Roswell Flower, "that the time would not be long and what was done must be done quickly."

Church planting in America didn't demand ordination and ministerial credentials, or a Bible school or a high school or even a grade school education. But it did require faith and lots of grit. Pentecostals seemed to thrive on proving God. When George N. Eldridge, a former pastor in the Christian and Missionary Alliance, and his wife, Anna, felt directed of God to pioneer a church in Los Angeles, they "hadn't a dollar in sight" or anyone to back them financially. George remembered that "for two years Mrs. Eldridge would rise at six o'clock in the morning, go out on the hillside at the back of our house, and there for two hours she would lift her hands to heaven and claim the money with which to build this church in obedience to God's command." One day, while looking for suitable property, George "clearly heard the Lord's voice saying, 'This is the spot.'" Through a set of unusual circumstances, he purchased the property. "God did not let us see very far ahead, but He met us at every point so that when [Bethel Temple] was dedicated, it was free from debt."

Neither did finances deter Harry Bowley from building the Assembly of God in Thayer, Missouri. After months of revival, marked by many conversions, healings, exorcisms, Spirit baptisms, and other usual happenings, meeting in a tent began to take a toll on the new congregation. "We began to pray," he recalled, "and God laid the need upon a woman who gave us the first hundred dollars. We bought a little tract of land on the side of a hill, which was nothing but rock. It cost ninety-five dollars. By the time we fixed the deed for it, we had twenty-five cents left, but we spent

Harry Bowley

this money on nails and hired some men to start building the foundations."

After digging the trench and preparing the forms for the concrete, a construction worker said to Bowley, "Man, you can't build a church on twenty-five cents." To which he replied, "When these nails are gone, God will give us some more nails." Sharing the experiences of other pioneer pastors and their flocks who ardently trusted in God's provision, Bowley added: "Every ounce of the concrete, every bit of the lumber, was prayed in."

The evangelists and church planters in this chapter, as well as the mission strategist who trained Hispanic pastors, had what it took, coming from a variety of backgrounds and developing lasting ministries: Robert and Marie Brown, Henry C. Ball, Francisco Olazábal, Ethel Musick, Robert and Mary Craig, and Aimee Semple McPherson.

ROBERT (1872-1948) AND MARIE BROWN (1880-1971)

They were an unlikely couple. Marie Burgess grew up in Eau Claire, Wisconsin, as an Episcopalian, sensitive and contemplative. Robert Brown, forthright and uncompromising, was born in Northern Ireland, served four years as a London policeman, stud-

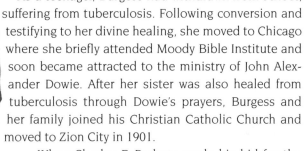

ied to be a civil engineer, and gained ordination as a preacher from the Wesleyan Methodist Church. After being baptized in the Spirit at Burgess's Glad Tidings Hall mission in New York City, he said to Burgess: "If you ever change your name, it will be to Brown."

As a teenager, Burgess had withdrawn from school, suffering from tuberculosis. Following conversion and testifying to her divine healing, she moved to Chicago where she briefly attended Moody Bible Institute and soon became attracted to the ministry of John Alexander Dowie. After her sister was also healed from tuberculosis through Dowie's prayers, Burgess and her family joined his Christian Catholic Church and moved to Zion City in 1901.

Marie and Robert Brown

When Charles F. Parham made his bid for the leadership of Dowie's organization by holding Pentecostal services there in the fall of 1906, Burgess attended and was baptized in the Spirit. She shook, spoke in tongues, and like other early Pentecostals, had visions of the nations of the world needing to hear the gospel message. Although not called to missions, she felt the heart cry for world evangelism, which never left her. In response to Parham's request, she headed for New York City in January to share the "apostolic faith."

Marie not only underwent a name change when she married Robert Brown in 1909, so did her "Hall." It became Glad Tidings Tabernacle. And so began a copastorate that lasted until his death in 1948 (she continued). The Browns and their growing congregation joined the Assemblies of God two years after it formed. Needing larger facilities, the congregation purchased the former Calvary Baptist Church in 1921 with a price tag of $105,000. Glad Tidings became a major center for Pentecostalism in the northeast, influencing the development of other congregations and supporting

Glad Tidings Tabernacle, New York City

many missionaries. Not only did it contribute to the Pentecostal witness among Ukrainian immigrants to the United States, but it also influenced Ivan Voronaeff, pastor of a Russian Baptist church in New York City. He eventually became the Pentecostal "apostle to Russia," returning to his homeland to evangelize in 1920.

Some pastors in urban areas, like Robert Brown, contended that a city needed only one Pentecostal church (perhaps believing it matched the New Testament pattern, e.g., the church of Ephesus and the church of Smyrna). Branch missions and other ministries would stem from this central congregation. For a time, Glad Tidings served as the hub for Pentecostal activities in New York City, but gradually unrelated Assemblies established themselves. In addition, the Browns held strongly to the notion that the Assemblies of God must remain a "voluntary cooperative fellowship" and never become a denomination. Yet they continued their membership in the General Council and Robert Brown served for many years as a general presbyter.

HENRY C. BALL
(1896-1989)

The Pentecostal faith among Hispanics in North America is usually associated with the ministries of George and Carrie Judd Montgomery, Henry C. Ball, Alice E. Luce, Juan L. Lugo, and Francisco Olazábal, among others.

"Hermano Ball" was born in Brooklyn, Iowa, in 1896, but grew up in Ricardo, Texas, cared for by his widowed mother. Though converted under the ministry of a Baptist preacher, he and his mother joined the Methodist Church in Kingsville, Texas, in 1910. Sometime after this, Ball was inspired by the message of a missionary from Venezuela and became burdened to minister to the Hispanics living in Ricardo.

Who Will Be the First To Come?

C. Stanley Cooke

C. Stanley Cooke, a noted evangelist in later years, suffered a rather embarrassing "Eutychus experience," while serving as song leader in a Swanton, Maryland, revival in 1922. The meetings were being conducted in a "glory barn" (and this was no mere euphemism). The top of a haystack was the only place young Cooke could find to be seated after his song-leading chore was finished. Edgar Barrick, missionary to India, preached the message and extended the invitation:

"Who will be the first to come?"

High on his lofty perch above the "platform," Cooke blinked sleepily. He shifted his position in the hay. To his consternation, he felt himself slipping. He could not stop his downward flight by digging his heels into the hay, and he would have dropped his guitar if he had tried to grab the hay with his hands. Faster and faster slid the song leader toward the unsuspecting audience below.

"Who will be the first to come?"

With a crash, Cooke hit the altar rail. No longer was "every head bowed and every eye closed." After all, it is not too often that one who sang like an angel should descend from above in such a startling manner to answer the altar call! Cooke was not only the first but also the last to respond to the invitation that fateful evening.

—*Carl Brumback, Suddenly . . . from Heaven (1961), 248–249.*

His inability to speak Spanish did not stop him. At age fourteen he began knocking on the doors of Mexican homes, telling the families the only words he knew: "El Domingo por la tarde en la escuela." When questioned about what would take place, he could only reply in his stumbling Spanish, "Sunday afternoon in the schoolhouse."

After ringing the school bell on Sunday afternoon, a man and woman arrived. He began the service singing the hymn, "We Praise Thee, O God," in Spanish. Ball then knelt and began to recite the Lord's Prayer. Halfway through the prayer, he peered cautiously through his fingers at his congregation; neither the man nor woman showed any emotion. He then sang the song again. Afterward, he asked the man to read from his Spanish New Testament; since he couldn't read, he handed it to the woman, who soon gave up due to her limited education.

A conversation then ensued between the woman and man that lasted for half an hour, leaving Ball wondering what was being said, except for the words Católico and Protestante. When it ended, the teenager smiled and sang the song for the third time. At the conclusion, he pointed to the door, signaling the end of the service.

For a while in his services, he read the sermons of John Wesley in a Spanish edition, learning the language as he went. Finally, after two months, he began preaching in Spanish and giving invitations at the end of the services for people to accept Christ. Eventually the woman who attended his first service came to Christ. Church attendance soon jumped from two to fifty, and the congregation became an established Methodist church.

When Felix A. Hale, an Assemblies of God evangelist, preached in Kingsville, Ball was baptized in the Holy Spirit. Although desiring to remain a Methodist, church officials sent him a letter of dismissal. In 1915, he gained ordination with the Assemblies of God and started a new congregation. As conversions among Hispanics increased, his activities grew to the point that he organized the first convention of Spanish-speaking pastors in 1918 in Kingsville. Later, he was elected as the first superintendent of the Latin American District Council in 1929.

Ball's commonsense approach to home and foreign missions constantly prompted him to seek new avenues for evangelism. He promoted annual conventions for Hispanic converts to provide fellowship and instruction. In 1916 while pastoring in Kingsville, he began publishing *La Luz Apostólica* (Apostolic Light); it later became the district's official publication. Designed as a tool for evangelism, it was enormously successful and helped growing congregations.

He also published a songbook in Spanish called Himnos de Gloria (Hymns of Glory), which was printed without musical notation. It became an instant success. In 1921, financed with money from his father's estate, he published a new edition with the notes included. Both editions were printed by the thousands. Knowing the Hispanic's love for music, other songbooks followed.

Interest in formal ministerial training led Ball to establish the Latin American Bible Institute (LABI) in San Antonio, Texas, in 1926. Faced with the same lack of curricular materials that Alice Luce struggled with in California, he wrote extensively to provide class notes for his students. Preparation was not easy, given his own lack of formal Bible training. Like other Pentecostals called to ministry, however, he confronted the problem and worked to resolve it. His notes became popular in other schools in Latin America and are still highly valued.

Henry C. Ball (first row center) and students at the Latin American Bible Institute in Texas

LABI graduates planted churches in many parts of the United States, Mexico, Spain, Nicaragua, Puerto Rico, and Cuba. Resigning as superintendent in 1939, the Balls went as missionaries to Chile for two years. By now his ministry had encompassed educational, editorial, and district responsibilities. For ten years (1943–1953) he served as the first field secretary for Latin America. In 1946, he founded what is now Life Publishers International, which produces gospel literature and textbooks in several languages. In many ways Hermano Ball proved to be one of the most far-sighted and creative missionary strategists that the Assemblies of God has produced.

FRANCISCO OLAZÁBAL
(1886-1937)

Many considered Francisco Olazábal to be the greatest Latin-American evangelist to emerge from Pentecostal Spanish-speaking churches. Called the "Great Aztec" because of his brown skin, large frame, and coal black eyes, he had "the blood of Montezuma in his veins." Olazábal was born in El Verano, Sinaloa State, Mexico, but at eighteen he went through a time of spiritual rebellion and left home to stay with an aunt in San Francisco.

Francisco Olazábal

Walking along the street one day, he was offered a tract informing him that Jesus Christ had come into the world to save sinners. Moved after reading it, Olazábal sought out the man who had given it to him, the wealthy businessman and gold miner George Montgomery. George and Carrie Judd Montgomery, devout members of the Christian and Missionary Alliance, operated several ministries in nearby Oakland. After Olazábal's conversion, the Montgomerys began to teach him basic Christian doctrines.

A few months later he returned to Mexico and began to prepare for the ministry. His calling confirmed to him a vision that he had had when he was twelve. He had seen a crack in the floor, and looking through it he had seen a large number of people dancing, drinking, and gambling. At that moment, a voice spoke to him saying, "They must be saved." With that in mind and his earnest desire now to preach the gospel, he enrolled at Wesleyan Methodist College in San Luis Potosí, Mexico, from which he graduated in 1910. He later studied at Moody Bible Institute in Chicago.

Ministry in the Methodist Church eventually took him back to California, southern California this time, where he worked for a time in the Compton area as an evangelist among railroad workers and farm laborers. He also ministered in planting Spanish-speaking Methodist churches in Pasadena, Los Angeles, and Sacramento. Becoming reacquainted with the Montgomerys in 1917, he was startled to learn that they had become Pentecostals and spoke in tongues. Convinced of the genuineness of this experience, he later attended a prayer meeting at their home, along with Alice E. Luce, Panchito Ortiz, and others, where he was baptized in the Spirit. As a result, he left Methodism to become a Pentecostal preacher.

Scum and Cream

Sometimes people would say that the Pentecostal meetings only attracted the "scum" of society. This was partially true for many times hardened sinners were completely transformed to new standards of living. Habitual drunkards, veteran gamblers and even immoral women and infidels were moved to God by a strange irresistible power. But "scum" was not all that was drawn into the Pentecostal camp. "Cream" too was likewise drawn to the Man of Calvary. Yes, some of the best people from many denominational churches were prompt to see the light and consecrate themselves for all that God had for them. Someone has said that both scum and cream are always on top. The Spirit of God is a wonderful equalizer, and where the Holy Ghost has His way nationality, race, age and social position are blended into one royal family of God.

—*Eugene N. Hastie*, History of the West Central District Council of the Assemblies of God *(1948), 71–72.*

Olazábal's new ministry soon bore fruit as young people who were Spirit baptized in his services entered full-time ministry, many joining the Assemblies of God. In 1918, he moved to El Paso, Texas, staying long enough to plant a church before traveling across the United States to hold revival campaigns. As more Hispanics were converted and joined the Pentecostal ranks, more of their ministers joined the "Mexican convention" of the Tristate district founded in 1918 under the leadership of Henry C. Ball.

Yet like many early Pentecostals, Olazábal felt restless within organizational boundaries. To him as well as others, Assemblies of God leaders, particularly Ball, had a limited understanding of Latin-American culture and could be insensitive at times. Some Mexican-American ministers felt they were governed by "gringos" in the predominantly Anglo Assemblies of God and wanted their own Latin American District Council. To further aggravate matters, Olazábal was ten years Ball's senior and had a superior education. Although Ball had completed a high school education, he had no formal ministerial training.

But whatever criticisms they may have had of Ball, none of them doubted the enormous contributions that he made over the years to Hispanic peoples. Nevertheless, the discontent finally boiled over in 1923 when Olazábal and other ministers met in Houston, Texas, and formed the Latin American Council of Christian Churches. Although he had held credentials with the Assemblies of God for only five years, his labors added to the growth of Hispanic congregations in the Council. Many years would pass before missionaries to ethnic populations in the United States or overseas would surrender control to talented indigenous church leaders.

ETHEL MUSICK
(1895-1989)

From Oklahoma (where Ethel was born) to Texas to California, Ethel and Marcus Musick held tent meetings and started new congregations. Their gifts were complementary: Ethel preached and Marcus worked as a carpenter to help support Ethel's ministry. Born Ethel Smith, her family suffered from the abuses of an alcoholic father. In her autobiography, she remembered that "quite often he came home so affected by the drink that mother and we children would steal away and hide until he became sober enough to lie down; then we would come from our hiding places and quietly go to bed."

Smith came to Christ in a holiness church, and eventually her entire family was converted. Under the influence of the pastor, a "Sister Tomson," she began holding evangelistic services as a teenager. Working out in the cotton fields from Monday to Saturday noon, she would then go to the woods "for a course in knee-ology" to pray, study the Bible, and prepare for preaching. Later with Marcus and their seven children (three died at early ages), they went on the road to hold services, often having significant results. In Cement, Oklahoma, one hundred came to Christ, sixty-five were baptized in the Spirit, and many reported being healed—a respectable result for a population center of eleven hundred.

Family life, however, often suffered. At times when Musick conducted services in various places, her husband or mother kept the children. When the family traveled, the children lacked a permanent home and attended school wherever they happened to be, if it was in session. They all felt the pain and awkwardness of this. Later, when the children were older, Marcus stayed at home with them while Ethel continued in evangelism.

As it was with other Pentecostal evangelists and missionaries, the call to ministry for Musick had priority. The life of the traveling evangelist not only severely tested the marriage bond, but the welfare of the entire family. Yet the Musicks persevered.

Being a female minister was a daunting task in other ways as well. Musick got into hot water with Assemblies of God district officials in 1934 when she pastored the church in Stecker, Oklahoma, for a brief time. Although the General Council finally ruled a year later that women could pastor churches, she resolved the conflict by returning to evangelistic ministry. She also hurdled other obstacles. When the Musicks arrived in Anadarko, Oklahoma, to hold meetings, they were surprised to find the Pentecostals holding services in an old saloon. After sizing up the situation, Marcus Musick told his wife, "Dear, if you will tell the people to buy a lot, we will put our tabernacle [tent] on the back of the lot and build a church."

But banks often refused to loan money to congregations that did not represent a mainline denomination. So Musick and her Pentecostal sisters resorted to canvasing the community for funds. After receiving three hundred dollars and a loan of a thousand dollars from a widow, they began construction. She later wrote that during the space of eighteen months, "God helped us to establish six new church works and build five new church buildings." In summing up what she had done, Musick was characteristic of Pentecostal women who were baptized in the Spirit and called to the ministry with few resources: "Although [I was] unlearned, God gave me this ministry and saved many souls."

How I Found Healing

If anyone asks me how I contracted the morphine habit I can only say: "'Through my fault, through my fault, through my most grievous fault."

I had been saved several years before, but, like Peter at one stage of his career, I was following afar off when I fell into this snare. It is a dangerous thing to follow afar off; I proved that to my cost.

Of course it is needless to say that nothing was further from my thought than becoming a "drug addict," . . . but I was engaged in very strenuous work, practicing medicine and surgery, and in times of excessive strain from anxiety or over-work, I occasionally resorted to morphine, singly or in combination with other drugs, to steady my nerves and enable me to sleep.

Knowing as I did the awful power of the habit-inducing drug to enslave and destroy its victims (I am a graduate of the University of Michigan Department of Medicine, Ann Arbor, Michigan), I was utterly inexcusable for daring to trifle even for a moment with such a destructive agent.

To ask me whether I had taken the drug on any particular day was as needless as to inquire whether I had inhaled atmospheric air; one seemed as necessary to my existence as the other.

Do you ask "Did you not pray?" Yes; I came to the place where I did nothing else. . . . Night after night I walked up and down our long drawing rooms calling on God, and sometimes almost literally tearing the hair out of my head. And you say "And you weren't healed after that?" No; I wasn't healed because I didn't believe the simple statement of the Word of God; rather, my healing could not be manifested, because of my unbelief.

"And why did you not have faith?" Simply because I did not have light enough to take it. . . .

I was getting very weak now and spent hour after hour in bed. . . . At last I drew my neglected Bible to me and plunged into it with full purpose of heart to get all there was for me, to do all that God told me to do, to believe all He said; and praise God! the insolvable problem was solved, the impossible was achieved, the deliverance was wrought. . . . The specific, irresistible, indescribable craving produced by demon power was gone.

And the best of all is that this healing was no happy accident, no special miracle on my behalf, but the working out in me of God's will for all of us, perfect soundness by faith in the Name of Jesus of Nazareth.

—*Evangelist Lilian B. Yeomans, M.D.,*
Healing from Heaven (1926), 8–15.

ROBERT (1872-1941) AND MARY CRAIG (1866-1943)

When early Pentecostals thought of winning souls for Christ in the power of the Spirit, they often set goals that humanly speaking could never be achieved. But better to expect great things from God than to be nearsighted in what might be accomplished. Thus, they made goals on the basis of expectant faith. This proved to be no less true for Robert Craig, a once ailing Methodist minister in San Francisco who had experienced healing and baptism in the Holy Spirit.

While praying at the home of friends ten miles from the city, Craig reported that

Mary and Robert Craig

"God put mighty intercession upon me in tongues and in English for various parts of this dying world, and one morning He called me definitely to return to San Francisco, assuring me that if I would return and be faithful to Him, that He would give me 100,000 souls to shine with Him in Glory, because of our cooperative labors." Starting a new congregation in San Francisco presented a great challenge. It had a cosmopolitan population of Italians, Irish, and Chinese, among others. The city had become famous because of the California Gold Rush and in pursuing material wealth. Its citizens had little time for religion. Craig's vision, however, enabled him and his wife, Mary—an emigrant from Denmark—to persevere and build a church that would eventually have a worldwide ministry.

For three months the young congregation met in an old saloon, and the Craigs lived on the second floor. It was a rough part of town, and sometimes street people and alcoholics wandered in. On more than one occasion, Mary Craig "sobered up the drunks with coffee, and prayed them through to salvation." Having limited finances, their lifestyle was simple. Mary would can fruits and vegetables to make ends meet.

Hazel Buel Miller recalled her water baptism in the first mission hall that Craig rented. To get into the baptismal tank "one had to climb up a ladder on the outside, over the top of the tank and down the inside. It wasn't very fancy, but it did the job, and God's blessings were evident and so real." Sunday evenings began with a street meeting. Afterward, people would follow the Craigs back to the church for another service. Miller's mother played the piano and sometimes led the singing. Mary Craig seated the three children, including Hazel, on the front row with several chairs in between them "to make it look like more people." (Another reason may have been to keep the children's attention on the service and off of each other.)

Students in bus from Glad Tidings Bible Institute advertising revival meetings with Evangelist John Goben (standing in front)

By 1922, Glad Tidings Temple had one of the largest congregations in the General Council. Three years later, the Craigs dedicated a new building with a sanctuary large enough to seat twenty-five hundred people.

But the goal of reaching one hundred thousand people with the gospel would require a team effort. So in 1919, largely through Mary Craig's vision for training Christian workers, the church opened Glad Tidings Bible Institute in the church office. The school was later relocated to Santa Cruz, California, ultimately becoming Bethany College of the Assemblies of God, which over the years has graduated thousands to minister at home and abroad.

AIMEE SEMPLE MCPHERSON
(1890-1944)

While some evangelists and church planters built their ministry in one location or traveled from state to state, Aimee Semple McPherson took hers around the world. Her creativity and dynamic ministry reflect the important role played by female evangelists and the differing views on culture within the Pentecostal movement.

In Canton, Ohio, the headlines screamed: "Cripples Are Cured When Woman Evangelist Prays," "Sick of Soul and Body Are Relieved," and "Two Hundred Men Answer Call to Pray." This northeastern Ohio city had never before seen anything like an Aimee Semple McPherson campaign. "Sister," as she came to be known, arrived with only the minimum of advance planning. So little in fact, that her recent convert and associate Charles S. Price—soon to become well known in his own right—had to play the piano during the services.

A picture of Aimee Semple McPherson preaching on the cover of her magazine, *The Bridal Call Foursquare*

Within days, testimonies of salvation and remarkable healings circulated widely. For two and a half weeks, the sick in soul and body, as well as the curious, packed the civic auditorium. Two daily newspapers printed the names and addresses of each person healed. Who could ask for better publicity?

Refusing to preach Jesus Christ as the great "I Was," Aimee proclaimed Him as "the same yesterday and today and forever" (Hebrews 13:8). Like other Pentecostals, she held that only doubt kept believers from seeing the same signs and wonders performed by Jesus and the apostles. The attention given the miraculous raised the interest of the ministerial alliance; they soon took their seats on the platform behind her. At the close of the campaign, over three thousand conversions had been recorded.

McPherson's methods of evangelism, especially the priority she placed on prayer for the sick, contrasted sharply with those of evangelist Billy Sunday, who had been there nine years earlier. His meetings had benefited from months of committee work, the construction of a large wooden tabernacle, the training of a six-hundred-voice choir, and the cooperation and promotion of the ministerial alliance. Thousands attended and "hit the sawdust" trail, which meant either to commit one's life to Christ, take the pledge not to consume liquor, or be a good American. His campaigns resembled pep rallies for the patriot more than rescue operations for the sinner.

Sunday's view of evangelism was a comfortable fit for the cultural values of middle-class America. On the other hand, McPherson's barnstorming techniques, reflecting her early experience in the Salvation Army, and anticipation of signs and wonders was something else: It was Pentecostal.

Salvation and Healing

Salvation for the soul and healing for the body have ever walked down through the ages together. Man tried to separate them but God didn't. Salvation and healing, hand in hand are walking through the corridors of God together. Can you hear Him say, "Thy sins be forgiven thee. Take up thy bed and walk"? They are yet together, aren't they?

—*Aimee Semple McPherson, "Council Jottings,"* Latter Rain Evangel *(October 1920): 23.*

Throughout her ministry, she dramatized the story of her life under the title "From Milkpail to Pulpit." Thousands drank in the details as she told of life on a small farm near Ingersoll, Ontario, Canada, with her Methodist father and Salvation Army mother. Audiences were charmed by her courtship of the six-foot, six-inch Pentecostal Scotch-Irish evangelist Robert Semple and their journey as young marrieds to Hong Kong as missionaries. They wept as she recounted his untimely death from malaria in 1910 and mourned with her as she told of the lonely return to America with their first child, Roberta Star, born six weeks after Robert's passing, and the uncertain future that awaited them.

They felt Aimee's struggle with obeying God's call until, when lying on her deathbed, she heard a voice say, "Now—will—you—go?" She told of her eagerness as a simple handmaiden to work for Jesus in any way possible. Therefore, it wasn't unusual to see her driving stakes into the ground for her tent meetings, praying for hours around the altar with seekers, feeding and clothing the hungry in Los Angeles, debating atheists, lending a hand in disaster relief efforts, and even selling war bonds during World War II.

Her listeners also empathized with the stings of persecution and criticism that came her way. With the threads of her story woven together, she then invited the unsaved to surrender their lives to Christ and challenged believers to commit themselves to His service.

In the Roaring Twenties, when mainstream Christians despised Pentecostals as heretics and cultists, Aimee Semple McPherson became North America's best-known evangelist. Denominational clergy and laity flocked to her services. On January 1, 1923, she opened her world famous Angelus Temple in Los Angeles, one of the first megachurches in the United States, including satellite congregations. The temple featured eight large stained-glass windows, fifty-three hundred seats, two balconies, and the largest unsupported dome in North America at the time. Furthermore, she dedicated it debt free, paid for by thousands of gifts from Protestants of almost every kind.

Angelus Temple

In the same year, she founded the Lighthouse of International Foursquare Evangelism (LIFE), now known as Life Pacific College, to prepare Spirit-filled pastors, evangelists, and missionaries. In the years when Pentecostal Bible institutes struggled for survival, LIFE started in a new building next to the temple. Frank C. Thompson, then retired from Methodist ministry and editor of the popular Thompson Chain-Reference Bible, taught Bible subjects and served as honorary dean. Although not a Pentecostal, Thompson shared her enthusiasm for divine healing. McPherson cherished unity and cooperation with other Christians.

Besides being ordained as a Baptist minister at the First Baptist Church of San Jose, California, and licensed as a Methodist exhorter, she held credentials for a short time with the Assemblies of God as an evangelist (1919–1922). Her stature became such in the denomination that at the 1920 General Council meeting in Springfield, Missouri, Sister preached in four evening services and held an afternoon healing service. In so doing, she became one of the few women to preach at a Council and the only one in the denomination's history to ever speak in more than one service.

Yet McPherson refused to limit her ministry to a single constituency. She boldly carried her "foursquare gospel" (a creative adaptation of the terms fourfold gospel and full gospel: Jesus as Savior, Healer, Baptizer, and coming King) wherever she went, to "red and yellow, black and white," as well as rich or poor.

What made her ministry so effective? There were many reasons. People flocked to her services around the country because they needed healing or simply went with friends and relatives who did. Preaching the great "I Am," she struck a responsive chord in audiences, resulting in thousands of conversions and stories of healing. She also engaged in interdenominational evangelism, a priority inscribed on the cornerstone of Angelus Temple.

McPherson's understanding of the dynamic work of the Holy Spirit enriched her creative talents. Though heavenly minded, she understood American culture and saw it as a bridge to take the gospel to humanity. So while other Pentecostals saw culture as the enemy, she took advantage of visual and audio means of communication, becoming famous for her illustrated sermons; wrote and produced sacred operas sung by robed choirs at the temple, accompanied by a large Kimball organ and a "Silver Band"; and founded KFSG, one of the oldest religious radio stations in the country.

Consequently, many Pentecostals in the Midwest and other parts of the country, including Assemblies of God leaders and church members, became scandalized at the worldliness of robed choirs and illustrated sermons. And, of course, as her star rose as a female preacher, that made some pastors and church officials uncomfortable. No one could deny, however, the evangelistic successes of her crusades and ministry. Tens of thousands visited Angelus Temple or heard her on the radio and came to Christ.

Although McPherson used cultural expressions for Christian witness, she did so critically. When hundreds of Ku Klux Klan members entered the temple expecting

Student Protest at Beulah Heights!

"Mother" Virginia E. Moss founded the Beulah Heights Bible and Missionary Training School at North Bergen, New Jersey, in 1912. The school became well known for the missionaries it produced. However, two years after her death in 1919, it became noted for something else: a student protest, caused by the school board's firing of the principal, E. L. Whitcomb. During this time, the school and its board had become deeply divided over the "whipped up," "militant" spiritual enthusiasm promoted by Whitcomb among the students. The students, nicknamed "the pounders," sometimes broke chairs they were kneeling at as they "pressed through" in prayer.

Things finally came to a head when the board decided to dismiss Whitcomb. However, the constitution required the reading of the resolution in an open assembly. By this time, a virtual state of siege had developed. When a board member attempted to read the resolution at the meeting, the students "whooped and hollered," pounded on the floor and the furniture, and yelled to the top of their voices. (Two of the "pounders" became well-known ministers in the Assemblies of God: Maynard L. Ketcham and Alfred N. Trotter.) Exasperated by this behavior, the board called the police and had the entire student body taken to the city jail. After the resolution was read, Whitcomb left and the students were released and sent home. The school reorganized and reopened in the fall but with only five students, down from eighty. Nonetheless, Beulah Heights grew once again, later changing its name to Metropolitan Bible Institute and coming under the auspices of the New York-New Jersey District Council of the Assemblies of God for many years.

—Interview with Maynard L. Ketcham, former Assemblies of God Field Secretary for India and the Far East, by the author, 13 July 1983, in Springfield, Missouri.

her blessing, she denounced their racism as contrary to the gospel. Even though the productions of her illustrated sermons had a Hollywood flavor (Charlie Chaplin reportedly gave advice on stage arrangements), she was quick to denounce the vices of society: alcoholism, prostitution, drug addiction, and anything else that kept people in the chains of sin.

She attacked police corruption (publicly denouncing corrupt officers by name), having recognized that evil in human structures crushes innocent and law-abiding citizens. Not surprisingly, the Los Angeles criminal underworld hated her. In Winnipeg and other cities, she visited houses of prostitution, distributing New Testaments and tenderly hugging the women and praying with them.

Sister McPherson also rejected the cultural norms that limited women, particularly the women called to ministry. On the Day of Pentecost the Spirit had been poured out on men and women alike. Even so, some Pentecostals sought to restrict the activities of women, particularly in pulpit ministry. She would have none of that. Undoubtedly, she had been influenced by other prominent women, including the colorful Evangeline Booth, Salvation Army commander for Canada (and daughter of founders William and Catherine Booth), and Maria B. Woodworth-Etter, the well-known evangelist who ministered from the 1880s to the 1920s. In turn, McPherson became a role model for other women, including Kathryn Kuhlman. Voting rights having been given to women in 1920, her ministry reflected the seemingly boundless opportunities that women could have in serving God.

Many have remembered McPherson for her flamboyant evangelism or for founding the International Church of the Foursquare Gospel or for being the subject of a controversial kidnapping (was she or wasn't she?). But her contribution to starting new churches still remains largely unnoted. In the wake of her campaigns across the nation, attended by mammoth crowds, hundreds and probably thousands of Pentecostal congregations took root. Some remained independent, but others joined the Foursquare Church and the Assemblies of God.

Whether she was preaching and praying for the sick in Denver, Wichita, San Jose, Baltimore, Philadelphia, Rochester, Tampa, or Toronto, revival followed. The impact of her campaigns also jump-started many struggling little Pentecostal churches.

Her journey "From Milkpail to Pulpit"—with its drama and pathos, its triumphs and failures, its laughter and tears—held her listeners at the edge of their seats because it resembled their stories too, or at least one they wished for themselves. But while she inspired their imaginations, she couldn't share the rest of her story.

At times, McPherson's public persona masked a painful loneliness. In 1911, a year after returning from China, she married divorcé Harold McPherson, who appeared to offer her the security she needed. Two years later, she gave birth to their son, Rolf. Domesticity, however, soon frustrated her intense burden for evangelism. When Harold agreed to travel with her in evangelistic ministry, she thought she had the best of both worlds. However, she was far more gifted than he. In the end, he couldn't live in her shadow, which was growing, and filed for divorce just as she was hitting her stride.

After the kidnapping, she was drained by a grueling schedule, sometimes preaching and teaching twenty-one times a week, dealing with the kidnapping court case and its negative publicity, as well as handling the temple's mounting financial troubles due to its large relief ministry. She suffered a nervous breakdown in 1930. Further, she became estranged from some of her family, and later, hoping for happiness, she entered into a marriage that seemed doomed from the start.

A national celebrity—truly remarkable for a Pentecostal at the time—she became a victim of the press as her every mistake received front-page coverage and every tidbit of gossip was put into print. No stranger to sorrow, she, nevertheless, contributed more to the expansion of Pentecostalism in North America than most. Sister died in 1944, twelve days away from her fifty-fourth birthday.

RECOMMENDED READING

Blumhofer, Edith L. *Pentecost in My Soul*. Springfield, Mo.: Gospel Publishing House, 1989.

———. *Aimee Semple McPherson: Everybody's Sister*. Grand Rapids: William B. Eerdmans Publishing Co., 1993.

De Leon, Victor. *The Silent Pentecostals: A Biographical History of the Pentecostal Movement Among Hispanics in the Twentieth Century*. Taylors, S.C.: Faith Printing Co., 1979.

Domínguez, Roberto. *Pioneros de Pentecostés*. Miami: By the author, 1977.

Eldridge, George N. *Personal Reminiscences*. Los Angeles: West Coast Publishing Co., n.d.

Epstein, Daniel Mark. *Sister Aimee: The Life of Aimee Semple McPherson*. New York: Harcourt Brace Jovanovich, 1993.

Espinosa, Gastón. "Francisco Olazábal: Charisma, Power, and Faith Healing in the Borderlands." In *Portraits of a Generation: Early Pentecostal Leaders*, edited by James R. Goff, Jr., and Grant Wacker, 177–197. Fayetteville: University of Arkansas Press, 2002.

———. *Latino Pentecostals in America: Faith and Politics in Action*. Cambridge, MA: Harvard University Press, 2014.

Gardiner, Gordon P. *Out of Zion Into All the World*. Shippensburg, Pa.: Companion Press, 1990.

McPherson, Aimee Semple. *This Is That*. Los Angeles: Echo Park Evangelistic Association, 1923.

Musick, Ethel. *Life and Testimony of Ethel Musick, Evangelist*. Tulare, Calif.: By the author, n.d.

Rosdahl, Bruce. "Whatever the Cost: The Formative Years of H. C. Ball, Pioneer of Hispanic Pentecostalism." *Assemblies of God Heritage* 31 (2011): 4-13.

Ruelas, Abraham. "An Under-Sung Heroine: Mary Craig, Founder of Bethany University." *Assemblies of God Heritage* 32 (2012): 52-59.

Wilson, Everett A. "Robert J. Craig's Glad Tidings and the Realization of a Vision for 100,000 Souls." *Assemblies of God Heritage* 8 (summer 1988): 9–11, 19.

CHAPTER 8

OBEYING THE MISSIONARY CALL

I n the months that followed the adjournment of the first General Council in April 1914, several hundred ministers joined its ranks. Among them were a sizable group of missionaries. The presence of missionaries and an enthusiasm for world evangelism commanded the Council's attention from the first. Early leaders wrestled with how to finance foreign missions. They were caught between strong antiorganizational sentiments at home and the often-desperate needs of missionaries abroad. Years of instability followed the Hot Springs meeting, despite earnest efforts to bring order out of chaos. The period from 1914 to 1927 represents the most unstable years in the history of Assemblies of God foreign missions.

For the most part, early General Council missionaries went to the traditional sites of Protestant missionary endeavor: China, India, and Africa. Others were scattered from Mexico to the Middle East. As a rule, they claimed to have received distinct calls from God to specific geographical regions. Blanche Trotter, an early missionary to Liberia, West Africa, reported that she saw "Africa" spelled out in letters of fire during a time of prayer.

Before 1919, the turnover in missionaries reflected the enormous difficulties of ministering on foreign fields. Many factors accounted for this. First, some died from old age since several who joined the Council were veteran missionaries. Second, sometimes they died from tropical fevers and diseases contracted while on the field.

What Makes a Poor Missionary

A poor, defective, inefficient missionary is a missionary who fails to acquire the native language, who lets down in his prayer life, who neglects the study of the Word, who refuses to cooperate and work in harmony with other missionaries already on the field, who disregards the fellowship of other missionaries, who is self-willed, bolshevistic in spirit, and lawless in his attitude to the District Council and the General Council. "Lord God help all such—they need Thee!"

— "What Makes a Poor Missionary," Pentecostal Evangel (April 5, 1924): 10.

Missionary Gottfried Bender attempting to cross the Monay River in Venezuela in his Ford car, which "refused to be turned into a boat."

For example, Henry B. Garlock, an early Assemblies of God missionary to West Africa, recalled that "during the first twenty-five years of the Pentecostal work in Liberia, no less than a missionary a year died of malaria or some tropical disease. And many others were sent home because of serious illness." Third, many of these women and men were not adequately trained and may have had only a naive view of what to expect. Confronted by harsh realities, they returned home. Such conditions discouraged others from remaining overseas. Fourth, some undoubtedly left the Council because of their intense desire to be governed exclusively by the Spirit's leading, unhampered by man-made policies. In the end, the missionaries who persevered on the foreign fields were rugged individualists who often remained skeptical of mission structures at home.

The missionaries in this chapter reflect a variety of backgrounds. Before joining the Assemblies of God to minister to Hispanic Americans, Alice E. Luce had served for many years with the (Anglican) Church Missionary Society in India as an educator. Baptized in the Holy Spirit in Hawaii, the Puerto Rican Juan Lugo received the missionary call and spurred the growth of Hispanic churches in Northern California, Puerto Rico, and New York City. Two weeks before the wedding, Lillian Trasher broke her engagement to follow God's call to Egypt. Ivan Voronaeff, who had served with the Cossacks (cavalry) in the army of Russian Czar Nicholas II, returned home in 1920. He arrived at a particularly dangerous time when the country was devastated by famine and civil war. And to the East, the young William E. Simpson grew up in China as a missionary kid.

ALICE E. LUCE
(1873-1955)

The first significant mission theorist in the Assemblies of God was Alice Eveline Luce. She carried unusual qualifications as a missionary in the early years of Pentecostal missions.

Reared in the home of a Church of England (Anglican) pastor in Gloucester, England, she attended the prestigious and exclusive Cheltenham Ladies College, where she studied nursing and theology.

Her early call to the ministry led to an appointment with the Keswick Convention Mission Council and being seconded by this agency to work with the Church Missionary Society (CMS) in India. She sailed there in 1896 and received appointment to teach at a Christian high school in Azimgarh, North India, and to evangelize

Alice E. Luce (center) with students at Latin American Bible Institute in California

Indian women in harems. Through the years, she became fluent in Urdu and Hindi, two of the chief languages of the country.

In 1905, Luce was transferred to Agra, onetime capital of the Mogul Empire where the famous Taj Mahal is located. There she served as principal of Queen Victoria High School. When the great revival started in India in 1905, she became actively involved, revealing her revivalist sentiments. Unfortunately, due to an attack of malaria, Luce returned to England seven years later. While it may have appeared to some that her contribution to missions was over, only the first chapter in her story had come to an end.

While in India, Luce had followed without hesitation the methods employed by the CMS, which focused heavily on schools, orphanages, and evangelism. But another Anglican missionary, Roland Allen, who worked in North China, soon challenged this comfort zone. Sharply criticizing traditional mission methods, he called for missionaries to follow the "Pauline methods" in evangelism and church planting. Allen recognized that missionaries needed to plant churches that would take responsibility for their life and evangelism themselves. To him, they should be self-supporting, self-governing, and self-propagating, rather than dominated by Western mission agencies, as was usually the case. Allen's *Missionary Methods: St. Paul's or Ours?* (first published in 1912) prompted many to rethink their approach to missions.

Although the famous "three selfs," or "indigenous church principles," as they are often called, were not original to Allen, his passionate critique of contemporary mission methods caught the attention of many, including Luce and her colleagues in India. At first, they thought he was a visionary and impractical. Luce, however, soon changed her mind. Having been baptized in the Spirit in 1910, she said *Missionary Methods* "opened my eyes to the diametrical distinction between our methods of working and those of the New Testament." With her renewed interest in the Book of Acts and Allen's exposition of how the apostle Paul had evangelized, she concluded, "There is such a thing as doing an apostolic work along apostolic lines."

As a Pentecostal, Luce went beyond Allen in her view of New Testament evangelism. She believed that apostolic methods should be followed by the power and demonstration of the Holy Spirit. When explaining indigenous church principles to the Assemblies of God constituency in early 1921, she pointedly asked: "When we go forth to preach the Full Gospel, are we going to expect an experience like that of the denominational missionaries, or shall we look for the signs to follow?"

After her resignation from the CMS, she entered the United States and began a lifelong ministry of training Hispanic Pentecostal pastors and evangelists. With her considerable missionary experience and ability to articulate the three "selfs," she had a profound influence on the home and foreign missions program of the General Council. Her three short articles in the *Pentecostal Evangel* in January and February 1921 prepared the Council to adopt a larger, more complete statement on its commitment to "New Testament Methods" (that is, indigenous church principles) at its meeting in September 1921. Her perspectives also shaped the thinking of other key missionaries and mission leaders: Henry C. Ball, Ralph D. Williams, Melvin L. Hodges, and Noel Perkin. More than any other single figure in the early years of the Assemblies of God, Luce shaped the future contours of the mission enterprise.

Luce, however, is best remembered for her many publications in English and Spanish. They served to assist in the spiritual and doctrinal formation of Spanish-speaking ministers, both in the United States and in Latin America. She also founded Latin American Bible Institute in San Diego (now located in La Puente, California) and taught there until she died in 1955. In addition to three books and a heavy teaching schedule, she wrote articles for Ball's *La Luz Apostólica* (*Apostolic Light*) and lesson comments for intermediate and senior Sunday School teachers' quarterlies for many years. Originally a missionary from England to India and then to the United States, her ministry profoundly influenced the course of Latino Pentecostalism.

Paul's Missionary Methods

Many say that these young assemblies need foreign supervision for a long time. Possibly so, but that is not because we are foreigners, but because we are older in the faith, and have experienced more of the Spirit's guidance than they have. If we guard our relationship with them as always of love and leading-not driving-not as being lords over God's heritage, but being examples to the flock, we shall find them very slow to disregard our counsel, when we offer it in the spirit of meekness. The babes in Christ always need the help of those who are older and more spiritual; but let us make our greater experience, or spirituality, or capacity for supervision, the criterion, and not our nationality. And when the Lord raises up spiritually qualified leaders in the native churches themselves, what a joy it will be to us to be subject to them, and to let them take the lead as the Spirit Himself shall guide them.

—*Alice E. Luce, "Paul's Missionary Methods" Part 3* Pentecostal Evangel *(February 5, 1921): 6–7.*

JUAN LUGO
(1890-1984)

Historians still track the stories of people filled with the Holy Spirit at the Azusa Street revival to see where they traveled across the nation and around the world sharing the news of the outpouring of the Spirit. On their way to Japan and China, several fledgling Pentecostal missionaries stopped in Hawaii and preached the gospel on the Island of Oahu. There the mother of Juan Lugo was converted and baptized in the Spirit. However, the young man resisted her newfound faith and continued in his worldly lifestyle, influenced in part by a coworker, Abad Velez.

Before long Velez became a Christian and his life was transformed, but being illiterate, he could not read his Bible. Taking it with him to work, he would ask Lugo to read it for him during their lunch break. One day while reading in the Gospel of John, Lugo surrendered his life to Christ. The night before his water baptism by his pastor Francisco Ortiz, Sr., at Waikiki Beach,

Juan Lugo and his
wife, Isabel

he had a vision of Christ appearing out of a cloud and calling Lugo to himself. A week later, he received Holy Spirit baptism when alone in prayer at his home.

In 1913 he traveled with Ortiz and his son to San Francisco, where he met George and Carrie Judd Montgomery. Just as they had mentored Francisco Olazábal, so they began to train him in the Scriptures; he later moved to Santa Rosa, California, where the mentoring continued under Sister Elsie Johnson, who took him into her home. Lugo and Ortiz soon joined the Assemblies of God and pioneered Hispanic churches in northern California.

Sensing the call of God to go to the Commonwealth of Puerto Rico and supported by Bethel Temple in Los Angeles, he stopped on his way at the General Council headquarters in St. Louis, Missouri, where he received the encouragement of J. Roswell Flower. Lugo then proceeded to his homeland in 1916. Initially unsuccessful in his efforts, things changed when his friends Salomón and Dionisia Feliciano Quiñones arrived from California.

In the city of Ponce on a Saturday night, they began by preaching on a street corner and found a ready response as hundreds of people gathered around them. Afterward, a man in the crowd invited them to his home where the service continued until two in the morning. "Without waiting, we went to his house, and nearly half of those who were [still] in the street followed us," Lugo remembered. "We started a meeting, God blessed us, and eleven souls were saved. . . . The owner of the house and his wife were the first to give their hearts to the Lord."

Incorporated with eleven churches and six hundred members in 1921, the work took the name Iglesia de Dios Pentecostal (Pentecostal Church of God) to insure that the word *church* would clearly identify it if legal questions arose. Lugo was chosen as leader, and the organization remained under the umbrella of the General Council. Certain pastors, however, preferred the name Asambleas de Dios (Assemblies of God). Division later arose when the Iglesia de Dios Pentecostal left the Council in 1956 to become a separate body.

With his wife, Isabel, Lugo left for New York City in 1929 to plant a church in Brooklyn. Eventually the congregation purchased a Jewish synagogue on 115th Street, and it became one of the largest Spanish-speaking churches in the region. From this initiative, as well as the activities of Francisco Olazábal on the East Coast, more than thirty Puerto Rican churches had been planted within ten years. From these beginnings emerged the Spanish Eastern district of the Assemblies of God.

At the urging of the Foreign Missions Committee in Springfield, Lugo returned to Puerto Rico to establish a Bible institute for training ministers. He chose Julia Valentine, a recent graduate of Latin American Bible Institute in California, and Johnny Perez to serve as instructors along with him and his wife. Mizpah Bible Institute opened in October 1937 with sixteen students.

Grateful for the opportunity to study the Bible, the students often had to overcome major obstacles to attend, including one poor young man who lived four miles away. Getting up at 4 a.m., he spent the next three hours delivering bread for a bakery.

North to Alaska

Bro. and Sister Personeus sent encouraging news from Juneau, Alaska. The tiny mission room where they have been holding services during the past three months proved unsuitable for the work as the people seemed to be afraid to enter the place.

They asked the Lord to give them a better location and they have succeeded in renting what was once a leaky, filthy saloon where many souls had been dragged down to ruin, and they have turned it into a large, clean, comfortable mission and meeting room and a lighthouse for the saving of precious souls for the full Gospel of Jesus Christ.

They have the mission open all the time so that the men who have no home, just "roomers," can come in at any time and read and write.

The Lord has opened a new home for them. A business man and his wife who have been attending the meetings became interested in the work and have given them the lower part of their house, free of rent.

God is blessing their services which they hold in the jail every Sunday morning. At the first the men seemed hardened and indifferent, but now many of them are showing a real interest, a number have raised their hands for prayer, and several are seeking the Lord. Pray for this pioneer work in Alaska.

—*Untitled news note,* Pentecostal Evangel
(March 30, 1918): 11.

He then walked to the campus for the 8 a.m. prayer meeting. He went home at noon—the school had no money to provide lunches—and then returned for the afternoon classes. "He is a very earnest student," said Lugo, "and the joy of salvation always shines on his face."

Because he obeyed the missionary call, Lugo became known as the "Apostle of Pentecost" to Puerto Rico.

LILLIAN TRASHER
(1887-1961)

Lillian Trasher

"We are fed like the sparrows who have no barns or storerooms," wrote Lillian Trasher in her diary twenty-five years after her arrival in Egypt. "My request is this: that the Lord will send the money needed for our food at least a day in advance." A typical entry reads: "We haven't 5¢ and I do not know where it can come from. . . . One hour later the mail came and there was an envelope with . . . a money order for $50. In the afternoon mail from America, we received $55. When I went to the bank to cash the money, a friend walked in and handed me $5. A stranger stopped me on the street and handed me 50¢." Caring for hundreds of orphans and widows at her orphanage at Assiout (Asyût) challenged her faith and stamina until she died at seventy-four years of age.

Lillian Hunt Trasher was born in Jacksonville, Florida, and grew up in Brunswick, Georgia, where she and her family were led to Christ by neighbors Ed and Anna Mason. Walking home from school one day, the nine-year-old knelt before an old log and prayed, "Lord, if ever I can do anything for you, just let me know and—and—I will do it." Little did she know at the time what that initial commitment would later require.

After the family moved to Asheville, North Carolina, she planned to return to her hometown to visit the Masons. Arriving early at the station, she found only a "sweet little lady"—evangelist Mattie Perry—waiting for a train. Trasher discovered that Perry operated an orphanage in Marion, North Carolina, that cared for one hundred children. The venture operated on faith in God's provision, a novel idea to the young woman. On the last day of her visit, she wandered down the same path and knelt at the same old log and said the same prayer, "If ever I can do anything for you, won't you let me know?" With tears coming to her eyes and rolling down her cheeks, she said, "I still mean it."

Trasher's love for children soon led her to accept Perry's invitation to join the staff. Life at the orphanage was a walk of faith, particularly since neither her parents nor her friends assisted her financially. When her shoes wore out, she asked permission to have a pair of men's shoes that had been donated along with some old clothes. Perry said, "My girl, they're just not your type." Trasher later wrote in her diary, "If I hadn't known it, it would not have taken long for me to find out as I walked into the classroom to teach the orphans and saw the drawing on the board of my feet with the toes sticking out—in men's shoes."

During her apprenticeship there, she "learned all the things that have been so very useful to me in my own work in Egypt—how to cut out clothes, sew, cook, take care of newborn babies, teach and oversee large numbers of children, and how to do without!" Perhaps most importantly, she learned the meaning and the challenge of the faith life.

Leaving the orphanage, she studied for one year at God's Bible School, a holiness institution, in Cincinnati, Ohio, before pastoring a church in Dahlonega, Georgia, and then traveling as an evangelist. Back at the orphanage in 1909, Trasher met a young preacher, Tom Jordan, who proposed marriage. But just ten days shy of being a June bride a year later, she heard a woman missionary tell of the great needs in India. Having prayed for several years that God would call her to a mission field, the burden of Africa suddenly redirected the course of her life: "While this lady was speaking, I suddenly felt the call of God!" Because her fiancé did not share the same calling, this energetic young woman for whom the whole world had suddenly opened up, broke off the engagement and made plans for travel to Egypt.

The New Policy of the Foreign Missions Dept.

First. The missionary work of the Council shall be on the "Co-operative faith" basis, viz., the missionaries, the Foreign Missions Committee and the home constituency shall look to God together to supply the needs of the work. . . . [T]he work at home and abroad shall be conducted on a cash basis. Debts will not be incurred, and work shall be undertaken only as funds are available.

Second. The Pauline example will be followed so far as possible, by seeking out neglected regions where the Gospel has not yet been preached, lest we build upon another's foundation (Rom. 15:20).

Third. It shall be our purpose to seek to establish self-supporting, self-propagating and self-governing native churches.

Fourth. The system of supporting missions and missionaries shall be based on the principle outlined in Acts 4:34, 35. . . .

Fifth. If funds are needed for the support of native workers, special arrangements should be made to meet these needs between the District Council on the field and the Foreign Missions Committee. No offerings for the support of native workers shall be sent direct to the natives, but to the missionaries in charge of the station. When necessary, the training of these native workers should include industrial or agricultural work so that they will not look to the missionaries for their support . . . .

Sixth. The Foreign Missions Committee shall define proper standards for the training and testing of candidates as to their call and qualifications for foreign service, as the needs of the work shall require.

—*General Council Minutes (1921), 60–61, 63.*

Though hoping to connect with Pentecostal missionaries home on furlough from Egypt by attending a missionary conference in Pittsburgh, she only had enough money to get by train as far north as Washington, D.C. Staying at the home of a friend of Perry's, she met G. S. Brelsford, a Pentecostal missionary working in Assiout, Egypt. Interested in her plans, he asked if she had the financial backing of a mission board or her family and if she had raised her fare for the trip. When she answered that she had no board appointment, that her family opposed her plans, and that she had only one dollar to her name, he advised her to go home to her mother. Not easily discouraged, she persisted until Brelsford invited her to work in Assiout. The gifts of friends and offerings received in churches where she preached finally enabled her to purchase the ticket. With the blessing of Robert and Marie Brown of Glad Tidings Tabernacle, she sailed out of New York City and arrived in Egypt in October 1910.

While having prayer in her cabin before the ship left the harbor, someone asked Trasher to open her Bible and ask God to give her a verse. The first verse to catch her attention was Acts 7:34 (KJV), "a verse that [she] had never noticed before": "I have seen, I have seen the affliction of my people which is in Egypt, and I have heard their groaning, and am come down to deliver them. And now come, I will send thee into Egypt."

"In this unmistakable way," she wrote, "God set His final seal upon my call."

Residing with other missionaries at Brelford's mission, she began to study Arabic and pondered the course of her ministry. Three months later, a tragic event resolved the question. Asked to visit a dying woman, Trasher and another woman missionary went to see how they could be of help. Entering a dimly lighted room that had no furniture, they discovered the young woman lying on the floor. After kneeling beside her, the woman opened her eyes and looked directly into Trasher's eyes and said, "Arjouky, arjouky." ("Please, please.")

Meanwhile, a neighbor held her three-month-old baby and was trying to feed it from a tin bottle. "It seemed that the bottle had been in use for some time, perhaps ever since the mother had been too ill to feed the baby, for the milk had become caked and green. Yet the child was trying to drink. I had never seen such a sight in my life—the darkness of the room, the suffering, the lack of just everything!" she confessed. "You see I was very young and had only just arrived from beautiful America; I had no idea of the suffering of others."

Before long, the mother died, but not without telling Trasher, "Arjouky takhdi-hom." ("Please take the baby home with you.") She then took the baby back to the Brelsford mission where it found a ready welcome from the missionaries, until it became ill and cried all night long for several nights. Grumpy after sleepless nights, the missionaries asked her to return the baby. Refusing to do so and with no one's approval, she walked out with the baby and enough money to rent a house. That was the beginning of what became the world-famous Lillian Trasher Memorial Orphanage. The first offering to support the new venture came from an Egyptian telegraph boy who gave her thirty-five cents.

It took dogged determination to survive as a faith missionary. Even though the faith principle rested on prayer and belief in God's miraculous provision, the missionary had to build a network of supporters. The faithful back home needed some direction as to where the Lord wanted their money to be spent. J. Hudson Taylor, founder of the China Inland Mission and one of the best-known advocates of faith missions, refused to let his missionaries tell church audiences in their homelands about their financial needs. Providing information about problems and triumphs, whether through personal testimony or the monthly *China's Millions*, would hopefully stir the hearts of believers to pray and contribute.

Lillian Trasher, helpers, and children at the orphanage opening barrels of supplies that had arrived from the United States

Trasher, however, never hesitated to share the needs of the orphanage, often riding her donkey into the villages requesting assistance. There were simply too many mouths to feed every day and too few resources, hence, "We are fed like the sparrows." Seldom returning to the United States, she depended on gifts from the local community, the charity of tourists, and responses to hundreds of letters of appeal. "My mail is very heavy," she wrote in 1934. "I find it very hard to write in the daytime as I am interrupted so often, and I have a difficult time sitting up late at night to answer it. That's why form letters work well for me—they are much quicker and cheaper. A form letter can be left open and sent home for 2¢ while a personal letter, if closed, costs 10¢. And I can send my booklets and tracts in the open letter at the cost of 2¢."

Thousands of Egyptian children and families received food, clothing, housing, spiritual nurture, and education in the ever-expanding number of buildings that Trasher constructed. This won her the respect of the Egyptian government, as well as the international community, and virtually raised her to sainthood among Pentecostals. The whole enterprise reflected her vibrant faith, compassion, courage, and business sense. A grateful Muslim village leader once said of her: "I believe that when she dies, in spite of the fact that she is a woman and a Christian, God will take her directly to paradise."

A year before Trasher died, Philip Crouch, a former associate, asked if she had ever had any regrets about breaking her engagement to Tom Jordan. She became very quiet and then responded, "When I think of Tom, if I had married him, what would have happened to all these children?"

IVAN VORONAEFF
(1886-1937)

Ivan and Katherine Voronaeff

Intense religious persecution from the Russian Orthodox Church forced Baptist pastor Ivan Voronaeff to migrate to the United States around 1911. Born in Central Russia, he had served as a Cossack in the Czar's army before entering the ministry. From Russia by way of Manchuria, he crossed the Pacific and settled in San Francisco to pastor a Russian Baptist congregation. Sometime later, the family relocated to New York City, where Voronaeff pastored the Russian church on Henry Street.

A spiritual crisis loomed when his daughter, Vera, was Spirit baptized and spoke in tongues while attending Sunday School at Robert and Marie Brown's Glad Tidings Tabernacle. To make matters worse, Voronaeff's congregation wondered what he would do. Speaking in tongues among some of the religious sects in Russia had made the Baptists deeply suspicious of anyone who claimed to experience the supernatural gifts of the Spirit. Upset by the news of Vera's testimony, deacons from the church visited Glad Tidings themselves to rescue any of their weaker members who might be there.

But due to Voronaeff's own spiritual hunger for the empowerment of the Spirit, he himself soon received the Pentecostal baptism. Leaving his Russian Baptist congregation in 1919, he founded First Russian Pentecostal Assembly in the city, beginning with almost twenty former parishioners who had also experienced speaking in tongues. The new congregation included Russians, Ukrainians, Poles, and other Slavic believers.

Gdansk Bible Institute

There is some indication that the Bible classes [at the Bible institute] often centered on a thematic approach in the early years, with doctrine classes on salvation, justification, law, grace, and the baptism of the Holy Spirit. Major changes in this approach did not come to the school until the arrival of [Assemblies of God and Russian and Eastern European Mission missionary] Nicholas Nikoloff as dean in 1935. Nikoloff was a highly trained educator with a strong background in methodological Bible study.

Nikoloff often lectured in four different languages, Russian, Bulgarian, German, and English, and would sometimes come home at the end of the day with severe headaches because of the intense concentration. . . .

Nikoloff also directed a male chorus and orchestra which were primarily developed as evangelistic outreach tools.

—*Tom Salzer, "The Danzig Gdanska Institute of the Bible," Assemblies of God Heritage 8 (Fall 1988): 11, 18.*

Before long, he felt impressed of the Lord to return to the newly established Soviet Union to evangelize and share the full gospel message. The call came initially through a prophetic utterance, or interpretation of tongues, by Anna Koltovich: "Voronaeff, Voronaeff, journey to Russia." Initially reluctant to accept this directive, he sought and received its confirmation in prayer. The Voronaeffs then resigned the church, packed their belongings, and sailed for Russia in 1920 assuming that the Russian propaganda about a new democratic government that guaranteed religious freedom was true.

Martha and Nicholas Nikoloff
and their children

Arriving first by way of the Black Sea at Varna in Bulgaria, Voronaeff held services and founded a number of churches, sparking the Pentecostal movement in that country. After journeying from Varna to Odessa, a busy seaport in the southern region of Ukraine, they were immediately arrested. After the Communist authorities confiscated many of their belongings, they were released several weeks later "half sick and starved."

Despite finding the Russian propaganda to be largely untrue, Voronaeff appreciated what little religious freedom the new atheistic government did allow. While the government severely persecuted Orthodox Christians, they allowed the "sects" (Baptists, Pentecostals, etc.) to flourish in order to further weaken the formerly established church. Nine years later, the tide would turn against those groups as well.

Even before official antagonism, Voronaeff's endeavors met hardship. Famines and civil war plagued the Soviet Union. In Odessa, his family suffered along with the rest of the population during the famine of 1921. The famine also took its toll in the village where his parents lived; from a family of twelve, only his mother and a sister survived. His son, Paul, remembered that men and women he saw in the streets resembled skeletons. The dead lay in the streets for weeks and months since the living were often too weak to bury them. "In desperation, many people ate [the] rotten flesh of animals, horses, dogs and cats." While weak from hunger himself, Voronaeff found "strength to kneel beside the sick and dying, to comfort and pray. Many made their peace with God just before their last breath and passing out of the sad, cruel world of suffering, pain and sorrow."

Because of the devastation of the civil war in other parts of the country, Voronaeff made Odessa his base of operation. He also hoped to officially enlist the Baptist churches in the Pentecostal movement. However, this brought a decisive parting: Voronaeff resigned and proceeded to found a Pentecostal church, half of whose membership came from Baptist and evangelical churches.

Pentecostalism largely spread from Odessa upward into Russia and Siberia. Voronaeff's travels took him as far north as Leningrad (present-day St. Petersburg). Before the passing of the antireligious law of 1929, evangelicals and Pentecostals had an unparalleled opportunity to evangelize. Traveling across the country for three months at a time, he found a positive reception to the full gospel. The first Pentecostal congress in the Soviet Union took place in 1927 and formed the Union of Christians of Evangelical Faith. Voronaeff was selected as president of the new association. Two years later, he reported that five hundred assemblies had come into being with twenty-five thousand believers. Voronaeff's own church in Odessa reached a thousand members.

Group of young evangelists on bicycles from Gdansk Bible Institute ready to take the gospel to nearby Poland

Along with several of his workers, he received monthly financial assistance from the Russian and Eastern European Mission (REEM), as well as Glad Tidings Tabernacle. REEM came into being in 1927 through the efforts of Paul B. Peterson, G. Herbert Schmidt, and C. W. Swanson. Peterson served as general secretary at the home office in Chicago, while Schmidt directed activities from the field office in Gdansk, Poland, where the organization also sponsored a Bible institute that trained students from Eastern Europe and Russia for ministry. Both Peterson and Schmidt had previously served as missionaries in Eastern Europe.

Since REEM enlisted Pentecostal members, for example, Schmidt and Nicholas Nikoloff, who were closely affiliated with the Assemblies of God, the General Council turned its work over to the new agency in the same year it was organized. This appeared to be a practical move, since REEM members had previously ministered in Europe and had a field council in Gdansk to care for the needs of the missionaries. The General Council and the Russian and Eastern European Mission entered into a unique cooperative arrangement, both recognizing the credentials of the other.

Originally the work encompassed Ukraine and Russia (where Voronaeff played a key role), Poland, Latvia, Lithuania, Bulgaria, Czechoslovakia, and Germany. Later it added Greece, Hungary, Romania, and Siberia. By the beginning of World War II, REEM claimed over eighty thousand believers in Eastern Europe and Russia, a significant accomplishment.

After the decree of 1929, ministry in Russia had become far more perilous. Baptist and Pentecostal churches were shut down and pastors sent to slave labor camps. There they continued to share the gospel, and more converts were gained. Shortly after this, the Cheka (the secret police) charged Voronaeff with espionage, and because of his financial support from the Russian and Eastern European Mission, they considered him to be a tool of "American imperialists" working against the Soviet government. Shortly thereafter, he was arrested, interrogated, and finally imprisoned in Siberia.

On the night of his arrest, Paul Voronaeff wrote, "We looked at him as if for the last time and tried to imprint every feature of his face in our memories. His head was bent forward. On his pale face was an expression of utter weariness. The corners of his mouth were twitching slightly. His hair had begun to turn gray. He had grown to be an old man during those last few days." The family had few contacts with him. Reports later circulated that he was shot and killed and his body torn apart by guard dogs in what was made to look like an attempted escape in 1937.

WILLIAM EKVALL SIMPSON (1901-1932)

William Ekvall Simpson in Tibetan garb

The unexpected death of young William Simpson at the hands of bandits near the Tibetan border in China was deeply mourned in the Assemblies of God and the Christian and Missionary Alliance. His father, William Wallace Simpson, was part of that hardy band of Alliance missionaries who arrived in China in 1892, intent on penetrating the "forbidden kingdom," Tibet, with the gospel message. Three years later, W. W. married Otilia Ekvall, another missionary whose family became well known in the Alliance for their missionary service in China. The couple had two daughters and a son, William Ekvall Simpson. Young William grew up speaking Chinese and Tibetan. This mission field became the only home he knew.

During a revival at the Alliance station in Taochow, China, in 1912, his father, W. W., was baptized in the Spirit, an event that ultimately led to his departure from the

Tribute to William E. Simpson

The gospel has not yet reached all of this region. People are still in darkness. For many years, this pastor who has come to our land from across the seas has preached the gospel in this mountain area. The Assemblies of God ministers have looked to him, this single young man who was completely dedicated to the gospel. He preached the Word of God, ministering to both the wise and the simple, and did the work of the Lord by helping the poor. Without warning, he came face to face with a bandit and was killed. Now he is with the angels in paradise. We are all bereaved. We have lost our teacher and friend. Now he has ascended, and our hearts are so stricken with grief that the tears stream down our cheeks like rain.

—*An excerpt from the banner prepared for the funeral of William E. Simpson in June 1932, written by the saints of Pekou Assembly, Wen County, in Kansu Province, China; "Tribute to a Martyr,"* Mountain Movers *(November 1983): 6–7 (contains full text).*

Finally, A Tibetan Convert

The missionary [Victor G. Plymire] made his first Tibetan convert ... in a remarkable way.

The husband of this [Tibetan] woman was a Chinese, and he had recently been saved at one of the chapel services. Returning to his home, he had broken the good news to his Tibetan wife. She was not pleased; rather she became enraged.

"I'll kill you and myself too, if you do not recant," she threatened. Her brother, a Tibetan priest, encouraged his sister in this opposition to her husband, so that day by day she became more unreasonable. In spite of her ranting, the husband remained unmoved. He purposed to be true to his new-found Saviour.

One day the wife yielded to the devil and became possessed. So violent was her behavior that her relatives called in several priests who chanted far into the night in an attempt to exorcise the evil spirit. The attempt failed. The

Victor Plymire and
a Tibetan tribesman

following day, after the priests had given up, the missionaries called on the family. Entering the room where the woman lay in a stupor, they battled with Satanic forces for the possession of a soul. Unbelieving relatives stood around to watch the results. The missionaries continued in prayer. Mr. Plymire laid his hands upon the woman: "In the name of Jesus," he fairly shouted, "I command you, evil spirit, to leave." And the demon left the body of its victim.

Several Tibetans claimed they saw a loathsome, beastlike creature come out of the woman on the floor. One bystander in the doorway was knocked down as the demon left the place!

Again Christ had triumphed. The Tibetan woman was now free-and converted at the same moment! Thus it was that after sixteen years of faithful labor the missionary had made his first Tibetan convert.

—*David V. Plymire*, High Adventure in Tibet *(1959), 64–65.*

Alliance three years later. Having returned to the United States, the deteriorating health of W. W.'s wife prevented any immediate mission work. He sent his son to study at an academy in Tennessee, W. W.'s home state. At fourteen years of age, the younger Simpson dedicated his life to missions.

In 1916, his father accepted the post of principal at the newly established Bethel Bible Training School in Newark, New Jersey. The school had been founded by Minnie T. Draper and other former members of the Alliance. After the death of his mother, W. E. enrolled at Bethel as a student for one year before returning with his father and sisters to China in 1918.

W. E. later applied for missionary appointment with the Assemblies of God in absentia in 1923. He then received a certificate granting him an initial term of seven years.

They located at the city of Labrang, near the Tibetan border. During his years there, W. E. traveled by horseback along the border and into the mountains of Tibet distributing gospel tracts and witnessing to Chinese and Tibetans, nomads, and priests at the Tibetan monasteries. In one year he traveled thirty-eight hundred miles, spending 185 days on the road. He became a familiar figure in the region and traveled in areas where others had been unable to go in safety.

Isaac Neeley and his wife, Martha, were the first African Americans appointed as missionaries by the Assemblies of God. They had served in Liberia since 1913.

After fourteen years of evangelism without a furlough, he lamented the small number of people that he had been able to lead to Christ. However, in countries where non-Christian religions were deeply entrenched and hostile to Christianity, some missionaries spent a lifetime without seeing a single convert.

In 1927 he wrote home, "I am the only one left in Tibetan work. I want to ask you to pray: first, that we may be enabled to preach the Word of God with boldness . . . ; second, that enmity of man may not hinder the work of God; third, that the power of God may rest on us and the work as never before; fourth, for protection in all kinds of danger, both spiritual and physical; and fifth, that a mighty revival may be sent to this part of Tibet." Journeying in this region, he faced constant danger.

Shortly before his death, he welcomed his father back from the United States; they hadn't seen each other in two years. A few days later, they parted, his father traveling on to Labrang and W. E. going to pick up supplies and his father's baggage, along with that of the other missionaries in the party. On the road home to Labrang, W. E. and a Russian friend were attacked on June 25, 1932, by bandits, Muslim deserters from the Chinese army. Firing on the truck on which Simpson and his friend were riding, the bandits killed them instantly. Like locusts, they stripped the truck and the bodies of the two men. Villagers nearby buried them and notified the Chinese authorities, who contacted Simpson's father.

The funeral service brought Assemblies of God and Alliance missionaries together, and William H. Christie, who had traveled with W. W. Simpson to China in 1892, conducted the service. Simpson recalled, "As I groped my way through blinding tears toward his grave, I thought, 'Oh for one last word from my boy, just one word to remember him by!'" Then he noticed a piece of paper on the ground. Picking it up, he saw the text from a Bible lesson: "In remembrance of Me." It was wrinkled in such a way that only those words could be seen. "Unfolding it I found it blotched and spattered with my son's blood! So the Lord arranged for this paper to convey my son's last word to me. His blood is my blood and was shed

The Poured-Out Life

He poured out his life and spared it not,
　　No cost seemed too dear to pay
To reach the souls on Liberia's shore,
　　Though his life was fast ebbing away;
Then the summons came from the Father above,
　　"Come higher, thou faithful one;"
And our brother was borne to the Father's arms
　　To receive the King's "Well done!"

　　—Excerpt from Wesley R. Steelberg, "The Poured-
　　　　Out Life," in memory of John Torta.

Missionary John Torta died from blackwater fever in Cape Palmas, Liberia, in 1934.

to help a party of missionaries locate on the Kansu-Tibetan border to preach the gospel to the unevangelized."

Only in a few countries did missionaries face hostilities as a direct result of preaching the gospel. Simply being in some countries exposed them to danger, a fate shared by other foreigners as well. Whatever the risks, missionaries saw themselves as entrusted with the gospel message: "All this is from God, who reconciled us to himself through Christ and gave us the ministry of reconciliation: that God was reconciling the world to himself in Christ, not counting men's sins against them" (2 Corinthians 5:18–19).

Whatever circumstances befell them were immediately understood as advancing or hindering the work of the Lord, the hindrances potentially representing the activities of Satan. After all, the apostle Paul had warned, "For our struggle is not against flesh and blood, but against the rulers, against the authorities, against the powers of this dark world and against the spiritual forces of evil in the heavenly realms" (Ephesians 6:12).

Assemblies of God congregations rejoiced at missionary stories of spiritual victories and growing numbers of converts. They also enthusiastically sang such triumphant missionary hymns as "We've a Story to Tell to the Nations" and "Bringing in the Sheaves." However, the death of William Ekvall Simpson and of others overseas painfully reminded them of the human cost in obeying the Great Commission.

RECOMMENDED READING

Alicea-Lugo, Benjamin. "Juan L. Lugo's Legacy: Puerto Rican Pentecostalism." *Assemblies of God Heritage* 32 (2012): 32-41.

Baron, Beth. "Nile Mother: Lillian Trasher and Egypt's Orphans." *Assemblies of God Heritage* 31 (2011): 30-39.

Blan, Nora. *Over Rugged Mountains: W. E. Simpson.* Springfield, Mo.: Foreign Missions Department, n.d.

Booze, Joyce Wells, ed. *Heroes of the Faith*. Springfield, Mo.: Assemblies of God Division of Foreign Missions, 1990.

Donev, Dony K. "Ivan Voronaev: Slavic Pentecostal Pioneer and Martyr." *Assemblies of God Heritage* 30 (2010): 50-57.

Durasoff, Steve. *Pentecost Behind the Iron Curtain*. Plainfield, N.J.: Logos International, 1972.

Hogan, J. Philip. "China Church Growth—A Story of Danger and Dedication." *Mountain Movers* (November 1983): 4–7.

Howell, Beth Prim. *Lady on a Donkey*. New York: E. P. Dutton and Co., 1960.

Luce, Alice E. "Paul's Missionary Methods." Parts 1–3. *Pentecostal Evangel* (8 January 1921): 6–7; (22 January 1921): 6, 11; (5 February 1921): 6–7.

Lugo, Juan. "Souls Being Saved in Porto Rico." *Pentecostal Evangel* (25 November 1916): 13.

———. "New Bible School, Puerto Rico [sic]." *Pentecostal Evangel* (15 January 1938): 9.

Salzer, Tom. "Danzig Gdanska Institute of the Bible." Parts 1 and 2. *Assemblies of God Heritage* 8 (fall 1988): 8–11, 18–19; 8 (winter 1988): 10–12, 17–18.

Trasher, Lillian. *Letters From Lillian*. Edited by Beverly Graham. Springfield, Mo.: Assemblies of God Division of Foreign Missions, 1983.

Voronaeff, Paul. *My Life in Soviet Russia*. Tulsa: Christian Crusade, 1969.

Wilson, Everett A., and Ruth Marshall Wilson. "Alice E. Luce: A Visionary Victorian." In *Portraits of a Generation: Early Pentecostal Leaders*, edited by James R. Goff, Jr., and Grant Wacker, 159–176. Fayetteville, Ark.: University of Arkansas Press, 2002.

CHAPTER 9

CONTENDING FOR THE FAITH

When the General Council of the Assemblies of God came into being in 1914, a large doctrinal consensus already existed among those who attended. They agreed on the historic points of Christian doctrine, intertwined with Wesleyan-holiness and Keswickian themes. Yet within a year, the unity and future of the new Fellowship would be jeopardized by a major doctrinal challenge.

Between 1914 and 1927, several disagreements arose; the most serious questioned the traditional understanding of the Godhead. Others included a renewed controversy over tongues as initial evidence. Sometime later, a prominent Pentecostal pastor claimed that all humanity would be saved whether or not every individual had accepted Christ in this life.

This chapter introduces three persons who engaged in these disputes: one who defended a key doctrine, another who questioned it, and finally, a non-Council pastor who provoked the Council to denounce his pet doctrine. These men, respectively, were Daniel W. Kerr, formerly of the Christian and Missionary Alliance; Fred F. Bosworth, a noted evangelist; and Charles Hamilton Pridgeon, a Princeton Seminary graduate who became Pentecostal.

DANIEL W. KERR
(1856-1927)

In the early years, "Elder" or "Daddy" (as he was sometimes called—he was almost sixty when he joined the Council in 1914) Daniel Kerr guided the Assemblies of God in defining its beliefs. A member of the Christian and Missionary Alliance, he epitomizes the enormous influence of that association on the Assemblies of God.

The Alliance's fourfold gospel—Christ as Savior, Sanctifier (Baptizer in the Holy Spirit), Healer, and coming King—formed the spiritual core of the Council. The fourfold gospel would become the four cardinal doctrines of the new Assemblies of God. Other former Alliance members also played key roles. Among them was John W. Welch, an early general superintendent; Frank M. Boyd and William I. Evans, educators; J. T. Boddy, an early editor of the *Pentecostal Evangel*; and Alice Reynolds Flower, one of the gifted spiritual writers that Pentecostalism has produced. None, however, occupied center stage with a more crucial role than Kerr. The Alliance legacy was far-reaching, impacting spirituality, doctrine, church structure, missions, and educational institutions.

Daniel Kerr and his wife, Mattie, had met in 1878 while students at North Central College in Naperville, Illinois, a school run by the Evangelical Association. After their studies, they pastored an Evangelical church in Northern Illinois. Sometime

Daniel and Mattie Kerr

later he joined the Alliance. He became a familiar figure in those circles as a member of the Ohio Quartet, which traveled to conventions every summer with Alliance founder A. B. Simpson.

When the Kerrs heard about the Azusa Street revival in Los Angeles, they were pastoring the Alliance Tabernacle in Dayton, Ohio. Both received Spirit baptism while attending the annual Alliance state convention in 1907 at Beulah Park campground, east of Cleveland. Its services proved eventful for more than one reason: A woman dropped dead while speaking in tongues. Jolted by this and shocked at what followed, one observer said, "Her body lay on the floor . . . while the worshippers, driven almost mad by strange religious zeal, prayed that God would perform a miracle and bring back life to the woman. Then a doctor was summoned."

The Kerrs and the Alliance did not approve of fanaticism. But like other radical evangelicals, they believed that expectant faith in God could bring about the seemingly impossible. After all, Jesus had raised the dead in His earthly ministry and told His disciples, "'I tell you the truth, anyone who has faith in me will do what I have been doing. He will do even greater things than these'" (John 14:12).

Four years later, the Kerrs moved to Cleveland to pastor the Alliance congregation; under his leadership, it would eventually join the Assemblies of God. Unable to attend the first General Council in Hot Springs, he supported it nevertheless, because he saw the value in organizing. Despite his absence, he was elected to a seat on the Executive Presbytery, given the delegates' esteem for him.

At the Council meeting in 1915, it became obvious to everyone that the "New Issue" might threaten the unity of the Assemblies of God. Kerr spent the following months examining the teaching with his Greek New Testament and books on theology and church history. E.N. Bell (who never accepted Oneness doctrine) had been rebaptized in the name of Jesus Christ as had other Trinitarians because they felt it might bring more power to their ministry; the majority of those rebaptized clearly rejected belief in the Trinity, contending that the Godhead had only one Person, the Lord Jesus Christ.

My Dear Brother Brickey:

Now it is true that the Lord blessed me in my personal attitude toward Him when I was baptized, but there was an element in that baptism that most of the brethren are totally unaware of. In addition to the matter of baptism in Jesus' name I had been half convinced that my baptism by the Baptists was unsatisfactory, and that possibly the Lord wanted me to be baptized in water by a man filled with the Holy Ghost, and that had bobbed up more or less during all the years that I have had the baptism [in the Holy Ghost] experience. It is possible that the Lord was seeking for me to obey Him in this matter all these years. . . .

Now this combined with the matter of being baptized in the name of the Lord Jesus Christ, and it is not possible even for me to-day to tell which of these lines of thought was uppermost in my heart. I feel at least you should know that the obedience had this additional element in it, so that you could see that a large measure of the blessing might have come entirely regardless of the formula which was used.

Had there not immediately been made an issue over the formula by both sides of the question, I could have gone on baptizing simply in the name of the Lord Jesus Christ. I believe still that where there is no issue, and no false doctrine connected with this formula in Acts, and no opposition to Matt. 28:19, that a person could be baptized simply in the name of the Lord Jesus Christ, and that it would be perfectly acceptable to the Lord. But, when an issue was made out of this matter, and many serious false doctrines associated with being baptized in the name of the Lord Jesus Christ, so that I could not baptize a man in that way without being understood as teaching and tolerating these false doctrines as the motive for my baptizing in this way, than I could not conscientiously baptize in this way alone. For to do so I would be misunderstood as to truths of far more vital importance than the matter of the baptismal formula. I was more concerned not to teach that Jesus Christ is the only person in the Godhead, not to teach that the name of Jesus is the Name of the Father, and of the Son, and of the Holy Ghost; not to teach that Jesus is the Father; not to teach that water baptism is necessary to salvation; not to teach that the baptism with the Spirit is the birth of the Spirit, etc., than I was to contend over a mere formula.

—*Personal letter from E. N. Bell to Brother J. C. Brickey (August 20, 1920).*

Meanwhile, John W. Welch, the general chairman, and J. Roswell Flower, secretary, struggled to keep the Council faithful to the historic doctrine of "One God in Three Persons." The central issues revolved around (1) the restoration of another apostolic pattern in the Book of Acts and (2) whether or not the Bible actually teaches the Trinity.

To most Pentecostals, the pattern of Spirit baptisms in the Book of Acts, marked by speaking in tongues, framed the doctrine of initial evidence. However, Oneness believers pointed to Acts 2:38 as the final restoration of the apostolic faith. Spoken to the crowd gathered on the Day of Pentecost, Peter said, "'Repent and be baptized, every one of you, in the name of Jesus Christ for the forgiveness of your sins. And you will receive the gift of the Holy Spirit.'" This seemed to replace and reinterpret what Jesus meant when He told His disciples to baptize "'in the name of the Father and of the Son and of the Holy Spirit'" (Matthew 28:19). As the redemptive name of God, the full benefits of God's power came when a person went into the waters of baptism in the name of Jesus Christ.

As their new understanding of the Godhead grew, Oneness believers testified to its truthfulness. Frank Ewart, a prominent leader, recalled tent services that he had held in Belvedere, California. "We purchased a baptismal tank," he wrote, and "candidates for baptism in the Name of Jesus started to flock to the tent." Persecution followed, as it often did when Pentecostal meetings were in progress. Rowdies threw stink bombs into the tent and finally burned it. They also intimidated Ewart and his wife as they walked home after services.

Despite all of this, he declared that "God was working after the pattern of the old-time apostolic order." But to Ewart, the most startling aspect of the meetings appeared when "the vast majority of the new converts were filled with the Holy Ghost after coming up out of the water . . . speaking in other tongues. Many were healed when they were baptized." But Trinitarian Pentecostals reported the same as they baptized in the name of the Father, Son, and Holy Spirit.

At the 1916 General Council in St. Louis, Kerr headed a five-member committee asked to prepare a statement of faith. Those who knew the members of the committee—Kerr, S. A. Jamieson, Stanley H. Frodsham, T. K. Leonard, and E. N. Bell—could have surmised that the Oneness doctrine would be condemned.

From their brainstorming came the *Statement of Fundamental Truths*, with the longest section upholding the historic Christian view of the Trinity. The committee maintained that the "Lord Jesus Christ" is a proper name given only to the Son of God. It is never applied in the New Testament to either the Father or the Holy Spirit.

At the same time, the committee contended that the *Statement* was "not intended as a creed for the Church, nor as a basis of fellowship among Christians, but only as a basis of unity for the ministry alone." Kerr himself, for example, held to a rather unusual view of the rapture of the Church and the Tribulation. Nevertheless, on the matter of the Trinity, the Council affirmed it by closing ranks. By the time all the Oneness ministers had left the Council, the ministerial roll had dropped from 585 to 429.

Like all other creeds churned up by controversy, the *Statement* highlights the disputed doctrine. Other doctrines, such as "Divine Healing" and "Baptism in the Spirit," are amazingly short. The *Statement* itself also bears a strong resemblance to the teachings of the Alliance.

Charges of "creed making" stung Council leaders. But their decisive action had kept Assemblies of God beliefs clearly within the traditional framework of evangelicalism. At the same time, enlarging the field of required beliefs ran against their desires. Cooperation of the Spirit-filled for world evangelism ranked above minor points. Hair splitting had characterized the denominational churches, which, they claimed, had forsaken Bible doctrines and become apostate.

FRED F. BOSWORTH
(1877-1958)

With broken health caused by a lung disorder, Fred Bosworth wandered into a Methodist church in the little town of Fitzgerald, Georgia. Evangelist Mattie Perry was conducting the meeting. Painfully coughing all through the service, he went to the front at the close of the service with other seekers for prayer. Perry prayed for his healing after telling him about the healing power of Jesus. He soon testified that he had indeed been completely healed.

Bosworth and his wife, Estelle, later moved to Zion City, Illinois, impressed by the teachings of John Alexander Dowie. Since Bosworth was a skilled musician who played the cornet, Dowie invited him to become the city bandleader. Along with others who lived in Zion and became Pentecostals, he received Spirit baptism in 1906 during a visit by Charles F. Parham. Afterward he became an evangelist.

As mentioned previously, persecution against Pentecostals could be severe. Bosworth faced this squarely while holding services in the east-central Texas town of Hearne. White believers there, not wishing to receive the baptism of the Spirit at a "colored altar," asked the black Pentecostals in the community to invite a white preacher to help them receive. Bosworth accepted the invitation. When he arrived, he preached to two large Saturday night audiences, one white and the other black.

He intended to stay longer, but several white bullies had got word that he had preached to blacks as well as whites. Claiming that was putting whites on the same level with "niggers," they cursed and threatened him at gunpoint. Bosworth told them he was ready to die but wanted to explain the circumstances of his invitation. After hearing him out, they decided not to kill him but ordered him to take the next train out of town.

He walked to the depot and purchased a ticket for Dallas. But before he could get on the train, a mob of twenty-five whites attacked him. They knocked him to the ground and beat him with heavy hardwood clubs made from boat oars. "I offered no resistance," he said, "but committed myself to God and asked him not to let the blows break my spine. God stood wonderfully by me and no bones were broken except a slight fracture in my left wrist." Since there weren't enough clubs to go around, the others beat him with their fists, knocking him down several more times, but without making him unconscious—"a miracle of God's care." Finally, to add insult to his very real injuries, they refused to allow him on the train. He then had to walk nine miles to the next town to board a train for home.

Fred F. Bosworth (r) standing with Elias Birdsall outside Bosworth's home in Dallas, Texas

Bosworth attended the Hot Springs Council in April 1914. At the second Council in November in Chicago, he gained a one-year appointment to the Executive Presbytery. Over the next few years, however, he rethought the doctrine of initial evidence, ultimately rejecting it. His change of mind reflects the atmosphere of tentativeness about the role of tongues before Pentecostals began publishing doctrinal statements separating themselves over it and other issues.

In his booklet *Do All Speak With Tongues?* he wrote: "We have no 'Thus saith the Lord' in the Scriptures that all are to speak in tongues." In his estimation, a distinction between "evidential tongues" (Book of Acts) and the gift of tongues (1 Corinthians 12) could not be supported biblically. He believed that many had been Spirit baptized without speaking in tongues. Furthermore, he pointed out the newness of the teaching by saying that "not one of the world's great soul winners ever taught it."

Council leaders defended the doctrine of initial evidence, among them Kerr and E. N. Bell stand out. Sharing the fears of many Pentecostals since his time, Kerr solemnly warned, "Whenever we . . . begin to let down on this particular point, the fire dies out, the ardor and fervor begin to wane, the glory departs."

In his study of the New Testament, Kerr observed that the writers had carefully selected the information they included for emphasis. The apostle John, for example, "made a selection of just such materials as served his purpose, and that is, to confirm believers in the faith concerning Jesus Christ the Son of God." In a similar vein, Luke chose "from a voluminous mass of material just such facts and . . . manifestations of the power of God as served his purpose. What is his purpose? No doubt, his purpose

Tarred and Feathered

It was in early 1918 that a wave of persecution was directed toward my father [Pentecostal preacher Frank Gray] by some of the neighbors in the farming area where we lived, about 20 miles west of Spokane, Washington. The hatred in these men increased until one evening a group came to the house and forcibly removed him, took him out and literally "tarred and feathered" him. I was sleeping at the time he came home, but I heard noises downstairs, and I came and saw my mother scraping the tar from his body and bathing him.

—*Harold F. Gray quoted in Carl Brumback,* Suddenly . . . from Heaven *(1961), 285.*

is to show that what Jesus promised He hath so fulfilled. . . . The 120 believed and, therefore, they [spoke] in other tongues as the Spirit gave them utterance. We also believe, and we speak in other tongues as the Spirit gives utterance."

"Is this not," said Kerr, "an altogether striking characteristic of the book of Acts?" The plain sense of the biblical text clearly showed that whether in Acts 2, 8 (by implication), 10, or 19, tongues occurred with Spirit baptism. Hence, the pattern itself amounted to a "thus saith the Lord." Nowhere, however, did Kerr attempt to refute Bosworth's claim about some believers who made "noise without the power" or sought tongues more than Christ. The founders of the Assemblies of God were not amused by those who spoke in tongues and lacked holiness of character. Neither were other believers. One such person was troubled enough to send an inquiry to Bell's "Questions and Answers" column in the *Pentecostal Evangel*. The letter writer asked if one could be baptized in the Holy Spirit and still "often get angry" as well as dislike others. Apparently, the writer had observed such a display when one woman was sat next to by "another sister . . . whom she does not like."

Bell responded that the erring sister may have genuinely repented at one time and been Spirit baptized. Nonetheless, she had not been weaned "from these fleshly ways, and this fleshly temper." If such behavior continued, she would grieve the Spirit (Ephesians 4:30–31) and "lose out with God."

"Having once received the gift of tongues," he lamented, "one may sometimes continue to so speak after the love of God has largely leaked out." He then referred to 1 Corinthians 13, where in verse 1, Paul warns, "If I speak in the tongues of men and of angels, but have not love, I am only a resounding gong or a clanging cymbal."

Extending Paul's instruction about the relative merit of tongues, Bell concluded, "Tongues without the love of God in the heart will not take one to heaven." Then he had some pastoral advice for the letter writer/observer: "But you must get your eyes off of others and on to the Lord."

However, Bosworth's concern that none of the great soul winners had ever taught initial evidence revealed the awkwardness of claiming a newly restored doctrine. Kerr, looking at church history through his Pentecostal lens, said, "During the past few

Taken from the cover of the *Weekly Evangel* (December 9, 1916).

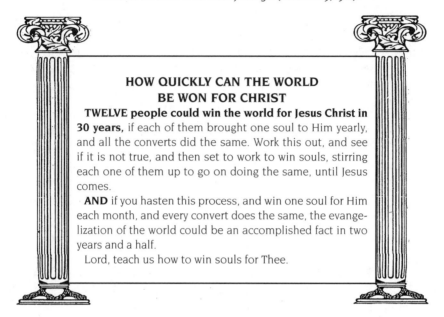

**HOW QUICKLY CAN THE WORLD
BE WON FOR CHRIST**
**TWELVE people could win the world for Jesus Christ in
30 years,** if each of them brought one soul to Him yearly,
and all the converts did the same. Work this out, and see
if it is not true, and then set to work to win souls, stirring
each one of them up to go on doing the same, until Jesus
comes.

    AND if you hasten this process, and win one soul for Him
each month, and every convert does the same, the evangelization of the world could be an accomplished fact in two
years and a half.

    Lord, teach us how to win souls for Thee.

years God has enabled us to discover and recover this wonderful truth concerning the Baptism in the Spirit as it was given at the beginning. Thus we have all that the others got [e.g., Luther, Wesley, Simpson], and we got this too. We see all they see, but they don't see what we see."

Delegates at the 1917 General Council meeting in St. Louis took notice of an oversight. On a nearly unanimous vote, they corrected Article 6 in the *Statement of Fundamental Truths* to read that tongues served as the "initial *physical* sign" (the word "physical" had been inadvertently left out). This highlighted that Holy Spirit baptism involves a vocal utterance that occurs with the spiritual dimension of the experience. Decades later, theologian Simon Chan would address the divine-human dimension of the Spirit-filled life: "Glossolalia . . . is the most natural and regular concomi- tant of Spirit-filling involving an invasive or irruptive manifestation of the Spirit in which one's relationship to Jesus Christ is radically and significantly altered." Hence, "when one experiences the coming of the Spirit in such a manner, the most natural and spontaneous response is glossolalia." In an insightful observation, famed British Assemblies of God leader Donald Gee wrote, "In the final analysis, the Baptism in the Spirit is not a doctrine, but an experience." And "the test of whether I have received is not a cleverly woven doctrine that will include me within its borders, but whether I know the experience in burning *fact* in heart and life."

In the following summer and before the next Council, Bosworth submitted a let- ter of resignation, but to avoid forcing the issue further he discouraged his friends from leaving the organization with him. Nevertheless, he went to Springfield for the meeting, spoke from the floor even though no longer a Council member, and voted on the resolution. Historian Carl Brumback noted that Kerr won the argument when he "drove home again and again that it is the Word of God . . . that is the touchstone" for the doctrine of initial evidence.

Overriding Bosworth's position, Council members chose to reaffirm allegiance to the doctrine of initial evidence, calling it "our distinctive testimony." All ministers and missionaries, therefore, were expected to adhere to it. Indeed, the *Statement of Fundamental Truths* had become a creed and "basis for fellowship."

After the gavel fell, Bosworth chose to identify with the Christian and Missionary Alliance, where some had affirmed tongues but not as initial evidence. Ironically, Kerr had left the Alliance for this very reason. The legacy of the naturally quiet and reserved Daniel Kerr continues in the doctrines he wrote and defended. It is also reflected in several Assemblies of God schools that he helped found: present-day Bethany College, Vanguard University, and Central Bible College.

CHARLES HAMILTON PRIDGEON
(1863-1932)

Though never a member of the Assemblies of God, a Pittsburgh pastor's belief about the destiny of non-Christians disturbed Canadian and American Assemblies of God leaders from Toronto to Springfield. What could Charles Pridgeon, head of a mission agency, have done to rattle them? He had said the unthinkable, challenging the very reason for being of the Pentecostal movement: the need to save sinners from eternal destruction.

Pridgeon had a distinguished academic background. He graduated from Lafayette College with BA and MA degrees. Somewhere in these years he assisted Dwight L. Moody in evangelistic work. He then enrolled at Princeton Theological Seminary, the Fort Knox of Calvinist theology. For a time, he and a classmate visited universities in Scotland and Germany where they studied under noted theologians. Returning to Princeton, Pridgeon then completed his seminary program and the required work for a doctoral degree in 1899.

Placing his quest for the "fullness" of the Spirit over completing his doctorate, he was ordained and called to be the founding pastor of First Presbyterian Church at Canonsburg in southwest Pennsylvania. His interest in the Holy Spirit centered on the Keswick emphasis of the higher life. Eventually, after coming into contact with A. B. Simpson and his teachings, he received the experience he had longed for since 1892. At the same time, he became an ardent preacher of faith healing.

Criticism soon followed within the Presbyterian Church over his praying for the sick. On one occasion during the controversy, he attended special meetings at Carnegie Hall in New York City, led by former Presbyterian, A. B. Simpson. "Mr. Pridgeon," Simpson said, "I understand that you have been going through the fire."

"Just a little," he responded. Pridgeon finally submitted a letter of resignation to his presbytery and resigned his church in 1901.

Hell Not Eternal, Minister's Interpretation of the Bible

That hell, made necessary by the sins of man, is a place of limited duration, through which man, having learned his lesson and suffered the due penalty of his sins, is finally brought to a realization of the love of God, is a Scriptural interpretation being made by the Rev. Charles H. Pridgeon, in his Tuesday night lecture before the Pittsburgh Bible Institute on "The Purpose of God for the Ages."

In making such an interpretation, Mr. Pridgeon says he is advancing nothing controversial, but is holding a view embraced by many of the church fathers between the time of John and St. Augustine.

"I believe in a real heaven and a real hell," said Mr. Pridgeon, "but I do not believe that evil is eternal as God is eternal. Therefore, I believe that the duration of the place of punishment will be finite and that God will be Victor. I believe in a conscious existence hereafter, both in heaven and in hell, but I believe that God has a loving and a corrective purpose, even in punishment.

[Mr. Pridgeon] accepts the full inspiration and authority of the Bible, but does not ignore the claims of conscience, reason, and the best thought of writers ancient and modern.

—*Comments cited in Grace D. Clementson,* Charles Hamilton Pridgeon
(1963): 131–2, 134–5.

Moving to Pittsburgh, he founded the Wylie Avenue Church as an independent congregation. A year later he established the Pittsburgh Bible Institute to prepare Christian workers. The doctrines taught there bore strong resemblance to those of the Alliance. Later, to scout for possible mission sites, he traveled abroad. By the time he incorporated his Evangelization Society in 1920, Wylie Avenue Church and the Pittsburgh Bible Institute had become powerhouses of evangelism and missions.

Pridgeon's acceptance of Pentecostal doctrines began the same year that he attended an Aimee Semple McPherson crusade in Dayton, Ohio. Responding to an invitation to help pray for the sick and believing that he had already received the fullness of the Spirit, he went to Dayton and witnessed a greater dimension of the power of God than he had ever seen. Upon his return to Pittsburgh, he closed the school to any who had been attending Pentecostal meetings or claimed the Pentecostal experience "so that a true test case might be demonstrated."

Historian William W. Menzies, whose mother was an eyewitness of the revival, states that "nightly 'tarrying' services were conducted within the student body, except on Sunday nights when evangelistic meetings were held in the city." Conservatively estimated, over fifteen hundred people received Spirit baptism and spoke in tongues over the next two to three years.

Despite the organization of the Evangelization Society and his reception of the Pentecostal message, Pridgeon had already begun preaching a new doctrine at the school in 1918, specifically, that God's great love would eventually lead to the "restoration" or "restitution of all things." Following a lengthy time of judgment and purification after death (a virtual purgatory), unbelievers and even Satan and his angels would be reconciled to God. He authored a treatise on the subject; Funk & Wagnells published all 333 pages of Is Hell Eternal? or Will God's Plan Fail? in 1920. Having mulled it over for twenty years and after much prayer, "God [spoke] to him and gave him liberty to give out what had become a very precious truth to him." Critics could only wonder, however, whose voice he had heard.

Pridgeon was not the only Pentecostal to raise questions about the final destiny of the wicked. Charles F. Parham had once taught that God would annihilate all unbelievers in the final judgment. Later he changed his mind to say that hell's eternal flames would reach only those who had become "utter reprobates." Neither Pridgeon's nor Parham's views represented the vast majority of Pentecostals. Max Wood Moorhead, a former missionary to India and like Pridgeon a former Presbyterian, challenged Pridgeon's argument. "If all men are by nature children of God and are not children of wrath as the Bible declares," he asked, "where is the need of vicarious sacrifice [Christ's death on the cross]? And if hell is not eternal, why warn men to flee from the wrath to come?"

Faced again by a troublesome teaching, the General Council condemned the "restitution of all things" in 1925. Pastor Robert Brown from New York City forthrightly reminded the delegates that "'He that believeth not shall be damned,' and that means that he shall go to hell." In a reminder of how seriously Assemblies of God leaders took the authority of Scripture and the importance of correct doctrine, he added, "I don't believe that means that we will go to purgatory, but it means that we will go to h-e-l-l, HELL! And once you get into that place you will never come out. There is only one way that you may escape, and that is to turn away from your sin, and get back to God. REPENT!"

When a constitution and bylaws passed two years later, it was listed in the bylaws under "heresies disapproved." Rather than updating or expanding the Statement of Fundamental Truths, lest this generate more charges of "creed making," Council leaders chose censure as a means of disapproving questionable teachings. This then made disavowal of certain teachings as binding as allegiance to the Statement of Fundamental Truths.

Everlasting Punishment

The first Bible reference given in the Statement of Fundamental Truths [in #15 "The Final Judgment"] —Matthew 25:46—uses the phrase "everlasting [Greek, aionion] punishment." Some have denied that this means eternal in the sense of absolutely unending. In the same verse, however, Jesus used the same word of life "eternal" (aionion) in a manner that is directly and exactly parallel. In other words, the punishment will be as eternal as the eternal life. This leaves no room for any later restoration of the wicked. In Matthew 25:41 the punishment is defined as "everlasting [Greek, aionion] fire."

—Where We Stand: The Official Position Papers of the Assemblies of God (1994), 84.

As time passed, other means of protecting cherished doctrines were employed. After the Executive Presbytery wrestled with the danger of the anti-Pentecostal notes in the *Scofield Reference Bible* in 1924, they banned advertisements of it in the *Evangel*. Two years later, they concluded that the acceptable notes outweighed the unacceptable ones and allowed its advertisement again.

Gospel Publishing House produced a variety of popular-style books with doctrinal themes in addition to publishing the *Evangel*, Sunday School lessons, and tracts. These included *Healing from Heaven*, written by Lilian B. Yeomans, a Canadian medical doctor who had been converted and delivered from morphine addiction. Former Presbyterian pastor and Lane Seminary graduate S. A. Jamieson wrote a manual on Bible doctrine called *Pillars of Truth*. It contained chapters on the Bible, Christ's ascension to heaven, tithing, and other topics. Frank Lindblad wrote *The Spirit Which Is from God*, the Council's first major theology of the Holy Spirit.

RECOMMENDED READING

Barnes, Roscoe. F. F. *Bosworth: The Man Behind "Christ the Healer."* Newcastle upon Tyne, England: Cambridge Scholars, 2009.

Bell, E. N. *Questions and Answers.* Springfield, Mo.: Gospel Publishing House, 1923.

Bosworth, F. F. "Beating in Texas Follows Ministry to Blacks." *Assemblies of God Heritage* 6 (summer 1986): 5, 14.

———. "Do All Speak With Tongues?" New York: Christian Alliance Publishing Co., n.d.

Brown, Robert A. "The Way of Salvation." *Pentecostal Evangel* (17 October 1925): 2–3, 10.

Chan, Simon. *Pentecostal Theology and the Christian Spiritual Tradition.* Sheffield, U.K.: Sheffield Academic Press, 2000.

Clementson, Grace D. *Charles Hamilton Pridgeon.* Gibsonia, Pa.: Evangelization Society of the Pittsburgh Bible Institute, 1963.

Ewart, Frank J. *The Phenomenon of Pentecost.* Rev. ed. Hazelwood, Mo.: Word Aflame Press, 1975.

Jacobsen, Douglas. *Thinking in the Spirit: Theologies of the Early Pentecostal Movement.* Bloomington, Ind.: Indiana University Press, 2003.

Kerr, D. W. "The Bible Evidence of the Baptism with the Holy Ghost." *Pentecostal Evangel* (11 August 1923): 2–3.

McGee, Gary B., ed. *Initial Evidence: Historical and Biblical Perspectives on the Pentecostal Doctrine of Spirit Baptism.* Peabody, Mass.: Hendrickson Publishers, 1993.

Menzies, Glen. "Tongues as the Initial Physical Sign of Spirit Baptism in the Thought of D. W. Kerr," *Pneuma: The Journal of the Society for Pentecostal Studies* 20 (Fall 1998): 175–189.

Menzies, William W. "The Non-Wesleyan Origins of the Pentecostal Movement." In *Aspects of Pentecostal-Charismatic Origins*, edited by Vinson Synan, 83–98. Plainfield, N.J.: Logos International, 1975.

Moorhead, Max Wood. "Pridgeonism." *Pentecostal Testimony* (November 1923): 7–8.

Perkins, Eunice M. *Fred Francis Bosworth: His Life Story.* 2d ed. River Forest, Ill.: F. F. Bosworth, 1927.

Wilson, Lewis. "The Kerr-Peirce Role in A/G Education." *Assemblies of God Heritage* 10 (spring 1990): 6–8, 21–22.

Scofield Bible To Be Sold Again

Two years ago [1924] the Executive Presbytery decided that advertisements for the Scofield Bible should not be printed in the *Evangel*. There were some things in it they felt they could not endorse. At this meeting, Brother [J. R.] Evans brought up the matter, saying that he felt it was not well for us to refuse to sell this book, because it contained much that was most helpful....

The matter was discussed very fully. Most of those present were very appreciative of the many good qualities of the Scofield Bible. They mentioned, however, some things they could not endorse in his notes. The notes in the Scofield Bible designate the sermon on the mount as "pure law" and teach that the primary application of the words of Christ on this occasion are "neither the privilege nor the duty of the church." This cannot be right for the Lord in His great commission [Matthew 28:19-20] told His disciples to go into all the world and preach the gospel to all nations, "teaching them to observe all things whatsoever I have commanded you."

There is another teaching in the notes . . . that no Pentecostal believer can endorse, that "every believer is born of the Spirit, indwelt by the Spirit, and baptized in the Spirit." We know a great many believers who have not received the Baptism of the Spirit in the scriptural way. In our fundamentals we state that "all believers are entitled to and should ardently expect and should earnestly seek the promise of the Father."

There is a theory in the notes . . . that the kingdom of heaven is "postponed," which we believe is contrary to the teaching of Rom. 14:17; 1 Cor. 4:20; and Col. 4:11. There is also somewhat extreme teaching on eternal security, that most of our people hesitate accepting.

In view of the many valuable things that are taught in the Scofield Bible, and that in the main it is perfectly sound, it was agreed to restock this book again, provided that in every advertisement we plainly point out the errors mentioned above.

— *"Scofield Bible To Be Sold Again," Pentecostal Evangel (May 1, 1926): 3.*

The Scofield Reference Bible

THE

HOLY BIBLE

Containing the Old and New Testaments

AUTHORIZED VERSION

With a new system of connected topical references to all the greater themes of Scripture, with annotations, revised marginal renderings, summaries, definitions, chronology, and index, to which are added, helps at hard places, explanations of seeming discrepancies, and a new system of paragraphs

EDITED BY

REV. C. I. SCOFIELD, D.D.

CONSULTING EDITORS:

REV. HENRY G. WESTON, D.D., LL.D., President Crozer Theological Seminary.
REV. JAMES M. GRAY, D.D., President Moody Bible Institute.
REV. WILLIAM J. ERDMAN, D.D., Author "The Gospel of John," etc., etc.
REV. ARTHUR T. PIERSON, D.D., Author, Editor, Teacher.

REV. W. G. MOOREHEAD, D.D., President Xenia (U.P.) Theological Seminary.
REV. ELMORE HARRIS, D.D., President Toronto Bible Institute.
REV. ARNO C. GAEBELEIN, D.D., Author "Harmony of Prophetic Word," etc., etc.
REV. WILLIAM L. PETTINGILL, D.D., Author, Editor, Teacher.

New and Improved Edition

NEW YORK
OXFORD UNIVERSITY PRESS

Minion 16mo, Black-faced—References   *Scofield Facsimile Series No. 1*

CHAPTER 10

DIFFERENT KINDS OF GIFTS

There are different kinds of gifts, but the same Spirit," so wrote Paul to the church at Corinth (1 Corinthians 12:4). To understand the growth of the Assemblies of God, one must look at the various efforts of many people. J. Roswell and Alice Reynolds Flower represent one notable instance of mutual dependence in ministry, in their case, as a married couple. While J. Roswell met with other Pentecostal leaders to found the General Council, Alice stayed at home with the baby in Indiana. With him keeping her informed of the happenings in Hot Springs, she wrote the material for that week's edition of the *Christian Evangel* and had it typeset and printed by a local newspaper. Overseeing its mailing to subscribers, she also sent copies to Hot Springs, where it was distributed on the Council floor.

It took countless believers to make it work. Local pastors and families sacrificed to house and feed evangelists and missionaries when they came through to hold services. Church members willingly gave up evenings at home to participate in street meetings to reach the lost for Christ. Volunteers worked in hot kitchens at camp meetings to feed the faithful. For every missionary who asked for financial support, hundreds of men, women, and children prayed and emptied their pockets into offering plates.

As Lillian Trasher saw it, "God has one to preach and one to rock babies and another to get up in the night and give them milk, another to write about them, another to send money and another to work in the shop and earn money to send." When Trasher told of the children's need of clothing at her orphanage, Etta Calhoun and her Pentecostal sisters in Houston, Texas, got out their sewing machines and set to work.

Thus with "different gifts, according to the grace given us" (Romans 12:6), leaders and committed laypersons together contributed to the dynamic that made the Assemblies of God thrive. Several Pentecostals with unique gifts receive attention in this chapter. George S. Montgomery, a wealthy businessman, owner of a gold mine, and layman, became burdened for the evangelization of Mexico. With his wife, Carrie Judd Montgomery, he initiated several important ministries. Alice Reynolds Flower wrote Sunday School lessons, devotional books, poems, songs, and with her husband, J. Roswell Flower, reared six children. Pentecostals have always maintained that spiritual leadership doesn't emerge simply as a result of human selection, but through enrollment in the "school of prayer." Garfield T. Haywood, an African-American Oneness Pentecostal, strummed the heartstrings of the faithful with his songs. Last but not least, Smith Wigglesworth, the plumber-turned-evangelist, traveled around the world preaching on faith and praying for the sick.

GEORGE S. (1851-1930) AND CARRIE JUDD MONTGOMERY (1858-1946)

In a room at the American Exchange Hotel in San Francisco, George Montgomery downed a bottle of brandy and put a gun to his head three times but didn't have the nerve to pull the trigger. The owner of silver mines in Nevada and part of a gold mine in Mexico by age twenty-nine, he had amassed a worth of sixty thousand dollars by the 1880s. But on one wild day of trading on the stock exchange, he lost everything, including the fortunes of his business associates.

The Montgomery family, Scottish Presbyterians, migrated to America from Tyrone County, Ireland, beginning in the early 1860s. At fifteen and on his own, George left home and sailed all the way around South America to California to join his two brothers in San Francisco. Like others in that era, he caught the gold fever and went to Mexico in hopes of making a fortune. Realizing his hopes, he had returned to California to

R. W. GREENMAN
TRAVELING RAILROAD EVANGELIST
1404, 6TH AVE. NORTH
GREAT FALLS, MONT.

Railroad Evangelism

This is my fourth year in the railroad work. There are some missions at various Divisional points, but very little work outside. Some think the railroad men are a rough class, but I find them different. They seldom have a chance to go to church as they are likely to be called at any hour of the day or night. Therefore I feel we must go to them at our Master's bidding, and in these last three years many have found the Lord through the simple Gospel; I know no other.

I have just been holding meeting[s] in Winnipeg, amongst the men, wives and children, and I never saw them so interested as when they saw the power of God falling. If any feel led to go in for this work I would like to hear from them and all about them. They are going to appoint me a traveling railroad evangelist out of Chicago through the Pentecostal Herald. If all is well I will hold a convention there in October, as this is the largest railroad center in the United States. Any who would like to correspond can address me as follows: R. W. Greenman, Traveling Railroad Evangelist, 1404 6th Ave. N., Great Falls, Montana.

—Weekly Evangel (July 7, 1917): 16.

live the good life, only to lose everything. After faltering at suicide, he mustered his resolve and made his way back to Mexico to duplicate his success.

After several more years there, he returned to California with another fortune and began to move in high society. Suc-

cess seemed sweet until the effects of his bouts with tropical fevers, diabetes, and drinking caught up with him. Doctors from San Francisco to Europe offered him little hope. Finally, while on a cruise to Japan, he heard the voice of God speak for what he thought would be the last time: "My spirit shall not always strive with man. If you do not yield now, I shall never come again." He

Carrie, Faith, and George Montgomery

then fell to his knees and repented of his sins.

Montgomery's illness, however, continued to worsen. After returning home, the doctors labeled his condition incurable. As it happened, John Alexander Dowie was in the city holding services. Granted a rare personal visit with the famous faith healer, Montgomery asked him to pray on his behalf. The next day he testified to complete healing.

In June of 1889, he traveled to Western Springs, Illinois, where he met Carrie Judd at the Western Convocation of Christian Workers. Engaged by the end of the year, they were married the following spring at Buffalo, New York, by her lifelong friend A. B. Simpson. She hadn't given much thought to marriage, "except to ask the Lord not to let me be troubled with the attention of anyone who was not the Lord's choice for me."

"O Lord," she prayed, "if Thou didst create anyone on purpose for me let him find me, but if not, I do not want anyone."

Judd had been reared in an Episcopalian family. At eighteen she had become an invalid due to a severe back injury. Some months later, her father noticed in a newspaper the story of Mrs. Edward Mix, an African American who had been healed of tuberculosis. Mix herself now prayed for the sick but at her home in Connecticut. Judd corresponded with Mix, who instructed her to discontinue her medicines and quoted the promise of James 5:15: "The prayer offered in faith will make the sick person well."

Mix set a date and exact time when she and her friends would pray for Judd and asked her to join them. At the agreed-upon moment of prayer, Judd asked her nurse to read something from the Bible. "It was something on the line of the Lord's healing ministry while on earth."

"Suddenly," Judd remembered, "words she was reading arrested my attention: they seemed to be illuminated with a light from heaven, gaining entrance into my heart in such a way as to create a new faith within me. Without waiting for the special season of prayer, which we expected to have together, I interrupted my nurse and called her to my side, saying quietly and without excitement, 'Clara, I will get up now.'"

When George Montgomery died in 1930, someone paid tribute to him as the man "raised up of God to take care of the Lord's little ambassador," referring to his wife who had become well-known in holiness and Pentecostal circles. Though written with good intentions, this failed to adequately describe the partnership that George and Carrie enjoyed. Wealth from his investments did not keep them socially aloof from caring for the drunkards and the down-and-out. Within weeks of setting up house-keeping in San Francisco, they started their first ministry: a rescue mission. The People's Mission opened in September 1890 in one of the worst parts of the city, the infamous Barbary Coast.

As time went on, they joined the Salvation Army and the Christian and Missionary Alliance. For George, proceeds and ventures in serving the Lord went hand in hand. His businesses grew to include hotels, restaurants, real estate, and more mining operations. He felt that God had given him the expertise to make money to help in Christian humanitarian endeavors and in world evangelism. In one enterprise, the La Trinidad Mining Company, Montgomery and his two partners promised God that all the profits would go to missions.

Carrie became a highly sought after conference speaker and writer in the broader holiness movement. She also fervently taught on faith healing. Beginning the periodical *Triumphs of Faith* in 1881, she edited it for sixty-five years. It became a favorite in the Alliance and among Pentecostals, as well as other believers.

In 1889, George purchased Park Place, sixty-seven acres of land in Oakland. He gave a portion to the Salvation Army for its Rescue Home, Beulah Orphanage, and Home of Rest. He also provided space for the establishment of the Home for Aged

An Ideal Pentecostal Church

I want to say that an ideal Pentecostal church is not only comprised of born-again believers, is not only a holiness church, and not only a church that believes in and enjoys the Baptism of the Holy Ghost, but an ideal Pentecostal church is a demonstrative church.... Now I have declared myself very emphatically, taken off my gloves and told you exactly how I feel about it. Many Pentecostal churches are dying from propriety. I do not believe in wildfire, nor do I encourage fleshly manifestations, and I know there are plenty of folk who will demonstrate in the flesh unless you have enough of the power of God in your service to keep the flesh in subjection.... On the other hand, you cannot have the mighty operations of the Holy Ghost in your midst without demonstrations. In many places they are trying to be so nice and proper that a lot of those professing Pentecost look like marble slabs in a cemetery and act as though they had spiritual rheumatics.

—A. G. Ward, *The Whirlwind Prophet and Other Sermons* (1927), 73.

and Infirm Colored People, the first in California. Finally, Park Place became the site of Carrie's healing home, the Home of Peace.

The Montgomerys strongly supported foreign missions; George was determined to evangelize all of Mexico. For a time he considered buying a large section of land to set up a "Protestant" colony. In 1905 he purchased several mines in Nacozari, across the border from Arizona. On his many trips there, he distributed Spanish-language gospel tracts and New Testaments.

Later, after George and Carrie had been baptized in the Spirit, they were among those who preached the Pentecostal message in Nacozari. Services were held in an empty store beginning in 1911, and two years later Carrie conducted an evangelistic campaign there. Through their efforts, both in Mexico and San Francisco, they influenced three outstanding evangelists to Hispanics: Chonita Howard, Francisco Olazábal, and Juan Lugo. Later the Montgomerys joined the newly organized Assemblies of God, with Carrie as a charter member. Despite their allegiance to the Council, their continued association with the Salvation Army, the Christian and Missionary Alliance, and a wider swath of evangelicals kept them above the narrow sectarianism that had come to flourish in Pentecostal ranks.

During his lifetime, George Montgomery made vast sums of money and spent a fortune in many Christian endeavors. An obituary in the *Oakland Tribune* referred to him as a "one-time millionaire mining man, who became a religious worker and gave his fortune for the benefit of mankind." His life and that of his wife had been interwoven with a passion for evangelism.

J. ROSWELL (1888-1970) AND
ALICE REYNOLDS FLOWER (1890-1991)

People never visited the home of J. Roswell and Alice Reynolds Flower at 430 West Woodridge Street in Springfield, Missouri, without her praying for them before they left. "Mother" Flower's ministry stretched from her home and individuals she personally mentored to audiences of her speaking engagements across the country and her writing assignments. Members at Central Assembly of God in Springfield still remember her Sunday School class that she taught until she was ninety, as well as her prophetic inspiration in the worship services. This gentle but resolute woman authored sixteen books and more than one hundred poems and became a spiritual mentor or, as some called her, a "matriarch" in the Assemblies of God.

Alice Reynolds and
J. Roswell Flower

Alice Marie Reynolds grew up in Indianapolis, Indiana, the daughter of parents having Quaker and Methodist connections. The family became part of the Christian and Missionary Alliance after the dramatic healing of her mother in 1882. From the nucleus of a prayer group that her mother was a member of, the Alliance Gospel Tabernacle came into being; people soon called it the "Power

House." A. B. Simpson often spoke at its annual missionary conventions, and his teaching made a deep impression on Reynolds.

When Glenn Cook arrived from the Azusa Street revival in January 1907, Pentecostal revival began at the Tabernacle. Reynolds received Spirit baptism on Easter Sunday in 1907 at a special "tarrying" meeting. As she lifted her hands and began to

The Fullness of Pentecost

What is the fullness of true Pentecost—
  What does the Latter Rain bring?
Heart-thrilling moments of worship and praise
  Unto our glorious King!
Blessed revealings that God doth prepare
  Thus to unfold to His own;
Glimpses of Christ in His beauty most rare
  Unto our hearts clearly shown.
Fullness of joy,
  Blessings untold
Jesus thy Lord
  Thus to behold.
What more does the Spirit's fullness embrace?
  A vision of Calvary~
The cross in its fullness of Love's sacrifice,
  The measure of agony;
The Garden, the Judgment, the Passion's full pain
  Are felt in their darkest hour;
Then beyond their shadows our hearts rejoice
  In full Resurrection pow'r.
To suffer with Him
  The secret we gain,
Fullness of Glory
  Thus to obtain!
What of the fullness the Comforter brings
  To witness for God each day?
Emboldened like Peter, Christ's name to declare
  The Life, the Truth, and the Way.
The power of Christ promised we thus may receive,
  Anointed to sound His name;
To men of all nations and tribes and tongues
  His marvelous grace to proclaim.
Spirit of God,
  This very hour
Breathe upon us
  Fullness of pow'r.

—*Alice Reynolds Flower, A Barley Loaf (1938), 28–29.*

praise the Lord, "for the first time in my life I felt the physical manifestation of God's power all through my being, and I sank to the floor. . . . Wave after wave of glory swept over me until there seemed to be a shining path reaching from my opened heart right into the presence of God." As her chin began to tremble, "the praise that was literally flooding my soul came forth in languages I had never known." (Two of the people praying with her, George and Bethia Flower, commented, "We wish God would give Roswell a girl like that for a wife.")

The revival also stirred the heart of young Flower, an employee of the Indiana Seed Company who had begun to read law in preparation for a legal career. A backslider, he began attending the meetings sometime later. During one service, six people, including Reynolds, began to "sing in rich harmony a song in the Spirit."

"The sensation was like being a pipe organ from which poured forth the wonderful melody from deep within my being," she remembered. "Without effort the heavenly music flowed freely, reminding us of the words of Jesus when he said, 'Out of his belly shall flow rivers of living water' (John 7:38 [KJV])." Standing in amazement at the back of the crowded hall, Flower knew that this was a work of God.

He soon surrendered his life to Christ and a year later received Spirit baptism. For a time, he assisted in a church pastored by A. S. Copley in Kansas City. While there he coedited an early Pentecostal periodical called *The Pentecost*, one of many such publications that kept Pentecostals in touch with each other through news notes as well as testimonies and editorials.

Returning to Indianapolis, Flower and Reynolds married in 1911. "We were thrown together in public meetings, cottage meetings, factory and street meetings," she recalled, "until we almost took each other as a matter of course, so intent were we with fulfilling the service God had laid upon our hearts. Perhaps we did not realize how much our dependence upon each other for the task God had assigned us was actually becoming a close-knit heart attraction." Afterward, they began traveling and preaching in northern Indiana. Two years later, they began the *Christian Evangel* (later *Today's Pentecostal Evangel*). When the General Council organized at Hot Springs in 1914, the Flowers became members, and for the rest of their lives, their names and those of their children would be closely attached to it.

Like the Montgomerys, the Flowers respected and depended on each other's gifts. J. Roswell pastored and served in district and national leadership capacities, while Alice became a prolific author. Her many publications reflect the strong Christ-centered piety of A. B. Simpson and the Alliance. She wove insights into victorious Christian living with homespun illustrations. Chapters from her books, such as "Threads of Gold," "Playing Second Fiddle," "Replenishing Your Fire," and "Soul-Erosion," offered struggling believers comfort and instruction. In *Open Windows*, she wrote, "Where the language of love might fall short of its full end, the deeds of love will carry the message across. . . . I doubt if Dorcas ever dreamed how far her loving ministry was reaching. She lived day by day to reach the needs of others; and into the coats she made, her needle was ever stitching love, love, love."

Though critics charged that Pentecostals sought more for the gifts than the Giver, Mother Flower and a host of other Pentecostal writers pointed to Christ being formed in the believer's heart through the work of the Holy Spirit. In commenting on the meaning of spiritual victory, she noted, "Christ lives within, and as we recognize His sweet and holy presence, evil thoughts, selfish desires, unholy purposes must wither and die. In the person of Christ, you died on the cross, which means that the things of the old life belong back there, and you are living in holiness and love unto God alone."

However, it wasn't her speaking and writing that she wanted to be remembered for. "When people remember me," said Mother Flower at a General Council prayer breakfast in her ninetieth year, "I don't want them to say, 'Well, Mother Flower could talk; she could write poetry.' I want them to say, 'Mother Flower knew how to touch God.'"

GARFIELD T. HAYWOOD
(1880-1931)

At one point, during the intense debate over the New Issue at the 1916 General Council, T. K. Leonard referred to the Oneness doctrine of Garfield T. Haywood and his colleagues as "hay, wood, and stubble," alluding to 1 Corinthians 3:12. The influence of Haywood on the Assemblies of God, however, could not be put down so easily.

Pentecostal revival came to Indianapolis when Henry Prentiss and Glenn A. Cook brought news from Los Angeles of the outpouring of the Spirit. Prentiss, an African

Garfield T. Haywood

American, became pastor of a small integrated congregation; one member said that "to hear him pray was like listening to an angel talk to God." A friend invited Haywood to attend one of the services; he was consequently converted and baptized in the Spirit. Later, Haywood became pastor of the growing congregation and received ministerial credentials in 1911 with the Pentecostal Assemblies of the World (PAW).

Despite this affiliation, he traveled in larger circles through camp meetings, revivals, and even as a featured speaker at early General Councils of the Assemblies of God. Reflecting the high esteem held for him, he was granted the privilege of speaking from the floor. But his rebaptism in the name of Jesus and adoption of Oneness theology reduced his movement within the Assemblies of God. For the remainder of his life, he served in leadership capacities in the PAW.

Gifted and creative, Bishop Haywood had a voice that "rang like an expensive cathedral bell when he spoke under God's unction." He also painted, wrote extensively, and composed poetry and music. For decades, Oneness and Trinitarian Pentecostals sang his hymns. Two in particular were favorites: "I See a Crimson Stream of Blood" and "Jesus the Son of God."

In the course of his ministry, Haywood often fasted and prayed. It was after a week of prayer and fasting that he was inspired to write "I See a Crimson Stream of Blood." As he stepped to the pulpit and began singing it, "a new vision of Calvary

Sacred Songs the Lord Has Given

I Fell in Love with the Nazarene
The Bridal Song
Keep Step My Brother
God's Grand Triumphant Army
Spiritual Israel
Dear Heart, Take Heart
What Hast Thou Gleaned Today?
Father, Lead Me to the Pearly Gates
The City of Our God
Behold, I Come Quickly
The Magdalen
The 144,000
When Jesus Swings the Great Gates Wide
The Islands Are Calling for Thee

Two new ones soon to be out:

Daughter of Spiritual Israel and *In His Name.*

Any of the above songs can be obtained at 25 cents each from the composer, who is open for invitations to speak or sing. Address: Sarah Haggard Payne, Sacred Song Writer, Box 44, Ocean Park, Calif.

> — *"Sacred Songs the Lord Has Given" (Advertisement),*
> Pentecostal Evangel *(November 1, 1919): 29*

gripped the hearts of those who heard. No wonder sinners wept their way to salvation." The words speak of the redemptive work of Christ in His sacrificial death on the cross. For the repentant sinner, this means justification by faith and cleansing from all transgressions.

But the next verse speaks to the struggle the new believer might experience after conversion, supplying these words of assurance:

> When gloom and sadness whisper
> You've sin'd no use to pray,
> I look away to Jesus,
> And He tells me to say:
> I see a crimson stream of blood,
> It flows from Calvary,
> Its waves which reach the throne of God,
> Are sweeping over me.

His song spoke not just of the past and the present, but also to the future of salvation, "when we reach the portal, where life forever reigns."

The evangelical nature of this gospel song paralleled that of "Jesus, the Son of God." In it Haywood spoke to sinners, inquiring if they had received His grace. To those who had rejected this gift, the Suffering Savior continues to offer love and forgiveness so that in heaven they might be "His jewels, most precious and holy." What made this grace possible? Haywood pointed to the "sweet wonder," the mystery of redemption in Jesus Christ (Romans 16:25–27). Because human reason falls far short of understanding the magnitude of the divine love, the soul can only cry out, "O sweet wonder! How I adore thee! O how I love Thee! Jesus, the Son of God."

Haywood was not the only or even the most prominent Pentecostal songwriter. That honor goes to Thoro Harris, whose many compositions were published by Nazarene Publishing House, Haldor Lillenas, Gospel Publishing House, and other evangelical music presses. His songs include "Jesus Loves the Little Children," "All That Thrills My Soul Is Jesus," and "He's Coming Soon." Harris also wrote songs about the Spirit-filled life, such as "More Abundantly." Holiness, Trinitarian Pentecostal, and Oneness Pentecostal beliefs were common enough to allow Nazarenes and other Wesleyans, Assemblies of God, and Oneness congregations to sing them—each group making a slight adjustment in interpretation to accord with its doctrinal distinctive.

SMITH WIGGLESWORTH
(1859-1947)

In Washington, D.C., at a Smith Wigglesworth meeting in 1934, a young girl on crutches entered the auditorium with the help of two other people. Having no muscular ability, her legs dangled like a rag doll's. When Wigglesworth invited those who wanted prayer for healing to walk to the front, she struggled to go forward. He then said, "You stay right where you are. You are going to be a different girl when you leave this place." Upon asking about her physical condition, he found that she had never walked before. Laying his hands on her head in prayer, he commanded, "In the name of Jesus Christ, walk!" Suddenly, she dropped her crutches and began to walk.

Smith Wigglesworth

To an unparalleled extent, Pentecostals grabbed the apostolic banner and marched down the parade route of the Great Commission testifying to God's miraculous power as they preached the gospel. Wigglesworth was no exception, but in fact modeled the uniquely Pentecostal approach to evangelism. In Sweden, he created such a furor among the medical doctors and clergy in the Lutheran state church that he was denounced for his practice of praying for the sick. As a result, the government forbade him to lay hands on anyone as he prayed for their healing. When a crowd of twenty thousand assembled at an outdoor service, he stayed within the law by asking the sick to stand and lay their hands on their afflicted parts while he prayed for them. Many claimed healing, as they did in his campaigns elsewhere around the world.

Those who knew him in his earlier years couldn't have imagined that he would one day see thousands converted, crutches and braces discarded, and himself described as an "Apostle of Faith." Certainly they wouldn't have imagined that a government would consider his ministry a threat.

Converted at eight years old through contact with the Methodists, Smith Wigglesworth was confirmed by a bishop in the Church of England, immersed in water as a Baptist, and received biblical instruction from the Plymouth Brethren. In Wigglesworth's early years, George Müller, another product of the Brethren, modeled the faith life at Bristol, a seaport in southwestern England. Thus Wigglesworth's early association with the Brethren helps to explain his radical concept of faith.

While preparing to become a master plumber in his late teens in Bradford, England, Wigglesworth became attracted to the Salvation Army. There he met the woman who would become his wife, Polly Featherstone. After their marriage in 1882, they shared in ministry by opening Bowland Street Mission in Bradford. Polly, however, became the main preacher. Because of Smith's lack of self-confidence, he could speak for only two to three minutes at a time in the pulpit before breaking down in tears and asking someone to finish for him.

Two dramatic spiritual experiences changed him and his ministry forever: sanctification while attending a Keswick conference in 1893 and baptism in the Spirit at Sunderland, England, in 1907. "The power of God fell upon my body with such ecstasy of joy," he recalled, "that I could not satisfy the joy within, with the natural tongues, then I found the Spirit speaking through me in other tongues." Returning home and entering the pulpit, he preached with surprising boldness and fluency. Sitting in the back, Polly said in a voice loud enough that those around her could hear, "That's not my Smith, Lord, that's not my Smith!" Thus began an international ministry. While holding services in America, he obtained credentials with the Assemblies of God.

Wigglesworth's beliefs mirrored in part those of others in the Pentecostal movement. Together, he and Polly agreed never to seek the help of doctors or take medicine but to trust Christ as their healer. Suffering had no place in God's plan for the believer. He saw praying for the sick as a contest between God and the devil: "I have no word for rheumatism only 'demon possessed.' Rheumatism, cancers, tumors, lumbago, neuralgia, all these things I give only one name, the power of the devil working in humanity. When I see consumption, I see demon working power there. All these things can be removed." His concept of spiritual warfare going on when praying for the sick helps account for his occasional rough handling of people early in his ministry. When he hit a person where they hurt, he saw himself as hitting the devil.

In one service, however, he met his match. At Glad Tidings Tabernacle in New York City after he had struck an Irish immigrant woman who had gone forward for prayer, she immediately drew back her fist and shouted, "Begorra, if it's a fight you want, it's a fight you'll get!" Fortunately, calm prevailed, and the service proceeded without further incident.

Robust faith characterized Wigglesworth's life, and he became widely known for certain quotations. In reference to faith in God's promises, he said: "The Word of God has not to be prayed about; the Word of God is to be received and obeyed." To those who repeatedly asked God for healing, he announced, "If you ask God seven times for the same thing, six times are in unbelief."

Nevertheless, Wigglesworth himself mourned the early death of his wife and a son, and prayed many times for his daughter to be healed of deafness but to no avail. He also experienced excruciating pain for three years because of kidney stones, after which he expressed more compassion to the suffering. In this respect, his ministry of healing was nagged like others with the question, Why isn't everyone who is prayed for healed?

In the Pentecostal movement, when evangelists closed revivals and moved on to preach and pray for the sick elsewhere, pastors remained to console those who

The Gift of Weather Forecasting

The pages of the *Evangel* carried some curious prophetic speculations in its earliest years. However, an announcement carried in three consecutive issues of January 1916 proposing a "Weather Department" column must top the list. Editor John W. Welch ran the "Special Notice" on the strength of respect for Texas Assemblies of God minister Warren F. Carothers (1872-1953)—that God had given him "a most wonderful discovery by which it is possible to predict weather conditions." By the third issue to carry the notice, however, Carothers was displaying some caution by writing in his new "Grapes and Pomegranates" column (January 15, 1916) that he "would not think of launching a new doctrine or new 'movement' without consulting the brethren" (p. 9).

In keeping with this concern, the notice sought an expression of interest in such a column by "one hundred or more . . . subscribers." In that Carothers could supposedly predict the weather "two weeks or more in advance," his predictions would have been current when the magazine went to press since the lead time for preparing and printing each issue was probably two weeks. After the third appearance of the notice, however, nothing more is mentioned about Carothers's "'discovery" and weather predictions (indeed his "Grapes and Pomegranates" column, which appeared at the time of the first notice, disappears with the third notice).

Even after the founding of the General Council of the Assemblies of God and the adoption of the Statement of Fundamental Truths in 1916, a tension between freedom and order continued. Belief in the restoration of apostolic power, coupled with expectant faith that God could do the unusual and impossible (John 14:12-13), sometimes led to extravagant claims. Council leaders and ministers struggled to accept the validity of spiritual "'gifts" and other practices that lacked biblical warrant. As time passed, such novelties were ignored.

continued to suffer. Ultimately, the pastor was the person who went with the family to the cemetery to bury a loved one, possibly to sing with them the words of the song-writer Albert E. Brumley: "I'll meet you in the morning, . . . in the sweet by and by."

RECOMMENDED READING

Bundy, David. "G. T. Haywood: Religion for Urban Realities." In *Portraits of a Generation: Early Pentecostal Leaders*, edited by James R. Goff, Jr., and Grant Wacker, 237–253. Fayetteville, Ark.: University of Arkansas Press, 2002.

Flower, Alice Reynolds. *Grace for Grace: Some Highlights of God's Grace in the Daily Life of the Flower Family.* Springfield, Mo.: By the author, 1961.

Frodsham, Stanley H. *Smith Wigglesworth: Apostle of Faith.* Springfield, Mo.: Gospel Publishing House, 1972.

Golder, Morris E. *The Life and Works of Bishop Garfield Thomas Haywood (1880–1931).* Indianapolis: By the author, 1977.

Hywel-Davies, Jack. *The Life of Smith Wigglesworth.* Ann Arbor, Mich.: Servant Publications, 1987.

Miskov, Jennifer. *Life on Wings: The Forgotten Life and Theology of Carrie Judd Montgomery (1858-1946).* Cleveland, TN : CPT Press, 2012.

Montgomery, Carrie Judd. *Under His Wings: The Story of My Life.* Oakland: Office of *Triumphs of Faith*, 1936.

Ringer, David. "J. Roswell Flower: Pentecostal Servant and Statesman." *Assemblies of God Heritage* 32 (2012): 14-23.

Stock, Jennifer. "George S. Montgomery: Businessman for the Gospel." Parts 1 and 2. *Assemblies of God Heritage* 9 (spring 1989): 4–5, 17–18; 9 (summer 1989): 12–14, 20.

Wigglesworth, Smith. *The Anointing of His Spirit.* Compiled and edited by Wayne E. Warner. Ann Arbor, Mich.: Vine Books, 1994.

———. *Ever Increasing Faith.* Springfield, Mo.: Gospel Publishing House, 1972.

UNIT THREE
1928-1947

TIME LINE 1928-1947

1929—E. S. Williams, Philadelphia pastor, elected general superintendent; Stock market crashes, the Great Depression begins. Charles F. Parham dies.

1931—First General Council held outside Midwest (Glad Tidings Temple, San Francisco).

1933—First General Council held in the East (Highway Tabernacle, Philadelphia).

1935—What becomes Minister's Benefit Association (MBA) organizes; Dallas welcomes General Council; Council approves ordination of women as pastors.

1937—Fred Vogler appointed to head newly organized Home Missions and Education Department.

1939—Southern California Bible College inaugurates first baccalaureate program in the Assemblies of God.

Springfield hosts Council for first time since 1927. Sunday School Counselor introduced as a monthly periodical. General Presbytery rules against credentialing of African Americans.

1941—Japanese attack on Pearl Harbor brings America into World War II. Military Chaplaincy Department developed; Reveille for military personnel introduced.

1943—National Christ's Ambassadors Department established. General Council approves becoming a charter member of the National Association of Evangelicals. Missionary conference at Central Bible Institute in Springfield.

1944—Aimee Semple McPherson dies.

1945—General Council conducted in Springfield a month after World War II ends. Radio Department starts with Thomas F. Zimmerman as director. General Council leadership reorganized to include four assistant general superintendents.

1947—Berean School of the Bible established; report given that Sermons in Song radio program had been inaugurated and the Spanish Literature Department (now Life Publishers International) created.

CHAPTER 11

TEAMWORKING FOR THE TASK

P entecostals had railed against creeds and human organization because in the quest for order and uniformity, the freedom to be led by the Holy Spirit might be curtailed. But after thirteen years, the need for accountability and teamwork convinced a majority of Assemblies of God ministers to approve a constitution and bylaws. In other words, they now realized that the Spirit could also speak through Council votes and committee decisions. Indeed, the increasing number of church structures, whether at local, district, or national levels, were justified to aid in the development and effectiveness of various ministries. Districts grew rapidly during this time.

Therefore, the constitution in 1927 marked a milestone in the evolution of the General Council. Although insiders have preferred terms like *cooperative fellowship* and *the Fellowship*, this decision pushed the organization ahead to denominational status. Like other human institutions devoted to doing the Lord's business, the Council has moved from simplicity to complexity in its operation.

After the controversy over initial evidence, the Assemblies of God faced no more disputes that could disrupt its doctrinal identity until after World War II and the coming of the New Order of the Latter Rain. Small issues arose, but were addressed through passing bylaws, which saved the Council from enlarging the *Statement of Fundamental Truths*. "Pridgeonism" and other heresies received swift condemnation.

On the other hand, the Council allowed ministers some diversity in their view on the timing of the rapture of the Church. While the majority held to a pre-Tribulation Rapture, others maintained that the Church would be taken up in the middle of the Tribulation period, and still others looked for that to happen at the end of the period. Since everyone professed that Christ would come for His church before the literal one-thousand-year millennial period, a measure of tolerance for the mid- and post-Tribulation views was granted. In this way, the literal interpretation of the prophetic books of the Bible would remain largely unchanged. Those who leaned toward the post-Tribulation view, however, were ordered not to preach or teach it publicly. Again, unity among the Spirit-baptized for the task of world evangelization still ranked above requiring strict adherence to one view of the timing of the Lord's return.

Important advances had to do with the increasing number of national programs, the founding of the Home Missions and Education Department, the rapid growth of Bible institutes, more publications from Gospel Publishing House, changes prompted by World War II, and the long-awaited recognition of the Assemblies of God and other Pentecostal organizations by evangelicals. Other significant events included the decision to ordain women as pastors in 1935, as well as the refusal of the General Presbytery to grant credentials to African Americans four years later.

Growth continued in the grassroots through these years. While pastors and evangelists conducted evangelistic campaigns here and there, laypeople shared the burden of gospel witness. Mrs. Alloe Taylor, pastor of First Assembly of God in Walhalla, South Carolina, crisply reported to the *Evangel* that she had "held services in homes and brush arbors since Christmas, with great success. Have found many who are hungry for the full gospel. About 25 believers. Plans are being made to build a church soon. A lot has been donated. We need your prayers in this needy pioneer work."[1] Evangelist Charles Hurst of Stonewall, Mississippi, held a revival in Samburgh, Tennessee, where eighteen people were converted and others Spirit

Women in Ministry

Diversity of opinion on the issue of women in the ministry has always existed in the Assemblies of God. From the holiness movement, which long championed women's rights, came early Pentecostal evangelists Maria Woodworth-Etter and Carrie Judd Montgomery. Others reflected traditions disapproving of female ministers, as did the first general chairman of the Assemblies of God, E. N. Bell of the Southern Baptist Convention.

The ideal of the male pastor was brought into Pentecostalism from existing religious traditions, but widespread lay ministry blurred such gender distinctions. At the center of Assemblies of God growth was intensive lay evangelism; every believer was called to minister. Nevertheless, when the Assemblies of God began, the Council ordained women only as evangelists and missionaries. Even so, female evangelists and missionaries found they had to pastor their fledgling flocks.

Much of early Pentecostal growth was due to the efforts of women ministers. Through the 1930s, one out of every five ministers was a woman and two out of every three missionaries.

As Bible institutes were established, young female students spent summer holidays holding daily vacation Bible schools and establishing Sunday schools in unreached communities. Female graduates who married a pastor would co-pastor the church, and those who married non-pastors generally limited themselves to a particular ministry in a local church.

Although women were leaders at the local level, they rarely held district posts or national executive offices.

—Darrin J. Rodgers

baptized. A Sunday baptismal service at the lake concluded the meetings, with saints shouting the praises of God on the hillside.[2] Finally, Ida Hamilton, director of a Daily Vacation Bible School in the little town of Brimson, Missouri—population 143 in 1934—joyfully noted that fifty-seven children had been enrolled; some walked two and a half miles to attend. "We are grateful most of all [for] the warm place for the full gospel program which it created in their hearts," she added.[3] Pentecostals like Taylor, Hurst, and Hamilton, today largely forgotten, labored to make the Assemblies of God what it is today.

COUNCIL LEADERS

The small size of the General Council operation at the national level from 1914 to 1918 required only two officers at the top: the general superintendent and the general secretary. Changes began in 1919 with the addition of the Missionary Department and the office of missionary secretary. A year later, the editor of the *Pentecostal Evangel* also gained executive status. Pastor David McDowell, a graduate of A. B. Simpson's school at Nyack, New York, became the first assistant general superintendent in 1923 when the Council established the office. However, he continued to serve his pastorate in Pennsylvania.

A long period of stability began in 1929 with the election of Ernest S. Williams as general superintendent. Although surprised by his election and not really wanting to move to Springfield, Missouri (it took him fourteen months!), he served in the post for twenty years. With the increasing size of the organization, four assistant general superintendents were elected at the General Council meeting in Springfield in 1945: Ralph M. Riggs, Gayle F. Lewis, Fred Vogler, and Wesley R. Steelberg. The resolution stated that "it is physically impossible for the General Superintendent and Assistant Superintendent to take care of all the field work and yet to meet the demands of the headquarters office."[4] The assistant superintendents administered different facets of the operation in Springfield.

Ministers at the Santa Rosa camp meeting: (l to r) Ira Surface, Howard Carter, J. Narver Gortner, Emma Taylor, Mark T. Draper, Robert H. Moon

The national leaders, along with many evangelists, traveled widely across the country speaking at local churches, conventions, and camp meetings. The Northern California camp held at Santa Rosa in 1934 boasted three general superintendents as guests: E. S. Williams, Howard Carter (Assemblies of God in Great Britain and Ireland), and C. L. Greenwood (Assemblies of God in Australia). Other featured speakers included Emma Taylor, who spoke in the evening evangelistic services that attracted two thousand people. "What unction! What zeal! And with what power she

Rambling as the Spirit Leads

My husband sometimes rebukes me for taking a text and then never coming back to it. Never mind, as long as men and women ramble along in sin, I'm going to ramble after them from Genesis to Revelation, as the Spirit reveals the need and gives utterance at any moment in my sermon.

—*Evangelist Emma Taylor quoted in "Nuggets,"* Pentecostal Evangel *(December 7, 1935): 11.*

did speak, as she poured out her very soul to the multitude," wrote R. H. Moon, the "camp reporter." Ira Surface taught on the Old Testament tabernacle with an "illuminated model . . . of his own construction. . . . He made Christ more real to us, as he explained the typical and prophetic meaning of this earthly pattern of things heavenly." The camp ended in a "blaze of glory" with the best possible results: "100 received their Baptism, while many others were saved," and the "camp meeting was initiated, and conducted without calling upon the district treasury for help."[5]

CREATIVE VENTURES OF FAITH

Structural growth did not stifle individual initiative; in fact, much of the growth came as a result of initiative. Elsie Peters related that "in 1924, the year of my ordination to the ministry, God called me to minister to the deaf. . . . After my testimony [at the 1925 General Council], 'Daddy' (J. W.) Welch arose and told the congregation he felt the blood of the deaf would be upon the hands of the Assemblies of God if the gospel was not presented to them."[6] Etta Calhoun's vision for women helping home and foreign missions led to highly effective district and national programs.

In New York City, Bartholomew Hutzaluk, pastor of First Ukrainian Evangelical Pentecostal Church (Assemblies of God) became burdened to provide literature for Ukrainian people. He was the first to produce Sunday School literature and also published the hymnal *Songs of Joy*. In 1941, Hutzaluk inaugurated *Evanhelski Palomnyk* (*Evangelical Pilgrim*), a bimonthly magazine sent to Ukrainians around the world.[7]

Bartholomew Hutzaluk

In another vital area of ministry, Marion Wakeman established a mission station at Pence in the mountains of Kentucky. Inspired by her work, Pastor Oscar E. Nash of First Christian Assembly in Cincinnati, Ohio, spearheaded an effort to take the message of Christ into the region.[8] Life proved challenging for the growing cadre of women and men who went as missionaries. Much of the travel had to be done on horseback. In one day, Elsie Elmendorf rode fifty-one miles to reach her destination. Housing often meant living with a mountain family in a ramshackle log cabin. Sometimes their lives were endangered, as when Elva Hoover conducted a revival in the schoolhouse at Wide Creek. Fearing that a mob would disrupt the meetings, the local believers promised that a man would sit by her every night with a gun to protect her. "I didn't like that idea," she insisted. "We shouldn't have to shoot the gospel down their throats."[9]

Mushrooming endeavors on the home front caught the attention of church leaders. Due to limited finances and authority, the Missionary Department simply could not fulfill its original mission of directing both foreign and home missions. After many years of discussion, the General Council finally authorized the establishment

Features of Pentecostal Prayer and Praise

Oral prayer–collective oral prayer, all praying at once, mostly vernacular or mostly glossolalic or some mix of the two. This pattern expresses the personal experience of each.

Raising of hands–joint or individual prayer [that] reflects literal response to biblical precedents (Exod. 17:11-12) and commands (1 Tim. 2:8). One or two hands may be used. Pentecostals are more likely to extend the arms fully upward, palms forward.

Dancing in the Spirit– Always individually done, never in couples, always unplanned and never scheduled, at almost any point in the service. During hymns or during the sermon, a believer so moved will leave the seat and move up and down the aisles of the church, eyes often closed, arms usually uplifted, lost in abandon to the worship of God. This practice more often appears among black Pentecostals, where usually purer forms of Pentecostal worship survive. . . . Was it not David himself who "danced before the LORD with all his might" as the Scriptures say (2 Sam. 6:14)?

Jericho March–named from the march of the children of Israel seven times around the city of Jericho till the walls fell down (Joshua 6:1-27). In an atmosphere of high enthusiasm, a congregant may rise and make for the aisles, possibly inviting others to join. Around the perimeter of the place of assembly they go, gathering more worshipers till a full column is formed. . . . During the march, there is much singing, maybe some shouting (as happened also in the Bible, and at the bidding of the leader: Joshua 6:10, 16, 20). The whole affair might last as long as an hour or two, and it might even displace the preaching. Afterwards, the marchers return to their seats and the service goes on. . . . Pentecostals . . . never thought it wrong for worship to be fun.

Falling under the power–[presently known as] being "slain in the Spirit"—a virtual faint, almost always supine, sometimes accompanied by soft glossolalic prayer, sometimes conspicuously silent, sometimes with arms fully raised from the lying position accompanied with loud prayer. In this posture many early Pentecostals received the baptism in the Holy Spirit and, for the first time, spoke in tongues. In later Pentecostalism, "falling under the power" came to be associated with certain ministers credited with having a gift that led to the phenomenon.

—*Russell P. Spittler, "Spirituality, Pentecostal and Charismatic,"*
New International Dictionary of Pentecostal and Charismatic Movements:
by Stanley M. Burgess and Edward M. van der Maas, 1099–1100.
Used by permission of The Zondervan Corporation

of the Home Missions and Education Department in 1937 to promote church plant-ing and oversee the Bible institutes (a separate education department came in 1945).

Consequently, the Council elected Fred Vogler to provide leadership over home missions and education. Vogler, a native of Australia who immigrated to the United States, was converted and baptized in the Spirit during the Pentecostal revival at Zion City, Illinois, in 1907. He planted numerous churches, supporting his family of five children through his skill as a carpenter. Vogler later served as the Kansas district superintendent before working at the national office.[10] While still living in Kansas, he visited the campus of Central Bible Institute (CBI) in Springfield. Hav-ing had the district purchase twelve tents for church plants, he invited students to evangelize during the summer, assuring them that none of them would starve before the fall semester began.

Despite grand hopes, the Home Missions and Education Department found itself only coordinating the growing number of specialized ministries among foreign lan-guage groups in the United States (e.g., Hispanic, German, Ukrainian), Native Amer-icans, blind and deaf, prison inmates, and Jews. Neither the General Council nor its Home Missions and Education Department had the authority to plant churches or tell the constituency how it should be done. From the beginning, churches had been pioneered by individuals with or without the help of local churches or districts. The progress of the districts, however, did bring more oversight (though not necessarily more financial assistance).

Another venture focused on the need of local congregations to increase their giving to missions. Since only 25 percent of Assemblies of God churches made meaningful contributions through the Springfield office to foreign missions, the time had arrived for a new promotional plan. Arthur F. Berg, a former missionary to Africa, proposed the "Busy Bee" plan in the late 1920s. In his estimation, "to have and maintain a strong 'foreign missions base' simply means that we must have a strong and expanded 'home missions base.'"[11] The program involved a missionary visit to a local assembly and the dispensing of small wooden beehive banks to those in attendance. Everyone had the opportunity to "make honey" for God. A slip of paper handed out with the bank read: "I shall honestly endeavor with the help of the Lord to lay aside out of my income regularly as I receive it the sum under which I have marked X."[12] Monthly collections would then be placed in the missionary offering to the General Council. The offerings sent under this arrangement were then divided: 25 percent to home missions for the pioneering of new churches and 75 percent to foreign missions. However, 5 percent of each of these percentages went to pay for office expenses.

Interest in a youth program captured the attention of California pastors. Under the name Pentecostal Ambassadors for Christ, youth rallies were held in Oakland and Stockton under the leadership of Wesley R. Steelberg. But it was a youth pas-tor in Los Angeles, Carl Hatch, who coined the term Christ's Ambassadors, taken from 2 Corinthians 5:20. After Verona Wagner Lyden composed "We Are Christ's Ambassadors," youth leaders usually began their "C.A." services with this song. Taking the lead, the Southern California district began publishing Christ's Ambassadors Herald in the early 1930s (later a national publication, the CA Herald). In 1943 the General Council authorized the national CA Department (later the Department of Youth Ministries).

It is to the credit of its first director, former Michigan pastor Ralph W. Harris, that the youth of the Assemblies of God adopted the ambitious Speed the Light project in 1944. By today's standards, starting a new program at that time was incredibly simple. Harris simply walked into the office of Ernest S. Williams, the general superintendent, and proposed the idea. After inviting Missionary Secretary Noel Perkin into the discussion, Speed the Light was approved within an hour.[13]

Speed the Light served as a key component in a wider headquarters' effort

Gladys Hinson with children at Hillcrest Children's Home

to prepare for the postwar period in missions. Channeling the efforts of youth into raising funds for missionary transportation and equipment proved remarkably successful. Challenging every young person to contribute one dollar, the response resulted in one hundred thousand dollars. Whether airplanes, boats, bicycles, cars, trucks, or ox carts and mules, Assemblies of God missionaries were among the best outfitted to make unprecedented progress after the war's end. The funds enabled the Foreign Missions Department to purchase seventy-one vehicles in the first year.

Assemblies of God people created an array of ministries, including benevolent institutions at home and abroad. Gladys Hinson dreamed of going to China as a missionary to start an orphanage. When World War II prevented this, she gained permission from the General Council to establish one in Hot Springs, Arkansas, in 1944, now known as Hillcrest Children's Home. Although she died from cancer three years later at the age of thirty-six, her legacy lived on in the care of hundreds of boys and girls.

MINISTERIAL TRAINING

Ministerial training underwent dramatic changes between 1928 and 1947: Several older schools ceased to operate and new ones took their place. Strong leaders usually guided these schools, including Frank J. Lindquist (North Central Bible Institute), P. C. Nelson (Southwestern Bible School), Dorothy Locke (Peniel Bible Institute), and Henry Ness (Northwest Bible Institute). The urgency to train workers before Christ's return and the need for them to remain within their geographical areas for pastoring and church planting led to the founding of such schools. Started as ventures of faith on shoestring budgets, some survived to become strong and enduring institutions, others collapsed or merged, and still others remained in stringent circumstances for decades. Alice E. Luce at the Latin American Bible Institute in California viewed the school as an "adventure in faith." She shared that "with no funds and no promises at hand, the Lord gave . . . the assurance with a promise found in Isaiah 60:22 [KJV]: 'A little one shall become a thousand, and a small one a strong nation: I the Lord will hasten it in his time.'"[14]

These schools were joint efforts in faith: Students, staff, faculty, and administrators often made great personal sacrifices to keep them going. Students sometimes enrolled with only the call of ministry on their lives and a robust faith in God's provision for the necessary fees. Men and women were equally welcomed, and acceptance did not depend on a high school diploma. To help keep tuition low, students were assigned chores that ranged from serving in the kitchen to caring for farm animals. Students at the Latin American Bible Institute in San Antonio, Texas, paid two dollars a month for tuition, which covered their room, board, and studies. When the school purchased a farm on the outskirts of the city, called "Canaan Land" by the students, they raised vegetables and tended dairy cows to get milk, butter, and cheese to insure a healthy diet. Outside

Peniel Hall, the girl's dormitory at Peniel Bible Institute at Campton, Kentucky (c. 1940). The school billed itself as the "Only Mountain Bible School of the Assemblies of God."

assistance was gratefully accepted: Peniel Bible Institute in Kentucky received furniture from T. K. Leonard of Findlay, Ohio, after his own school closed.

Teachers like Myer Pearlman wrote Sunday School lessons and other materials for Gospel Publishing House to keep food on the table. Faculty members received no salary during the long months of the summer recess. Instructors at Midwest Bible School in Auburn, Nebraska, the first school started by the General Council, received less than ten dollars a month in 1920 and 1921, not nearly enough to cover expenses. Students worked in the summer wheat harvest for five to seven dollars a day to save for school costs.[15] Although Midwest was in existence only one year, it still produced an impressive number of ministers.[16]

Bible institutes shared several characteristics. Most had enrollments of fifty students or less. The size encouraged personal contact between students and teachers both in classes, the dining room, and chapel. Spiritual mentoring was always available, and guidance in the operation of the gifts of the Spirit in chapel services—often called the "classroom of the Holy Spirit"—prepared students for spiritual leadership.

The facilities varied: Midwest Bible School occupied the former Avenue Hotel in Auburn. T. K. Leonard's Gospel School operated in a former tavern. J. Roswell and Alice Reynolds Flower began Maranatha Summer Bible School at the Eastern district's campground, Maranatha Park, at Green Lane, Pennsylvania. Others enjoyed better facilities: Glad Tidings Bible Institute in San Francisco occupied a six-story building. Pastor

CBI men's volleyball game in the 1930s

Henry Ness opened Northwest Bible Institute at Hollywood Temple (now Calvary Temple) in Seattle, Washington, in October 1934 with eighteen students. "There was no equipment, no faculty, no money for either, and no experience in the administration of an educational institution," said Maxine Williams about the founding of the school. Nevertheless, "the new school began with three assets: a man of vision and energy, a roof overhead, and a conviction that this was the will of God."[17] Later renamed Northwest College of the Assemblies of God, its graduates pioneered many churches in the Pacific Northwest.

Bible courses formed the core of the curriculum. Other courses included soul winning, dispensational truths, music, and missions. A full course of study could be completed in three years. Libraries were usually small, and teachers often had little formal academic training. Accreditation did not interest leaders (even if it had been available and accessible). Student life consisted of chapel services, classes, prayer, Bible study, chores, and student ministry on weekends. The latter activities included conducting street meetings, holding services in rescue missions, and planting churches within a radius of the school. Many churches owe their origins to the work of student ministry teams.

Hazel and Philip Crouch

Amid severe restrictions, romance often flourished in the schools. At CBI where formal dating did not exist, male and female students could sit together at one meal a day, but only with another couple present. In other contexts, private conversations were simply not allowed. As students walked about, one could look at the other, but not talk. Yet love managed to blossom. Hazel Conway from North Little Rock, Arkansas, and Philip Crouch, the son of missionaries to Egypt, fell in love. After graduating together in 1937—they were both class speakers at the commencement—Philip went to serve with his parents as a missionary. Hazel received missionary appointment and itinerated to raise her financial support. When Andrew Crouch had a heart attack and needed to return to the United States, the Missions Department asked Philip to take his father's place in directing the work. The department then gave Hazel permission to join him; she traveled alone from Arkansas to Egypt. He met her at the dock, and they were married on July 24, 1938. Her mother had hand sewed her wedding dress, and Philip had a tuxedo and wedding cake made in Alexandria.

If an instructor fell in love with a student, the courtship required great discretion, as in the case of Myer Pearlman and Irene Graves. Enrolled in Myer's Spanish class, Irene received a letter from him sent through his secretary. This initiated a

correspondence between them that lasted for some weeks. Happy to be matchmakers, Frank Boyd (the CBI "principal") and his wife, Helen, contacted Irene and invited her to their home for dinner during the Christmas break. Myer joined them, and that evening when he proposed marriage, she accepted. With their engagement kept secret, they continued to correspond during the spring semester with no further personal contacts outside the classroom. News of the coming wedding circulated after school was out, and they were married in August.

Despite their limited resources, Bible institutes made major contributions to the Assemblies of God. What they lacked in academic standing, they made up for in channeling the energies of enthusiastic students into spiritually disciplined ministry. Graduates often proved capable of adjusting to new situations and demands: Their endurance of hardships at home, in Bible school, and abroad testified to deep-seated commitments made as students.

Myer and Irene Pearlman

In 1947, the General Council established Berean School of the Bible under the leadership of long-term educator Frank Boyd. A graduate of A. B. Simpson's Missionary Training Institute at Nyack, New York, he began teaching at Bethel Bible Training School in Newark, New Jersey, and then at CBI in Springfield, and later at Southern California Bible College in Costa Mesa. In Springfield, students fondly remembered him as a caring teacher, for his interest in prophecy, and for his annual singing of a favorite song (part of a poem written by Simpson) as he slowly marched back and forth across the chapel platform to emphasize the importance of faithfulness in following the Lord:

P-L-O-D, plod.
    So le-e-t us plod,
Steadily plod
    All along the way.
Zeal may fire
    And hope inspire,
But plod will win the day.[18]

Frank M. Boyd

In the years that followed, Boyd produced textbooks for correspondence courses that prepared men and women to meet district ministerial training requirements. In later years, Berean School of the Bible enlarged to become Berean University without losing its nontraditional approach to training, before merging into Global University, which serves the same purpose.

MUSIC AND PUBLICATIONS

Donald Gee, who wrote materials for both the Assemblies of God in Great Britain and Ireland and the Assemblies of God (U.S.A.), said the "glory of a true Assembly of God" centers on the exaltation of the Lord Jesus in both song and sermon. "One pretty noticeable trait in such assemblies is the added zest that occurs whenever the words of a chorus, or a hymn, a testimony, or an address magnify some attribute of the Glorious Redeemer," he observed. "I noticed it again the other day when, after a time of intercession, we began to sing that true chorus—'What the world needs is Jesus.'"[19]

For the discipling of believers in local churches, Gospel Publishing House (GPH) printed tracts, booklets, and books, in addition to the *Pentecostal Evangel* and an increasing number of Sunday School materials. Since Pentecostals expressed their faith in vibrant singing and testimony, GPH, as well as private publishers like Seeley Kinne, produced songbooks with favorites from the nineteenth-century holiness movement (e.g., "Pentecostal Power" and "Old-Time Power") and others produced by evangelical revivalism. Pentecostals added their own songs: Alice Reynolds Flower wrote "Far and Wide" ("Souls are struggling, drifting, dying; send the gospel far and wide"). Kinne penned "Pentecostal Backsliders" ("Fight the fight 'gainst self and sin: Trust in Christ, you're sure to win"). And reflecting on the nearness of the Lord's return, one Pentecostal put these words to song: "When you see Jesus coming in the sky, Good-bye, hallelujah! I'm gone."

GPH had begun publishing doctrinal manuals in the mid-1920s. This continued with Peter C. Nelson's *Bible Doctrines* (1934), written in "plain, everyday speech" for use in "short-term Bible Institutes, for studies in fundamental doctrines, and for young people who are unable to attend Bible School, that they may obtain a working knowledge concerning what we believe."[20] Pearlman's *Knowing the Doctrines of the Bible* followed three years later. Focusing exclusively on the baptism in the Holy Spirit and speaking in tongues, Carl Brumback authored *What Meaneth This?* (1947). Billed as "A Pentecostal Answer to a Pentecostal Question," it represented the most in-depth exposition on the doctrine to date by a Pentecostal.

WORLD WAR II

As international tensions intensified in the 1920s and 1930s, and it became obvious once again that the leading industrial nations would likely go to war, preachers across the Assemblies of God warned the saints of the Lord's soon return. Harry J. Steil, one of the best-known pastors, pointed to two key passages of Scripture that speak of end-time events: Luke 21:28, "When these things begin to take place, stand up and lift up your heads, because your redemption is drawing near.'" And Luke 21:36, "'Be always on the watch, and pray that you may be able to escape all that is about to happen, and that you may be able to stand before the Son of Man.'"

"If we determine that the nations are trending toward another world conflict, toward Armageddon, and every statesman and world leader believes this to be inevitable," he wrote, "then how imminent, how very near, must His coming be for His saints."[21]

When thou prayest, enter into thy closet, and when thou hast shut thy door, pray to thy Father which is in secret; and thy Father which seeth in secret shall reward thee openly. Matt. 6:6

Pentecostal Evangel art by Charles Ramsay

The Gospel to Servicemen

Thousands of American youth are being called into training camps. Gospel services are prohibited in these camps. However, you can preach to these men by the distribution of gospel literature. We have the literature and will send it to you in five-pound packages of choice back-dated quarterlies, 150 per five-pound package.

Let your young people, especially your young men, roll and wrap these quarterlies in red cellophane paper. Let them approach a serviceman and gently speak to him, saying, "This is not a stick of candy. Please put this in your pocket until you return to your place of abode. In your quiet moments, you may unwrap it and enjoy the contents of this package." The happy faces of your Christian workers will add to the value of gospel literature thus distributed. The good seed prayerfully sown may win the hearts of those who are prohibited to be ministered to in gospel services.

—Pentecostal Evangel *(April 26, 1941): 12*

Early on, Pentecostal pacifists had ranked the need to evangelize on behalf of the heavenly Kingdom above the need to fight on behalf of the kingdoms of this world—they would soon fall anyway. As Ralph M. Riggs, an influential leader and later general superintendent, stated: "To the Church of the last days is given the exalted privilege of gathering in the balance of the quota to make up the bride of Jesus Christ. . . . Perhaps it will be some humble soul from the mission field who will complete the number. Then the trumpet will sound and the Bride will rise to meet her Bridegroom."[22]

Pacifist sentiments, however, had changed considerably by 1941. Democracy appeared to be wimping out as totalitarianism bullied its way around the world. Then the Japanese attack on Pearl Harbor shattered isolationist sympathies in the United States and rallied patriotic enthusiasm for war. For the most part, Assemblies of God church members supported the war effort, determined to keep religious freedom and other cherished liberties. Some served as combatants, others as noncombatants, and many more worked in war-related industries. Approximately seventy-six thousand men and women from the Assemblies of God served in the military.

The 1941 General Council committed itself to ministering to military personnel. It made a major contribution by publishing the small nondenominational periodical *Reveille*. It was edited by Myer Pearlman, a veteran of World War I, and illustrated by artist Charles Ramsey. Hundreds of denominational chaplains recognized its value. On one occasion, a thousand uniformed men and women were reported to have read a single copy.[23] In 1944, the Servicemen's Department came into being to develop a Servicemen's Directory, coordinate the more than forty Victory Service Centers around the country, direct the activities of eleven field workers, and publish *Reveille*.[24]

The war effort also brought out the need for higher academic standards in the denomination's ministerial training schools. Some ministers had sought appointment as military chaplains only to discover that requirements called for four years of college work and three years in a standard seminary program. Fortunately, the government made exceptions, and thirty-four experienced pastors gained commissions. For training, they attended special chaplaincy schools held at various institutions. R. Stanley Berg, pastor of the Assembly of God in Pocomoke City, Maryland, attended a ten-week school at Harvard University in 1941. (Educational requirements for chaplains eventually prompted, in part, the founding of the Assemblies of God Theological Seminary.)

Landing at Utah Beach in France, "smoke still consumed the air," Berg recalled. "The smell of blood and death lingered, though the battle had been fought several weeks earlier."[25] As his regiment moved through Normandy, "I began to realize my calling. I worked tirelessly, holding services wherever we could assemble men—in barns, fields, jeeps, and thickets. We were able to lead many soldiers and officers to Christ. . . . The hearts of these men were ripe for the gospel during those tension-filled days."[26]

Assemblies of God chaplains, like Berg, learned to work in a broader religious context given the needs of the soldiers they accompanied. Becoming friends with

Colonel Levy, a Jewish lieutenant colonel, Levy asked him: "Chaplain, if we ever find a Jewish synagogue that is still intact, let's take it and have a service for our Jewish soldiers."[27] Berg found a synagogue that had remarkably remained intact in the bombed-out center of the city of Rheims. Since the Germans had used it to store engines for their fighter planes, he had the army clear the building and with Levy arranged a special Hanukkah service.

THE 1943 MISSIONARY CONFERENCE

Because a third to a half of the missionaries were forced to stay in the United States during World War II, the Foreign Missions Department convened a special conference in 1943 in Springfield, Missouri. With the war's outcome now certain, the time had come to plan for the future. Next to founding the department in 1919 and publishing a mission policy manual in 1930, calling this meeting would prove momentous. Before this, mission strategy had generally been in the hands of individual missionaries and overseas district councils. The missions department had primarily distributed funds and appointed missionaries. Now for the first time, in consultation with the missionaries, the department took the lead in strategizing for the future.

The conference set several goals for the war's end: the addition of field secretaries (regional administrators), the recruitment of five hundred new missionaries, the creation of advisory committees of ministers and missionaries, a program at CBI for advanced training of missionaries, and regional missions conventions in the United States.

Raising five million dollars to support the program after the war constituted the final objective. Actually, the conference had suggested a goal of one million dollars. But after listening to the speakers, General Superintendent Ernest S. Williams stood to the pulpit and challenged the figure. He proposed that the sum be increased to five million. In typical Pentecostal fashion, he feared that a low figure might indicate a lack of faith and thus limit what God could do. His suggestion won approval (no one was going to challenge the general superintendent over a matter of faith in God's provision). By war's end, about a half million dollars had been given—still a considerable sum of money for the time.

EVANGELICAL IDENTITY

When Pentecostals couldn't satisfactorily prove that speaking in tongues constituted languages for missionary preaching, skeptical holiness believers and fundamentalists howled in condemnation. In the view of many, Pentecostal tongues-speaking was of the devil. Others, while not detecting a conspiracy of evil, judged that Pentecostals suffered from some kind of disorder of the mind. In any event, both within evangelical circles and in the larger society, Pentecostals found themselves dismissed as part of the troublesome religious fringe.

Faith healing also generated criticism. During the early years, Pentecostalism was known almost as much for its strong emphasis on healing as for speaking in tongues. In campaigns led by evangelists Aimee Semple McPherson, Smith Wigglesworth, Charles S. Price, and Lilian Yeomans, attention centered on prayer for the sick. For example, in a two and a half week campaign, McPherson might only preach one night on baptism in the Holy Spirit. Yet the healing ministry could be easily justified as a vital part of evangelism in "signs and wonders." Few could doubt the impact that such meetings had in starting new congregations. When McPherson died in 1944 and Wigglesworth and Price three years later, many Pentecostals nervously thought the "glory has departed" (1 Samuel 4:22), an era had ended.

During the famed "fundamentalist-modernist" controversy that rocked mainline Protestantism in the 1920s and early 1930s, Pentecostals remained on the sidelines. As the fundamentalist movement fragmented, the Federal Council of Churches remained as the only umbrella organization to speak for American Protestants. But with the Federal Council's emphasis on social causes—the "social gospel"—many conservatives became wary of its liberal agenda. Some conservatives saw the need for a unified voice to speak for their interests.

Two chief initiatives appeared in response, largely by those outside the mainline churches: the American Council of Christian Churches and the National Association of Evangelicals. The American Council was founded in 1941 and directed by Carl T. McIntire, a veteran of the fundamentalist conflict within the Presbyterian Church, U.S.A.

Along with a small band of others, he had bolted the denomination. Fiercely separatistic, McIntire's organization refused admission to any organization that still belonged to the Federal Council. His interpretation of 2 Corinthians 6:17, "come out

Organizational meeting of the National Association of Evangelicals
at the Coronado Hotel in St. Louis, Missouri

from them and be separate," excluded any individual or any organization he chose to brand as liberal. He viewed Pentecostalism as a sign of evil and apostasy in the last days. The next year, however, Pentecostals found an alternative in the formation of the National Association of Evangelicals (NAE). The NAE's origin can be traced to J. Elwin Wright and the New England Fellowship of Evangelicals. Wright's father, Joel A. Wright, had been a Pentecostal preacher, and the family had strong contacts with other Pentecostals in New England.[28] However, he and his family gradually put distance between themselves and Pentecostalism.

The New England Fellowship had brought a measure of unity and cooperation to a broad group of conservative Christians in the region, including Pentecostals. Believing that such an agency could unite evangelicals nationally, Wright traveled widely to survey interest and gather support.

Although far more inclusive than the American Council, the NAE did have serious doctrinal concerns among its delegates at the organizational meeting. In preparation for that event, leaders insisted that despite a likely Calvinistic majority, Wesleyan

J. Roswell Flower and the NAE

Brother Flower made an explanation [at the September 1943 General Council in Springfield] concerning an association of Fundamentalists that has been formed, which has given a very cordial invitation to the brethren of the Assemblies of God fellowship to become associated with them in the drawing up of a constitution of a simple organization that would express the voice of Evangelical Protestantism . . . .

Brother Flower stated that in response to the invitation, a number of brethren from headquarters attended a meeting in St. Louis last year [1942] for the purpose of considering the advisability of forming this association . . . . At this meeting a statement of fundamentals, upon which all agreed, was drawn up, and also a suggested constitution.

At the meeting held in May of this year in Chicago, over seven hundred evangelical ministers met, including 104 ministers of the Assemblies of God, among whom were a number of District Superintendents who had been sent by their Districts. At this special meeting in Chicago the organization was perfected. . . . Brother Flower was elected to be one of the nine executives of this new National Association of Evangelicals for United Action.

At this [General] Council, Brother Flower stated, we should consider whether it would be worth our while to become part of such an organization. [He] stated how absolutely necessary it was for evangelical Christians to have a voice in this country. . . .

Recognizing the need for a united voice to speak authoritatively for Evangelical Protestantism in America, and so that we can identify ourselves with other Fundamental Evangelical groups without jeopardizing our denominational identity, it was agreed to become a part of this Evangelical fellowship.

—*Stanley H. Frodsham, "The Diary of a Delegate,"* Pentecostal Evangel (September 23, 1943): 4–5.

*The sequence of sentences has been altered slightly to better clarify the order of events.

holiness churches and Pentecostals would be welcomed and given equal standing. Ironically, many Wesleyans (along with Calvinists) openly questioned whether the NAE umbrella should be opened enough to include Pentecostals. At an early conference, a featured speaker challenged the propriety of a Pentecostal girls' trio being on the program; by this means, he criticized the presence of Pentecostals in the organization. Whereupon, Harold J. Ockenga, NAE president, and other leaders made it clear to everyone that the speaker's opinions were his own and not those of the leadership.

Pentecostals themselves wondered if the relationship would actually work; some General Council members denounced the proposed affiliation, fearing that they might at last have come to the point of trading their spiritual birthright for respectability. Nonetheless, the association of evangelicals and Pentecostals has worked well, far better than anyone may have expected.

Before the General Council voted to join the NAE at its biennial meeting in 1943, J. Roswell Flower, the general secretary, spoke strongly in favor; evangelical Christians needed a voice before the government. If evangelicals and Pentecostals were to preserve their enormous investments in gospel radio programs, they needed to take action as efforts were being made to limit religious broadcasting. Furthermore, a representative of the NAE had already done much to keep their voice "on the air," and a permanent office was being opened in Washington, D.C., to serve the interests of conservative evangelicals in broadcasting, missions, and other areas of concern.[29] After heated debate, the resolution passed.

Membership brought several valuable benefits. Foremost, the NAE conferred recognition as evangelicals on Trinitarian Pentecostals. No longer to be viewed as sectarians or cultists, they could now take their seats with other evangelicals. Although other members strongly disagreed with distinctive Pentecostal teachings, they no longer considered them heretical. After all, each body within the NAE had its own doctrinal distinctives. At the same time, membership centered on confession of historic doctrines of the Christian Church, to which all declared fidelity. "Jesus Name," or Oneness, Pentecostals, on the other hand, have yet to receive any such doctrinal "pat on the back" for their view of the Godhead.

Second, Pentecostals profited from the work of various NAE agencies set up to assist with mission endeavors, Sunday Schools, radio evangelism, and accreditation for Bible institutes and Bible colleges.

Third, Pentecostals recognized the value of dialogue with other believers. In fact, contact among Pentecostals at NAE meetings led directly to the founding of the Pentecostal Fellowship of North America in 1947.

Notwithstanding, the new relationship with conservative evangelicals not only led the Pentecostals to embrace their issues and concerns, but also isolated them from other evangelicals who stayed in the mainline churches. Pentecostals had always been evangelical in doctrine, teaching, among other doctrines, the infallible authority of Scripture, justification by faith, the Virgin Birth, the substitutionary atonement of Christ, and the Second Coming. Yet their emphasis on Holy Spirit baptism with speaking in tongues, belief in the full restoration of the gifts of the Spirit, and prayer for the sick set them apart.

It is important to remember that while Pentecostals often cheered fundamentalist attacks on liberal theology and the historic churches, they themselves responded somewhat differently. For example, fundamentalists reacted to philosophical and religious skepticism with rational proofs. Pentecostals, on the other hand, pointed to the demonstration of divine power.

As early as 1924, Stanley H. Frodsham, editor of the *Pentecostal Evangel*, gushed, "'I praise God that I am a Fundamentalist, and that I am a Pentecostal Fundamentalist. That is what we all are.'"[30] Another Council leader, David H. McDowell, said later that the Pentecostal movement as a whole might be termed *Fundamentalism Plus*. By this, he meant "a movement standing solidly for the plenary and verbal inspiration of the Scriptures as the Living Word of God; and standing for all the fundamental teachings of this sacred and Holy Book."[31]

But more cautious, Donald Gee detected that although fundamentalists defended the miracles in the Bible, they also insisted that those miracles had ceased with the Early Church. "They boldly affirm," he wrote, "that the Church has grown beyond the 'childish' need of occasional manifestations of the Spirit in her midst, and assume a development to have taken place that puts them [on the same side as] their Modernist opponents!"[32]

RECOMMENDED READING

Berg, Stan, with Jamie Bilton. *Called, Chosen, Faithful: The Memoirs of Rev. R. Stanley Berg*. Springfield, Mo.: By the author, 2000.

Celebrando Mas de Seis Decados, 1928–1992. Bronx, N.Y.: Distrito Hispano del Este de las Asambleas de Dios, 1992.

Declare His Glory: Speed-the-Light—40th Anniversary. Springfield, Mo.: Youth Department of the Assemblies of God, 1983.

Jacobsen, Douglas. "Knowing the Doctrines of Pentecostals: The Scholastic Theology of the Assemblies of God, 1930–55." In *Pentecostal Currents in American Protestantism*, ed. by Edith L. Blumhofer, et al., 90–107. Urbana: University of Illinois Press, 1999.

Evans, Elizabeth. *The Wright Vision: The Story of the New England Fellowship*. Lanham, Md.: University Press of America, 1991.

Gilbert, Bodie. "A Short History of Congregational Song in the Assemblies of God." *Assemblies of God Heritage* 28 (2008): 32–39.

Lyon, Ruth A., comp. A *History of Home Missions of the Assemblies of God*. Springfield, Mo.: Division of Home Missions, 1992.

Marsden, George. *Fundamentalism and American Culture: The Shaping of Twentieth-Century Evangelicalism, 1870–1925*. New York: Oxford University Press, 1980.

Menzies, William W. *Anointed to Serve: The Story of the Assemblies of God*. Springfield, Mo.: Gospel Publishing House, 1971.

Murch, James DeForest. *Cooperation Without Compromise: A History of the National Association of Evangelicals*. Grand Rapids: William B. Eerdmans Publishing Co., 1956.

Palmer, Leonard. "The Story of a Song: Composer of 'Christ's Ambassadors' with the Lord." *Assemblies of God Heritage* 14 (winter 1994–95): 16–17.

Wilson, Dwight. *Armageddon Now! The Premillenarian Response to Russia and Israel Since 1917*. Grand Rapids: Baker Book House, 1977.

Ziefle, Joshua R. "Missionary Church Planters and Developers: An Entrepreneurial Heritage." *Assemblies of God Heritage* 33 (2013): 26–35.

ENDNOTES

1 Mrs. Alloe Taylor, untitled news note, *Pentecostal Evangel* (6 October 1945): 14.

2 George Preslar, untitled news note, *Pentecostal Evangel* (6 October 1945): 13.

3 Ida Hamilton, "Daily Vacation Bible School," *Pentecostal Evangel* (4 August 1934): 12.

4 "Diary of a Delegate," *Pentecostal Evangel* (6 October 1945): 1.

5 R. H. Moon, "Northern California Camp," *Pentecostal Evangel* (25 August 1934): 13.

6 "Pioneer to the Deaf," *Silent Ambassador* (August 1963): 4.

7 Fred Smolchuck, *From Azusa Street to the U.S.S.R.: A Brief History of Pentecost Among Slavic Immigrants, 1900–1991* (Springfield, Mo.: North American Slavic Pentecostal Fellowship, 1992), 27.

8 Ibid., 13–14.

9 Ruth A. Lyon, comp., *A History of Home Missions of the Assemblies of God*, (Springfield, Mo.: Division of Home Missions, 1992), 13–14.

10 Edith L. Blumhofer, *Pentecost in My Soul* (Springfield, Mo.: Gospel Publishing House, 1989), 101–116.

11 Arthur F. Berg, "WORLD MISSIONS! How It Started—And WHY?" (Typewritten, n.d.), 2.

12 "The Busy Bee World-Wide Missions Program," *Pentecostal Evangel* (9 November 1929): 6.

13 Gary B. McGee, *This Gospel Shall Be Preached: A History and Theology of Assemblies of God Foreign Missions to 1959* (Springfield, Mo.: Gospel Publishing House, 1986), 183–184.

14 Alice E. Luce quoted in Victor De Leon, *The Silent Pentecostals: A Biographical History of the Pentecostal Movement Among the Hispanics in the Twentieth Century* (Taylors, S.C.: Faith Printing Co., 1979), 69.

15 Glenn Gohr, "The Midwest Bible School," part 1, *Assemblies of God Heritage* 10 (summer 1990): 14.

16 Glenn Gohr, "Fruit of the Auburn School," *Assemblies of God Heritage* 10 (summer 1990): 14.

17 Maxine Williams quoted in Marjorie Stewart, "A Story of Pentecost in the Pacific Northwest," *Assemblies of God Heritage* 7 (summer 1987): 16.

18 For the full text, see A. B. Simpson, "Plod," *Pentecostal Visitor* (August 1937): 1.

19 Donald Gee, *The Glory of Assemblies of God* (Luton, Beds, U.K.: Executive Council of Assemblies of God in Great Britain and Ireland, n.d.), 17.

20 P. C. Nelson, *Bible Doctrines*, rev. ed. (Springfield, Mo.: Gospel Publishing House, 1971), 6.

21 "The Trend Toward Armageddon," *Pentecostal Evangel* (18 July 1936): 2.

22 Ralph M. Riggs, "Missionary Enterprise in the Light of the Soon Coming Christ," *Pentecostal Evangel* (18 July 1936): 2.

23 Wayne Warner, "The Assemblies of God and World War II," part 1, *Assemblies of God Heritage* 10 (summer 1990): 8.

24 Wayne Warner, "The Assemblies of God and World War II," part 2, *Assemblies of God Heritage* 10 (fall 1990): 16.

[25] Stan Berg, with Jamie Bilton, *Called, Chosen, Faithful: The Memoirs of Rev. R. Stanley Berg* (Springfield, Mo.: By the author, 2000), 43.

[26] Ibid., 44.

[27] Ibid., 50.

[28] Elizabeth Evans, *The Wright Vision: The Story of the New England Fellowship* (Lanham, Md.: University Press of America, 1991), 6–7.

[29] Stanley H. Frodsham, "Diary of a Delegate," *Pentecostal Evangel* (25 September 1943): 4.

[30] Stanley H. Frodsham, "Dear Evangel Reader," *Pentecostal Evangel* (5 April 1924): 15.

[31] David H. McDowell, "The Pentecostal Outpouring of the Last Days," *Pentecostal Evangel* (17 April 1943): 2.

[32] Donald Gee, *Why Pentecost?* (London: Victory Press, 1944), 28.

CHAPTER 12

HARVESTING IN THE FIELDS OF THE LORD

Strong individualists, Pentecostal missionaries often remained suspicious of organizational controls. Sometimes skeptical of committee decisions made by mission leaders in the Ozark Mountains of Missouri, they preferred the Spirit's direct guidance. The hope that the General Council could improve the financial base of missions and bring about closer cooperation among the missionaries took many years to achieve.

Yet a bond of loyalty existed between the saints at home and the missionaries, reflected in informal networks that extended around the globe. For example, George R. Wood had been converted under the ministry of Ben Mahan, who pioneered a church in Jeannette, Pennsylvania, in 1914. Wood then went to Beulah Heights Bible and Missionary Training Institute in North Bergen, New Jersey. Like many students who enrolled there, he felt called to missions, specifically China.

He later married Elizabeth Weidman from First Pentecostal Church (now First Assembly of God) in Cleveland, Ohio. She had studied at A. B. Simpson's school at Nyack, New York, and shared the call to China. Ten years older than George, she had already served there as a missionary for eight years and had returned home on furlough. They met as he prepared to go for his first term and she for her second in 1932. Courting on the ship, they married after arriving in Shanghai and on the next day began the arduous trek into the interior. The Woods labored in China with the support of the Jeannette and Cleveland churches, among others. Such "ties that bind," in this case stretching from local churches in Pennsylvania and Ohio to Kansu Province, have been characteristic of many relationships built on a mutual commitment to the Church's worldwide mission.

Missionaries kept busy overseas with open-air preaching, tract distribution, Bible school teaching, and directing schools, orphanages, and homes for widows. With the delay in Christ's return, they usually followed the lead of other Protestant missionaries. This meant raising funds in America to pay pastors and evangelists who worked under their watchful but beneficent gaze. Though formally committed to indigenous church principles (i.e., churches should be self-governing, self-supporting, and self-propagating), few knew how to implement them. In effect, potential church leaders were often denied exercise of the gift of leadership (Romans 12:8).

Life on the mission field could be risky for various reasons, ranging from the whirlwind circumstances of political upheavals and war to sickness. Lillian Trasher dodged bullets to save two toddlers at her orphanage in Assiout, Egypt, having been caught in a cross fire between Egyptian and British troops during an insurrection.

Twenty-nine-year-old Eric Booth-Clibborn, a grandson of Salvation Army founders William and Catherine Booth, received missionary appointment on February 24, 1924, sailed with his wife, Lucile, and their little girl to Upper Volta (now Burkina Faso), French West Africa, and died of dysentery and malaria on July 8. Before leaving the United States, he had written these words to his mother: "And now as we turn to Africa . . . I know how hard it will be for us to part, but our Lord bade us to occupy till He comes, and we are obeying His command without reasoning till our work is done." Lucile, pregnant with their second child at the time of his death, reflected, "Oh for more of that implicit trust, that exquisite faith! What a difference it would make for Africa and for every other . . . land if those called responded joyfully, without 'reasoning' or 'questioning' till their work was done."

In the same year, Clarence and Dorothy Radley arrived in Nicaragua with their four-year-old daughter, Evangeline. Clarence died soon afterward from malaria and blood poisoning. With the country caught up in the throes of a civil war, Dorothy found herself isolated in the village of Esteli and largely without help for the burial.

On February 14, 1947, twenty Assemblies of God missionaries and their children boarded the Marine Lynx in San Francisco bound for China. They are mingled with other evangelical missionaries in the picture below. J. Philip Hogan stands in the top row (third from the left).

With the aid of some Nicaraguan believers, she made the casket, conducted the service, and sang a solo. Since the village would not permit his burial in the cemetery, he was buried in a field known as the "Dung Heap." Later, with the construction of the Pan American Highway that came within ten feet of his grave, local believers erected a ten-foot-high marker with the words: "He sowed the Word at the cost of his life." Eventually, he was reburied in a prominent location in the cemetery with the marker moved next to the grave.

Grave site of
Clarence Radley

Yet others were more fortunate. "Knowing that I was going to the border of Tibet and not expecting to have any doctors in case of sickness," remembered Grace Agar, "I definitely took the Lord as my Physician. He has kept me in health and strength for the past 38 years. He has protected me from all harm, from accidents on ice, slippery roads, from robbers, wild beasts and from epidemics so common in China. I have proved it true that the 'Angel of the Lord encampeth round about them that fear Him and delivereth them' (Ps. 34:7 [KJV])."

During World War II, four Assemblies of God missionaries had booked passage on the ill-fated voyage of the Zamzam. Shelled by a German raider ship in the South Atlantic, the missionaries and other passengers were transferred from the sinking vessel to the Dresden and then taken to Nazi-occupied France. Because the United States would not enter the war for eight more months, the American missionaries were allowed to return to neutral America, while the British missionaries were sent to concentration camps. Paul Kitch and his son, however, spent ten days in a lifeboat after German torpedoes sank their ship on their return to America from Africa.

The Nazis severely persecuted Pentecostals in Europe. In a narrow escape from the Gestapo, missionary G. Herbert Schmidt, a founder of the influential Danzig Institute of the Bible, smuggled on board a merchant ship leaving Danzig (Gdansk) for Sweden. Only after the close of the war was he reunited with his daughters who had been left behind (his wife did not survive the war). Pentecostal missionaries suffered most in the Far East, with more than a few interned by the Japanese both in China and the Philippines. Paratroopers rescued Rena Baldwin and Blanche Appleby, along with 2,145 other starving civilians, at the Los Banos internment camp forty miles southeast of Manila. Missionaries liberated from the Old Bilibid Prison in Manila included Leland and Helen Johnson and their children, Gladys Knowles, and others. In a noteworthy twist, members of the Juergensen family (missionaries to Japan since 1913) ministered at internment camps in the United States for Americans of Japanese descent—Minidoka Relocation Center near Twin Falls, Idaho, and Topaz Relocation Center in Utah—while at home in America during the war, a noble witness to the integrity of their calling.

"The Vision" is a song that calls for the total commitment of one's life to Christ. Oren Munger, a missionary to Nicaragua who later died from a fever at age twenty-five,

Oren Munger—Surrendered to God

Oren and Florence Munger

Oren Munger possessed unusual scholastic and musical abilities. . . . His life was surrendered to God and the call of foreign missions throbbed in his soul. . . .

After his marriage in May 1942 to Florence Tiahrt, they were accepted by the Missions Board of the Assemblies of God. In July 1942 they set their faces toward Central America.

After study of language and methods in El Salvador, the Mungers were asked to consider ministering in Nicaragua. Three missionaries had been laid beneath its soil. How many more would it take before Nicaragua would come to God? Oren Munger heeded this call. Although weary in body from the tremendous amount of work, many hours of earnest intercessory prayer went up. The answer came in November 1944 when God met them in a sweeping revival which stirred every church. . . .

Brother Munger gave himself to spreading the gospel in the jungle, this meaning many hours of travel by mule over rocky trails and living in the dangers of the tropical climate. Coming home from one of these trips Brother Munger contracted typhoid fever, which was followed by malaria, tropical dysentery and finally abscess of the lungs. His words to those at home were, "Tell them I am passing thru deep waters, but that the Lord is the Lord of the deep waters."

In August 1945, after six months of illness, he laid down his life at the age of 25. One more labourer had finished his part of the harvest. He went to join the company of the redeemed of those who loved not their lives unto the death. Matt. 10:39. "He that findeth his life shall lose it; and he that loseth his life for My sake shall find it."

—Oren E. Munger, Songs of the Savior (1950), preface.

composed the music for the words written by Harold McKinney, another Assemblies of God minister. Its stirring words have inspired an untold number of Pentecostals to dedicate their lives to missions (verse 3, chorus):

> Ev'ry dream and ev'ry burning longing,
>> I surrender to their [the heathen's] crying need;
> I am leaving ev'ry hope behind me,
>> To follow anywhere my Lord may lead.
> Take me, Master, break me, use me,
>> I am leaning on Thy breast,
> All ambitions fast are dying,
>> From their pain now give me rest;
> On the altar I have lain them,
>> Now to Thee I give my heart,
> Fill me with the fire of vision,
>> Let my passion ne'er depart.

The missionaries introduced in this chapter illustrated this passion and labored in a variety of contexts. In different ways, they were all pioneers. Noel Perkin served in Argentina for several years, became the missionary secretary, and published a policy manual for missionaries to improve working relationships. In Burkina Faso, Arthur E. Wilson helped lay the groundwork for a strong national church. Ralph D. Williams started a model Bible institute in El Salvador. Jessie Wengler evangelized in Japan, a non-Christian country noted for its resistance to the gospel. Finally, drug addicts and other needy persons heard the gospel from Marie Stephany in North China.

NOEL PERKIN
1893-1979

Noel Perkin

That Noel Perkin flunked his Latin exam proved fortunate for the Assemblies of God. Otherwise, he might have spent his life as a dentist in England. Perkin was born into a moderately well-to-do English family who were members of the Wesleyan Methodist Church. Although his parents had sent him to a church boarding school at Cambridge, he rebelled against their faith. Now with a career in dentistry doomed, he turned to banking. Like other young Englishmen of his day, he left England to seek his fortune in some outpost of the British Empire. He got as far as Canada, where he settled in Toronto to work at the branch office of the Bank of Montreal.

Unfortunately, he made friends with other young men of his standing and lived "a careless life, drinking and smoking as was customary among that group." But after being diagnosed with tuberculosis, he began to think about the welfare of his soul. Taking up residence in a boarding house run by a former missionary, he knelt in prayer one day in his room, "telling the Lord that I believed He was alive and if this were true, He was interested in those who are sick and needy, and I asked Him to heal me of my disease. I felt that was a turning point and believe that at that moment I was born into a new life."

After his conversion and healing, he attended services at the Christian and Missionary Alliance church in Toronto. His fellowshipping with Pentecostal believers who had formerly belonged to the Alliance, however, led to his Spirit baptism. He was then spiritually mentored by the leader of the group, Christian Schoonmaker, a missionary to India residing in Canada at the time.

Harry Turner, an Alliance missionary who had received the Pentecostal baptism with speaking in tongues, invited Perkin and another friend to join him in Argentina. So in 1918 Perkin did just that. Since the three missionaries worked with little pledged support, they decided on chicken farming for additional support. Apparently they were not called to be chicken farmers; the hens died from an amoebic disease.

After three years and a diminished savings account, Perkin returned to Canada. While visiting the Rochester Bible Training School in Rochester, New York, he met Ora Blanchard, who later became his wife. After several years of pastoral work, Perkin moved to Springfield to work at Gospel Publishing House and the Foreign Missions Department. The Council needed his expertise in bookkeeping. The department had previously forwarded designated offerings to the intended missionaries and then sent small yellow receipts to the donors. Duplicates were filed in alphabetical order in an envelope box. Incredibly, hundreds of thousands of dollars were processed by this means. Obviously, the time had come for a more efficient and reliable procedure. When Perkin arrived, he installed a proper bookkeeping system with an account for every missionary.

At the time of his permanent appointment as missionary secretary in 1927, Assemblies of God missions showed remarkable growth. Giving since 1925 had jumped 28 percent, reaching three hundred thousand dollars, and the missionary roster had gone up 18 percent to 277. Although only thirty-four years old, Perkin brought several strengths to the office: missionary and pastoral experience, financial skills, a warm and winning personality, and a capacity to adjust to new situations and move ahead with the times.

His first major achievement appeared with the publication of a policy manual in 1931. Though only twenty-eight pages long, it contained a philosophy of missions, a brief historical sketch, and a statement of departmental policies. When listing the qualifications for missionary appointment, it stipulated that priority went to those having definite calls from God, proven effectiveness in ministry, and commitment to "scriptural" methods of missions. But regardless of all these factors, life in the Spirit and holiness of character remained foremost.

The host of people who entered the Assemblies of God from the Alliance were among A. B. Simpson's best pupils, having been schooled in his vision for missions

Missionary Policies

Term of Service:

It should be the resolution of the missionary, God permitting, that his entire life shall be spent in missionary service. . . . Should it be necessary for the missionary's health or for the good of the work to return to the homeland, a furlough will be considered on the advice of the Field Council. However, the nature of our organization does not permit the guaranteeing of a furlough after any definite length of time. . . .

Marriage:

It is desirable that engaged couples should not marry until the completion of two years from the date of arrival of the one who last reaches the field, and the successful passing of both parties of such examinations in the language as are prescribed for that period by the field concerned.

—*Missionary Department of the Assemblies of God,*
Missionary Manual (1931), 19–21.

Haven't You Heard about Pearl Harbor?

I was speaking in a Milwaukee church [December 7, 1941], giving my farewell messages before leaving for my third term in India. After the last service, someone came to me and said, "You won't be able to leave for India; haven't you heard about Pearl Harbor?" No, I had not heard.

Two days later I received a letter from the State Department in Washington, D.C., asking me to return my passport at once [because] overseas civilian travel had been cancelled....

It was a traumatic experience, and for the next year and a half I tried every possible way to get back to India. Then I heard of a shipping company in Argentina; so I wrote asking for a booking to India, but the reply came that it would not be safe. I replied that I was not afraid [since] the Lord would be with me and that I wanted to get back. "The Lord may be with you," they replied, "but the devil is surely down here. No booking."

Finally I was able to sail on a Portuguese ship from Philadelphia to Portugal. After more than 3 weeks of waiting, I boarded another Portuguese ship which traveled down the west coast of Africa (struck by lightning enroute), then around Capetown and up the east coast. After another month's delay, I was able to board a warship at Durban, East Africa, for Bombay, India.

It took 4 months from Philadelphia to Bombay, but God protected me and brought me safely to my destination.

—Hilda Wagenknecht, "Four-Month Return Trip to India"
Assemblies of God Heritage 11 (winter 1991–92): 15.

and Christ-centered piety. Along with Simpson, Perkin and the vast majority of Pentecostals considered the touch of the Spirit on a person's life to be more important than educational preparation. Although such preparation carries certain advantages, it can never replace the Spirit's power. To Perkin, a barely educated person preaching under the anointing of the Spirit would more likely bring a university professor to Christ than could the university graduate without the assistance of God. "If we have to choose between the two," he maintained, "let us take the Spirit."

Dependence on the Spirit, however, was not without qualification. According to the manual, missionaries were now to undergo physical examinations before leaving for the field. Sparks flew from those who held that consulting doctors was a denial of their belief in divine healing. One veteran missionary, Hilda Wagenknecht, simply refused to have a checkup. Confronted with her objection as well as her claim to good health, the Foreign Missions Committee swallowed hard and allowed her to return to India. But candidates who couldn't pass the examination were simply advised to go home and "pray through" until healed. Appointment would then be forthcoming.

The curious importance attached to a medical checkup in a denomination that stressed divine healing points to the pragmatism underlying Assemblies of God missions. Common sense dictated that little could be expected from a missionary in poor health. If medical treatment resolved the problem, they could resume their ministry. But if God healed them directly, so much the better—the doctrine still stood.

Perkin did not visit any of the mission fields until nine years after taking office. Two reasons account for this: the department's financial straits and Perkin's commitment to administrative duties. By 1936, however, the financial picture had changed, and he made his first trip to Puerto Rico, Santo Domingo (present-day Dominican Republic), and Cuba.

The membership of the Assemblies of God in the Foreign Missions Conference of North America brought many benefits. At one of the gatherings, Perkin became friends with Emory Ross, a noted missionary and mission leader with the Disciples of Christ. Ross urged him to continue traveling abroad, both to encourage the missionaries and to gain a better understanding of their situations and problems. He accepted the advice, and by the time of his retirement in 1959, he had gone around the world three times and visited nearly every country in the world.

During his thirty-two year tenure, Perkin became well known in the U.S. postal service because of the huge volume of mail he received from overseas. On one occasion, a postcard arrived from Africa addressed only "Noel Perkin, America."

ARTHUR E. WILSON
(1892-1984)

While the saints back home were singing "When We All Get to Heaven" and "I'll Fly Away," Arthur Wilson and other Assemblies of God missionaries were hard at work in Africa laying the groundwork for a strong national church. Though it might appear that the folks back home thought only of the Second Coming, they shared the

conviction with the missionaries that the second coming of Christ was at hand and believed that the mission fields were ripe for the great end-time harvest. As partners, missionaries and supporting congregations knew that the task ahead might take time and would not be easy. Missionaries, therefore, had to translate, teach believers to read, and train workers because, as Jesus said, "'Night is coming, when no one can work'" (John 9:4).

Wilson, a member of the first graduating class at Central Bible Institute, represented the new generation of missionaries (at least the majority) that had received spiritual formation in Bible institutes. In part, their student experi-

Arthur E. Wilson and his second wife, Elizabeth. She had served as a missionary to the Philippines before they were married.

ence contributed to the long-term appeal of teamwork: Coming from many churches, Bible school students lived, studied, prayed, and ministered together. Their loyalties grew broader than to simply the home congregation. Indeed, as mission expenses increased over the years, the networking among graduates—many of them now pastors—enabled missionaries to raise support more easily.

When Arthur and Jennie Wilson arrived in Burkina Faso in 1926, they joined efforts with other pioneers already there. Plans were laid in 1928 for reducing the Mossi language to writing and then for translating the New Testament, Sunday School lessons, doctrinal studies, and gospel songs. (Fellow missionaries John and Cuba Hall spearheaded the translation of the entire Bible into More, the language of the Mossi people. In his translation work, John personally typed the Bible six times.)

In the early 1930s, the Foreign Missions Department began publishing booklets that highlighted various mission fields. Each described the country and its residents, as well as the work of the missionaries. Wilson wrote A Visit to Mos[s]iland (about 1932). In describing the people, he noted, "the Mos[s]ies are of negrotic stock. Mentally, they are not the equal of some other tribes, but they are not of such low mentality as some have supposed. They can be trained to a very satisfactory degree." Unwittingly, Wilson had carried an American racial myth in his cultural baggage to Africa. Like other missionaries, he was a child of his time. Fortunately, as the years passed, such attitudes receded, due in part to changing racial attitudes in the United States and growing appreciation of cross-cultural differences.

At the same time, Wilson also recognized the insights of the Mossi culture and concurred with the saying, "'The white man's sense is in his books, but the black man's sense is in his head.'" He agreed, saying, "I have met some old men who, though they knew nothing of books, yet they were filled with wisdom."

Wilson proved to be one of the best missionaries sent to Africa. His love for the Mossi people grew over his many years of service. Unlike earlier missionaries who often had no strategy beyond tongues and prayer for the sick, he understood indigenous church principles. With other missionaries, he looked ahead to a self-supporting, self-governing, and self-propagating national church. In his estimation, this necessitated a "trained native ministry," one not dependent on American money. "The time has come," he wrote, "to divorce the preaching of the gospel in foreign countries from home finances."

The preparation of locals as Christian workers offered crucial advantages: "The natives know their own people as no white man will ever know them . . . , can endure hardships that would kill a white man," and "are given more liberty to preach." With proper training and mentoring, they could carry on in the event that the missionaries were forced to leave. In 2001, the Assemblies of God of Burkina Faso celebrated its eightieth anniversary with over 547,000 members and adherents in a nation of 12.5 million people. Its impressive growth can be attributed to revival, mature leadership, and the combined "senses" of the black person and the white person.

RALPH D. WILLIAMS
(1902-1989)

Revisiting her native England, Alice E. Luce met Ralph and Richard Williams and became acquainted with their plans to study at Glad Tidings Bible Institute in San Francisco. Welshmen with a Methodist background, they had been converted and baptized in the Spirit during a Pentecostal revival in 1919. They had dedicated their lives to Latin-American missions. The Williams brothers and Alice Luce became life-long friends and, for a time, colleagues.

Through Luce's mentoring and their studies at Glad Tidings, the Williams brothers became familiar with Roland Allen's *Missionary Methods: St. Paul's or Ours?* Not without controversy in some missions circles, Allen's message challenged missionaries to follow Paul's methods for church planting. In 1926 the brothers received missionary appointment and went to San Diego to assist Luce in her church and at Berean Bible Institute.

When Richard and his wife left for Peru, Ralph and his wife, Jewyl, went to Mexico to work in a Bible institute. At the invitation of Salvadoran Pentecostals, they journeyed to El Salvador in 1929. Having little money and only their luggage, they had no alternative but to live very close to the level of the people. Their diet consisted mostly of black beans, rice, and tortillas. For housing, they rented "some 'almost bare rooms' in town which they abandoned occasionally to scrimp on money."

Visiting the churches with Francisco Arbizú, a Salvadoran evangelist and teacher, the Williamses were surprised at the worship they observed. With spontaneous expressions of tongues, testimonies, and praises, the services went on for hours. Congregations "seemed untiring, always ready to sing, to pray and to testify." But the "mixture of zeal and ignorance" and erroneous teachings, which negatively affected the moral behavior of believers, deeply troubled Williams. Nevertheless, he respected the freedom they felt in "praying aloud, praying in tongues, or [giving] spiritual utterance in prophecy. And they were never hesitant about praying for the sick with genuine expectation of being healed."

Arbizú and Williams worked together to establish a doctrinal standard for the churches and arranged meetings for discussing the issues. Getting church representatives to cooperate was no easy task. But a constitution did win approval in 1930 that placed the churches on an indigenous footing. A year later, Williams began a Bible institute and introduced, with Arbizú, the *Reglamento Local, A Standard of Christian Doctrine and Practice*. Those who sought church membership had to be knowledgeable of it as well as demonstrate a godly lifestyle. This worked so well in El Salvador that Assemblies of God churches in many Latin-American countries adopted it.

Williams's contribution to foreign missions centered on his applying indigenous church principles and pioneering quality training for pastors and leaders. Bible institutes were made successful by at least three characteristics: adaptability, a direct connection to evangelism and church planting, and a growing curriculum. Because national churches and missionaries had limited financial resources, adaptability was essential to overcoming problems of geography, resources, and facilities.

Years later, when teaching at a Bible school in Barquisimeto, Venezuela, Williams learned there were people who wanted to attend classes, but lived too far away. The answer lay in starting night schools in Maracaibo and Cabimas, a combined population center of over one million. All ten Assemblies of God churches in the area sent students to the two schools. Those without cars could walk to the schools. The school in Cabimas saved students a two-hour ride and payment of expensive tolls on a bridge six miles long.

The sponsoring committee in Maraca- ibo had resources to provide classrooms and equipment, but the one in Cabimas was not so fortunate. "There were no desks," Wil- liams reported. "Some used iron chairs purchased from an old theater. Also the church designated for the classes had no roof. There was, however, a lean-to-annex running down one side of the building which was to serve as the classroom.

Ralph D. Williams

With the large number of students, this narrow annex proved to be too hot and stuffy, so we moved out into the roofless auditorium. We now hold our classes under the starry sky, except for those nights when the rain chases us back under cover."

Much to the surprise of Williams and his colleagues, when the schools opened, forty-six students enrolled in Maracaibo and twenty-eight in Cabimas. The consecra- tion of students and teachers and the ministry of God's Word—not the facilities—led

Highway in the Sky

World War II had hampered all missionary activities in most parts of the world. One of the more visible efforts to increase missionary effectiveness was to buy a trans-oceanic type airplane.

Following World War II, commercial flights were not readily available. The first *Ambassador* was a modified army surplus Highway in the Sky C-46. It had been con- verted from a cargo plane and could hold 40 passengers. Later, realizing that four motors are better than two—especially when there is nothing below except the ocean— the C-46 was sold, and a converted B-17 bomber was bought.

Although the air service lasted only 3 years (1948–51), the two *Ambassadors* brought prestige and glamour to the missionary efforts—or as George Carmichael described it, "The heavens have become a highway."

Converting the C-46 cargo plane was no small task. The original surplus cost of $5,000 quickly jumped to an investment of $20,000. But still the *Ambassador* was con- sidered a bargain because the plane had cost the government more than $200,000.

Paying for it was not so hard either. Assemblies of God youth caught the spirit of the project and helped pay for the Ambassador through Speed the Light projects.

—*Wayne Warner, "Flying Ambassadors of Goodwill"*
Assemblies of God Heritage 5 (winter 1985–86): 3.

to the success of such institutions. Modest beginnings would eventually be superseded by improvements, as they trusted God.

Like other Assemblies of God missionaries, Williams found that building an indigenous church meant training potential leaders. Upon arriving on the mission fields, missionaries quite naturally assumed they would continue to focus their energies on pulpit ministry. Much to their surprise, however, they found themselves behind lecterns much of the time, teaching classes in Bible institutes. Since 1922, when Assemblies of God missionaries founded their first overseas Bible institute in North China, the denomination has made enormous investments in personnel and monies for training national leaders. Indeed, it was far greater than Ralph Williams or anyone else could have imagined. Mission statistics for 2002 revealed 1,893 Bible schools and extension programs with over 90,534 students, supported by the General Council and its fraternally related constituencies worldwide.

JESSIE WENGLER
(1887-1958)

Women were indispensable to the growth of Assemblies of God missions, and for decades married and single women made up two-thirds of the missionary personnel. While often inaccurately stereotyped as simply workers in mission schools and orphanages, many, like Jessie Wengler and Marie Stephany, evangelized and taught prospective pastors. They served in the ranks of many other missionaries who pioneered on the "stony ground" of non-Christian countries. Along with those who

Jessie Wengler

labored in the Middle East, India, Sri Lanka, and Indonesia, they rejoiced in what appeared to others as "small harvests."

On her application for endorsement as a missionary, under "experience" Wengler had listed teaching music, working in the office of a Pentecostal publisher, participating in jail and hospital ministry, and handing out tracts. In addition, she had studied at a teacher training college in Colorado, Moody Bible Institute in Chicago, and Brooks Bible Institute in St. Louis. Without having been a pastor or evangelist, she received appointment in 1919, but for whatever reason she waited thirty years for ordination.

Pentecostal missionaries had worked in Japan since 1907. When Wengler arrived at the turn of 1920, she joined the Carl and John Juergensen families and others already there. In addition to evangelism, she later threw her energies into teaching at the Bible institute in Tokyo.

Along with others who anticipated the soon return of Christ, she interpreted natural calamities as divine judgments, prophetic "signs of the times" (Matthew 16:3). Through a revelation, Wengler declared that the devastating earthquake that hit Japan in 1923 signaled God's wrath on the country. On the night of September 1, 1923, from her home in an outlying district, she saw the red horizon over Yokahoma and Tokyo,

Waiting for the Ambassador

I was superintendent for Gold Coast [present-day Ghana] when the *Ambassadors* were operating, and no one was happier than I was when the planes were sold. It was said that they flew "on a song and a gallon of gas."

I was responsible for booking flights in Africa, and they were always late. That meant entertaining missionaries for days while we waited for the plane.

Two days after we sent our boys home on the *Ambassador*, we received a telegram from Brother Perkin who asked if we had any news concerning the *Ambassador*. We learned that it had been sitting at Roberts Field in Liberia for 2 days!

I never rode the *Ambassadors* and wouldn't for all the tea in China.

Eric M. Johnson

— "Letters from Our Readers,"
Assemblies of God Heritage *5 (spring 1985–86): 15.*

which stretched for miles. "As I sat there in the dark with the Japanese people all around me," she wrote, "I saw something in the clouds . . . , the form of a cherub; in the hand of the cherub was a vial, and he was pouring that vial upon the earth. That scripture which tells of the wrath of God being poured out on the earth came to my mind" (Revelation 16). At that moment, she didn't know that hundreds of thousands were being burned to death because of fires sparked by the earthquake.

"As I looked," she recounted to a wide-eyed gathering of believers at Central Assembly of God in Springfield, Missouri, "this cherub seemed to change, and it was Jesus Himself. He was standing with His hands outstretched, and I cannot describe the awful agony on His face. It seemed as though He were pleading with the people. When I afterwards learned of the awfulness of that calamity, I knew that God had shown me that He was moving in the earth, and I believe that that calamity was one of the signs of the time in which we are living. Of all the missionaries of the many denominations that were on the field, only one was killed. God protected His people at that time."

Little did she realize that a greater holocaust was not much more than twenty years ahead and that she would experience it firsthand. Before the United States would be engulfed in a world war for the second time, Noel Perkin notified the missionaries to return home at the department's expense. The year was 1941. Unfortunately, Wengler had been confined to a hospital bed for several months. By the time she was well enough to be released, the Japanese navy had attacked Pearl Harbor and brought the United States into the conflict. Even after her release, she remained partially paralyzed on her left side, and she was suffering from heart trouble so was unable to travel. Though she grew stronger in some respects, her health remained fragile throughout the war.

The Japanese authorities kept her under house arrest but allowed her to walk to the market when she needed to buy food. As conditions worsened, the government rationed food and charcoal. The uncertainty of daily living severely tested her faith, but she found comfort and strength in prayer. It was dangerous for Japanese Christians to be seen with an American; occasionally they sneaked food to Wengler at night. "Once a Japanese doctor sent me a big bag of bones," she remembered. "The bones were full of marrow, so I made nourishing soup from them." Yet because of the general food shortage, her weight dropped from a normal 124 pounds to just under 90 pounds. When she had no food, she drank tea.

Unable to receive money from America, she asked the Swiss legation to intervene for her with the Japanese government. It had confiscated and sold two pieces of property she owned and kept the money. When the authorities reversed themselves and allowed her to draw monthly from the account, she considered it nothing short of a miracle.

The bombing of Tokyo intensified in November 1944. Hundreds of American B-29s, B-24s, and P-51s flew nightly sorties over Tokyo, dropping their loads of incendiary bombs. During these months, the police moved her from suburb to suburb and finally housed her with five American Baptist missionaries who had also not been interned. One night, bombs rained around them and they fled for their lives. Running through a wall of fire, they found refuge in a school compound. Frightful sounds of bombs coming through the air terrorized them: "You thought it was coming straight for you when actually it was falling some distance away." She said, "I was not afraid to die, yet the screams of thousands of people burning to death and the sound of the raging fires was the most terrible thing I have ever heard."

The Miracle Cow

In 1941, Robert and Mildred Tangen, missionaries to China, transferred to Baguio, Philippines, to escape the impending war. When the Japanese invaded the Philippines in December 1941, the Tangens once again found themselves in "harm's way." Five hundred civilians, including the Tangens who were expecting their first baby, were interned near Baguio. Forced to live in deplorable conditions and subjected to mental cruelty, they faced a starvation diet of wormy rice gruel. Six months later, little "Bobby" Tangen was born. Although the internees repeatedly asked for milk for the babies and nursing mothers in the camp, their captors ignored the requests. As the situation worsened and Mildred's milk began to dry up, a miracle happened. A cow with a young calf suddenly appeared at the camp and stood by the fence. That cow faithfully supplied milk for the internees until the day before their transfer to a prison in Manila where they were rescued by the American forces.

—Annette Newberry

Wengler's relatively benevolent treatment by the Japanese contrasts sharply with that endured by missionaries held in internment camps. When the war ended, she continued her ministry and served as the Assemblies of God representative to the Allied Powers during the occupation of Japan. With other missionaries, she envisioned the postwar period as "an unparalleled opportunity for the uplifting of the Christian faith, which makes it possible for the Church in Japan to rise up out of her despair and live anew in Christ." Wengler was in Japan working toward that goal when she died at seventy-one.

MARIE STEPHANY
(1878-1963)

In the 1920s and 1930s, the government of Shansi province in North China struggled with the rise of opium addiction and the climbing crime rate that came with it. To stamp out the problem, they first prepared places for addicts to live in order to provide a positive atmosphere in which they could break the habit. Despite the provision of food and kind treatment, they turned to opium again when they were released. In frustration, the authorities then ruled that every drug dealer should be beheaded; the warning had little effect. Finally, they decreed that all who sold opium, as well as those who smoked it, should be taken outside the gates of the cities and shot. Though hundreds of people were executed in this fashion, the slavery of drug addiction increased. Into this context of suffering came thirty-eight-year-old Marie Stephany.

Marie Stephany

Born in Hungary, Stephany and her family had immigrated to the United States and taken up residence in Cleveland, Ohio. From her early years, life had been difficult, often requiring hard work and long hours to support herself. After conversion, she received Holy Spirit baptism at the Christian and Missionary Alliance church in Cleveland (later First Pentecostal Church) and felt called to China. She then went to Beulah Heights Bible and Missionary Training Institute to prepare for ministry. In 1916, Stephany received missionary ordination from the Assemblies of God and sailed for China. As with many other Pentecostals who traveled overseas in mission, she received formal missionary appointment after the fact, in her case three years later.

Stephany made her home in Taiyuan, the capital of Shansi province, where she spent two years in language study. In 1919 she moved twenty-five miles outside the city to the village of Huei Ren with just two hundred dollars in her purse. There she opened a chapel in a building located between a theater and a temple and began preaching the gospel. She later moved to Ta Ch'ang, where she continued her ministry. When the great famine of 1920 and 1921 devastated this region of China, she took children into her home to share her food with them.

Like other Pentecostals who believed in the priority of evangelism over charitable endeavors, she found herself caught with the need to help the hurting. "I must tell you a little about my orphanage," she wrote in a book entitled *The Power of the Gospel in Shansi Province*. "Although I am not called to this kind of work, I am praying that the Lord will definitely call a missionary to take it upon her heart so that we may be able to take in more children." Already assisted by Alice Stewart, the arrival of Henrietta Tieleman shortly after the book's publication in 1934 must have seemed like an answer to prayer.

Stephany needed all the help she could get. Not only did she and her coworkers administer an orphanage and conduct evangelistic meetings, but they also ran a Bible school and ministered to drug addicts. The strategy of training Chinese believers paid rich dividends in church planting. "Thank God, we have seen signs following the preaching of the gospel in China," she reported. "The Lord has given the gift of healing to some of the native evangelists and pastors. A native pastor who has charge of one of the outstations has prayed for hopeless cases, one a man who had been an invalid from rheumatism for five years. After he was prayed for he was able to get up and make his own living." Stephany, Stewart, Tieleman, and other female missionaries who taught in Bible institutes often proved to be effective mentors to young men training for the ministry, in some cases, more successful than male missionaries.

During Stephany's twenty-six years in China, many people testified to being delivered from the "devil's smoke" under her ministry. In some respects, her approach could be compared to an early kind of Teen Challenge ministry (an Assemblies of God program that began in the late 1950s). No one could deny the courageous achievements of this woman—affectionately known as "Mother Peace"—who served in China during turbulent times.

The "girls" at the beach, missionaries attending missionary conference on the Chinese coast: (l-r) Marie Stephany, Martina Kvamme, Alice Stewart, Palma Ramsborg, Irene Larsen, Ruth Melching, Helen Gustavson, Pansy Blossom

Out of Revulsion, Love

After the chanting ceased, the lamas welcomed us and asked us to be seated. A servant passed around a large bowl to each guest. I asked David, "What kind of soup is this?"

David replied, "'It is Tibetan tea with yak butter. The hot drink will do you good!"

As the bowl of brown liquid was placed in my hands as a gesture of hospitality and friendship, I noticed some hairs floating gracefully on top, along with a chunk of yak butter-and even a few lice. The rancid odor of the butter made me feel sick. I realized that I must drink; to refuse would seriously offend our hosts.

Desperately, I prayed two prayers: first, after blowing off some of the top layer that included the hairs and lice, I said, "Lord, thank You! Help me to accept their hospitality and to drink this stuff"; then, after gulping most of it down, "Lord," I pleaded, "help me now to keep it down!". . .

We took the path down the mountain to La-p'u to spend the night in the dirty inn. But I could not sleep. The Tibetans in this area appeared to me even more filthy than any of the Lisu I had met. A revulsion was rising up and growing stronger within me, undoing all the progress I had made in adjusting to the cultures. I felt myself drawing back, not wanting to mingle with these people any more. But how could I minister to the people when I felt I could never love them? Praying desperately, I cried, "Lord, help me!"

That night the Lord spoke to me in a dream. I saw a filthy individual standing before me, draped in an assortment of rags. I exclaimed, "This must be one of the filthiest persons I've ever seen!"

Then the Lord Jesus spoke softly, "Leonard, that is how you appeared in My sight. But I loved you when you were unlovely. I died on the cross for you. Before My precious blood was applied to you, you were just as unclean as any of these people who have never washed. But I loved you. Can you not love these less fortunate people for Me?"

Then I awoke. As I prayed, I experienced a baptism of love; His love was shed abroad in my heart by the Holy Spirit. From that time on my attitude changed completely. God gave me such a love for the Tibetans and the Lisu that I was able to eat with them, sit with them, sleep in their homes, and accompany them for days at a time. Out of my revulsion the Lord planted His love.

—*Leonard Bolton, China Call (1984), 64, 66–67.*

RECOMMENDED READING

Agar, Grace C. "Tibetan Border of Kansu Province." 1940. Typewritten.

Carlow, Margaret. *The King's Daughter: Jessie Wengler*. Springfield, Mo.: Foreign Missions Department, n.d.

Cavaness, Barbara. "God Calling: Women in Assemblies of God Missions." Pneuma: *The Journal of the Society for Pentecostal Studies* 16 (spring 1994): 49–62.

Derr, Paul K. "The Zamzam's Last Voyage: 4 A/G Missionaries Rescued After Germans Sink Ship in 1941." *Assemblies of God Heritage* (fall 1987): 3–6.

Johnson, Elva. *Through Deepest Waters: Oren Munger*. Springfield, Mo.: Foreign Missions Department of the Assemblies of God, n.d.

Kitch, Paul L. "The Days in a Lifeboat." *Assemblies of God Heritage* 5 (winter 1985–86): 8–10.

McGee, Gary B. *This Gospel Shall Be Preached: A History and Theology of Assemblies of God Foreign Missions*. Vols. 1 and 2. Springfield, Mo.: Gospel Publishing House, 1986, 1989.

Stephany, Marie. *The Power of the Gospel in Shansi Province*. Springfield, Mo.: Foreign Missions Department of the Assemblies of God, ca. 1934.

Warner, Wayne E. "1945 Philippine Liberation Creates Emotional Scenes." *Assemblies of God Heritage* 5 (spring 1985): 6–11.

———. "The Dramatic 1945 Liberation at Los Banos, Philippines." *Assemblies of God Heritage* 5 (summer 1985): 7–8, 10–11, 16.

———. "Missionaries Caught in the Crossfire." *Assemblies of God Heritage* 11 (winter 1991–1992): 4–7, 9, 26–27.

———. "An American Missionary in Nazi Hands." Parts 1–3. *Assemblies of God Heritage* 11 (winter 1991–1992): 10–11, 27; 12 (spring 1992): 3–5, 24; 12 (summer 1992): 24–27.

Wengler, Jessie. *Letters From Japan*. Pasadena, Calif.: By the author, 1955.

Williams, Ralph D. "Night Bible School for Venezuela," Key 3 (1966): 11.

Wilson, Everett A. "Identity, Community, and Status: The Legacy of the Central American Pentecostal Pioneers." In *Earthen Vessels: American Evangelicals and Foreign Missions, 1880–1980*. Grand Rapids: William B. Eerdmans Publishing Co., 1990.

Wood, George O. "Their Last Full Measure." *Enrichment Journal* (fall 1999): 66–71.

Zongo, Etienne. "Bible College Lectures on the History of the Assemblies of God in Burkina Faso." D. Min. diss., Assemblies of God Theological Seminary, 2003.

COOPERATIVE FELLOWSHIP

Pioneering churches in the decades of the 1930s and 1940s required the same faith, stamina, and commitment that earlier Pentecostals had needed. Next to a highway on the outskirts of Little Rock, Arkansas, in 1933, evangelist Roy Gilliam started a revival "under a tree, with nothing but his Bible and a determination to go on. Things looked very gloomy but he did not give up." Within months an Assemblies of God church had been established. District Superintendent David Burris preached on "The Foundation of Pentecost" at the first anniversary of the new congregation. For the saints who gathered on that occasion, it all fit together: Pentecost, grace, and grit.

The Pentecostal tradition in evangelism continued to thrive in the Assemblies of God: "We had no publicity chairman," remembered Walter Higgins about his tent campaigns. "Nor did we hire an agency to announce our meetings. Our publicity was the Power of God in action. When the Lord began to work, somebody would get the Baptism, or some vile sinner became converted, or a miracle of healing would take place, then we would let out a shout, and the crowds would come to see what was taking place."

Walter Higgins

Over the years, the benefits of cooperative fellowship became more apparent. The scope of ministries also enlarged to encompass Jews, Hispanics, Native Americans, and other language groups, as well as those who were deaf and blind. In 1934, Nick and Arvilla Sivonen began working among Native Americans in Washington State, "visiting numerous reservations as well as ministering . . . along the highways and rivers." In addition to preaching and teaching, they distributed clothing, bedding, and doing "what we can to win the confidence of the Indian people." To provide them with proper housing, *Evangel* readers were asked to send offerings for the purchase of a "good lightweight house trailer." Cooperation took many forms.

The diversity of ministries, personalities, and creative methods enriched the growth of the Assemblies of God. This chapter investigates the endeavors of several individuals in different parts of the country who impacted the denomination in various ways. Baptized in the Spirit at the Azusa Street revival, Ernest S. Williams became a leading pastor in the General Council and served as its general superintendent. In the north-central part of the United States, Frank J. Lindquist shaped much of the early history of the Minnesota and outlying districts and founded North Central Bible Institute in Minneapolis. Little known to people outside Ohio and West Virginia, Elva K. Stump and a band of friends sacrificed to pioneer churches.

From Texas to Colorado, Demetrio Bazán, Sr., pioneered Hispanic congregations and later became superintendent of the Latin American District Council. Two prominent evangelists from drastically different backgrounds are introduced: Edith Mae Pennington, a one-time beauty queen, and Anna B. Lock, a former drunkard and drug addict. William J. Mitchell, a seaman and drunkard whose life was transformed at conversion, did much to encourage the Pentecostal movement in New England.

ERNEST S. WILLIAMS
(1885-1981)

William J. Seymour, the well-known leader of the Azusa Street revival, doubted whether Ernest Williams was made of "ministerial timber"; at least that was Williams's interpretation of the look he got from Seymour when he told Seymour he "felt called to the ministry." Whether an accurate interpretation or merely projection (Williams described himself as a "timid soul"), Williams proved to be an enduring leader.

His parents were devout members of the First Holiness Church, a Wesleyan-holiness congregation in San Bernardino, California. Williams was working on a ranch in Colorado when his mother sent word about the Azusa Street revival in progress. After arriving there in October 1906, he was baptized in the Spirit and called to the ministry.

First Native American Convention

History was made when the First Indian Convention ever to be held in the Assemblies of God convened early in February on the San Carlos Reservation in Arizona. The five-day session brought together a large group of Apache Indians and missionaries who are working among various tribes. In addition to the staff of Arizona missionaries, a delegation came from Washington and Idaho.

The blessings and benefits of the meetings were beyond description as the workers and Indian Christians fellowshiped together in prayer and worship. What a joy to the missionaries to see the large company of Indians, cleansed by the blood of Christ and anointed by the Holy Spirit! Testimonies with true ring were given by the Indians, as well as the missionaries, some telling of their salvation experience, some relating marvelous healings, still others witnessing to being baptized with the Holy Spirit. In the course of the meetings, God graciously spoke through the Indians with other tongues, and interpretations were given. . . .

— *"Our Home Frontiers,"* Pentecostal Evangel *(April 10, 1948): 10–11.*

He traveled as an evangelist for several years before marrying Laura Jacobson. They moved east, pastoring churches in Ohio, New York, New Jersey, and finally in Pennsylvania. His ministry at Philadelphia's Highway Mission Tabernacle began in 1920, and the congregation grew rapidly. Williams began out-door services in parks and on streets, utilizing a "gospel car" for a traveling platform and pulpit for the meetings. He added jail and hospital ministries, and encouraged a strong youth program. The tabernacle also had a thirty-piece orchestra that played at church services and street meetings. Crowds at the church grew until they had to enlarge the former Pres-byterian church where they met. Williams was generous to those in need. On one occasion his wife remarked, "I have to hide the table money, or he would give it away to any person approaching him with a financial need."

Ernest S. Williams

Recognition of his leadership led to his election as an executive presbyter of the Eastern district and finally as general superintendent of the Assemblies of God in 1929. After twenty years of service in this capacity, he announced he would not be a candidate for reelection.

Williams and other leaders kept a close eye on the General Council's financial operation. Funds were always tight, and every dollar had to be carefully spent. He was particularly concerned about his stewardship of the "Lord's money." As he trav-eled by train across the United States to speak in churches, conventions, and district councils, he never paid the additional fee for a sleeping compartment when traveling overnight. He preferred to sleep sitting up in the coach in order to save money. When traveling through Europe with Noel Perkin, the missionary secretary, to visit mission-aries, Williams charged Perkin to spend as little as possible on their meals. Perkin, however, knowing that Williams did not understand the currency transactions, made certain that they had a full meal at least once every day. When Williams wondered if the meal appeared to be too expensive, Perkin could still assure him that he was being frugal.

Momentous changes took place during his long administration. The lists of min-isters, church members, and congregations more than tripled. New departments and programs emerged: national Christ's Ambassadors (CA) Department, Speed the Light, national Sunday School Department, and Boys and Girls Missionary Crusade (BGMC). He also encouraged the development of the Radio Department and became the speaker on the program *Sermons in Song*, first aired in 1946. The Assemblies of God entered the National Association of Evangelicals (1942), Pentecostal World Confer-ence (1947), and the Pentecostal Fellowship of North America (1948). He played key roles in the founding of the last two organizations.

Over the years, Williams wrote extensively on doctrinal and devotional subjects. Many of his articles appeared in the *Pentecostal Evangel*, which also included his pop-ular "Questions and Answers" column (a service to readers that had originated with

E. N. Bell). While remaining a popular speaker around the country after his retirement, he taught for several years at Central Bible Institute (present-day Central Bible College). His classroom theology notes took form in his three-volume *Systematic Theology*, published in 1953.

This text added significantly to the doctrine books already printed by Gospel Publishing House, notably Peter Nelson's *Bible Doctrines* (1934) and Myer Pearlman's more extensive *Knowing the Doctrines of the Bible* (1937). Each one presented Pentecostal doctrine within the theological tradition of evangelicalism.

Thomas F. Zimmerman, an associate of Williams and later general superintendent, commented that "it was characteristic of Brother Williams, that whenever a new situation presented itself, he would rise to the challenge and put his whole effort into the work."

FRANK J. LINDQUIST
(1898-1989)

"The test of a leader is not what he can do himself, but what he can inspire other men to do." It was a motto Frank J. Lindquist lived by, and his achievements reflected it. Raised in a predominantly Swedish-American community near Pittsburgh, Pennsylvania, the family held membership in the Evangelical Free Church. When Pentecostal evangelists came to hold meetings in the community, the entire family and

The Saints Declare

"Many a four-star general in God's army, in the eyes of the saints down here, will leave the Judgment Seat of Christ as a 'buck private'; and many a 'buck private,' in the eyes of the saints down here, will be revealed as a four-star general at the Judgment Seat of Christ. Man looketh on the outward appearance, but God looketh on the heart."
—*H. B. Kelchner, evangelist*

"When preaching [Smith Wigglesworth] became entangled in long, involved sentences. Then he would relieve our perplexity by speaking angelically in tongues which he always interpreted himself. It was all part of the sermon. Explain it how you will, there were some remarkable flashes of revelation."
—*Donald Gee, British Pentecostal leader*

"At the present time the dictator of Italy [Benito Mussolini] is the head of 'the confederation of the west' [Daniel 7:23-25]. Whether or not he is the anti-Christ will never be known until the Holy Spirit, the great restrainer, is taken out of the world and the identity of the man of sin is finally revealed [2 Thessalonians 2:6-10]."
—*Charles S. Price, evangelist and author of* Mussolini: Is He the Anti-Christ?

"I know a lot of men preached that Mussolini was the anti-Christ. I wonder what those poor fellows are preaching now."
—*Jack Coe, evangelist*

about thirty others from the congregation were baptized in the Spirit. Forced to leave their church, they rented an auditorium and began to hold Pentecostal services.

Frank J. Lindquist

Inspired by the ministry of evangelist Ben Hardin, Lindquist and close friend James Menzie joined him in 1920 in conducting a tent revival in Gary, Indiana. A year later, the two young men set out for Minnesota, having been told by Hardin that it was one of the neediest areas for the gospel. Taking their tent from town to town, they planted new churches as they went. Their successes in evangelism, combined with those of others, led to the forming of the North Central district in 1922. Both received ordination at the inaugural meeting. The district encompassed five states: Wisconsin, Minnesota, (eastern) Montana, and North and South Dakota. When the first superintendent, C. M. Hanson, left office a year later, Lindquist became the second and held the position for twenty-two years. But his longevity was not inspired by the perks. Like other district officials of the time, he pastored a church, Minneapolis Gospel Tabernacle (1924–1967), due to the financial limitations of the district.

To the hats of pastor and district officer, he added that of president in 1930, founding North Central Bible Institute (now North Central University) in the church basement. Seven years later they purchased the Asbury Hospital in downtown Minneapolis. Valued at $469,000, it was purchased for $125,000 during the Depression. Evangelist Watson Argue, Sr., visiting the school, observed: "It has been [my] privilege to visit many Bible school buildings, but none has impressed [me] more than this: . . . spacious classrooms, reception rooms, libraries, offices, dormitory rooms, an elevator, and quarters for the Northern Gospel Publishing House."

Although lacking formal ministerial training, Lindquist strongly supported it. But reflecting the long-standing tension between reliance on education and divine empowerment in one's ministry, he told the students: "You've got to have more than a degree to go into the ministry. You've got to have an anointing. You've got to have a call of God. You must experience the anointing of the Holy Spirit in public, private, and family life."

No account of Frank Lindquist would be complete, however, without mention of his wife. Irene Gunhus had been converted and baptized in the Spirit during a Charles S. Price crusade at the Skating Arena in Minneapolis, an event that boosted attendance at the Gospel Tabernacle. Joining the congregation, she met Lindquist, and they were married in 1928. Irene was a major contributor to her husband's ministry and took an active role in pastoring the church.

ELVA K. STUMP
(1885-1985)

"Sister Stump" died at one hundred years of age in 1985, and her name appeared in an obituary list of ministers in the *Pentecostal Evangel*. But few in the General Council recognized her name, and of those who did, probably most of them knew little of her remarkable ministry in Ohio and West Virginia. Like the vast majority of workers in the Lord's vineyard, she died in relative obscurity.

Elva K. Stump

She was born Elva Klingler in Somerset, Ohio. Moving to the neighboring state of Pennsylvania, she enrolled in a nursing program at an Episcopal hospital in Philadelphia. She and her husband, Thomas, were members of the ("Dunkard") Brethren Church. Although he never became a Pentecostal, after Elva was baptized in the Spirit he supported her call to the ministry. For this—not having his wife "in subjection" according to 1 Timothy 2:11–12—the Brethren excommunicated him.

During her pastorate of the Maple Avenue Mission in Canton, Ohio, in 1928, she testified to being healed one evening. She had been diagnosed with a terminal spinal infection and had taken to bed in an upstairs room of the home of friends. While downstairs they mourned that she wouldn't make it through the night, Stump got out of bed and began to walk. "When they saw and heard [me and the nurse] walking and shouting and praising the Lord," she wrote, "I guess it was something like the lame man at the gate who was healed. . . . The telephone was kept busy that evening, witnessing and testifying. Many people came in, even until midnight, and joined us in our praises."

In the midst of other responsibilities, Elva and Thomas found time to adopt and raise thirteen children. The number jumped from six to thirteen when the children's home they directed near Canton closed. Because the last seven children could not be placed, the Stumps made them part of their family.

Elva Stump and a "Sister Coltharp" felt led of the Spirit on August 12, 1937, to plant a church in Shadybrook, a village on the outskirts of Weston in the mountains of West Virginia. Although the community had a public school, it had no church. Apparently no one had been successful in establishing one there. Renting an unfinished second floor area above a garage, they worked hard to get it ready for services. Eight days later, they began a Vacation Bible School and discovered that the children who came had little or no Christian training. At the first announced church service, seventeen people went to the altar for salvation. "The place was very crude," Stump wrote to supporters, "but people came because a crucified risen savior was preached."

As the weather turned colder in the autumn, they found larger and better quarters for the congregation. Except for time off at Christmas, the two women and visiting preachers held evangelistic meetings every night (Tuesday to Sunday) for months at a time. Stump wrote that at the Shadybrook Gospel Mission of Weston, "we are holding up a high standard and people are cleaning up from their filthy habits and being transformed by the power of God. Eight confessed to the use of tobacco and asked for prayer to be delivered. God answered prayer, delivered and filled some of them with the Holy Ghost." Before she resigned the church years later, it had grown to two hundred believers.

Among others, she and "the Elliott Sisters, Bro. & Sis. Stewart, Bro. & Sis. Allison, Bro. Kirkpatrick, Bro. & Sis. Hart, Bro. & Sis. Berquist and Sis. Coltharp" made up the "Pioneer Mission Workers of West Virginia." This loose-knit association worked within the Assemblies of God to evangelize the region. It is not known if all of them had ministerial credentials; Stump, however, had been ordained in (what was then) the Central District Council in 1934 at age forty-eight.

Without formal financial backing from churches, they went to unchurched areas, holding "tent meetings, camp meetings, street meetings, jail services and opening new fields." In 1939 she reported, "We know what it is for the larder to be empty and [to] boil the potatoes and turnip peelings for soup and live on skimmed milk for three days, [to] not even have money to buy a postage stamp." Finding an abandoned church, schoolhouse, or hall, they would begin holding revival meetings and Vacation Bible Schools.

To train workers, they started their own Bible school. Still, more were needed: "Our greatest need is laborers, I say 'sweaters,' who are not afraid of the 'summer's noonday sun,'" she wrote. "Yes, there are opportunities on every hand. Calls come but

Deutscher Zweig der Assemblies of God

The German Branch of the Assemblies of God (renamed German district in 1973) was formed in 1922 to meet the needs of German-speaking Pentecostals in the U.S. Hugo A. Ulrich, at the urging of E. N. Bell, invited fellow German-speaking pastors to New Castle, Pennsylvania, in November 1922 for the purpose of organizing the German Branch. Seven of the sixteen participants hailed from Michigan; others were from Illinois, New Jersey, New York, Ohio, Pennsylvania, Wisconsin, and Canada. The scattered German-speaking congregations overcame their isolation and worked together to effectively minister in their native tongue.

By the 1930s, churches were added in California, Nebraska, North Dakota, South Dakota, and Washington. The German Branch and the Russian and Eastern European Mission (R.E.E.M.) jointly published *Wort und Zeugnis (Word and Witness)*. The German Branch began publishing a Sunday School quarterly in 1932. After the Assemblies of God and R.E.E.M. parted ways in 1940, the German Branch began publishing *Licht und Leben (Light and Life)* in 1942. Annual camp meetings were held in various churches and camps (including at Lake Odessa, Michigan) until the German Branch established Bethel Camp at Bridgman, Michigan, in 1944. The German Branch began sending missionaries in the 1930s, resulting in outreaches in Yugoslavia, Poland, India, Mexico, and a substantial work in Brazil. German Pentecostals in the U.S. and Canada maintained close fellowship.

Like other immigrants, many German-speaking Pentecostals clung tenaciously to their culture and language.

Over time, many German churches were Americanized and transferred to English-language districts. By the late 1970s, most German district churches had made the controversial choice to switch to English-language services.

—*Darrin J. Rodgers*

no one to go and [it's] better not go than see souls born into the kingdom and left by the wayside to perish because there is no faithful pastor."

Asked to explain why she could send only an offering of one dollar to headquarters for the renewal of her credentials in 1939, Stump assured the brethren in Springfield that she had not "spent money on fine automobiles, pianos, fine clothes, [perms], jewelry and many other things that I see in our Pentecostal ranks." Then bringing the Word to bear on herself, and expressing the matter-of-fact pluck of a Pentecostal pioneer, she concluded: "But I hear Jesus say, 'What is that to thee, follow thou me' [John 21:22]. So I turn my eyes to Him and He supplies."

DEMETRIO BAZÁN, SR.
(1900-1976)

Demetrio Bazán was so admired by some Hispanic pastors that in addition to imitating his mannerisms and preaching, many began wearing crew cuts just like his. Bazán's legacy, however, rests on a stronger foundation than hero worship. Pastors respected him, for they knew that he shared their struggles.

Manuelita and Demetrio Bazán

Born in Mexico in 1900, he was adopted at age nine by a well-to-do family who had no children of their own. This insured that he would receive an education. When the family later moved to Kingsville, Texas, he was converted under the ministry of Henry C. Ball, who discipled him in the faith. He married Manuelita (Nellie) Treviño in 1920, and both received ordination from the Assemblies of God. Afterward, they went to El Paso to work with Francisco Olazábal.

Two years later, Bazán joined Olazábal and others in withdrawing from the Assemblies of God to form a competing organization. They had become frustrated with the decision of the General Council's leadership to delay the establishment of a Latin American district with Hispanic leaders. At a time when U.S. relations with Mexico were severely strained due to recent American military intervention in Mexican affairs, emotions ran high. Ball, the leader of the "Mexican convention" of the Texico district, had to break the bad news of the delay; this triggered the separation. The Hispanics who remained (likely out of esteem for Ball) waited until 1939 before one of them took office as district superintendent of the Latin American district.

Bazán's departure was brief, however, and he reaffiliated a year later. After returning, he pastored churches in Kingsville, Houston, and Denver, Colorado. When called to pastor in Denver, he lacked any promise of funds for food and clothing. Furthermore, he didn't know where his large family of nine would stay once they arrived. They went with only the address of someone living in Denver who knew a member of their former congregation in San Antonio. Upon arriving, they met José Arroyo, who immediately told them, "I have the house for you to live in." He told them that he had been led by a dream to contact the owner of a certain house. With his consent, the Bazáns set up housekeeping.

The honor of being the first Hispanic superintendent of the Latin American district fell to Bazán himself in 1939. His contributions to the district included its restructuring, recommending the formation of the Spanish Eastern district (originally with Puerto Rico), and training. Many pastors received their only formal instruction in Scripture and doctrine from the ministers' institutes he conducted in various places. Bazán's concern for the welfare of the ministers and their families led him to have the new Social Security Act (1935) translated into Spanish in order for them to enroll and understand the benefits.

EDITH MAE PENNINGTON
(1902-1974)

Voted "Most Beautiful Girl in the U.S." by the judges in a national competition in 1921, Edith Mae Patterson became a celebrity overnight. This award transformed the young schoolteacher from Pine Bluff, Arkansas, into a beauty queen and led her to Hollywood for a promising career in motion pictures. It was the Roaring Twenties

My Trip to the Holy Land

They called for everybody [on the ship] to register. You were to register what State you were from, your occupation, your business on this trip, and so forth. I registered as a "Pentecostal evangelist," and the purser on the boat said, "A—a what?" I told him. He said, "What does that stand for?" "We're Full Gospel folks," I replied. He said, "What do you mean by 'Full Gospel folks'?" I said, "We believe in salvation holiness, the soon coming of the Lord, Divine healing, and the baptism in the Holy Ghost." Everybody was listening, but nothing stayed with them except the words, "divine healing." After we had registered I went back up [on deck]. Pretty soon they had to lead me to my room. I was deathly sick. I was in my room for about two hours with my first hard seasickness. It makes you so sick that you do not want to see anybody. There came a knock at the door. Mr. Graham said, "Mrs. Taylor, my wife is awfully sick. Didn't you say you believe in divine healing?" I said, "Yes sir."

He said, "Will you come and pray for her?"

I thought if it were anything else but seasickness! I tried to look pleasant; I did not want her to see I was seasick. I went in, and without an introduction said, "O God, touch her! Heal her." My eyes began to draw shut, and something caused me to get up. I said, "I'll be back." I went back to my room—and for about three and a half hours in came the sick calls! And the devil said, "Physician, heal thyself. Why don't you do something for yourself?" I said, "I'm too sick to pray for myself. The reason I prayed for the other folks was because I had to!"

—*Evangelist Emma Taylor, "My Trip to the Holy Land,"*
Pentecostal Evangel *(July 11, 1936): 8–9.*

in America, and the dazzling lights of Hollywood enticed many young women, who would have given anything for the opportunity handed Edith.

Although she enjoyed the limelight for a time, she became disillusioned with the glitzy lifestyle and the lack of moral values in what she came to see as a modern Sodom. "What is wrong with me?" she asked her mother. "Most young girls would be thrilled with all these honors and publicity, to have their names in electric lights, newspaper write-ups, et cetera. Mother, why am I not happy?" Finding only emptiness, she began to read her Bible and finally severed her contact with Hollywood. Sometime after, she knelt at an old-fashioned altar in a Pentecostal church in Oklahoma City and surrendered her life to Christ: "The Light from the Cross exceeded the bright lights of the stage. I exchanged the glamour of the world for the glory of the Cross. I pledged my irrevocable word to Christ to forsake all and follow Him." The turnabout brought an end to her marriage with her business manager, J. B. Pennington, who wanted nothing to do with her faith.

Advertisement for services with Edith Mae Pennington

Later baptized in the Spirit, she heard the call to preach and received ordination from the Arkansas-Louisiana district in 1930. For the next twenty years, Pennington became a highly successful evangelist and then pastor in Shreveport, Louisiana. Her celebrity status and decision to forsake the lights of Hollywood for ministry on the sawdust trail captured the interest of newspapers across the country, which retold her story and highlighted her meetings. Reporters eagerly sought for interviews and pictures.

Another aspect of Pennington's fame came from her calling as a female preacher. Although the General Council had earlier given credentials to women as evangelists and missionaries, ordination as pastors didn't come until 1935. Many questioned the place of females in the pulpit, except when a male minister was not available. This artificial difference couldn't last, for too many women had been active in ministry from the beginning of the Assemblies of God, and few could deny the fruit of their labors. In regard to the outpouring of the Spirit on men and women (Acts 2:16–18), she demanded: "If God calls a woman to preach the gospel, and His blessings are upon her, 'in confirming His Word with signs following,' whose right is it to question her right to preach the gospel, pastor a church, or lead a movement under God?"

ANNA B. LOCK
(1890-1952)

"Now I lay me down to sleep, I pray the Lord my soul to keep" was the only prayer that Anna B. Lock could remember. Trapped in a sinful lifestyle and chemically addicted, she recited this in moments of great loneliness and despair; there were many such times. She knew that Jesus had died on the cross, but didn't know how to get saved. No one ever invited her to church—good and upstanding people would have flinched at the sight of her entering their church.

Like other children growing up in the home of an alcoholic parent, she had more than one strike against her. When her father brought his buddies home and mixed

Anna B. Lock

drinks for them, he gave Anna whiskey to drink when she asked for it. She was only seven or eight years old.

Her mother took the children to Sunday School, but had to endure the curses of her husband. Added to other abuses, she finally left the faith and moved to another town to rear her children in safety. Unfortunately, it was too late for Anna. At fourteen years, she had already become an alcoholic and left home. Two years later, she gave birth to a baby girl out of wedlock and left her in the care of family members. Anna was in the fast lane to a dead end—skid row.

Never able to keep a job, Lock drifted to Los Angeles and then to San Francisco. While in California, she nearly died several times from her drinking and drug overdoses. By the time she came into contact with the Salvation Army, her weight had dropped from 163 pounds to 107 pounds. The Army helped arrange for her return home to Illinois. At long last, she was reunited with her daughter, mother, and older sister. For a time, she managed to keep away from liquor and drugs. During this time, she married and promised her husband that she would remain off drugs. Her drinking, however, resumed. "I made home brew by 20-gallon lots and drank it the same way," she wrote. "My husband furnished a lovely home for me but I didn't take care of it. All I wanted was drink and cigarettes."

When her aunt arrived for a visit in 1931, she encouraged Lock to attend a revival at a local Pentecostal church. Finding herself strangely drawn to the meetings, she attended almost nightly for two weeks. One night, sinners were invited to the altar while the congregation sang:

> I've wandered far away from God,
>> Now I'm coming home.
> The paths of sin too long I've trod,
>> Lord, I'm coming home.

Approaching her, one of the preachers put her arm around Lock and said, "Jesus loves you. He needs you."

Moments later Lock went to the altar and wept in repentance. "O God, I've been so wicked and low," she prayed. "Could You do anything with a wreck like me? Here I am, Lord. If You'll forgive me, I'll live the rest of my life for You."

Then began a remarkable change in her life: She led her family to the Lord, and two years after her conversion, she began pioneering a church there in Galva, Illinois. It began meeting in the basement of the post office, and within six years grew to a congregation of eighty people. Understanding the needs of the poor during these Depression years, she organized a sewing circle to make clothes. The services at the Galva Assembly were marked by preaching, "shouting, singing, and dancing in the Spirit." At the annual Illinois district camp meetings, "[Lock] could always be seen on the platform with her tambourine and usually led at least one 'Jericho March' during the meetings."

In the late 1930s, she felt led to become an itinerant evangelist and journeyed across North America holding services and sharing her testimony. Even with only a third-grade education and no formal ministerial training, her campaigns led to many conversions and Spirit baptisms. In addition, she frequently went to Chicago's skid row to evangelize on the streets and in the bars. "It takes no more of His precious blood to cleanse a poor, drunken, cigarette-smoking, dope-using sinner," she wrote, "than it does the haughty, high-minded, stiff-necked church member who has a form of godliness, but denies the power thereof."

Her own dramatic conversion provided her with a special understanding of the transforming power of God's love: "[Jesus] lifted me from the underworld and prepared me for the upperworld." Often Lock would begin the process for her converts in a similar fashion, removing them from skid row and taking them home to live with her family until they were able to stand on their own feet as Christians.

I Listened to Myself Preach

In 1922, I was in my first pastorate at Puxico, Missouri, which is in the southeastern part of the state. I was a real novice in the ministry, pastoring a small congregation in a town of only 700.

Evangelist Maria B. Woodworth-Etter was at that time closing out an outstanding ministry. I had read a lot about her but had never been in one of her meetings. When I heard that she would be conducting services in Sikeston, I told one of the women in the church that I would like to attend a service and hear Sister Etter preach.

I didn't have a car at that time, but the woman in the church told me her sister had a car and would be happy to take us.

When we walked into the open-air meeting at Sikeston, we looked at the biggest church crowd we had ever seen. I thought it looked like 10,000 people, but it was probably more like a thousand.

I Listened to Myself Preach, continued

Before the service started, several people on the platform were talking with Sister Etter. We learned later that the song leader's mother had died so he had gone to the funeral. They were looking for a song leader.

Soon a woman on the platform walked into the audience and came straight toward my wife and me. We then discovered that we knew the woman.

She said, "Brother Aaron, Mrs. Etter wants you to come to the platform."

But I didn't think I belonged on the platform. The woman insisted, so I went. After I met Sister Etter, they asked me to lead the singing. I answered that I had never led a song service for such a big congregation. I hadn't been preaching very long, and the crowds at Puxico were very small compared to this one.

Mrs. Etter answered my objection. "You'll do all right. The Lord will help you."

With fear and trembling I accepted the responsibility and talked with Sister Etter about the type of songs she wanted.

Aaron A. Wilson

After I had led a verse of the first song and was into the second verse, I felt a light tap on my shoulder. It was Mrs. Etter. She said, "Brother, the Lord would have you preach here tonight."

I was stunned. I had reluctantly accepted the invitation to lead the song service. Now Sister Etter wanted me to preach!

I went on with the singing and got into the second song. I felt that little tap on my shoulder again. This time Sister Etter was more forceful. "Brother, don't fail God. He wants you to preach here tonight."

I hardly knew what to say. I had come to hear this great woman preach, and now she was asking me, a novice, to preach to this huge crowd.

I finished the song service and sat down.

When the time came for me to preach, I had decided I would preach along the line I had preached the previous Sunday night in my church—on the coming of the Lord.

But the Holy Spirit had other plans.

After Sister Etter announced that I would be speaking, I stood to my feet and walked toward the pulpit. I had only taken a few steps when suddenly a passage from the 5th chapter of John flashed through my mind: "Wilt thou be made whole?"

I took the passage for my text, and the Spirit of God preached that whole sermon through me. I really listened to myself preach. God moved through the audience in a miraculous manner.

It wasn't me. It was the Holy Spirit. I was just a young preacher and didn't know how to handle a crowd like this one. The Spirit moved!

That service has been one of the mountain peaks of my Christian experience.

—*Aaron A. Wilson, "A Mountain Peak of My Spiritual Experience"*
Assemblies of God Heritage 4 (winter 1984–85):12.

WILLIAM J. MITCHELL
(1878-1958)

The testimony of many Pentecostals who entered the ministry involved several common ingredients: salvation, healing or deliverance from a chemical addiction, Spirit baptism, and a divine call to evangelism. Pentecostals believed this made up for whatever shortcomings one might have had in upbringing, education, or social graces. William J. Mitchell, born and reared in Newfoundland in eastern Canada, left school while in the third grade and went to sea as a cabin boy at eleven. It was far from a promising start.

Susanna and William Mitchell

Sailing around the world with hard-drinking crews, he became an alcoholic while still a young man. Desperate to overcome his addiction, according to his son, Allen, once Mitchell even made a "blood vow," cutting his wrist and "then writing in his own blood, he vowed never to drink again. But it was to no avail."

In 1900 he met and married Susanna Patience Curnew in St. John's, Newfoundland, and a year later, she gave birth to the first of their thirteen children. Following the large migration of Newfoundlanders to New England and especially to Massachusetts, the Mitchells settled in Chelsea, where he began work as a carpenter. After the birth of their second daughter, they discovered that she had epilepsy, so they moved to Zion City, Illinois, noted for John Alexander Dowie's healing ministry. The timing of Mitchell's salvation and the move were very close. The Zion saints prayed for the girl, and she never again experienced a seizure. The family remained there until 1905, when Dowie had a stroke and the community entered a period of turmoil.

Returning to Chelsea, Mitchell started an independent mission on Park Street in a former saloon. When news of the Pentecostal outpouring began to circulate in New England, he sent out an appeal for workers who had experienced speaking in tongues according to Acts 2:4 to visit them. Several responded, including two women, Mabel Smith and Jean Campbell (and possibly Charles F. Parham himself). Smith and Campbell had been baptized in the Spirit during the Pentecostal revival in Zion City under Parham's ministry. An outpouring of the Spirit in Chelsea, however, eluded them. But when Brother and Sister Sankey Lee came from Texas in the spring of 1907, Mitchell and others were baptized in the Spirit. After the Lees departed, Mitchell said, "I continued to carry on the meetings the rest of the year, besides working at my trade as a carpenter. The news spread that the Lord was blessing, so that people came from everywhere, making it necessary for us to move into a larger building."

A Few Hints to Preachers

Make no apologies. If you have the Lord's message, deliver it; if not, hold your peace. Have [a] short preface or introduction. Say your best things first, and stop before you get prosey. Do not spoil the appetite for dinner by too much thin soup. Leave self out of the pulpit and take Jesus in....

If you do not want to "'break," make your shirt collar an inch larger, and give your blood a chance to flow back to the heart. Don't get excited too soon. Do not run away from your hearers. Engine driving-wheels fly fast with no load, but when they draw anything they go slower.

Do not scold the people. Do not abuse the faithful souls who come to meeting [on] rainy days, because of the others who do not come. Preach the best to small congregations. Jesus preached to one woman at the well, and she got all Samaria out to hear Him next time.

Do not repeat, saying, "'as I said before." If you said it before, say something else after. Leave out words you cannot define. Stop your declamation and talk to folks. Come down from stilted and sacred tones, and become a little child. Change the subject, if it goes hard. Do not tire yourself and every one else out. Do not preach till the middle of your sermon buries the beginning, and is buried in the end. Look the people in the face, and live so that you are not afraid of them.

Take long breaths, fill your lungs and keep them full. Stop to breathe before the air is exhausted. Then you will not finish each sentence-ah, with a terrible gasp-ah, and so strain the lungs-ah, as if you were dying for air-ah, and never find it out-ah, because their friends dare not tell them-ah, and so leave them to make sport of the Philistines-ah. Inflate your lungs. It is easier to run a mill with a full pond than an empty one. Be moderate at first. Hoist the gate a little way; when you are half through, raise a little more; when nearly done, put on a full head of water.

Aim at the mark. Hit it. Shoot, and see where the shot struck, and then fire another broadside. Pack your sermons, make your words like bullets.

—*Burt McCafferty, "A Few Hints to Preachers,"*
Weekly Evangel (January 27, 1917): 7.

As the revival continued, participants started new missions in different parts of New England. This dispersion was reinforced by the great Chelsea fire of 1908, in which half the city—including Mitchell's mission and all the family's possessions—was destroyed.

Providing for such a large family was no small task. When Mitchell started Glad Tidings Tabernacle in Everett, Massachusetts, he continued working at his trade to increase his income. However, it also gave him valuable contact with other men on the job. One acquaintance remembered: "Many of his parishioners were carpenters, painters and iron workers. Hence, he had contact with them during working days and situations. He . . . was the example which led so many of them to salvation and membership in the church."

His reputation for evangelism, church planting, and prayer led to his election in 1936 as superintendent of the New England District Council. Mitchell served in this capacity for two years. Throughout his ministry, he kept contact with other Pentecostals in the region as well, including Christine Gibson, founder of Zion Bible Institute in Rhode Island. The advance of Pentecostalism in New England is part of the legacy of William Mitchell and other pioneers who believed the reports about the outpouring of the Spirit, experienced it for themselves, and declared it to others.

RECOMMENDED READING

Bazán, Demetrio, Sr. *Autobiographia de Demetrio Bazán*. Unpublished ms., 1975.

Bazan, Nellie. *Enviados de Dios: Demetrio Y Nellie Bazan*. Miami, FL: Editorial Vida, 1987.

Blumhofer, Edith. "The Role of Women in the Assemblies of God." *Assemblies of God Heritage* 7 (winter 1987–1988): 13–17.

Gohr, Glenn. "Ben Hardin: A Man with a Heart for Evangelism." *Assemblies of God Heritage* 15 (winter 1995–1996): 7–11, 23.

———. "A Dedicated Ministry Among Hispanics: Demetrio and Nellie Bazán." *Assemblies of God Heritage* 9 (fall 1989): 7–9, 17.

———. "A Harvest in Minnesota: The Story of A/G Pioneer Frank J. Lindquist." *Assemblies of God Heritage* 10 (spring 1990): 10–13.

Janes, Burton K. "William J. Mitchell: A Pentecostal Pioneer in New England." Parts 1 and 2. *Assemblies of God Heritage* 12 (winter 1992–1993): 10–12, 24–25; 13 (spring 1993): 22–24, 33–34.

Lock, Anna B. "From the Underworld to the Upperworld." *Assemblies of God Heritage* 14 (summer 1994): 19–21.

Pennington, Edith Mae. *From the Footlights to the Light of the Cross*. Shreveport, La.: Plant of Renown, n.d.

———. Should Women Preach the Gospel? Shreveport, La.: Plant of Renown, 1982.

Stump, Elva K. "A Miracle of Healing." *Assemblies of God Heritage* 14 (spring 1994): 14–15.

Saggio, Joseph J., and Jim Dempsey. *American Indian College: A Witness to the Tribes*. Springfield, MO: Gospel Publishing House, 2008.

Warner, Wayne. "From the Footlights to the Light of the Cross: The Story of Evangelist Edith Mae Pennington." *Assemblies of God Heritage* 7 (winter 1987–1988): 6–9, 20.

CHAPTER 14

TEACHING THE SAINTS

I n late summer 1930, William I. Evans, the "principal" of Central Bible Institute (CBI) announced that the school year would begin on September 26, and there was still room for more students. "We are looking for Jesus to come and, in consequence of that glorious event, we may never conduct the [term]," he remarked. "We thank God for the blessed hope. . . . However, we are occupying till He comes. That occupation with us is making this Institute count for the very most in the advancement of the Kingdom." The school preferred mature and "diligent students of the Word," nineteen years of age and older. Accepting applicants below this age might mean that at graduation three years later, they could still be "too young to be trusted with the responsibilities involved."

Evans lamented that finding students with the "highest type of consecration among us is getting rarer." Life at a Bible institute contrasted sharply with campus life at colleges and universities. Preeminently an experience in spiritual formation, it demanded a high level of dedication to stay the course.

The "standards of holiness" required separation from worldly values. "It grieves our hearts and we could weep," he added in disappointment, "when we see world conformity among Bible school graduates!" Women especially seem to have been the culprits: "We have seen pastors' wives and lady pastors and leaders dressed so much like the world as to show no line of separation." Hence, "short skirts, low necks, sheer clothes, adornments, and worldly style of hair dress, are inexcusable. Certainly religion does not consist in what we wear, but genuine religion of the kind we profess will show itself in these matters." Hopefully, "only . . . serious-minded youths will care to apply themselves to [the school's] rigor."

Although strict discipline characterized all the schools, the atmosphere could hardly be described as dull or without humor. Instead, both students and faculty members shared a common commitment for the evangelization of the world. Reflecting the desire of church leaders and grassroots believers alike, Evans pleaded, "We want all its facilities from walls and roof to the services of consecrated instructors to produce the very utmost in lives for the Kingdom."

Alumni from Assemblies of God schools often recall classroom instructors who profoundly impacted their lives. Since these institutions were ventures of faith, faculty members worked long hours, struggled with low pay, and frequently received little recognition for their sacrificial efforts. In a report published in the *Pentecostal Evangel* about the 1937 commencement at Latin American Bible Institute in San Antonio and the thirty-five men and women who graduated, the writer attributed the success of the school to the sacrifices of the staff: "Much credit is due to Brother Ball and the group of workers who have been assisting him as teachers in the school, since funds have never been very plentiful so as to enable anyone to be really remunerated for his services; but each has given his time and effort willingly as unto the Lord, trusting God for the supply of his individual needs."

Most churches did not financially support these schools for several reasons: First, they sometimes preferred spending their monies on local church ministries and/or foreign missions. Second, a long-standing fear of educational preparation made many wary of Bible institutes. Third, since the schools operated on faith, God would somehow provide for them; indeed, strong financial backing might jeopardize their spiritual vigor. Despite the handicaps that worked against their effectiveness, teachers contributed heavily to the spiritual formation of thousands of pastors, evangelists, missionaries, and other church workers.

Classes Start at LABI

In about a month the Latin-American Bible Institute in Saspamco, Texas, will open its doors again for another school year. From all along the Mexican border and also from several states of this country, young men and women will gather in for another year of study and training for the ministry among their own Spanish-speaking people. Year after year the institute turns out Spirit-filled and trained workers who are doing effective work in bringing the gospel to the Latin-American fields.

The Bible Institute is located on a large farm near Saspamco, where the students help with the raising of produce for the table as well as feed for the cows

Classes Start at LABI Continued

and pigs. Mr. Einar Peterson, a worker in the institute, has just been visiting the Missions Department. From him we learn that the school will be opening under a serious handicap this fall in that there are no crops this year because of drought. The same condition at the homes of the students will prevent many of them from coming to school unless funds can be provided from some other source.

As we bring this urgent need before our *Evangel* readers, we trust the Lord will lay it upon some hearts to help, for we believe that funds invested in the school will yield good dividends in the Kingdom of God. Offerings may be sent to the Foreign Missions Department, 336 West Pacific Street, Springfield, Missouri, designated for the Latin-American Bible Institute in care of H. C. Ball. They would also be grateful for farm produce or canned goods sent direct to the Latin-American Bible Institute, Post Office Box 113, Saspamco, Texas.

— *"Missionary School Opening,"* Pentecostal Evangel *(September 23, 1939): 8.*

Educators presented in this chapter include Peter C. Nelson, Myer Pearlman, Marcus L. Grable, Christine Gibson, and Stanley H. Frodsham. Gibson, founder of the independent Zion Bible Institute in Rhode Island, never held credentials with the General Council. Yet hundreds of Assemblies of God ministers received their training there; her story deserves to be told. Stanley H. Frodsham, long-time editor of the *Pentecostal Evangel*, has also been included. While he did some teaching at CBI, his contributions lie in his editorial work and many books. Through these means, he contributed to ministerial preparation formally and informally. Many who couldn't attend the Bible institutes depended on the *Evangel* for instruction, sermon ideas, and Sunday School lessons.

PETER C. NELSON
(1868-1942)

Generally, Pentecostals looked down on academic degrees as more of a hindrance than help for Spirit-filled ministry. For example, one early Council leader recalled,

Peter C. Nelson

"the use of 'big' words was generally detested. The preachers were never called 'Reverend.' Everybody was brother and sister so and so. D.D. [doctor of divinity] was invariably interpreted to mean 'Dumb Dogs' [Isaiah 56:10, KJV]."

"P. C." Nelson, however, knew the value of formal preparation for ministry. An American Baptist pastor who became a Pentecostal in 1920, he had graduated from Denison University in Ohio and studied under one of America's foremost theologians, Augustus H. Strong, at the Rochester (New York) Theological Seminary. Yet such training had not been an easy thing for him to acquire.

Nelson's family migrated to Iowa from Denmark. At twenty he felt called to the ministry, but his early attempts at preaching were so discouraging that he renounced his call and he despaired spiritually. "The difficulties and ridicule to which [I] was subjected were too heavy for [me] to bear alone," he wrote, "being without a spiritual adviser, and without anyone to encourage [me] to go forward." This proved to be the darkest time in his life: "All hope of Heaven being gone, [I] wandered in darkness, in the blackest darkness."

Morning dawned at last, however, when he met J.F. Bryant in 1888, a Baptist pastor in Harland, Iowa. Although Nelson thought he had committed the unpardonable sin against the Holy Spirit (Matthew 12:31), his faith and calling were renewed under

Bryant's influence. Enrolling at a Baptist seminary in the Chicago area a year later, he found that without an undergraduate degree he was not prepared, so he switched to Denison University in Ohio. To cover his expenses, he worked as a manual laborer. While there he met his wife, Myrtle Garmong, who then helped him complete the program (in seven years).

Still feeling unprepared, he enrolled at Rochester Seminary in 1899. Augustus H. Strong, the president and professor of theology, taught the courses in systematic theology, and Nelson became one of his students. *Strong's Systematic Theology*, first published in 1886, had gone through seven editions and reached nearly twelve hundred pages by the time he got there. "I have discarded none of the Baptist doctrines," he reminisced many years later, "but have built a story or two on the good solid foundation laid for our faith."

Following graduation, he evangelized and pastored several churches before being called to pastor Conley Memorial Baptist Church in Detroit. His contact with Pentecostals began in 1920, but they failed to impress him. Nevertheless, a healing from a serious and possibly life-threatening infection led him to begin preaching on divine healing. But the congregation refused to accept this new teaching, and before long he resigned. Shortly after, he was baptized in the Spirit and joined the Assemblies of God.

By now over fifty years old and a seasoned minister, he detected that many young people in the Assemblies of God were entering the ministry just like he had: with little preparation. In 1927 he moved to Enid, Oklahoma, where he founded a church and opened Southwestern Bible School. Like Alice E. Luce and Henry C. Ball, Nelson recognized the need for Pentecostal curricular materials. This led him to write several books, including *The Young Minister's Guide* (1932) and *Bible Doctrines* (1934), his best known. Before his death, Southwestern Bible School merged with two other schools

Commencement Exercises

April 14th the second annual commencement exercises of Southwestern Bible School, Enid, Okla., were held in the First Methodist Episcopal Church. A class of nine young men and thirteen young women—gathered from all over this country—received diplomas. The musical numbers, both vocal and instrumental, as well as the [student] addresses were of high order. . . .

On Sunday, the 12th, General Superintendent

E. S. Williams [had] preached the baccalaureate sermon in Enid Gospel Tabernacle, from 1 Thess. 2:8. In the evening he delivered a missionary address after which Pastor Nelson asked all the students who felt the call of God upon their lives to foreign missionary service, to come forward, and fifty-five responded. The missionary spirit in Southwestern has been growing, and many are now ready to go to distant lands as soon as they can be sent forth.

—*P. C. Nelson, "Commencement Exercises at Southwestern Bible School,"*
Pentecostal Evangel (May 16, 1931): 12.

(Shield of Faith Bible School and Southern Bible College) to form what is now known as Southwestern Assemblies of God University in Waxahachie, Texas, a fitting legacy for a man who knew what it was to be ill prepared for the ministry.

MYER PEARLMAN
(1898-1943)

The personalities in this chapter came from widely different backgrounds, and Myer Pearlman was no exception. The eldest son of a Jewish family, he studied at a synagogue school in Birmingham, England. In school he remembered learning the Jewish version of the three R's: the Jewish faith, the Torah (Old Testament), and the Hebrew language. "I was taught," he recalled, "that while I was to be a patriotic Englishman, I was also a Jew, a member of the nation, and that I was different from other people. I remember passing meat markets, and inwardly thanking God that I did not eat unclean meat."

Myer Pearlman

The economic situation in England forced his father to move the family to the United States in hopes of gaining employment and improving their living standard. After settling in New York City in 1915, the younger Pearlman eventually enlisted in the U.S. Army and served eighteen months in the medical corps in France. His proficiency in French helped him in this capacity. After the war, he traveled to California where "groping for light I began to read religious books and attend services."

Sometime later, walking by a mission in San Francisco, he noticed a crowd gathered at the entrance and stopped to listen to the music. On another evening, he stood outside again. Mustering his courage, he entered and took a seat. He was particularly impressed by the music, especially the song "Honey in the Rock," written by F.A. Graves. Based on Deuteronomy 32:13 ("he nourished [Israel] with honey from the rock"), it tells of God's grace and provision from an unexpected source. Verse two asks, "Have you 'tasted that the Lord is gracious?' Do you walk in the way that's new? Have you drunk from the living fountain? There's Honey in the Rock [Jesus Christ] for you." Attending nightly, he eventually confessed his sins and became a Christian, praying "in the name of Abraham, Isaac and Jacob."

In 1922, Pearlman enrolled at Central Bible Institute, where he later met his wife, Irene Graves, daughter of the songwriter. A brilliant student and self-taught in many areas, he read the Scriptures in Hebrew, Greek, Spanish, French, and Italian. At graduation time, the principal, Frank M. Boyd, invited him to join the faculty. Pearlman accepted and taught there from 1924 until his death in 1943. Since teachers were not paid when classes were out in the summer, he wrote materials for Gospel Publishing House to earn additional money. Before long, he became the writer of *Adult Sunday School Teacher* and *The Adult and Young People's*

Doctrinal Knowledge Is Essential

Strong beliefs make for strong character; clear-cut beliefs make for clear-cut convictions. Of course, a person's doctrinal belief is not his religion any more than the backbone is the man's personality. But as good backbone is an essential part of the man's body, so a definite system of belief is an essential part of a man's religion. It has been well said that "a man does not need to wear his backbone in front of him, but he must have a backbone and a straight one or he will be a [shapeless], if not a humpbacked, Christian.

—*Myer Pearlman*, Knowing the Doctrines of the Bible *(1937)*, 9–10.

Teachers' Quarterly. With his increasing responsibilities, he divided his days between classroom instruction in the morning and writing in the afternoons at the publishing house.

Over time, he became a widely read author in Pentecostal circles, producing Sunday School materials as well as a number of books. In 1937, he wrote his most enduring work, *Knowing the Doctrines of the Bible*, a four-hundred-page survey of doctrine. Theologian Russell P. Spittler has described it as "the theological jewel of classical Pentecostalism's middle period—written after the era of tracts, at the throes of self-conscious polemic, and before the 'evangelicalization' of Pentecostalism led to the training of its teachers in places like Wheaton College and the interdenominational theological seminaries." He notes in particular Pearlman's careful reflection, balance, nontechnical language, and irenic tone.

Pearlman's workload continued to grow: more writing, teaching, camp meetings. World War II being in progress, he was approached about starting a publication for servicemen. Having been a serviceman, feeling he could identify with them, he accepted. What seemed to be a modest effort became the well-circulated paper called *Reveille*; it grew into the Servicemen's Department. But the pace was beginning to tell on Pearlman; he was encouraged to slow down and rest. The assistant general superintendent, Ralph M. Riggs, wrote him, "You could coast . . . from now on and still come out ahead of the rest of us." Eventually his health broke, and he died in a veteran's hospital; he was forty-five. Among the floral arrangements at his funeral, two symbolized his spiritual pilgrimage: a large Star of David made of blue flowers sent by Jewish friends and a cross made of white flowers from his Gentile friends.

MARCUS L. GRABLE
(1891-1970)

At an interdenominational revival held at the Shrine Mosque in Springfield, Missouri, in 1933, Marcus Grable first encountered Ralph Riggs, then pastor of Central Assembly of God. Area pastors had been invited to give the invocation at the meetings, and one evening Riggs offered the prayer. Afterward, Grable turned to his wife and said, "That man knows God." Before long, the Grables joined the Assemblies of God. Riggs and Grable, a minister and a layman, soon found they shared a common concern: promoting Sunday Schools and teacher training. Little did Riggs know when he prayed that night that he would inspire another Sunday School enthusiast like himself.

Grable had been converted at the Christian Church in Egerton, Missouri, in 1901, and through the years worked in different leadership roles in local Sunday Schools. After moving to Springfield and joining Central Assembly, he started working as a janitor at Gospel Publishing House. In his spare time, he assisted in the opening of three branch Sunday Schools in the community. At work, he asked for a desk and typewriter to answer inquiries about Sunday School matters that arrived from around the country.

Recognizing the need for better training and standardizing Sunday School programs, and noting the obvious skills and enthusiasm of Grable, the Executive Presbytery appointed him in 1935 to lead and develop the newly established Sunday School Promotion Department. His office began with a steel table, a chair, and a typewriter. From modest beginnings, this devoted layman aggressively built a national program that saw phenomenal growth before his resignation from office fourteen years later. He became the General Council's "Mr. Sunday School." During his years in office, Assemblies of God Sunday Schools expanded by 300 percent, leading all other church groups in growth.

Two chief objectives guided his plans: teacher training and Sunday School conventions. For example, shortly after taking office, he sent every pastor a complimentary copy of Riggs's *Successful Sunday School*. In conjunction with this, he introduced a "Training for Christian Service" course that laid the groundwork for the national Workers Training program. Standards for local Sunday Schools were also set. To offer further assistance, he launched *Our Sunday School Counselor* in 1939, the official publication for Assemblies of God Sunday Schools, and later the [Sunday School] *Superintendent's Assistant*.

Grable's second objective focused on sponsoring national and regional Sunday School conventions. The first of eleven national conventions gathered in Springfield, Missouri, in 1940. Near the end of his tenure, the Sunday School Department introduced the Boys and Girls Missionary Crusade (BGMC) at the National Sunday School Convention in Springfield in 1949 to promote missions among the children and raise funds for various projects.

With failing health he resigned in 1949, but remained in Springfield. Ironically, he felt that a minister would serve the office better. In retirement, his

Early in 1942 the national Sunday School Department mailed this Lighthouse Sunday School poster to 5,000 AG Sunday Schools. Promoting the Lighthouse idea are (l to r): J. Z. Kamerer, general manager of Gospel Publishing House; Loine Honderick, Sunday School representative; and Marcus L. Grable, "Mr. Sunday School."

Why a National Sunday School Convention?

The evangelistic use of the Sunday School (and oh, what an evangelizing agency a Sunday School is!) is discovered to be not just an available means for the growth and extension of our own Sunday School and church, but it becomes a path of duty and obedience. The sheep and lambs out there all around us are His sheep and lambs, and He says He (and we) must bring them in. Our determination to succeed in our Sunday School work deepens into a solemn resolve to obey our Master at any . . . cost. He will be with us in this as in every other phase of obedience to the Great Commission.

—*Ralph M. Riggs, "Why a National Sunday School Convention,"*
Pentecostal Evangel *(February 24, 1952): 5.*

interest in Sunday Schools never flagged. Four days before his death in 1970, he participated in a parade that was part of a kid's crusade at Calvary Temple Assembly of God. Dressed as a farmer, he pushed a wheelbarrow on the three-mile parade route with a display he had made himself. The sign on it summed up his life's work: "Pushin' for Our Kids."

CHRISTINE A. GIBSON
(1879-1955)

At the dinner hour at Zion Bible Institute in East Providence, Rhode Island, barely enough food to eat could be found in the pantry. Zion's stance as a "faith school" would again be tested. "Mother" Gibson rose to the occasion and led the students in singing the Doxology. As they sang "Praise God from whom all blessings flow," a truckload of canned goods, fruits, vegetables, and staples arrived, along with a cash offering. It had come as a gift from friends in western New York. Dinner was soon on

Christine A. Gibson

the table. The story of Christine Gibson abounds with such stories of faith, divine guidance through visions and dreams, and the pursuit of the ministry to which God had called her.

Her parents having died when she was quite young, Christine Eckman was reared by her grandmother in Georgetown, British Guiana (present-day Guyana in South America). She attended a Presbyterian school. As a young adult, her life and enjoyments were similar to those of other young women her age. One evening while on her way to a dance, a girlfriend asked her if she would mind going with her to visit briefly a Salvation Army officer who had become ill. When he learned of their plans to go dancing, he looked at Christine and said, "A little dance, a little hell; a little dance, a little hell." She took offense, but his words haunted her.

On her way home from work a few days later, she felt compelled to enter a nearby Roman Catholic Church. Kneeling before the altar, she experienced a vision of Christ's crucifixion and heard the words: "Do you see that Man on the cross? He took the sinner's place. He became sin for a lost world. You are a sinner. He died in your stead. You can have His righteousness, for He is your salvation." This brought about her conversion; soon after, she affirmed her faith at the Salvation Army "barracks" (chapel).

Feeling called to mission work two years later, she went into the interior of her own country to take over the mission station of a missionary who had become too ill to continue. Unfortunately, Christine quickly felt the ravages of malaria, but trusting in Christ as her Healer, she refused to take quinine. With her health broken, she had no alternative but to return to Georgetown. Then, leaving a failed marriage behind, she immigrated to the United States and began preaching in holiness circles before settling in East Providence, Rhode Island. There she joined Alpheus Angel Cleveland's Church of the First Born (later Zion Gospel Temple).

Christine heard about the Pentecostal revival from several friends. One of them, Reuben A. Gibson, a Christian and Missionary Alliance pastor, had attended the revival that took place at the Missionary Training Institute in Nyack, New York, in May 1907. Several weeks later, she visited the Rochester Bible Training School directed by Elizabeth V. Baker and her four sisters. During a morning devotional hour, she was baptized in the Spirit.

In 1920 Christine and Reuben were married and worked together in ministry. Eventually, she became pastor of the church in East Providence and director of its faith home. Four years later (and just months after the death of her husband), she opened the doors of Mount Zion Bible School. She renamed it the School of the Prophets a year later; in 1936 the name changed again to Zion Bible Institute. (In 1999, Zion Bible Institute, now located in Barrington, Rhode Island, became an endorsed college of the Assemblies of God dedicated solely to ministerial training.)

NCBI Announcement

North Central Bible Institute and Business College, Minneapolis, Minn., will begin its 10th year [on] Sept. 18. It offers thorough training in Bible subjects in a three year, two year, or one year course. A. G. Ward, formerly of Toronto, Canada, has now joined our Faculty. Thorough training in Secretarial, Accounting, Bookkeeping, Shorthand, Typesetting, Business English, and Commercial Law, with actual office practice is offered. Dormitory and class rooms in modern fire-proof building in the heart of the city. Splendid opportunities for part time employment for students, and also for practical Christian work in the Twin Cities. Only Christian students accepted.

For catalogs and literature write to 900 Elliot Ave. S., Minneapolis, Minn.

—Frank J. Lindquist,
"North Central Bible Institute and Business College,"
Pentecostal Evangel *(September 16, 1939): 15*

Founded on faith in God's provision, the institute's operation was described by Mary Campbell Wilson, Gibson's biographer: "No charges of any kind were placed upon the students. They came, and everyone trusted God to supply the needs of Zion. Were it not for the stand that she took, many would have been denied the privilege of Bible school training. Sister Gibson championed the rights of the poor, and the rights of all men to study the Word of God."

After the closing of Rochester Bible Training School and Bethel Bible Training School in the 1920s, and the gradual decline of Beulah Heights Bible and Missionary Training Institute, other schools appeared on the scene. These included Metropolitan Bible Institute in Suffern, New York, and New England Bible Institute in Framingham, Massachusetts.

In response to the need for training, even more schools came into being, this time in Pennsylvania. After becoming superintendent of the Eastern district in 1929, J. Roswell Flower and his wife, Alice Reynolds Flower, started a summer Bible school three years later at the Maranatha Park campground in Green Lane. In 1938, a permanent institution began at the same site, Eastern Bible Institute (present-day Valley Forge Christian College in Phoenixville, Pennsylvania), with former missionary Allan Swift as its first president. Each of these schools prepared men and women who became Assemblies of God ministers, missionaries, and trained laypersons.

President Milton T. Wells teaching a class at Eastern Bible Institute in Green Lane, Pennsylvania

STANLEY H. FRODSHAM
(1882-1969)

"We are praying for God's man; are you that man?" asked John W. Welch, the general chairman of the Assemblies of God in 1916. While thanking Stanley H. Frodsham for three articles that he had submitted to the *Pentecostal Evangel*, Welch took the opportunity to ask him about being its editor. Frodsham's acceptance of the invitation propelled this Britisher into a national leadership role in the Assemblies of God that would continue for the next three decades.

Stanley H. Frodsham

Few people were better qualified than Frodsham. In his native England he had edited *Victory*, a monthly periodical that reported Pentecostal revivals around the world. Besides his skillful writing and absolute dedication to the task of publicizing the Pentecostal message, he also had friendships and contacts with other first-generation Pentecostal leaders.

Frodsham had been baptized in the Spirit since 1908 when he visited the (Anglican) All Saints Church pastored by Alexander A. Boddy in Sunderland, England. All Saints had been the scene of Pentecostal revival for over a year. But it had been Mrs. Boddy, rather than the pastor, who had laid hands on Frodsham. He was kneeling at the exact spot where Smith Wigglesworth had been baptized a year earlier, and as she prayed, Frodsham reported, "it seemed as if a thousand strong electric batteries came into my legs, and then a lot more came into my vocal organs—and volumes, torrents of tongues, poured from my lips. Thus began a full six months of heaven upon earth."

With his wife, Alice, they moved to the United States. At Welch's request, they attended the 1916 General Council in St. Louis. There Welch chatted with Mary Arthur from Galena, Kansas, a woman he greatly respected. "Have you been praying as I requested you to do for God's man to be the editor of the *Evangel*?" he asked. "Yes, and every time I pray," she replied, "the Lord shows me that the man who wrote this article is the one He has chosen." She pointed to an article by Frodsham in a recent issue of the *Pentecostal Evangel*. The Frodsham family then moved to Springfield, Missouri. For five years before assuming the position of senior editor, he worked as the Council's general secretary and missionary secretary in addition to his responsibility as assistant editor.

Like other early Council leaders at the headquarters, the Frodshams had little choice but to live frugally; his beginning salary was five dollars per week. Never purchasing a car, they preferred to walk or take public transportation in order to have more money to send to missionaries.

In 1921 the General Council selected him to be the senior editor and, by virtue of that office, a member of the Executive Presbytery. He was thirty-nine years old. Over time, he became a prolific writer. In addition to editorials and articles, he wrote Sunday

School quarterlies and papers. Fifteen books came from his pen, including a children's book, *The Boomerang and Other Stories* (1925), which was serialized in four periodicals with a combined circulation of one hundred thousand. He also wrote *With Signs Following: The Story of the Latter Day Pentecostal Revival* (1926), the first world survey of the Pentecostal movement. Two others about his friend Smith Wigglesworth became immensely popular: *Ever Increasing Faith* (1924), stories from his ministry, and *Apostle of Faith* (1948), a biography. Along with Alice Reynolds Flower and Carrie Judd Montgomery, he stands as one of the most prominent spiritual teachers in the Pentecostal movement.

As editor, Frodsham exercised charity in responding to the critics of Pentecostalism. In 1928, a convention of fundamentalists broadly denounced the Movement, accusing it of fanaticism and unscriptural teachings—"a menace in many churches and a real injury to sane testimony of Fundamental Christians." Publishing the statement in the *Pentecostal Evangel*, he replied: "Although we Pentecostal people have to be without the camp, we cannot afford to be bitter against those who do not see as we do." Rather, "our business is to love these Fundamentalists and to pray, 'Lord, bless them all.'"

Boys Plucked from a Life of Crime

Philomena M. Trocine

After graduating from Eastern Bible [Institute] [now Valley Forge Christian College], I began working in Gwinhurst, Delaware. My co-worker and I had no funds to rent an apartment for us nor to rent a building to use as a church.

Praise God He answered our prayers with an old bus on a large lot! We slept and ate in this cold bus and almost froze in the winter. Neighbors brought us tomatoes and we ate tomato sandwiches for some weeks. God was with us. One night after midnight a loud knock woke us and there was one of the brethren of the Lord with boxes and bags of food.

After canvassing the community, we had many parents consent to send their children to our Sunday school and vacation Bible school. On commencement evening, every seat in the YMCA was filled with children and their parents, including the parents of some incorrigible boys who were already at ages 5, 6, and 7 stealing, smoking and cursing. The parents asked us, "How did you do it?" It was worth all the efforts we put forth.

Though we were very tired from working with these children, and from walking long distances, neither the weariness nor the cold bothered us because Jesus blessed. Children were being saved, and mothers were being touched by God's Spirit. I can say without hesitancy those days were our happiest, despite the hardships.

A few years ago, I saw in the *Pentecostal Evangel* one of our "boys" now ministering as a missionary in a foreign country. Only eternity will tell how many of the children to whom we ministered were plucked from a life of crime and drugs. Praise be to God!
—*Philomena M. Trocine*, Reflections of Faith *(1992), 74–75.*

At sixty-seven Frodsham was still spiritually alert to and eager for the moving of God's Spirit. His daughter described him as "a man of intense passion for the supernatural" and "always eager to attend services where people were praying and being brought into vital contact with the Lord." Such a disposition led him to identify with a move that would become known as the New Order of the Latter Rain. At the same time, he was aware of his visibility and identification with the Assemblies of God, which the new move was challenging. In good conscience he could not be identified with both. So on November 5, 1949, after almost thirty years as the editor of the *Pentecostal Evangel*, Stanley Frodsham offered his letter of resignation, which was reluctantly accepted by the executive brethren. Not only did the new movement affect him, it would soon impact the spiritual identity of the Assemblies of God itself (as a later chapter will recount).

RECOMMENDED READING

Burke, Bob and Viola Holder. *The Whole Gospel for the Whole World: The Life of P. C. Nelson.* Oklahoma City, OK: Commonwealth Press, 2008.

Campbell, Faith. *Stanley Frodsham: Prophet with a Pen.* Springfield, Mo.: Gospel Publishing House, 1974.

Evans, William I. "The Standards of the C. B. I." *Pentecostal Evangel* (9 April 1930): 8.

Kendrick, Klaude. "A Pioneer Pentecostal Educator." *Assemblies of God Heritage* 2 (spring 1982): 2, 4.

Lee, Sylvia. "Sunday School Conventions—A Quest for Quality." *Assemblies of God Heritage* 12 (summer 1992): 15–19.

———. "Marcus L. Grable: 'Mr. Sunday School' for the Assemblies of God." *Assemblies of God Heritage* 21 (winter 2001–2002): 4–7, 10–11.

Nelson, P. C. *Autobiography of P. C. Nelson.* Unpublished ms., 1928.

Pearlman, Irene P. *Myer Pearlman and His Friends.* Springfield, Mo.: By the author, 1953.

Spittler, Russell P. "Theological Style Among Pentecostals and Charismatics." In *Doing Theology in Today's World*, edited by John D. Woodbridge and Thomas Edward McComiskey, 291–318. Grand Rapids: Zondervan Publishing House, 1991.

Wilson, Mary Campbell. *The Obedience of Faith: The Story of Rev. Christine A. Gibson, Founder of Zion Bible Institute.* Tulsa: Victory House, 1993.

CHAPTER 15

SPIRITUAL MENTORS

I n Christian history, certain teachers have stood out for their spiritual wisdom. Although some have been teachers in the formal sense of classroom instruction, all have been identified as people of prayer and valued for their insights into the divine dimension of Christian living. They have received respect not because of human selection or their own theoretical knowledge, but on the basis of what they have personally "seen and tasted." In a true sense, they function as theologians, not in the modern academic sense, but as a result of time spent in the school of prayer.

John Wright Follette, an Assemblies of God minister and one of the best-known spiritual teachers in early Pentecostalism, aptly expressed such passion in his poem "Breath of God:"

O Breath of God, I need Thee so!
Apart from Thee I cannot live.
I seek no other life to know
But that which Thou alone canst give.
In me no goodly thing I find,
I sink in utter helplessness.
By Thee I live, O Breath divine—
So full of life and blessedness.
And if the embers of my love
Should smolder in the ashes gray,
And only in my memory
Should burn the love of yesterday,
Come, Holy Breath, and breathe once more
Upon this fainting heart of mine
Until it bursts into a flame
To burn for Thee with love divine.

In Methodism and the broader holiness movement, leaders such as John Wesley, Phoebe Palmer, William E. Boardman, Hannah Whitall Smith, A. B. Simpson, Andrew Murray, as well as the Christian Brethren philanthropist George Müller, inspired the faithful to seek to become more Christlike. Pentecostalism, built in large part on their foundational work, has also produced remarkable spiritual mentors. They have modeled the faith life in one way or another, offered guidance on the ministry of the gifts of the Spirit, and taught believers how to pray and sense the moving of the Holy Spirit in worship. Joseph and Helen Wannenmacher pastored for decades in Milwaukee, but their ministry extended far beyond the city limits. Zelma Argue and Charles S. Price each traveled as evangelists across North America. Robert Cummings served for many years as a missionary to India and as a teacher at Central Bible Institute (CBI). Known for her teachings on the "deeper life," evangelist Hattie Hammond became one of the most prominent speakers in the Pentecostal movement.

Since mentoring in Pentecostal spirituality can hardly be separated from worship in music, Herbert Buffum, the itinerant composer of ten thousand gospel songs, has been included. Finally, the chapter ends with W. I. Evans, the revered dean of Bethel Bible Training School and CBI.

JOSEPH (1895-1989) AND HELEN WANNENMACHER (1890-1985)

At the conclusion of a Sunday morning sermon at First Assembly of God in Elyria, Ohio, in the fall of 1954, Pastor Robert Graber began preparing to serve Communion to the congregation. Because Pentecostals believe the atonement of Christ provides both spiritual and physical healing, they have often prayed for the sick when celebrating the Lord's Supper. Graber then recounted a story of healing that his father-in-law, Joseph P. Wannenmacher, had shared with him.

Wannenmacher had been born into a German Catholic family in Hungary in 1895. As a teenager, the family left for the United States and settled in Milwaukee, Wisconsin. For a time, he worked as an apprentice mechanic and later as a foreman in a tool shop. A diseased foot, two operations, and the remaining possibility of amputation forced him to change professions. A skilled violinist, he began to play in restaurants, theaters, and concert halls to make a living.

Joseph and Helen Wannenmacher

A friend suggested that he seek healing through the assistance of a Christian Science practitioner. But instead of improvement, his condition became worse. Fortunately, he began to read a Bible that someone had given the family. In 1917, the Wannenmacher family learned about a church that preached "Jesus Christ was the living Saviour and the healer of men today—in this present day and age." Visiting the German Pentecostal mission, he responded immediately when the pastor,

Pastoring Elder Bates

It was my joy to pastor Elder Bates in the last years of his life. While he was able to drive, I could always count on him driving his Chrysler Imperial ("the only car worth driving") down to the church to pray over his pastor ("pastah"). He would lay his big hands on my head and call on God for the Holy Ghost anointing on his pastah. He was a very tall and lean man. He liked to refer to his height as 5 feet and 18 inches tall.

His deep concern for the welfare of the ministers of our fellowship prompted him to start Christian Fidelity Insurance Company. He served as the president for many years and the company prospered and blessed many of our Assemblies of God ministers and churches through insurance and church loans.

When physical weakness overcame him and he was hospitalized, he called for me to come and discuss his funeral with him. He had asked me to bring Pete Pulley, one of our ministers and musicians. He gave Brother Pete a chorus he wanted sung. Pete asked what he wanted after that. Elder Bates said, "Pete, if you don't know what to do after you sing that song, just sit down." Then he instructed me with great earnestness: "Don't let them put on a dead funeral for me; I want a celebration! If you don't have a glorious celebration, I will come back and do it myself." The Southwestern Assemblies of God College (now University) Chapel was full and I assured them he meant business about his funeral. He no doubt was proud, for we had a celebration, not a dead funeral.

Over 60 years ago, A.C. Bates started the Southwestern Prayer and Bible Conference, which continues today without a break. Elder Bates was concerned to maintain Pentecostal fervor, worship, and Pentecostal doctrines and practices. This meeting was designed to promote the apostolic and prophetic gifts and ministry that gave birth to the Pentecostal Movement. It continues today to draw a large attendance from across the nine districts that make up the region.

On one occasion, he was preaching in a West Texas town on the courthouse steps when a heckler kept disturbing the meeting. He stopped preaching and asked the crowd to wait a moment for him. Dragging the fella around to the other side of the courthouse, he "whipped the tar" out of him. He then returned and finished his preaching. I asked him about this story once and he just smiled with a measure of delight on his face.

—*James K. Bridges*

Hugo Ulrich, asked: "If there is anyone here who is sick and wishes to be prayed for, come to the front."

"No sooner had I bowed my knees before the Almighty God and His Son Jesus Christ—even before the preacher or anyone else could pray with me," Wannenmacher remembered, "than the power of God fell upon me in mighty dynamic healing streams surging through my entire body." Two weeks after his conversion and healing, he received Holy Spirit baptism.

In 1921, while preparing for ministry at the Zion Faith Homes in Zion City, Illinois, he met and married Helen Innes. Her family had moved there twenty years earlier to sit under the ministry of John Alexander Dowie. Converted while attending a service at one of the Faith Homes, she received Spirit baptism soon afterward. While on her way to another service, God assured her that he had a greater blessing for her. "After it was over I was aware that I still had not received all that He had for me," she remembered. "So while others visited in the vestibule, I quietly knelt down in an inner room by myself. No sooner had my knees touched the floor than the Spirit began flooding my soul with the glory of the Lord. . . . The power of God was so mightily upon me that before I realized it, I was lying prostrate on the floor, with my hands outstretched to heaven and at times shaking mightily under its power." Before long, "such a joy of surrender filled my soul that I began to laugh and weep at the same time. . . . At that moment I began to speak in other tongues as the Spirit gave utterance. For some time I lay praising God in tongues and weeping with tongues of intercession." Innes then ministered in the Faith Homes before helping to pioneer Pentecostal churches in nearby Waukegan, Illinois, and Kenosha, Wisconsin.

How Can We Have a Revival?

When you think that a revival means going out and bringing sinners to the altar, you are wrong. You will never be able to drag sinners to the altar over a bunch of icebergs. Pentecostal people are the best people in the world but all some of them ever do is to warm eighteen inches of a bench, say "Glory" once in a while, and when church is over make a dash for home. God's people need to pray. The doors of the house of prayer need to be repaired. The fire of God needs to be re-kindled. All that defiles must be put away. The saints must fully consecrate themselves. We need to let the Holy Ghost work in us as individuals and as a congregation until the beauty of God's holiness is manifest. Then the outsider will say, "That is what I have wanted all my life; let me get to the altar."

An old-fashioned Holy Ghost revival starts right behind the pulpit, works out into the pews, gets hold of the deacons, Sunday School teachers, and all the church members. All the big I's are erased, and all the little u's are lifted up. Everyone falls on his face, prays through, gets in a good humor with everyone else and gets a new infilling of the Holy Ghost.

—*Aaron A. Wilson, "How Can We Have a Revival?"*
Pentecostal Evangel (September 30, 1939): 1.

Joseph and Helen spent more than sixty years in Milwaukee pastoring Calvary Assembly and planting new churches in the city. (They began their ministry by going door-to-door offering to pray for anyone in the home who might be sick.) Genuinely partners in ministry, their endeavors influenced a broad audience in America and Europe. In addition to her role as copastor, Helen became popular as a retreat speaker and wrote many articles for Bread of Life magazine. Joseph served as the first superintendent of the Hungarian district of the Assemblies of God and also assisted Assemblies of God relief efforts in Central and Eastern Europe. Despite all of these activities, prayer and keen insights into the ministry and gifts of the Holy Spirit marked their ministries.

Graber proceeded to tell the Elyria congregation that on one occasion when Wannenmacher was on his way by train to New York City, he felt led of the Lord to make an unplanned stop in Lorain, Ohio, to visit the home of a Hungarian pastor. A conductor assured him that he could still arrive on time by getting on board another train that would come two hours later.

Arriving by taxi at the parsonage, he found the home filled with relatives who told him that the daughter was gravely ill and near death. "The atmosphere in that house was so filled with unbelief and fear, you could have cut it with a knife," Wannenmacher told his son-in-law. He then announced to the family, "I am on my way from Milwaukee to New York City. While traveling past Toledo, God told me I should stop in Lorain, pray the prayer of faith, and the Lord would heal your daughter." Leaving the unbelieving relatives downstairs, he went up to her bedroom where he found twenty-two-year-old Elizabeth Urban on her deathbed. Surprised to see "Pastor Wannenmacher," she too expressed her belief that she was dying.

While tuning up his violin (he always carried it with him), he told her, "Nonsense, honey. If the Lord never wanted to heal you, He would not have told me about your illness, and would not have asked me to come and pray the prayer of faith." As he played "What a Friend We Have in Jesus," the "room was filled with God's presence, and the power of God touched Elizabeth so that she jumped out of bed with the sheet wrapped around her." Before he could anoint her with oil and pray for her, "she was instantly healed and strengthened. As she came down the steps, the family thought she was out of her mind, but she wanted food." After lunch together, they drove him back to the train station.

When Graber finished telling the story, he stepped out of the pulpit and down to the Communion table. As he did, a woman raised her hand. Since he didn't know her, he was reluctant to let her speak and delay the Communion service any longer. But when a parishioner next to her nodded in approval, he addressed her by saying, "Would you like to say something?"

She replied, "Yes, Pastor Graber. I am Elizabeth Urban. I am the young woman you spoke about. God healed me instantly. I was completely restored to full strength and I have not been sick from that day to this. Shortly after my healing I married, helped my husband pastor, [and] moved to California." Not having been back to Ohio since the healing, she had returned to visit friends from her father's Hungarian congregation and just happened to visit First Assembly in Elyria with the friend who was sitting next to her on that Sunday morning.

Graber, who had no idea that the woman was still alive or that she was sitting in the service, said, "You can imagine the kind of communion we had after that!"

As John Wright Follette said, "In the new creation we are blest with wonderful capacity for the deep things of the Spirit and fuller revelations of God. That is why, after real prayer for a closer walk and fuller knowledge of Him, He begins uncovering, as it were, and digging down into the inner life, to make room and enlarge our powers of apprehension and appreciation. There are potential powers for God waiting to be released and set free."

ZELMA ARGUE
(1900-1980)

"When a meeting seemed locked tight, fasting and secret prayer would bring a break," so wrote Zelma Argue.

Zelma Argue

"Souls are not melted to weeping and groaning in anguish for their sins" unless believers intercede with God in prayer for their conversion. She knew the truth of this from evangelistic campaigns across the United States and Canada. At Topeka, Kansas, when the expected results were slow in coming, she and another female evangelist called the congregation to set aside a day of fasting and prayer. She recalled that "hours were spent in waiting there upon God, and a spirit of victory seemed to come to the praying ones."

At the close of the next service, while the faithful sang invitation choruses for sinners ("Jesus Is Passing This Way" and "What Will Your Answer Be?"), something unusual happened. A woman with both arms raised and crying at the top of her voice made her way forward. Her husband soon followed and also confessed his need of salvation. They were new to the church and had attended only to pacify their seventeen-year-old son, who had repeatedly asked them to accompany him. Argue declared that their conversions had "brought a break in that campaign. . . . Our day of prayer was more than repaid, and the campaign went forward in real victory."

Pentecostal evangelists claimed that successful soul winning required preparation in prayer as well as the ministry of the Holy Spirit. It was far more than an exercise in rational persuasion: The power of the Spirit was expected to break the chains of sin that enslaved people and set them free. Such scenes of conviction and deliverance were not uncommon. (The husband found the next day that the mere thought of his old smoking habit made him sick to his stomach.)

Argue's ministry was intertwined with those of other family members. Her father, Andrew H. Argue, a businessman in Winnipeg, Canada, received the baptism in the Holy Spirit at William H. Durham's North Avenue Mission in Chicago in 1907. This experience led him and his children to become one of the best-known Pentecostal families dedicated to evangelism. In 1920, Argue invited twenty-year-old Zelma to join his evangelistic party. For sixty years, she traveled at different times with her father, her brother, Watson, and her sister, Beulah. Sometimes she traveled alone, but always with her trombone (a favorite instrument among Pentecostal preachers).

Her piety, like that of other Pentecostals, centered on "communing with Jesus, holding a feast with Him . . . , worshiping Him, loving Him, adoring Him, [being] conscious of His presence more strongly than of our surroundings." Life in the Spirit of Christ meant the continual "inflowing and outflowing" of the water of life (John 7:38). As long as the believer had her or his eyes on Jesus, taught Argue, the troubled sea of life would not cause them to sink beneath its waves. And when distractions would come and the breaking point was reached, looking upward in trust, she wrote, "We fall back on Jesus. . . . Our hearts rise in adoration, in worship."

Argue remembered the great meetings of Maria B. Woodworth-Etter. There she heard the "heavenly chorus" in worship and received her "first vital taste of the reality of spiritual things." It is somewhat unclear whether the chorus was the congregation's singing in tongues united with the heavenly choir or miraculously hearing heaven's choir. Nonetheless, she recognized "a beauty, a harmony, beyond that of earth." Watching "Sister Etter" praying, she wondered if she was about to be "translated before our very eyes." Sensing the dynamic presence of the Holy Spirit in worship, Argue expressed the sentiments of other Pentecostals when she said: "The veil between heaven and earth becomes very thin at such times." It is easy to see how she gained a reputation as otherworldly. Be that as it may, she was known as a powerful intercessor.

Women in Missions

Jesus Christ's first coming was revolutionary for all, but especially for women—who were for the most part excluded from Jewish ritual. Baptism was open to everyone, as was the call to share the Good News. The woman at the well was perhaps the first female missionary to bring a town to Christ. The first to be given the mission of spreading the news of the resurrection was a woman. And, on the day of Pentecost—traditionally celebrated only by Jewish males—both men and women received the outpouring of the Holy Spirit. Peter's message from Joel 2:28-29, that "sons and daughters" would prophesy, has since been the anchor for many women in ministry, particularly for those with roots in the holiness movement of the nineteenth century.

—*Barbara Cavaness, "God Calling: Women in Assemblies of God Missions,"*
Pneuma: The Journal of the Society for Pentecostal Studies
(spring 1994): 50–51.

CHARLES S. PRICE
(1887-1947)

"Charles, she is calling for *sinners*," a Presbyterian minister said as he put his hand on the shoulder of Charles S. Price. "She is calling for people who *need to be saved*." Aimee Semple McPherson had said: "I want every man and woman in this audience who will say, 'Sister, I am a sinner and I need Jesus and I want you to pray for me,' to stand to your feet." The one-time law student at Oxford University, lecturer on

Charles S. Price

the Chautauqua circuit, and now the distinguished pastor of First Congregational Church in Lodi, California, Price stood to confess his need of the Savior. His conversion turned out to be a highlight of McPherson's 1921 campaign in San Jose, California.

A native of England, Price had immigrated to Canada in search of his fortune and peace, for he was a restless soul. Sometime after living in British Columbia, he moved to Spokane, Washington. There he visited the Life Line Mission, a Free Methodist ministry. Following this, he entered the Methodist ministry.

Reports eventually reached the mission about the outpouring of the Holy Spirit in Los Angeles. Consequently, he decided to attend a Pentecostal prayer meeting. But on his way, he met a minister who invited him to his home. During their conversation, his host discouraged him from having anything to do with Pentecostals: "Price, I cannot let you go. You will wreck your future—your life. You are young and inexperienced. If you take this step you will regret it as long as you live."

As a result, Price did not go and began to study the writings of "modernist" theologians and to preach on humanitarian concerns. Eventually, his prestige as a preacher grew, and he came to enjoy the benefits of pastoring affluent congregations. So when an excited parishioner at his church in Lodi returned from the McPherson campaign in San Jose, telling him that he had been "saved—saved—through the blood," Price credited the thousands of testimonies of conversion and healing to "mob psychology" and "mental and physical reactions."

Reluctantly, however, he accepted the invitation of a friend to attend. Following his experience at the San Jose service and Spirit baptism, his life and ministry dramatically changed. After briefly traveling with the McPherson party, he started on his own in 1922. He held many meetings across the United States, especially in the Pacific Northwest, as well as in British Columbia. Miraculous healings highlighted his services, and newspapers readily reported such happenings. In 1923, he conducted a particularly successful campaign in Vancouver, British Columbia, where the total attendance at the civic arena reached 250,000 in three weeks. The Vancouver Daily World reported: "People in all walks of life, business men, professional men, laborers and tradesmen were packed elbow to elbow in the boxes and balconies."

From Vancouver, the Price evangelistic party went to Edmonton, Alberta. His preaching and praying for the sick again attracted large crowds. On one occasion, the ice arena that seated twelve thousand was so crowded that "people climbed onto the roof and tried to break their way in. They even smashed windows and then threw money into the arena to pay for the damage they had done." When he tried to rent the building a year later, the city council said it would approve only if Price took out an accident insurance policy that covered everyone who attended.

The Saints Declare

"The seraphs are not sitting up nights measuring God's servants by their salaries."
—A. G. Ward, early Pentecostal leader

"Cook your sermons in the oven of prayer."
—Pentecostal Evangel

"Would it not be better if instead of multiplying organizations we could go back to God's simple, original plan—one soul ablaze for God setting another soul on fire?"
—Alice E. Luce, founder of Latin American Bible Institute (California)

"Whilst on my knees, this Scripture was given, 'Faith without works is dead' (James 2:20b). . . . I was then shown that my work was to obey the word of God to me—whenever it was given, and whatever it required me to do. I got no further light that day, but I rose up with a determination to obey God at any cost."
—Christine A. Gibson, founder of Zion Bible Institute

"Enoch conversed with God. I want to live in constant conversation with God. I am so grateful that from my youth up, God has given me a relish for the Bible. I find the Bible food for my soul. It is strength to the believer. It builds up our character in God. And as we receive with meekness the Word of God, we are being changed by the Spirit from glory to glory. And by this Book comes faith, for faith cometh by hearing, and hearing by the Word of God."
—Smith Wigglesworth, evangelist

"We can be absolutely certain that if we speak as the oracles of God, as we are directed to, He will not let any of our words fall to the ground, but will confirm them with signs following, setting the seal of Heaven on our utterances."
—Lilian B. Yeomans, M.D., evangelist

At a later campaign in Winnipeg, the *Winnipeg Free Press* reported that over eight thousand jammed the city auditorium on the last night to hear the evangelist. Price later recalled, "What the paper did not know was that I had to climb in through the kitchen window to get into the building, for the crowd was so great at the door that I could not make my way through the throng." It was not uncommon for one hundred to four hundred people to kneel at the altar during a single service. As he continued in itinerant evangelism, he often had to construct wooden tabernacles to hold the crowds in smaller communities; he thus contributed to Pentecostal church growth in the Pacific Northwest.

Besides being a prolific writer, turning out many books, Price also edited the periodical *Golden Grain*. Although he never held credentials with the Assemblies of God, the faithful held his ministry and spiritual writings in high esteem. His most influential book may have been *The Real Faith*, first published in 1944. In this book, written near the end of his life, he shared his frustration over the vast numbers of people who left his services not healed. "I have gone home with the faces of poor supplicating people haunting me," he wrote. "I have seen them do their best to rise from the wheel chair, only to sink back again in sorrow and disappointment. I have been moved by the groans, cries, and intercessions around altars, until they have lingered with me for days after the services were over."

In the unsuccessful quest for healing, most healing evangelists pointed to the failure of the seeker. Price's contemporary Fred F. Bosworth wrote the popular *Christ the Healer* in 1924. Entitled "Why Some Fail to Receive Healing From Christ," the last chapter listed twenty-two reasons, ranging from ignorance about the healing power of Christ, to unbelief, to demon possession, to poor stewardship of one's body, to unconfessed sin. When all is considered, according to Bosworth, the seeker is at fault since God never intends for his children to experience physical suffering. Not surprisingly, the meaning of *faith* in the Pentecostal tradition has been problematic, leaving the saints with gripping questions about the promise of divine healing in the atonement of Christ: Is there any purpose in suffering? Why doesn't God heal everyone? What accounts for people dying, even those of great faith?

In attempting to answer the question of why God doesn't heal everyone, Price took a more positive stance than Bosworth. He suggested that the problem centers on the difference that many believers make between "faith" and "belief": "To believe in healing is one thing; but to have faith *for* it is altogether something else." Accordingly, "that is why so many needy people, who believe, come to the Lord on the basis of His promises in the Word and *try* and *try* and *try* to affirm that they are healed." Here lies the difficulty: faith has been made a condition of the mind.

"Real faith," however, is a gift from God himself, "a divinely imparted grace of the heart. . . . Whenever and wherever this *faith* is in operation," he declared, "we shall no longer be standing around poor, sick folk hour after hour, rebuking, commanding, demanding, struggling, and pleading as in the days of yore. There may be a place for intercession, but it is not in the exercise of faith. . . . The full realization—that it was not our ability to believe that made the sickness go, but rather that the faith which is of God was imparted—will steal over our soul, like a morning daybreak, to bid the night shadows flee away."

Price initially brought comfort to the seeker by saying that human strivings for the needed gift of faith will not bring healing. Although he struck a delicate balance between human effort and divine grace, he only partially resolved the dilemma.

ROBERT W. CUMMINGS
(1892-1972)

Director of a missionary language school in British India (he had studied twelve languages himself), having master's degrees in theology and oriental missions, a Presbyterian army chaplain in World War I, Robert (Bob) W. Cummings was an unlikely candidate for missionary appointment with the Assemblies of God. Yet his spiritual journey, complicated by mental illness, changed his life and the lives of many others.

The son and grandson of Presbyte-rian missionaries to India, Cummings and his wife, Mildred ("Mid"), began their first term of service in India, the land of his birth, in 1920. He went there with "many modernistic leanings," but soon realized his lack of spiritual power. While seeking for the baptism in the Holy Spirit, he also came to a new understanding of Calvary. As a result, he made a complete surrender to God: "My whole being seemed to be so purged of sin and selfishness that for four or five months there seemed to be nothing in me that could respond to temptation." In 1925, both he and Mid were baptized in the Spirit and led others into the same experience.

Robert and Mildred Cummings

Cummings became interested in the meaning of Christ's agony in the Garden of Gethsemane. This was prompted in part by Muslim objections that Christ had appeared unwilling to do the will of God because he had prayed, "'Father, if thou be willing, remove this cup from me: nevertheless not my will, but thine, be done'" (Luke 22:42, KJV). (The name of the Muslim faith, Islam, means "submission" [to God's will].) How then could Jesus Christ be divine and bring atonement for the sins of humankind? Cummings grappled for answers, but found none that did justice to the biblical record. He struggled to understand why Christ initially recoiled from the will of His Father: "What did that cup contain to make the Strong Son of God shrink from it in sorrow and amazement and horror?" This led him to pray, "God, . . . give me an understanding of the agony in the garden, and of the cross, so that I might be able to answer the questions of the inquirers."

The doctors said overwork caused his physical and mental breakdown in 1932, which required him to leave India. To this could be added the toll on his health taken by malaria. Without doubting the truthfulness of these explanations, he also knew "that God allowed me to pass through a nervous breakdown, and immediately after delivering me, illuminated my mind to picture and understand something of our Lord's experiences in the garden, and their bearing on the nature of redemption's victory."

Like John of the Cross, a sixteenth-century mystic, Cummings began to experience the descent into the "dark night of the soul." For the first three months, he seemed to lose all willpower and "became the prey of the most terribly vile and blasphemous evil powers. . . . Horrible and obscene suggestions and imaginations poured in an unceasing flood through my consciousness." Sleep became impossible without medication. Finally, "I felt as though I had been dragged through the sewers of hell." All of the joys he had experienced in the Holy Spirit had now left him.

His worst fears were soon realized: The devil seemed to ask him, "Do you think, after the Lord has filled you once, and now that I have trapped you and flooded your soul with all this evil, that the Lord could ever cleanse you and take you back again?" Reluctantly, he agreed, believing that he had committed the unpardonable sin; all hope had vanished. In the words of John of the Cross, "The soul feels itself to be so impure and miserable that it believes God to be against it, and thinks that it has set itself up against God . . . that God has cast it away."

After two years of suffering, which included time spent in New York mental hospitals, Cummings began to listen and internalize the Scripture promise pressed on him by several friends: "I will never leave thee, nor forsake thee" (Hebrews 13:5). For the first time in two years, on October 4, 1934, he fell to his knees and began to pray: "'Lord,' I said, 'I am ashamed even to get into an attitude of prayer. I have been so resentful. My mind and heart and being have been so filled with things which must be more repulsive to Thee than they are to me. I know now that there is no hope for me. I don't believe you could ever take me back. But, Lord, I wonder if I could be wrong? You see in what terrible darkness and hopelessness every moment of my experience is spent. Lord, if there is anything you can do for me, won't you do it? I would pray if I could, but I can't pray. There are no words to describe what I feel. Anyway, I don't even feel. My heart is like a lump of stone.'"

He remembered that deep in his consciousness "a chorus began to sing." It was line 2 of the song "In Jesus" that suddenly became illuminated with meaning. Written by James Procter, a former atheist who became a Christian, it reads:

> My soul is night, my heart is steel;
> I cannot see, I cannot feel;
> For light, for life, I must appeal
> In simple faith to Jesus.

Then, "as the last word sang itself out in the silence of my heart, I knew HE stood with me. He gathered me in His arms and brought me into a place of nearness that I had never known before. His precious blood cleansed away all the stain and sin, all the feeling of evil, all the effect of that terrible experience. . . . The fetters snapped and I was free. O the unspeakable joy of that deliverance!"

Sometime later, while staying in New York City, Cummings rose early one morning. "While I was praying," he recalled, "it seemed as though God took me by the hand into the garden of His agony, and showed me His Son there. My mind was astonished at what I saw. The Son of God appeared to be crushed. It seemed that He could not stand the horror of the thing that confronted Him." Asking God what could have been in the cup that nearly overwhelmed Jesus, the Lord replied, "Do you not remember the terror through which you passed during the first months of your nervous breakdown? Do you not remember calling out, 'O God, it is impossible for me to endure another moment of this awful horror'? I was allowing you to taste a little, a very little, of the cup that My Son drank to its dregs, the cup of the world's iniquity and sin."

In the early 1940s the Cummingses became affiliated with the Assemblies of God and were invited to join the CBI faculty, Bob as director of missions and Mid as an instructor in English and Hindi.

For the rest of his life and ministry, Cummings shared his insights into Christ's sufferings in Gethsemane. Along with his uncommon discernment in the operation of the gifts of the Spirit in worship, his message of Christ as the sin-bearer for the redemption of lost humanity left a deep imprint on many Pentecostals, especially his students.

HATTIE HAMMOND
(1907-1994)

While Hattie Hammond was speaking at a Deeper Life convention in Indianapolis, a minister on the platform stood to his feet, raised his hands, and with tears rolling down his face, cried out: "O God, curse everything within me that will not yield to you!" Not only were many people converted in her services, but thousands went away inspired to completely consecrate themselves to Christ.

"Ultimately we shall be brought into the immediate presence of God," she said. "But how precious is the foretaste now, when we can enter in behind the veil into the presence of God, there to live, there to move, and there to abide—living in the heavenlies with God, with the Lord Jesus Christ." Pentecostals

Hattie Hammond

flocked to hear Hammond preach as she traveled across the country from her home in Maryland.

Ordained in 1927 at age twenty, her ministry lasted an incredible sixty-seven years. Though healed of typhoid fever as a young girl, she had struggled spiritually as a teenager until she visited a tent revival sponsored by Bethel Assembly of God in Hagerstown, Maryland. While sitting on the back row, she heard the pastor from the front of the tent praying, "Ooooh God, Ooooh God."

"Every time he would say [this,] it would go through every part of my being. It just seemed to feed me somehow, bring something to me. And I said, 'That's what I want, whatever that man has, that's what I want.'" Observing her interest, the visiting evangelist, John J. Ashcroft, went and sat beside her and prayed with her. Her conversion and Spirit baptism at that meeting changed her life. She began to witness to her friends and, at age sixteen, she dedicated her life to full-time ministry.

Ashcroft and his wife began to mentor Hammond and invited her to accompany them to Martinsburg, West Virginia, where he was scheduled to preach. By Pentecostal standards, the services seemed dry and without demonstration of the power of God. Finally, before a Saturday evening service, he invited her to preach. While the congregation sang, Hammond desperately prayed to receive a message from the Lord. He "dropped into her heart" the verse, "O foolish Galatians, who hath bewitched you, that ye should not obey the truth [?]" (Galatians 3:1, KJV).

Stepping to the pulpit, she quoted the verse, paused momentarily, and then quoted it again. Without being able to launch into a sermon, she looked at the congregation and said, "Friends, if you get nothing else from this service tonight except the word of God, I want you to get the Word of God, so I am going to read this again."

After the third reading, a backslidden woman cried out, "O God, have mercy on me!" The woman went forward for prayer; her repentance brought a revival that lasted for several months.

While still in her twenties, Hammond became one of the best-known spiritual mentors in the Pentecostal movement. She eventually spoke in churches of many denominations, camp meetings, Bible institutes, Deeper Life conventions in North America, and more than thirty countries overseas. In Oakland, California, she told an audience that there were seven in her evangelistic party: "Father, Jesus, Angel of the Lord, Holy Spirit, Goodness, Mercy, and Self!"

HERBERT BUFFUM
(1879-1939)

His songs were sung by Nazarenes, Baptists, Methodists, Presbyterians, and Pentecostals, among others. Upon his death, the *Los Angeles Times* called him "The King of Gospel Song Writers," saying that "what Stephen Foster did for American folklore, Herbert Buffum did for its homely religious sentiments; he expressed it in simple musical strains that all could understand." Although many people having a variety of gifts have enriched Pentecostal spirituality, music has always been central.

Indeed, while others refused the use of musical instruments in their services in an attempt to restore the New Testament church (e.g., the noninstrumental Churches of Christ), Pentecostal congregations became noted for orchestras and skilled musicians.

No one denomination can claim Herbert Buffum. Both Herbert and Lillie had Methodist backgrounds and identified variously with the Nazarenes, Volunteers of America, and the Church of God in Christ. Herbert never joined the Assemblies of God, but Lillie did. Yet his was a familiar name from the many songbooks that carried his more than one

Herbert Buffum

thousand published compositions. Always on the move—every five weeks for many years—the Buffums sang and preached across the country in churches, camp meetings, and skid row missions. By 1918, their diaries revealed that ten thousand people had come to Christ in their services.

Among Buffum's many songs were "Lift Me Up Above the Shadows," written after the death of his mother; "I'm Going Thro', Jesus," when he had doubts about

Demon-Inspired Music

Arthur Rodzinski, conductor of the New York Philharmonic Orchestra, has made this statement: "The style of boogie-woogie which appeals to hep cats is the greatest cause of delinquency among American youth today."

Why is this? It is because there is a strong demon influence, without a doubt, behind modern jazz and the jitterbug frenzy which it produces. Musicians have traced its origin to the drum-beating, dancing demon worshipers of pagan jungles. An authority declares that to achieve the height of jazz perfection the player must be in a trance in which he wanders off into a world of his own. Anyone with spiritual discernment can sense the demonic power behind it when he hears some of this swing "music" come over the radio, and it is little wonder that young people who listen to it by the hour drift into all kinds of sin.

— *"Demon-Inspired Music,"* Pentecostal Evangel *(May 27, 1944): 12.*

continuing in the ministry; and the popular "I'm Going Higher," after seeing an airplane overhead (an uncommon sight in 1923). This last song became popular in youth services. The song leader would sometimes have the audience sing the chorus of the song seated, then standing, and finally mounted on their chairs (on outings, they might stand on picnic tables).

Buffum's compositions touched the chords of joy and sorrow in the Christian life and often reminded believers of their heavenly hope. In many ways, he shaped early twentieth-century evangelical and Pentecostal worship patterns. He had no formal training in music; nevertheless, his self-instruction and unusual ability enabled him to learn virtually any keyboard or stringed instrument.

With enormous powers of concentration, Buffum could write songs (music and lyrics) during church services, in hotel lobbies, on trains, and in train stations, even while his four children climbed all over him. According to his daughter Lois, only one thing could throw off his concentration: singing another song. If no piano was available, Buffum would improvise on a table or another piece of furniture and tap out the song. He would even invite congregations to get into the act. First, he would have them suggest song titles. Writing the suggestions on a chalkboard, he would then have them vote on their top choice. Finally, he would compose a matching song on the spot.

In Huntington Beach, California, an eleven-year-old girl suggested the title "When I Take My Vacation in Heaven." Although the congregation didn't choose this one, Buffum was intrigued by it. By the next morning, he had composed the song. Although he usually sold the rights to a song for five dollars—just enough for food and basic expenses—he sold this one for one hundred dollars; it became immensely popular, moving into the secular market.

The life and ministry of Herbert Buffum epitomizes the church's troubadour, those who itinerated with the gospel in song. Their melodies and choruses not only enriched worship, they also influenced day-to-day life, leaving a lyric in the heart that enabled the believer to maintain a walk of faith. Their legacy of music blessed generations of people in all walks of life in congregations around the world.

WILLIAM I. EVANS
(1887-1954)

"We looked to him as a champion of our movement in the things of the Spirit and of the old paths of Pentecost," wrote Milton T. Wells on behalf of the faculty of Eastern Bible Institute in Green Lane, Pennsylvania, after hearing of the death of "W. I." Evans. "One of his greatest joys in the eternal world will be to see the stamp of the Spirit which under God he left upon so many thousands of lives either directly or indirectly." Few have had a greater formative influence on the Pentecostal spirituality of Assemblies of God ministers than "Brother Evans."

Born in Philadelphia, Pennsylvania, to devout Methodist parents, he came to Christ at age eleven while kneeling at his mother's knee in the kitchen of their home.

After his conversion, however, he became attracted to the Christian and Missionary Alliance. Called to the ministry, Evans enrolled at A. B. Simpson's Missionary Training Institute in Nyack, New York, in 1906. The next year at the Alliance's convention in Nyack, he and many others were baptized in the Spirit and spoke in tongues.

Like other Alliance Pentecostals who remained, he went on with his ministry of preaching. While pastoring in Richmond, Virginia, he also studied for three years at the University of Richmond. During this time, he met his wife, Hilda Mae Lindberg; they were married in 1914. In the same year, he left the Alliance due to its rejection of the doctrine of tongues as initial evidence. After pastoring the Ossining (New York) Gospel Assembly, he moved to Newark,

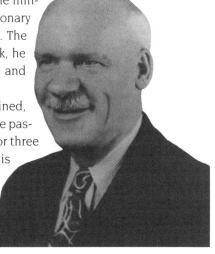

William I. Evans

New Jersey, where he joined the faculty of Bethel Bible Training School. Although the board of the independent Bethel Pentecostal Assembly in Newark sponsored the school, many of its faculty members and students were members of the Assemblies of God. Evans served as principal in the last years of the school's existence (1923–1929).

Had I But One Hour to Live

What in all the realm of life is worthy of attention except the personal constant presence of the Lord Jesus Christ! Only those things which contribute vitally toward seeking Him and discovering new beauties in Him are worth- while. If in this fleeting ephemeral day called life, we can reach Him in a mighty grasp of faith that brings Him intimately near and makes Him supremely real, we have wrung from earthly walking the only thing worthy of attention.

To apprehend Him in faith's close grip, to be apprehended by Him in love's strong grasp, to be constrained then in the embrace of His mighty anointing, urged by an unquenchable zeal, to rescue others from the night and present them complete in God's salvation, this is the sum of life below.

The heart cries for adjustment to God and His will with a passion that blinds the eyes to all human standards and to every admirable achievement or apparent success of our brethren. Nothing short of Christ Himself becomes the pattern, nothing less than all the fullness of God, abiding, pulsating, motivating, accomplishing, can stay the longing or still the crying. The soul chafes at every earthly bond and, awakened to a strength hitherto unrealized, presses out in quest of [the most intense] reality and highest, holiest, satisfying achievement.

—W. I. Evans, "Had I But One Hour to Live," Pentecostal Evangel (April 26, 1941): 5.

Your Questions

Will the little children of unsaved parents go to heaven when they die?

We believe that children who die before they reach an age of moral consciousness will be saved. We will be judged for our own sins, not for the sins of our parents. "So then every one of us shall give account of himself to God" (Romans 14:12).

What is meant by 1 Corinthians 15:50—"Flesh and blood cannot inherit the kingdom of God"?

It means that, in our present natural state, we cannot inherit the kingdom. We will be given spiritual bodies in place of our present bodies which are material.

When Jesus comes and catches us away, will we leave our clothing as Jesus left His when He rose from the dead? Is it scriptural to sing, "This robe of flesh I'll drop and rise"?

I think it is in harmony with scripture to sing, "This robe of flesh I'll drop and rise." The meaning is that we will no longer be robed in a mortal and corruptible body, but we will be robed with a glorified body. This does not refer to clothing.

Will Old Testament believers be caught away with the Church when Jesus comes?

I believe so, for does not the Church (the "called-out ones") include faithful believers of all the ages? Abraham "looked for a city that hath foundations." God will not disappoint him. We are told that Abraham, Isaac, and Jacob will be seen in the Kingdom (Matthew 8:11). On the gates of the New Jerusalem will be the names of the twelve tribes of Israel (Revelation 21:12-13). I expect the entire Church of Old Testament and New Testament believers will be included in the Rapture. What a great family reunion that will be!

The question and answer column for readers of *Today's Pentecostal Evangel* first appeared in the January 1, 1916 issue of the *Weekly Evangel*, during a time of doctrinal strife in the Assemblies of God over the correct understanding of the Godhead. Questions had to be sincere ("not for controversy"), brief, and about religious matters "that can be answered from the Bible and History." Inquirers were told specifically not to ask for the interpretation of dreams and visions since "we do not have the gift to interpret these."

E. N. Bell provided the answers until his death in 1923; Gospel Publishing House then made them available in book form as *Questions and Answers*. E. S. Williams later wrote the columns and his "Your Questions" appeared in 1968. Years later, the column resurfaced with Stanley Horton as the writer. It has been a popular means of providing spiritual advice for believers.

When Bethel "merged" with CBI (that is, the Evans and Ralph M. Riggs families moved to Springfield), he continued his training of Spirit-filled young people. Evans is remembered for his life of prayer and keen insight into the moving of the Spirit, including the operation of the Spirit's gifts in worship.

One of his favorite illustrations, which he shared with freshmen, referred to a trip he had taken through Kansas. He had observed that the "wheat stalks yielded even to the slightest moving of the air. To him, this was a picture of what should be true in a Christian's life. It should be yielded to God, and so sensitive to Him, that the slightest movement of the Spirit would be obeyed." Evans himself modeled this life in the Spirit.

His daily schedule began early with extended prayer, Bible study, and meditation. Next, he went to his office to pray with the faculty before the chapel service. He was always there thirty minutes ahead of his colleagues and never looked up as they came into the room. However, he sensed that the spiritual atmosphere intensified as the number increased: "As each digit is added, the power is multiplied."

Prepared now for the morning chapel, the faculty and Dean Evans took their seats on the platform. In leading the service, he encouraged times of prayer and "waiting before the Lord." When revival came, he kept things moving in the right direction by urging the students to "hold steady." One student said this "brought many a service of victory and blessing." Hence, when problems arose, he was able to keep the Spirit from being "quenched" (1 Thessalonians 5:19, KJV). Evans also understood the meaning of "the joy of the Lord." There were times of Pentecostal blessing when he would begin to "laugh in the Spirit." Students recalled how the chapel reverberated with his hearty laugh.

For W. I. Evans, affectionately known as "Pop" Evans, holiness and spirituality went hand in hand. Those who claim Spirit baptism but haven't submitted their wills and ambitions to Christ will never have "a Holy Ghost ministry."

"You may have a spurt here and there," he wrote, "like the shooting off of a firecracker, or the detonating of a skyrocket, but it will fizzle out and come down with a thud. Holy Ghost ministry is by Christ's Lordship.

RECOMMENDED READING

Argue, Zelma. *Contending for the Faith*. 2d rev. ed. Winnipeg: Messenger of God Publishing House, 1928.

————. *Garments of Strength*. Springfield, Mo.: Gospel Publishing House, 1935.

Blumhofer, Edith L. "Life on Faith Lines: Early Homes and Early Pentecostal Values." Parts 1 and 2. *Assemblies of God Heritage* 10 (summer 1990): 10–12, 22; 10 (fall 1990): 5–7, 21–22.

Craig, Marion. Prepared by God: Robert Cummings. Springfield, Mo.: Foreign Missions Department, n.d.

Cummings, Robert W. *Gethsemane*. Springfield, Mo.: By the author, 1944.

————. *Unto You Is the Promise*. Springfield, Mo.: Gospel Publishing House, n.d.

Enloe, Tim. "Dr. Charles S. Price: His Life, Ministry and Influence." *Assemblies of God Heritage* 28 (2008): 4–13.

Evans, Paul A. *Letters from "Pop" Evans.* Springfield, Mo.: Central Bible College Alumni Association, 1973.

Evans, W. I. *This River Must Flow!* Springfield, Mo.: Gospel Publishing House, 1954.

Follette, John Wright. *Arrows of Truth.* Springfield, Mo.: Gospel Publishing House, 1969.

Gohr, Glenn. "Two Pioneers of Pentecost in Milwaukee: Joseph and Helen Wannenmacher." *Assemblies of God Heritage* 9 (spring 1989): 11–12, 20.

Hammond, Hattie. "Christ Bringing Us to God." *Pentecostal Evangel* (24 April 1937): 2–3.

Price, Charles S. *The Real Faith.* 1940. Reprint, Plainfield, N.J.: Logos International, 1972.

———. *The Story of My Life.* Pasadena, Calif.: By the author, 1935.

Shearer, Sheryl. "Zelma E. Argue: Handmaiden of the Lord." *Assemblies of God Heritage* 22 (spring 2002): 18–23.

St. John of the Cross. *Dark Night of the Soul.* New York: Doubleday, 1990.

Warner, Wayne E. "Herbert Buffum: The King of Gospel Song Writers." *Assemblies of God Heritage* 6 (fall 1986): 11–14, 16.

UNIT FOUR
1948-1968

TIME LINE 1948-1968

1948—"New Order" of the Latter Rain begins; State of Israel established in Palestine. Healing movement begins to impact Pentecostalism at home and abroad through the ministries of evangelists like William Branham, Oral Roberts, Clifton Erickson, T. L. Osborn, and Kathryn Kuhlman.

1949—Wesley R. Steelberg succeeds E. S. Williams as general superintendent. New printing plant built on Boonville Avenue in Springfield. Boys and Girls Missionary Crusade (BGMC) begins. Council approves AG as charter member in the Pentecostal Fellowship of North America (PFNA).

1951—Women's Missionary Council (now Women's Ministries) recognized. Radio Department report tells of broadcast renamed *Revivaltime* and lengthened to 30 minutes.

1953—Ralph Riggs elected general superintendent. Approval given for Evangel College (1954), a new headquarters administration building (1961), and *Revivaltime* (1953) to go on ABC Radio Network (with C. M. Ward as speaker). Report given that Men's Fellowship (now Honor Bound) was established in 1952.

1955—Missionettes program launched.

1956—Music Department established.

1957—GPH publishes Melodies of Praise songbook.

1959—San Antonio council names new officers: Thomas F. Zimmerman, general superintendent; Bartlett Peterson, general secretary; J. Philip Hogan, executive director of foreign missions. Missions department introduces Global Conquest program.

1960—Dennis Bennett announces to his Episcopal congregation in Van Nuys, California that he has been baptized in the Holy Spirit and has spoken in tongues.

Zimmerman becomes first Pentecostal to serve as president of the National Association of Evangelicals.

1961—Light for the Lost founded. Council meets in Portland, Oregon.

1962—Johnnie Barnes begins working to create Royal Rangers program for boys.

1963—Mobilization and Placement Service (MAPS) started.

1964—J. W. Tucker and other missionaries martyred in the Congo.

1965—Advance magazine for ministers and leaders introduced. Disaster Relief established.

1966—Ambassadors in Mission (AIM) begun by the national Youth Department.

1967—Executive Presbytery appoints fifteen-member Committee on Advance to conduct a self-study of the AG. International Correspondence Institute (later Global University) founded.

1968—Council on Evangelism meets in St. Louis, Missouri. Assassination of Martin Luther King, Jr. Growing conflict in America over Vietnam War.

CHAPTER 16

TESTING AND GROWTH

Nearly a half-century after the Topeka revival, many Pentecostals began to wonder if the "fire" of the Movement had gone out. For insiders, any perceived slackening of spiritual fervor, any apparent reliance on the natural instead of the supernatural, and any absence of spiritual gifts spelled disaster. Some predicted that the Holy Spirit would do even greater things than had been seen before. "This revival we have had is nothing to what God is yet going to do," prophesied Smith Wigglesworth.[1] The Canadian Pentecostal pioneer R. E. McAlister predicted that the "coming great revival" would be characterized by divine healing.[2]

Speakers at Assemblies of God Bible institutes, conventions, and local churches exhorted the faithful to seek for demonstrations of God's power. Harold Horton, a prominent British Assemblies of God teacher and author, shared this sentiment with the students at Central Bible Institute (CBI) in 1948: "The Lord has brought us into this supernatural experience," he avowed. "Indeed, our only excuse for existing as a separate movement is that we believe in the supernatural."[3]

A year later at the General Council meeting in Seattle, the national youth director and keynoter Wesley R. Steelberg preached on "Our Place in the Supernatural Line": "I believe that the young people of our Pentecostal fellowship, having heard the testimonies of the fathers, having listened eagerly to the accounts of the yesterdays that are past, are rising to cry with new fervency, . . . 'Give us a double portion of the Spirit . . . that it may rest upon us, and that we may go forth in the courage, in the faith, in the determination, in the spirit of sacrifice that our fathers have manifested for us.'"[4] Steelberg captured the longing of the younger generation to experience the same measure of power that the first generation had experienced. Indeed, this has been the heart cry of every generation of Pentecostals.

Sermons at General Councils and reports from churches published in the *Pentecostal Evangel* in the years immediately following World War II not only reveal intense longing for revival, but remarkable spiritual and evangelistic vitality in the grassroots. At the same Council where Steelberg preached, the *Evangel* reported that "God manifested His presence in every service. There were prophecies, messages in tongues, and interpretation of tongues in nearly every meeting as the Holy Spirit moved upon the congregation."[5]

Other evidences of spiritual zeal included increased student enrollments and candidates for missionary service. Ralph Riggs informed delegates at the 1949 Council gathering that "out of 14,000 returned servicemen attending theological schools in the U.S.A., 1,050 were studying at Assemblies of God Bible schools!"[6]

Nevertheless, since the level of revival fervor and the frequency of manifestations of the gifts of the Spirit in church services varied across the Assemblies of God and other Pentecostal denominations, a perception grew that the Movement had become a shadow of its former self. In addition, some Pentecostals were attracted to the notion that the offices of apostle and prophet (Ephesians 4:11) had yet to be restored. This would then complete the return of apostolic Christianity, free from the shackles of humanly conceived church structures.

"In the beginning of 'Pentecost' we were deathly afraid of 'denominationalism,'" wrote A. W. Rasmussen, "and we never failed to lift up our voice and proclaim that we were . . . a movement. How is it today? Pentecost is divided up into many camps of denominationalism. It has gone the way of every preceding Spiritual revival."[7] Certainly the Pentecostal movement, and the Assemblies of God in particular, had changed in important respects by midcentury; it had become more comfortable with American culture and benefited from shedding its factional image for alliance with evangelicals. Threatened by new trends, Rasmussen and other leaders of the new revival movement, the New Order of the Latter Rain, sharply condemned what appeared to them as spiritual compromise.

J. Roswell Flower on the Latter Rain

With the passing of the first phase of the latter-day outpouring of the Holy Spirit, a new generation was born within the ranks of the Pentecostal Movement. To this new generation, the truths proclaimed and the experiences received did not appeal as the "latter rain" as much as to the spiritually hungry who had first received. The message of the baptism in the Holy Ghost, in its second phase, was appealing to an entirely different class of people. Consequently, the term "latter rain" fell into more or less disuse. It is not surprising, therefore, that a revival of emphasis with the use of the term should result in a new acceptance of the truth of the dispensational outpouring of the Holy Spirit as the "latter rain." This does not change the fact, however, that we have been in the time of the (spiritual) "latter rain" since the turn of the century, and the conviction received in the beginning has been confirmed again and again that we are now in the end of the last days, in the time of the harvest, and that the coming of our Lord is rapidly drawing nigh.

Let us guard our heritage with all diligence, praying with all prayer and supplication in the Spirit, that the purpose of God in this great Pentecostal fellowship shall not be frustrated or destroyed.

—J. Roswell Flower, "The Early and the Latter Rain," Pentecostal Evangel (June 11, 1949): 5–6.

To the majority of Pentecostals, however, the Movement had matured, despite the ongoing need for more revival. T. H. Spence, for one, worked to prevent stagnation during these years. Elected the Alabama district superintendent in 1948 while still an evangelist, he served a twenty-five-year tenure that saw the district grow from 175 to 313 churches. In these years he also served on the board of South-Eastern Bible College (later Southeastern College) in Lakeland, Florida, and supported the school as it prepared ministers for the rapidly growing southern districts.

T. H. Spence

Obviously, the power of Pentecost was alive and well. Pastor Gordon Kampfer of Eugene, Oregon, wrote to the *Evangel* about a recent ten-week meeting at his church with evangelist Velmer Gardner: "It was a time of visitation from God, a season of ingathering of precious souls. Over 170 sought salvation. . . . About 50 were baptized with the Holy Ghost according to Acts 2:4." Moreover, "the power of the Lord was present to heal, and as faith reached out to the Lord during the Divine Healing services, many were instantly healed of afflictions, such as deafness, arthritis, asthma, tumors, and so forth."[8] From Hawaii, District Secretary Alfred Morrison announced, "We have just experienced the greatest thing any of us has ever seen, and something exceedingly above that which we dared to expect here in Hawaii—a sweeping revival."[9]

In the southeast, District Superintendent R. C. "Keetah" Jones rejoiced about the moving of the Spirit in his churches: "It seems that everyone in Georgia has had the vision to fast, pray, preach, and let God work." Reflecting the widely held concern for spiritual balance, he added, "A spirit of prayer and consecration has come into our hearts; . . . worship is deeper and more sincere. Our people definitely desire something in a service other than just a song, a shout, and a sermon."[10]

Finally, many accounts of local revivals tell the same story of the saints being revived. When "Sister Floyd Reeves" of Shamrock, Texas, held a revival in Midwest City, Oklahoma, "fourteen were saved, seven filled with the Holy Ghost, and the entire church was moved toward God."[11]

Yet more than other organizations, the General Council of the Assemblies of God suffered the criticisms of those who were convinced of its having strayed from the Pentecostal path. Beginning with the crisis of the New Order in 1948 to the reassessment of its world mission in 1968, the Assemblies of God faced new challenges. During this twenty-one-year period—and indeed to the present day—it has sought how best to balance its uniquely Pentecostal and evangelical identity.

THE NEW ORDER OF THE LATTER RAIN

The number of Pentecostals involved in the New Order of the Latter Rain was never large. Still, the long-range influence of the movement far exceeded its actual size. At least four factors triggered its reactionary stance. First, membership of the

Leaders of the New Order of the Latter Rain in the "Cloud Room" at the Sharon Orphanage and Schools: (l to r) Ern Hawtin, Percy Hunt, George Hawtin, and George Warnock

Assemblies of God and several other Pentecostal bodies in the National Association of Evangelicals brought with it newfound respectability. For those who had championed their otherworldly status as God's "peculiar people" (1 Peter 2:9, KJV)—believers whose lives and ministries more closely resembled the apostolic ideal than other Christians—this could only mean compromise.

Second, new programs and the growing size of the church constituency naturally brought more policies and regulations. The increasing numbers of staff members at the district and General Council levels were quite obvious. The missions program required more officers (for example, the appointment of field secretaries over geographical regions) and more effective fund-raising techniques. This too earned criticism. For example, in 1950, one missionary resigned from the Council in protest of administrative red tape. Martha Schoonmaker wrote to the field leadership, "We are so highly organized now . . . that if God were to lead an individual to go to a certain place for evangelistic work, he or she would have to first of all consult with three committees. . . . As a missionary of the Lord Jesus, I want to be allowed to be led by His Spirit and do whatever He may want me to do."[12]

Third, along with the new evangelical connections and growing size of denominational operations, improvement in the quality and length of ministerial training became a priority. When the possibility of starting a national liberal arts college in Iowa temporarily surfaced, one pioneer grumbled that it had originated "with certain ones in Springfield, who want to compare favorably with other denominations in high education."[13] In 1945, the General Council called for CBI (now Central Bible College) to "provide a Full Theological Seminary Course" in addition to its other programs.[14]

This would be of particular value to those preparing as hospital, institutional, and military chaplains or Bible college teachers. Nonetheless, to many the notion of a seminary—an institution usually ridiculed by Pentecostals as a "cemetery"—seemed to indicate that students would rely more on reason than on faith and the guidance of the Holy Spirit.

Four years later, after the General Council in session voted to allow CBI to apply for membership in the Accrediting Association of Bible Colleges and offer academic degrees, heated discussion followed over the idea that a degree might become necessary for ordination. To appease such protest, a resolution passed that the Council would forever oppose the idea of demanding academic degrees for ordination.[15]

Fourth, several of the most important Pentecostal evangelists died in the 1940s: Aimee Semple McPherson (1944), Charles S. Price (1947), and Smith Wigglesworth (1947). Their passing heightened fears that the glory and power of Pentecostalism had waned, the days of "signs and wonders" had passed. Who would "stand in the gap" (Ezekiel 22:30, KJV) and take their place?

The "New Order" began with a revival at the Sharon Orphanage and Schools in North Battleford, Saskatchewan, Canada. Believers there claimed in February 1948 that the "latter rain" had begun to fall once again in fulfillment of Joel's prophecy. They also believed the present-day Church should have in operation the New Testament offices of apostles and prophets. In this way, they championed an open-ended

The Most Serious Implication of the New Order

The most serious aspect of the "new order Latter Rain Movement" in our opinion is the assumption that God is NOW setting in the body of Christ the members thereof, through the ministry of the laying on of hands and prophecy: that He is, through this means, confirming the ministry gifts of first apostles, secondarily prophets, thirdly teachers, etc. The ordination of our ministers through the laying on of hands of the Presbytery is discounted by these brethren, that is, discounted if it was not accompanied by the prophetic gift designating to what ministry the minister has been called and with prophetic confirmation of the gifts with which he is endowed. It has been stated repeatedly that God is now doing something new and this is a new spiritual body being formed. The members of the body are being confirmed in their gifts, so that many members of the local church are receiving the gifts of healings, miracles, prophecy, casting out of demons, etc., etc. Then, when these ministries are needed in the church, the members of the body who have received these gifts are called forward to minister for the particular need.

It was stated to us that there should be an apostle and prophet present for the ministry of laying on of hands. The apostle and prophet have, of course, been confirmed as such by the laying on of hands of other apostle and prophets, tracing back to the brethren of North Battleford, [Saskatchewan] where the movement started....

—*From a letter from the Executive Office of the General Council of the Assemblies of God (April 20, 1949).*

view of the Spirit's gifts and workings, one not chained to denominational—and what appeared to many to be even biblical—restraints.[16]

At the Assemblies of God National Sunday School Convention in Springfield in 1949, news circulated that the "end-time Revival has started" in Canada and Detroit, Michigan. Former CBI student Bill Britton asked one of the speakers who had just been to Detroit, "I hear there is a new thing going on, and Revival breaking out. Show it to me in the Bible; where is it in the scriptures?" He then concluded, "There it was . . . all through the Bible. Scripture after scripture testifying to the truths of the One Body of Christ and the sin of denominationalism, the ministry of Apostles and Prophets in the Church today, the gifts of the Holy Spirit in the members of the church, imparted by the laying on of hands with prophecy. It was there! Why hadn't they seen it before? It was time for Revival."[17]

North Battleford became a magnet for those seeking revival. From there the movement quickly spread to Portland, Oregon; Los Angeles; Detroit; Memphis; St. Louis; Beaumont, Texas; Lima, New York; and even Springfield, Missouri. Controversy brewed over actions that Assemblies of God leaders considered contrary to scriptural teaching: Erroneous views included the impartation of the spiritual gifts through the laying on of hands, restoration of apostles and prophets as part of local church leadership, personal prophecies of guidance given to individuals, and expectancy of the Spirit's dispensing languages for missionary evangelism.

"The 'new order' Latter Rain Movement in reality is giving us nothing that is new in spite of the claims of its advocates," wrote General Superintendent Ernest S. Williams.[18] For Williams and his colleagues, Latter Rain practices pointed backward to

problems that had once vexed the stability, unity, and spiritual integrity of the Pentecostal movement. Neither could the proper interpretation of Scripture justify the teachings of the new movement.

Opinions on the revival's genuineness varied. The new teachings and the (at times harsh) reactions and counter-reactions revealed a growing gap between establishment Pentecostals and grassroots Pentecostals in some quarters. Although believers in the Latter Rain differed in their teachings to some extent, the General Council listed abuses in the movement and condemned them all in 1949.[19]

Myrtle Beall founded the Bethesda Missionary Temple in Detroit, Michigan, a church that soon became a center for the Latter Rain movement and attracted thousands of visitors. Beall and the congregation left the Assemblies of God in 1949.

Latter Rain leaders cried foul. Like the historic churches' condemnations of earlier Pentecostals, so now the Assemblies of God had denounced fellow Pentecostals.

Nevertheless, the movement had created serious problems and divisions in local congregations in some areas that could not be ignored. North Dakota Superintendent Robert L. Brandt told district ministers, "[We] Pentecostal people should be prudent, but often there are those among us who are victims of rank deception. Today there is an alarming increase in the number of men who prey upon our people and get by with it because they set themselves forth as great spiritual leaders."[20] Pastors who refused to accept the new teachings felt the sting of being told they were unspiritual and were preventing their flocks from receiving the blessings of the latest outpouring of the Spirit.[21]

But in the minds of Council leaders—most of them first-generation Pentecostals—such new teachings would only hinder spiritual growth and evangelism, not enhance them. In a special edition of the Quarterly Letter to the clergy of the Assemblies of God, Williams said, "The true test of any movement is whether or not it will stand up under the light of the Word of God." Just as the 1916 Council had judged Oneness teachings about the Godhead "not on the testimony of spiritual blessing, but on its adherence to the Scriptures," so the present Council would do the same regarding the New Order of the Latter Rain; the Council still stood for sound doctrine.[22]

THE HEALING MOVEMENT

Parallel to the New Order of the Latter Rain and in some respects influenced by it, renewed interest in divine healing led to a dynamic new surge in healing ministries. It began in 1947 and peaked in 1958. Well-known healing evangelists included William Branham, Oral Roberts, Jack Coe, T. L. Osborn, Kathryn Kuhlman, and A. A. Allen. A native of Zion City, Illinois, Gordon Lindsay publicized their campaigns in the (independent) *Voice of Healing* magazine, published in Dallas, Texas. Issues also highlighted testimonies. In many ways, the healing movement focused on evangelism in the Pentecostal tradition: preaching, praying for the sick, and expecting signs and wonders. Lindsay summed up the vigor of the new movement in the title of his book *Bible Days Are Here Again* (1949).

Before long, however, healing evangelists became swirled in controversy. At times, their methods provoked debate. For example, Branham exercised the "word of knowledge" (1 Corinthians 12:8, KJV) in diagnosing people's illnesses and announcing their healings—an unusual phenomenon among Pentecostals at the time. Jack Coe sometimes handled people roughly when praying for them in healing lines (which Smith Wigglesworth had also done). Others, however, avoided such tactics. Regardless of the approaches, thousands testified to healings and conversions.

By 1958, the movement had crested. Its momentum had been slowed by the questionable lifestyles of some evangelists, unusual methods and claims, and the competition and saturation of healing evangelists on the sawdust trail. In addition, nagging questions never received the answers they deserved: Why weren't more people healed? Does God allow Christians to suffer?

In a blunt challenge to what he considered as misguided beliefs and practices, Donald Gee contended that "gifts of healing and of working of miracles have their true sphere in evangelism rather than among the saints. . . . Miracles of healing are signs to follow them that believe as they preach the gospel to every creature." Furthermore,

Dixie's Healing

The summer before my daughter Dixie started to Kindergarten she...had a severe case of Whooping Cough. Dixie seemed to [get] worse...she would have spasms and struggle for her breath. The Doctor told us this had damaged her ears. We didn't realize this until one day her teacher called me in for a conference. She had detected a hearing loss; Dixie didn't respond to instructions but did better if she was on the front row.

I took her to the Doctor; her hearing chart and test revealed she had 80% hearing loss. Our pastor's wife told me she had attended a Revival in Riverside. The Evangelist [Oral Roberts] gave teaching and instructions on healing in the afternoon classes. Our Faith was increased, but we did not realize we had to fill out a card in order to be called to the platform for prayer.

That night the Evangelist announced he was only praying for people who had some need for their five senses. How thrilled I was, for we had a need, but we didn't have a card filled out. I prayed, "Lord you know this is the only day we can be here, do help us." I was overjoyed to hear the Evangelist say he felt such an urge to pray for people who didn't have a card—if they had a hearing loss. Praise the Lord! So Dixie and I joined the long line that was making their way to the platform. After the Evangelist had laid his hands on Dixie she left the platform saying, "I can hear...I can hear!"

I took Dixie back to the Doctor, another hearing chart was made, and this time it revealed she only had a 20% hearing loss, almost on the normal line. The Doctor read the chart and nearly jumped out of his chair as he compared it with the last chart. He said he didn't know what had happened to Dixie, but she had certainly had a big improvement.

[Dixie] went through school with flying colors and won an award in High School for outstanding scholarship for which we praise the LORD. To God be the GLORY.

—*Dixie's mother Elsie M. Bonds Stockton, California (c. 1948)*

"all who have had experience with great evangelistic and Divine healing campaigns will have noted that the majority of outstanding miracles of healing occur upon those attracted for the first time: and not upon faithful members of churches, and 'chronic' cases among Christians."[23]

The faithful often tried to find a middle course between the claims of the evangelists and the cautions of Gee. This dilemma arose at a time when Americans, including Pentecostal Christians, were becoming enamored with the advances of medical science. It is not without significance that America's foremost healing evangelist, Oral Roberts, would later build the City of Faith Hospital in Tulsa, Oklahoma, to emphasize both the spiritual and medicinal aspects of healing.

Evangelists frequently held healing campaigns overseas, some of which had long-lasting effects on the growth of Assemblies of God constituencies. T. L. Osborn preached in open-air services to tens of thousands and prayed for the sick in countries around the world.[24] In Chile in 1951, thousands attended the meetings of evangelist Clifton Erickson. Hundreds were converted and testified to healings of various ailments. Significant church growth followed.[25] Along with Lester F. Sumrall, he held another noteworthy campaign in Manila, the Philippines, two years later.

A spectacular crusade with evangelist Tommy Hicks took place in Buenos Aires, Argentina, in 1954. Reports of dramatic healings drove the revival, leading to ever-larger crowds. Attendance totaled nearly two million during the two months of services. Thousands of conversions impacted both Pentecostal and evangelical churches and led to a major breakthrough for Protestantism. Conservative Baptist missiologist Arno Enns noted a sharp increase in church membership among evangelicals and Pentecostals —especially in the Assemblies of God. "An intangible but nonetheless solid result of the campaign was a new spirit of faith and spiritual optimism which pervaded the entire Evangelical community," he added. "Humble and fearful Christians were made aware of their latent potential which could be released in saving power through the exercise of faith. Among the population in general, the prestige and appreciation of the Evangelical Churches increased noticeably."[26]

Although some campaigns resulted in church growth, problems arose in the early 1950s. They centered on the financial policies of certain evangelists, spectacular and questionable claims, and promotion of direct support to sympathetic national pastors and evangelists. Placing such workers on the payrolls of American evangelists appeared to flout the process of making national churches self-supporting, self-governing, and self-propagating. However, others, such as Gordon Lindsay (Native Church Crusade) and T. L. Osborn (Association for Native Evangelism), made positive contributions by offering equipment, building materials, and financial resources to foster the growth of indigenous churches.

With the heightened emphasis on healing, mission leaders openly wondered if gospel proclamation had become secondary to praying for the sick. "In numbers of instances healings that have been reported have not been

Evangelist Tommy Hicks (l) with missionaries Lillian and Louie Stokes on the platform at Hicks's evangelistic campaign in Buenos Aires in 1954. In addition to occupying the 45,000 seats in Huracan Stadium (top), other thousands stood in the aisles to hear Hicks preach and see him pray for the sick.

lasting and the number of souls actually saved and added to the church in such meetings has frequently been quite small in comparison with the magnitude of the meeting," wrote Noel Perkin to the district missionary secretaries. "The adverse reaction in the thinking of many who crowd to these meetings for healing when disappointed in their hopes is impossible to calculate. . . . Our commission is to preach the gospel. It is the Lord's work to confirm the Word with signs following."[27]

THE BLESSINGS OF PROSPERITY

As the nation's economy boomed in the years after World War II, church members experienced economic and social lift. New church buildings regularly graced the covers of the *Pentecostal Evangel* throughout the 1950s and 1960s. The saints were moving out of their storefronts, tents, and old theater houses, places not architecturally designed for worship. They could now afford to erect brand-new buildings having large sanctuaries, choir lofts, offices, Sunday School rooms, and—with some controversy—kitchens. They often constructed all or much of the buildings themselves and sacrificed financially to make it happen.

No longer just confronting the prevailing culture with the gospel, they now began seeking to transform it with Christian values. Southern California Bible College (later Vanguard University of Southern California) led the way in 1939 by offering

Congregation and building of Gospel Tabernacle, La Grande, Oregon

the first four-year program with degree-granting status. Along with ministerial programs, it added arts and science majors and training for public schoolteachers. Irvine J. Harrison, a later president of the school, completed the first academic-level history of the Assemblies of God as a doctoral dissertation in 1954.

With the encouragement of Ralph M. Riggs, the general superintendent (1953–1959), the General Council established Evangel College (later Evangel University) in Springfield, Missouri, as a national college of arts and sciences in 1955. It has the distinction of being the first Pentecostal liberal arts college chartered in America. Vanguard and Evangel received regional accreditation (the highest available) in 1964 and 1965, respectively, an accomplishment that many conservative evangelical colleges had only just begun to realize.

In the same period, most Assemblies of God Bible institutes changed their names to colleges and began to broaden their curricular offerings to include students who were preparing to enter vocations other than ministry. Even the Arkansas district's short-lived South Central Bible College provided a junior college program for those seeking a liberal arts education.[28]

Comfortableness with the culture also led to the decline of some holiness taboos: women started cutting and curling their hair and wearing makeup and jewelry. The younger generation began to participate in sports events and other forms of leisure. Televisions could now be found in Pentecostal homes. When urgent requests were issued for the financial needs of the growing cadre of foreign missionaries, the faithful increased their giving. At the same time, however, they spent more money on themselves, evident by the cars they purchased, the homes they built, and the neighborhoods they chose to live in.

Pentecostals also entered the professions. Formerly congregations were made up of working-class people; now lawyers, doctors, educators, and business leaders gradually found their place in the pew. With other evangelicals in the postwar period, they began working to bring Christian values into the marketplace for the improvement of society. Examples include Arnold Cheyney, a public school administrator from Canton, Ohio, who earned a PhD in education from Ohio State University and later served as professor of education at the University of Miami and wrote curricular

Strongly and Relentlessly Opposed . . .

Question: What is the attitude of the Church toward liquor, tobacco, dancing and cosmetics?

Riggs: With that array which you've given us, . . . we are strongly and relentlessly opposed. We are deeply convinced these things are inherently evil. One of the chief evils of America at the present time is liquor. Tobacco we don't hesitate to include in the taboos, for that, also, is thoroughly detrimental to the human body. Dancing, too, is under condemnation as far as we are concerned.

Question: And cosmetics?

Flower: There's been a frowning on cosmetics, generally, over the Movement. But there may be people who are slipping over a little bit into that realm. Some of our preachers are preaching against it very strongly.

Riggs: Nine-tenths of our preachers are opposed to cosmetics, and the other ten per cent is silent.

Lewis: It's felt that cosmetics are associated with many other things that one might term to be distinctly wrong.

Riggs: We have membership cards on which a person who has joined the Church declares that he will not use liquor, or tobacco, or engage in dancing. That's mentioned as well as the sins of the world. However, that list does not include cosmetics, or jewelry, or short hair. But, in a general way, those things do come under condemnation.

From an interview of Ralph M. Riggs, general superintendent;
J. Roswell Flower, general secretary; and
Gayle F. Lewis, an assistant general superintendent
—*Irwin Winehouse,* The Assemblies of God: A Popular Survey *(1959), 84–85.*

Pulitzer Prize-winning cartoonist
Vaughn Shoemaker

materials. The Pulitzer Prize–winning cartoonist Vaughn Shoemaker worked to shape public opinion through his political cartoons in the *Chicago Daily News*.[29] Kansas businessman and millionaire Henry Kraus, as well as California farmer and business entrepreneur Bryan S. Smith, took their faith to the workplace and gave generously to their churches, Assemblies of God schools, and missions. Although not a layman, J. Roswell Flower served for eight years on the city council of Springfield, Missouri, at a crucial juncture in the city's history.

THE CHANGING OF THE GUARD

Like Ernest Williams, the general superintendents who succeeded him—Gayle Lewis and Ralph Riggs—were first-generation Pentecostals, or as in the case of Wesley Steelberg, an early second-generation Pentecostal. That would change within a decade. Steelberg served only briefly (1949–1952) before an untimely death from a heart attack. A man of boundless energy, he had become known as the "boy preacher" at age sixteen and, just three years later, received ordination in 1919. Pioneering churches took him from Arizona to Los Angeles and to Stockton, California. While in Stockton, he spearheaded the "Pentecostal Ambassadors for Christ" program for young people in the Northern California and Nevada district. It became so popular that the General Council decided to establish a national program known as Christ's Ambassadors for the denomination's youth.

A pastorate in Philadelphia then catapulted him to the office of superintendent of the Eastern district, followed by his move to Springfield as an assistant general superintendent. He then succeeded Williams as general superintendent. Despite growing problems with his heart, he ignored the advice of doctors and friends and refused to slow his pace. After Steelberg's funeral, a eulogy in the *Evangel* stated: "He displayed a rare combination of faithfulness to the old paths of the Pentecostal movement and aggressiveness to meet the challenge of the days in which he lived. His daring faith to push ahead and risk all for God was tempered by sincere humility and dependence on God."[30]

To fill his unexpired term, the General Presbytery chose Gayle F. Lewis, a former Central district superintendent who had served as one of the four assistant general superintendents since 1945. At the General Council meeting in Milwaukee in 1953, the delegates elected Ralph M. Riggs, the longest serving assistant general superintendent, to the post of general superintendent.

Riggs had attended the organizational meeting at Hot Springs in 1914 and studied both at R. B. Chisholm's Nashoba Bible School in Mississippi and Rochester (New York) Bible Training School. As a missionary, he worked in South Africa under the auspices of the Pentecostal Mission in South and Central Africa and later taught at its Bethel Bible Training School in Newark, New Jersey. In 1929, he and his family moved to Springfield where he taught at CBI. He then pastored Central Assembly—for many years considered the "headquarters church"—during a time of unprecedented growth. In 1943, he succeeded Fred Vogler as assistant superintendent.

When he became general superintendent, he brought to the office the insights of a first-generation Pentecostal, a missionary, a pastor, and a Sunday School enthusiast. While a church executive, Gospel Publishing House published several books that he authored, including *The Spirit-Filled Pastor's Guide* (1948) and *We Believe* (1954). His most enduring work came with *The Spirit Himself* (1949), designed to provide instruction on Pentecostal distinctives to ministers and laypersons alike.

When he took office, the Assemblies of God was still feeling the effects of the Latter Rain controversy, as well as those of the troublesome healing movement. Despite the popularity

Ralph M. Riggs

of new programs, many still wondered if organization and education were weakening the Council's spiritual vigor. One rather humorous story illustrates the fear of change: When concern prompted one minister to ask if the Council was pulling away from its roots, Riggs reassured him that "Sister Riggs and I are 'holding the line' in Springfield."

Anxiety over change, however, led in part to Riggs's being voted out of office in 1959. At the Council in San Antonio, Texas, two other first-generation Pentecostals retired from office: J. Roswell Flower (general secretary) and Noel Perkin (director of foreign missions). The Council elected Thomas F. Zimmerman as general superintendent and J. Philip Hogan as executive director of Foreign Missions. Two unusually strong leaders, they were second generation, nevertheless. They had reached the pinnacle of leadership in the Assemblies of God before fifty years of age. Their leadership styles, administrative policies, and visions for church planting and missions would dominate the national scene of the Council for the next three decades.

MOBILIZING THE SAINTS

The Assemblies of God became adept at implementing new programs to include virtually everyone in a congregation. Women's Missionary Councils (WMC) in local churches thrived with the initiative, becoming a national department in 1951. Local chapters served in many ways. Paul and Kathern Carlstrom pioneered Calvary Temple Church for the Deaf in Seattle, Washington. In 1964, its WMC chapter began to support the ministry of missionary Betty Haney, who worked among the sixty thousand deaf in South Korea. In two months time, the women "made 50 toys and cleaned, mended, packed, and shipped 279 pounds of clothing." They also sent financial support to missionary Wayne Shaneyfelt in the Philippines, who worked with the deaf in that country.[31]

WMC chapters were also popular in the Hispanic districts. One of the best-known leaders, Frances Figueroa, WMC director for the Latin American district, traveled widely in promoting the program in the United States and Latin America. "I rode a burro all day long through some steep trails in the mountains, and worst of all, without a saddle," she remembered about visiting churches in the Mexican state of Veracruz. "I fell off of the burro twice and crossed one particular river 28 times. I thought I wouldn't make it back." WMC leaders like Figueroa displayed strong commitment to assisting in the Church's worldwide mission.

The Men's Fellowship Department gained recognition in 1951. Charitable ministries also grew beyond the Hillcrest Children's Home to include Highlands Child Placement Services and Maternity Home in Kansas City, Missouri, as well as the Aged Ministers Assistance program and efforts to provide relief to disaster victims.

Having discovered that the growth rate of converts, new churches, and ordinations had slowed in the 1950s and 1960s, leaders called for intensified spiritual activity in the ranks. (The Hispanic districts, however, continued to grow at a fast pace.) The General Presbytery approved the formation of a committee in 1962 to study the problem, make recommendations, and review the work of the Department of Evangelism.

Several significant changes had occurred: the number of women pastors had sharply declined as well as that of men and women evangelists traveling throughout the constituency. Even so, numerous husband and wife evangelistic teams still crisscrossed the country. In a career that spanned over fifty years, Paul—"Cowboy Smiley"—and Myrtle Hild traveled about two million miles, conducting more than twelve thousand services while visiting 870 cities. Their ministry focused on children—"Kids Crusades."[32] Child (preteen) evangelists like Little David Walker, Uldine Utley, Mary Louise Paige, Charles Jaynes, and Dolores Lee Dudley, also traveled widely, preaching in their own evangelistic campaigns and on occasion baptizing new converts.[33]

Cowboy Smiley in kids' parade

The gravity of one major change, however, eluded the committee's notice: the waning of single-women evangelists on the sawdust trail. More than one thousand women, both single and married, had served as evangelists in the Assemblies of God before 1950. Women like Blanche Brittain—known as the "sod buster" for having planted over forty churches—had largely passed off the scene. G. Raymond Carlson, a native of the state and later general superintendent, said of her, "The name of Blanche Brittain is synonymous with the Assemblies of God in North Dakota. She pioneered many churches. . . . From these churches a goodly number of converts [including Carlson] became pastors, evangelists, and missionaries."[34] The contributions of well-known women like Brittain and

Anna Lock, as well as lesser-known figures like Naomi Blaylock, Pauline Sawyer, and Norma Elliott became invisible to the next generation.

When the General Council met in 1963 to hear the report and recommendations, the committee affirmed that "prior to any Pentecostal organization, God indicated that evangelism is the whole work of the whole church, and Holy-Ghost-filled people [are] the evangelistic agency of God. True spirituality and evangelism are inseparable."[35] Furthermore, the great achievement of the Day of Pentecost was not speaking in tongues, but the three thousand people who became believers. Therefore, financial gains or new buildings could not measure advancement. "Success in the spiritual realm is determined by the souls set free from the power of Satan."[36]

In response to the committee's report, the Council resolved to make evangelism the top priority for every department at the headquarters and assigned this responsibility to the general superintendent. Two years later, the Council abolished the Department of Evangelism and replaced it with the Spiritual Life–Evangelism Commission. Two initiatives became especially popular and have made significant contributions to home and foreign missions: Mobilization and Placement Service (MAPS) and Ambassadors in Mission (AIM).

The larger of the two programs, MAPS had actually begun in 1964 and was designed "to ascertain areas of need and opportunity in the United States for . . . individuals who can assist districts, churches, and institutions on a short term, temporary, or permanent basis."[37] In addition, it provided opportunities overseas for short-term missions work (two years or less).

This new door of ministry for laypersons in the Assemblies of God afforded college students, retirees, business and professional people, teachers, technicians, office workers, and other adults opportunities to work in home missions, including Native American ministries, literature and media ministries, and building construction. Foreign missions opportunities embraced, among others, office work, media ministries, printing and publications, and construction. Specifically, MAPS hoped to maximize the participation of the laity "in ministry and evangelism, church planting, and strengthening existing congregations."[38]

In 1968, MAPS workers began the pilot project: a new church building on Grand Bahama Island in the West Indies. Missionary Robert E. Ferguson, "construction missionary" Gordon Weden, and MAPS representative Norman L. Correll directed the operation. Volunteers—working as carpenters, electricians, plumbers, painters, and laborers—paid their own expenses.[39] With this successful effort, lay and professional talents were joined, becoming a premier achievement of the Assemblies of God.

Evangelist Jimmy McClellan, seen here at age 16, spent a total of 53 years in the ministry as an evangelist, church builder, and presbyter in the South Texas district.

The call for intensified spiritual and evangelistic vitality in the ranks also prompted two new publications. *Advance* (later replaced by *Enrichment Journal*) functioned to serve ministers with promotional materials and information on denominational programs. In addition, the Council launched *Paraclete*, a journal containing articles and book reviews focusing exclusively on the person and work of the Holy Spirit.

COUNCIL ON EVANGELISM

The need for an in-depth self-study of the General Council and its headquarters operation led the Executive Presbytery in 1967 to set up the Committee on Advance. Its assignment was to analyze reasons for the downturn in growth and develop a five-year plan of advance. As part of the study, a specially called Council on Evangelism met on August 26–29, 1968, in St. Louis, Missouri, to articulate the world mission of the Assemblies of God. It attracted some seven thousand ministers and laypersons.

In the keynote address, "The Mission of the Church," Thomas F. Zimmerman charged them to fulfill the threefold task of the church: ministry to the Lord, to other believers, and to the world. The last point placed heavy emphasis on winning the lost to Christ. Although he lauded the heritage of the Assemblies of God, Zimmerman counseled, "Let us never get the idea that God has brought us to our present plateau to terminate progress—His command is, 'Go *forward*.'"[40]

At the conclusion of the meeting, the Council issued the "Declaration of St. Louis," representing the work of the Committee on Advance. Noting that the Assemblies of God was brought into being by the Spirit "as an instrument of divine purpose in these end times," it stated (1) God's purposes for humankind, (2) the triune mission of the Church, and (3) the importance of strongly encouraging believers to be baptized in the Holy Spirit. Only Spirit baptism would enable them to evangelize accompanied by supernatural signs as in the Book of Acts, worship in the fullness of the Spirit, and respond to the "full working" of the Spirit in building the body of Christ.[41]

To those in attendance, compromise on the last point could only weaken spiritual energy; Spirit baptism as an entry to the deeper work of the Spirit had to remain a cardinal teaching if revival and evangelization were to happen. Although Donald Gee had died two years earlier, those present would have shared his sentiments: "To surrender [baptism in the Spirit] would be to surrender a sacred trust from the Most High and renounce a testimony of great value even to those who reject it. The Pentecostal revival performs its true function within the whole Body of Christ while it keeps unimpaired its own distinctive testimony. The Church needs a Pentecostal revival."[42] The Council, therefore, appealed to its spiritual heritage as the key to fulfilling its divine calling.

Although the papers read at the Council on Evangelism were published in *Our Mission in Today's World* (1968), they basically restated priorities in place since 1914. In Cyril Homer's address, "The Ministry of the Church to the World," he voiced the opinions of Anglo-Pentecostals, conservative evangelicals, and fundamentalists alike in regard to the Church's involvement in society: "The great danger of this church

Council on Evangelism (1968) Declaration at St. Louis

Recognizing the end times in which we live and the evident hand of God which has rested upon the Assemblies of God for these times, and having engaged together in prayerful study in this Council on Evangelism concerning God's purpose in the world today and our place in His purpose, we make the following declaration.

Because the Assemblies of God came into being as the Holy Spirit was poured out in prophetic fulfillment at the turn of the century and a body of like-minded Pentecostal believers voluntarily joined together in worship, ministry, and service; and

Because the Assemblies of God has accepted the Bible as the inerrant Word of God and has declared it as the whole counsel of God, giving emphasis to the full gospel; and

Because the Assemblies of God has grown rapidly both at home and abroad and has continued to experience the blessing of God as it has sought to do His will and to be an instrument of divine purpose; and

Because the Assemblies of God determines to remain a body of believers responding fully to the divine working in these last days; therefore, be it

Declared, That the Assemblies of God considers it was brought into being and built by the working of the Holy Spirit as an instrument of divine purpose in these end times; and be it

Declared further, That the Assemblies of God recognizes God's purposes concerning man are:

1. To reveal Himself through Christ to seek and to save that which was lost,
2. To be worshiped in spirit and in truth.
3. To build a body of believers in the image of His Son; and be it

Declared further, That the Assemblies of God recognizes that its mission is:

1. To be an agency of God for evangelizing the world,
2. To be a corporate body in which man may worship God,
3. To be a channel of God's purpose to build a body of saints being perfected in the image of His Son; and be it

Declared further, That the Assemblies of God exists expressly to give continuing emphasis to this mission in the New Testament apostolic pattern by encouraging believers to be baptized in the Holy Spirit, which enables them:

1. To evangelize in the power of the Holy Spirit with accompanying supernatural signs,
2. To worship God in the fullness of the Spirit,
3. To respond to the full working of the Holy Spirit in expressing His fruit and gifts as in New Testament times, edifying the body of Christ and perfecting the saints for the work of the ministry.

—*Richard Champion, et al., eds.,* Our Mission in Today's World: Council on Evangelism Official Papers and Reports *(1968), 212.*

generation," he insisted, "is that it can become so busy with the social and material-istic problems it neglects the one great work committed to it."

For the largely white and upwardly mobile constituency of the Assemblies of God, nothing more needed to be said about church and society. After all, Homer noted, "a man's soul is infinitely more important than his body. It is a simple fact that once a man's soul is in right relationship with God, divine provision is made for body, soul, and spirit."[43]

At the same time the Council met, however, America's major cities were seething with racial discontent; in fact, some were burning. The great leader of the civil rights movement in America, Dr. Martin Luther King, Jr., had been shot dead that spring. The Vietnam War, then at its height, was ripping through the fabric of American society. In 1965, the General Council had passed a resolution favoring civil rights and condemning any kind of discrimination. Yet no agency within the denomination was added to work toward those ends. White Pentecostals rarely became involved in any prophetic witness against the injustices of the prevailing culture (e.g., racism, poverty).[44] Twenty-five years would pass before white and black Pentecostals themselves would begin the painful process of repentance and reconciliation.

A respected longtime pastor and educator in the General Council, Cyril Homer served in many capacities including the presidencies of South-Eastern Bible College and North Central Bible College.

Despite such shortcomings, the Council on Evangelism had successfully clarified the mission of the Assemblies of God. It assured the faithful that the denomination had remained committed to its original vision of evangelizing the world in the last days. Kansas District Superintendent Paul Lowenberg summed it up best in his evening address entitled "The Mandate of the Church": "The end is in sight. We must redouble our efforts; we must renew our consecration; we must revive our zeal; we must hasten the return of our Lord. Every sign points to His soon coming," he charged the delegates. [45]

From the crisis over the Latter Rain to the Council on Evangelism, major challenges confronted the Assemblies of God. Committed to using all possible means to win the world for Christ, new and more effective programs were started. Council leaders also cooperated with the various agencies of the National Association of Evangelicals, including the National Sunday School Association, Evangelical Foreign Missions Association (present-day Evangelical Fellowship of Mission Agencies), National Religious Broadcasters, and Accrediting Association of Bible Colleges.

After World War II, the living standard of the faithful improved. As this took place, questions arose about the role of the Christian in society, the meaning of holiness, and the very nature of Pentecostal spirituality itself.

The U.N., America, and Armageddon

According to the present trend of events it is apparent that we shall see a further step taken beyond that of the United Nations . . . to that of a WORLD GOVERNMENT. That which has made America great—yes, the greatest nation under the whole heavens—is the fact that she was wrapped in the swaddling clothes of Eternal Truth, based upon the Word of Almighty God, and her faith in the Lord Jesus Christ as the Savior of mankind. . . . America may be far away from the path of righteousness, and there is great room for improvement in her religious life, but one thing can be said to her everlasting credit—she is not Anti-God. If the plans for One World Government succeed, Christianity will take its place alongside that of the religions of heathen nations.

That we are nearing the great battle of Armageddon there can be very little doubt.

—*D. P. Holloway, "Russia and Armageddon,"*
Pentecostal Evangel *(June 4, 1949): 5.*

RECOMMENDED READING

Champion, Richard, Edward S. Caldwell, and Gary Leggett, eds. Our Mission in Today's World: Council on Evangelism Official Papers and Reports. Springfield, Mo.: Gospel Publishing House, 1968.

Cheyney, Arnold B. People of Purpose: 80 People Who Have Made a Difference. Glenview, Ill.: Good Year Books, 1998.

Gee, Donald. Trophimus I Left Sick: Our Problems of Divine Healing. London: Elim Publishing House, 1952.

God's Plowman: The Story of Henry Krause. Los Angeles: Full Gospel Business Men's Fellowship International, 1966.

Harrell, David Edwin, Jr. All Things Are Possible: The Healing and Charismatic Revivals in Modern America. Bloomington, Ind.: Indiana University Press, 1975.

Harrison, Irving John. "A History of the Assemblies of God." Th.D. diss., Berkeley Baptist Divinity School, 1954.

Lindsay, Gordon. God's 20th Century Barnabas. Dallas: Christ for the Nations Institute, n.d.

Riss, Richard M. Latter Rain: The Latter Rain Movement of 1948 and the Mid-Twentieth Century Evangelical Awakening. Mississauga, Ontario: Honeycomb Visual Productions, 1987.

Robeck, Cecil M., Jr. "The Assemblies of God and Ecumenical Cooperation: 1920–1965." In Pentecostalism in Context: Essays in Honor of William W. Menzies, edited by Wonsuk Ma and Robert P. Menzies, 107–150. Sheffield, U.K.: Sheffield Academic Press, 1997.

Rodgers, Darrin. "The Assemblies of God and the Long Journey toward Racial Reconciliation." Assemblies of God Heritage 28 (2008): 50–61.

Warner, Wayne E. Kathryn Kuhlman: The Woman Behind the Miracles. Ann Arbor, Mich.: Servant Publications, 1993.

Weaver, C. Douglas. The Healer-Prophet, William Marrion Branham: A Study of the Prophetic in American Pentecostalism. Macon, Ga.: Mercer University Press, 1987.

ENDNOTES

[1] Smith Wigglesworth quoted in Stanley H. Frodsham, "The Coming Revival," Pentecostal Evangel (13 November 1948): 4.

2 Ibid.

3 Harold Horton, "Miracles and Ministry," *Pentecostal Evangel* (17 July 1948): 2.

4 Wesley R. Steelberg, "Our Place in the Supernatural Line," *Pentecostal Evangel* (8 October 1949): 3.

5 "Diary of a Delegate," *Pentecostal Evangel* (15 October 1949): 8.

6 "Diary of a Delegate," *Pentecostal Evangel* (1 October 1949): 2.

7 A. W. Rasmussen, "Scriptural or Unscriptural Church Order," *Sharon Star* (1 February 1948): 1.

8 Untitled news note, *Pentecostal Evangel* (17 July 1948): 14.

9 Alfred J. Morrison, "Hawaiian Revival," *Pentecostal Evangel* (22 October 1949): 8.

10 R. C. "Keetah" Jones quoted in Edgar R. Lee, *Our Golden Heritage: Georgia District of the Assemblies of God* (Macon, Ga.: Georgia District of the Assemblies of God, 1984), 8.

11 Untitled news note, *Pentecostal Evangel* (22 October 1949): 14.

12 Letter from Martha Schoonmaker to Maynard L. Ketcham and Members of the Executive Committee, 29 July 1950.

13 Eugene N. Hastie, *History of the West Central District Council of the Assemblies of God* (Fort Dodge, Ia.: Walterick Printing Co., 1948), 203.

14 General Council Minutes, 1945, 25.

15 General Council Minutes, 1949, 30.

16 Richard M. Riss, *Latter Rain: The Latter Rain Movement of 1948 and the Mid-Twentieth Century Evangelical Awakening* (Mississauga, Ont.: Honeycomb Visual Productions, 1987), 95–96.

17 Bill Britton, *Prophet on Wheels: The Life Story of Bill Britton* (Shippensburg, Pa.: Destiny Image Publishers, 1987), 19.

18 Ernest S. Williams, *Quarterly Letter* (20 April 1949), 3.

19 Edith L. Blumhofer, *The Assemblies of God: A Chapter in the Story of American Pentecostalism* (Springfield, Mo.: Gospel Publishing House, 1989), 2:57–67.

20 Robert L. Brandt quoted in Darrin J. Rodgers, *Northern Harvest: Pentecostalism in North Dakota* (Bismarck, N.D.: North Dakota District Council of the Assemblies of God, 2003), 22–23.

21 George O. Wood, "Workers for the Lord," interview by Wayne Warner, *Assemblies of God Heritage* 14 (winter 1994–95): 22, 33.

22 Williams, *Quarterly Letter*, 3.

23 Donald Gee, *Trophimus I Left Sick: Our Problems of Divine Healing* (London: Elim Publishing Co., 1952), 9.

24 T. L. Osborn, *Believers in Action* (Tulsa: OSFO Publishers, 2000), 94.

25 *Field Focus: Chile* (Springfield, Mo.: Assemblies of God Division of Foreign Missions, n.d.), 3.

26 Arno W. Enns, *Man, Milieu and Missions in Argentina* (Grand Rapids: William B. Eerdmans Publishing Co., 1971), 79; see also, Louie W. Strokes, *The Great Revival in Buenos Aires* (Buenos Aires: Casilla de Correo, 1954).

27 Noel Perkin, "Introduction to the Missions Seminar," *Key* (July–August 1956): 6.

28 "Serving the Youth of Arkansas," *Pentecostal Evangel* (3 August 1952): 7.

29 Robert Walker, "Vaughn Shoemaker: Pulitzer Prize–Winning Christian Cartoonist," *Assemblies of God Heritage* 22 (spring 2002): 4–8.

30 "All for Jesus," *Pentecostal Evangel* (10 August 1952): 4.

31 "Joyfully They Serve," *Pentecostal Evangel* (31 May 1964): 18.

[32] Patti Lindsay, "'There's No Place Like Home,'" *Assemblies of God Heritage* 20 (spring 2000): 20–21.

[33] Wayne Warner, "A Child in the Pulpit," *Assemblies of God Heritage* 16 (spring 1996): 3, 16–17.

[34] G. Raymond Carlson, "When Pentecost Came to the Upper Midwest," *Assemblies of God Heritage* 4 (spring 1984): 5.

[35] General Council Minutes, 1963, 15–16.

[36] Ibid., 17.

[37] Spiritual Life–Evangelism Commission, "Mobilization and Placement Service of the Assemblies of God," (1966, mimeographed), 1.

[38] MAPS Committee Meeting Minutes, 3 June 1964, 1.

[39] "MAPS Pilot Project," *Pentecostal Evangel* (10 March 1968): 16–17; David A. Womack, "Our First Construction Missionary," *Pentecostal Evangel* (12 May 1968): 21.

[40] T. F. Zimmerman, "The Mission of the Church," in *Our Mission in Today's World: Council on Evangelism Official Papers and Reports*, ed. Richard G. Champion, et al. (Springfield, Mo.: Gospel Publishing House, 1968), 17.

[41] Ibid., 212.

[42] Donald Gee, *Toward Pentecostal Unity* (Springfield, Mo.: Gospel Publishing House, 1961), 33.

[43] Cyril Homer, "The Ministry of the Church to the World," in *Our Mission in Today's World*, 64.

[44] General Council Minutes, 1965, 60–61.

[45] Paul Lowenberg, "The Mandate of the Church," in *Our Mission in Today's World*, 24.

CHAPTER 17

MOVERS AND SHAKERS

I n the 1960s, the Assemblies of God began to emerge as a major American denomination. Coming out of its isolation as a "peculiar people" through membership in the National Association of Evangelicals (NAE), it enjoyed the dawning respect for its fast growth and unusually successful missions program. Over the years, the General Council had developed into an elaborate organization through a unique combination of Presbyterian and Congregational models.

Third-generation believers were now enrolled in the Council's Bible colleges, liberal arts colleges, various Christian colleges and seminaries, and secular institutions of higher learning. The church constituency became increasingly comfortable with American culture. Declining expectancy of the imminent return of Christ became evident as ministers and laypeople adopted more comfortable lifestyles and invested monies to cushion their retirements.

The times called for strong leadership to guide the Assemblies of God through a new maze of problems and issues in a context very different from that faced by first-generation Pentecostals. Yet leadership in the Council and the broader Pentecostal movement has never been limited to elected officials. Individuals with prophet-like ministries have called the faithful back to the spiritual roots of Pentecostalism. In so doing, new and sometimes controversial ministries have been created.

The five leaders introduced in this chapter served in different ways. However, lest too great a difference be made between them, it should be noted that all of the following were dynamic leaders whose agendas reflected those of grassroots constituencies. During the twenty-six-year tenure of Thomas F. Zimmerman as general superintendent, he helped shape the denomination as it now stands and became the best-known Pentecostal ambassador to the evangelical movement.

Although Pentecostals have highlighted Spirit baptism for power in evangelism, the work of the Holy Spirit centers on glorifying Christ in holiness of character and behavior (John 15:26). Thus repentance and reconciliation lay at the heart of spiritual renewal. Indeed, great spiritual awakenings have always had social and even political consequences. Evangelist Bob Harrison confronted racism in the General Council;

Juan Maestas (far left), deacon in the Chama, New Mexico, church, with the first three superintendents of the Latin American District Council of the U.S. (left to right): José Girón, third superintendent; Demetrio Bazán, second superintendent; Henry C. Ball, first superintendent

his determination to remain opened doors for other African Americans to minister in the denomination.

A farsighted leader, José Girón played a leading role in the emerging maturity and organizational development of several Hispanic districts. With the breakup of the Latin American district, he wrote the constitutions and bylaws for the new districts.

No less important were charismatic leaders whose activities opened new vistas for ministry but sometimes clashed with the church hierarchy. David J. du Plessis became the foremost Pentecostal in the charismatic renewal, known worldwide as "Mr. Pentecost." Burdened by the need of the cities, David Wilkerson called for the saints to repent and evangelize the masses, particularly the outcasts of urban ghettoes.

THOMAS F. ZIMMERMAN
(1912-1991)

When Pentecostal leaders met with conservative evangelicals at the Coronado Hotel in St. Louis, Missouri, in 1942 to organize the NAE, a young Assemblies of God pastor from Granite City, Illinois, drove across the Mississippi River to join them. Along with such luminaries as Ernest S. Williams, J. Roswell Flower, Ralph M. Riggs, Noel Perkin, and Stanley H. Frodsham, there sat Thomas F. Zimmerman, having just turned thirty. The NAE's welcome to Pentecostals was a turning point in his ministry as well as in the history of American Pentecostalism. Eighteen years later, he would become the first Pentecostal to be elected president of the organization.

Zimmerman's parents, Thomas and Carrie Zimmerman, were devout members of a Methodist Protestant congregation in Indianapolis when he was born in 1912. Five years later, Carrie was diagnosed as terminally ill, a result of tuberculosis, and given only six weeks to live. Initially she was shocked at the news; then she remembered visiting a local Apostolic Faith mission where the sick were prayed for, a practice that had been explained to her by a cousin, Alice Reynolds Flower. With little time to waste, the Zimmermans asked Daniel Rickard, the pastor of the mission, to come and pray for Carrie. With members of his congregation, he went to their home. Gathering around her bed, they anointed Carrie with oil and asked God to heal her. After a medical examination several weeks later, the doctor declared her cured. However, news of her healing, precipitating cottage prayer meetings with members of their church, prompted the pastor to ask them to leave.

The Zimmermans' move to Rickard's congregation allowed young Thomas to grow up in the stirring atmosphere of an early Pentecostal mission. There he not only prayed for the sick but led in singing and preached at street meetings. Rickard's

The Fellowship

Our fellowship is the outgrowth of a realization that we can do far more together in reaching the world than we could accomplish through many unassociated, individual efforts. It has been blessed to see what God had wrought through the sincere efforts of many hearts bound together by a common desire to reach this generation. However, we should beware lest we fall prey to a trend which would fragmentize our efforts and cause us to be less effective separately through the multiplying of machinery and a duplication of organizational efforts. God has given us a means by which all of us can find complete expression for our God-given ministries within the framework of our movement.

Thomas F. Zimmerman

We ought to hold steady and thank God for the vehicle He has given us for the communication of our message to the lost and dying world. Within this glorious movement there is complete liberty given for all our ministries. There is a diversified opportunity for each to find his niche and function within the fellowship.

By many hearts working together in accomplishing the purposes of the Church, God will fulfill His Word with signs following. All can feel confident in investing time and talent and finance in the work of our church where there is spiritual emphasis, moral integrity, and fiscal responsibility. To me these are blessings that accrue to us from associating ourselves together.

—*Thomas F. Zimmerman, "Fervent in Spirit,"*
Pentecostal Evangel *(October 8, 1961): 13.*

successor, John Price, profoundly influenced Zimmerman's spiritual formation by inviting him to serve as assistant pastor. After graduating from high school, he enrolled at Indiana University. But when his father died two years later, Thomas gave up his studies and returned home to help support his mother in the family's bakery business. All the while, he continued as Price's assistant.

In the midst of the Great Depression in 1933, he married Price's daughter, Elizabeth. Although Zimmerman now had a better job with a good salary, his call to the ministry finally led him to resign and pastor a small struggling congregation in Harrodsburg, Indiana. Despite the poverty of the congregation and their own restricted resources, the church grew within two years to 250 and moved into a former Presbyterian church building.

Since the town itself had a population of only two hundred, the growth of the congregation reflected his vigorous ministry. While living in Harrodsville, he received ordination from what was then known as the Central district of the Assemblies of God.

From there, the young couple moved quickly from one congregation to another, invited to ever-larger and more influential pulpits. Finally, he answered the call to pastor the Assembly in Granite City, Illinois, and then Central Assembly of God in Springfield. His rapid rise to prominence advanced as he became increasingly involved in executive tasks: He established the national Radio Department in 1945 and produced its *Sermons in Song* broadcast. Responsibilities as Southern Missouri district secretary-treasurer followed his ministry at Central Assembly before moving to Cleveland, Ohio, in 1951 for a short stint as pastor of another prestigious church: First Pentecostal Church (pastored many years before by Daniel W. "Daddy" Kerr).

The Zimmermans moved back to Springfield after his election as one of the four assistant general superintendents at the 1953 General Council. Within a few years, he had worked in every phase of the headquarters operation and also helped in the founding of Evangel University. At the 1959 General Council in San Antonio, Texas, he was elected to replace Ralph M. Riggs on the ninth ballot. Along with that of J. Philip Hogan's as executive director of foreign missions, Zimmerman's election clearly showed that the second generation had taken the reins of leadership. His vision would focus on using every available means to evangelize the United States and the world. Years later, he reflected, "It is not given to us to choose the time in which we live and serve. But we are given the choice as to how we will respond to the challenge and opportunities that are ours."

Seizing the opportunity to prepare the Assemblies of God for unprecedented evangelism, he led the Council into a major self-study to clarify its mission in the world and then worked to make that possible. "I see the denominational structure as providing a support system for the local church," he wrote. "Among the supports are materials and programs which help the church accomplish its ministries. I believe the denominational structure should provide an overall umbrella for the church, while at the same time remaining fluid enough to allow for a variety of expressions of ministry."

In the same years, Zimmerman's stature among evangelical church leaders continued to grow. His engaging personality and organizational skills served the Assemblies of God and the wider Pentecostal movement well as he became their best-known leader. He faithfully attended annual NAE conferences, served on various boards and committees, such as the Lausanne Committee for World Evangelization, organized large gatherings for the NAE, and held membership on the executive committee of the National Religious Broadcasters (1944) for over forty years. He became friends with well-known figures such as Billy Graham and Bill Bright. For many of them, friendship with Zimmerman became their primary link to the Pentecostal movement.

From his attendance at the first NAE meeting, Zimmerman valued closer identification with evangelicals, a conviction shared by a growing number of Council members. His election as president in 1960 illustrated that commitment. During his long years as general superintendent, the relationship grew until the Assemblies of God came to be viewed as one of the major conservative evangelical denominations in the country. Commitment to this alliance appeared in his address before the World Congress on Evangelism in Berlin in 1966: "Because Christ commissioned the Church to evangelize the world, we must faithfully and concertedly carry out his Word, if we are to receive him with joy when he returns!"

Zimmerman's twenty-six years in office made him the longest serving general superintendent since Ernest S. Williams (twenty years). A deeply respected international Christian leader, he worked as chairman of the Pentecostal World Conference and as a Pentecostal ambassador to the evangelical organizations previously mentioned. Beyond all this, he deeply impressed others with his personal concern for the individual. Many remarked, "Once you had met Brother Zimmerman, he never forgot your name." His leadership raised the stature of the Assemblies of God in the world Christian community; and his pastoral care for persons, passion for excellence, and Pentecostal spirituality endeared him to the Fellowship.

ROBERT E. HARRISON (1928–2012)

A look at the beginnings of American Pentecostalism, the revival in Topeka, Kansas (1901), and the Azusa Street revival (1906–1909) in Los Angeles, reveals that participants had world evangelization on their minds. Both revivals focused on the restoration of tongues as evidence of Spirit baptism and preaching in the last days. The fact, however, that Azusa Street was interracial adds a dimension that neither Topeka nor many other such revivals enjoyed. One might say that the broader implications of the Spirit's work became visible at 312 Azusa Street.

Unfortunately, Pentecostals often failed to see the contemporary relevance of the reconciling work of the Spirit as found in the Book of Acts (Acts 8 and 10 through 11). Despite testimonies of sanctification and Spirit baptism, they generally remained children of their time in racial attitudes. Division began to appear as early as 1906. Pentecostal denominations were clearly distinguished as either white or black.

Although the General Presbytery had disapproved credentials for African Americans in 1939, the action left some ambiguity. Northern districts quietly continued the practice as the General Council, General Presbytery, and Executive Presbytery debated the issue in the decades that followed. Events, however, forced the Council to resolve the issue. In 1951 the Northern California–Nevada district's refusal to license Robert "Bob" Harrison as a minister because of race contributed to the change. (Harrison was the first African American to attend the district's Bethany Bible College [now Bethany College].) The refusal itself proved particularly awkward since the district had ordained his grandmother, Cornelia Jones Robertson, many years before. She had pastored churches in San Francisco and Oakland. After an appeal to the Executive Presbytery, Harrison received a license to preach—six years later.

Robert E. Harrison with Billy Graham
Compliments of the Billy Graham Evangelistic Association

But it was Billy Graham's decision to invite Harrison to join his crusade team in 1962 that embarrassed the General Council into revising its policy. Church leaders then approved Harrison's ordination. "In a very definite sense he might be considered to have broken a 'color line,'" wrote Howard N. Kenyon, "for his high-visibility ordination and ministry effectively ended once and for all the ongoing ambiguities of the General Council on the matter of inclusion of American blacks." Harrison continued in fruitful ministry as an evangelist and missionary.

In 1965, the General Council officially condemned racial discrimination: "Resolved, That we reaffirm our belief in the teachings of Christ including His emphasis upon the inherent worth and intrinsic value of every man, regardless of race, class, creed, or color, and we urge all our constituency to discourage unfair and discriminatory practices wherever they exist."

While white Pentecostals have been quick to condemn drinking alcoholic beverages, smoking, pornography, and abortion as personal sins, they have been slower to recognize and address the evil that works through human institutions. Racial inequities, hunger, poverty, and injustice need the prophetic witness of the gospel as well. Charles G. Finney's *Lectures on Revival* has long been a favorite among Assemblies of God preachers because of its uncompromising emphasis on individual repentance and revival. However, they have often been unaware of Finney's social activism: "The fact is," declared Finney, "that ministers, and all other men, not only have a right but are bound to expose and rebuke the national sins."

The Pentecostal Curtain

To bring the Pentecostal message and experience to all believers, and thus, through the entire Church, to evangelize the entire world, is the divine purpose of the Pentecostal Movement. It was not intended that all who receive the Pentecostal blessing should be required to go behind the "Pentecostal Curtain." While it has been necessary to set up organizations and to provide a haven for those who were forced out of unsympathetic groups, we must be careful that we do not seek to direct this mighty move of God exclusively into organizational channels. We must fulfill the divine purpose.

.—*Carl Brumback*, Suddenly . . . from Heaven *(1961), 353.*

Church leaders recognized that while working to evangelize other groups across the nation and around the world, they had largely ignored African Americans. Since Harrison's ordination, the Council has worked to build an African-American clergy, as well as evangelize this important sector of the population.

JOSÉ GIRÓN
(1911-2001)

Far from NAE conventions in plush hotels, José Girón received the mantle of Demetrio Bazán, Sr., to lead the Latin American District Council. Girón grew up in Del Norte, a community in the San Luis Valley of Colorado. His parents were members of a Presbyterian church and taught him the doctrines of the faith. As he neared his high school graduation, the church offered to pay all of his expenses for seminary training, no small offer in light of the Great Depression having just begun. It was then that he encountered P. V. Jones, a Pentecostal evangelist holding a revival in Del Norte. Visiting one of the services, he and a local

José Girón

Methodist pastor were baptized in the Spirit on the same night.

Recognizing the young man's call to the ministry and potential, Jones wrote to H. C. Ball, superintendent of the Latin American district, and asked him to issue credentials to Girón. Sensing that this was of the Lord, Ball sent him ministerial papers without having met him. Girón immediately began holding revivals and in 1932 started a new Pentecostal church in his hometown.

He eventually pastored eight churches and twice served as a district presbyter. "I would write to the pastors whose churches I planned to visit ahead of time and ask them to sell me a certain number of sacks of potatoes," he reminisced. "I would load my pickup truck, pray to the Lord that it wouldn't break down, and start my presbyter's trip. When I arrived, all the potatoes were sold [by Girón]; I preached for the pastor, dealt with the problems of the church, many times held elections, continued on my way visiting churches, until I had just enough money to return home."

Opposition to Pentecostal preachers among Hispanics sometimes became intense and dangerous. In the spring of 1936, while a presbyter in the New Mexico Conference, he traveled to the church at Gallina to visit the pastor and preach in several services. Local opponents, however, had threatened to kill the minister and his flock if they held another service. As a group of believers walked to the pastor's home after the evening service, three shots rang out and Girón and Miguel Sanchez, a layman, were hit.

Although Girón survived the wound to continue preaching in Gallina, Sanchez died several months later. Such persecution did not deter Pentecostal evangelism and church growth, but spurred it on.

After serving as district secretary for eleven years, Girón succeeded Bazán as superintendent in 1959 and remained in office until 1970. Through these years, he promoted ministerial training at the Latin American Bible Institutes in Texas and California and praised those who pursued seminary education. Since the district was organizationally weak, Girón encouraged each regional conference within it to adopt constitutions. In this way, they could better conserve their work, coordinate their efforts more effectively, and stand in closer harmony with the General Council. By 1960, the statistics demonstrated that the Latin American district led all others in planting new churches. The Spanish Eastern district, having already separated from the Latin American district, began to make great strides in church growth as well.

At his retirement in 1970, the district subdivided into four new districts: Gulf Latin American, Midwest Latin American, Central Latin American, and Pacific Latin American. With the Spanish Eastern and the later creation of the Puerto Rico and Southeastern Spanish, this brought to seven the number of Hispanic districts in the

A Supporter of Education

Girón loved education. . . . He graduated from Del Norte Colorado High School in 1930, studied at a later period at Castillo, New Mexico, taking postgraduate commercial courses that developed in him a business mind. In 1946 he received a Graduate of Theology degree from Light House Bible College of Rockford, Illinois. With a mind that believed in education, and being aware of the change of the times, Girón emphasized education by his very presence. One reason that undoubtedly played an important role was the fact that he had been a school teacher in Taos County elementary schools in New Mexico in 1943, and being himself a Mexican-American, he saw the problems that minority children had in acquiring their education. . . . Girón emphasized education wherever he could. He wrote articles in the official organ of the district (*La Luz Apostolica*) about the benefits of seeking better education and requesting the youth of the district to go and study at the Bible schools of the district. To those that were going to colleges and universities, he would give special recognition. He especially praised the [ministers who] pursued seminary degrees.

—*Victor De Leon, The Silent Pentecostals (1979), 124–5*

Council. Girón's leadership proved vital in the maturing and growth of this important sector of the Assemblies of God.

DAVID J. DU PLESSIS
(1905-1987)

As the Assemblies of God basked in its postwar recognition, the winds of the Spirit began blowing in new directions. In May 1960, Episcopal priest Dennis Bennett announced to his Sunday morning audience at St. Mark's Church in Van Nuys, California, that he had been baptized in the Spirit and spoken in tongues. This signaled that the charismatic movement had begun in earnest. In the 1960s, charismatic renewal occurred not only among Episcopalians, but Presbyterians, Baptists, Methodists, Mennonites, Disciples of Christ, and Lutherans as well.

David J. du Plessis

Charismatics in the historic and "respectable" churches that had formerly dismissed Pentecostals as misguided enthusiasts now prayed in tongues and sought to lead their friends into the baptism in the Holy Spirit. To further complicate the picture for evangelicals and Pentecostals, charismatic renewal followed in the Roman Catholic Church on the heels of Vatican Council II. Starting at the famous "Duquesne Weekend" in mid-February 1967, thirty students and two theologians from Duquesne University in Pittsburgh, Pennsylvania, met for a retreat and read David Wilkerson's *The Cross and the Switchblade.* Inspired by its testimony to the power of Spirit baptism, each of them experienced a new outpouring of the Spirit with many speaking in tongues. Charismatic renewal also began in the Greek Orthodox Church.

Who would speak to the charismatics on behalf of classical Pentecostals? Thomas Zimmerman represented institutional Pentecostalism and faced the unenviable task of maintaining the evangelical connection while at the same time trying to affirm what the Spirit was doing outside the circle of the NAE. However, this did not keep him from affirming the significance of the newest wave of Pentecostal outpouring: "The rise of the Pentecostal movement came under conditions which existed prior to revivals both in Bible times and in later Church history. The rise of the present-day move of the Spirit is directly attributable to believers who fulfilled God's conditions for revival."

Although not an elected officer representing the denomination, David J. du Plessis observed, "When I got out of my Pentecostal shell, I found the Holy Spirit was at work in other churches all over the world with the same blessing and the same

Finding Fellowship with Pentecostals

About a year ago we became acquainted with the leaders of the major denomination of the Pentecostals. I went to Springfield, Mo., headquarters of the Assemblies of God, accompanied by Russell T. Hitt and Walter Martin of the Evangelical Foundation and George Cannon of the Christian and Missionary Alliance.

About twelve of the top leaders of the Assemblies of God met with us in one of their beautiful air-conditioned glass and steel buildings. . . .

Our conference began with prayer, and long before the last man had prayed I was convinced that these were Christian brethren. No matter what differences might develop in our conversations, I was sure that these men were fully committed to the Lord Jesus Christ, and that they honored, worshipped and owned Him as Lord of all.

During our entire first day, we discussed things upon which we agreed. As the hours passed all of us felt that marvelous unity that comes only from the Holy Spirit.

We agreed that the Lord Jesus Christ is God, the eternal Word, second person of the Godhead; that He came into the world without a human Father by the divine intervention of the Holy Spirit; that He went to the cross to die as our Savior, and by the pouring out of His life we were redeemed from sin. We agreed that He arose from the dead on the third day in the same body in which He had lived; that He ascended into Heaven and is there at the right hand of God, interceding for us. We agreed that His promised return is sure, and that He may come at any moment.

As time passed all of us felt increasingly the oneness that is ours in Christ. . . .

The next day we began to discuss the things on which we differ, beginning with the subject of divine healing. . . .

There was considerable discussion . . . . Nevertheless, as one of the Pentecostal brothers said, "We are in agreement in 95 percent of our positions."

But that five per cent covers an area of frank disagreement. . . . Pentecostals hold that about the year 1905 God began a special work looking toward the end of the age. . . .

This latter rain they hold to be a special work of the Holy Spirit. They believe (but we do not) that, in addition to the work of the Lord in regeneration, there is "the baptism of the Holy Spirit." They believe that at a certain stage of his spiritual development the Holy Spirit comes upon a believer and "baptizes" him, and that he then speaks in tongues. . . .

So strong was our agreement on essential truths, however, that before this article appears in print I shall have held a week of meetings in the Central Church of the denomination in Springfield, Missouri. It is good for the whole body of Christ to notice that a Presbyterian minister who adheres to the Westminster Confession is an acceptable guest in a Pentecostal Assembly.

—Donald Grey Barnhouse, "Finding Fellowship with Pentecostals,"
Eternity (April 1958): 8–10.
(Barnhouse, a prominent leader in the NAE and editor of Eternity
*magazine, had strenuously opposed membership for Pentecostals in
the organization in its early years.)*

manifestations." The church scene was quickly changing as traditional walls of separation began to crumble. It was a new and challenging day for Pentecostals.

Du Plessis was born near Cape Town, South Africa, to parents who became Pentecostals through the ministry of John G. Lake and Thomas Hezmalhalch. As early Pentecostal missionaries from Los Angeles and Zion City, Illinois, they established the Apostolic Faith Mission (AFM) there before returning to the United States. Converted in 1916, du Plessis was baptized in the Holy Spirit two years later. In the same year, the family moved to Basutoland (present-day Lesotho), a tribal enclave in South Africa.

His ministry began with street preaching while still a teenager. Eventually, he was ordained and moved into the higher offices of the Apostolic Faith Mission, serving in the post of general secretary for eleven years (1936–1947). Because of the intense opposition to Pentecostals by the Reformed churches in South Africa (the AFM was not allowed to be incorporated as a "church"), du Plessis bitterly denounced them as spiritually dead. Yet at the annual conference of the AFM in Johannesburg in December 1936, the visiting preacher, Smith Wigglesworth, prophesied over him that a great revival was coming—even greater than the Pentecostal revival, then in its third decade. Furthermore, du Plessis would play a major role if

The Holy Spirit and the Great Commission

Today, we are witnessing an outpouring of the Pentecostal experience on groups and individuals that our prejudices and our provincialism are sometimes slow to accept. I have just returned from the heart of Latin South America where my brethren confronted me directly to say, "What should our attitude be toward hundreds of Catholic priests who are testifying to the reality of the baptism of the Holy Spirit?" They said, "These men, five years ago, were throwing rocks at us and doing everything possible to contain the Protestant message. Now they have covered up the Stations of the Cross in their cathedrals and have in turn emblazoned the message of Pentecost."

What can I say when priests and bishops and powerful leaders of liturgical groups around the world tug at my sleeves in airports or in other crowded areas of the world to confidently whisper, "Brother Hogan, you will be surprised to know that I pray in tongues every day."

If I had been designing the persons or groups upon whom I felt the sovereign Spirit would fall, some of these are the last ones that my provincialism would have dictated should receive this blessing. However, thank God, the essential optimism of Christianity is that the Holy Spirit is a force capable of bursting into the hardest paganism, discomfiting the most rigid dogmatism, electrifying the most suffocating organization and bringing the glory of Pentecost.

Stand in awe, my friend, and witness in these days the wonder of the ages. The Spirit of God is being outpoured upon persons and in places for which there is no human design and in which there is not one shred of human planning.

—J. Philip Hogan, "The Holy Spirit and the Great Commission,"
World Pentecost (1970): 5.

Practical Unity

There is a path of practical unity for us in evangelism. In preaching the gospel we find a wonderful unity. I will not conceal the fact that we have different ideas about some things. I am glad that we have in the body of Christ not one member but many. But when it comes to preaching Jesus Christ we are absolutely one. When it comes to believing in the Bible as the Word of God, we are one. When it comes to preaching redemption through the precious blood of Jesus Christ, we are one. When it comes to the baptism in the Holy Ghost for power, we are one. I am here to thank God for all the essential unity in fundamentals which we have. And in the outward urge of Pentecost we shall find our true unity.

—*Donald Gee at the 1952 Pentecostal World Conference in London;*
in "Gems of Truth," Pentecostal Evangel *(November 30, 1952): 4.*

he remained faithful and obedient. Little did he realize what a change of heart that would require.

When the inaugural meeting of the Pentecostal World Conference took place in Zurich, Switzerland, in 1947, church leaders chose du Plessis to be the organizing secretary for future gatherings. He then resigned his position with the AFM and moved his wife, Anna, and their children to Basel, where he hoped to open the Conference headquarters. But with their congregational church polity, the Europeans, led by Lewi Pethrus, leader of the Swedish Pentecostal churches, resisted any formal organization. Consequently, du Plessis planned the triennial conferences in Paris, London, Stockholm, and Toronto without benefit of office space or salary.

The next year, in 1948, du Plessis and his family moved to the United States. At first, he taught at Lee College (now Lee University) in Cleveland, Tennessee, then worked for Far East Broadcasting Company, and in 1952 he accepted the position of interim pastor of the Stamford Gospel Tabernacle (Assemblies of God) in Stamford, Connecticut. Three years later, he affiliated with the General Council as an ordained minister. At the same time, he traveled widely in Pentecostal circles and came to know many leaders on a first-name basis. Obviously as secretary of the Pentecostal World Conference, he was concerned with spiritual unity among Spirit-filled believers. His horizons, however, soon began to widen.

While living in Stamford, he felt the Lord direct him to visit the offices of the World Council of Churches (WCC) in New York City and share his Pentecostal faith with its leaders. Not having been invited, he would arrive unannounced. It was not an easy step for him. "Lord, I have preached so much against them. What do I say to them now?" he prayed beforehand. "They will not listen to me. Their churches have put our people out of their fellowship." Before getting an early train into the city, he told Anna, "I will be back by lunch." When he arrived, he introduced himself and made it clear that he was a Pentecostal, indeed "one of the worst, actually the world secretary."

Yet he received a warm welcome and stayed through the afternoon. Leaders in the WCC had observed the growth of Pentecostalism in countries such as Chile and

Brazil and noted the strong missionary movement of the Pentecostal churches. This led to important invitations to speak in circles normally inaccessible to Pentecostals. In the years that followed, he lectured and testified to his Pentecostal faith at Princeton Theological Seminary, Yale Divinity School, Union Theological Seminary (New York City), Colgate-Rochester Divinity School, and the Ecumenical Institute in Bossey, Switzerland. In addition, he was reporting that an outpouring of the Spirit had begun in the historic churches.

EVANGELICAL IDENTITY VERSUS THE ECUMENICAL MOVEMENT

Pentecostalism never had a better prepared "goodwill ambassador" to the wider Church world than du Plessis. And he never compromised his Pentecostal faith. Nevertheless, by 1961, NAE leaders began to criticize his connections to the World Council. Although he never claimed to be an official representative of the Assemblies of God, when reporters and others asked his church affiliation, he would say the Assemblies of God. Obviously, his position could be easily confused in the public eye.

When ordered by the Executive Presbytery to cease his ministry within ecumenical circles, du Plessis chose to continue, a decision he defended as a personal leading of the Spirit. As a consequence, in 1962 he was asked to surrender his credentials. Even so, he and his family remained members of First Assembly in Oakland, California, where they then resided. (In 1980 the General Council restored du Plessis's credentials.)

Concerns about the ecumenical movement led delegates at the 1963 General Council to condemn the movement and forbid ministers to participate in any of its local, national, or international events, despite the charismatic renewal being experienced in many of the member churches. Doctrinal inclusiveness in the mainline churches, the focus on social concerns over individual salvation, and the anticipation that the World Council of Churches would turn into a world superchurch made it appear to be a harbinger of prophetic events described in the Book of Revelation.

Zimmerman and other Assemblies of God leaders understood the advantages to membership in the NAE and sought to preserve the relationship. It had brought not only theological respectability to Trinitarian Pentecostals, but enormous benefits through its agencies. The relationship had also opened new opportunities for broader cooperation in evangelism. Thus, the General Council's affirmation of the charismatic movement in the historic churches—denominations connected to the National and World Councils—was given with reluctance.

While no less interested in evangelism, du Plessis recognized that God had begun to renew the historic churches through individuals being baptized in the Holy Spirit. While some Pentecostals warmly accepted charismatics and ministered to them in various ways, others became irritated when they didn't renounce their church membership and join Pentecostal denominations. Du Plessis himself encouraged them to remain in their churches to evangelize and bring renewal. Many of the historic Protestant denominations and the Roman Catholic Church gradually endorsed the renewal and recognized the contributions of charismatics.

In these years, du Plessis had ranged widely in ecumenical territory, had attended Vatican Council II, and had spoken at conferences around the world. He, thereby, led thousands of people into the baptism in the Holy Spirit marked by speaking in tongues. With Catholic Father Kilian McDonnell, O.S.B., he cofounded the international Roman Catholic and Classical Pentecostal Dialogue in 1972.

In 1970, du Plessis noted "a tendency among our people to go the way others have gone. Gradually we are preaching more and more doctrine and have less and less demonstration of the power of the Spirit. It is a great tragedy when the Spirit becomes 'a displaced person' in the Church, and all kinds of substitutes are introduced." Mr. Pentecost died in 1987.

DAVID WILKERSON
(1931–2011)

If David J. du Plessis challenged Pentecostals to look for the Spirit's outpouring beyond their denominational confines, David Wilkerson called them to repent of their material comforts and look to the unevangelized cities. His story became known worldwide, how he, a rural Pennsylvania preacher, traveled to New York City to share the gospel with seven gang members on trial for beating and stabbing to death a disabled youth. Whether through the book or the movie *The Cross and the Switchblade*, millions have heard the story. It is the stuff of legend.

The Truth on Fire

Then there came a question [at a conference of ecumenical church leaders in Connecticut] that presented an opportunity to be devastatingly frank, but I had no desire to belittle or criticize or hurt anyone. Silently I prayed. The question was: "Please tell us what is the difference between you and us. We quote the same Scriptures as you do, and yet when you say those words they sound so different. We say the same things that you do, but there seems to be a deeper implication in what you say." What was I to say? The Spirit came to my rescue, and I said: "Gentlemen, comparisons are odious, and I do not wish to injure anyone's feelings or hurt your pride. But the truth as I see it is this: You have the truth on ice, and I have it on fire."

"That is too deep for me; please explain," said one.

".... I submit there was a Pentecostal experience of the baptism in the Holy

Ghost in the lives of the Apostles before they ever developed or framed the doctrine and the theology. They had experience and no doctrine. Today most people have doctrine and no experience."

"My friends," I said, "if you will take the great truths of the Gospel out of your theological deep freezers and get them on the fire of the Holy Spirit, your churches will yet turn the world upside down."

—David J. du Plessis, The Spirit Bade Me Go (n.d.), 16–18.

A third-generation Pentecostal preacher, Wilkerson and his wife, Gwen, lived in Philipsburg, Pennsylvania, where he pastored the local Assembly of God. One night in 1958, he had broken off praying in his study and his attention was drawn to a story in *Life* magazine: seven teenage boys were on trial for murder. Inexplicably he began to cry, and a thought "full-blown, as though it had come into me from somewhere else" said, "Go to New York City and help those boys."

When he shared the *Life* article at the Wednesday evening service, "I told them how I had burst into tears and how I had got the clear instruction to go to New York, myself, and try to help those boys. My parishioners looked at me stonily," he recalled. "I was not getting through to them at all and I could understand why. Anyone's natural instinct would be an aversion to those boys, not sympathy. I could not understand my own reaction." Nonetheless, when he told them he had no money to make the trip, this congregation of farmers moved forward to the Communion table and laid seventy-five dollars down for his expenses.

David Wilkerson preaching outdoors

Like other Pentecostals who stepped out on faith to answer God's call, he had no idea how events would unfold. After arriving in New York, Wilkerson was told that he would need the permission of the trial judge to visit the jail. Contacting the judge, however, proved difficult since threats had been made on his life and he had had his telephone disconnected. The only alternative would be to attend a session of the trial and afterward ask to speak with the judge in his chambers. But when he stepped out into the aisle of the courtroom to address the judge, he ducked behind the bench and guards hustled Wilkerson out before any contact could occur between them. The reporters had a story. They also had a picture. When asked if he was ashamed of the Bible he had in his hand, he held it up. And so the country preacher appeared on the front page of the *New York Daily News* on March 1, 1958.

Although Wilkerson never did gain access to the seven, the picture gave him an open door to the gangs, who called him "the guy the cops don't like." With the heart of an evangelist, he resigned his church and moved his family to New York City to preach to the gangs. He had made the transition without pledged support or a salary. Twenty New York City Assemblies of God pastors gathered at Glad Tidings Tabernacle to discuss his ministry. They each pledged to give him five dollars a week to cover his expenses. The success of his street ministry and the support of these pastors led to the founding of Teen Challenge, now a worldwide ministry.

R. Stanley Berg, pastor of Glad Tidings, recalled: "I proceeded to tell him how we'd been praying that God would send someone with this burden to our city. . . . I told this young man, David Wilkerson, 'We've talked long enough; we know the problem is real. Now instead of talking, let's start doing something about it.'"

An evangelist rather than an administrator, Wilkerson relied on the assistance of several gifted persons to develop and mature the ministry. Wilkerson's brother, Don, assisted in managing the Brooklyn Teen Challenge center as a place where converted drug and alcohol addicts could be sheltered and receive intense discipleship training.

Frank Reynolds, pastor of El Bethel Assembly of God in Staten Island, and his wife, Gladys, moved to Pennsylvania to found the Teen Challenge Training Center in Rehrersburg. There they pioneered a residential program for male converts from the streets. The Walter Hoving Home in Garrison, New York, offers an equivalent program for female converts.

As time passed, Teen Challenge offered the most successful drug rehabilitation program in the country. Contending that addictions resulted from spiritual alienation from God, Wilkerson wrote: "It is impossible to cure a drug addict without God. Those who refuse God's power and the simple Bible way of salvation soon land in jail. When they are desperate enough they will call on God." Many believers caught his vision and soon Teen Challenge centers were opened in cities across the United States and overseas. Wilkerson's citywide crusades and summer street evangelism assisted in the starting of many of these centers.

Through his preaching and more than a score of books, Wilkerson has stirred Pentecostals and evangelicals to minister in the cities to the outcasts of society. Through *The Cross and the Switchblade*, particularly, he stirred ministers and laypeople of mainline denominations, from the United Methodist Church to the Roman

Catholic Church, to consider the miraculous, ultimately drawing them into charismatic renewal. Leaving the Assemblies of God in 1987, he went to New York City and founded the nondenominational Times Square Church in the historic Mark Hellinger Theater in Manhattan at 51st and Broadway.

Church growth in the Pentecostal tradition has always been influenced by the presence of charismatic leaders, whether holding formal church offices or not, clergy or laity, men or women. This dynamic has been a chief characteristic of the Pentecostal movement, bringing with it unique strengths, as well as weaknesses.

RECOMMENDED READING

Bennett, Dennis J. *Nine O'Clock in the Morning*. Plainfield, N.J.: Logos International, 1970.

Blumhofer, Edith L. "Thomas F. Zimmerman." Parts 1–4. *Assemblies of God Heritage* 10 (winter 1990–1991): 3–5, 21–22; 11 (spring 1991): 13–15; 11 (fall 1991): 12–14, 20–21; 12 (summer 1992): 9–12, 30–31.

Christenson, Larry, ed. *Welcome, Holy Spirit: A Study of Charismatic Renewal in the Church*. Minneapolis: Augsburg Publishing House, 1987.

Du Plessis, David J. *The Spirit Bade Me Go*. Rev. ed. Plainfield, N.J.: Logos International, 1970.

Harrison, Robert, with Jim Montgomery. *When God Was Black*. Grand Rapids: Zondervan Publishing House, 1971.

Hocken, Peter. *The Glory and the Shame: Reflections on the 20th Century Outpouring of the Holy Spirit*. Guildford, Surrey, U.K.: Eagle, 1994.

Kenyon, Howard N. "A Social History of the Assemblies of God: Race Relations, Women and Ministry, and Attitudes Toward War." PhD diss., Baylor University, 1987.

Laurentin, René. *Catholic Pentecostalism*. Garden City, N.Y.: Doubleday & Co., 1978.

McDonnell, Kilian, ed. *Presence, Power, Praise: Documents on the Charismatic Renewal*. Collegeville, Minn.: Liturgical Press, 1980.

_____. "The Death of Mythologies: The Classical Pentecostal/Roman Catholic Dialogue." *America* (25 March 1995): 14–19.

Quebedeaux, Richard. *The New Charismatics II*. San Francisco: Harper & Row, 1976.

Reid, Thomas F., with Doug Brendel. *The Exploding Church*. Plainfield, N.J.: Logos International, 1979.

Robeck, Jr., Cecil M. "Roman Catholic-Pentecostal Dialogue: Some Pentecostal Assumptions." *Journal of the European Pentecostal Theological Association* XXI (2001): 3–25.

Sherrill, John L. *They Speak With Other Tongues*. New York: McGraw-Hill, 1964.

Slosser, Bob. *A Man Called Mr. Pentecost*. Plainfield, N.J.: Logos International, 1977.

Wilkerson, David, with John and Elizabeth Sherrill. *The Cross and the Switchblade*. N.p.: Bernard Geis Associates, 1963.

Ziefle, Joshua R. *David du Plessis and the Assemblies of God: The Struggle for the Soul of a Movement*. Leiden ; Boston: Brill, 2013.

Zimmerman, Thomas F. "The Reason for the Rise of the Pentecostal Movement." In *Aspects of Pentecostal-Charismatic Origins*, ed. by Vinson Synan, 7–13. Plainfield, N.J.: Logos International, 1975.

CHAPTER 18

LOCAL ASSEMBLIES AND LEADERS

Within a few weeks of the organizational meeting of the Assemblies of God in Hot Springs, Arkansas, the *Christian Evangel* carried an article entitled "The Assembly of God," which defines the term as "an assembly, called by God, and belonging to God." It should be the "light and salt of the earth, . . . a dwelling in which God lives by his Spirit," and led according to the will of God by "certain men (and women) who are specially chosen to act for the assembly in discharging various parts of its service."

The emphasis on the presence and manifestations of the Spirit's gifts set an Assemblies of God church apart from an evangelical church. "I want to say that an ideal Pentecostal church is not only comprised of born-again believers, is not only a holiness church, and not only a church that believes in and enjoys the Baptism of the Holy Ghost, but an ideal Pentecostal church is a demonstrative church," remarked A. G. Ward, an early leader. "You cannot have the mighty operations of the Holy Ghost in your midst without demonstrations [of supernatural power]." Regrettably, "In many places, [Pentecostals] are trying to be so nice and proper that a lot of those professing Pentecost look like marble slabs in a cemetery and act as though they had spiritual rheumatics." Although written in 1927, his ideal of what made a service Pentecostal lived on in the postwar period.

Pentecostals placed great value on Paul's description of the participatory worship at Corinth: "When you come together, everyone has a hymn, or a word of instruction, a revelation, a tongue or an interpretation. All of these must be done for the strengthening of the church" (1 Corinthians 14:26). In this context, the Spirit glorifies Christ through the preaching of the Word, worship, prayer for the sick, and manifestations of the gifts of the Spirit in ministry to the saints.

Mildred White of Stone Lake, Wisconsin, told of asking for prayer for healing during a revival meeting at the Signor Indian Mission. "I mentioned only my spine, not my hip, which had begun to pain because of the way I was walking to ease the hurting in my back," she recounted. "God touched my spine, and a few nights later as I stood at the altar God completely healed my hip also. I surely praise His name." Pentecostal periodicals like the *Evangel* have published thousands of such testimonies through the years, reflecting the ongoing expectancy of supernatural manifestations of power in the churches.

The ministry of Hispanic evangelist José Rojas also illustrates the anticipation of the Spirit's power. Since he had not attended a Bible school, his preaching was limited to his testimony about his own personal conversion out of a life of wickedness. During revivals he would spend most of the nights in prayer. When the time came to preach, he began by singing a Spanish chorus "Dios te ve." ("God sees you.") In many of his services, he never got further than the song because people would begin to feel remorse for their sinful lives and make their way to the altar to repent. Hundreds came to Christ in this fashion. Rojas became so well known for singing this song that many people knew him only by the name "Dios te ve."

Churches generally exhibited a high level of audience involvement through song, choirs, vocal and instrumental ensembles, expressive worship (clapping, raising hands, shouting the praises of God, and, occasionally, dancing), testimony, and the gifts of the Spirit. Exuberant singing marked the services, sometimes with people in the congregation taking the liberty to lead out in a favorite song at an appropriate time in the service when they felt the Spirit prompt them. Otherwise, the song leader—usually the key worship leader next to the pastor—selected the songs. Still the features of Pentecostal worship varied across the country due to cultural differences, ranging from lively Southern-style worship to more staid worship to the exuberant services of the Hispanic churches. (An Assembly of God without a pianist or guitarist, however, presented no small challenge to a worship leader.)

Dancing in the Spirit

It was not unusual for the altar services on Sunday evening [at First Assembly] to last at least several hours. No one seemed anxious to leave the presence of the Lord. Men and women would stand, sit, or lie slain in the Spirit, worshipping God. A symphony of praise would rise and fall in tides. After I had finished praying, I turned in my seat and quietly worshipped with my eyes open. There were people slain in the Spirit all over the altar area. A woman at the far left of the altar area began gracefully dancing in the Spirit. She had her eyes shut and her hands were lifted high to the Lord. She began moving slowly across the altar area and my first thought was, *Oh, no, she is going to step on someone's hand or foot...or even worse yet, trip over someone and land right on them!* In total amazement, I watched her gracefully dance all over the altar area from one end to the other without ever touching a hand, foot, or body. I knew that what I was seeing was totally impossible for a human being to do...a supernatural dance was being performed before my very eyes. Even though I was only in my early teens, I will never forget that supernatural performance.

—Adeline Emery Worthley, Ferndale, Michigan

Perhaps reflecting the influence of the Salvation Army on early Pentecostals, churches often had orchestras; consequently, many young people became skilled musicians. Aimee Semple McPherson's Angelus Temple in Los Angeles, California, sported a large "Silver Band." Most orchestras, however, were much smaller.

Church choir and musicians with speaker Carl Stewart from Boulevard Assembly of God in Ft. Worth, Texas, broadcasting over KWBC

The musicians at Bethel Temple Assembly of God in Canton, Ohio, had a ministry both within and far beyond the walls of the church sanctuary. Bob Vance, a steelworker and elder in the church, served as the director and played the guitar. Velma McGee was the equivalent of first violinist, assisted by the church custodian, Ed Jensen, and Gene Kulik. Kermit Snyder, an elder, played the drums. David McNeilly and his son played trumpets, Gary McGee made sounds on the baritone horn, and several other youths played clarinets. George Hartzell strummed the bass fiddle, and Lucille Kempthorn played the piano. They ministered in Sunday evening services and traveled several times a year in the surrounding area to church dedications and revivals and to hold services at nursing homes and county homes. This lay-driven ministry exemplified similar efforts across the country.

Unique to Pentecostal churches, the vocal utterances of the Holy Spirit (gifts of tongues, interpretation, and prophecy) played an important role in worship. Sovereignly distributed like the rest of the nine gifts (1 Corinthians 12:7–11), Pentecostals viewed their manifestation as indispensable to Spirit-filled worship. However, it was clearly understood that Paul's instructions about the exercise of these gifts (1 Corinthians 14) had to be followed to insure that the work of the Spirit would not be jeopardized by poor judgment. At the Council on Spiritual Life in Minneapolis in 1972, California pastor Dwight H. McLaughlin cautioned, "The gifts of the Spirit must be balanced by the fruit of the Spirit. Speaking in tongues, the gift of prophecy, all knowledge, all faith, even though seeming to help others, will not profit their users without love (1 Corinthians 13:1–3)."

The vision, dynamism, and growth of Pentecostal churches have been determined to a great degree by the pastor, aided by committed church workers. Assemblies of God congregations have always expected much from their pastors: They should be Spirit-led worship leaders, powerful preachers, prayer warriors, competent administrators, skilled counselors, devoted marriage partners, caring parents with perfect children, and models of integrity. If all this were not enough to age one prematurely, "the minister [also] runs into unseen opposition," wrote Ernest S. Williams. "Often Satan opposes and other things may contribute. . . . At such times he must 'fight

Forrest Bridges

While the word "mentor" was not in vogue, this is what my dad became to many young men in his pastorate as well as in the section of which he was the presbyter. At his funeral, those young ministers served as pallbearers and mourners for an elder who had invested his life in them.

—*James K. Bridges*

the good fight of faith,' seek to avoid self-consciousness, maintain poise and perseverance."

Such expectations have sometimes overwhelmed pastors and led to their departure from the ministry, while most steadfastly remained at their posts. At age eighty, Texas minister Forrest Bridges accepted another pastorate, a church on the brink of closing its doors. When asked about the wisdom of taking on such a responsibility in his senior years, he responded by saying, "Retire? . . . [Not] until the One who called me tells me that it's time to retire." Fred Henry, a blind musician who ministered in evangelistic campaigns across the nation, shared the same sentiments in his later years as full-time organist and pianist at Renton (Washington) Assembly of God. (At age eighty-two, he played the organ for a church cantata, which required him to memorize all of the songs.)

In the postwar period and especially after 1960, a number of congregations grew to megachurch status, with fleets of buses scurrying through communities to bring visitors and the faithful to church. A strong leader pastored each one, a charismatic figure capable of inspiring people to work together in evangelism. The stories of their growth and methods increasingly set the pattern for success in the denomination. In many respects, they resembled Baptist megachurches that developed at the same time.

It is significant that early Pentecostal church growth had depended on preaching accompanied by signs and wonders, usually miracles of healing, to attract the unsaved. Assemblies of God churches now

Hear... **REV. JOHN PEEL**
VANCOUVER, B. C.
Pastor and Youth Leader

Sunday, Sept. 18th, to Oct. 2nd

KINGSTON TABERNACLE

Fred Henry often provided the special music during evangelistic campaigns. Here his picture appears on a handbill announcing meetings for John Peel.

added attractive programs appealing to the entire family. Obviously, the times were changing.

In fact, transmitting the spiritual heritage to the next generation had become a challenge. Someone sent the following query to Williams, who penned a column for the *Evangel* entitled "Your Questions": "Why is it that so many people (especially the young people) now want to sit in the back seats in church and refuse to do differently when the pastor asks them to? We used to want the front seats and we entered into the services with all our hearts." Williams bewailed young people "sitting listlessly" in the back of the church as "mere spectators." Nevertheless, he suspected that the real reason could be the lack of spiritual vitality in the church, since "when God sends revival all wish to be near the front to participate in the service."

The persons introduced in this chapter all attained success, but of various kinds. Among the best-known church administrators, James Hamill pastored First Assembly of God in Memphis, Tennessee, for thirty-seven years and watched it grow from ninety-nine to twenty-eight hundred members. Tommy Barnett left the evangelistic field to pastor Westside Assembly in Davenport, Iowa, and spearheaded its dramatic growth through soul-winning and dazzling promotion. Among Native Americans, Navajo artist Charlie Lee became the first appointed national home missionary and pioneered the Assembly of God in Shiprock, New Mexico.

Different in many respects from the churches above, Alexander H. Clattenburg's Trinity Assembly of God in Baltimore, Maryland, became a pillar congregation on the East Coast. And different yet again, Daena Cargnel shepherded small congregations in Ohio.

Georgia pastor Edgar Bethany remarked: "Nobody is complete without eyes for vision, ears for hearing, nose for discerning of pleasant or foul odors, mouth for expression and communication, arms and feet for erect locomotion." Indeed, "every member is needed in the Body of Christ." Voicing the same concern, evangelist Gladys Pearson admitted, "There is a great burden on the hearts of evangelists today—we need help from among the lay members. For evangelists to assume the whole responsibility of winning souls is impossible. Each person has a sphere of influence that no other reaches. He is therefore responsible before God for the souls within that sphere." Thus, congregations could not have grown without the work of dedicated believers like Charlie Holdock, Hugo Cargnel, Bob Vance, Velma McGee, Melvin Pridemore, Mrs. Venezia, and Michael Cardone, all laypersons mentioned in this chapter.

JAMES HAMILL
(1913-1994)

In his long ministry at First Assembly in Memphis, James Hamill became a virtual institution in the city, widely known among religious and civic leaders. Like other Pentecostal pioneers who reached success after years of labor, he grew up in hard times. His father, a timber contractor in Pughs Mill, Mississippi, died when Hamill was six years old. Although the family had been unchurched, he was converted and called to the ministry at age seventeen. Without the benefit of either formal training or spiritual heritage, he began preaching two years later and pastored churches in Arkansas, Oklahoma, and Mississippi before moving to Tennessee.

It took a strong individual to hurdle what Hamill encountered in his ministry. In his first year as an evangelist, his income was $172. The next year, $258. He was philosophical: "Poor preach, poor pay. If I ever learn to preach, maybe they'll pay me."

At thirty-one he accepted an invitation to pastor First Assembly and moved to Memphis with his wife, Katheryne. "The church was poorly located, small . . . and

James Hamill (right) speaking with General Superintendent Ernest S. Williams (center) and neighboring pastor Paul McKeel (left) at the dedication of Hamill's First Assembly of God in Memphis, Tennessee

discouraged," he later wrote. "But God laid that congregation and city on my heart. And I obeyed." In the succeeding years (World War II had just ended), he led the church into six building programs and founded a Christian school along with other ministries.

Related to the growth of the church, Hamill held a strong, virtually patriarchal view of the pastor's authority. In his estimation, serious problems arose when a congregation suffered from poor leadership. Instead, "the successful pastor must lead with authority. To exercise [it] does not mean to dictate, to be a tyrant. It means rather to lead and guide in one's work with individuals, committees, boards, as well as with the congregation." He also taught tithing and believed that each member of the congregation should pledge an annual amount of money to finance the church budget. When he retired in 1981, the budget had reached two million dollars.

Blackwood Brothers Quartet (l to r): Roy, James, and R. W. Blackwood and Don Smith with Hilton Griswold at the piano.

Well-known personalities attended First Assembly. James Blackwood of the famous Blackwood Brothers Quartet and a member of First Assembly was baptized in the Spirit under his ministry. Elvis Presley, early in his career, also attended services there, but never joined the church. In addition to pastoral responsibilities, Hamill served in many district and General Council leadership capacities and for many years as an executive presbyter. While offering advice to youth and undoubtedly reflecting on his own long ministry, he wrote: "Jesus Christ needs men and women with strong wills and clear vision, who dare to be different, who rouse the church to its sense of purpose. Such people are on course to the maximum."

TOMMY BARNETT
(1937-)

Tommy Barnett

"Any church might have a few treats for the kiddies now and then," wrote columnist Clay Thompson in a Davenport, Iowa, newspaper, "but only Tommy Barnett would oversee construction of a 500-foot-long banana split. . . . Any church might schedule some religious entertainment," he added, "but only Tommy Barnett would persuade Johnny Cash to sing for free." An old river town on the Mississippi, Davenport had never seen anything like Barnett and his expanding Westside Assembly of God.

The son of H. W. Barnett, a prominent Assemblies of God pastor in Kansas City, Kansas, he became an evangelist at sixteen. Beginning with a revival in Seminole, Texas, in 1953, he then traveled extensively across North America and to several foreign countries. With enormous personal charisma, he became a popular evangelist and stayed in this ministry for sixteen years.

On one occasion in the early 1960s, while preaching in Northern California, an elderly and well-educated businessman challenged him after an evening service: "Look here, sir! There are hundreds of religions in this country, and the followers of each sect think theirs [is] the only true one. How can a man like me discover the real truth?" After a pause, Barnett replied: "Hundreds of religions, you say? That's strange, I've heard of only two."

Contesting that he certainly must know of more than two, Barnett responded, "I admit that I find many shades of difference in the opinions of those comprising the two great schools. However, there are but two. The one covers all who expect salvation by their doing; the other, all who expect salvation by something being done for them. So you see, the whole question is very simple. . . . If you can be your own savior," he added, "you do not need my message. If you cannot, then you may well listen to it." Such has been Barnett's enthusiasm and quick thinking in witnessing for Christ.

Bringing his itinerant ministry to a close, he and his wife, Maria, joined the staff of his father's church in Kansas. Restless to pastor his own church, two years later he began seeking one. Above all else, he wanted to raise up a strong evangelistic church where conversions would be the norm, rather than the exception.

After much effort and many letters, he finally received an invitation in 1971 to pastor the small, struggling Westside Assembly in Davenport. It had averaged seventy-two in Sunday School and never kept a preacher for more than one or two years. To make matters worse, the church building stood in an unpromising part of the city. After three weeks of preaching salvation messages, not a single person came to Christ. He then wondered if he had made a mistake in moving there.

Finally, a woman approached him and said, "Brother Barnett, I've been saved for a year, and although I've never won anyone to the Lord since I have been saved, I have been going out every Friday for two hours and witnessing. I believe God has led you to this city to win people to Christ."

He then went with her and another friend knocking on doors and sharing the gospel. As a result, an elderly man came to Christ. Inviting him to church the next Sunday, Barnett had him sit on the front row and give his testimony. Following the same procedure with other converts in the following weeks, enthusiasm grew for outreach

Voices of Harmony: Gospel Quartets

With the rise in popularity of the all-male quartet in the early 1930s, gospel music seemed captivated by the timbre of the male voice. Quartets formed around the country, singing in churches, schools, civic centers, conventions, and revival meetings. Soon, the quartet sound flooded the airwaves, first on radio and then on television. During the late 1940s and early 1950s, the ABC (radio) Network broadcast the Old Fashioned Revival Hour, which featured its own popular quartet singing such favorites as "Jesus Saves" and "The Love of God."

This new singing style found immediate acceptance among the music-loving Pentecostals, including James Blackwood, Connor B. Hall, J.D. Sumner, and Eva LeFevre (one of the few female soloists). Early on, groups began to form on Bible school campuses. In 1933 four Central Bible Institute students organized a group called the Singing Parsons (originally the Couriers). Although the group saw several personnel changes over the years, it always had the same first tenor, Edwin P. Anderson. The rest of the group, which sang at four General Councils, included second tenor Marcus Gaston, bass Donald Waggoner, and baritone Elmer Bilton.

In the midst of this male-dominated genre, four young women, known as the Light Bearers Quartet, began to shine. Following their graduation in 1935 from Glad Tidings Bible Institute, Katherine Lehto, Mary Filardo, Laurette Searles, and Ida Conduits left San Francisco in an old Chevrolet for what was to be a summer of singing ministry. That summer lasted for 11 years. During that time the Light Bearers Quartet lived a life of prayer, earnestly desiring to see souls saved and believers filled with the Holy Spirit. In some meetings they did not sing or preach, but just prayed and sought God. One meeting in Minnesota lasted for seven weeks as the power of God fell and touched many lives.

—*Kenneth A. Worthley*

to unbelievers. This began to transform the congregation. "People are being saved every week; something has to be done for their transportation," he told the faithful. After an attempt at carpooling, the church began to purchase buses, finally assembling an entire fleet of them.

While driving one of the buses, a deacon stopped to pick up some children for Sunday School and noticed a young man of about thirty years of age sitting in a nearby front yard. After being invited to church, Melvin Pridemore told the deacon that he would attend on the following Sunday. Faithful to his promise, Pridemore visited and confessed Christ as his Savior. Before long, Pridemore asked to become a "bus captain." Later, he broke all records in the United States for the number of people he brought to Sunday School. On one Easter Sunday, he brought 676 people to church in numerous bus runs.

To attract interest in the Quad Cities (Davenport and Bettendorf, Iowa; Rock Island and Moline, Illinois), Barnett creatively used publicity and every conceivable program to reach the lost for Christ and to disciple them. When he left Davenport in 1979 to pastor in Phoenix, Arizona, Westside Assembly averaged forty-four hundred.

CHARLIE LEE
(1924-2003)

An echo came back as a boy shouted across a small New Mexico canyon. "Who is talking to me?" he wondered. "Who dares to mock Yel Ha Yah?" Childhood experiences like this showed Charlie Lee's determination to find the purpose of life.

At seven years of age, he left home to attend a Christian boarding school where he learned the "white man's language." This introduced him to the Christian faith and a whole new world of learning. Returning home in the summers, he remained aloof from the practices of the Navajo religion even though conversion came later. His artistic interests flowered in high school as he studied silversmithing and painting. Encouraged to attend the Santa Fe Indian School because of its art program, he soon found a market for his pictures. A visiting art student from the University of New Mexico purchased his first painting, a boy straddling a palomino horse. The principal of the art school bought his second painting. After that, virtually every painting was sold almost as soon as he finished it.

Charlie Lee

After graduation, Lee supported himself by painting. His prize-winning pictures were placed on exhibit at the New Mexico State Fair, State Art Museum, DeYoung Art Memorial in San Francisco, and elsewhere. Arizona Highways magazine featured his sketches and paintings, and the Smithsonian Institution purchased one for its Navajo art collection. Despite his growing fame and success, he felt a restlessness in his soul.

In 1947, an Apache friend invited him to his home in San Carlos, Arizona, and to visit the Apache Assembly of God. "For the first time in my life I saw a group of Indians worshiping God with enthusiasm and sincerity," he remembered. After attending more services, he concluded, "I knew I was a sinner. But to me this salvation . . . was more than a thing just for me. I began to reason this way: I want to help my people; lift them out of their ignorance and darkness. The best thing I can offer them is the story of Jesus because it is of eternal value. . . . I was more concerned with their needs than my own. I felt that I had been chosen as an instrument through which God could reveal His salvation to them." Consequently, "when I finally gave myself to Christ, I was not only saying 'Yes' to Him as my Savior, but as the Savior of my people."

Shortly after his conversion, he felt called to be a missionary to the Navajo people and enrolled at Central Bible Institute in 1948 to prepare for ministry. Graduating three years later, he and his bride, Coralie, moved to Shiprock, New Mexico. Finding no suitable house to rent, they stayed with friends seventy miles away in Cortex, Colorado, and commuted back to the reservation to visit families and conduct services. When they permanently settled in Shiprock, they initially camped with the people, using their station wagon for living quarters. After a year's labor, they had their first converts.

It took three appearances before the Tribal Council to get permission to build a home. After gaining approval, Lee built a two-room house (fourteen by twenty-eight feet) in which he also held services. Sometimes forty-five people crammed into the small space; in pleasant weather, they met outside.

His plan to build a church, however, met resistance—apparently council members felt that Shiprock had enough churches. Finally, the council ruled in his favor after a member stated that their refusal had seemed inconsistent with the hope that educated Navajo young people would return to the reservation and help their own people: "Now this young man has returned and wants to start a church, and we are fighting him. He is entitled to have a piece of land, but he has been considerate enough of our authority to channel his request through our Tribal Council. I think we ought to let him have his request." This carried the argument, and the vote gave unanimous approval.

Ruth Lyon

Home Missions Editor

Ruth Lyon, who wrote 176 articles on the ministries of home missionaries for the *Pentecostal Evangel*, had served as an evangelist and also as a missionary among the Chippewa people in Minnesota. During her 33 years at the headquarters, she worked for the Sunday School Department and then spent the last 25 years as editor and promotions coordinator for the Division of Home Missions.

For Yel Ha Yah—Lee's Navajo name that means "he ascended in anger," referring to a warrior going to war—his patience positively witnessed to his faith.

In 1957, the congregation moved into a new thirty- by sixty-foot building. Within three years, it had grown to two hundred in attendance and space was once more at a premium as he and the saints evangelized the area. The local Men's Fellowship chapter had a Sunday afternoon jail service every week, and Lee journeyed to distant parts of the reservation to hold services in hogans (family dwellings built of earthen walls and supported by timbers). Home missions editor Ruth Lyon remarked, "Although he still enjoys painting when time permits, he gets a greater thrill out of observing the 'Master Artist' at work painting the beauty of salvation upon the canvas of human lives."

ALEXANDER CLATTENBURG
(1902-1972)

Alexander Clattenburg

Despite the impressive statistics of the megachurches, most Assemblies of God churches have never been large. Though people often believe that numbers measure success, pastors have achieved significant ministry through their pastoral care, discipling believers, mentoring young ministers, mothering new churches, serving in sectional and district leadership posts, and building community relationships.

Trinity Assembly of God in Baltimore, Maryland, never averaged more than 250 during the thirty years that Alexander Clattenburg pastored it. Yet he touched the lives of many parishioners over those years, as well as a host of pastors and missionaries. Although not especially gifted in administration, he preached and mentored and promoted foreign missions with distinction.

The story of Trinity Assembly dates back to its being the Baltimore Branch, or church, of the Christian and Missionary Alliance. After the Pentecostal message reached Baltimore, the church became a hotbed of revival. Relations grew strained though due to "the failure of the Alliance to keep pace with the 'Latter Rain' outpouring" and its refusal "to see in the Bible that speaking in tongues was the only evidence of the baptism of the Holy Spirit." Consequently, pastor E. F. M. Staudt and his congregation reorganized as the Full Gospel Church of Baltimore in 1923.

Clattenburg had been born into a family that emigrated from Nova Scotia at the turn of the century to settle in Lowell, Massachusetts. As a boy, he was invited to Sunday School by a woman from a local Alliance church. As a teenager, he joined the merchant marine. While stationed in Halifax, Nova Scotia, in 1917, he escaped injury after a Norwegian steamer collided with a French munitions ship carrying TNT, explosive acid, and benzene. The explosion—the largest recorded man-made blast in history until the dropping of the atomic bomb—destroyed the harbor, killing two thousand people and injuring six thousand.

Immediately afterward, Clattenburg went to the Alliance church in Halifax and surrendered his life to Christ. Eventually, through contact with Pentecostals, he received Spirit baptism and a call to ministry. To prepare himself, he enrolled at Bethel Bible Training School in Newark, New Jersey, and graduated with the class of 1923. The school had been founded seven years before by the board of the independent Bethel Pentecostal Assembly, many of whom had formerly been members of the Alliance.

Although not a typical Pentecostal church, Bethel had become one of the strongest Pentecostal congregations on the East Coast, sponsoring, for example, its own missions agency. Leading ministers of the Assemblies of God served as pastors there in the early years.

Rare among early Pentecostal congregations, its membership included several wealthy believers. The building itself had been constructed as a church and even had carpet, a clear exception to the usual storefronts, tents, and makeshift accommodations that characterized early Pentecostalism. Spiritually formed in this atmosphere, Clattenburg matured in his love for preaching and missions.

He pastored six churches and spent three years on the evangelistic field. At his first church—in Oxford, Pennsylvania—he met and married Sylvia McNamee, a schoolteacher, in 1928. Moving to Baltimore in 1942, he began serving the Full Gospel Church and became the first Pentecostal pastor to join the city's ministerial alliance. At various times he did additional course work at nearby Johns Hopkins University.

Five years later, the congregation dedicated a new building and took the name Trinity Assembly of God. With colonial architecture, steeple, and split chancel (later removed after protests), it represented a conscious move toward the religious mainstream of postwar America. The "Order of the Dedication Service" read: "The Congregation, led by the minister, the clergy, and the choir, shall proceed into the church, singing the doxology." Most Pentecostals had denounced what appeared to be the dead formality of the historic churches. Clattenburg, however, appreciated the value of ceremony as found in the Christian tradition. One can assume, however, that

On to a Million!

An estimated 28,600 different persons attended the six 1955 Regional Sunday School Conventions. There were 16,915 delegates registered according to final reports.

Delegates around the nation were challenged by the fact that the Assemblies of God Sunday Schools can reach a million members by 1960 if every Sunday School worker, every Christian, will do his or her part in reaching the lost.

The task was presented as not just the burden of the Sunday School, but as the responsibility of every department of the church. The Men's Fellowship, the [Women's Missionary Council], the Christ's Ambassadors, the Foreign Missions, the Radio Departments—all must work together in the reaching of this million souls! . . . .

—Guy Davidson, "On to a Million!"
Pentecostal Evangel (May 15, 1955): 10–11.

the procession scandalized many of the Pentecostals present. If not, then surely the singing of the "Gloria Patria" set them off.

Although an innovator, he remained devoted to the meaning and significance of the twentieth-century Pentecostal revival. He upheld the vision of the original congregation, when they had left the Alliance. In the last twenty-five years of his ministry, he became concerned that the next generation of Pentecostals might not experience the supernatural power of Pentecost. In this respect, "he was concerned that history would record a generation [that] missed the glory of God and knew nothing of the special moving of the Holy Spirit."

When the General Council of the Assemblies of God condemned the New Order of the Latter Rain in 1949, Clattenburg nearly turned in his ministerial credentials. He felt the sweeping condemnation seemed to ignore the positive aspects of a movement that sought the return of the Spirit's power to the churches.

When the charismatic movement began in the 1960s and the Catholic renewal emerged later in the decade, he joined their prayer meetings and retreats at the St. Joseph Spiritual Center in the city. And he attended not simply as an observer but as a Pentecostal. He resonated with the emphasis on Spirit baptism and the ministry of the Spirit's gifts.

His contributions could also be found outside of the local church in his work as district missionary secretary. For fifteen years, Clattenburg acted as a cheerleader for foreign missions in the Potomac district, booking services for itinerating missionaries hoping to raise their financial support and housing them at his home whenever necessary—no small accomplishment given the space needed for his brood of six children.

DAENA CARGNEL
(1911-2006)

Born in Trento, Italy, just months before her family moved to the United States, Daena Cargnel was reared in a devout Catholic home. At a Catholic school in Denison, Ohio, she completed her high school education. Seeing her religious commitment and spiritual searching, a Catholic sister encouraged her to become a nun. Accepting this as God's will for her life, she made plans to enter the Carmelite convent in Nazareth, Kentucky.

Everything seemed on schedule for her move into the cloister when her father became reacquainted with a man at work, Gentilini, who had been on the same ship to the United States. Over time this Pentecostal layman asked her about being born again and encouraged her to begin reading the Bible. His patient testimony led to her conversion and Spirit baptism. She also began attending the Assembly of God in nearby Uhrichsville, Ohio.

Cargnel's initiation into ministry differed greatly from that of the other pastors in this chapter. At a Wednesday night service and with no speaker available because the church had not yet found a new pastor, members devoted themselves to prayer. All at once, she heard the booming voice of Brother Charlie Holdock say, "Sister Daena, you

Let Everybody Sing!

In most Assemblies of God churches today, it is hard to imagine a service without a song leader. Nonetheless, early Pentecostal meetings often did not have designated song leaders. In fact, no one selected songs ahead of time, the instrumentalists did not rehearse, and no one bothered to write an "order of service." Members of the congregation were free, if led by the Spirit, to lead out in any song they wished. Special musical numbers took place on the spot, with no rehearsal. Pentecostal gatherings were intentionally informal to allow for maximum participation of the congregation in the worship service through songs, testimonies, and manifestations of the Spirit. In all, the Spirit was the guide.

As congregations grew in size and respectability, many among both leaders and laity viewed the "chaos" of their heritage as unsophisticated and wanted more structure and dignity in worship. This required a greater degree of leadership in the area of music. As a result, volunteer worship leaders or a member of the pastoral staff selected songs and led the congregation in singing. Eventually, the full-time "minister of music" emerged, with song styles and singing methods related to his or her age and level of training.

In this way, they influenced tremendously the beliefs and understandings of the congregation. Besides leading in worship, the music minister may be responsible for directing a choir as well as organizing Christmas and Easter productions.

Today, the term "worship leader" not only refers to a song leader or minister of music, but to the leader of a "worship team." The leader may be the minister of music or a layperson. Worship teams lead congregations in singing and praise by their singing and playing musical instruments on the platform with the assistance of microphones. The words of the songs are often shown to the congregation through the use of a projector.

With increasing demand by parishioners for freedom in worship, the worship leader is now faced with balancing freshness in worship with excellence in music. Many are finding a fine line between entertainment and worship. With well-organized, well-rehearsed worship teams, it is a challenge to "flow in the Spirit" or allow room for manifestations of the Spirit.

—*Kenneth A. Worthley*

pray." She had never prayed in public before. But, she recalled, "the Spirit of the Lord came mightily upon me and words just flowed out. It was like I was someone else, and I found myself startled and amazed at the prayer of supplication and intercession coming forth. I prayed on and on, finally the words stopped."

Holdock, the chief deacon, then went over to her and laid "a heavy hand upon me, telling me the Lord had his hand upon me and was calling me forth to preach the gospel. I was going to go to all parts of the world and proclaim his word." Going home that night, she felt a deep joy and peace. Yet as a young woman and having just been converted six months earlier, she could hardly have understood all the implications of his statement. Nevertheless, she began studying her Bible with more intensity and hoped to enroll at a Bible institute, but finances were such that she had to stay at home and support her family.

Before long, Holdock told Cargnel to be ready to preach, since the church still lacked a pastor. "What! me preach! I hardly know the Old Testament from the New Testament—are you kidding me? I can't preach," she protested. Telling her to go home and study her Bible and pray, he gravely cautioned: "Woe, Woe, unto you if you don't preach," referring to Paul's statement in 1 Corinthians 9:16. "God has called you, you must obey." With knees shaking, she stood behind the pulpit on the following Sunday, read her text, and preached. Pleased with her preaching, he told her to prepare another sermon, adding the same solemn "Woe, Woe."

Daena Cargnel

Holdock had attended the 1921 Aimee Semple McPherson crusade in Canton, Ohio, where he had been baptized in the Spirit. Forced out of his church when it refused to accept his Pentecostal message, he left and founded Uhrichsville Assembly of God. To disciple Cargnel and instruct her in the Scriptures, he invited her and her sister to visit his home once a week with their parents' permission. "He took his large Bible in his hand and began to teach the word to us," she recounted years later; "it was like sitting at the feet of Gamaliel."

As she continued preaching and with no other minister yet in sight, the congregation unanimously voted her in as pastor. She was seventeen. Shortly after, she received a ministerial license from the district and began taking correspondence courses to further her preparation. Like many Assemblies of God pastors, she learned to minister while on the job. In the earlier years of the General Council, gaining ministerial credentials was a relatively short process.

First Gypsy Convention

The first Gypsy Convention ever held in the United States convened in Texarkana, Ark., in December 1964. The meetings were held in the only active gypsy church in America according to present knowledge.

As many as 100 gypsies crowded into the little church. . . . Gypsy ministers were able to witness to many of the 300 who joined the camp whether they attended services or not. . . .

The purpose of the first American convention was to bring all the gypsy workers together to plan activities for the coming year, to promote the gypsy work as a whole, and to strengthen the ties with the Assemblies of God. . . .

The outstanding feature of the convention was the New Year's Day service when five brethren were dedicated to the work of evangelism.

—*Ruth Lyon, "Pentecostal Fire Burns in Gypsy Camps,"*
Pentecostal Evangel *(March 7, 1965): 3, 14.*

With the support and encouragement of her husband, Hugo, she eventually pastored several small churches, the largest in Newcomerstown, Ohio, which averaged eighty-five in Sunday attendance. Hugo worked in secular employment until he became disabled. Daena later reflected that "in revivals and in pastoral work, my husband was with me. Together we worked for God." After his death in 1973, she continued in ministry as an evangelist and spoke at Full Gospel Business Men's Fellowship conventions, overseas as well as in the States. Becoming increasingly well known, she also preached on the radio and appeared as a guest on the PTL Television Network in Fort Mill, South Carolina.

MICHAEL CARDONE, SR.
(1916-1994)

"Walking in the Spirit is being receptive to God's will in our lives, being open to His 'nudges,' seeking His guidance in everyday circumstances. Walking in the Spirit is

Michael Cardone, Sr.

listening to God's inspiration instead of giving in to one's mortal negativism," wrote Michael Cardone, Sr. At first glance, one might think these are the words of a Pentecostal preacher. Cardone, however, was a devout layman, a leading industrialist and inductee into the Automotive Hall of Fame.

Cardone's story is part of the larger American drama. Born in Hughestown, Pennsylvania, the son of an immigrant Italian coal miner, he reached the pinnacle of success through hard work and ingenuity. Different from industrialists like Henry Ford II and Lee Iacocca, Cardone combined his faith and his business skills. "It was the Lord's guidance that sustained him through crises, such as devastating fires, recessions, and other calamities," wrote Norman Vincent Peale in the foreword to Cardone's autobiography *Never Too Late*.

The Cardone family came into the Pentecostal movement through the testimony of a midwife, "Mrs. Venezia," whom they noticed standing out in the street near their house preaching on a cold winter night in January 1927. This was a novelty, so Joseph and Concetta Cardone went outside to listen. Before long, they were kneeling on the pavement, praying to receive Christ as their Savior. Since Venezia belonged to a local Assemblies of God church, they joined it.

When Cardone began to seek the will of God for his life, his pastor, "Brother Antonio" Baglio, said, "Mike, just keep asking God for direction. . . . It may be His will for you to become a missionary or a preacher. . . . Or He may want you to become a good businessman, a Christian businessman." He added, "God knows the world needs more of them." Through a chain of events, Cardone began remanufacturing automobile parts. Eventually, A-1 Remanufacturing, now known as M. Cardone Industries, Inc., became the largest privately owned automotive remanufacturer in the world.

Appalled by the crude conditions and unsafe practices in the coal mine where his father worked, Cardone determined to provide the workers at his plant in Philadelphia with a safe and comfortable environment. Beyond this, he also cared for their spiritual condition. Without making attendance a requirement, the company began to sponsor early morning chapel services in 1979. Because seeking God's guidance had always been a vital part of running the business, he felt led to make prayer and worship a formal part of the operation. This led to hiring a full-time chaplain and then seven more to serve the multiethnic community employed by Cardone Industries.

Cardone and his son, Michael Cardone, Jr., as Christian businessmen, testified to their faith in other ways as well. The company added programs to help employees prepare their income tax, improve home maintenance, gain college scholarships for children, learn foreign languages, study the Bible, and enjoy themselves, adding the Factory Fun Center.

"I began to see the real reason God wanted me to start this business," he concluded. "He wanted to be invited to work in every phase of it, in every square inch of the plants, in every

Cardone Media Center, Springfield, Missouri

assembly line process, in the life of every employee. He would be our senior partner." Cardone shared his financial blessings by becoming a founding regent of Oral Roberts University in Tulsa, Oklahoma, and an international director of Full Gospel Business Men's Fellowship International, and by contributing generously to the building of the Assemblies of God's Michael Cardone Media Center and Assemblies of God Theological Seminary. In the first four years of the denomination's Decade of Harvest program for the 1990s, Michael and Frances Cardone contributed to the starting of seventeen new congregations.

"One day after attending Chapel services and noticing an employee huddled in consultation with one of our chaplains, I remembered back to when I was a youngster and wondered if God wanted me to become a minister," Cardone wrote in 1988. "I smiled when I thought of what happened when one gives oneself completely to God. He not only made me a businessman but helped me start a ministry with a parish of some twelve hundred people."

All of the persons in this chapter approached their tasks with limited resources and then faithfully and sacrificially worked hard to achieve their goals. Successful leadership has often been equated with natural endowments, administrative expertise, force of will, and enthusiasm. However, within the Pentecostal tradition, these pale in importance to the ideal attribute. Marcus Gaston, a leading pastor, explained it well at the 1968 Council on Evangelism: "True spiritual leadership . . . [comes] to those who are filled with the Spirit and who walk daily in the Spirit, so that their intellect and emotions and will all become available to God for the achieving of His purposes. Under the Holy Spirit's control, natural gifts of leadership are sanctioned and lifted to their highest power. The spiritual leader influences others, not by the power of his own personality alone, but by that personality irradiated and interpenetrated and empowered by the Holy Spirit."

All the same, the combination of God's call with hard work, gutsy determination, and creativity continued to account for the progress of the denomination.

For many years, issues of the *Pentecostal Evangel* routinely included classified advertisements. This one promoted the sale of bonds for the building of the new headquarters administration building in Springfield, Missouri (dedicated in 1962), sales opportunities for believers in Christian companies, information about companies that sold church furniture, musical instruments, and musical cowbells, among other items.

RECOMMENDED READING

Cardone, Michael, Sr. *Never Too Late: For a New Beginning.* Old Tappan, N.J.: Fleming H. Revell Co., 1988.

Cargnel, Daena. *Although the Fig Tree Shall Not Blossom: Personal Experiences and Writings.* N.p.: By the Author, 1976.

Gaston, Marcus. "The Place of Leadership in Revival." In *Our Mission in Today's World*, edited by Richard Champion, Edward S. Caldwell, and Gary Leggett, 45–48. Springfield, Mo.: Gospel Publishing House, 1968.

Gohr, Glenn. "Walking by Faith . . . Not by Sight: The Story of Blind Musician Fred Henry." *Assemblies of God Heritage* 14 (spring 1994): 11–13, 31.

Hamill, James E. *Pastor to Pastor: Insights From a Lifetime of Experience.* Springfield, Mo.: Gospel Publishing House, 1985.

Hembree, Charles R. *The Westside Story.* Grand Rapids, Mich.: New Hope Press, 1975.

Lebsack, Lee. *10 at the Top: How 10 of America's Largest Assemblies of God Churches Grew.* Stow, Ohio: New Hope Press, 1974.

Lee, Charlie. "Charlie Lee's Testimony." *Pentecostal Evangel* (17 August 1952): 10–11.

Lyon, Ruth. "Navajo Artist Builds a Church for His People." *Pentecostal Evangel* (24 April 1960): 8–9.

Tarango, Angela. *Choosing the Jesus Way: American Indian Pentecostals and the Fight for the Indigenous Principle.* Chapel Hill, NC: University of North Carolina Press, 2014.

Ward, A. G. *The Whirlwind Prophet and Other Sermons.* Springfield, Mo.: Gospel Publishing House, 1927.

Williams, Ernest S. *A Faithful Minister.* Springfield, Mo.: Gospel Publishing House, 1941.

CHAPTER 19

BUILDING THE CHURCH OVERSEAS

By midcentury, the worldwide expansion of the Pentecostal movement began to catch the attention of outside observers. Its growth interested church leaders, missiologists, historians, sociologists, and other analysts. While fundamentalists and evangelicals grimaced at this development, the facts could not be denied.

In 1953, Bishop Lesslie Newbigin of the Church of South India, a well-known evangelical and ecumenical leader, identified a "third stream of Christian tradition," which he labeled the "Pentecostal stream." He noted its emphasis on "that which is to be known and recognized in present experience—the power of the ever-living Spirit of God." Five years later, Henry P. Van Dusen, then president of Union Theological Seminary in New York City, also referred to a "third force" in Christendom in an article in *Life* magazine. Van Dusen noted the mission successes of Pentecostals as well as the growth of Holiness, Adventist, and Church of Christ. This positive reference encouraged Pentecostals to refer to themselves exclusively as the third major segment of Christianity.

Factors driving Pentecostal church growth included more than spiritual dynamics alone; strategic planning and implementing indigenous church principles figured in as well. Assemblies of God constituencies overseas mushroomed as missionaries trained nationals and then turned control over to them. Still, changing the relationship from the paternal control of missionaries to partnership did not always come easily. As Morris Williams, missionary field director for Africa stated, "It will take

Where Is the Church?

Let me . . . characterize this [third] stream by saying that its central element is the conviction that the Christian life is a matter of the experienced power and presence of the Holy Spirit today; . . . that if we would answer the question "Where is the Church?", we must ask "Where is the Holy Spirit recognizably present with power?"
—*Lesslie Newbigin*, The Household of God *(1953)*, 94–5.

grace, wisdom and determination to produce a truly indigenous church, but it is the only hope of reaching all of the lost in our generation. Sending churches can never supply enough missionaries to get the job done."

Working to develop the indigenous church had many facets, sometimes even

the bricks and mortar side of the endeavor. In Fiji, Adrian and Charlotte Heetebry reported that in constructing a church building in the village of Lami, "We cannot afford a builder, so we have to do the work ourselves. A friend attending our Sunday night services has offered to draw the plans for our building as a gift to the mission, thus saving us several hundred dollars. This is most appreciated as building materials will cost far more than we anticipated. Pray with us that

Missionary Adrian Heetebry (upper left) laying hands on newly credentialed ministers and praying for them

every need will be supplied." Of course, their call for prayer implied the hope that God would lay it on the hearts of *Evangel* readers to contribute the necessary funds.

In other places, believers had the resources and the initiative to build their own churches. Missionaries Florence Christie and Karlene Burt felt "an overwhelming 'hallelujah' come to our lips" at the dedication of the new Sohag Assembly of God in Egypt. "Today, we stood . . . before a crowd of possibly three hundred well-dressed,

Evangelizing the Cities

Heeding the injunction, "arise . . . go to that great city," our missionaries and evangelists have conducted large-scale campaigns in many major cities. Tokyo, Naples, Montevideo, Rome, and numerous other cities have been the scenes of revival. Often the results can be followed up by establishing a large church or evangelistic center.

Global Conquest and Light for the Lost have joined forces to make possible a new approach to evangelism. Global Conquest funds cover the cost of renting halls, purchasing time on radio and TV stations, etc. Light for the Lost funds provide literature for saturation campaigns preceding the preaching crusades and for follow-up programs, such as correspondence courses.

. . . . As a result of revival campaigns in Seoul, Korea, a building was constructed in 1961 to seat 1,500 people. This was later enlarged to seat 2,500. Now the church has multiple services on Sundays in order to accommodate its 4,000 members. The Seoul Revival Center [now known as Yoido Full Gospel Church pastored by David Yonggi Cho with nearly three quarters of a million members] has become the base of revival for all of South Korea.

—Christine Carmichael, "Arise . . . Go to that Great City," Pentecostal Evangel (October 23, 1966): 21–22.

educated young women in a beautiful and modern church building. . . . erected mainly with Egyptian money, the sacrifice that comes with fruitful Christian lives."

Naturally, the prayer and financial support of the home constituency was vital to the mission enterprise. When missionaries had only limited funds and needed to return home, the *Evangel* would ask its readership to send in special offerings. An announcement in 1956 said that eighty-eight-year-old Frederike Juergensen, a missionary to Japan with her late husband Carl since 1913, needed to return to the United States for retirement: "The record of Mrs. Juergensen is one of loyal service and sacrifice for the cause of Christ and we believe her eternal reward in souls will be great. . . . Now it is necessary that this beloved servant return . . . and we appeal to all the friends of our sister and the work she has been doing to assist in bringing her home." And reflecting that she had no pension, it added: "There will be subsequent living expenses in addition to her fare."

Remarkable stories of sacrifice appear in the grassroots. In her retirement years, Flora Massey, a schoolteacher and later church planter in Texas, "lived on the minimum—oatmeal in the mornings and beans and cornbread—when there was no company." Grandson Kerry Wood recalled, "She did it so she could support missionaries and ministries—$5 here and $10 there, out of her social security checks." The financial sacrifices of church members in the Latin American district became evident when Augusto and Evelyn Vereau became the first missionary couple to raise most of their budget from Spanish-speaking congregations. They went to Peru in 1966.

Missions conventions became popular in churches and received the encouragement of the Foreign Missions Department. Eleanor Johnson, pastor of First Assembly in Berkeley, California—a congregation that averaged a hundred in attendance—described its 1956 convention: Despite the fact that "ours is not a large church, nor

Augusto and Evelyn Vereau
with family

Speakers at the 1971 missionary convention at First Assembly of God, Long Beach, California, pastored by Wesley P. Steelberg and his wife Earline (center): (l to r) foreign missionaries John and Cuba Hall, Bob and Hazel Hoskins, the Steelbergs, Harold Calkins, Melba and Don Ulman, and home missionary Don Ramsey

are our people particularly prosperous," she concluded that such an effort was definitely worthwhile. She told of planning for five months, enlisting the support of the church board, sending invitations to missionaries, borrowing a set of flags of the nations from the district office, using the mission convention bulletins provided by the Foreign Missions Department, and advertising in the local newspaper. Church members provided housing for the missionaries.

The meetings lasted for two weeks with thirteen missionaries present representing nine mission fields. On the final Sunday, three hundred people attended and watched a "colorful missionary parade with the missionaries in their native costumes." Johnson observed, "Our people are impressed with a new vision, determination, and conviction for godliness, and there is in our midst a new sense of reality and stability in spiritual interests."

The efforts of the seven missionaries in this chapter denote the changing scene in Assemblies of God missions: Missionaries trained in Bible institutes—more loyal to the Foreign Missions Department and with broader exposure among the churches—gradually replaced those whose loyalties had been tied to a particular sponsoring congregation. Melvin L. Hodges became well known for his popular exposition of indigenous church principles. In Indonesia, Margaret J. Brown and Marcella Dorff trained national church leaders. J. W. Tucker suffered martyrdom during the Congo uprising of 1964, a somber reminder of potential dangers in overseas ministry. Adele Flower Dalton made significant contributions to the development of Sunday School literature and teacher training in Latin America.

The last two missionaries devoted their lives to reaching marginalized peoples with the gospel: lepers and the Jews and Gypsies of France. Florence Steidel earned the gratitude of the Liberian government for her founding of New Hope Town for lepers. Finally, during the Nazi occupation of France in World War II, Kenneth Ware helped Jews escape the country and later ministered to the Gypsy population.

MELVIN L. HODGES
(1909-1988)

People walking down the street in Greeley, Colorado, probably wondered who the young man was playing the trombone and preaching at a street corner to anyone who would listen. Leading people to Christ and going places where no Pentecostal had ministered or started a church set Hodges's agenda. Lois Crews shared this vision, and they were married in 1928.

Ordained a year later by the Rocky Mountain district, Hodges pastored churches and served as a district youth leader and presbyter. Although Latin America was foremost in his mind, he remained uncertain where the Lord would have him do foreign missionary work. Inspired by the example of Gideon, who sought the Lord's will before going into battle, he laid a fleece before the Lord. In a letter to Henry B. Garlock, a former Colorado pastor then serving in the Gold Coast (present-day Ghana), Hodges shared his interest in missions. As he sent it, he prayed, "'Lord, if you want me to go to the mission field have Brother Garlock say something about this to me in his reply.' To my dismay, Garlock did not mention the subject."

Melvin and Lois Hodges in Central America

Two years later, however, he received another letter from Garlock, who now urged him to apply for appointment to Africa. Because this raised his hopes, he now faced the dilemma of where God wanted him to go, Latin America or Africa. He applied for the Gold Coast because at long last the question behind the fleece seemed to have been divinely answered. That was before Noel Perkin's visit in 1935 to Fort Morgan, Colorado, where Hodges pastored at the time. Perkin, a former missionary to Argentina, challenged him with the need for missionaries in Latin America. "Everyone feels good about your being a missionary," he told Hodges, "but not about your going to Africa." At last, his intense desire to work in Latin America would be realized.

On April 5, 1936, their ship neared port, or perhaps it would be more accurate to say was shipwrecked outside the harbor of Acajutla, El Salvador, in Central America. Despite this perilous incident, Hodges wrote, "Once again in this experience, we have witnessed the truth of the scripture 'that all things work together for good to those that love the Lord' [Romans 8:28]." As it had turned out, the immigration officers waived the landing fees and duty charges, saving these financially pressed missionaries a considerable sum of money.

China Missionary with Christ

B Martin Kvamme, 80, of Tacoma, Washington, went to his eternal reward [on] July 21, 1966. Born in Bergen, Norway, in 1886, Brother Kvamme was married in 1912 and ordained to the ministry in 1914. After moving to Tacoma, Washington, he became a member of the Northwest District Council of the Assemblies of God and received his appointment for missionary service in China in 1921.

The Kvammes labored for the Lord in North China from that time until 1946, coming home for furlough only in 1928 and 1937, and were in North China during the difficult years of World War II.

When missionaries could no longer go into China, Brother Kvamme organized the Oriental Relief Agency at Tacoma. This was a blessing to the work in the Far East in the years after World War II and the Korean War.

The steel barrels, which he packed with a hydraulic press, were often so full of clothing that they would nearly explode when opened in the Orient.

Customs officials learned to leave his barrels alone, for they could not begin to refill them after inspection.

He was also very helpful to the missionaries of the Northwest District in packing and shipping their equipment. He would always remind them that when he went out to China, a few suitcases had been sufficient for all he and his wife carried with them to the field.

During his last years he worked among the shut-ins of Tacoma's First Assembly. He was only sick for a few days before he passed on to be with the Lord.

He is survived by his wife, Martina; a brother; four sisters; and several nieces and nephews.

—Pentecostal Evangel *(October 23, 1966): 15.*

Before his departure, Perkin had recommended that he read two books by Roland Allen, *Missionary Methods: St. Paul's or Ours?* (1912) and *The Spontaneous Expansion of the Church and the Causes Which Hinder It* (1927). Hodges's assignment to work with Ralph D. Williams, an understudy of Alice E. Luce, afforded him the opportunity to learn first-hand within a context already being fashioned by the teachings of Allen. Eventually, El Salvador became a showcase of church planting.

After ten months there, Melvin and Lois and their family moved to Matagalpa, Nicaragua. They traveled extensively to survey the churches, often living in primitive conditions. Convinced that training would best equip national ministers to reach their own people, he founded a Bible institute in Matagalpa. Those who enrolled were required to combine their studies with evangelism and church planting.

After Hodges's arrival in Central America, his penchant for writing became evident: A steady stream of letters and reports flowed from his pen to church publications. Using a simple style, he wrote in English and Spanish to the common person.

At the close of their second term in 1944, the Hodgeses returned to the United States physically exhausted. He accepted an invitation to the headquarters in Spring-field, Missouri, and worked for five years as editor of mission publications. In 1948, he became the founding editor of *Missionary Forum*, an in-house publication for missionary personnel. Using this as his pulpit, Hodges heralded the values of building self-supporting churches. In this, he joined with the missionary secretary, Noel Perkin, who cautioned the missionaries about the growing expenses of maintaining and enlarging the many orphanages and charitable institutions they supported. Perkin reasoned that "the material and physical need of the people in many lands is relatively unlimited, so that all available missionary funds could readily be absorbed in such work." Still, he credited the home constituency with a continuing interest in the needy, observing that financial appeals from these efforts consistently gained responses when others failed. For Hodges and Perkin, both of whom deeply cared about suffering people, charitable ministries represented by-products of evangelism, not primary means to that end.

Yet it is fair to say that mission leaders sometimes misjudged the value of charitable institutions in countries like Egypt and India for training church leaders. In Ted and Estelle Vassar's orphanage in South India, young men who desired to enter the ministry were encouraged to "learn a trade along with their Bible training. They were admonished not to rely solely on the Western Church for their support. From childhood, the orphans had chores for which they received an allowance and they were taught to tithe." Notable Indian church leaders emerged from this institution with an abiding appreciation for their tutelage.

In 1951, the Foreign Missions Department invited Hodges to address a special gathering of missionaries. His lectures formed the basis for what would become his best-known book, *The Indigenous Church*, published two years later. Noting one of the key ingredients for Pentecostal church growth, he declared, "The faith which Pentecostal people have in the ability of the Holy Spirit to give spiritual gifts and supernatural abilities to the common people, even to those who might be termed 'ignorant and unlearned,' has raised up a host of lay preachers and leaders of unusual spiritual ability—not unlike the rugged fishermen who first followed the Lord."

After a third term in Central America, Hodges again returned to Springfield, this time to become field secretary for Latin America and the West Indies. He began his job by overseeing the activities of nearly two hundred missionaries, planning strategy, and developing specialized ministries in radio, literature, and ministerial training. Over the years he and other leaders retrained the entire missionary force in understanding the nature of indigenous church principles and how to apply them. Not surprisingly, this changed the relationship of missionaries with national church leaders from one of paternal control to partnership.

At the same time, charitable institutions continued and new ones developed; gradually the Assemblies of God developed a holistic theology of mission. In this respect, the practice of its mission program has been a pilgrimage: a long-standing resolve to be true to the Great Commission, along with a search to understand its implications for caring for the impoverished and despised.

Hodges contributed to the education of thousands of missionaries (both Pentecostal and non-Pentecostal), who in turn prepared many more thousands of pastors, evangelists, and church workers. In addition, he became the leading Pentecostal missiologist and the first to be published outside of denominational publications; his public became worldwide.

At sixty-four years of age and after twenty years' service as field secretary, he retired from office in 1973 to begin another career as professor of missions at the Assemblies of God Graduate School (later Assemblies of God Theological Seminary) in Springfield. J. Philip Hogan said it well when he announced that Hodges had laid down "his briefcase, his passport, and his Dictaphone" to teach "a fledgling army of new missionaries." Four years later, he published another first, this time his *Theology of the Church and Its Mission*, a theology of Assemblies of God missions. Hodges illustrates the typical pioneering Pentecostal of his time. Having little more than the call

First Bible School

When the first Assemblies of God missionaries came to Indonesia, they quickly realized it would be impossible for them to reach every person individually with the gospel. With great foresight they started Bible schools to train the Indonesian Christians to reach their own people

. . . . The first Bible school in Indonesia opened in 1947, shortly after World War II ended. Missionaries Raymond and Beryl E. Busby started a night school in [Djakarta], the capital of Indonesia. Most of the men who pastor the 80 to 85 Assemblies of God churches on the island of Java were trained at this original night school and a school established later in Malang.

—*Leonard Lanphear, "Bible Schools Train Nationals,"*
Pentecostal Evangel (February 29, 1979): 17.

of God (he never finished high school), he took up the missionary task—including writing about it because no one else was—reshaped it, and then returned home to administer the program and instruct others in what he had learned firsthand. In the process, he became the best-known missionary educator of the Assemblies of God. (At age forty, while living in Springfield, Hodges successfully passed an examination for a Missouri "Certificate of High School Equivalence.")

MARGARET J. BROWN (1922-) AND MARCELLA DORFF (1923-1987)

Women have made enormous contributions to the progress of Assemblies of God missions. Notable women served as role models, including Florence Steidel (Liberia), Hilda Olsen and Peggy Anderson (Southern Africa), Lillian Trasher (Egypt), Doris Edwards (India), Lula Bell Hough (Hong Kong), and Eva and Sadie Bloom (Hawaii).

Women in local congregations worked to support the mission of the church both at home and abroad. Sandra G. Clopine, a former women's leader in the Council and missionary to Africa, said: "Women not only pray, they also help supply books, furniture, and appliances for missionary families, Bible schools, and other missions institutions overseas. Every woman who involves herself feels a keen sense of partnership with the missionary process." For example, many local chapters of the Women's Missionary Council in Assemblies of God congregations spent hours tearing sheets into narrow strips for bandages, rolling them up, and packing them with other supplies in large metal (oil) drums for shipment to New Hope Town for the lepers.

Sometimes single women missionaries teamed up for a work. Such was the case of Margaret J. Brown and Marcella Dorff, long-term missionaries to Indonesia. Margaret Brown arrived first, in 1945, along with her brother Elbert and his wife, Frances. After graduating from Northwest Bible Institute in Seattle, Washington (later Northwest College in Kirkland), Brown helped a classmate, Marie Dressler, in ministry in Idaho. A heart ailment, however, forced Brown's return to Seattle. One night, struggling with her call to Indonesia, but aware that her heart condition disqualified her for appointment, she recommitted her life to Christ. "That night the Lord definitely healed me," she wrote. "I returned to the doctor who was astounded by my apparent good health!"

Margaret Brown

From the beginning of her ministry in Djakarta, Brown became involved in Bible school teaching. "A regular day's work begins early," she remembered, "usually around 6 a.m. after breakfast, studying, paper correcting, visitation (if assisting a church and its pastor), lunch and a short siesta, bath and light supper and classes." Each morning began with prayer with the students, then supervising the work around the school, and finally teaching in afternoon Sunday Schools in different parts of the city and the adjoining villages. If this was not enough to break one's health, "there

[were] lesson stencils to run and prepare, report cards to keep up-to-date and all of the regular chores of school life."

Marcella Dorff

Marcella Dorff grew up in Fargo, North Dakota, and enrolled at North Central Bible College in Minneapolis, Minnesota. From the time of her conversion, she heard the call to missions. While still in Fargo, she had a vision while in prayer and saw "brown skinned people coming down a mountain to hear the Word and they were so happy." At North Central her interest grew, but she hesitated to tell anyone lest her dream not come true. She asked the Lord to give her a sign by having someone else confirm the call to her.

During her junior year, the Lord impressed on her the spiritual needs of Indonesia. Reminding Him of her request, she suddenly remembered the fate of Zechariah, father of John the Baptist, who also demanded a sign (Luke 1:18–20). "Icy chills ran down my back," she remembered, "and I said, 'Lord, I can't be stricken dumb, I am in school and I must earn my living.' In a flash it was made plain what God was trying to show me and I said 'Yes, [that] I believed it was God's will and I would tell others about my call.'"

Finishing her studies, Dorff went to Owatonna, Minnesota, and spent five years pioneering an Assemblies of God church. Lessons of faith learned there prepared her for the mission field. On one occasion she asked a real estate agent to help her find a new place of worship with only ten dollars "between [me] and the church." A house was purchased, and nine months later so were several lots for the construction of a church building—"God helped us to meet every payment."

Dorff departed for Indonesia in December 1952. Visiting Gambangwaluh in a remote area sometime later, she saw people walking down mountain paths to attend the church there. Observing this, she said, "I was reminded of what I had seen when I was first saved."

In 1955, she opened a Bible institute in Malang, East Java. Several months later, Margaret Brown joined her and thus began a successful partnership. In addition to the normal activities required in such schools, they supervised student church planting in the area. Spending almost forty years each in Bible school teaching and administration, they trained hundreds of pastors and church leaders and left their mark on the Indonesian Assemblies of God. When it was decided that a male national minister would direct the school, Brown and Dorff moved to a different region and established another thriving school.

J. W. TUCKER
(1915-1964)

"The missionary outlook is bright. Nothing is being done to hinder the missionary program," reported J. W. "Jay" Tucker, a missionary to the Belgian Congo (now the Democratic Republic of Congo), in a 1961 issue of the *Pentecostal Evangel*. "Never, since my first contact with The Congo in 1939 have I had reason to be more hopeful for what can be accomplished." Three years later, however, as an American perceived to be a threat to a rebel cause, he was clubbed to death, his body taken fifty miles into the jungle, and thrown into the crocodile-infested Bomokandi River.

After the Belgian Congo was granted independence, civil war had broken out. Well aware of the risk involved, Jay and Angeline Tucker left the capital, Leopoldville (now Kinshasha), where it was safer, and returned with their children to the city of Paulis (now Isiro). Both had been hesitant about returning. But one night while still in the capital, Angeline had gone into the room where their children were sleeping. "Lord, what shall we do?" she prayed, "What about taking them into this area?" At that moment, she heard His answer: "I promise to deliver these children, not from, but out of the den of lions." Angeline and Jay did not yet know that the rebels called themselves "simbas"—Swahili for "lions."

The rebel Simbas eventually took control of Paulis, placing the Tuckers and other Westerners under house arrest. Then the rebels took Jay into custody and held him, with other hostages, in a Catholic mission. Fearing an attack by American and Belgian paratroopers, the insurgents hardened their attitudes toward the prisoners. Several days passed. Angeline had received no word about her husband. Finally she telephoned the mission to inquire about his welfare. In guarded words, "the Mother Superior . . . said, 'Well, things are going along.' I said, 'How is my husband?' She answered in French, 'He is in heaven.'"

Shortly afterward, in a joint operation, American and Belgian paratroopers rescued Angeline, her children, and other missionaries. The Tucker family returned to America and settled in Springfield, Missouri. Angeline later served in the national Women's Missionary Council (later, the Women's Ministries Department).

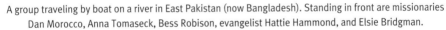

A group traveling by boat on a river in East Pakistan (now Bangladesh). Standing in front are missionaries Dan Morocco, Anna Tomaseck, Bess Robison, evangelist Hattie Hammond, and Elsie Bridgman.

Years later, Derrill Sturgeon, Assemblies of God missionary to the Democratic Republic of Congo, reported the spiritual aftermath: In the rebels' attempt to conceal their carnage, they had unwittingly served the Lord's purposes. He said that a convert of Jay Tucker's was persuaded to be police chief in Nganga, the homeland of the Mangbetus, a tribe that had been very unresponsive to the gospel for years. Their new police chief began to tell them of the missionary who "had been thrown into 'their' river" and that his "blood had flowed through 'their' waters." This arrested the attention of the Mangbetus, proving to be "the key to their hearts." Because this man had been thrown into their waters, the Mangbetus believed "now they must listen to the message" he carried. Ultimately, "a great revival began as thousands were saved, hundreds were healed, and some were even raised from the dead."

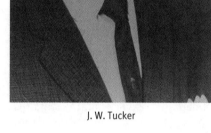

J. W. Tucker

In a eulogy entitled "Love's Summit Reached," J. Philip Hogan wrote, "[L]ove taken to its limits means a life outpoured. For some this becomes a total life span lived out day by day in giving, yielding, and sacrificing. For some it may mean a sudden final investment." The brutal murder of this gentle veteran missionary rocked the Assemblies of God as well as its missionary personnel around the world, reminding them that martyrdoms could still occur in the twentieth century. At the same time, his death prompted the dedication and rededication of many to world evangelization, as well as the response of a people who had appeared to be gospel resistant.

ADELE FLOWER DALTON
(1915-2006)

When Alice Adele Flower applied for missionary appointment in 1943, someone noted that her qualifications included being a high school and Central Bible Institute graduate; experience in writing Sunday School lessons at Gospel Publishing House; ability to play the piano, accordion, and violin; and involvement in several ministries. Her application to serve in Guatemala was accepted.

Shortly after arriving in the country in 1945, Adele was invited to speak in an adobe chapel in an Indian village, lit only by several candles. "As I looked into those hungry dark faces," she recalled, "I suddenly felt overwhelmed by the fact that this group of people was looking to me to feed them spiritually. How inadequate I felt to feed their need! Almost panic-stricken, I looked to God for help. In that moment, I felt His presence drop over me like a mantle. As I began to speak, I was lifted out of myself. Never, in English or in Spanish, have I felt greater liberty or anointing in ministering than I felt that night. I even found myself quoting Scriptures that I had never memorized in Spanish. Without a shadow of doubt, I knew that someone, somewhere, had in that moment touched God for me. And just as surely as I was ministering there in Guatemala, they also were ministering through me by their prayer."

Having known and worked with H. C. Ball, field secretary for Latin America and the West Indies at the time, she was appointed by him as the Sunday School coordinator for the region. For many years she traveled thousands of miles training leaders, speaking at Sunday School conventions, translating materials into Spanish, and writing lessons and Sunday School papers. It was a daunting task for a young single missionary.

Adele Dalton teaching Sunday School workers in the Dominican Republic

In 1950, she met Roy Dalton, a veteran missionary to Cuba and later Spain. She was thirty-five; he was thirty-four. Both had more on their minds than marriage. In the years that followed, Roy served in Spain as Adele crisscrossed Latin America. By 1957 they had become reacquainted in Springfield. With little time for courtship (less than three weeks), Roy proposed to her at the General Council meeting in Cleveland, Ohio, in 1957 in the hallway of a hotel. "With the whole world (it seemed) hurrying by, he asked me if I did not realize what God had done by bringing us both back to Springfield at the same time."

Adele and Roy Dalton

"Nodding my assent," she wrote, "I was ready for his next question: 'Will you return with me to Spain?' There was no reason for us to hesitate or think it over; both of us knew it was right."

So Roy and Adele became partners in ministry as well as in marriage. But it was an all too brief partnership. Eleven years later Roy was dead from cancer. Nevertheless, Adele stayed in Spain, working in Ronda for another eight years before returning to the United States. She joined the editorial office of the Division of Foreign Missions. Publicizing missions required interviewing scores of missionaries and writing extensively in such periodicals as Field Focus (providing information on specific mission fields), Good News Crusades, Mountain Movers, Pentecostal Evangel, and books such as Heroes of the Faith (1990).

Her personal wealth of information about the history of Assemblies of God missions enriched these publications. When missionary records (for example, letters) were being discarded to provide more space in the missions department, she took it

Such Big Feet!

My feet were not according to the fashion when I went to China. All young ladies my age, and older, had bound feet, and that made them foot-conscious. I was at a great disadvantage, for even if one is not beautiful they can improve the situation usually with a smile, but what can you do with big feet? They would measure with the thumb and index finger the size of theirs, and then have to use both hands to measure mine. I wanted to ask the Lord, "Why, when you wanted to call me to China, did you give me such big feet? However since I have a moon face and have, often been taken for a Chinese, feet notwithstanding, I let it suffice.

One day I was reading my Chinese New Testament, and the answer was found in Romans 10:15. It says, "How beautiful are the footprints of them that preach the Gospel of Peace, and bring Glad Tidings of good things." Then the Lord whispered to me, "You have preached my Gospel in many lands, and wherever you have done this, you have left a footprint that will glow throughout all eternity." Then said I, "Thank you, Lord, for giving me a big one."

—*A. Ruth Melching, Pearls by the Way (1976), 37–8.*

upon herself to collect and preserve what she could. Had it not been for her efforts, knowledge of the accomplishments of many early missionaries would have been lost.

FLORENCE STEIDEL
(1897-1962)

After World War II, the missions department discouraged the founding of new charitable institutions. They wished to invest more monies in direct evangelism. Even so, ministries of compassion continued. Furthermore, the faithful in America took great interest in them and sent funds their way.

Florence Steidel, raised in the Ozark Mountains of Missouri, grew up on a farm. Since there were no churches or Sunday Schools in the area where the family lived, they attended summer revivals held in brush arbors. At seventeen, after reading the Gospel of John, she surrendered her life to Christ.

Because there was no high school close to home, she moved to St. Louis and worked to support herself while attending school.

Kneeling in prayer at her home in 1924, the Holy Spirit showed her a foreign country in a vision. Wherever she looked, she saw dark-skinned people, needy and crying out in suffering. Wondering why no one helped them, she then understood God's call on her life and cried out, "I will go, Lord. Take me and make me a blessing to those needy ones." Another dream revealed the house where she would live in Africa: the woven floor mats, the stairway leading to the attic, and the layout of the rooms.

The missionary call changed her life. Dropping out of law school, she enrolled for nurse's training at Missouri Baptist Hospital in St. Louis, where she graduated in 1928. She then went on to the Southern Baptist Woman's Missionary Union Training School in Louisville, Kentucky, and finished a degree there three years later.

Preparing to go to Africa, possibly with Southern Baptist appointment, she stayed at the Mizpah Missionary Rest Home in New York City. While waiting for her ship to sail, she discovered that most of the missionaries in residence were from the Assemblies of God. Indeed, Mizpah was supported by the General Council, but served missionaries from other denominations as well. While fellowshipping with these Pentecostals, she became spiritually hungry and was baptized in the Spirit on November 4, 1934.

Florence Steidel welcoming Liberian President William Tubman on a visit to New Hope Leprosy Mission

Steidel received missionary appointment while still in the city. J. Roswell Flower, representing the Eastern district, recommended her because of her "high-grade" potential as a missionary. At thirty-seven she sailed for Liberia. (Ordination with the Assemblies of God, however, would come twenty years later.) When she arrived at the Palipo mission station, missionary Ada Gollan showed her the house they would share. "I have seen this house before," said Steidel. "I saw it in a vision or dream nine years ago. There is an attic, isn't there? I have been up there."

Missionary Ella Marie McCormick teaching school in Newaka, Liberia.

After working eleven years at the girls school in Newaka, she returned home infected with tuberculosis. Entering the Missouri State Sanitarium at Mt. Vernon, she resided there for a year and a half before the disease was completely arrested. After taking a course in elementary building construction at nearby Central Bible Institute in Springfield, she returned to Liberia in November 1944. Two years later, Steidel turned her full attention to her heart's desire: building a home for those with the dreaded Hansen's disease (leprosy). Evangelism and a greater ministry of compassion could now join hands.

The years that followed proved the most demanding of her life. Carving out New Hope Town in the jungle over several years, she supervised the construction of more than one hundred buildings: houses, separate schools for children with leprosy and those without, storerooms, a carpentry shop, three residences for missionaries, a thousand-seat chapel, and a Bible school. In addition to all this, she was responsible for the building of a road eighteen miles long to the nearest government road to expedite delivery of supplies. This was accomplished by cutting through the jungle, filling swamps, and erecting twenty-five bridges.

The lepers never stopped coming to the community, and she never stopped building. By her death in 1962, New Hope Town had hundreds of residents, and five hundred patients received treatment daily. Every year approximately one hundred lepers departed symptom free, about 90 percent converted to Christ before leaving the community.

Recognition of her efforts came from the American Leprosy Mission and from the government of Liberia. During the national centennial celebration in 1957, Liberian President William V. S. Tubman, who had visited New Hope Town himself, announced in a public meeting at Cape Palmas, "There is a lady in the audience who is worthy of decoration." Walking up to the surprised Florence Steidel, he conferred on her the award "Knight Official of the Humane Order of African Redemption." She became the first female missionary in the country to receive this honor.

KENNETH WARE
(1917-2005)

Although born in Memphis, Tennessee, Ware as a child returned with his mother to her homeland, Switzerland. His father, an American military officer, had lost his life in France one day before the Armistice of 1918.

Because his mother never recovered from the loss of her husband, Kenneth had been a neglected child and stuttered so badly that he couldn't pass an oral examination in school. At fifteen, running down a street in Vevey, Switzerland, he passed Smith Wigglesworth, who called out to him, "Come here, boy! Put out your tongue!"

"My mother had a lot of English-speaking friends so I thought at once that [he] was such a friend, probably an American doctor," explained Kenneth Ware. But no; it was the famous evangelist who had come to the French-speaking part of Switzerland to hold meetings. Taking hold of Kenneth's tongue, Wigglesworth abruptly said,

"Lad, this tongue will preach the gospel." From that moment, Kenneth's stuttering ceased.

Converted a year later at sixteen years of age under the ministry of Douglas R. Scott, the pioneering figure in French Pentecostalism, Ware soon felt called to preach. Ordained in 1935 he moved to Toulon, France, to minister. He later married Suzy Vinitzki, the daughter of Max Vinitzki, an orthodox Jew who had been converted while reading the Hebrew Scriptures.

In 1942, during the Nazi occupation of France, Ware noticed blood on the street. (During a raid on a Jewish home, Nazis had thrown a little Jewish girl from a third-story window.) Inquiring about the bloodstains, someone retorted, "It isn't human blood. It is Jewish blood." Outraged by this, Ware, along with his father-in-law, sheltered Jewish refugees as they attempted to escape to Spain or Switzerland. A year later, Kenneth and Suzy learned the Nazis had targeted them for arrest. Because of the impending danger, they fled to Switzerland.

On their way by train, informers spotted Ware on board, and he was arrested at the border. Knowing of his aid to Jews and connection to the French Resistance, the Nazis beat him, repeatedly knocking him to the floor. Worse yet, the authorities sentenced him to die the next day. Picking him up from the floor, the guard who had been brutally hitting him felt a package inside his coat. Reaching for it, he discovered a New Testament. With his hands shaking, the guard asked, "Are you a pastor?"

"Yes, I am," Ware responded. Silently the guard returned the New Testament to the pocket, after which he took Ware down an unused corridor and ordered him out of the prison.

Reunited with his wife and infant son in Lausanne, Switzerland, they found themselves penniless and without food. Ware heard Suzy pray in desperation early one

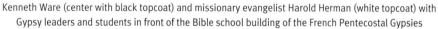

Kenneth Ware (center with black topcoat) and missionary evangelist Harold Herman (white topcoat) with Gypsy leaders and students in front of the Bible school building of the French Pentecostal Gypsies

morning, "Jesus, I need 5 pounds of potatoes, 2 pounds of pastry flour [mentioning the brand], apples, pears, a cauliflower, carrots, veal cutlets for Saturday and beef for Sunday. Thank you, Jesus." Later that morning, a man appeared at their door with the exact list of groceries that she wanted, including the brand of flour. Since they hadn't shared this request with anyone and didn't see him leave the building, they assumed that his appearance had been an angelic visitation.

Moving to Paris in 1948, Ware opened a mission in one of the worst slums in the city, where thousands of refugees and homeless people had crowded after the war. There he ministered to Jews, North African Muslims, and other needy persons. Over one hundred Jews came to Christ through his ministry. Later, he established a Bible school in Paris and worked on a new translation of the French Bible. Although a member of the French Assemblies of God, Ware received missionary appointment with the American Assemblies in 1953.

A new phase of his ministry began when evangelism and revival occurred among the despised Gypsy population in France. It started in 1954 when a Christian worker

All in a Day's Work for a Missionary

Everett L. Phillips

After arriving in Jos, Nigeria, I made a trip to Togo and Dahomey [now Benin] where I had been invited to speak at their annual convention. I flew to Lagos and then rode by bus to Lome on the coast where our mission plane in Togo-Dahomey was to pick me up. I cabled the brethren there that I would be a little late, inasmuch as I had to stop in Lagos and wait over until Monday morning to get a re-entry visa into Nigeria.

The all-night bus ride is an experience I would just as soon forget.

We went into the ditch twice, as some part of the steering kept breaking. We had to go through customs and immigration, leaving Togo and entering Dahomey, and there simply was no rest during the night. I even got fleas, which didn't make that night's journey very pleasant.

When I arrived after the all-night trip from Lagos to Lome, I saw our plane flying overhead. When I got to the airport about 20 minutes later, the airport manager told me that [our missionary] had just left to return to Natitingu. He had waited from the evening before and then decided that I wasn't coming and left. There wasn't anything to do but to turn around and head back to Lagos. So I had to rent a taxi and go back to Lagos.

Again, we went into the ditch on the way back. Our lights failed; the brakes failed; and I just about failed. We got back to Lagos about 1 a.m. but found the hotels filled. I finally got to one stinking hotel in downtown Lagos. I simply walked in with my suitcases and told them I was spending the night. There was no room, but I sat up in the vestibule with my feet on a chair and was literally chewed alive by mosquitoes all that night.

Anyway I got back to Lagos and eventually back to Jos and took up our work again.

—*Everett L. Phillips, Africa Field Director (1954–1971).*

visited an open market to sell Bibles, give out tracts, and distribute handbills inviting people to attend gospel services. One day, an illiterate woman took a tract, but didn't know its contents until four months later. When her son became seriously ill, she asked a neighbor to read it and learned the name of the local pastor and his address.

Accepting her invitation to visit her home, the pastor prayed for the boy's healing, which followed immediately. The boy then received Christ as Savior.

Word spread quickly among the Gypsies, and by 1965, over seven thousand had been baptized in water and fifteen thousand attended Pentecostal meetings. In the same year, Gypsy Pentecostal leaders invited Ware—"a man they knew loved God and the people to whom he ministered"—to represent, teach, and oversee their ministries. The Movement continued to grow as Gypsy missionaries took the gospel to other countries, including Spain and Belgium. The impact of their evangelization resulted in such a moral change in their communities that in 1968 the French government removed the laws against Gypsies and then registered them as French citizens.

Assemblies of God missionaries in the period from 1948 to 1968 transferred power to national church leaders, established Bible institutes, and wrote curricular and other materials as the need arose. They also ministered to marginalized peoples. Moving from oversight to partnership brought many changes in missionaries' lives and activities. Their motivation and commitment to missions, however, remained the same.

RECOMMENDED READING

Bolton, Leonard. *China Call: Miracles Among the Lisu People*. Springfield, Mo.: Gospel Publishing House, 1984.

Heetebry, Adrian, and Charlotte. "Fiji Island Advance." *Pentecostal Evangel* (15 January 1949): 9.

Johnson, Eleanor. "Big Missions Convention in a Small Church." *Pentecostal Evangel* (17 June 1956): 12–13.

McGee, Gary B. "Saving Souls or Saving Lives? The Tension Between Ministries of Word and Deed in Assemblies of God Missiology." *Paraclete* 28 (fall 1994): 11–23.

———. "The Legacy of Melvin L. Hodges." *International Bulletin of Missionary Research* 22 (January 1998): 20–24.

Newbigin, Lesslie. *The Household of God*. New York: Friendship Press, 1953.

Plymire, David V. *High Adventure in Tibet*. ev. ed. Springfield, MO: Gospel Publishing House, 1997.

Spence, Inez. *These Are My People: Florence Steidel*. Springfield, Mo.: Foreign Missions Department of the Assemblies of God, n.d.

Van Dusen, Henry P. "Force's Lessons for Others." *Life* 9 (June 1958): 122, 124.

Williams, Morris O. *Partnership in Mission: A Study of Theology and Method in Mission*. 2d ed. Springfield, Mo.: By the author, 1986.

Wood, Kerry. "A Legacy of Prayer, Tenacity and Faith (Flora Massey: 1896–2002)." *Assemblies of God Heritage* 22 (summer 2002): 27.

CHAPTER 20

COMMUNICATING THE GOSPEL

Pentecostals have been willing through the years to try any available means for communicating the gospel and the principles of Christian living. With or without the needed resources, they took the initiative and went forward. Sometimes they embraced unusual tactics to dramatically call attention to their message. Risking censure from the church establishment and polite society, they boldly pursued God's call on their lives. "The great accomplishments during the Church Age," wrote the well-known Pentecostal author Gordon Lindsay, "have been made by men [and women] who have prayed through and received a personal revelation of what God wanted them to do. They went ahead regardless of obstacles, and God saw them through."

In looking at the outcome of such determination, historian Grant Wacker says, "Pentecostals transcended one of the fundamental problems that had engaged the entire history of Christian thought and pastoral concern—what we might call the 'Mary and Martha' problem." They bridged their spiritual zeal—the belief that everything depends on the power of the Holy Spirit—to hard work—the notion that everything depends on human effort.

From the beginning, Pentecostals successfully used print media to spread their message. In this regard, they followed in the steps of their holiness forebears. Literature production has long been a preferred means of communicating the gospel and discipling believers. Radio and televangelism followed.

In local churches, visiting evangelists-teachers sometimes utilized large charts to instruct the saints. H. B. Kelchner of Flintstone, Maryland, who traveled across the country speaking in churches and at camp meetings, focused on the sanctified life. His chart read at the top: "Living Your Christian Life NOW in the Light of Eternity." When asked why his sermons always centered around this theme, he stated that he intended "to help . . . [the] saints to see the need of Living our Christian Life NOW as we shall have wished we

H. B. Kelchner

Evangelist John G. Hall has taken his 30-foot chart with him across North America and in countries overseas to teach on "God's Dispensational and Prophetic Plan."

had lived it when we all as Christians stand before the Judgment Seat of Christ, when we shall be unable to change the past or to do those things which we have left undone."

With a much larger chart stretched across the platform of a church—thirty feet long and in full color—John G. Hall from Newcastle, Oklahoma, taught on "The Eternal Program of God of the Ages and Dispensations." For believers in the pew, the chart projected the entire sweep of redemption from the dispensation of innocence in the Garden of Eden to the Great White Throne Judgment as depicted in the Book of Revelation, followed by the new heaven and the new earth. Other evangelists drew chalk drawings while they preached, often a scene of Christ's second coming.

The persons introduced in this chapter creatively used their talents, and as a result, "the word of God grew and multiplied" (Acts 12:24, KJV). C. M. Ward understood the value of newspaper advertising, realized the vital importance of building relationships in a community, and knew how to capture the attention of radio listeners. Mildred Whitney, a housewife in East Jordan, Michigan, prayed that God would use her in reaching others for Christ. From this humble beginning came the Assemblies of God mission to the blind. Devoted to ministry to the deaf, Lottie Riekehof penned the highly regarded *Joy of Signing*, a textbook for learning sign language.

A businessman in California who recognized the need for the distribution of gospel literature, Sam Cochran took the challenge and led the way to the Light for the Lost ministry. With the advent of the charismatic renewal in the '60s and '70s, navy chaplain Stanford E. Linzey not only preached to military personnel on the high seas, but also led thousands of people into receiving Spirit baptism in various contexts. Arvid Ohrnell, the first national prison chaplain, came to the United States from Sweden determined to win prisoners for Christ and befriend them. Finally, Ira Stanphill, a 1981 inductee into the Gospel Music Hall of Fame, warmed the hearts of millions with his many songs, reflecting the value that Pentecostals have placed on music and oral communication.

The *Pentecostal Evangel* routinely included a column announcing the scheduling of evangelists in local churches with all the pertinent information for interested readers. This announcement appeared in the May 24, 1964, issue.

EVANGELISTIC EVENTS

STATE	CITY	ASSEMBLY	DATE	EVANGELIST	PASTOR
Ariz.	Mesa	First	May 31-June 14	Gladys Voight	Vernon L. Hertweck
Ark.	Huttig	A/G	May 31-June 5	Erling Saxelid	J. O. Belin
	Pine Bluff	First	May 26-June 7	Maurice & Mrs. Lednicky	Ray Thompson
Calif.	Burbank	First	May 24-29	Christian Hild	H. P. Wilde, Jr.
	Long Beach	First	May 23-31	Hart R. Armstrong	Fulton Buntain
Colo.	Denver	First	May 24—	Musical Nathans	V. J. Crews
	Pueblo	Central	May 27—	James Black	C. F. Ferguson
Fla.	Bonifay	First	May 27—	David Grant	Arthur Moore
	Brandon	First	May 27-June 7	L. M. Addison	William Wynn
	Plant City	Turkey Creek	May 18-31	Don & Sharon Parker	H. Thomas
Idaho	Eden	A/G	May 26-June 7	C. M. Smitley	Mervin Baldwin
	Weiser	A/G	May 24-29	Dave & Sherry Harrison	Kenneth Lindgren
Ind.	Bloomington	First	May 26-June 7	Watson Argue	Robert J. Ferguson
Kans.	Ellwood	A/G	May 31-June 14	K. E. & Mrs.Matschulat	R. I. Phillips
	Topeka	Faith	May 27-June 7	Jerry & Mrs. Roberts	O. W. Hollis
La.	Alexandria	First	May 24-June 6	Ansley Orfila	Gayle Erwin
Mich.	Sault Ste. Marie	A/G	May 26-June 7	Arnold & Anita Segesman	C. C. Hanson
Minn.	Granada	A/G	May 26-29	Joel & Mrs. Palmer	Don L. Shoff
	Minneapolis	Fridley	May 19-31	W. S. Bragg	G. Mark Denyes
Mo.	Duenweg	A/G	May 25-June 8	Loyd Middleton	J. L. Hinson
	Florissant	A/G	May 26-June 7	Wesley F. Morton	Lester E. Shockley
	Liberty	A/G	May 31-June 14	Ward & Mary Popejoy	Herschel Phillips
Mont.	Billings	Parkhill	May 31-June 5	Charles Senechal	Robert Ross
Nev.	Fallon	A/G	May 26-June 5	Lynn & Becky Wickstrom	T. E. Fourt
N. Y.	Rochester	Bethel Full Gosp.	May 26-29	Warren Litzman	Phil Wannenmacher
N. C.	Charlotte	First	May 27-June 8	Ernie Eskelin	Charles Cookman
Ohio	Delta	*A/G	May 31-June 5	Dave & Pat Johnson	James E. Rickman
	Louisville	First	May 26—	Quentin Edwards	James W. Millsaps
	Johnsville	A/G	May 31-June 14	Daena Cargnel	Terry T. Diehl
	Painesville	A/G	May 26-June 7	W. W. & Mrs. Martin	Mircia Saghin
	Uhrichsville	A/G	May 26-June 7	Jerry & Joy Spain	Ronald Riley
Okla.	Shawnee	Glad Tidings	May 27—	David O. Bunch	B. E. Potter
	Wilson	First	May 31-June 14	Ervin & Mrs. Asiatico	J. R. Fuller
Oreg.	Portland	Evangel Temple	May 28—	Diehl Evangelistic Team	Joseph Dunets
Pa.	Huntingdon	**A/G	May 31-June 21	Paul Olson Party	Edward B. Berkey
Va.	Lee Mont	Faith	May 31-June 14	L. K. Dodge	Sam C. Rust II
Wash.	Colfax	A/G	May 31-June 5	Lowell & Andrea Wood	Stanley Jacobsen
	Omak	A/G	May 26-June 7	Lloyd Perera	Melvin Veland
	Sedro Woolley	A/G	May 26-June 7	Tanner Team	Carl O. Gunderson
Wis.	S. Milwaukee	A/G	May 20-31	G. A. & Mrs. Snavely	A. F. Sandell
Colombia	Bogota	Evang. Center	May 20-31	Bob Hoskins	Harry Bartel

* Children's Revival   ** City-wide Tent Crusade

Due to printing schedule, announcements must reach The Pentecostal Evangel 30 days in advance.

C. MORSE WARD
(1909-1996)

At the end of every *Revivaltime* radio broadcast, evangelist C. Morse "C. M." Ward extended an invitation to sinners to come to the "long, long altar" that stretched around the world. Thousands came to Christ, attracted to the message of the gospel through his crisp and clear sermons. A newscaster described Ward's voice as "a blend of Arthur Godfrey's one-on-one styles, Paul Harvey's pauses, and Walter Winchellian's staccato phrasing."

Sprinkled with skillfully told stories from the Bible, biographies, literature, and history, he held the attention of the sophisticated and the common person as well. Ward's radio audience crossed denominational lines, and his voice became familiar to English-speaking peoples overseas.

Born in 1909 in Toronto to Alfred G. "A. G." and Mary Ward, young Morse had a unique Pentecostal heritage. His father was a circuit-riding Methodist preacher who became attracted to the teachings of A. B. Simpson and joined the Christian and Missionary Alliance. When A. H. Argue returned to Winnipeg, Manitoba, from the Azusa Street revival, A. G. Ward was baptized in the Holy Spirit in 1907. Mary Ward came into the Movement when the Mennonite community in Ontario experienced a Pentecostal revival. "Elder" A. G. Ward, an honored title given to early Pentecostal leaders, became one of the founding fathers of the Pentecostal Assemblies of Canada (PAOC).

Although Morse had a burning desire to play professional hockey, his conversion and call to ministry took him in a different direction. Shortly after enrolling at the University of Toronto in 1925, his father and mother accepted the pastorate of Central Assembly of God in Springfield, Missouri. Moving with them, he then attended Central Bible Institute. Later, while ministering in Kansas, he met and married Dorothy Hymes. They subsequently returned to Canada to pastor a struggling congregation in Woodstock, Ontario. Like other Pentecostal preachers who lived through the Great Depression of the 1930s, the Wards barely kept bread on the table.

ON THE AIR

WITH D.V. HURST
SECRETARY
OF RADIO

GOD IS MOVING BY HIS SPIRIT! This is an inescapable fact! Hungry hearts across America are finding a satisfaction of soul in the blessed infilling of the Holy Spirit.

This, I believe, is another sign *we are in the end times*. We do not have long in which to work. The Good News must be "published" in every way possible. Every "crash" program available must be used. A sense of *extreme urgency* must grip the believing church. It cannot be "business as usual." The "ends of the world" are upon us!

This is why evangelism by radio is so important *now*. Radio "fills the air" and "gives the winds a mighty voice." It makes the gospel available to all who *want to hear* and all who *must hear*. The church has no alternative but to use the fastest and most encompassing means of communication available. Radio is as a gift from God to the church today!

And *Revivaltime* is as a gift of God to our movement. A great foundation has been laid with this service. It is time now to alert ourselves to the possibilities available and to increase the outreach of this service in a marked way. *Revivaltime can get the attention of the nation if we will give it the coverage of stations it deserves.* But not until every church shares each month in a *Revivaltime* missionary offering can this be done.

We now have 350 stations—but over three thousand are available. *Revivaltime* should be on one thousand stations! Will your church help to make this possible?

* * *

I continue to be impressed by the *home missions beachheads* being established by *Revivaltime*. For example, Northern New England is one of our most needy home missions areas. One of *Revivaltime's* good releases is in Portland, Maine. Within the radius of this outreach there are eight cities or towns in which there is already an Assemblies of God church. But there are twenty-six more cities or towns in this same radius from which *Revivaltime*

September 24, 1961

D.V. Hurst had a regular column in the *Pentecostal Evangel* promoting the activities of the *Revivaltime* broadcast.

Following a campaign held by Charles S. Price in Victoria, British Columbia, the congregation of Metropolitan Church where the services had been held requested a pastor from the PAOC headquarters in Toronto. With no one else to send, leaders there recommended Ward, who by this time was becoming known as a zealous evangelist. They added, "He doesn't know a great deal, but he is hot!" When the Wards arrived in Victoria, they found that the congregation met in an upstairs hall just a half-block from Chinatown. On the third floor, church members had placed a pulpit, a wooden platform, and old theater seats. From below they smelled the fumes from a fish-and-chips restaurant. Longshoremen, noted for their profanity, met in another part of the building.

Wondering how to attract people in this rough part of the city to his services, Ward decided to take the gospel to them through street meetings. The combination of music and testimonies with his preaching soon drew large crowds. In a story reflecting his sense of humor and unflappable nature, an alcoholic approached him during a Saturday night street meeting. "He reached me and put an arm around me and sang," Ward remembered, "bellowing out off-key an old-fashioned hymn that had come to his memory. Instead of being resentful, I took advantage of it. I put my arm around him and joined in the duet. We sang till our hearts were full. This brought a crowd like a fire. . . . I learned that the Lord sanctions and employs strange methods to bring attention to the Gospel. . . . From such street scenes it was not difficult to lead people up the steps to our hall."

Revivaltime evangelist C. M. Ward spoke to millions of listeners on the ABC Radio Network

Ward also rented a large flatbed trailer. With his singers and orchestra on board (he played the trombone), they headed down the streets into the nightlife "to serenade all of the saloons in the city."

"Sailors and B-girls and all kinds of riffraff" met them in front of the first saloon they arrived at. Gaining the manager's permission to sing and preach outside, "it was like magic," he recalled. "The drinking stopped; the dancing stopped; and the bar emptied. Many people left the nightclub first to see what was happening. Others departed to find another bar where this challenge wasn't present, because darkness can hardly exist where there is light. But others were . . . saved that night." After this, a newspaper headline read: "Pentecostal Preacher Serenades Nightclubs," featuring pictures of Ward and his musicians.

After brief stints working in Toronto as editor of the PAOC's *Pentecostal Testimony* and in Minneapolis on the faculty of North Central Bible College, Ward devoted himself to full-time evangelism and moved permanently to the United States. Beginning in 1943, he spent ten years pastoring the Full Gospel Tabernacle in Bakersfield, California. There he began radio ministry, using three and a half hours every Sunday. The success and the sparkle of his preaching earned the attention of denominational officials, who invited him to Springfield to begin their new *Revivaltime* radio broadcast on the ABC Network. "There were no material inducements," he recalled, "Springfield [headquarters] would pay me $150 a week—no housing, no utilities, no expenses. . . . All I knew was something within my soul said it was right . . . and the will of God."

Purchasing airtime on the network strained the financial resources of the denomination. Nevertheless, because their earlier *Sermons in Song* had failed to win a wide audience, a larger effort had to be made. Ward quickly became a familiar voice in homes across the country. *Revivaltime* began with the song "All Hail the Power of Jesus' Name," sung by the *Revivaltime* Choir (students from Central Bible Institute). After this came the reading of the biblical text, the sermon, and the invitation to the "long, long altar" as the choir sang Ira Stanphill's "There's Room at the Cross for You."

In his first half-hour broadcast on Christmas weekend in 1953, Ward preached on "The Big Birthday." Never once in his thirteen hundred broadcasts stretching over twenty-five years did he ever repeat a sermon; neither did a guest speaker ever preach in his place. The national Radio Department printed his sermons for interested listeners; eventually, they became available in bound annual volumes.

His early booklets offered to listeners included "The Dr. Jekyll and Mr. Hyde of the Old Testament," "Ten Year Olds in Hell?" and "The Three Big Lies of Communism."

The Quotable C. M. Ward

C. M. Ward saw Thomas Zimmerman in the headquarters lobby after the General Council executives had renegotiated health insurance. He said, "Tom [he always called Brother Zimmerman "Tom" in informal settings], if you raise Blue Cross Blue Shield another five percent, the whole General Council is going to have to go back to divine healing.

C. M. Ward went into Central Assembly in Springfield, Missouri, for a wedding and said it warranted the general superintendent, the assistant general superintendent, and "yours truly." He said there were enough flowers to feed your allergies for a hundred years and enough candles to pray the entire General Council out of purgatory.

When C. M. Ward was pastoring, it was not unusual for him to use unusual tactics to get his way. One time he wanted to renovate the restrooms. The church board did not want to have them done, so Ward found a sympathetic city official who had them condemned.

—*Charles T. Crabtree, Assistant General Superintendent*

Story of Juan Francisco, Sr.

Juan Francisco, Sr., born in 1923, was only 23 years old in 1944 when he gave his life to Jesus. The story about his conversion, however, was far from ordinary. As a youth, he had been introduced to the black art of spiritism. He became adept in this practice to the point where he was able to make money at it, revealing personal information and making predictions for his clients.

All that took a dramatic turn when he was 23 years old. In that year he had a vision that would forever change his life. He saw himself in a most unfamiliar surrounding where a man dressed in white was speaking. There were four elderly women in the audience. At the end of his speech, the man called to him, "Come and follow me." He found himself crying and the four elderly women around him saying, "Ask the Lord to forgive you of your sins."

The impact of the dream caused him to wake up. While meditating on what all it could mean, he heard a voice say, "Repent of your sins and follow me." Shortly afterward, he went to a store and bought some rum and headed for his favorite swimming hole with some friends. His intent was to drink, have fun, and forget this very disturbing chain of events. Diving deep into the water, he again heard a voice that said: "Repent and follow me."

A spiritist friend convinced him that what he saw in the dream was a Pentecostal church. She also suggested that he read Psalm 91. Tears began to flow as he read the psalm.

She then suggested that they visit a few such churches. But it wasn't until he visited the third church that he knew he was in the place he had seen in his vision: The man dressed in white was preaching and there were four elderly women in the audience. And exactly as it had occurred in the dream, when the man finished and opened the altar for prayer, he made a direct call to Francisco to repent and follow Jesus. One of four women who were around him told him to confess his sins to the Lord, which he willingly did. The church was an Assembly of God.

After some time of preparation, Rev. Francisco was sent to study at the first AG Bible Institute in the Dominican Republic. At a conference there, he met his future wife, Carmen Ramona Ramirez. Immediately upon graduating, they were sent out to plant new churches in various parts of the country. They planted five churches and each of their children was born at a different church plant. However, in their fifth assignment, his wife Carmen became ill; he was then commissioned to be an evangelist. His work for the Lord became very fruitful and widely recognized by the AG in the Dominican Republic. Later in life, Francisco moved to the United States and planted Door of Refuge Pentecostal Church (Assemblies of God) in Providence, Rhode Island, in 1974.

—*Juan Francisco, Jr.*

Catchy titles also marked the later ones: "Walking in White" touched on the theme song of the Broadway musical Carousel, and in "Love Letters in the Sand," he told the story of the woman taken in adultery and Jesus' writing in the sand (John 8:3–11).

For a quarter of a century, Ward preached weekly to a vast audience. The *Revivaltime* office eventually received eleven thousand letters a month, from common people to W. C. Hamby, composer of "St. Louis Blues," and Queen Juliana of the Netherlands. Sometimes he received letters from children addressed simply to "Preacher Ward," and they arrived in Springfield. No one took Pentecostal evangelism more successfully to the airwaves than C. M. Ward.

MILDRED WHITNEY
(1910-1994)

Far from the headlines and notoriety given to well-known evangelists, Mildred Whitney, a housewife and mother of nine, prayed, "Lord, what can I do for Thee?"

Mildred Whitney using her Braille typewriter

One Sunday during morning worship at the Assembly of God in East Jordan, Michigan, she suddenly lost her sight. "I sat as one in a trance, with the Word of God opened upon my lap, while the Lord spoke to my heart," she wrote. "For an entire hour He dealt with me showing me what it would be like if I could not see to read His precious Word."

Like many other endeavors, the Assemblies of God ministries to the blind and deaf did not originate through denominational planning or committee actions. It emerged through persons who sensed a divine call and willingly took the initiative.

Inspired by reading the story of another housewife in the Allegheny Mountains who transcribed Christian literature into Braille, Whitney wrote to her and received a copy of the Braille alphabet. With this and other information, she searched to find any organization that published Pentecostal literature for the blind. She found none, including Gospel Publishing House. At this time, she still hadn't made the acquaintance of a single blind person.

Whitney began her ministry in 1949 at nearly forty years of age. Raising nine children, including one with leukemia, and taking care of the usual household responsibilities left her little time for anything else. Furthermore, Edward Whitney, her husband, used their car for his well-drilling business during the day; this left her without transportation during normal working hours. Yet when she finished her tasks in the evening, she continued her study of the Braille characters. Two years later, she began transcribing Pentecostal literature into Braille.

Transcribing and printing Braille was a difficult task with limited resources. Nevertheless, Mildred and Edward made their own type press and drying racks. The process required making a Braille master copy for each page and punching every dot individually with a platen stylus. The backside then had to be lacquered and hardened to insure that the raised Braille letters would not be crushed when she ran them and the paper for copies through the wringer on her washing machine. Afterward, they were hung up to dry. From this painstaking procedure, Whitney began producing Sunday School quarterlies and the monthly *Pentecostal Digest*, made up of selected articles printed in the *Pentecostal Evangel*. Copies were soon mailed across North America.

Supportive of his wife's growing ministry, Edward kept the equipment in repair. Because of the growing demand for these publications, he gave her a Braillewriter on their wedding anniversary in 1954. As the work increased, members of First Assembly in Waukesha, Wisconsin, where they had relocated, began sharing her burden. Several learned Braille to help in transcribing and helped in the monthly mailings, which exceeded six hundred pieces by 1964. The church later provided office space and a voluntary staff.

As the ministry grew, the national Home Missions Department of the Assemblies of God provided assistance and gave her appointment as a home missionary in 1961. More publications followed, including books, taped materials, and other items available free of charge through the Assemblies of God Library for the Blind in Springfield, Missouri, later renamed the Whitney Library for the Blind. Funds from the Boys and Girls Missionary Crusade (BGMC) purchased computerized equipment to provide more efficient Braille production. It became the second largest denominational library of its kind by 1997, serving over fifteen hundred people. After living in Springfield for several years, Whitney returned home to Waukesha where she continued publishing the *Pentecostal Digest* until her death at eighty-three years of age.

LOTTIE L. RIEKEHOF
(1920-)

"I have three deaf children, all attending the special school in West Virginia. When they are at home with me in the summer I would like to be able to tell them about God but I cannot even sign to them," said a mother to Lottie Riekehof at a Potomac district camp. "Where can I learn?" The answer to that question began an individual quest for Riekehof to cross the language barrier that separates the deaf from hearing people. In turn, that calling became the seed that produced an international ministry.

Assemblies of God ministry to the deaf dates back at least to the early ministry of Elsie Peters beginning in 1919. However, a new chapter opened in 1947 when the Christian Deaf Fellowship of the Assemblies of God was organized in Tulsa, Oklahoma. With both deaf and hearing present, delegates established it "for the purpose of banding our Christian deaf together to evangelize the deaf and to establish full gospel churches among them." Officers were then selected to promote evangelism and church planting. A coordinated ministry to the deaf would lay the basis for further progress.

Training the deaf for ministry and teaching sign language to the hearing now required another important step. In 1948, Lottie Riekehof pioneered the deaf program at Central Bible College by teaching a course on sign language. In the years that followed, a school for the deaf was established at the college, and she trained a generation of ministers in the art of sign language.

Previous to her joining the faculty as dean of women and instructor, Riekehof had become acquainted with a deaf woman. "She took an interest in teaching me the manual alphabet and signs and also told me about Gallaudet College (now University) in Washington, D.C., which I visited shortly thereafter." But when Riekehof asked to study sign language there, she was denied permission—the school educated only deaf students. Persistently she appealed the denial, until Dr. Elizabeth Peet, one of the foremost authorities on sign language in America, relented and allowed Riekehof to sit under her instruction. This led to contacts with deaf persons around the world.

Leaving Central Bible College in 1967, Riekehof moved to New York City where she earned an MA and PhD at New York University and became an associate research scientist at the institution. She later joined the faculty of Gallaudet University. Over the years, she became one of the few internationally recognized Pentecostal scholars. The scope of her instruction in sign language multiplied when she published the best-selling *Talk to the Deaf* in 1963. Together with an updated and expanded version of *The Joy of Signing*, which first appeared in 1978 through Gospel Publishing House, her books have sold in the hundreds of thousands.

Among other dignitaries, she interpreted for former President Gerald Ford, Vice President Nelson Rockefeller, and Pat Nixon. Despite these honors, her scholarship and speaking has focused on ministry to the deaf population. After all, she asked,

Lottie Riekehof teaching sign language to students at Central Bible Institute in 1949

"How shall the deaf know the way of salvation . . . except it be preached to them by someone who knows their language?"

SAM COCHRAN
(1925-2006)

The story of the Assemblies of God's Light for the Lost program began with a layperson, Sam Cochran, a successful insurance broker who attended First Assembly in Santa Ana, California. While praying after a Sunday evening service at the church, he had a unique experience: "I saw a great multitude of people standing, looking up," he recounted. "A large hand out of heaven was hold-

ing a Bible toward the people. [They] were all reaching up as far as they could, stretching out their hands to take the Bible. As the hand and Bible came down, a trap door opened beneath them, and flames and smoke shot into the air as the people dropped screaming into the pit." It was at that moment that he realized God's purpose for his life: "to send the Word of God to every soul on earth as long as He gave me breath."

Sharing his vision with several other men in the church, Cochran pledged to set aside a certain amount of money each week to purchase gospel literature for distribution; each man agreed to do the same. Among

Sam Cochran

them were members of a quartet that sang in churches in the surrounding area, and through this ministry they shared their burden. Refusing to accept remuneration for their expenses, they simply requested that offerings be taken for their project. Before long, the monies purchased Gospels of John for Mexico; later, shipments were sent to Central America, Peru, Argentina, Brazil, Italy, and Sri Lanka.

So zealous was Cochran for this ministry that he pressed pastors for invitations to share his burden. During the week, he worked at his business, but devoted the weekends to raising funds. Eventually he and his committed band of men realized the need for more organization and petitioned the Southern California District Council for recognition. Consequently, they created a board of directors and chose the name Missionary Gospel Society. Cochran served as chairman along with other elected officers. By 1959, the program had become so popular that the General Council incorporated it into its Men's Ministries Department and renamed it Light for the Lost (LFTL).

Within the next two years, the endeavor sent more than three million Gospel portions to the mission lands to be used in evangelistic endeavors. In the years to come, LFTL councilmen would give millions of dollars in dues and raise even more for literature ministry at home and abroad. "It has been thrilling to watch a vision become a reality," wrote Everett James, an early leader. "'Light for the Lost' began with a burden and continues because dedicated laymen of the Assemblies of God are willing to shoulder this burden for lost men and women around the world."

STANFORD E. LINZEY, CAPTAIN, USN (1920-2010)

"Abandon ship!" Fearing that the aircraft carrier USS Yorktown might quickly capsize and that all hands would be lost, Captain Elliott Buckmaster gave his final order to the crew. It was the Battle of Midway in 1942; the Japanese and American navies had clashed in the Pacific. Hit by torpedoes and bombs, the Yorktown now listed twenty-seven degrees. Down inside the ship, Linzey and his comrades, with battery-powered battle lanterns, had to climb up the sloping third deck to the bulkhead hatch (a small door in a wall separating compartments). Two more such climbs and they reached the top deck. At any moment, the ship could have rolled over and sunk to the bottom three miles below.

Warned not to dive off the deck, the sailors climbed down ropes thrown over the side. "Oil got in our hair, our eyes, our noses, and our ears," Linzey recalled. "We tried to keep it out of our mouths, though some failed to do so and became nauseous and vomited." Their next concern was to get as far from the ship as they

Navy chaplain Stanford E. Linzey and Army chaplain Duie Jernigan

could so that when it capsized, it wouldn't take them with it. Finally, after hours in the water, they were rescued by the destroyer USS Balch. Given the amount of oil in the water, they were fortunate that it never caught fire. Although the Yorktown was sunk, the battle went to the U.S. forces.

"When I think back to those moments when I lay in that third-deck compartment at about water level and waited for the torpedoes to strike, I realize but for the grace of God one of those Japanese torpedoes could have sent me down with the ship," said Linzey. "I do not know why some men died and others survived; I only know God had a purpose for my life that was not yet fulfilled, and for that I praise His holy name and commit my life totally to His command."

Born in Houston, Linzey grew up in south Texas and graduated from high school in the small town of McAllen. A skilled clarinetist in the high school band, he gained admittance to the U.S. Navy School of Music and the navy band. Although a Christian before joining the navy, he rededicated his life to Christ and felt called to preach. On

Bible Quizzing

The concept of young people learn- ing and memorizing the Bible in an enjoyable manner began to materialize in the mid-1940s. Youth for Christ, founded with the help of Billy Graham, first intro- duced Bible quizzing. Assemblies of God youth participated with Youth for Christ in their quiz meets until the Iowa District Council of the Assemblies of God began their own quizzing in 1958. The Potomac District soon followed their example.

In 1962, the national Youth Department initiated the first official Bible Quiz curricu- lum, "Action in Acts." The first national championship (using questions taken from the Gospel of Luke) took place the next year at the General Council in Memphis, Tennes- see. The team from Bouldercrest Assembly of God in Atlanta, Georgia, won the first of its three national championships. This record for the most wins by one church stood until Orange Hills Assembly of God, Orange, California, tied it in 2003 with their third championship.

George Edgerly has played a leading role in Assemblies of God quizzing almost since its inception. After coaching for several years, he began to write the national Bible Quiz questions in 1969. Four years later, he started writing the study guides for each season. Edgerly instituted the Junior Bible Quiz program in 1975. In 1984, he also helped imple- ment the eight-year cycle of Gospels/Acts and Epistles currently in use.

A Bible Quiz match consists of twenty questions, with varying degrees of difficulty, taken from a book or books of the New Testament. Two teams of three contestants compete to be the first to "buzz in" and gain points by correctly answering the ques- tion. Players must be familiar, not only with the actual scripture, but also the people and places mentioned in it. To compete successfully, many quizzers memorize the entire book or books for that year!

This intense study and memorization of God's Word by Bible quizzers prompted Gen- eral Superintendent Thomas E. Trask to call Bible Quiz one of the most beneficial min- istries of the national Youth Department. He sees it as "an anchor stone" that provides guidance through the troublesome and tumultuous teenage years. Quizzers heartily agree with Trask's assessment and add making lifelong friendships, learning teamwork, using decision-making skills, and practicing good sportsmanship as secondary benefits. One quizzer even uses his Bible Quiz scripture portion as a witnessing tool!

Bible quizzing is contagious. Once a quizzer, always a quizzer. Some compete year after year until they reach the age limit. Many team coaches have previously been on a Bible Quiz team. Military personnel, former participants, have started Quiz teams on their bases overseas. Often several children in a family will be involved. The older quizzers even mentor their younger siblings until they are old enough to participate. Anyone involved in this program will agree: The Word works! Bible Quiz will change your life!

—*Robert C. Phraner and Annette Newberry*

board the Yorktown and other ships, he organized Bible studies and despite some persecution stayed with this ministry.

While stationed at Pearl Harbor, he discovered a Bible study group at his base and found they had not received an official okay to meet. Volunteering to get them the needed permission, he met with the senior chaplain. With approval secured, he started for the door when the chaplain asked, "'By the way, Linzey, what church do you belong to?'

"'The Assemblies of God,' I replied.

"'Well, that's fine,' he said. 'We don't want any holy rollers down there.'

"'Don't worry about that, Chaplain,' I responded. 'We've got it under control.' I had to smile to myself as I left his office."

Like other military personnel who have returned to their branch of service as chaplains, Linzey enrolled in college and then seminary after separating from naval service in 1947. While a student, he pastored several Assemblies of God churches. After graduating from American Baptist Seminary of the West in California in 1954, he became a chaplain the following year. He was the first from the Assemblies of God to enter the regular navy officer corps.

His last tour of duty before retiring in 1974 was aboard the USS Coral Sea, named after another Pacific naval battle Linzey had been in. "History will have forgotten that the Coral Sea became known as 'the Pentecostal ship' because more than one hundred officers and seamen were baptized in the Holy Spirit and spoke in their spiritual prayer language. . . . We had a weekly charismatic service in addition to the Protestant Divine Services and noonday devotions," Linzey wrote. "Of those who later went out of the Navy, twenty-eight to thirty became pastors or evangelists in various Evangelical and Pentecostal churches. Four became Pentecostal military chaplains, and one is a Bible college president."

Since that time, Linzey traveled the world preaching and praying for believers to receive Spirit baptism. Whether sharing his Pentecostal testimony with the brass at the Pentagon or with a congregation of the local church, his ministry continued to widen through the years.

C. ARVID OHRNELL
(1891-1963)

"This riot never would have happened," said the warden of the state prison in Monroe, Washington, "if you had still been with us. You knew these men and you knew how to work with them." Concern for the outcasts of society and a desire for justice marked the ministry of Carl Arvid Ohrnell, the first national prison chaplain of the Assemblies of God.

Ohrnell was born in Sweden and reared a Baptist. As a young man, he detested injustice and oppression, whether the ill-treatment of tenant farmers or the cruelties of prison life. He received Spirit baptism in 1916 in Göteborg at a time when Pentecostal revival swept through many Baptist congregations under the leadership of the Stockholm pastor Lewi Pethrus.

A year later he moved to Uppsala, where he opened a butcher shop. One day a man entered the store who had just been released from prison after serving a four-year sentence. Although a hard worker, his prison record left him with little hope of employment and support for his family. Taking an interest in his welfare, Ohrnell provided food for his family and eventually got him a job. As a result of this encounter, he became a student of penology, the branch of criminology that deals with prison management and treatment of prisoners.

C. Arvid Ohrnell (left) praying with a man in prison uniform at a banquet

Pethrus ordained him to the ministry in 1919 at the Filadelphia Church in Stockholm. In the succeeding years, he pastored several congregations, but continued studying prison life. During the early 1920s, he wrote five books, two of which were used in European universities as textbooks in criminology. Leaving the pastorate, he moved to Germany and later to Czechoslovakia (present-day Czech Republic) to minister to prisoners. In Prague, a friend advised him that his work would be much more productive if done in a democratic state. Thus, he immigrated to the United States in 1925 and pioneered a Philadelphia Church (that is, a Scandinavian congregation) in Chicago; eight years later he moved to Seattle, Washington, and became pastor of another Philadelphia Church.

Ohrnell's continuing interest in prison ministry led to his appointment as a state prison chaplain in 1935. In this capacity, he worked for the next sixteen years in Washington prisons. He also took keen interest in securing paroles for prisoners whom he believed had been wrongfully sentenced. On several occasions, his efforts were successful.

When he moved to the headquarters in Springfield, Missouri, in 1951 to become the General Council's national prison chaplain, his ministry became nationwide. This entailed promoting the need for prison and jail ministries, preparing and grading correspondence courses for prisoners, and obtaining books for prison libraries. By the time of his death in 1963, he had mailed out over eighty thousand courses. As he toured prisons and jails, he counseled men, helped them find jobs after their release, and walked alongside those sentenced to die to their executions.

Although some Assemblies of God congregations conducted services in local jails, Ohrnell detected hesitations about the value of ministering to just one or two inmates in small community jails. "Remember, dear friend," he responded, "every man serving time in Alcatraz, Sing Sing, San Quentin, or any other state or federal institution was first in a police station, or possibly a long time in a county jail before being convicted and sentenced to another institution." He emphasized the importance of such opportunities. In a day when capital punishment was common for serious offenses in the United States, he declared, "If they are not won to Christ they may possibly some day even face the chair, the gallows, the gas chamber, or a firing squad."

IRA STANPHILL
(1914-1993)

What did Elvis Presley, Pat Boone, Johnny Cash, Kate Smith, Gordon McRea, Red Foley, and Tennessee Ernie Ford have in common? Among whatever other traits they may have shared, it happened that they all recorded songs composed by Ira Stanphill. Though the present generation of young people may not recognize the names of some of these recording artists, they were among the best-known popular vocalists of the twentieth century. Through his own itinerant ministry in churches and camp meetings, as well as through the many other persons who sang his songs, Stanphill brought hope to millions of people through songs like "I Know Who Holds Tomor-

Ira Stanphill

row," "He Washed My Eyes With Tears," "You Can Have a Song in the Night," "Supper Time," and "Jesus and Me."

In Pentecostal worship services, the faithful sang a combination of gospel songs and hymns along with many choruses that were learned by memory. (Sometimes visitors hurriedly thumbed through songbooks trying to locate the words of a song being sung, but ultimately to no avail.) People looked forward to a visiting evangelist teaching them the latest chorus.

While Pentecostalism has produced few if any lengthy creedal statements compared to the Lutheran and Reformed confessions, the saints have memorized scores of songs. In fact, when one looks at the aggregate words of these songs, they not only testify to the provision of God's grace for daily living (the major focus), but uniquely affirm belief in doctrines like the Trinity, salvation by faith, the authority of Scripture, divine healing, Spirit baptism, and the Blessed Hope. In this way, musicians like Stanphill, Herbert Buffum, Thoro Harris, Doris Akers, and Audrey Mieir through their constant production of new songs served as popular theologians across a wide spectrum of evangelical and Pentecostal audiences.

Born in Bellvue, New Mexico, to Andrew and Maggie Stanphill, musicians who were always active in church work, he spent most of his youth in Oklahoma and Coffeyville, Kansas. He had a happy childhood; the more difficult times came later.

At eight years of age, Stanphill's giftedness in music had become evident. A local radio station recognized his talent with the ukulele and gave him a fifteen-minute program, playing songs that people called in and requested. Before long, he could play the piano, organ, accordion, guitar, saxophone, clarinet, and xylophone. Converted at age twelve, he ministered in revivals, in tent campaigns, in jails, and in street meetings. After graduation from Chillicothe (Missouri) Junior College at age twenty-two, he began to devote his life to ministry.

While holding a revival in Springfield, Missouri, he met Zelma Lawson, daughter of K. H. Lawson, a Southern Missouri district official whose family had a musical ministry and a radio program. She accompanied her parents on the piano. For their wedding at Central Assembly of God in 1939, Stanphill composed the song "Side by Side with Jesus." During their years together, they wrote the well-known song "There's Room at the Cross for You." Unfortunately, it was not a marriage made in heaven. After nine years of evangelistic and pastoral work, the stormy relationship ended when Zelma filed for divorce.

His hopes for reconciliation ended when she remarried. During this time of sadness, he wrote more than 150 songs, including "We'll Talk It Over" (verse 1 and chorus):

Tho shadows deepen and my heart bleeds,
I will not question the way He leads;
This side of heaven, we know in part—
I will not question a broken heart.
We'll talk it over in the bye and bye,
We'll talk it over, my Lord and I,
I'll ask the reasons, He'll tell me why,
When we talk it over in the bye and bye.

Despite loneliness and the care of his son, Raymond, he decided not to remarry while Zelma lived. With renewed faith, he knew that God would help them.

One morning, not too long afterward, he began singing a new song as he drove to church. He later published it as "I Know Who Holds Tomorrow" (verse 1, chorus):

I don't know about tomorrow,
I just live from day to day.
I don't borrow from its sunshine,
For its skies may turn to gray.
I don't worry o'er the future,
For I know what Jesus said,
And today I'll walk beside Him,
For He knows what is ahead.
Chorus:
Many things about tomorrow,
I don't seem to understand;
But I know who holds tomorrow,
And I know who holds my hand.

Meanwhile, Stanphill discovered that Zelma had left her second husband and worked as a nightclub singer in Troy, New York. In February 1951, he learned that she had been severely injured in a car accident. Without knowing that she had died within a few hours, he rushed to New York hoping to see her before she died.

Several months later, he married Gloria Holloway, daughter of a Cleveland, Ohio, pastor. They found joy in the years that followed as their family grew and his fame increased. "The basic reason I have written songs is that I love God, and Christ has loved me," wrote Stanphill. "Most of my songs are the outgrowth of real experiences with Christ. I think they appeal to people, because I have had trials, heartaches, and sorrow in my own life, and I know what I write about." Little wonder that he entitled one of his songs "Happiness Is the Lord."

RECOMMENDED READING

Conner, Carl. "Prisons Were His Parish." *Pentecostal Evangel* (12 May 1963): 18–19.

"Editors Interview Dr. Riekehof." *Radiant News* (winter 1977–1978): 1–2, 4.

Goff, Jr., James R. *Close Harmony: A History of Southern Gospel.* Chapel Hill, N.C.: University of North Carolina Press, 2002.

Gohr, Glenn. "A Woman with a Vision: Mildred Whitney." *Assemblies of God Heritage* 16 (summer–fall 1996): 35–39, 48.

————. "This Side of Heaven: The Story of Ira Stanphill and His Popular Gospel Songs." *Assemblies of God Heritage* 14 (summer 1994): 5–6, 8, 24–26.

Grant, Steve. "C. M. Ward: Voice of the Assemblies of God for 25 Years." *Assemblies of God Heritage* 16 (summer–fall 1996): 41–43.

James, Everett. "It Began with a Vision: The Story of Light for the Lost." *Pentecostal Evangel* (2 December 1962): 10–11.

Kircher, Leon G. "The History of the Organizational Development and Ministry to the Military by the Assemblies of God, December 1941–December 1979." Unpublished paper, 1979.

Linzey, Stanford E. *God Was at Midway: The Sinking of the USS Yorktown (CV-5) and the Battles of the Coral Sea and Midway.* San Diego: Black Forest Press, 1996.

————. *Pentecost in the Pentagon.* Hicksville, N.Y.: Exposition Press, 1975.

Mieir, Audrey. *The Laughter & the Tears.* Wheaton: Tyndale House Publishers, 1971.

Segrist, Jesse. "Fine Arts Festival: Fifty Years of the Arts in Ministry." *Assemblies of God Heritage* 33 (2013): 46–53.

Stanphill, Ira, with Earl Green. *This Side of Heaven.* Fort Worth: Hymntime Ministries, 1983.

Wagner, Benjamin. "C. M. Ward: The Voice of Revivaltime, 1953-1978." *Assemblies of God Heritage* 33 (2013): 16–25.

Ward, C. M., with Douglas Wead. *The C. M. Ward Story.* Harrison, Ark.: New Leaf Press, 1976.

————, with Jeffrey Park. *Things I Didn't Learn in Bible School.* South Plainfield, N.J.: Bridge Publishing, 1982.

UNIT FIVE
1965-1992

TIME LINE 1969-1992

1969—GPH publishes *Hymns of Glorious Praise*.

1971—Council in Kansas City streamlines headquarters operation. Four assistant superintendents replaced with one assistant, G. Raymond Carlson. Departments regrouped into divisions of Christian Education, Church Ministries, Communications, Foreign Missions, Home Missions, Publications, and Treasury.

1972—Council on Spiritual Life meets in Minneapolis, Minnesota.

1973—Assemblies of God Graduate School (now Assemblies of God Theological Seminary) and Maranatha Village open in Springfield.

1974—Lausanne Congress on World Evangelization held in Lausanne, Switzerland.

1975—*Turning Point* television ministry introduced at Denver council.

1977—Assemblies of God Archives (now Flower Pentecostal Heritage Center) established. Mark and Huldah Buntain open Assembly of God Hospital and Research Centre in Calcutta, India. Kansas City Charismatic Conference convenes.

1978—C. M. Ward retires after twenty-five years as *Revivaltime* speaker. Dan Betzer succeeds him as speaker.

1981—International Media Ministries and Center for Ministry to Muslims founded.

1982—Conference on the Holy Spirit meets in Springfield.

1983—HealthCare Ministries established.

1985—Thomas F. Zimmerman (who was first elected in 1959), retires. G. Raymond Carlson elected to succeed him.

1986—First North American Congress on the Holy Spirit and World Evangelization meets in New Orleans.

1987–1988—Media attention focused on the AG because of scandals surrounding televangelists Jim Bakker (1987) and Jimmy Swaggart (1988).

1988—First International Decade of Harvest conference held in Springfield.

1989—AG celebrates 75th Anniversary at Indianapolis council and formally launches the Decade of Harvest for the 1990s. J. Philip Hogan retires as executive director of foreign missions; Loren Triplett succeeds him.

1991—Charles E. Hackett elected to serve as national director (later executive director) of Assemblies of God Home Missions.

CHAPTER 21

RENEWED MISSION IN AMERICA

When the Assemblies of God marked its seventy-fifth anniversary at the General Council meeting in Indianapolis, Indiana, in 1989, nostalgia carried the day. Delegates celebrated the denomination's remaining faithful to the vision originally articulated in April 1914 at Hot Springs. Recalling the spiritual roots of the denomination and looking toward the future, Charles Crabtree, the keynote speaker, preaching from John 4:34–38, told his audience that the Holy Spirit was saying three things to the Church: "It is time for a spiritual harvest, it is time for a biblical Pentecost," and "it is time for fervent prayer."

As everyone knew, momentous changes had taken place. For some years, the Assemblies of God had been the fastest-growing church in the United States and constituted one of the largest Pentecostal denominations in the country. Leaders celebrated its status as a major evangelical denomination. Church growth experts studied the causes behind the rapid Pentecostal expansion overseas. In his book *Look Out! The Pentecostals Are Coming*,

C. Peter Wagner reflected on the impact of prayer for the sick on the mushrooming of Pentecostalism in Latin America. "When common people . . . hear that faith in God alone can produce healing without electrocardiograms, prescriptions, injections, or even fetishes, it is no wonder they are attracted," he noted. "The physical suffering that is so much a part of today's Latin America becomes a strong motivating force to bring men and women under the hearing of the message the Pentecostals

Yoido Full Gospel Church in Seoul, Korea

preach."[1] In a notable development in Seoul, Korea, David Yonggi Cho's Yoido Full Gospel Church (Korea Assemblies of God) became the world's largest congregation, approaching three quarters of a million members.[2]

Many Americans discovered that their Pentecostal neighbors didn't fit the old stereotype of ignorant and emotional holy rollers. In many respects, their services closely resembled those of Baptist and other evangelical churches.[3] The Assemblies of God had clearly come of age. By the time the Council convened in Indianapolis, statistics for the United States showed 2,137,890 members and adherents, 30,471 ministers, 11,192 churches, and world ministries giving for domestic and overseas ministries of $155,828,125.[4] Nevertheless, it would become increasingly apparent that the growth of the denomination had leveled off.

Although speaking in tongues had declined in the ranks, observers noted that church members held a rock-ribbed confidence in the authority of Scripture, exhibited love for God and a burden to evangelize others, and had an ardent belief that biblical miracles have continued to the present day.

Most of the saints were in the middle class, and the number of professional people in the ranks continued to grow.[5] Several gained national status. President Ronald Reagan tapped an Assemblies of God layman, James Watt, to serve as his secretary of the interior. Missourian John Ashcroft served two terms as governor of the state and went on to the United States Senate before becoming attorney general in the administration of President George W. Bush. In the conservative evangelical orbit, Don Argue, formerly president of North Central University in Minneapolis, gained election as president of the National Association of Evangelicals.[6]

During the same period (1969–1992), the denomination suffered acute embarrassments involving prominent ministers, such as televangelists Jim Bakker and Jimmy Swaggart. The popular Pentecostalism they modeled revealed how much the landscape in the Assemblies of God had changed. Bakker's headquarters at Fort Mill, South Carolina, blended church services with the comfort of a luxury hotel, timeshare arrangements, and an amusement park. "Bakker modeled what many classical Pentecostals had come to suspect," wrote historian Edith Blumhofer. "One could speak in tongues and exult in the thrill of a sense of power while embracing much more of this world than had previously been supposed. His was a mellowed brand of Pentecostalism . . . devoid of much of the rhetoric that nurtured understandings of the personal and public meaning of Pentecostal experience for generations."[7]

But Swaggart's concern for world evangelism and his harsh criticisms of anything that to him smacked of compromise with the world (for example, Christian rock music, Christian psychologists and counselors, and the charismatic renewal) also charmed the faithful, at least another segment of it. Many had become uncomfortable with the growing alignment of the Pentecostal movement with the surrounding culture. Still, Swaggart's own wealth and power reflected their dilemma: being squeezed between the American dream of financial gain and the older certainty that life on earth provided just a short time to prepare for heaven.

Indeed, by the last decade of the century, the saints differed considerably from those at Hot Springs who expected that at any moment the trumpet call would sound and the Church would be caught up to be with the Lord in the clouds (1 Thessalonians 4:16–17). Ministers now invested in retirement annuities, fretted over rising costs of hospitalization, scrutinized fringe benefits, and kept a close eye on IRS policies that affected housing allowances.

Missionaries whose counterparts had gone overseas on faith and limited finances now took nearly two years to raise required budgets, itinerating among the churches to raise monthly pledges of thousands of dollars to support themselves and fund projects helpful to national churches. The headquarters in Springfield grew in size and scope of operation, while districts began building multimillion-dollar facilities to improve the efficiency of their own operations.

ORGANIZATIONAL CHANGES

The growing size of the denomination required a streamlining of its national operation, according to the Committee on Advance, which had been working on a self-study of the organization since 1967. With its recommendations in hand, the 1971 General Council in Kansas City, Missouri, adopted major changes. The five assistant general superintendents were replaced with a single assistant general superintendent who would serve without a specific administrative portfolio—G. Raymond Carlson won the vote for this office. The portfolios on home missions, church ministries, Christian education, and publishing, previously held by four of the assistants, went to "national directors," elected by the Executive Presbytery and ratified by the General Presbytery. Without the title of assistant general superintendent, J. Philip Hogan retained his unique post as executive director of foreign missions.

Focusing so much attention on institutional structure, however, caused some alarm. To alleviate fears that the Assemblies of God had taken the path of other denominations, the delegates adopted a resolution to reassure church youth that

Korean District

Responding to an invitation from General Superintendent Thomas Zimmerman, some 89 AG Korean Christians met in Springfield, Missouri, in February 1982 to form the Korean district. Representing 26 states, they adopted a provisional constitution to guide them until its council could formally meet in March 1983.

Pastor Nam Soo Kim's Full Gospel New York Church is a thriving and vibrant example of Koreans not only evangelizing fellow Koreans but reaching out to the world. The majority of the 4,000 attendees are Korean immigrants. Pastor Kim has identified two major goals in ministry for the churches: children and international missions. They have reached out to India, Cambodia, Honduras, Ecuador, Kenya, Bolivia, Brazil, and North Korea. Their mission giving to support children reaches $500,000 annually.

—*Warren Newberry*

they had remained true to their spiritual heritage: "In a time when religious structures are being exposed as so rigid and inflexible as to discourage any hope among the young that the organized Church can be a viable structure through which the love and life of God in Christ can flow toward human need, the Assemblies of God has demonstrated to its youth once more that we are determined to resist the historical face of denominationalism. We are determined to stay a revival movement."

Streamlining, however, did not mean a reduction of programs or employees, but an attempt to improve efficiency. Indeed, the size of the headquarters operation in Springfield continued to expand as programs grew. District offices also added personnel and expanded their scope of activities. More Hispanic districts were formed because of rapid growth, and the Korean district came into existence in 1982.

The 1973 General Council in Miami made significant decisions as well. First, it changed a long-standing policy of forbidding ministers from performing the wedding of a divorced person whose spouse was still living. Though not approving divorce, the decision was designed to assist ministers to help people who had marital entanglements prior to their conversion.[8] Yet despite the rising divorce rate in the culture, the Council did not change its refusal to credential a person with a living former spouse. (That came at the 2001 General Council in Kansas City with the following resolution: "We disapprove of any married person holding ministerial credentials with the Assemblies of God if either marriage partner has a former companion living, *unless the divorce occurred prior to his or her conversion* or except as hereinafter provided."[9])

Second, the delegates in Miami implemented a rehabilitation program for ministers, which had been in the works for some time. To be redemptive in orientation, it required the minister to cease ministerial activities for a period of time; with acceptable conduct and progress, the minister could apply for the reinstatement of credentials and continue in ministry. No one could foresee how severely the policy would be tested in a few short years.

Another important change came several years later in 1991 when the denomination restructured the popular Mobilization and Placement Service (MAPS) between home and foreign spheres of activity. For the Division of Foreign Missions, it became Mission Abroad Placement Service; for Home Missions, Mission America Placement Service. "MAPS is not diminishing," said Lamar Headley, director of Mission Abroad. "In fact, we expect it to grow. As home and foreign missions efforts place emphases on their own areas, there should be an increase in participation from Assemblies of God people across the nation."[10] The growth of both programs proved him right.

CALLING THE SAINTS TO REVIVAL

If the Council on Evangelism in 1967 clarified the mission of the denomination, the Council on Spiritual Life in Minneapolis in the summer of 1972 highlighted the necessity of spiritual renewal to carry it out. For three days, several thousand people listened, prayed, and worshiped. Just a few days before it convened, the first International Lutheran Charismatic Conference on the Holy Spirit took place in the city and drew an even larger crowd.[11] Both events illustrated how the face of Christianity was being transformed in the last half of the twentieth century. Pentecostalism had challenged virtually every branch of Christianity to rethink its understanding of the ministry of the Holy Spirit as it relates to the life and mission of the Church. Now the Pentecostal movement itself and the Assemblies of God in particular stood in need of

Prayer at the Council on Spiritual Life in Minneapolis. Noel Perkin stands behind the podium with G. Raymond Carlson on the left and Thomas F. Zimmerman on the right.

revival as the delegates in Minneapolis clearly realized.

Thomas F. Zimmerman gave the keynote address entitled "Be Filled with the Spirit" that set the tone for the conference. This was followed by two more evening services with evangelist Robert ("Bob") Harrison preaching the closing sermon. After morning Bible studies, the attendees could choose from a considerable variety of forums to attend. The choices ranged from "Beyond Church Walls," to "Biblical Psychology of Christian Experience," "End-Times Prophecies," "How Music Contributes to Worship," "The Charismatic Renewal in Your Community," "The Jesus Movement," "The Gifts and Fruit of the Spirit," "The Significance of the Altar Service," and "The Pastor's Wife," among others.

While most of the speakers drew attention to the work of the Holy Spirit in a person's life or that of the family and the local church, Harrison concentrated on the ministry of the Spirit in reconciliation. In his sermon "The Believer's Relationship to the World," he boldly referred to the problem of racism in the culture. "The black man is a product of his environment. Therefore, when God the Holy Spirit takes up His abode within the black man. . . . His potential is untapped because he has been kept from experiences, organizations, and places whereby he could learn, grow, mature into an effective witness and servant of Jesus Christ."[12] Among the ways to remedy the alienation, he recommended that local churches encourage discussions and offer training classes to enable believers to learn about black Christians, black culture, and black literature. "Flush from your minds those tricky theological rationalizations

Robert Harrison

about the curse of the black man," he charged. "Stop calling the black Christians 'Our dear colored brothers' as if they were a separate category of Christian. There is oneness in Christ that overshadows all other differences." Finally, "every evangelical organization should have a strong recruitment program to include blacks."[13] Harrison's call reflects the long-standing connection between revival movements and the transformation of societies.[14]

In 1978, the Executive Presbytery announced that a special church growth convention would meet in Kansas City. This meeting aimed to study the biblical pattern of church growth, to emphasize the "ministering gifts of the Holy Spirit in church growth," to share ideas, to explore resources, to train in "workable methods," and to

receive inspiration through testimonies and reports. Fifty-eight workshops presented a wide range of practical topics, from the session on church growth led by John Wimber, founder of the Vineyard Christian Fellowship, to two sessions on "Building Bridges of Fellowship to Charismatics," to starting Christian schools, building an effective bus ministry, and developing a small groups ministry. District Superintendent José Girón called for the evangelization of the millions of unchurched Hispanics in the United States and attributed the current success to the power of the Holy Spirit.[15]

John Wimber

As the charismatic renewal impacted the Assemblies of God and the faithful prayed for a fresh outpouring of the Spirit, the Conference on the Holy Spirit took place in Springfield in the summer of 1982. "In His sovereignty God is moving mightily by His Spirit throughout the earth today, bringing spiritual life to multiplied millions," declared General Superintendent Zimmerman. "The coming of the Holy Spirit upon so many and in such a broad sweep of the church world is God's way of counteracting the liberalism, secularism, humanism, and occultism that plague our society. It is His way of preparing the harvest for end-time reaping and empowering laborers to reap that whitened harvest."[16]

The audience resonated when keynoter Dennis Bennett, the pioneer figure in the Episcopal charismatic renewal and one of the best-known charismatic leaders in the world, said, "The baptism in the Holy Spirit takes place when you decide to open the

rest of your house to the Holy Spirit. To be baptized in the Holy Spirit means that our souls and bodies, as well as our spirits, are drenched and overwhelmed by God's Holy Spirit." Furthermore, "When that takes place, we become vastly more aware of God. We are able to know that He is in us, to feel His presence, both in our souls and in our bodies, and we become much more aware of the spiritual world, both good and bad."[17]

Bennett then warned against two extremes that reflected a long-standing debate among evangelical Christians: withdrawing from the world because of its evil or plunging so deeply into

Dennis Bennett

social activism as to leave the gospel behind. But with a balanced ministry, "the love of God can come through [the Spirit-filled Christian] to help meet the natural needs of mankind (to feed the hungry, clothe the naked, and take care of the sick) and also the supernatural power of God can come through him to heal the sick, cast out evil spirits, raise the dead (physically and spiritually), and change circumstances through prayer so that the will of God can be done on earth. Thus the good news will be proclaimed, that God is real and that His full Kingship is at hand."[18] Like Harrison, Bennett closely related Spirit baptism to holistic ministry at a crucial time when Council members were increasingly recognizing the need to proactively bring their Christian witness to bear in the marketplace of society.

G. RAYMOND CARLSON
(1918-1999)

G. Raymond Carlson

Born in the small town of Crosby, North Dakota, G. Raymond Carlson once remarked, "Crosby isn't the end of the world, but you can see it from there!" His conversion at a young age came during a revival held by evangelist Blanche Brittain. One evening after she concluded her sermon, George Carlson took seven-year-old Raymond to the altar where they both made a profession of faith. The Pentecostal faith of the family was affirmed not only by the elder Carlson's healing from sciatica, but his son's later healing from partial paralysis after a farming accident.

For some time the fifteen-year-old Carlson had pondered a divine call on his life and finally dedicated himself to ministry at 3 a.m. in the prayer room at Lake Geneva Bible Camp in Minnesota. He then began to preach at his home church, area churches, and in jails. In 1934 he received ministerial credentials from what was then known as the North Central district. In the same year, he enrolled at Western Bible College in Winnipeg, Manitoba, the first full-time Bible school sponsored by the Pentecostal Assemblies of Canada and modeled after Wycliffe College in Toronto. There he sat under the ministry of the revered J. Eustace Purdie, an Anglican-turned-Pentecostal who founded the school and is credited with laying much of the foundation for the doctrinal stability of the denomination.[19]

Carlson's stay at the school lasted for only one year when he returned home to work on the farm. There in the midst of the Great Depression, he labored in the harvest, hauled grain, drove tractors, milked cows, and did all the other chores that running a farm required.[20] During this time he married Mae Steffler, who also attended the Assembly of God in Crosby. Wondering about their future, they prayed for the Lord's direction. It came with a letter from his mother telling him about an announcement in the *Pentecostal Evangel* that the church in Thief River Falls, Minnesota, needed a pastor.

Soon afterward, he received an invitation from the church to hold revival services; these meetings then led to his election as pastor. The years there proved to be a time of testing, but also of great satisfaction. In her biographical sketch, Fannie Mae Hall draws attention to the qualities for which he became widely known: "Carlson's keen sense of humor, coupled with an extremely high code of ethics won him the respect of old and young alike. At one wedding he teasingly told the groom that the bride had not showed up yet."[21] More than his humor, however, people remembered his spiritual insights and integrity.

His sensitivity to the leading of the Holy Spirit became evident during one Sunday evening service before he introduced a guest speaker. "The Spirit spoke to me, not audibly, but in a very real way. 'You're going to have a funeral, and you're to use John 11:25 as your text.' The impression was very strong and kept repeating itself. Now, I knew of no one in the area of my pastoral responsibility who was ill at the time, to say nothing of anyone dying. At that moment I noticed a lady stepping into the sanctuary. She spoke briefly to my wife who was seated at the back. Shortly my wife beckoned to me; and, after presenting the speaker, I slipped out a side door to get the message." The woman asked him to go immediately to visit her father who was dying in a nursing home. That night Carlson led the man to Christ.

The next morning, the woman visited the parsonage to tell them that her father had died just minutes after they left the nursing home. She then asked, "I'd like you

The Saints Declare

"When we all get to heaven and lay our plaques at Jesus feet . . . we won't be able to see Jesus!"

—*C. M. Ward*

"As I was sitting on this thought, a bench went through my mind."
—*Delegate speaking before a General Council meeting*

"Time was when you measured a man's ministry—if not by the number of poles in his revival tent—then, by the loudness of his voice. What you lacked in content you could make up in volume. There's the story of the preacher's outline found with scrawled marginal note: 'Meaning unclear, shout here!' No longer."
—*Russell P. Spittler*

"Every time I used to hear someone sing that song about the woman with the issue of blood spending all her substance on physicians 'yet grew worse, so to Jesus she came,' I thought people were looking back at me. But medicine is much improved from the simple herbs-and-spices type of those days!"
—*K. Dewayne Piker, M.D., at the 1982 Conference on the Holy Spirit*

"We have PowerPoint in our computers to enable us to get fancy in our singing and 'current' in our preaching. But, let me tell you, if you don't have power in your soul, PowerPoint in your projector is not going to be worth a hoot. . . ."
—*Gene Jackson, former Tennessee District superintendent*

to conduct the funeral. Now I know I shouldn't tell you what to take as a text, but could you use John 11:25, 'I am the resurrection, and the life: he that believeth in me, though he were dead, yet shall he live.'?" Carlson added, "And that's the story of my first funeral service."[22]

A rising star in the North Central district, he served as district Sunday School director and missionary secretary. On his trips by train to Springfield, Missouri, for conferences during the war years, he vividly remembered the pain and suffering of the wounded soldiers on board being transported to the U.S. Army O'Reilly General Hospital, the future location of Evangel University. He became district superintendent in 1948 just as the controversial teachings of the New Order of the Latter Rain brought division within the district. Carlson's "cool head and God-given wisdom guided the district through this troubled time," according to longtime friend and colleague John Phillips.[23]

In 1961, he followed Frank Lindquist as president of North Central Bible College in Minneapolis. Students from that era remember the insights and warmth of his Wednesday morning chapel sermons.

As the decade ended, Carlson was elected one of the five assistant general superintendents. To assume his post, he and his family moved to Springfield. When the Council reorganized its national structure in 1971, it elected him to be the sole assistant superintendent. Ministers gravitated to him because of his gentle manner, common touch, and spiritual leadership.

Carlson's contributions to the denomination extended well beyond executive responsibilities. He wrote extensively for church periodicals and Sunday School literature and authored fifteen books on doctrinal subjects and Pentecostal distinctives. In *Spiritual Dynamics*, written in 1976, he warned, "The hour demands from the Church two essentials: powerful evangelism without and personal holiness within. The Pentecostal experience is the God-provided dynamic to fulfill both essentials, but it needs to be a continuous experience. When Spirit-baptized persons fail to live in the Spirit, discredit is brought upon the Spirit and His experience."[24]

Elected general superintendent in 1985 to replace Thomas F. Zimmerman, Carlson said that God had given him a threefold burden for the Assemblies of God: to seek for a "renewed sense of the holiness of God . . . a renewed fervor to win the lost . . . and discipleship with servanthood."[25] These qualities in his life would prove decisive for the denomination as it faced the scandals of the 1980s.

COUNCIL LEADERS

The twenty-six-year tenure of Thomas F. Zimmerman stretched from his election in 1959 to his departure from office in 1985 at the San Antonio Council.[26] More than any other leader in the postwar period, he had forged the alliance of Pentecostals with evangelicals and shepherded the largest expansion of programs in the denomination's history. His broader responsibilities had included chairing the International Advisory Committee of the Pentecostal World Conference, being the Protestant vice-chairman

John Ashcroft, Missouri's governor at the time, speaking at the memorial service for Thomas F. Zimmerman at Central Assembly of God in Springfield, Missouri, in 1991

for the Year of the Bible in 1983 (announced by President Reagan), and working on the executive committees of the National Association of Evangelicals and National Religious Broadcasters.[27] After leaving the superintendency, he continued serving on the Lausanne Committee for World Evangelization. For his many contributions to the local community, he received the award "Springfieldian of the Year" from the Springfield (Missouri) Area Chamber of Commerce in 1974.

Other well-known leaders in the General Council in the years from 1969 to 1992 included Theodore Gannon, Kermit Reneau, Martin Netzel, Bartlett Peterson, Charles W. H. Scott, Raymond Hudson, Norman Correll, Joseph Flower, Everett Stenhouse, and Loren Triplett.

Joseph Flower

Eldest son of J. Roswell and Alice Reynolds Flower, Joseph Flower had been strongly influenced as a youth by the ministries of William Booth-Clibburn and Charles S. Price; he graduated from Central Bible Institute (CBI) in 1934. Six years later, he married Mary Jane Carpenter. On the way to their honeymoon cottage at a lake, they stopped in Bridgeport, Connecticut, to visit a friend, Charles Greenaway, whose wife had recently died. Still grieving, the newlyweds felt sorry for him and invited him to join them on their honeymoon. Mary Jane remembered that Joseph and Charles had a great time fishing! Such kindness on the part of the Flowers characterized their ministry. (Greenaway and his second wife, Mary, became missionaries to Senegal, and he later served as field director for Eurasia.)

After serving churches in the Northeast, Flower worked as New York district superintendent and as the nonresident executive presbyter for the Northeast before moving to Springfield in 1975 to serve as general secretary. He held this post until retirement in 1993 at age eighty. He is also remembered for his advocacy of women in ministry and a privately published paper he wrote titled "Does God Deny Spiritual Manifestations and Ministry Gifts to Women?" (1979).

Before taking office as assistant general superintendent in 1985, Everett Stenhouse had been an evangelist, pastor in California, missionary to Greece, and district superintendent of Southern California. He and Carlson served concurrently, weathered the crises of the 1980s together, and led the denomination into the 1990s Decade of Harvest endeavor. Calling for renewal at the seventy-fifth anniversary in Indianapolis, he charged: "As an organization, we must acknowledge that the Assemblies of God cannot do some of the things it once did through the vitality that comes with newness. That is not to say we cannot be on the cutting edge of what God wants to do in our world today. We can! But we must recognize the source of our strength. Let us realize with Paul, 'I can do everything through him who gives me strength' (Philippians 4:13)."[28]

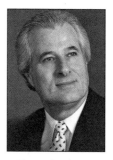

Everett Stenhouse

Born in a parsonage in San Jose, California, Loren Triplett remembered, "My father carefully divided his [income] into three parts: his tithe, his missionary commitment, and what was left for the family. The regions beyond were never far from our minds. Naturally a great deal of faith was involved in praying for a lost world, so big and unreachable."[29] From the year before his birth in 1926, his parents, Otis and Gladys Triplett, began to minister across North America to Alaska, Hawaii, and Ghana, West Africa. Growing up with such a strong mission heritage, it is not surprising that the younger Triplett felt called to be a missionary.

After eight months of Spanish language school, he and his wife, Mildred, launched their ministry in Nicaragua. Speaking the new language, however, led to occasional blunders. At one camp meeting, he invited everyone to sing "Jesus Breaks Every Fetter." But what he actually said was, "Let's sing that wonderful chorus 'Jesus Breaks Every Head.'" After fruitful years of ministry there, they moved to Miami where he directed Life Publishers International, an important literature ministry of Assemblies of God foreign missions. In 1973, he followed Melvin

Loren Triplett (r) preaching with an interpreter at the World Assemblies of God Congress in Seoul, Korea, in 1994

Hodges as field director for Latin America and the West Indies.

With the retirement of J. Philip Hogan in 1989, the General Council selected Triplett to replace him. When he began his eight years as executive director, he superintended the activities of 1,588 missionaries working in 121 countries, the largest organized mission endeavor in the Pentecostal movement. In a 1994 article in *Advance*, formerly the minister's magazine of the Assemblies of God, he laid out the basic fourfold strategy of the agency as the achievement of

1. The widest possible evangelization of the spiritually lost through every available means.

2. The establishment of indigenous churches after the New Testament pattern.
3. The training of national believers to proclaim the gospel to their own people and to other nations.
4. The showing of compassion for suffering people in a manner representing the love of Jesus Christ.

"These four statements," he added, "enfold the mission of our church overseas. Valiant missionaries have dedicated their entire lives to fulfilling these God-given responsibilities."[30]

DECADE OF HARVEST

Many evangelical denominations and parachurch agencies chose themes for the projection of their activities in the nineties, including the Assemblies of God. In January 1989, seven months before the seventy-fifth anniversary Council would meet in Indianapolis, the Executive Presbytery proclaimed the coming ten years to be the Decade of Harvest and published the goals for the United States set by the General Presbytery: "To enlist 1 million prayer partners . . . reach and win 5 million persons to Christ . . . train and disciple 20,000 persons for ministry . . . [and] establish 5,000 new churches."[31] G. Raymond Carlson admitted, "These goals are staggering if we compare what we have done during our 75 years of existence to what we are working to achieve in the next ten years. . . . During the coming decade we are talking of planting almost 50 percent more churches than the current number . . . , doubling the number of conversions each year, and increasing our ministerial force by more than 65 percent."[32]

In the previous summer of 1988, leaders from sixty nations had met in Springfield to form the International Decade of Harvest network among national churches to boost cooperation to a higher level for global evangelization. A second conference,

Surrounded by the Executive Presbytery, G. Raymond Carlson signs
the declaration announcing the Decade of Harvest.

meeting in conjunction with the Council in Indianapolis, led to the formation of the World Assemblies of God Fellowship.

Across the denomination, from the headquarters departments to the districts, schools, and local churches, leaders mobilized for evangelism and church planting. Southern California District Superintendent Ray Rachels said, "Through the burdened leadership of local pastors, we believe the greatest work of church planting will happen by using the mother church principle. Godly pastors must catch the vision and make it a reality."[33] Officials at Western Bible College in Phoenix, Arizona, devoted one chapel service each month to focus on soul winning, prayer, and establishing churches. They also introduced a new course entitled "New Church Evangelism" to train students in door-to-door evangelism and pioneering churches.[34] Finally, to develop and oversee the national program, the Executive Presbytery tapped California pastor Charles Crabtree to become director of the U.S. Decade of Harvest.

CROSS-CULTURAL MINISTRIES

Beginning in the 1970s, many avenues of cross-cultural ministry in the United States developed or were reformulated in their strategy, among them the evangelization of Jews and Muslims. Gospel witness to the Jews began early in the history of the Assemblies of God with "Hebrew missions" organized in cities like Chicago with large Jewish populations. After World War II, evangelicals and Pentecostals began to look at new ways to contextualize the gospel among the Jews. From this came the development of "Messianic synagogues," congregations of Jewish Christians retaining the Jewish cultural atmosphere and adhering to the Jewish religious calendar. Essential components include Jewish-style music, use of Hebrew and Yiddish expressions, and sermon references to Jewish history, folklore, and Yiddish proverbs. Freedom of worship in the services may include spontaneous group dancing. The congregations also emphasize strong family relationships among believers.

Two of the first home missionaries in the Assemblies of God to promote Messianic synagogues, Raymond and Kassiani Gannon moved to Los Angeles after study at Bethany College. Jewish home Bible studies and testimonies to the power of the Holy Spirit sparked the growth of their ministry. In these gatherings, Gannon prayed for the sick, and the news of remarkable healings drew interest. As a result, Jews began to attend the Thursday night services at Temple Beth Emmanuel. "[They] continued to flock in large numbers (by conventional standards)," he reported. "Statements like, 'I never felt God at the synagogue but I sure feel Him here!' punctuated their conversations."[35]

The power of the Holy Spirit prompted Jewish people to hear the gospel of the "Messiah Jesus." When they converted, Gannon encouraged them to witness to their newfound faith. In one instance, eighty-two-year-old Murray Cantor, living in Hollywood at the Knickerbocker Hotel, visited a Bible study. "After attending three meetings and coming to understand the utter Jewishness of our messianic faith," Gannon acknowledged, "he prayed to receive 'Yeshua' (Jesus) into his life. Cantor

Azusa Street and Jewish Ministry

As the "signs and wonders" people, Pentecostals are uniquely equipped to reach the Jewish people with the life-transforming gospel. . . . In our zeal, however, let us not neglect our obligation to evidence the fruit of the Spirit in our lives. The reconciliation factor present at Azusa must find expression in Jewish ministry. Walls should come down and stereotypes be set aside. Missionary fervor without godly character, true Christian love, and an educated sensitivity to Jewish-Christian history and relations will be fraught with trouble and doomed to fail.

—*Lois Olena, MAPS Associate with Jewish Ministries*

then began to testify of his faith at the hotel and pray for the sick. When word began to spread about healings, people would even stop him while walking down Hollywood Boulevard to ask him to pray for them on the spot."[36] Through the years, the Assemblies of God has remained committed to the evangelization of the Jews, in large part now through the ministry of Messianic synagogues.

The evangelization of Muslims in America has been a relatively recent ministry of the Assemblies of God. With Islam claiming to have over five hundred thousand adherents in the United States, it is currently the fastest growing major religion in the country.[37] For missionaries, ministry to Muslims has been a pilgrimage of prayer, friendship, and patience.

"Two main reasons we need to communicate with you right now," wrote Trey and Becky Hancock, appointed missionaries to the Arab Muslims in Dearborn, Michigan, in their July 2002 newsletter to supporters: Metro Outreach—a yearly outreach ministry of the Michigan District Youth Alive—would soon be sending forty students to "share the Love of Jesus and to give the Good News" in some of the parks of this heavily Muslim community. There would also be two Pinewood Derbies for the kids and three "evening cafes," sporting Arabic music, along with testimonies and human videos. "We need to ask God to draw kids and young adults out to be involved and hear the Gospel. . . . We really need God to do something supernatural. Honestly, we have never been involved with something that we have experienced so much spiritual frustration with." The reason? "Planning has been difficult: city permission has been hesitant; finances are tight, our teammates have had to be out of town at this critical time, and generally it has been difficult for us to be certain of what God wants to be done."[38]

The burden of the Hancocks for Muslims came about in an unexpected way at the Family Worship Center in Baton Rouge, Louisiana. Hancock, who played football at Auburn before transferring to Evangel University, now served on the pastoral staff. When Pastor Jimmy Swaggart invited people who wanted prayer to move forward to the altar, Hancock met an Iranian man named Shura. After sharing the gospel with him, Hancock then began to pray for him. When Shura said, "'In Jesus name' . . . his hands . . . wouldn't let go of mine," he remembered. "Big tears started coming down his face. He was sensing the reality of the living God. It was like he was coming alive."[39]

This experience stirred his interest in evangelizing Muslims. He resigned his position, thinking that God wanted him to apply for missionary appointment overseas. Attendance at a two-week summer training school in Dearborn convinced him that his mission field would be there instead. In the fall of the year, the family moved to Dearborn with only two pledges of a hundred dollars a month each from sympathetic churches. To meet their financial obligations, Hancock worked for five years as a home repairman.[40]

Working with a team of other home missionaries, they host Dearborn Assembly of God in their home, an international and multicultural congregation that works to make Muslim visitors feel comfortable. Sunday activities begin at 5 p.m. with a program for the children, dinner for all at 6 p.m., and worship at 7:30. Royal Rangers and Missionettes, which attract neighborhood boys and girls, meet on Wednesday nights.

These weekly ministries, along with Hancock's coaching a high school wrestling team, "Metro Outreach," a book table at the June Arabic Festival, and sundry other efforts have slowly born fruit.[41] "We fight the entertainment philosophy of outreach, and yet we know that something appropriate needs to be done to draw them," insist the Hancocks.[42]

This mosque in Toledo, Ohio, is representative of the growth of Islam in the United States. Courtesy of Dale Fagerland

Yet, as with all Assemblies of God mission endeavors, missionaries speak of their dependence on the work of the Holy Spirit to draw converts to the gospel, hence, the appeal to the supernatural dimension of ministry that has marked Pentecostal missions. Hancock recalls a nightmare. When he awoke he saw a "terrifying apparition" hovering above him." Ephesians 6:10 (NASB) then brought comfort: "Be strong in the Lord and in the strength of His might."

"I had to call out to the Lord, and it finally fled. . . . It was here to scare and intimidate people so they will leave the Muslims alone. I think the Lord put me through that to let me see the reality of this thing."[43] To highlight the importance of prayer for the conversion of Muslims, the Center for Ministry to Muslims, located in Springfield, sponsors the Jumaa Prayer Fellowship—Arabic for "Friday," the day for Muslim community prayer—with a membership now numbering over a hundred thousand people in forty nations.

GRIPPING THE PROBLEMS

Contrary to the stereotype that Pentecostals have valued subjective religious experiences over biblical teachings, the Hot Springs General Council in 1914 called for a network of believers who would "recognize Scriptural methods and order for worship, unity, fellowship, work and business for God, and to disapprove of all unscriptural methods, doctrine and conduct, and approve all Scriptural truth and conduct, endeavoring to keep the unity of the Spirit in the bonds of peace."[44]

In early 1915, J. Roswell Flower responded to fears that the existence of the General Council might lead to the evil of "centralization" of power in the Pentecostal movement. At the same time, doctrinal controversy was brewing over water baptism exclusively in the name of Jesus and over the Trinitarian nature of the Godhead. "We are determined to get back to Apostolic standards of order, both in doctrine and in ministry, and we believe that God is with us and will make the way plain for us," he wrote in the *Christian Evangel*. "There are dangers all about us, we are fully aware, but that is no reason why we should turn into cowards and run from the dangers, allowing someone else, more courageous in character, to step forward and overcome the foe. Mistakes will in all probability be made—we are but weak vessels of clay—but, by the grace of God, they will be corrected as fast as discovered and God sheds further light on our pathway."

Then, appealing for the faithful to stand with their leaders, he added: "May everyone of us, praying with all prayer and supplication in the Spirit, and with a firm faith which will not falter, grip the problems as they are presented and go through with God for a greater fellowship and co-operation in the work of the Lord and a greater evangelism which will not be checked until the clouds roll back, revealing the coming Son of Man in His power and glory, coming to take His beloved out of the world to be forever with her Lord."[45]

Hence, the fathers and mothers of the new organization desired integrity in doctrine and practice. The leadership, then and now, have known that the Church must respond to new challenges as they arise. To put it another way, they have wanted to insure that above all else biblical and spiritual balance would be the norm in church life, whether among ministers or people in the pew. Looking toward the fall semester at CBI in 1924, Frank Boyd shared the sentiments of leaders across the Assemblies of God when he reported to the *Evangel*, "The purpose of the Bible school was not to turn out a lot of dried up students." In marked contrast, "all the students [should] be more filled with fire and love and zeal and more filled with the Spirit when they left than when they came." Pointing to the core issue, he noted: "When men had the Word without the Spirit they were often dead and dull and dry; and when men had the Spirit without the Word there is always a tendency towards fanaticism. But where men had the Word and the Spirit, they would be equipped as the Master wants His ministers equipped."[46]

Over the course of the century, the General Council made decisions over numerous issues, beginning with the question about the Godhead in 1916, initial evidence in 1918, universal salvation in 1925, the timing of the rapture of the Church in 1937, and the teachings of the New Order of the Latter Rain in 1949. The Council chose to respond to these and other questions through resolutions and bylaws without amending the *Statement of Fundamental Truths*.[47]

Issues troubling the churches, however, eventually required further official exposition. In 1970, the General Presbytery approved the publication of "The Inerrancy of Scripture," the first of twenty-five position papers produced before 2003. Covering a wide variety of concerns, they include abortion, assisted suicide, the restoration of apostles and prophets, baptism in the Holy Spirit, creation, qualifications and responsibilities of deacons and trustees, the discipleship and submission ("shepherding") movement, divorce and remarriage, gambling, homosexuality, ordination, positive confession teachings, transcendental meditation, the role of women in ministry, among others.[48]

"To [prevent] deviations from the *Statement of Fundamental Truths* and proliferation of unscriptural teachings," the 1979 General Council authorized the establishment of the Commission on Doctrinal Purity.[49] Far from the court of inquisition that some feared, the pastors, church executives, and theologians on the panel prepare position papers at the request of the Executive Presbytery. Along with the latter, the Commission endorses denominational opinions, known as "AG Perspectives"—"commonly held beliefs"—on what the Bible teaches on such topics as "AIDS/HIV (Is It God's Judgment?)," "Capital Punishment," "Lotteries," "Pornography," "Drugs," "Racism," "Secret Societies," "Suicide," and many more. The authoritative weight of position papers and "AG Perspectives" stand second and third, respectively, to that of the *Statement of Fundamental Truths*.

In recent years, the labors of Assemblies of God scholars have significantly contributed to the better understanding of Pentecostal distinctives. To expedite their work, Gospel Publishing House created an academic imprint, Logion Press, to produce textbooks from a Pentecostal slant for the denomination's schools.

Maintaining the balance between Word and Spirit that so concerned early believers would continue to challenge church leaders and scholars as the Assemblies of God entered the twenty-first century.

HEALING THROUGH COUNSELING

"Is any one of you sick?" wrote James (5:14–16). "He should call the elders of the church to pray over him and anoint him with oil in the name of the Lord. And the prayer offered in faith will make the sick person well; the Lord will raise him up. If he has sinned, he will be forgiven. Therefore confess your sins to each other and pray for each other so that you may be healed. The prayer of a righteous man is powerful and effective." When it came time to pray for the sick in churches, Pentecostals often understood these verses more in physical than psychological terms. Yet, James included more than the physical dimension of the needy person.

In the latter half of the twentieth century, the emotional and spiritual welfare of believers—pastors, missionaries, and laypersons—suffering from personal, marital, and family problems gained more attention among evangelicals and Pentecostals. When it comes to the ministry of counseling psychology in the Assemblies of God, the names of two pioneers stand out: the late Raymond Brock and Richard Dobbins.

Coming from different ministry backgrounds, Brock and Dobbins provided leadership at a crucial juncture, promoting healthy relationships through their personal counseling, teaching seminars, and publications. Both men related scriptural wisdom to the problems that Christians face, taking them beyond the "ought to's" of the Bible to show them practical "how to's." While the insights of psychology could not substitute for theology, they could help in the application of biblical truths in daily living. Thus, counseling ministry represents another vital component of the Church's mission.

Raymond Brock

Brock's path to counseling came through his ministry as an educator and missionary. After a term of service in Nigeria, he and his wife, Lynita, moved to Springfield where he served as editor of publications for the Division of Foreign Missions. During this time, he began writing a column entitled "Dear Ray" in Christ's Ambassadors Herald, the denominational youth magazine. The question-and-answer format addressed problems that troubled teenagers. The column reappeared in the *Pentecostal Evangel* for young adults and families. He later spent many years on the faculty of Evangel University and as chairperson of its behavioral sciences department. Outside the classroom, thousands of people became familiar with his teaching on marriage and the family through marriage enrichment seminars that he conducted in churches from coast to coast.

The taproot for Dobbins's interest in counseling goes back to a painful episode in his life. When his first wife, Dolores, was expecting their first child during the late 1940s, complications arose that required a Cesarean-section birth. This led to severe postpartum depression and a period of six months in which she was suicidal. "When we looked to the medical world for help," Dobbins recalled, "they blamed her problem on religion and urged us to get out of her 'crazy religion,' reassuring us that this would result in her recovery. On the other hand, when we looked to the church for help, her devotional life came under scrutiny. We were told that she needed to spend more time in prayer and reading God's word every day.

"Delores was always a very devout person. All during this time, she was spending from 30–45 minutes a day reading her Bible and praying, even though she believed she was condemned and abandoned by God. She had no conscious awareness of God's presence in her life. But from her exemplary devotional habits, I knew her symptoms were not the result of neglecting this area of her life."[50]

The ordeal ended on a happy note: Months afterward, when the Dobbinses were praying together, she testified to being healed. From this painful experience grew an intense compassion for Christians suffering with problems of mental health.

While pastoring Evangel Temple Assembly of God in Akron, Ohio, his counseling ministry moved beyond the congregation to parishioners from other churches in northeast Ohio. Academic training in counseling psychology took him to the

University of Akron where he earned a PhD; he then became a licensed psychologist. A staff member remembers "Doc," as he is affectionately called, sitting on the corner of a desk and thumping his fist on the desktop, saying, "Someday we're going to have a place where people in pain can come. I don't know yet when or where, or what we'll call it, but we're going to have such a place someday!"

Richard Dobbins

The dream became a reality in 1973 when he founded EMERGE Ministries as an evangelical Christian mental health center. Incorporated independently of Evangel Temple, he resigned as pastor three years later to direct the program full-time. The ministry blossomed as the clientele grew and the center added more Christian therapists. Fleming H. Revell Company published Dobbins's first book in 1975: *Train Up a Child*. Other books and audiocassette series followed.

The activities of EMERGE have extended to audiences across the nation and overseas through seminars, the Institute of Pastoral Counseling, publications, and many other initiatives. In 1995, the Assemblies of God instituted a confidential hotline to EMERGE—"HelpLine"—for ministers and missionaries home on furlough, along with their families, in need of counseling. Dobbins and Pastor Jerry Qualls of Glad Tidings Church in Norfolk, Virginia, went on the radio in 1999 with *From This Day Forward*, to "share the good mental health news of the gospel."

Another ministry came with the beginning of Assemblies of God Marriage Encounter through the efforts of Wesley and June Hurst and Mark and Rebecca Rhoades and other friends in 1981.

By 2003 more than thirty-five thousand couples worldwide had participated in the program. Two new initiatives have been added: Engaged Encounter for a couple preparing for marriage and MarriageRestored to help a couple whose marriage is in crisis. Indicative of the value now placed on mental health care for believers and the need to build strong marital and family relationships, the Assemblies of God Theological Seminary began offering the first graduate degree in counseling among the denomination's institutions of higher education in 1984.

RECOMMENDED READING

Batty, David and Ethan Campbell. *Teen Challenge: 50 Years of Miracles*. Springfield, MO: Teen Challenge USA, 2008.

Blumhofer, Edith L. *Restoring the Faith: The Assemblies of God, Pentecostalism, and American Culture.* Urbana, Ill.: University of Illinois Press, 1993.

Carlson, G. Raymond. *Spiritual Dynamics: The Holy Spirit in Human Experience*. Springfield, Mo.: Gospel Publishing House, 1976.

Hall, Fannie Mae. "G. Raymond Carlson." Parts 1 and 2. *Assemblies of God Heritage* 13 (summer 1993): 5–8, 31; 13 (fall 1993): 11–15, 27.

Jansen, Harris, Elva Hoover, and Gary Leggett, eds. *Live in the Spirit: A Compendium of Themes on the Spiritual Life as Presented at the Council on Spiritual Life.* Springfield, Mo.: Gospel Publishing House, 1972.

Jones, Gwen, ed. *Conference on the Holy Spirit Digest.* Springfield, Mo.: Gospel Publishing House, 1983.

Jones, Gwen, Ron Rowden, and Mel Surface, eds. *Higher Goals: National Church Growth Convention Digest.* Springfield, Mo.: Gospel Publishing House, 1978.

Molenaar, William, "Intercultural Ministries." In *U.S. Missions: Celebrating 75 Years of Ministry.* Springfield, MO: Gospel Publishing House, 2012.

Poloma, Margaret M. *The Assemblies of God at the Crossroads: Charisma and Institutional Dilemmas.* Knoxville: University of Tennessee Press, 1989.

Spittler, Russell P. "Are Pentecostals and Charismatics Fundamentalists? A Review of American Uses of These Categories." In *Charismatic Christianity as a Global Culture,* edited by Karla Poewe. Columbia, S.C.: University of South Carolina Press, 1994.

Wagner, Benjamin. "Cautious Embrace: The Assemblies of God and the Charismatic Renewal." *Assemblies of God Heritage* 29 (2009): 34–43.

Walker, Ken. "Detroit's Soul-Winner." *Charisma & Christian Life* (December 2001): 54–55.

Where We Stand: The Official Position Papers of the Assemblies of God. Springfield, Mo.: Gospel Publishing House, 2001.

ENDNOTES

1 C. Peter Wagner, *Look Out! The Pentecostals Are Coming* (Carol Stream, Ill.: Creation House, 1973), 127. (Later reissued as *Spiritual Power and Church Growth: Lessons From the Amazing Growth of Pentecostal Churches in Latin America* [1986]).

2 For the dynamics behind its growth, see Karen Hurston, *Growing the World's Largest Church* (Springfield, Mo.: Chrism, 1994).

3 Edward E. Plowman, "Assemblies of God: On the Way Up," *Saturday Evening Post,* July/August 1982, 72.

4 "Statistics on the Assemblies of God (U.S.A.), 1989" (Springfield, Mo.: General Council of the Assemblies of God, 1989).

5 Grant Wacker, "America's Pentecostals: Who They Are," *Christianity Today* (16 October 1987): 16–21.

6 "An Interview With Don Argue, New President of National Association of Evangelicals," *United Evangelical Action* (May–June 1995): 1–2.

7 Edith L. Blumhofer, *Restoring the Faith: The Assemblies of God, Pentecostalism, and American Culture* (Urbana: University of Illinois Press, 1993), 257.

8 Edith L. Blumhofer, *The Assemblies of God: A Chapter in the Story of American Pentecostalism* (Springfield, Mo.: Gospel Publishing House, 1989), 2:181.

9 General Council Minutes, 2001, 44.

10 "Foreign MAPS ministry joins Division of Foreign Missions," *Pentecostal Evangel* (23 June 1991): 29.

11 Larry Christenson, ed., *Welcome, Holy Spirit: A Study of Charismatic Renewal in the Church* (Minneapolis: Augsburg Publishing House, 1987), 354.

12 Robert Harrison, "The Believer's Relationship to the World," in *Live in the Spirit: A Compendium of Themes on the Spiritual Life as Presented at the Council on Spiritual Life,* ed. Harris Jansen, Elva Hoover, Gary Leggett (Springfield, Mo.: Gospel Publishing House, 1972), 41.

13 Ibid., 43.

14 See W. G. McLoughlin, Jr., *Revivals, Awakenings, and Reform: An Essay on Religion and Social Change in America, 1607–1977* (Chicago: University of Chicago Press, 1978).

15 José Girón, "Reaching the Hispanic Population," in *Higher Goals: National Church Growth Convention Digest*, ed. Gwen Jones, Ron Rowden, Mel Surface (Springfield: Gospel Publishing House, 1978), 230.

16 Thomas F. Zimmerman, "Statement of Purpose," in *Conference on the Holy Spirit Digest*, ed. Gwen Jones (Springfield, Mo.: Gospel Publishing House, 1983), 1:5.

17 Dennis J. Bennett, "Baptized in the Holy Spirit," in Jones, *Conference on the Holy Spirit Digest*, 1:14.

18 Ibid., 1:15.

19 Ronald Kydd, "The Contribution of Denominationally Trained Clergymen to the Emerging Pentecostal Movement in Canada," *Pneuma: The Journal of the Society for Pentecostal Studies* 5 (spring 1983): 17–33.

20 Fannie Mae Hall, "G. Raymond Carlson: The Early Years in the Upper Midwest," *Assemblies of God Heritage* 13 (summer 1993): 7.

21 Ibid.

22 G. Raymond Carlson, *Spiritual Dynamics: The Holy Spirit in Human Experience* (Springfield, Mo.: Gospel Publishing House, 1976), 50.

23 Hall, "G. Raymond Carlson," 8.

24 Carlson, *Spiritual Dynamics*, 61.

25 Hall, "G. Raymond Carlson," 12.

26 "Thos. F. Zimmerman Steps Down as General Superintendent of the Fellowship," *Pentecostal Evangel* (29 September 1985): 23.

27 The National Religious Broadcasters paid tribute to Zimmerman after his death in 1991; see Richard G. Champion, "Religious Broadcasters Emphasize Character, Commitment at Convention," *Pentecostal Evangel* (24 March 1991): 27.

28 Everett Stenhouse, "Spiritual Renewal for the Harvest," *Pentecostal Evangel* (10 September 1989): 9.

29 "The Executive Director, D. F. M. Speaks," AGAMA *News and Notes* (Jan–April 1990): 1.

30 Loren Triplett, "Celebrating 80 Years of Strategic Missions Ministry," *Advance* (January 1994): 22.

31 "Declaration of a Decade of Harvest," *Pentecostal Evangel* (1 January 1989): S-2.

32 G. Raymond Carlson cited in "Our Mission for the 90s," *Pentecostal Evangel* (1 January 1989): S-3.

33 T. Ray Rachels, "Facing a Raging Inferno—Wake up the Sleeping Firemen," *Pentecostal Evangel* (1 January 1989): 8–13.

34 Lester G. Searles, "Western Bible Institute Pioneers New Work," *Pentecostal Evangel* (1 January 1989): S-14.

35 Raymond L. Gannon, "Temple Beth Emanuel: The First Messianic Synagogue in the Assemblies of God," (research paper, Assemblies of God Graduate School, 9 March 1982), 5.

36 Ibid., 7.

37 *Intercultural Ministries* (brochure) (Springfield, Mo.: Assemblies of God Home Missions, n.d.).

38 Trey and Becky Hancock, newsletter, July 2002, 1–2.

39 Hancock cited in Ken Walker, "Detroit's Soul-Winner," *Charisma & Christian Life* (December 2002): 55.

[40] Ibid.

[41] See Yousef and Patricia Habibi, "The Watchman's Report" (newsletter), summer 2002, 1–4.

[42] Hancock newsletter, 2.

[43] Hancock cited in Walker, "Detroit's Soul-Winner," 54.

[44] Combined Minutes of the General Council, 1914, 4.

[45] J. Roswell Flower, "Editorial Note," *Christian Evangel* (30 January 1915): 1.

[46] "Opening of the Central Bible Institute," *Pentecostal Evangel* (25 October 1924): 8.

[47] See Gary B. McGee, "Historical Background," in *Systematic Theology: A Pentecostal Perspective*, rev. ed., ed. Stanley M. Horton (Springfield, Mo.: Gospel Publishing House, 1995), 9–36.

[48] See *Where We Stand: The Official Position Papers of the Assemblies of God* (Springfield, Mo.: Gospel Publishing House, 2001).

[49] General Council Minutes, 1979, 26–27; see also Blumhofer, *The Assemblies of God*, 2: 183–185.

[50] "The Emerge Story" from the Emerge website.

CHAPTER 22

MISSIONS ON THE WORLD SCENE

By the 1980s, outside observers discovered that Pentecostals formed one of the largest segments of modern Christianity. On the world scene, four streams of Pentecostals in the broadest sense could be found: (1) classical Pentecostal denominations, (2) charismatic renewal movements in and outside the historic churches, (3) independent congregations and movements resulting from schisms in churches at home and overseas, and (4) indigenous nonwhite churches and movements with an evangelical witness. Classical Pentecostals (that is, those originating from the nineteenth-century holiness movement and generally insisting on the doctrine of tongues as initial evidence) reportedly accounted for one of the largest families of Christians.

With this development came recognition and appreciation of Pentecostal contributions to evangelism and church life. An editorial in *Christianity Today* stated, "[W]e owe the Pentecostal church an immense debt of gratitude. It has reminded us that the Holy Spirit makes worship come alive, that the Holy Spirit is not the power stored in unused batteries, but a live current running through our every action." A leading evangelical missions scholar, David Hesselgrave noted that Pentecostalism "has usually produced a deep-seated missionary motivation, and it is this motivation that has propelled it to its present role as perhaps the most missionary-minded segment of world Christianity."

MOBILIZING FOR MISSIONS

The Assemblies of God has played an important role in the global upsurge of evangelism. After the Council on Evangelism in 1968, many new and creative initiatives were adopted to expedite evangelism, including publications, highly coordinated task forces to promote evangelism and church planting, and MAPS volunteers and construction teams. The Spanish Literature Division, founded in 1946 by Henry C. Ball, became Life Publishers International to furnish gospel literature in many languages.

Four new international ministries also gained approval: International Correspondence Institute (ICI [now Global University]) to provide worldwide distance education for evangelism, discipleship, and training; International Media Ministries to witness for Jesus Christ through video presentations, etc.; Center for Ministry to Muslims "to be a facilitating ministry to assist the Church worldwide in providing an adequate witness of Jesus Christ to every Muslim by every means possible"; and HealthCare Ministries. The latter represented a new venture in ministering to the physical needs of people, moving beyond the traditional model of medical missions. Medical professionals and nonmedical helpers work on short-term assignments to give an evangelistic witness through offering medical treatment, providing medical assistance to disaster victims, teaching health care professionals in many countries how to improve their skills, and supporting the work of field missionaries, among other goals.

Donald C. Stamps

In an important publishing strategy, Donald C. Stamps edited the *Life in the Spirit Study Bible*, published by Zondervan Publishing House under the sponsorship of the Division of Foreign Missions. Stamps, a former Nazarene missionary who joined the Assemblies of God and remained in Brazil as a missionary, saw the potential benefits that a study Bible could have in that country. When the complete Bible rolled off the presses in 1992, it had become a global project with translations not only in English and Portuguese, but with plans for many other language editions.

Construction teams from local congregations crisscrossed the globe building churches and schools. The sponsoring churches usually paid for the materials, while workers paid their own way and often used their vacation time to work. Crossroads Cathedral (First Assembly of God) in Oklahoma City, pastored by Daniel Sheaffer, sent scores of teams to the African country of Malawi to assist in building churches, as well as the Assemblies of God School of Theology in Lilongwe. The church has also supported evangelistic crusades and other projects in cooperation with the national church. Since 1982, it has invested over $7 million in Malawi. With fewer resources, most congregations tackled smaller projects (for example, building a church in Mexico) or worked on a larger project in league with other congregations (for example, building an apartment building at Continental Theological Seminary near Brussels, Belgium).

Pentecostal Paradigm of Missions

Many believers within the Pentecostal-charismatic tradition have come to see that experience-oriented religion becomes self-centered. The present emphasis upon the biblical theology of missions comes as an answer to this problem. A Pentecostal paradigm of missions, anchored in a biblical theology of missions, thus stands as today's "means" to accomplish the mission of the Church. It looks to the future success of God's stated mission revealed throughout Scripture, culminating in a Spirit-filled Church expecting Christ's imminent return as it makes disciples from among all nations.
—*John V. York, Missions in the Age of the Spirit (2000), 163.*

PENTECOSTAL MISSIOLOGY

On another front, Assemblies of God mission scholars increasingly made academic contributions to the study of missions. The venerable Melvin Hodges continued to write books in his later years, most notably A *Theology of the Church and Its Mission* (1977). As required reading for mission courses in many of the denomination's Bible institutes and colleges, it was later surpassed by John York's *Missions in the Age of the Spirit* (2000). Another important milestone appeared in 1991 with the publication of *Called & Empowered: Global Mission in Pentecostal Perspective*, edited by Murray Dempster, Byron Klaus, and Douglas Petersen.

Through their research for advanced degrees in missiology, history, anthropology, and education, missionaries enhanced their skills, laid plans for the future, and provided insight into Pentecostal missions. Published dissertations included Petersen's *Not by Might Nor by Power: A Pentecostal Theology of Social Concern in Latin America* (1996). Other notable dissertations have come from the pen of Barbara Cavaness, who explored the decline of single women missionaries in the Assemblies of God; Beth Grant, theological leadership training in India; Warren Newberry, Pentecostal distinctives in missions; and Wardine Wood, continuing education for missionaries. Outside the formal academic context, missionaries home on furloughs not only received inspiration at the annual summer School of Missions in Springfield, but practical instruction as well.

Following the lead of evangelicals after World War II, Assemblies of God biblical scholars (for example, Gordon Fee) and missiologists (for example, Peter Kuzmič) began to explore the meaning of the kingdom of God (the rule of God in the hearts and behaviors of believers) as a present reality for the mission of the Church, but without discounting the future millennial reign of Christ in His restored kingdom. "For the followers of Jesus who believe the 'whole/full gospel,'" writes Kuzmič, president of Evangelical Theological Seminary in Osijek, Croatia, "the commission to preach the good news of the kingdom of God is linked with the equipping power of the Holy Spirit to overcome the forces of evil. . . . The manifestation of biblical charismata, the experience of 'joy in the Holy Spirit' (Rom. 14:17), and the anointed ministry in which signs and wonders confirm the proclamation of the Word are the distinguishing marks of the kingdom of God at work. In the age of

Peter Kuzmič (second from left) with friends in war-torn Bosnia

rationalism, theological liberalism, and religious pluralism, Pentecostals and charismatics believe that evidential supernatural activity of the Holy Spirit validates Christian witness."

While full-scale exposition of the Kingdom from a Pentecostal missiological standpoint began with the work of former missionary Paul Pomerville in his *Third Force in Missions* (1985), others also contributed, including the late Ruth Breusch, sometime missionary to India and professor at Southeastern College, through articles written for *Mountain Movers*, a monthly publication of the Division of Foreign Missions.

Ruth Breusch

Accordingly, any suggestion that Christians are passive observers in a world characterized by injustices, discrimination, and hunger, but active participants only in world evangelism, represents a split-mindedness for Christian living and limits Christian witness. While Assemblies of God missionaries have avoided politicizing their activities, their ministries have included feeding the hungry and helping improve the quality of life of the people they serve, without diminishing the importance of gospel proclamation.

More and more, ministry abroad necessitated that missionaries work as partners with fraternally related national organizations. The change from paternal control to partnership led to spectacular growth in many countries, but remained a challenge for missionaries (bringing needed monies) and national leaders (working with limited resources). To address this problem, Morris Williams, field director for Africa, wrote *Partnership in Mission* (1986) to build bridges between the Assemblies of God (U.S.A.) and national churches. "Love is absolutely essential to successful partnership," he stressed. "You can have one hundred constitutions and three thousand policies . . . you can make job descriptions until you run out of paper, but if [the American Assemblies of God] and national churches do not trust each other . . . if there is no desire to make the team effort a success . . . if love is not the glue that holds the agreements together . . . then partnership will fall flat on its face."

While life in many countries improved for missionaries and their families, political upheavals, poor medical facilities, and the cultural challenges of living abroad could still make life difficult. After the Cuban revolution ended in 1958, Floyd Woodworth was jailed by Fidel Castro's army as a spy; after twenty days he was released in an unusual set of circumstances. During the civil war in Nigeria

Morris Williams teaching on partnership principles at a seminar for missionaries in Springfield, Missouri

Missionary Floyd Woodworth (r) and a student (left, inside building) liberating turkeys from a room in the Bible school chapel where they had been put for safety during a hurricane in Cuba

(1967–1970), missionaries had to flee the state of Biafra (and were divided in their opinions about the war).

Health care continued to be chancy in many places. In the Philippines, Gerald Johnson had to be hospitalized for a potentially fatal infection caused by an amoeba, a microscopic organism that attacks the lining of the stomach. Since the hospital had no dietician, it served all the patients the same food. His first two meals consisted of the wrong foods for his condition: a cold greasy egg, a pineapple ring, old crunchy rice, and fish heads and more rice. Fortunately, he regained strength through medication, his wife bringing him food free of acid and grease, and absolute confidence that someone was interceding for him in prayer. However, for some missionaries, such illnesses broke their health and forced them to return to America and minister there.

SIGNS AND WONDERS

Missionaries occasionally testified to divine interventions on their behalf. Driving an old Cadillac down a mountain road in Uruguay, Anthony and Rita Giordano and their two children cried out, "Dear God, help us!" when the brakes failed. Just twelve inches from slamming into a herd of cows crossing the road, the car hit something soft, jolted to a stop, and the motor stalled. "We were convinced that Jesus sent angels to ride in the car with us on that trip," Rita recalled. "The proof was evident. Because of them we are alive today!"

Eugene Grams concluded that a policeman he met near the South African parliament building and who directed him to the appropriate government office for his inquiry was really an angel. The policeman seemed to know all about Grams's desire to ask permission to establish a racially integrated Bible school during the time when apartheid policies still existed; the policeman assured him of God's blessing. "My mind was going in 40 different directions," he remembered, "and I glanced toward the building for a moment. Then I thought I would ask the policeman if I could meet him for lunch. I wanted to ask him how he knew these things. But when I turned back, he was gone. The courtyard was large, and there was no place he could have stood without being seen. Nor could he have taken leave of me without my noticing. 'Thank You, Lord,' I prayed. 'I never realized what great importance You placed upon this project.'" In an unusual gesture, the government gave a nonrestrictive permit to establish such a school (Cape Theological Seminary) in a designated white area of Cape Town.

In equally remarkable ways, missionaries reported how the Holy Spirit opened new doors for ministry in sectors of Christianity influenced by the charismatic

Missionary Paul Dear (r) praying with a Catholic charismatic believer (l) in Ireland.

renewal. While pastoring Calvary Assembly of God in Youngstown, Ohio, a parishioner told Pastor Paul Dear about a Catholic neighbor interested in the Holy Spirit. He then accepted an invitation to visit the woman's home and spoke for four hours from Genesis to Revelation on the ministry of the Spirit to the five women who assembled. On the following Friday at 8 p.m., he spoke to a larger group of Catholics from several parishes; by 5 a.m., eight or ten had been baptized in the Spirit and spoken in tongues. As many as twenty received Spirit baptism a day later. This opened a door of witness in the rapidly growing Catholic charismatic renewal.

In 1978, Dear and his wife, Norma, moved to Ireland to minister to Catholics with an unusual combination of blessings from Thomas F. Zimmerman, J. Philip Hogan,

We Can't Go Back to Egypt!

While preaching with an interpreter in Eastern Europe, missionary Charles Greenaway declared that just as the Israelites had left Egypt to enter the Promised Land, so Christians had left the old life of sin to live victorious lives in Christ. To emphasize faithfulness despite difficult circumstances, he exhorted the congregation with the American expression, "Hang in there!" The interpreter, not understanding the expression, translated it as "Go out and hang yourself!" Soon realizing that something was wrong, he stopped Greenaway and said, "Brother Greenaway, wait, we must go back! We must go back!" To which Greenaway shot back, "No, my brother, we can't go back to Egypt!"

and Bishop James Malone of Youngstown. With the Catholic renewal in full swing, they had a remarkably fruitful ministry during an unusual time of revival among Catholics. Before leaving to work full-time with the ICI operation headquartered in Brussels, they had inaugurated the Irish Assemblies of God, Irish Bible College, Teen Challenge, and the ICI program in that country.

Meanwhile, in Latin America, missionary Richard Jeffery saw signs and wonders in his open-air crusades that resulted in many new and sometimes large churches com-

ing into existence. Jeffery and his wife, Elva, would stay from three to five months in one location to gather and train a strong nucleus of new believers. Their legacy of focusing on salvation and prayer for the sick continues in the Assemblies of God denominations of Nicaragua, Costa Rica, and other Central and South American countries.

During an outdoor service in Chile, Richard Jeffery (center) invited "Sister Fresia" (left) to testify that her husband and daughter, both deaf, had been healed in one of the first days of the evangelistic campaign in Antofagasta.

In Assemblies of God foreign missions after midcentury, the name of J. Philip Hogan stands out. Indeed, one may refer to the years 1960–1989 as the "Hogan Era." Missionaries Mark and Huldah Buntain began the Assembly of God Hospital and Research Centre to minister to the spiritual and physical needs of people in Calcutta, India. After World War II, military personnel stationed in Europe benefited from the work of missionaries like Eddie Washington.

To provide distance-education learning for thousands of students and church leaders abroad, George M. Flattery founded International Correspondence Institute. Louise Jeter Walker left a remarkable legacy in Sunday School literature for Latin American Pentecostals, Bible school teaching and administration, and curricular materials. Finally, missionary-evangelist Morris Plotts—"Bwana Tembo"—raised large sums of money to build churches and schools in East Africa.

J. PHILIP HOGAN
(1915-2002)

At Bethel Assembly of God in Lincoln Park, Michigan, during a missions convention, missionaries Leonard Bolton of China and Willis G. Long of India challenged the congregation to support missions with their prayers and offerings. But unexpectedly, God called the pastor and his wife, J. Philip and Virginia Hogan, to go to China as missionaries.

After Bolton preached, a woman offered to take care of the Hogan's young daughter in the church nursery to give Virginia the opportunity to pray at the altar. While praying, she heard the Lord say to her, "This [China] is the place." She responded with some hesitation, hoping that her husband would hear the same call. Since Bolton was staying with them, Hogan talked with him at length about China—Hogan too had been stirred in his heart. In the following months, he avidly read every book on China that he could find in the Detroit public libraries.

At Christmastime in 1945, the Hogans traveled to Springfield, Missouri. His parents had moved there from their ranch near Olathe, Colorado. However, they also wanted to consult with Noel Perkin, the missionary secretary. After meeting with the Hogans for less than thirty minutes, Perkin gave them tentative appointment to China. Resigning from their church, they enrolled at the Chinese language institute at the University of California at Berkeley to study Mandarin.

J. Philip Hogan

Notice of their formal appointment arrived in December 1946, and two months later they sailed to the Far East. After arriving at the Chinese coastal city of Ningpo, they worked at the Bethel Mission founded in 1912 by Nettie Danks Nichols. Eighteen months there tested their faith and commitment. Reflecting the paternalism still widespread in Assemblies of God foreign missions, Bethel depended heavily on American funds and little attempt had been made to restructure according to indigenous principles.

Compounding the problems, the Communist revolution raged against the Nationalist government of Chiang Kai-shek, throwing the future of the mission, along with the entire work in China, into great uncertainty. Communist activities in the Ningpo area became ever-more menacing. Before the defeat of Nationalist authorities on the mainland and their flight to Taiwan, they summarily executed many Chinese youths who were known or suspected Communist sympathizers.

Having seen some of the executions firsthand, Hogan reflected, "I saw them stacked up like cordwood beside the road. I saw their bodies strewn across the green rice fields. As I stood over them, moved with great emotion, I said to myself, 'What is the strange god of these young people that will cause them to make this kind of sacrifice?' It is going to cost us something to preach Jesus around the world in this hour." The Church's responsibility for wholehearted commitment to the Great Commission would become an overriding theme in his writings and sermons.

Having fled China for Taiwan, the Hogans ministered there for a brief time before Virginia and the two children returned to the United States in 1949. Six months later, they were reunited. After a year of preaching in churches on behalf of missions and a short stint in a pastorate in South Carolina, they returned to Springfield. Missions was in their blood, and Hogan could

Hogan homestead in Olathe, Colorado

now direct all his energies to heralding the urgency of missions. He traveled widely, speaking in churches and regional missions conventions. Whether through preaching and showing missionary films (some grumbled about his showing "movies" in

A Legacy in Kerala and the World

John Burgess (1903–2001) was born into a Christian Reformed family in Muskegon, Michigan. As a young teenager, he heard about the Azusa Street revival from family who had experienced renewal on the West coast. The Burgess family joined the Assemblies of God immediately after its formation in 1914. During the First World War, John received the baptism of the Holy Spirit in a small storefront church in Muskegon Heights, Michigan. He attended Rochester (N.Y.) Bible Training School (1924–25) where he received a divine call to become a missionary to India during a literature course — and Bethel Bible Training School, Newark, N.J. (1925–26).

In 1926 Burgess sailed for India, having been appointed by William Faux, Assemblies of God foreign missions director, to establish a Bible school. In June 1927 Burgess founded Bethel Bible School (later College) in Mavelikara, Travancore (now Kerala). The school was relocated in 1940 to Punalur. Outside the United States, Bethel Bible College is the oldest Assemblies of God institution for ministerial training in the world. Burgess's dream of developing native leadership in the Indian church has been realized, for the Assemblies of God church in Kerala now functions without Western missionaries. Currently, the Keralite church sends missionaries to other sections of India, to numerous countries in Asia, the Middle East, and the United States.

—*Stanley M. Burgess*

churches) or writing his influential "Call to Action" column in the *Pentecostal Evangel*, he highlighted world evangelization.

When Perkin retired from office in 1959, the General Council entrusted the missions department to the leadership of the forty-three-year-old Hogan. His contributions as director centered on his pragmatic consideration of new and creative initiatives in evangelism and accented on building strong national mission churches capable of aggressive evangelism themselves. It is hardly incidental that the four international ministries mentioned earlier were birthed during his tenure and have made far-reaching contributions. A cornerstone of his leadership was his earnest desire to follow where the Holy Spirit seemed to be leading.

By selecting associates who supported indigenous church principles, Hogan contributed, along with the grassroots efforts of hundreds of missionaries, to the rapid growth and maturation of national churches. As an administrator, he exhibited the concerns and flexibility of a practitioner.

The constituency demonstrated their confidence in Hogan's leadership by reelecting him fourteen times. Similarly, with his long years in office, evangelicals accorded him prominence as a mission leader: On three occasions, he received election as president of the Evangelical Fellowship of Mission Agencies. Before his retirement from office, Hogan worked toward the establishment of the World Assemblies of God Fellowship to foster cooperation between the Assemblies of God (U.S.A.), several European Pentecostal denominations, and its daughter churches overseas.

Leaving office in 1989, he "simply bowed in amazement and unqualified admiration before what God had done—as often as not—despite his and his colleagues' best efforts," wrote historian Everett Wilson. "Initially inclined by his training and assumptions to believe that the destinies of the Christian church lay in the hands of highly motivated, visionary, and resourceful men and women, he admitted at the end of his administrative career to be perceiving more clearly the deft hand of God, the facile coordination of the Spirit, behind what on the face of the enterprise appeared to be the achievements of missionaries and their sending churches." Wilson adds, "After all, he and his colleagues in the global venture were simply 'unprofitable servants,' the meek and humble from every nation, whom God used on a historically discernible scale to accomplish his purpose among the nations."

MARK (1923-1989) AND HULDAH BUNTAIN (1924-)

In Calcutta, the once proud capital of the British Empire in India, millions of refugees and the urban poor live in squalid poverty. There in 1954 in a tent on Royd Street, Mark and Huldah Buntain began their work. It was apparent from the beginning of the church that it would have an unusual ministry. Surrounded by a steadily growing population that overwhelmed the meager medical and humanitarian services available in the city, the Buntains were daily confronted by the hungry and the hurting.

Today their legacy appears in the Mark Buntain Memorial Church, the Assembly of God Hospital & Research Centre, a school of nursing, a teacher's training college, elementary and secondary schools, and West Bengal Bible College. Tens of thousands of people are fed every day through the feeding programs. And these are only the major parts of the current operation; the Buntains started many churches as well as other significant ministries in the region.

In looking back over his ministry, Buntain said that when he arrived in Calcutta, "My heart broke to pieces. When I saw the hunger and destitution, I could not close my eyes to the city's decaying human conditions. The words of Jesus came to me, 'Give them something to eat.' Everywhere I looked I could only see hungry people." Always active in evangelism, he was distributing tracts in a crowded railway station when three young men said to him: "Sir, give us something for our hungry stomachs; then you can give us something for our hungry souls."

Mark, Maureen, and Huldah Buntain

Shaken by their response, he was later galvanized into action by the Bengali famine of 1964. On his own, he opened food kitchens for its victims and then added a hospital for medical treatment. (The Assemblies of God had never sponsored such a sizable charitable ministry before, and leaders initially feared that it might consume funds needed for direct evangelism.) Many years later, the University of Missouri recognized his contributions to humanity by conferring on him an honorary doctorate of humane letters. Yet Mission of Mercy in Calcutta was always a shared ministry. Huldah, known as "Auntie Buntain," shouldered much of the administrative load, a load that grew heavier when Mark was away for long months raising funds in America.

Over the years, the feeding ministry received financial assistance from the Canadian International Development Agency, the governments of Alberta (Canada) and Sweden, UNICEF (United Nations International Children's Emergency Fund), Assemblies of God, Pentecostal Assemblies of Canada, Bethesda Foundation, Jimmy Swaggart Ministries, and World Council of Churches, among many others. Indeed, an unlikely combination of agencies and people stirred by compassion for those unable to help themselves has blessed the people of Calcutta with financial gifts.

Buntain had little sympathy for the notion held by many Pentecostals that missions should only relate to spiritual needs. "If God became man [on] the first Christmas," he said in an interview with Tom Harpur, religion editor of the *Toronto Star*, "it means that nothing human is beyond God's concern. The good news is for the whole person."

Observing the complex of ministries administered by the Buntains, Harpur remarked, "Small wonder they call him St. Mark of Calcutta, the Protestant equivalent to Mother Teresa whose name is now revered around the world for her work in the same sprawling city." When he asked Buntain what he thought of this accolade, he "grinned and roared above the crazy din of traffic outside his office: 'Brother, I'm just a sinner saved by grace.'"

Whenever the Roman Catholic Church canonizes the late Mother Teresa, they will do it based in part on her heroic faith. Though Pentecostals don't confer sainthood on their own heroes, many observed heroic faith in the lives of the Buntains. Their extraordinary vision and compassion reflect that expectation of God's provision so characteristic of the Pentecostal tradition, assisted by successful fund-raising and promotion before the saints back home.

EDDIE (1916-2008) AND
RUTH WASHINGTON (1924-2011)

In 1991, Ronda Curtis, who lived at 519 Dogwood Street in Troy, Illinois, sent a letter to the officers of the Division of Foreign Missions in Springfield and enclosed a high school term paper written by her daughter Kristine. Asked by an English teacher to write on someone who had influenced her life—an "unforgettable character"—Kristine chose Pastor Edward Washington. As a military family, the Curtises had been stationed in Germany from 1983 to 1987 and attended services conducted by "Ruth and Eddie."

Hoping that something would be published to honor their ministry from the information in Kristine's paper, Curtis added, "You never realize how much of an affect you can have on people. I think it would be wonderful to show the good fruits of this couple, who have dedicated their whole life to serving the Lord and people." Military personnel and Europeans who knew the Washingtons would have concurred.

On the European scene, the Washingtons worked as missionary evangelists and touched many people, including the Curtis family. Eddie and his twin brother, Billy, were born at Central Falls, Rhode Island, and at age fourteen both of them came to Christ at Christine Gibson's School of the Prophets, later Zion Bible Institute. Both were baptized in the Holy Spirit at the same time at Zion. Raised in an orphanage, the institution eventually placed them in a home just three houses from the school. Mother Gibson loved the two teenagers and took them with her on preaching trips and to her cottage at Old Orchard, Maine, a popular camp meeting site.

Graduating in 1937, the "Sunshine Twins," as they were called, traveled holding evangelistic campaigns in New England and Pennsylvania. Eddie married Ruth Washington (no relation), and she joined the team. After Billy married, the couples eventually parted their ways in ministry, and Eddie and Ruth joined the Assemblies of God.

They continued in evangelism in the United States and Canada before receiving missionary appointment in 1966 and moving to Kaiserslautern, West Germany. This city had the largest settlement of service personnel outside of America, over seventy-five thousand by 1979. While on occasion they pastored a church at a military base, most of their work was on the road preaching at various military installations from Germany to the Azores. The Washingtons also ministered among European Pentecostals, preaching at a family camp in France, a youth camp in Yugoslavia, revivals in Spain and Austria, and at Full Gospel Business Men's conventions. They also participated in the annual servicemen's retreats at Berchtesgaden in the Alps of southern Bavaria, the location of Hitler's former home.

For a month in 1973, they were assisted by a musical trio of young blind students from Bethany College in Santa Cruz, California, known as the "Braillettes." Together they ministered with the Washingtons in fourteen military chapels in

Ruth and Eddie Washington

Austria, Germany, and Holland. "Their ministry of music and testimony is terrific," Washington reported. "There were people lined up at each altar call."

Ministry to Military Personnel

Following World War II, the Assemblies of God did not forget the servicemen and women stationed around the world. It encouraged qualified pastors to consider military chaplaincy and sponsored the Servicemen's Department that corresponded with soldiers, airmen, and sailors. It also continued to publish Reveille (twenty-six issues from the war to 1956, totaling nearly 17 million copies) and encouraged other forms of ministry.

"Mom" Mincey ministering to a young sailor

Servicemen's correspondent Warren McPherson promised that everyone on the mailing list would receive four letters a year, along with tracts, booklets, and other items. He and his helpers answered letters, providing comfort and counsel as well as explaining the path of salvation.

In Tokyo, "Pop and Mom" Mincey provided a "Christian home" for military personnel stationed in Japan and for those on leave for R and R (rest and relaxation) from assignments in Korea, Taiwan, Okinawa, or aboard ship. After twenty-five years of ministry in the United States, the Minceys felt directed of the Lord to open Tokyo Home. Beginning in 1952, it offered a home atmosphere, family altar, recreational activities, home-cooked meals—two thousand a month and free of charge—and Christian fellowship. The endeavor grew and required the assistance of others. In 1960, they became appointed missionaries and moved on to new ministry in Korea.

Young Kristine Curtis wrote in her paper that "everyone is Pastor Washington's friend because of the loving spirit that he exerts. . . . No one is allowed to walk by [him] without receiving a huge bear hug. . . . He uses the experiences from his past to relate to and help people who are lonely and hurting." To this impressionable teenager, to lonely soldiers, and to the thousands who were "touched by his energy and love of people," he was an unforgettable servant of the Lord.

GEORGE M. FLATTERY
(1936-)

For many years, Assemblies of God missionaries had developed correspondence courses to nurture new converts. Stateside, the General Council launched the Berean School of the Bible in 1947. Under the direction of Frank M. Boyd, it offered Bible and doctrinal training for adults and potential ministerial candidates who were unable to attend the denomination's residential schools. A standardized international program tailored for overseas students, however, had not yet appeared.

The vision for what became Global University originated in part with George M. Flattery, the son of missionaries to West Africa. His interest in nontraditional distance education dated back to his boyhood experiences of receiving his education through correspondence courses. Later academic training, particularly a doctorate in education from Southwestern Baptist Theological Seminary in Fort Worth, Texas, amply prepared him as a specialist in religious instruction, enabling him to lay groundwork for an international program.

George M. Flattery

A six-month's vocational requirement for completing Flattery's doctorate took him and his wife, Esther, to Springfield in 1966, where they assisted in a research project on overseas Bible institutes. This involved traveling to Europe and the Middle East to survey the Bible schools there. After gaining a clearer picture of such institutions, he explored the potential for correspondence study. The timing of this project significantly coincided with efforts in other mission circles to promote training by extension.

After two more years of research, Flattery opened the International Correspondence Institute with several "Christian life" courses and an evangelistic tool entitled "The Great Questions of Life." As time passed, ICI became headquartered in Brussels, Belgium, then moved to Fort Worth, Texas, and finally to Springfield, Missouri, where it was renamed Global University. A long-time colleague, Robert Love remembered, "By long tradition ICI had a company picnic in the spring or summer. It usually happened at some point in the festivities that President Flattery would be pelted with water, or with water balloons. At one picnic, George and I had been talking, so I was near enough to him to hear a stifled groan as it became clear that the missionary kids were massing, with water balloons on the ready. George was thoroughly wet down, but was as always a great sport."

Global also developed collegiate and graduate programs for students around the world. J. Philip Hogan, a strong supporter, rightly observed that "wherever Assemblies of God missionaries have gone, they have established some kind of systematic training program almost immediately. . . . Versatility has been the hallmark."

Over the years, skilled MAPS volunteers have assisted in accounting, graphic arts, editing, photography, printing, audiovisual technology, writing, and secretarial help. Through their commitment to missions, they have saved the program millions of dollars. The close relationship between Global University and MAPS shows laity's ongoing enthusiasm for missions.

Like others in this chapter, Flattery reflects the willingness among Pentecostals to take bold and sometimes risky initiatives to do the Lord's work. In his case, it also reveals the benefits of higher education to the cause of missions.

LOUISE JETER WALKER
(1913-1998)

In September 1993, Loren Triplett, then executive director of the Division of Foreign Missions, honored Louise Jeter Walker for sixty years of missionary service. One could have assumed it was a retirement ceremony. But it wasn't—far from it—she was in the midst of writing a three-volume history of the Assemblies of God in Latin America. "Louise is married to her typewriter," her husband, Alva Walker, once said. "She will tie it on her back for the Rapture." Living at Maranatha Village in Springfield, the General Council's retirement center, she continued writing and editing Global University courses past her official retirement in January 1996.

Louise Jeter was born into the home of a devout Presbyterian family, the third of seven children. Shortly after her birth, her parents were sent as "Sunday School missionaries" to the Ozark mountains of northwestern Arkansas. Later joining the Pentecostal movement, her father, John E. Jeter, pastored Assemblies of God congregations in the area.

In her first year in college, she studied Spanish, "just in case the

Louise Jeter Walker

Lord should call me to Latin America." Later, while enrolled at Southwestern Bible School in Enid, Oklahoma, she received her call to preach and to missions. Following graduation, she hoped to join her brother Hugh and his wife, Gertrude, in their missionary work in Peru. Unfortunately, she was too young. Furthermore, it was 1933, the height of the Great Depression; the missions department was making few new appointments.

"I received a gift of one dollar," she later said, "and dedicated that to start my fund for fare to Peru." The dean of women and her secretary at the school, along with Jeter, prayed that God would multiply the gift abundantly. Three months later Louise had the necessary money. So at nineteen, a third-class ticket in hand, she boarded a Japanese steamer leaving California for Peru. (She was, however, in the company of another missionary and her two daughters.) A little ahead of schedule, she would not receive ordination and formal missionary appointment for six years.

After reaching the mission station, she was surprised to find that everyone attended a single Sunday School class and that the children had no literature in Spanish. It was a plight faced by other Protestant mission agencies as well. "If the children . . . were to have literature," she wrote, "someone would have to write it." Like other Pentecostal pioneers, she rose to the occasion; she found a typewriter in a pawnshop and bought it. Still struggling with her first year of Spanish, she began writing and publishing a Sunday School paper, *Joyas Escogidas* (*Chosen Jewels*), with stories from the Bible and applications for everyday life. A children's teacher's quarterly and visual aids followed. Determined to provide Christian education for children, she kept the keys of the typewriter clacking even after she contracted tuberculosis. (When she had enough strength, she would get out of bed and type.) A long and distinguished career had begun.

On Christmas night in 1938, a widowed missionary from the Belgian Congo, sixteen years her senior and a father of four, proposed. She recalled being "flabbergasted, dumbfounded, speechless." The math didn't compute. "I [had] prayed that if it was the Lord's will for me to get married, if I could serve Him better married than single, that He would work things out and give me the husband of His choice, but if I could serve Him better single . . . that He would keep me from getting emotionally involved and making a mess of my life." The next year, Louise became a wife and mother, marrying her suitor, Alva Walker.

After their marriage, Alva transferred to Peru, and they spent five years there. Later, Louise received appointment as coordinator for Bible schools in Latin America and the West Indies. She also served as director of the Cuban Bible Institute, Alva assisting her as business manager. Although he technically retired in 1960, he continued to help in her many assignments for Global University, as well as in other projects.

Alva and Louise Walker enjoy a time of food and relaxation at a training conference in Bolivia.

Louise Jeter Walker set a challenging pace. Her *Faculty Training Program for Overseas Bible Schools* (1965) became an essential guide for Assemblies of God Bible institutes. At the same time, as with the other couples in this chapter, their happy marriage modeled partnership in ministry.

MORRIS PLOTTS
(1906-1997)

"The Lord has given me a new set of tires, tuned up my engine and filled my tank with New Jerusalem octane gasoline!" declared missionary-evangelist Morris Plotts at age sixty-seven. "I am ready to go out and on for God." No one who knew about his ongoing quest to plant churches in Africa could doubt his renewed commitment to the task. Indeed, when he finally retired at eighty-three, he had traveled over two million miles, preached more than forty-one hundred sermons, and raised over three million dollars in the cause of missions. He built thirty-eight churches—mostly in Africa—and three Bible schools and contributed to numerous other projects. All of this he accomplished after he became a missionary at age forty-nine.

Born in Omaha, Plotts began his ministry there in 1925. Three years later he married Neva Holdiman. His first pastorate was at the Methodist church in Wilcox, Nebraska. After receiving the baptism in the Holy Spirit in 1932, their lives dramatically changed. Evangelistic ministry and church planting followed. "I never enjoyed anything better than starting from nothing," he remembered. "When it is going well I want to turn it over to someone else and start again."

His revivals in south central Iowa during the Great Depression in the early 1930s brought blessing to some and roused hostility in others in the rural towns where he preached. From New Sharon to Oskaloosa to Montezuma and other communities, the responses to his fiery preaching and the loud music in the services seemed to turn these towns upside down. Someone even composed a ballad about the zealous young preacher:

One day to our little town
    God sent the Word of life,
Through a brash young man in overalls,
    With a family of six and a wife.

Those Disruptive Pentecostals!

The [fundamentalist] American Council [of Christian Churches] . . . let it be known through its leaders that it considered the Pentecostal, or Tongues, groups outside the classification of the historic position of the Christian church. The Tongues groups never had, historically, been counted among the Protestant churches, and to recognize them would promote and advance their error of tongues which depreciates so much [of] their testimony. Undoubtedly, there are many splendid people in the Pentecostal groups; and these groups have been growing rapidly in this country, mainly because of their "life," in contrast to the deadness and coldness of so many of the [National] Council denominations. Nevertheless, they are a most disruptive force.

—Carl T. McIntire, *Twentieth Century Reformation* (1944), 195.

This bold young preacher, with his
    guitar, stood out on the street to sing,
And folks would listen,
    embarrassed like,
To the gospel he wanted to bring.
    Night after night, they filled the tent
While spectators laughed
    or complained.
But nothing could stop this
    new-found joy,
Nor the inner peace they had gained.

Hundreds of people flocked to the meetings from miles around, and many conversions followed. Stories circulated about penitents making restitution for past wrongs, among other things returning stolen animals; one person gave back a gun. Others attended to see the unusual happenings and sometimes to stir up trouble for the preacher. When ordered by the mayor of New Sharon to leave town on the threat of being tarred and feathered, local rowdies who disliked the mayor protected Plotts and the tent after the services ended.

At Searsboro, a gang threw so many eggs at him that he joked about looking like a "walking omelet." In a case that won newspaper coverage across Iowa, a Montezuma court convicted him of being a public nuisance because of the loud music and singing in his services that sometimes lasted until 3 a.m. He served thirty days in the local jail. Undaunted, he went on to hold more meetings and plant more churches in other communities.

After conducting revivals from coast to coast, he finally settled down to pastor Lake Charles Revival Center in Lake Charles, Louisiana. Originally ordained with the Independent Assemblies of God in 1942, he later joined the General Council's Louisiana district.

The burden for missions began with meetings he held in Japan in 1951. But the "Macedonian call" came while visiting Kenya a few years later. After arriving by train from Nairobi to Kaimosi, he asked the missionaries there if they could arrange for him to preach in a place where the gospel had never been heard. They sent him several miles away to the Muslim village of Mumias. News that a blind beggar had regained his sight after Plotts prayed for him led to an audience with Ali Wamakoya, chief of the Wanga tribe. He initially expressed little interest until Plotts told him, "Chief Wamakoya, Jesus can cast out demons." He immediately invited the tall white stranger to return and promised to give him land for a church. (Plotts later returned and prayed for the chief's sister, who was delivered from the torment of evil spirits. With the help of missionaries, a church was built and an African installed as pastor.)

He subsequently returned home, resigned his church, and applied for missionary appointment. Mission leaders in Springfield, however, refused to accept his application because he was forty-nine years old, well past the limit for new candidates. Fortunately, this did not prevent him from traveling to Africa for evangelistic campaigns. Yet, in trying to raise his support, he recalled that nine out of ten pastors he contacted declined to invite him for services, in part because without appointment local congregations could not receive world ministries credit for their offerings.

Morris Plotts

Searching for help, he turned to another Pentecostal denomination with which he had some ties, but it would not support him because he was ordained with the Assemblies of God. Another organization said they would sponsor him if he left the Assemblies. Some questioned if he had made a mistake and missed God in the venture. Finally, for tax purposes, he established World Missionary Evangelism as a private corporation to give his endeavors legal status. Despite difficulties and challenges, his trips to Kenya began to bear fruit.

Not easily discouraged, Plotts persevered until—with the support of several Louisiana pastors—he received missionary appointment from the Assemblies of God in 1962.

J. Philip Hogan recognized his proven missionary work and welcomed him aboard. Always a trailblazer, Plotts began to raise large sums of money in American churches for mission projects from Guyana in South America to Africa to Iran, while concentrating his efforts in East Africa.

Plotts held audiences in rapt attention as he vividly described Africa and asked for their support to advance the gospel. "He made missions real," his daughter Marilyn Ford remembered. "Elephants trumpeted, lions roared and hippos splashed in the rivers of his stories. African people came alive through his words. People knew them by name, saw their spears, felt the pressures of their culture and their crying needs."

An approachable person whose genuine warmth was not missed by the Africans, Plotts became known as "Bwana Tembo"—"Lord Elephant"—because of his big feet, a term of endearment. Like the other missionaries in this chapter who left footprints around the world, his legacy lived on in the people he served.

RECOMMENDED READING

Booze, Joyce, ed. *Jesus! A Collection of Testimonies From People Around the World Who Have Experienced Firsthand the Power in the Name of Jesus.* Springfield, Mo.: Assemblies of God Division of Foreign Missions, 1995.

Buntain, Huldah, as told to B. W. Corpany and Hal Donaldson. *Treasures in Heaven.* Springdale, Pa.: Whitaker House, 1989.

Burke, Bob, with David A. Womack. *Push Back the Darkness: The Story of Don Stamps and the Full Life Study Bible.* Springfield, Mo.: Lumina Press, 1995.

Cavaness, Barbara Liddle. "Factors Influencing the Decrease in the Number of Single Women in Assemblies of God World Missions." PhD diss., Fuller Theological Seminary, 2002.

Fee, Gordon D. *God's Empowering Presence: The Holy Spirit in the Letters of Paul.* Peabody, Mass.: Hendrickson Publishers, 1994.

———. "The Kingdom of God and the Church's Global Mission." In *Called & Empowered: Global Mission in Pentecostal Perspective,* edited by Murray W. Dempster, Byron D. Klaus, Douglas Petersen, 7–21. Peabody, Mass.: Hendrickson Publishers, 1991.

Flattery, George W., Sr. *Pentecostal Pioneering: An Autobiography.* Springfield, Mo.: By the author, 1992.

Grant, Alice Elizabeth. "Theological Leadership Education in India: Leadership Development for the Indian or Western Church?" PhD diss., Biola University, 1999.

Harpur, Tom. "St. Mark Lights Up the Earth's Darkness." *Toronto Star* (22 December 1979): A1, A10.

Hesselgrave, David J. *Today's Choices for Tomorrow's Mission: An Evangelical Perspective on Trends and Issues in Missions.* Grand Rapids: Zondervan Publishing House, 1988.

Jeffery, Richard, with Gerald Robeson. Put the Coffin Back . . . I'm Healed. N.p., n.d.

Kuzmic, Peter. "Kingdom of God." In *Dictionary of Pentecostal and Charismatic Movements,* edited by Stanley M. Burgess and Gary B. McGee. Grand Rapids: Zondervan Publishing House, 1988.

Muck, Terry. "Spiritual Lifts." *Christianity Today* 16 (October 1987): 15.

Newberry, Warren Bruce. "Major Missiological Motifs in North American Classical Pentecostal Missions." D.Th. diss., University of South Africa, 1999.

Peters, James E. *Prevailing Westerlies (The Pentecostal Heritage of Maine).* Shippensburg, Pa.: Destiny Image, 1988.

Plotts, Morris, with Robert Paul Lamb. *Bwana Tembo: A Prince with God.* Baton Rouge, La.: Jimmy Swaggart Evangelistic Association, 1980.

Warner, Wayne. "Pioneering Churches in South Central Iowa." Part 1. *Assemblies of God Heritage* 8 (spring 1988): 8–11, 20; "The Montezuma Showdown" (Part 2), 8 (summer 1988): 3–6.

Wilson, Everett A. *Strategy of the Spirit: J. Philip Hogan and Growth of the Assemblies of God Division of Worldwide* (1960–1990). Irvine, Calif.: Regnum Books International, 1997.

Wood, Wardine P. "Identification of Perceived Need of Assemblies of God Missionaries for Continuing Education and a Strategy for Developing a Continuing Education Program Plan." Ed.D., Nova Southeastern University, 1997.

CHAPTER 23

INTO THE HOMES
OF MILLIONS

W hatever will help spread the good news, try it!" Through the years, Pentecostals have used every possible means to reach the masses: print, open-air meetings, music, slides and films, radio and TV. And they have used any available site: on street corners, from "gospel cars," in stadiums and auditoriums, under brush arbors and tents, at truck stops, at rodeos, at racetracks, and in roller rinks.

On the sawdust trail, evangelists had to adapt to changing times and changing expectations of local churches. Congregations wanted forceful preaching under the Spirit's anointing but often preferred evangelists with musical talent or other special abilities. Well-known leader Bert Webb said that when he started out as an evangelist in the 1920s, he couldn't have made it "without a Ford car and a trombone."

In fact, to attract crowds and unbelievers, evangelists often learned to play more than one instrument—favorites were trombones, accordions, guitars, and pianos. Evangelist Lorne Fox also composed his own music. He gained a certain notoriety while holding meetings at Central Assembly of God in Springfield, Missouri, around 1950. His playing of "The Fall of Jerusalem" became so loud at one point that one member of the congregation said to another, "It sounds like another chariot wheel just fell off!" Indeed, as he continued the number, his aggressive style actually broke the piano.

Lorne Fox

Some illustrated their sermons with colored chalk drawings or taught from large dispensational charts, taking the faithful across the platform from Genesis to Revelation. Yet, print media remained a favorite among Pentecostals, and the Assemblies of God has excelled in publications. The *Pentecostal Evangel*, recently renamed *Today's Pentecostal Evangel* and now the nation's foremost Christian weekly, has entered into the homes of countless Pentecostals, and thousands of unbelievers have come to Christ through its gospel witness. Some of the faithful never threw copies away, always saving them to distribute to friends and acquaintances or at retirement homes. Editors like J. Roswell Flower, Stanley Frodsham, Robert Cunningham, Richard Champion, and more recently Hal Donaldson have profoundly influenced the Assemblies of God.

RICHARD "DICK" CHAMPION
(1931-1994)

After his appointment as editor of the *Pentecostal Evangel* in 1984, a friend inquired about how Richard "Dick" Champion would be able to write a fresh and creative editorial every week. With barely a pause, he eagerly said he was up to the challenge. By the time he died, he had written more than four hundred insightful columns.

Richard Champion and Robert Cunningham

Champion was born in Elkhart, Indiana, but grew up as a Michigander. Called to the ministry early in his life, he enrolled at Central Bible College, where his budding editorial ministry began as yearbook and campus newspaper editor. There he met Norma Black, and they were married in 1953. After graduation, they went to Illinois to pastor and pioneer new churches.

In 1955, Robert Cunningham invited Champion back to Springfield to join the staff of the *Evangel*. After two years, he became editor of youth publications, a post he held until 1964 when he returned to work with Cunningham. In the succeeding years, both Dick and Norma would become experts in different fields of communications. She would become a local television personality with her own children's show, earn a PhD in communications and serve on the faculty of Evangel University, and work in the Missouri House of Representatives and later in the Missouri Senate.

Over the course of years, he authored three books, wrote hundreds of articles for the *Evangel* and other headquarters' publications, and became a popular speaker at writers' conferences around the world. Like the Old Testament prophet Habakkuk, he told his staff, as well as aspiring writers, that the nature of their work required them to "write the vision, and make it plain" (Habakkuk 2:2).

Those who knew Champion remember his ability to affirm those with whom he worked. When staffers submitted poor articles, he would meet with them personally and review the problems. They would not only leave knowing how to make the needed changes, but also feeling positive about themselves and their skills. Friends also remember his keen wit.

Champion's editorials spoke to the common person on the meaning of the Christian life and suggested ways to put their faith into action. In one incisive editorial that talked about the kind of spiritual decline that can take place in a local church, he asked, "We pride ourselves on being Pentecostal, but what changes has the infilling of the Spirit made in our lifestyles? We have learned the right words to say, the right places to add a 'hallelujah,' the right time to clap or bounce to the music's beat. We can cry on cue when caught in wrongdoing, but we do not repent, admitting we have sinned and need to change our way of living. We don't even apologize to those we have hurt." The time had come to take inventory, he insisted, lest the witness of evangelical Christianity be damaged by "Pentecostal pretenders." Fortunately, "saints exhibiting and worshipping in the reality of the Spirit demonstrate that Jesus Christ really does make a difference in their lives."

Although most of the editorials focused on personal piety, they occasionally addressed larger issues in the culture. When Congress passed the Americans

The Saints Declare

"Television will bring the saloon, the brothel, the gambling room, the burlesque show, with all their suggestiveness and veiled obscenity, into the homes of millions."

—*Russell Taylor Smith (1950)*

"Have you ever considered what part television may have in fulfilling Revelation 11:9? Not many years ago the scoffer would ask, 'How is it possible that the dead bodies of the two witnesses will be seen lying in the streets of Jerusalem by people all over the world?' Television has rendered the problem elementary."

—*Pentecostal Evangel (1951)*

"Someone may say, 'Television is here to stay, so we might as well get used to it.' So are the movies here to stay, but so far we have never become used to them. We have barred them from our ranks. If they can wedge their way in via the TV set, it will not be long until we stop preaching against the theater—and we dread to think of the final results."

—*Gordon F. Preiser (1952)*

"Twenty years ago, when I first came into the Assemblies of God, I heard our ministers denounce radio, even as I am hearing some denounce television today. I heard them say, in speaking of radio, 'I would not have one of those ungodly things in my home. They bring Hollywood into the home,' etc. But those same ministers have radio in their homes today. Perhaps it would be better not to make emphatic statements about television in case they should change their minds later."

—*Lillian B. Rogers (1952)*

"For the church to come out with a blanket condemnation of television would be unfortunate, I believe. Electronic media can be great purveyors of good. Think of the great blessing television has been in spreading the gospel. This positive effect will not decrease but increase if the Lord tarries."

—*Del Tarr (1981)*

with Disabilities Act in 1990—requiring accessibility for the physically challenged to places of "public accommodation"—he noted that the new law did not apply to churches. While affirming the need to keep church and state separate, he forthrightly said: "I hope churches and religious organizations will not hide behind this and fail to comply with the spirit of the law." He admitted that modifications of existing church structures could be expensive, but the church should follow the instructions of Jesus: "'I tell you the truth, whatever you did for one of the least of these brothers of mine, you did for me'" (Matthew 25:40).

In his last years, Champion suffered from a malignant brain tumor that proved to be fatal. He shared his struggle with the readers of the *Evangel*. When the doctor informed him about the malignancy, he asked himself, "*Why me*? But as soon as the question came, it was answered *immediately* by another question: *Why not me*?"

Though recognizing the promises of God to heal the sick, he observed, "God in His love for us, and His grace extended to all people, has put us on display in the world [Ephesians 2:4–7]. We are the epitome of the message. People will watch our lives who will not come to our churches or read God's Word for themselves. What they know of the gospel is what they see in us." Thus, "there are times when the world must see grace under difficulty. . . . As those who watch us see that God is able to help us, it provides a testimony of His power, love, and grace."

Despite radiation treatment, Champion's condition worsened. Yet, he stayed at his work as long as he could. In an editorial calling the Church to balance the provision of physical resources for the needy with spiritual provision in witnessing the love of Christ, he used a personal illustration to drive home the point: "It can be discouraging to spend a few minutes on the closet floor because you don't have the balance to get up." He then added, "It is . . . more discouraging to realize the church may be on the floor because it lacks balance." He concluded, "We need both, or we will not arise to meet the needs of our generation." With a warm heart and pen in hand, he modeled this balance in his own life.

Champion and his colleagues understood the weighty responsibility for integrity in their labors: "What a communications opportunity is ours. We can rely on the Spirit

Pentecostals and Culture

There was a time when Pentecostals warned themselves and anyone else who would listen not to become entangled and dependent on the 'things of the world'. Pentecostals were suspicious of the passing fads of stylish clothings, the latest hair-do, glitzy new consumer products. They were also—as it turns out rightly—suspicious that the powerful new mass media could be a seductive lure, tricking people into the empty values of the consumer market culture. Perhaps it is time for a rebirth of that ethic of simplicity, that suspicion of 'the things of this world', for which the early Pentecostals were so famous.

—*Harvey Cox, "Pentecostalism and the Global Market Culture,"*
in The Globalization of Pentecostalism: A Religion Made to Travel *(1999): 394.*

to empower us, to help us say the right words at the right time to the right people, people the Spirit of God is drawing to Christ." Unfortunately, not every Pentecostal who employed media to reach the masses reflected so deeply on how integrity could affect the message of the gospel.

THE CHALLENGE OF TELEVANGELISM

Despite criticizing modern culture and its many sins, Pentecostals sanctioned the use of new technology to advance the gospel. By the 1950s, television ministry had become a possibility. Though Oral Roberts's radio broadcasts could be heard on more than five hundred stations, he quickly put his healing ministry on television, a medium that seemed to have the potential for reaching ever-wider audiences.

This chapter includes the stories of two persons, Jim Bakker and Jimmy Swaggart, whose ministries epitomized all that was good and bad about the use of mass media in evangelism. Like other "televangelists" (an Americanism coined in the early '70s), they saw the value of television for calling America to its knees as well as reaching overseas audiences. Their control and misuse of two of the largest televangelism ministries in the United States placed severe pressures on the Assemblies of God.

Yet there were many other faces on the TV screen whose integrity matched their image. Pastor Owen Carr and the Stone Church (Assembly of God), having a vision to evangelize "Chicagoland," overcame great odds to found Channel 38. Jerry Rose, another ordained minister with experience in television production, joined Carr, later succeeding him at the station. And finally, best-selling author Betty Malz, a layperson, became an oft-featured TV guest with an unusual testimony of God's grace.

None of these ministries originated in the conference rooms of denominational planners, but bubbled up from the wellsprings of popular Pentecostal piety. They join a long line of Pentecostals who cut new channels of ministry.

JIM BAKKER (1940-) AND
JIMMY SWAGGART (1935-)

When G. Raymond Carlson became general superintendent of the Assemblies of God in 1985 at age sixty-seven, he reached the apex of a long distinguished service in the Council. At the same time, and representing a younger generation, Jim Bakker (forty-five) and Jimmy Swaggart (fifty) were also at an apex, having become two of the most visible and influential Christian leaders in America.

"Heritage U.S.A. was 'heaven on earth,'" mused Roy Wead, an executive presbyter, "but oh how I love to hear Jimmy Swaggart preach!" In one short remark, Wead summed up the larger dilemma that has increasingly challenged the identity of the denomination since the end of World War II: growing comfort with American culture and its material rewards, but still restless from a heritage that denounced worldliness. Together, Bakker and Swaggart embodied this tension, which had begun to polarize the church constituency.

As private corporations, Bakker's PTL Television Network and Jimmy Swaggart Ministries had multimillion-dollar budgets. Furthermore, they had developed as private corporations, uniquely beyond the control of the Council's governance. Because of their triumphs in televangelism and fund-raising, Bakker and Swaggart appeared to be untouchable. But to the surprise of millions, their empires collapsed within a few months of each other. In the aftermath, Carlson and other leaders led the constituency in weathering the storm and upholding the reputation of the denomination.

Between 1987 and 1988, discredit multiplied as the Bakker and Swaggart scandals negatively impacted Christian witness in America and overseas. Despite Carlson's warning, the divorce of power from holiness, magnified in these circumstances, cost the Assemblies of God dearly.

JIM BAKKER

Heritage U.S.A. at Fort Mill, South Carolina—the sprawling retreat center, television studios, and Christian theme park built by Jim Bakker just south of Charlotte, North Carolina—offered Christians the ultimate camp meeting experience. "I recognized that the drab, outmoded campgrounds I had attended as a child," Bakker wrote, "would no longer appeal to a generation accustomed to vacationing at clean hotels and theme parks and other recreational centers, a generation to whom 'roughing it' meant the hotel had only an outdoor pool."

Responding to never-ending telethons, tear-jerking appeals for money to avert impending financial disasters, and time-share offers, viewers of Bakker's popular *PTL Club* talk show sent millions of dollars to make it all possible. "God birthed within me a vision to build what I called a twenty-first-century, total-living community modeled on the old-time camp meetings, but where the entire family could come and enjoy a beautiful park and plentiful opportunities for spiritual growth."

Jim and Tammy Faye Bakker had come a long way from their evangelistic ministry in the early 1960s and their children's show on Pat Robertson's fledgling Christian Broadcasting Network (CBN). With his boyish good looks and easy manner on the 700 *Club*, Bakker proved himself an unusually successful fund-raiser. After CBN and work for a brief time with Paul and Jan Crouch of Trinity Broadcasting Network in California, the Bakkers moved to Charlotte, North Carolina, in 1974.

One view of Heritage U.S.A. with construction project in the background

Their new ministry there expanded quickly as one project after another was conceived. Reluctant to focus just on evangelism, Bakker wanted to permeate the culture with Christian values. Whether at the dinner theater, where PTL singers belted out songs from Broadway musicals, or at the spectacular water slide, Heritage U.S.A. gave the saints an opportunity to enjoy and show off God's blessings. Those who could afford to stay at the Heritage Grand Hotel and shop in the stores revealed just how well-heeled Pentecostals had become.

Despite Bakker's grandstanding promises to forward designated gifts to charitable endeavors and overseas television ministries (for example, Brazil), he diverted funds to his own pet projects at Heritage U.S.A. as well as to a sumptuous lifestyle. While some assistance did get to intended mission projects, it paled in comparison to the amounts promised. These actions eventually led to an investigation by the Federal Communications Commission.

Tammy Faye and Jim Bakker
AP/Wide World Photos

Bakker's television image masked unresolved personal conflicts, a failing marriage, unbridled greed, and unscrupulous treatment of staff. It must be said, however, that most of the people who worked for him as paid staff or as volunteers were dedicated believers who championed the spiritual ideals that had been the basis of the ministry. Over the years, some who became aware of the problems left. Bakker's ministry foundered in 1987 on allegations of an extramarital affair and deliberate mishandling of funds. Before the end of his trial on financial irregularities—PTL partners had been defrauded of millions of dollars—the Assemblies of God defrocked him as a minister for sexual misconduct.

In a statement issued by the Executive Presbytery and reflecting prophetic witness against the culture, the leadership expressed sadness that "convictions of holiness and personal piety have been eclipsed with self-interest and prosperity." Moreover, "creature comforts have become the idols of too many today. Even the religious communities have been invaded by an emphasis on pleasure, prosperity, and personal gain."

After his conviction in court, Bakker spent several years in prison before his release. During his incarceration, he issued a letter of apology for preaching the "prosperity gospel." Excerpts of the letter were published in *Charisma* magazine. "I ask all who have sat under my ministry to forgive me for preaching a gospel emphasizing earthly prosperity. . . . [Jesus] wants us to be in love with only Him," he wrote. "If we equate earthly possessions . . . with God's favor, what do we tell the billions of those living in poverty, or what do you do if depression hits?"

It would be unfair, however, to write off PTL and Heritage U.S.A. as a sham and Bakker himself as just another swindler preying on people's dreams. There had always been a measure of sincerity in his ministry, even though the lure of success gradually corrupted it. Vast numbers of television viewers were encouraged or found Christ through the ministries of Bakker and a host of guests on the PTL *Club*. Visitors at Heritage U.S.A. went home spiritually uplifted along with memories of family fun in a Christian environment. The numbers of those turned off to the gospel by the moral and financial betrayals, however, will never be known.

JIMMY SWAGGART

A most painful heartbreak for the cause of world evangelization came on Sunday, February 21, 1988, when Jimmy Swaggart confessed on his television show to moral failure. The pain and sadness deepened when he refused to accept the terms of rehabilitation expected of other Council ministers facing similar charges. He too was defrocked.

Shock waves rippled through the Assemblies of God. His public confession embarrassed national churches overseas as well, churches who had both supported and received assistance from his ministry.

Jimmy Swaggart
AP/Wide World Photos

From the standpoint of missions, J. Philip Hogan lamented, "Though time has a way of healing many of these matters, it is my judgment that in some areas the whole foundation of gospel witness has been severely eroded and it is one of those things [for which] we simply must bow our heads in humble contrition and pray that God will keep all of us from being an embarrassment and an offense to the worldwide body of Christ."

Unlike Bakker, Swaggart contributed millions of dollars to designated projects of the Assemblies of God Division of Foreign Missions (DFM). These ranged from feeding and educating over two hundred thousand children in Latin America to medical ministries to buildings for Bible institutes to Buntain's Mission of Mercy. With funds being routed through DFM, they reached their intended destinations. By 1987, contributions had reached one million dollars a month.

"My confidence in Assemblies of God missions is such that we have, without reservation, thrown the full weight of our efforts behind this great work of God," the Louisiana evangelist said in 1985. He had done so "with full confidence that the monies we donate are being maximized through its very able offices." Unfortunately, neither his generosity nor the General Council's fiscal accountability for these funds gained an adequate hearing in the negative publicity that swirled about the scandal.

As an evangelist, Swaggart had come to prominence in the mid-1960s. At the end of the decade he began singing and preaching on the radio, attracting a considerable

One building in the Assembly of God Hospital and Research Centre complex in Calcutta, India

following. His popularity grew to such proportions that before long he was preaching to people in packed-out auditoriums all over North America and intensifying an overseas campaign schedule. Seeing the potential of television, he later stopped his radio programming and began investing his money and energies in televangelism.

Swaggart's telecasts, bolstered by the finest technology available, reached millions around the world. With the help of skilled translators, viewers in Italy thought he was preaching in Italian; Brazilians thought he preached in Portuguese. By 1986 he had become an internationally known television personality whose organization's annual receipts had grown to $186 million. But like Bakker, behind Swaggart's carefully manicured media image, he had deep personal conflicts. Unlike Bakker, he also masked an opulent lifestyle.

With his loud and dramatic preaching, denouncing the world and its values, he touched a resonant chord in Pentecostal spirituality. And then with his country music gospel and honky-tonk style piano (similar to that of his entertainer cousins Jerry Lee Lewis and Mickey Gilley), he endeared himself to millions. Because of thousands of recorded conversions in his crusades, a high public visibility, and a seeming ability to work by the Council's rules, Jimmy Swaggart Ministries enjoyed a special latitude with the Assemblies of God.

For vast numbers of Pentecostals (including the Assemblies of God), Swaggart seemed to model the ideal Pentecostal evangelist. In actual fact, however, his approach to evangelism was closer to that of Billy Graham. Like Graham's, Swaggart's campaign services included a musical package, a simple gospel message, and an altar call. At the same time, his program differed in musical and preaching style, occasional sermons on Spirit baptism, and sometimes a blistering rhetoric. But signs and wonders hardly surfaced in Swaggart's crusades—no healing line, no "power encounters." Instead, he would offer a brief prayer for anyone needing healing. In the days of Maria B. Woodworth-Etter, Charles S. Price, and later Reinhard Bonnke, signs and wonders had held center stage in demonstrating God's power to save and heal, paying rich dividends in evangelism.

In the mid-1980s, serious strains developed between Council leaders and Jimmy Swaggart Ministries. Some missionaries complained about certain practices in the overseas campaigns. When asked why the musicians sang almost exclusively in English before non-English-speaking audiences, a top Swaggart aide replied: "You must know that the anointing of the Holy Ghost is so strong on the music that the people will receive the message

Jimmy Swaggart's Family Worship Center in Baton Rouge, Louisiana

without knowing the words." (The real audience was the TV cameras in front of the crusade platform videotaping the services for American audiences.)

For his part, Swaggart increasingly criticized church officials and, alleging spiritual compromise, spoke of purging the Assemblies of God. Like fundamentalist Carl McIntire before him, Swaggart condemned any group he viewed as a threat. Certain practices of his overseas campaigns and his claim that the world could be won to Christ only through his efforts also offended many in the Council. Finally, observers noticed that Swaggart had seeded a schism by establishing from his Family Worship Center in Baton Rouge a network with other Assemblies of God congregations and by founding a Bible college and seminary, institutions competing with those of the denomination.

THE STAND FOR INTEGRITY

At the beginning of April in 1988, a strange sight appeared on the south parking lot of the headquarters complex in Springfield. Satellite trucks filled the area as reporters waited for the decision of the General Presbytery on the Swaggart case. Despite interviewing everyone they could find, things became rather boring for some. On a local nightly news program, one reporter interviewed another on what it was like to be outside the building waiting for the decision.

The decision was not about whether to discipline Swaggart, but the length of time he would be banned from the pulpit. Ron Davis, a reporter for the Springfield *News-Leader*, wrote, "The 19 words that shook the church's foundation center on who has the power to punish preachers." Swaggart's district, the Louisiana district, had chosen to recommend a three-month absence from the pulpit, instead of the usual longer requirement. It based this decision on a General Council bylaw that stipulated: "The extent to which he (the preacher) may be permitted to minister, if any, shall be determined by the district presbytery." With only a three-months leave, Swaggart thought he stood a much better chance of retaining his vast television audience and income.

Ironically, he had earlier affirmed the customary two-year policy in his *Evangelist* magazine: "We should forgive those who have trespassed us (Matt. 6:14, 15). But we aren't dealing with forgiveness here. This is a question of violating the God-anointed role of Christian leadership. This is a position where, if holiness, righteousness, and purity are not maintained, the whole church will be destroyed." In the same article, he continued: "After removal, the fallen clergyman must prove himself over a period of time. In the Assemblies of God (of which I belong) the prescribed period is two years. During the first year he can't preach at all, and during the second year he may preach only under the supervision of another minister. Only then, after two years probation, can he come back to a full-time ministry—as the Lord would lead."

The Executive Presbytery, however, announced that as the "General Council Credentials Committee" it held ultimate jurisdiction in disciplinary matters within the denomination. Assistant General Superintendent Everett Stenhouse stated that one could find "more than forty references in the bylaws that name the Executive

First Night on *Revivaltime*

I felt a sense of responsibility and urgency which has never left me to this day. Today, nearly a quarter of a century later, I still have the burden and heart for *Revivaltime*. Imagine this: in the 17 years I ministered on the broadcast, I received 1.25 MILLION letters from around the world. God had given me an open door to preach His glorious gospel to millions of people. I remember so well one letter from a prisoner on death row: "Dan, I heard your message today on *Revivaltime*. You told me God loved me. I believed you and accepted Christ into my life. I am scheduled to be executed Thursday night...."

I wrote most of the *Revivaltime* messages in the wee hours of the mornings. So many times the Lord awakened me with a thought and I would rush to my typewriter (later, a computer) to get the message on paper. I felt such an anointing as I would write—picturing the person on the other side of the radio who would be hearing God's Word through me. Oh, what exhilaration as I would pray and write! I only wrote for one person—and then spoke to one person over the mike.

—*Dan Betzer, "My Seventeen Years as Revivaltime Speaker,"*
Assemblies of God Heritage 23 (summer 2003): 16.

Presbytery" as serving in that capacity. It then ruled that like all other ministers in such circumstances, Swaggart would need to spend two years in rehabilitation.

To resolve any constitutional questions, the Executive Presbytery then convened in Springfield a meeting of the General Presbytery—the national body of representatives from each district that serves as a court of appeals in matters of ministerial discipline and establishes policy on major issues between General Council sessions. After considerable deliberation, the General Presbytery upheld the authority of the Executive Presbytery. Louisiana District Superintendent Cecil Janway graciously responded by announcing: "We do not agree with the decision of the General Presbytery, but we will not attempt to hinder them from carrying out their decision. . . . Nor will we cause division within the Assemblies of God fellowship."

Many of the reporters who covered the event assumed that the General Presbytery would buckle in their resolve because of pressures from Swaggart's organization, public opinion, or fear of losing his sizable contributions to Assemblies of God foreign missions. Reporters and other interested parties across the country were unaware, however, that severe strains between Jimmy Swaggart Ministries and the Division of Foreign Missions had reached the boiling point over several issues, among them statistical claims about television coverage and viewers, several months before the scandal broke out. The financial contributions had also radically dropped off in early 1988. Instead of letting money talk, the General Presbyters—most of whom handled disciplinary problems in the districts—stood their ground in maintaining the moral integrity of the Assemblies of God. Refusing to accept the two-year requirement, Swaggart replied that he would only consent to the three-month period. Failure to comply with the Executive Presbytery's decision then led to his being defrocked as a minister.

Although the denomination was shaken by the episode, it survived the test intact and won the praise of outside observers. Along with many Christian leaders, an editor of *Christianity Today* applauded the action: "Swaggart's scandal hurt the church—especially his erstwhile denomination, the Assemblies of God. But the Assemblies has shown itself a Christian body of truthfulness and grit. . . . It is not easy," it went on to say, "especially in a nation so given over to flash and cash, to confront one of your denomination's richest benefactors. The Assemblies did so anyway. And because the Assemblies stuck to the best of its biblical and denominational tradition, we can gladly expect it to heal."

In Pentecostalism, a charismatic quality of personal leadership has often been an agony and an ecstasy. Strong and dynamic leaders have undeniably been decisive forces in church growth, leading the faithful with a God-given vision. Their initiatives and pragmatic use of technology have made major contributions to the advancement of the kingdom of God. Regrettably, the concept of the anointed leader has sometimes led to a Lone Ranger kind of leadership, resistant to both counsel and accountability. In such cases, matters of holiness have sometimes been left behind in the pursuit of power.

The Assemblies of God acted swiftly in the Bakker and Swaggart cases when sexual immorality pulled issues out of the gray areas into the black and white of "thou shalt not." By taking action, "the Assemblies of God continues to stand tall today," wrote *Evangel* editor Dick Champion. "Principles of right and wrong are more clearly defined. And I think the cause of Christ will be stronger because of it."

Despite these highly publicized failures, Assemblies of God ministers did not lose confidence in the value of television for preaching and teaching the saints. Examples of successful endeavors, though on a smaller scale, were not hard to find.

OWEN C. CARR
(1923-)

Chicago, the Windy City, had never lacked for preachers and evangelists who prayed that it might be transformed by the gospel and "set on a hill" (Matthew 5:14, KJV). Owen Carr, a red-haired Kansas farm boy called to preach the gospel and lately the new pastor of the Stone Church, shared the dream. Overwhelmed by the size of Chicago, he determined to make a difference. Pastoring a congregation of four hundred people could not be an end in itself, the question blazed in his mind: How can this congregation fulfill the Great Commission in Chicagoland?

"In my mind's eye, I saw Chicago as a huge black kettle, like we used back on the farm in Kansas to make lard in the fall. But the kettle had no handles, and I couldn't get a grip on it. It was too big around." Carr could only weep and ask the Lord how. "You love them. You died for them. You've given me this love for them, but you haven't told me *how*." At that point, he recalled, "the Holy Spirit spoke" to his heart and said, "'If you had a television station, Owen, it would help.'"

Although he had considered a thirty-minute television program from Stone Church, the notion of a Christian television station surprised him. Through David Oseland, a media enthusiast who also shared the idea, Carr learned

Owen C. Carr

that the Chicago Federation of Labor (CFL) had decided to put its own Channel 38 and transmitter up for sale. Though the Federal Communications Commission had just granted its approval, CFL had come to doubt the market for the venture and decided to sell it before ever going on the air.

Presenting the opportunity to his congregation, Carr estimated that the cost could require an investment of $4 million up front. "The entire sanctuary was supercharged with the electricity of victory," said Carr. By the end of the two and a half hour meeting, the members gave and pledged $135,000. It was a small but significant beginning. With the church board becoming the directors for Christian Communications of Chicagoland, along with the able support of his colaborers, Carr faced long and tortuous months of fund-raising and cutting through governmental red tape.

Finally, on May 31, 1976, five and a half years later, they turned on the transmitter and WCFC–Channel 38 became a reality. The Windy City now had a Christian television station.

JERRY ROSE
(1941-)

From his previous broadcasting experience, Jerry Rose brought unique gifts to Channel 38. Born in Texas, he had worked at two TV stations, served in the Coast Guard, run cameras for ABC's Wide World of Sports, and then put together a station for Pat Robertson's Christian Broadcasting Network in Dallas. From there, at Carr's invitation, he went to Chicago.

Channel 38 began with a screen wide enough for Pentecostals, charismatics, and evangelicals to share the gospel. When Carr departed for a new ministry in 1978, Rose succeeded him as president, presiding over the station's development that followed. Ten years later, TV-38 ceased operation and Total Living Network (TLN), a cable Christian network, came into being. Today, TLN, now reaching a nationwide audience, offers a variety of programming. Apart from preaching services and teaching programs, it has come to include Christian music videos, family-oriented television series (e.g., "Little House on the Prairie"), and newsmagazine and talk shows.

Jerry Rose

Channel 38 grew out of the steady faith and persistence of a team of people who shared the vision. "While audience is the product in commercial television, the Gospel is the product in Christian television," Rose reflected. "Our message is not whatever will sell the most laundry soap; our message is the Good News that there is hope through Jesus Christ."

BETTY MALZ
(1929-2012)

"*Can this be death*? I wondered. If so, I certainly had nothing to fear. There was no darkness, no uncertainty, only a change in location and a total sense of well-being," wrote Betty Malz in her best-selling autobiography *My Glimpse of Eternity*. On a family vacation trip to Florida in 1959, her first husband, John Upchurch, had rushed her to a small hospital at Tarpon Springs with the symptoms of appendicitis. For this young vivacious Indiana homemaker, a pilgrimage of intense pain and suffering, as well as discovery, had begun.

Weeks later, at 5 a.m. on a July morning, Betty Upchurch was pronounced dead in a Terre Haute, Indiana, hospital from a burst appendix and complications. In her out-of-body experience (years before the term was coined and the experience commonly reported), "the transition [to heaven] was serene and peaceful. I was walking up a beautiful green hill. It was steep, but my leg motion was effortless and a deep ecstasy

Royal Rangers

As the Assemblies of God experienced growth in the 1950, Burton W. Pierce, then secretary of the Men's Fellowship Department, noticed a specific need: too many young boys were drifting away from the local church. Observing this disturbing phenomenon, he commented, "Our number one priority is to get men involved in soul winning and the discipling of boys."

In 1960, Charles W. H. Scott suggested the name, "Royal Rangers," for such a discipleship program. Two years of intensive research produced a plan that included four primary objectives: instruction in the Bible, motivation for Christian service, introduction to the basic beliefs of the church, and participation in various indoor/outdoor activities.

After receiving executive approval in late 1961, Pierce invited Johnnie Barnes to become the first Royal Rangers national commander. It was Barnes's responsibility to supervise the development and operation of the entire program. He assumed leadership on January 1, 1962, serving in this capacity until his death on June 15, 1989.

Johnnie Barnes, often called "Mr. Royal Rangers," personified the objectives of the Royal Ranger program as a man of integrity, discipline, and devotion to Christ. His outstanding leadership and charismatic personality allowed him to reach, teach, and keep boys for Jesus Christ. At his graveside service, General Superintendent G. Raymond Carlson, summed up the man and mission of Johnnie Barnes: "'There was a man sent from God, whose name was John.' We can also say that there was a man sent from God whose name was Johnnie."

The growth of Royal Rangers has been remarkable. After the first outpost was organized by Bob Reid in Springfield, Missouri, in 1962, it took only four years for the program to begin in Latin America and Australia. Four decades later, the program had grown to 5,140 outposts with 116,498 members in the USA and over 100,000 in 65 other nations. Since boys are naturally drawn to the outdoors, the Rangers have effectively used camping as a discipleship tool. The first National Camporama was conducted at the Air Force Academy in Colorado Springs, Colorado, in 1974. Another milestone occurred in 1985 when over 1,500 acres of land were purchased in Eagle Rock, Missouri, to establish the National Royal Rangers Training Center.

It has been said that Johnnie Barnes combined the best of all youth programs into the Royal Rangers program. He would say, "This is good, but it can be better." The national commanders who followed him, Ken Hunt (1989–1999) and Richard Mariott (1999–), have continued to develop and improve the program in order to prepare boys to be "Ready for Anything."

To meet the challenges of a new millennium, the Rangers introduced an exciting new award and advancement program: Kids Rangers, Adventure Rangers, Discovery Rangers, and Expedition Rangers. To fulfill the Great Commission, National Commander Mariott issued a challenge to the local commanders, both men and women, to win two- and-half million boys to Christ by 2021. While methods for reaching boys may have changed with the times, the goal remains the same: to reach, teach, and keep boys for Christ.

—*Robert C. Phraner and Annette Newberry*

flooded my body. Despite three incisions in my body from the operations, I stood erect without pain, enjoying my tallness, free from inhibitions about it."

In her conversation with the Lord, however, she asked to return to her family. At 5:28 a.m., she awoke in the hospital room, much to the surprise of her grieving father, Glenn Perkins. As an Assemblies of God pastor, he had nurtured his daughter in the faith and the possibility of miracles, but this was overwhelming. Testimonies to such experiences, though different in details, had been recorded long before that morning in Terre Haute. In New Testament times, Jesus had raised Lazarus from the dead (John 11:41–44). Even the apostle Paul told of a man who had been caught up into paradise, and heard unspeakable words (2 Corinthians 12:4).

Indeed, visions of heaven and hell circulated in sectors of the holiness and Pentecostal movements. Around 1907, the Nazarene Messenger (Los Angeles) reported

Betty Malz

that at age fifteen, a certain Eula Wilson had died and was laid out for burial. Hours later, she rose up suddenly and said to her mother, "'I have been in heaven and Jesus has healed me and told me to eat, drink, and walk.'" The writer added that Wilson had been completely healed and remained so.

From that July morning, Betty was a changed person. Overwhelmed by the love of God in her experience, relationships between her and others in the extended family changed. Her account of heaven prepared her husband, John, for death, which occurred unexpectedly four years later. "Why God chose me—a selfish, proud, unloving person—for this unusual experience I'll never know," she wrote. "Perhaps, just as Joshua and Caleb went out to spy the land and brought back the grapes of Eschol . . . , God let me spy out the heavenly city so that I could come back and tell everybody how great and beautiful it was." In the foreword to *My Glimpse of Eternity*, the celebrated author Catherine Marshall described it as "a ringingly triumphant book, a love letter from the Lord of glory to each one of us."

Years later Betty married Carl Malz, an Assemblies of God missionary, who later served as an executive officer at Trinity Bible College in Ellendale, North Dakota. Betty's testimony became well known through her appearances on TV talk shows and many books. In reflection, she said, "My life is testimony to the fact that I believe in the supernatural power of God to change people and to alter our circumstances today." Millions of Pentecostals and charismatics would probably shout, "Hallelujah, sister, preach it!"

RECOMMENDED READING

Bakker, Jim, with Ken Abraham. *I Was Wrong*. Nashville: Thomas Nelson Publishers, 1996.

Blumhofer, Edith L. "Divided Pentecostals: Bakker vs. Swaggart." *Christian Century* 6 (May 1987): 430–431.

Carr, Owen C., with Doug Brendel. *The Battle Is the Lord's*. Carol Stream, Ill.: Creation House, 1977.

Champion, Richard G. *Write the Vision*. Springfield, Mo.: Gospel Publishing House, 1995.

Clapp, Rodney. "Swaggart's Worst Enemy." *Christianity Today* (17 June 1988): 17.

Davis, Ron. "Scandal Resolved for All but Swaggart." *Springfield (Missouri) News-Leader* (3 April 1988).

Justice, Nancy. "Bakker Apologizes for Prosperity Gospel." *Charisma & Christian Life* (December 1992): 49.

Malz, Betty. *My Glimpse of Eternity*. Old Tappan, N.J.: Fleming H. Revell Co., 1977.

Paige, Vonda. "AG Official: No Choice on Swaggart." *Springfield (Missouri) News-Leader*, (2 April 1988).

Rose, Jerry. *On Wings of Victory*. Chicago: Christian Communications of Chicagoland, 1987.

_____. *Deep Faith for Dark Valleys*. Nashville: Thomas Nelson Publishers, 1999.

Schultz, Quentin J. *Televangelism and American Culture: The Business of Popular Religion*. Grand Rapids: Baker Book House, 1991.

Seaman, Ann Rowe. *Swaggart: The Unauthorized Biography of an American Evangelist*. New York: Continuum International Publishing Group, 2001.

Shepard, Charles E. *Forgiven: The Rise and Fall of Jim Bakker and the PTL Ministry*. New York: Atlantic Monthly Press, 1989.

Swaggart, Jimmy. *The Cup Which My Father Hath Given Me*. Baton Rouge: World Evangelism Press, 1991.

CHAPTER 24

WRITERS, TEACHERS, AND ACTIVISTS

Full-time ministry in the Assemblies of God has always appeared to be the domain of pastors, evangelists, and missionaries. On closer examination, the ministries of editors, writers, and educators have also been indispensable to the mission of the Church. Furthermore, whether working at the denominational headquarters in Springfield, Missouri, or teaching in colleges and seminaries, such people have played crucial parts in building the reputation for doctrinal stability that the General Council has enjoyed.

Over the years, Gospel Publishing House (GPH) and the headquarters operation have been lightning rods for the criticism of those who mistrust the work of church bureaucracies. Editors, writers, managers, printers, artists, secretaries, mail clerks, and food servers don't attain the kind of glamour that Pentecostals usually associate with power-packed ministry. Yet, such persons turn the wheels of church machinery that serve the churches in important ways. Editors like Ralph Harris and Harris Jansen

Sketches by Charles Ramsay were a regular feature in the *Pentecostal Evangel*. Here he is seated at the art board at Gospel Publishing House.

spent years writing and editing church publications to inspire and disciple the people in the pew and keep revival fires burning.

Church School Literature editors looking at curricular materials. (l to r): Ralph Harris, Zella Lindsey (seated), and Dorothy Morris.

The dedication required for their ministries compares favorably with that required of other endeavors in the General Council. Among those rarely in the limelight, Dorothy Morris and artist Norman Pearsall labored long in the preparation of Sunday School literature. (In a chapel service at Central Bible College, Pearsall once quipped, "God called me to preach until He heard me!" In any event, he became a gifted artist with a deep devotion to ministry.) Dorothy Kirschke, a secretary in the music department, played a major part in the preparation of *Hymns of Glorious Praise* (1969), the first hymnal (rather than gospel song-book like *Melodies of Praise*) produced by GPH. Joyce Wells Booze, Janet Walker, and Beverly Graham placed the urgency of missions before the denomination by editing *Mountain Movers*, formerly the monthly missionary magazine of the Assemblies of God. Juleen Turnage ably represented the Assemblies of God to its public constituencies through her service as director of public relations, gaining widespread respect for her work during the televangelist scandals of the 1980s.

The roll call gets much longer for church publications when one adds faculty members in Assemblies of God schools, many of whom have enlarged the scope of their ministries by writing as well as teaching at overseas training schools during the summers.

Charlotte Schumitsch Goble, national Missionettes coordinator (l), with Mildred Smuland, national secretary of the Women's Ministries Department (r), looking at a map showing chartered Missionettes chapters in the United States

When ministries to children are considered, two names stand out: Charlotte Schumitsch Goble launched the Missionettes program for girls in 1955; the first chartered girls' club came a year later. To follow Paul's instruction in Titus 2:4–5 that women should mentor young girls in the faith, Missionettes training stretches from age three to the high school years: Rainbows, Daisies, Prims, Stars, Friends, and Girls Only Clubs.

Johnnie Barnes blazed the path for Royal Rangers, a program for boys, in 1962. A favorite motto said, "A man never stands so tall as when he stoops to help a boy."

Little wonder that Barnes became a hero to the thousands of boys who entered the program. In its desire to spiritually motivate boys through Bible study and memorization, with their being mentored by mature Christian men, the program has spread to eighty countries. Weekly meetings, enhanced by training camps, mature them spiritually, physically, mentally, and socially.

Johnnie Barnes

The persons introduced in this chapter have functioned as role models for those who have followed them in different facets of Christian education. Though most of the church's rank and file have never met Gwen Jones, her editorial work at headquarters enhanced the myriad of publications designed for preachers and laity. Stanley M. Horton influenced the course of denominational doctrine after midcentury through his teaching ministry in print (produced by GPH and its academic imprint, Logion Press) as well as in the classroom.

Few excelled J. Robert Ashcroft as a visionary leader in Assemblies of God higher education and as an interpreter of Pentecostal spirituality. Besides writing the weekly Sunday School lesson in the *Pentecostal Evangel*, J. Bashford Bishop inspired students in his college courses. Fred Smolchuck, a district official and writer, has helped preserve the Ukrainian-American Pentecostal heritage. Three distinguished educators gained recognition for their skills and activism far beyond the walls of Assemblies of God classrooms: Billie Davis, Robert Cooley, and Jesse Miranda.

GWENDOLINE JONES
(1911-2005)

"Gwen, I believe the Lord has healed you," said evangelist Charles S. Price to the young legal secretary suffering from severe physical and nervous exhaustion. Within days her friends marveled at how healthy she looked. Jones's family had attended a Methodist church in Victoria, British Columbia, when Price arrived to hold an evangelistic campaign. As a result, her family came into the Pentecostal movement. Her father, baptized in the Spirit during the meetings, felt called to the ministry. He later pastored and served as a district official.

After her healing, Gwendoline (Gwen) Jones resigned her job and took up residence in Seattle, where she enrolled at Northwest Bible Institute (now Northwest College). Her music training and editing of the college yearbook reflected the two great interests of her life: music and journalism. After graduation in 1939, she moved to Springfield at the request of Noel Perkin, the missionary secretary, who had stayed in their home while preaching in her father's church. "She came [to Springfield], and what a ministry she has had," wrote Lee Shultz, a friend and church leader. "She doesn't carry any ministerial credentials, not even a specialized ministry license. But her ministry is far reaching and will live on for many years to come."

The offices of the missions department were located on the second floor of the old headquarters building on West Pacific Street. Given the cramped quarters, work could

Gwen Jones at her desk at Gospel
Publishing House

never be dull. Since two large oscillating fans provided the "air conditioning," this required "a good deal of time rescuing papers which escaped from the paper weights and blew around the room." A warm fellowship existed among the employees: Ignoring the greasy spoon next door, Jones and her coworkers would walk up to Commercial Street at noon to eat at "Joe's," where the regular lunch cost twenty-five cents and the deluxe, thirty cents.

When the General Council established the Servicemen's Department during World War II, Jones became its office manager. In this capacity, she also wrote tracts and helped edit *Reveille*, an enormously popular piece for military personnel. Printed in red and blue ink on 8½ by 11-inch white paper stock, its four pages were crowded with articles, a gospel message, items of humor, and cartoons that spoke to military personnel. During the war years, fifteen issues of a million copies each were mailed to soldiers around the world free of charge. Showing her versatility, Jones's later editorial responsibilities included work on the CA *Herald* for church youth, *Pulpit* magazine for preachers, *Paraclete* for students of the doctrine of the Holy Spirit, and several mission periodicals. When the General Council sponsored special convocations, church leaders often turned to her to edit the collection of commissioned papers. The *Editorial Procedures Manual* used at the headquarters illustrates her concern for excellence.

An issue of Reveille, the publication for
military personnel

In 1965, Jones became the founding editor of *Advance*, a new minister's magazine. Church leaders wanted a person who understood the various departmental programs at headquarters as well as Council policies and doctrines. Few could fill the bill better. In recognition of her accomplishments, the Evangelical Press Association elected her to its board of directors.

Over the years, Jones demonstrated the ministry that women could have in print media. She modeled effective leadership professionally and spiritually. "She demanded of herself the higher road of skills and efficiency; mediocrity was not in her vocabulary or behavior," remembers Projects Director Carol Ball. Women at the headquarters saw her as a mentor who enabled them to find their own way into productive ministry. "Observing Gwen, talking with her, seeking her counsel about routine questions," added Ball, "helped me define the importance of my calling, the direction of my profession, and the ingredients of practical applications of skills."

We Called Him T.J.

The words of our little old professor's prayer were always the same as, without warning, he bowed his snowy white head to commence class, "Open our eyes that we may behold wondrous things out of Thy Word and bless these precious students for Jesus' sake. Amen." As students at North Central Bible College there was no doubt in our minds that the Reverend T.J. Jones was deeply concerned about our hearts, our minds, and our ministry to a lost and dying world.

We students who were reared in Sunday school considered the first five books of the Holy Bible, known as the Pentateuch, to be extremely boring and nonessential. Most of us were completely unfamiliar with its content, except for a few action-packed stories. Our feelings about the Old Testament, and the Pentateuch in particular, soon began to change as this advanced student of the Word made these books come alive.

Nothing was omitted as T.J. read aloud every single verse, explaining each term and defining various individual words. A big, black Bible was always at his side, but he much preferred reading from small, separate paperback books of the Bible. They were much easier for him to hold close to his face as he sat on a high stool with both arms resting on the lectern.

Fifty years of strenuous preaching had greatly taxed the voice of our lovable instructor. It wasn't exactly melodious as he spoke into the small microphone clipped to his lapel. But, oh, the truths that came forth from that scholar of the Word! We considered him a scholar because he could tell us what was in every chapter of the Bible and could quote most of it, too. But T.J. thought of himself as "just a student" of God's precious Word.

Our predecessors frequently tried to tell us that we should have heard T.J. Jones 20 years ago or more when he was really fiery and full of life. Our retort was simply, "T.J. knows more now." We reasoned that a man would have to be wiser after studying the Bible every day for that many additional years. Besides, his brilliant mind was still as sharp as a tack.

The quaint old gentleman, who knew what he was talking about, often interspersed nuggets of personal wisdom in his teaching of the Scriptures. Since "One hamburger was cheaper than two," he didn't marry until after he had pioneered a few churches. Continually T.J. encouraged the young men to get their books first, then their Buick, and last of all their bride. Some advice was hard to follow.

T.J. wasn't able to move about as he wanted to when he became excited, but that didn't keep him from dramatizing Moses' reply to Pharaoh, "Not a hoof shall be left behind!" Not even Leviticus was dry after T. J. Jones got done with it. His words held true, "The drier the book, the more it burns."

The complex study of Daniel and Revelation was difficult for most of us, and even after weeks in the class many things weren't clear in our minds. Often T.J. asked a difficult question and no one was able to answer. His expression would change to one of despair

We Called Him T.J., Continued

as he asked, "Have I been with you so long and still you do not know?" After a lengthy pause he would begin to go through the material until our minds were enlightened.

The Jones' course in typology was considerably less difficult with the aid of a complete full-scale model of the tabernacle in front of the class. Sometimes he would get so thrilled while teaching that he'd start to sing. An original song of his was about going through the courtyard and Holy Place and into the Holy of Holies. His creaky singing was thoroughly enjoyed by all of us, but he would stop abruptly and blurt out, "You don't want to hear me sing." Not too many days passed, though, until he'd get the urge to sing for us again.

T. J. Jones lived to preach and teach God's Holy Word. He always came to class with an armful of books, including a notebook stuffed full with notes sticking out each side of it. His organization was such that only he could figure it out. When reading from one page fastened in the notebook, he would suddenly pull out a slip of paper from another part. Scribbled on it would be a continuation of what he was reading or an augmentation to it. When he finished with the piece he would jam it back in somewhere—or anywhere—who knows?

A "scrap" he pulled out one day was an old tattered Christmas church bulletin on which he had jotted some valuable notes. How he could figure out such a seemingly disorganized system was amazing to us.

Never was Brother Jones to be interrupted while teaching. When such an event happened, it was evident he was not pleased. Whenever a fellow walked into class late, T.J. would stop immediately and begin to question, "Young man, was your tea too hot or are you trying to impress the girls?" If T. J. then gave his unmistakable giggle with three fingers raised in front of his mouth, we knew everything was all right. But that wasn't always the case. Whenever he was late, though, he blamed it on the slow elevator.

Heartfelt concern for students marked the ministry of T. J. Jones at North Central Bible College. Besides increasing our head knowledge of God's Word, he daily encouraged us to hide it in our hearts that we might not sin against God. It was also this great man's joy to bear students' burdens whenever he was asked to pray in chapel. After reading the requests, he would place the cards in his hands and raise them high as he poured out his soul to the Lord. Prayers were answered.

Occasionally he spoke about getting old and assured us that the song "Beautiful Isle of Somewhere" was definitely not going to be heard at his funeral. In a determined voice he explained that he was not going to a beautiful isle somewhere, but he was going to heaven to see his Jesus!

On July 17, 1970, Jesus Christ became T.J.'s joy of heaven and no longer his hope of earth. Sure enough, not a strain of "Beautiful Isle of Somewhere" was heard at that glorious funeral. Instead the air was filled with the melodies of his favorite songs: "All the Way My Saviour Leads Me," "God Will Take Care of You," "Face to Face," and "Jesus Led Me All the Way."

We surely miss Rev. Thomas James Jones, but we know heaven is happier with the presence of such a saint.

—*Sheryl May Johnson, "We Called Him T. J.,"* Assemblies of God Educator
(July-August 1971).

Jones also became known for her wit. On one occasion, she told her colleagues that at her funeral she wanted only women pallbearers. Since men hadn't taken her out when she was alive, she wasn't going to let them take her out when she was dead! (Also in typical journalistic fashion, she acknowledges that she didn't originate the remark, but appropriated it for its humor.)

With great applause from church leaders and headquarters employees as well, Gwen Jones retired in 1990 after a record-breaking fifty years of service at headquarters.

STANLEY M. HORTON
(1916-2014)

Stanley M. Horton

During a Saturday children's service at Angelus Temple in Los Angeles, California, Aimee Semple McPherson invited a young boy to sit on her lap: Stanley Horton. On the way to becoming one of the nation's best-known evangelists, McPherson knew the power of Pentecost firsthand: Thousands found salvation, inspiration, and healing in her campaigns. Like other first-generation Pentecostals, she exhibited the restless and creative energy of a pioneer—endowed with the Spirit's power and determined to win the world for Christ.

Of course, McPherson couldn't know that the little boy on her lap would someday serve the Pentecostal movement as well, but in a different way. It fell to the second generation, like Horton, to conserve, define, and defend the revival. This agenda carried a certain peril: the work of preservation—enshrining tradition—can stifle the vitality and vision that brought the Movement into existence. Making the task more difficult, Pentecostals have generally feared that academic study of the Bible and theology will short-circuit ministry zeal.

With growing interest in improving the quality of training in Assemblies of God Bible colleges by 1950, faculty members were encouraged to further their education. As a result, Bible and theology instructors began to earn specialized degrees in their areas of teaching. A younger generation of students revered teachers like Horton and

Klaude Kendrick

Donald Johns (Central Bible College), who set a new standard of service in the church. The same was true for those teaching in the liberal arts, among them Alexander Vazakas (Evangel University), Klaude Kendrick (Southwestern Assemblies of God University), Marjorie Stewart (Northwest College), Betty Skipper (Southeastern College), and Everett Wilson (Bethany College). These were just some of the educational pioneers who early on pursued graduate studies with Pentecostal zeal.

Their achievements, however, do not diminish the important contributions teachers with less formal training made to their students. Widely known for inspirational instruction were T. J. Jones (North Central University), W. H. Kesler (Trinity Bible College), Walter Beuttler (Valley Forge Christian College), Esther Rollins (Zion Bible Institute), and Rodger Cree (American Indian College).

Horton's roots go deep in the Pentecostal movement. Elmer K. Fisher, his maternal grandfather and a Baptist preacher, had been baptized in the Spirit at First New Testament Church in Los Angeles in 1906. Afterward, he started his own congregation, the Upper Room Mission.

By age twenty-four, Horton had embarked on a career as a scientist. A graduate of the University of California at Berkeley, he worked at the laboratory of the California Bureau of Chemistry in Sacramento. Faithfully attending Bethel Temple Assembly of God in the city, he sang in the choir, led the youth group, visited the elderly in nursing homes, and taught a Sunday School class. Becoming a minister was not in the formula. That changed, however, one Sunday afternoon while he prayed alone in the church prayer room. "A marvelous sense of God's presence came upon me, and I heard a voice," he recalled. "I knew it was God's voice for I felt Him so near. It's the only time God ever spoke to me in an audible voice." The message? "Go back to school and prepare to teach in [a] Bible school."

Following this encounter, Horton resigned his job in Sacramento and moved to Massachusetts to enroll at (present-day) Gordon-Conwell Theological Seminary. After graduation, he entered Harvard Divinity School, where he earned a master of

Spiritual Growth in Seminary

A seminary without a deep concern for spiritual life is really a contradiction in terms, for spiritual growth must be vitally conjoined with intellectual growth in training for ministry. It was certainly not accidental that Mark noted Jesus "appointed twelve, that they might be with him" (3:14). Disciples learn fellowship with their Lord before they dare be His spokesmen to a lost world.

Assemblies of God Theological Seminary

Intellectual and spiritual growth must proceed on parallel tracks joined like a railroad with innumerable cross ties, thus comprising one avenue to meaningful life and service. Intellectual growth alone leads to rationalism; spiritual intensity alone to fanaticism. It is clear that our Lord never intended a bifurcation between mind and spirit—a stereotype allowed too long to flourish in our church. . . .

Devotion to Christ evidenced in a deep concern for Spirit-filled life and ministry must be the foundational heritage we bequeath to our students.

—*Edgar R. Lee in "Parameters for Seminary Education,"* Assemblies of God Educator, (January-March, 1989): 4–5.

sacred theology degree. In the 1940s, only a handful of Pentecostals had studied Hebrew and Greek at this level. Years later in 1959, he completed a doctorate in Old Testament at Central Baptist Theological Seminary in Kansas City, Kansas. By that time, he had taught at Metropolitan Bible Institute in New Jersey and Central Bible College in Springfield. When Assemblies of God Theological Seminary opened its doors in 1973, he received appointment to the new faculty. After retiring from the classroom, he served as the general editor for the Pentecostal Textbook Project of Logion Press, a GPH academic imprint.

Disregarding the widespread fear of seminary training among Pentecostals, Horton gained the necessary tools for Bible exposition and, within the framework of Pentecostal spirituality, penciled in the background of Assemblies of God doctrines. One finds in his ministry a rare combination of mature reflection and experiential piety. Whether writing the *Adult Teacher Quarterly* (which he did for twenty-five years) or one of his many books, whether teaching Bible in a classroom at home or overseas, his efforts have clearly influenced the wider Pentecostal movement.

J. ROBERT ASHCROFT
(1911-1995)

"Prayer is not what you say when you're on your knees or when you're in church," said J. Robert Ashcroft in a newspaper interview. "Prayer is the way you live. Your life is prayer. And if it isn't prayer, what you say doesn't make any difference anyway." "Bob" Ashcroft exemplified this kind of prayer through his many activities as educator, spiritual master, and civic leader.

The son of evangelists John and Elizabeth Ashcroft, he understood the passion of Pentecostals to evangelize the world in the last days. Later, as a graduate of Central Connecticut State University and New York University, he discovered the need for a broader witness in the American marketplace. After pastoring in West Hartford, Connecticut, he moved to Springfield, Missouri, in 1948 to join the faculty of Central Bible College. Five years later, he received appointment as national secretary of the Council's education department.

J. Robert Ashcroft

Believing in Christian involvement in the community, he encouraged J. Roswell Flower to run for the Springfield City Council. (Flower won and served for eight years.) He shared General Superintendent Ralph M. Riggs's vision of founding Evangel College as a senior school for arts and sciences and worked to make it a reality. From 1958 until 1963, he served as president of both Evangel College and Central Bible College and looked for the day when the schools could unite to train both clergy and laity in a shared Spirit-filled context.

Although he served as president of Evangel, Central Bible College, Valley Forge Christian College, and Berean University at different times, he is best remembered for his years at Evangel. Referring to the nineteenth-century Catholic intellectual John

Henry Newman, who wrote on the nature of a Christian university, Ashcroft conceived of a Christian college as a community: "the communion, the relationship of scholars, those that had information and those that were seeking information." To maximize the dynamic of such an enterprise, he added the Pentecostal dimension—a "Spirit awareness" that leads each one involved into taking all material, physical, and intellectual resources and using them for spiritual ends.

"Spiritual leadership is not managerial talent," he said at a time when institutional structures were flowering in the General Council. The model of the pastor and church leader increasingly resembled a CEO. Instead, said Ashcroft, it is to be marked by "God's approval, with modesty, no self-aggrandizement." To achieve this, "one must discover how to release [the love of Jesus] in the highest sense. This is beyond . . . the common human dimension. It is Calvary love."

Ashcroft became one of Missouri's better-known citizens. One of his sons, John Ashcroft, became governor of the state, then one of its two senators, and finally attorney general of the United States in 2001. Well into his retirement by 1989, the senior Ashcroft turned his energies to highlighting the need for prayer both within the denomination and in the city of Springfield. One of his last activities was to organize and lead a monthly interfaith prayer meeting for ministers, including Protestants and Catholics.

J. Robert Ashcroft teaching district Sunday School directors, sectional representatives, Christian education directors, and teachers at the Advanced Christian Training School (ACTS) held at Central Bible Institute. ACTS conferences began in the summer of 1954.

The Teacher's Reward

We educators are among the highest paid professionals around. What higher dividend is there than when the student academically surpasses the teacher? What greater compensation than comments like these: "Doc, I know I speak for both Renee and myself when I say you have had an awesome and long-lasting influence in our lives. We love you and Esther very much. Thank you again for everything you have done and been in our lives." What higher dividend than those thousands of students who are points of light shining in this world? Our hope rests in them.

—Dan Pecota, Northwest College of the Assemblies of God

J. BASHFORD BISHOP
(1913-2001)

Born in China and named after a famous Methodist missionary bishop, J. Bashford Bishop had a unique background. His mother and father met while in China, she as a Methodist missionary and he as an American diplomat stationed in Beijing. When the family left China in 1921, they moved to Washington, D.C., where the elder Bishop continued to work for the United States government.

Four sons and a daughter were born to their union; the daughter, however, was born with Down's syndrome and virtually helpless. Nonetheless, her condition brought the family into the Pentecostal movement. A woman coming to their door selling brushes and brooms noticed the child. She suggested that the Bishops take her to the mission she attended so the pastor and congregation could pray for her. Desperate to see their little girl become healthy, they mustered their courage and

J. Bashford Bishop (l) conversing with Stanley H. Frodsham (r) at Gospel Publishing House

drove over to Pennsylvania Avenue. There they found a shabby second-floor mission over an army-navy surplus store. Even though their daughter never received healing, the Bishops found a new spiritual dimension in their lives.

An ardent lover of sports, young "Bash" hoped to become a professional baseball player. But after a bout with tuberculosis at age thirteen, he felt called into the ministry. He enrolled at Central Bible College and after graduation in 1936 became an assistant pastor in Allentown, Pennsylvania. Visiting Springfield months later, Stanley H. Frodsham, editor of the *Pentecostal Evangel*, told him of the need for teachers at Peniel Bible Institute in the mountains of Kentucky.

Accepting this as God's will, Bishop drove his Model A Ford to Peniel and found the accommodations there to be primitive. Using creek beds that doubled for roads during the dry season, he preached in remote churches on weekends and helped students get to their preaching points as well. With the help of other CBC grads like Carl Brumback (who would write the first official history of the Assemblies of God, *Suddenly . . . From Heaven*) and Eleanor Parry (a later librarian who indexed the *Pentecostal Evangel*), Bishop set about his tasks with enthusiasm. After finishing a year's teaching at the institute, he realized that education had now become an important part of his life's work.

In 1939 he married Ruth Garvin and later joined the editorial staff at headquarters in Springfield, where, among other tasks (for example, teaching at his alma mater), he wrote the *Intermediate Teacher's Quarterly*. He also began writing the *Pentecostal Evangel*'s weekly Sunday School lesson, making his name known across the denomination.

Thousands of former students remember him for his years of instruction at Southeastern College in Lakeland, Florida. Every class he taught heard "Brother Bishop's confession of ignorance" several times: "There are two things that I can not understand: Why Ruth loves me, and why Jesus loves me." His happy marriage and concern for the students led him to counsel virtually every couple that became engaged at the college. At his own expense, he also presented them with a book or two on how to build a healthy Christian home. "Bash was not assigned by the college to do this; he just wanted young couples to know the kind of joy and unending love affair that he and Ruth shared," said R. Paul Wood, a close friend and colleague. "The hours of premarital counseling and books were his 'gifts' to the couples." And like other Assemblies of God faculty members, "The limits of [his] ministry were never determined by a contractual agreement with a college or a church. Neither was ministry confined to a job description."

On one occasion, Bishop realized that due to his great love for desserts he had put on too much weight. After a strenuous six-week's diet in which he denied himself all desserts and lost the weight, he decided it was time for a treat. Going through the cafeteria line, he selected eight of the biggest and richest desserts he could find, along with several cups of ice cream. Shocked by the sight of his food tray, one student chided him by saying, "Brother Bishop, don't you think that is gluttony?" Never at a loss for words, he responded, "Absolutely not! You just don't know how many I would eat if I really let myself go."

FRED SMOLCHUCK
(1917-2008)

While aware of the growing Hispanic districts, many today have not heard the story of the European and Russian immigrants who were evangelized and joined the Assemblies of God in its earlier years. Following the establishment of the first language district (Latin American District Council), the Assemblies of God also encouraged Germans, Italians, Ukrainians, and, more recently, Korean- and Portuguese-speaking Americans to form their own councils. Romanian-American and Swedish-American

Pentecostal churches joined the denomination as well. As time passed and the children of these immigrant groups became fluent in English, many of their congregations chose to switch their affiliation to the English-speaking districts.

Fred Smolchuck

Smolchuck's parents left the Ukraine before the close of World War I. A series of tragic events brought Kirylo and Sophia to Christ. Hope began to brighten when some-one gave them a five-cent New Testament, and Christian friends witnessed to them. They soon became members of the Russian, Polish, and Ukrainian Pentecostal Church of Chelsea, Massachusetts. Kirylo taught his son to read and write the Ukrainian language and familiarized him with the culture; this would pay dividends when he became a minister.

Growing up in Boston, a port of entry for many newcomers from across the Atlan-tic, he felt called to the ministry and enrolled at Christine Gibson's Zion Bible Insti-tute in East Providence, Rhode Island. After graduation and marriage to Stella Hanko, they began pastoring churches. After spending time as evangelists, they settled down to pastor a Pentecostal church in Claremont, New Hampshire, made up of Russians, Ukrainians, and Poles. With his fluency in Ukrainian and speaking ability in Russian and Polish, he adapted well to the needs of this multicultural congregation.

Missionary Steve Durasoff, author of *The Russian Protestants*, *Bright Wind of the Spirit: Pentecostalism Today* and *Pentecost Behind the Iron Curtain*, talking with a Russian university student in Red Square in Moscow

While living in New York City, he served as executive secretary of the Slavic Pentecostal Union and later as superintendent of the Ukrainian "Branch" (district) of the Assemblies of God for five years (1947–1952). After moving to Michigan to pastor a Slavic Pentecostal church in Detroit, he spent nearly twenty years as an executive of the Michigan district.

While missionary educator Steve Durasoff explored the Pentecostal movements in Russia and Eastern Europe, Smolchuck traced the evangelization of immigrants in North America and the church growth that resulted. His *From Azusa Street to the U.S.S.R.: A Brief History of Pentecost Among Slavic Immigrants* (1992) opens the door to this remarkable chapter of the Pentecostal heritage. Never content to simply preserve history, he has also written on the distinctives of Pentecostal spirituality, such as baptism in the Holy Spirit.

BILLIE DAVIS
(1923-)

Most of the children in the Sunday School class probably thought it sounded strange when the teacher read the Bible verse, "'It is more blessed to give than to receive'" (Acts 20:35). But not Billie Crawford, a migrant whose family followed the

Billie Davis

harvests from Iowa and Nebraska to the Imperial Valley of California during the Great Depression. "When what seemed to me like a huge, shiny car, filled with smiling, well-dressed people stopped before my ragged tent on the edge of a cotton field," she recalled, "I had to walk out in front of them, wrinkled and barefoot, to receive a Thanksgiving basket, and say, 'Thank you, ma'am.'" Obviously, they seemed happier than her. "Wouldn't it be neat to have something other people need, and be able to give it away!" Whether waiting in line for a food parcel at the Salvation Army or in a welfare office, she dreamed of being "a happy giver." The remarkable story of Billie Davis reveals how a young girl overcame seemingly impossible obstacles to receive an education and become a "real person."

Each child in the Crawford family was born in a different state and connected with a particular harvest. Davis's birth came during the Oregon hop harvest. The family moved across country in a Ford truck with a canvas top over the back. Because they lived and slept in tents, years passed before she set foot in a house. With the rest of the family, she picked everything from cotton to apples. Relief from this dreariness came only when she would go to nearby towns and villages to sell the baskets her father weaved.

As she ventured into these communities, she became conscious of public buildings: churches, post offices, government offices, libraries, schools. Since they were free and open to the public, each one made a profound impact on her life. Having gotten permission from her mother to attend a Sunday School class, Davis heard the teacher say that Jesus loved her. Now she had not only sat on a chair for the first time, she had found hope. "It was the first time I saw a way out of the fatalism of the campgrounds," she reflected. "The rich get richer, the poor get poorer, everybody pushes you down, you don't have a chance. But in Sunday School they said you *did* have a chance, because you're a child of God."

Libraries opened a whole new world for her, and the public school promised her the same education that every other child received. After Davis's family settled down during World War II, she graduated from high school as the valedictorian of her class and began working at an aircraft factory in San Diego. Having edited her high school paper, she dreamed of becoming a journalist and wrote to the national Sunday School Department in Springfield. Learning of her interest in writing and editing, Marcus Grable invited her to assist with the new *Sunday School Counselor* magazine.

Only nineteen and having a single change of clothes, she arrived in Springfield in the early 1940s to collect sixteen dollars a week at headquarters. Giving up plans to study at the University of Missouri School of Journalism, she began taking classes at

The Saints Declare

"Selling a college program is a lot like selling cars. We are furnishing transportation to young people to enable them to reach their God-given goals."
—*Dan Pecota, Northwest College of the Assemblies of God*

"A Christian college campus must not be viewed as a hothouse, nor should it be viewed as a museum where students are granted guided tours by teachers who preserve and polish the relics of past spiritual experiences."
—*Wayne Kraiss, Vanguard University*

"The admonishment to a Christian student to 'make your desk an altar' is just as valid as the college chapel being 'the classroom of the Spirit.'"
—*Malcolm R. Brubaker, Valley Forge Christian College*

"Critical thinkers, loyal to the church, offer a prophetic dimension to the process. They assist the church in standing outside of itself and seeing the 'cataracts' which have developed through time. With God's help, vision and life return, and the church renews its mission."
—*Benny C. Aker, Assemblies of God Theological Seminary*

"I conclude that both divine and human laws require majority persons to take more responsibility in matters of race and ethnic relations. We cannot hide behind general declarations of Christian love."
—*Billie Davis, Evangel University*

Drury College (now University). It was during this time that she met George Davis, a student at Central Bible College. Married in 1945, she was ordained three years later. They went to Costa Rica as missionaries in 1957 and eventually were assigned to promote Sunday Schools throughout Latin America. With George's skill as a pilot, they flew extensively about the region to workshops and conferences.

Years later, Davis graduated with highest honors from Drury and capped her training with a doctorate in education at the University of Miami in Florida. Hoping to enter a sociology program, she discovered that the university did not offer a doctorate in that area. Finally, she decided to visit the Education Department to see if they might have a program to suit her needs. Walking into the office of Professor Arnold Cheyney, he immediately remembered her address before the Ohio Education Association. Since he was directing a study on the education of migrants, he welcomed her into the department and invited her participation on the project.

While enrolled, she directed a federally funded High School Equivalency Program. The *Miami Herald* reported: "Mrs. Davis and her staff are helping 49 young people find their way out of the fields and into a college education, vocational training, or a job."

In 1952, the *Saturday Evening Post* carried her story, "I Was a Hobo Kid." *Readers Digest* soon reprinted it in condensed form. The account became so highly acclaimed that the National Education Association in 1957 produced a movie on her life called *A Desk for Billie* (now available on video). It was one of the earliest films ever produced on the life of a Pentecostal (*The Nile Mother* on the life of Lillian Trasher had come out two years earlier).

School children across the nation have learned and been inspired by her achievements and confidence in public education. When George and Billie made their residence in Springfield, she served for years as professor of behavioral sciences and chairperson of the department at Evangel University. As a scholar, she has received many awards, including the University of Miami's Distinguished Alumna award. The Council on Migrant Education honored two outstanding persons for their service to migrants: César Chávez and Billie Davis.

Sharon Ellard, promotions coordinator for the national Sunday School Department (r), reading a book, *Where Is Noah?*, to a young girl

In 1995, the Division of Christian Education of the Assemblies of God inaugurated an Award of Excellence for Sunday School teachers. There was no question who the award should be named for and who should be its first recipient. Davis was still serving the Sunday

School ministry as a columnist for the *Christian Education Counselor* (formerly *Sunday School Counselor*) when General Superintendent Thomas Trask presented the award to her at the St. Louis General Council. The plaque, which hangs in the division offices at the headquarters, is inscribed with her philosophy of education: "The best thing you can do for yourself is learn. The best thing you can do for others is teach." In accepting the award, she reminded the audience that Jesus first invited His disciples to "come and learn." Then He commanded them to "go and teach."

Through her many books, articles, and workshops, Davis's scholarship has influenced Christian education in the Assemblies of God as well as secular teacher-training programs across America. Whenever possible, she has emphasized holistic ministry. "People who are poor, sick, and hungry need more than money, health, and food," she wrote in 1990. "Like us all, they need meaning in life—a sense of order, a reason for living. This is where Christians have so much to offer. If you help people find the meaning of life while helping them find a home or get a job, you are helping them at the deepest level."

ROBERT E. COOLEY
(1930-)

A number of Assemblies of God scholars like Billie Davis have made significant academic contributions. To the hall of fame must be added the name of Robert E. Cooley. He was born into a pastor's home in Kalamazoo, Michigan, and his father later served as Michigan district superintendent. In 1952, he married Eilene Carlson and received ordination from the Michigan district six years later.

Robert E. Cooley

Academic training for the ministry took him from Central Bible College to Wheaton College. After gaining bachelor's and master's degrees, he finally entered New York University where he earned a PhD in Hebrew Studies and Near Eastern Archaeology in 1968. Only a relatively small number of Pentecostal educators in the '50s and '60s had attained such a high level of training. In this and other areas, he became a pacesetter for Pentecostal and evangelical educators.

Cooley's sweat and tears (from dust!) in excavating biblical cities (for example, Dothan and Ai) in Israel and Egypt, his reputation as a professor, his congenial manner, and his administrative skills caused his name to circulate in the corridors of the Evangelical Theological Society. This led to his selection as president of the society, the first (and only) Pentecostal to win this honor.

Always well-prepared for his lectures and deeply caring about his students, his teaching ministry took him from Central Bible College to New York University, Wheaton College, Dropsie University, Evangel University, Wheaton College, and back again to Springfield at Southwest Missouri State University. At the latter he founded the Center for Archaeological Research in 1973.

Russell P. Spittler

Cooley's inauguration as president of Gordon-Conwell Theological Seminary in 1981 marked a milestone in North American Pentecostalism. "'Historic' . . . seemed a tame term," mused Russell P. Spittler, a leading theologian in the Council. "A minister of the Assemblies of God becomes the head of a leading evangelical seminary reaching the conclusion of its first century of service." The welding of establishment Pentecostalism to evangelicalism, which had begun in 1942 with membership in the National Association of Evangelicals, appeared complete.

After retirement as president, Cooley was named chancellor of the seminary. Even so, from supervising archaeological digs in the Middle East to arguing for the historical reliability of the Old and New Testaments, he has not been an armchair scholar. In leading one of the major evangelical think-tank seminaries and serving on the boards of World Relief and other significant ministries, he has modeled the scholar-activist in serving the broader Christian community.

JESSE MIRANDA
(1937-)

Christianity Today magazine called Jesse Miranda "the granddaddy of U.S. Latino Protestantism." Founder of the National Alliance of Evangelical Ministries (AMEN, Alianza de Ministerios Evangélicos Nacionales), advisor to three American presidents on immigration issues and faith-based organizations, and executive presbyter of the Assemblies of God, Miranda has a distinguished record of service to church and society. Evangelism, reconciliation, and bridge building among different groups have marked his ministry.

Miranda grew up in an unpromising environment: a poor barrio in Albuquerque, New Mexico, one of five children born to a sawmill worker who had emigrated from Chihuahua State in Mexico and a mother of Spanish descent. He came to Christ at an early age after members of a nearby Pentecostal church, who had heard that his mother was sick, came to the house and prayed for her. Her healing had a dramatic effect on the family and young Jesse.

The church had been in contact with the family for two years before the healing. "This little Pentecostal church would come in an old broken-down-bus, pick us up, and take me to church—that made the difference," Miranda recalled. It was at church that he learned to write. At Christmastime, when his parents gave clothes as presents to him and his siblings, the church provided toys for the children.

While growing up, the disciplined lifestyle of his father and the spiritual encouragement of his mother strongly influenced him. On one occasion, during a church service, his mother put her arm around him and told him that she wanted him to become an educated man. She then pointed to a man kneeling at the altar in prayer as an example: Joe E. Martinez, an Assemblies of God layman and professor at the University of New Mexico. "That's the image that stuck."

The Larger Spiritual Conflict

The Kerygma [the proclamation of the gospel of Jesus Christ in the power of the Spirit] has a prophetic cutting edge. This means that the Hispanic Pentecostal church must not be content to preach and witness just to individual-personal sins, but must see the larger spiritual conflict. It must preach from the whole Bible to the whole person. No area is exempt in personal or social life from the Kerygmatic task. As the scope and depth of the Kerygma is discovered by the Hispanic Pentecostal church, they will join in solidarity with others and bring to bear a clear witness on the many ills that afflict their "barrios" and the world. The issues that the church must deal with in society are many and complex. . . In confronting these issues the church is cognizant of its weakness too. It must seek the leading of the Spirit as it endeavors to be a faithful witness.

—*Eldin Villafañe*, The Liberating Spirit: Toward an Hispanic American Pentecostal Social Ethic *(1993), 220.*

His parents—a Catholic father and mainline Protestant mother—also mentored him in the importance of reconciliation. "I remember I was 13 or 14, and I said, 'Dad, Catholics never read the Bible,' because I never saw him read it. 'Mother, you read the Bible but never come to the book of Acts.' And then they would turn around and say, 'And you Pentecostals never leave the Book of Acts.' So I saw my shortcomings and I saw differences. Yet we loved and respected one another so that we really enjoyed our fellowship. And we all affirmed one another."

At age sixteen, he began to attend Bible school, and his pastor assigned him preaching responsibilities a year later. Like other young people who demonstrated leadership abilities in Pentecostal churches, his pastor gave him opportunities to discover his gifts for ministry. Then came the big surprise: He was told to prepare "a lot of sermons" because he would plant a church on his own. The church rented a storefront building for him, nestled between a bar and a dance hall. In the summer months, this eighteen-year-old preacher established a church.

Miranda's educational preparation took him from Bible school to Vanguard University, Talbot Seminary, California State, and finally to Fuller Theological Seminary, where he earned a doctorate in ministry. His other activities have included time spent as superintendent of the Pacific Latin American District of the Assemblies of God, associate dean of urban and ethnic affairs at Azusa Pacific University, and currently

Jesse Miranda (r) speaking to Thomas E. Trask (l) and others at a meeting in Springfield

distinguished professor and director of the Center for Urban Studies and Ethnic Leadership at his alma mater, Vanguard University in Costa Mesa, California.

The National Alliance of Evangelical Ministries that he inaugurated includes Protestant laypeople and clergy of twenty-two nationalities from twenty-seven denominations and seventy parachurch organizations. In an unprecedented action among Hispanics, it has also established an alliance with Catholics to work toward the improvement of life and opportunities for this sector of the population. "There is no nationality group called Hispanics," Miranda wrote in the *Pentecostal Evangel*. "There are only Mexicans, Puerto Ricans, Cubans, Guatemalans, and others hailing from the various Spanish-speaking countries of the world. Hispanic is only an adjective describing a historical, cultural, and religious common denominator of a growing population in the United States."

Miranda urges Anglo Christians to understand the history and culture of this community, now the largest ethnic population in the U.S. "The church can neither evangelize nor serve effectively a people whose culture it rejects as inferior," he warns. "How long can a country survive with a permanent underclass? How can the body of Christ be built to maturity when within it lives a large number of underdeveloped members?"

Crucial to the growth of Hispanic churches is the challenge of Anglo-Hispanic relations. To illustrate the problem, he writes: "Too often, an Anglo church, in its desire to salvage an inner-city property, seeks Hispanic involvement, a tenant's investment. This is a relationship Hispanics understand. The Hispanic congregation may be expected to shoulder increasing fiscal responsibility, but it may not be allowed to share in the governance as an equal participant. In the final analysis, the relationship appears much like what we have known for too long: The Anglo-European in a dominant position continues to 'call the shots' in exchange for gratitude. Hispanics must decide to accede or depart. If they depart, they are called ungrateful and uncommitted."

Miranda not only calls the Church to repentance and reconciliation, but also works to bring about progress in both church and society. "The church can follow the nation's pattern of cultural self-preservation. Or it can work to dissolve racial prejudice and to reconcile social antagonism. The church may offer the world a privatized, personal, and 'spiritual' brand of Christianity, or it can provide leadership toward a more just and humane society exemplifying the kingdom of God."

Christianity Today noted, "Since the days of playing in backyard junk cars [in the barrio], he has not stopped envisioning a better future. Now, he says, his dream is that his children and grandchildren will live and work among a broader Christian community as a result of his bridge-building."

The varied endeavors of the persons introduced in this chapter represent the notable work of Christian mentors. Paul, too, recognized the value of mentoring when he advised his understudy Timothy to "be strong in the grace that is in Christ Jesus; and what you have heard from me through many witnesses entrust to faithful people who will be able to teach others as well" (2 Timothy 2:1–2, NRSV).

RECOMMENDED READING

Ashcroft, J. Robert. *The Sequence of the Supernatural and Other Essays on the Spirit-Filled Life.* Springfield, Mo.: Gospel Publishing House, 1972.

Davis, Billie. "Don't Throw Bread from the Truck." *World Vision* (August/ September 1990): 12–14.

_____. *Renewing Hope: Helps for Helping Others.* Springfield, Mo.: Gospel Publishing House, 1995.

Davis, Rodney. "'Just Call Me Johnnie': Remembering Johnnie Barnes, the First Royal Rangers Leader." *Assemblies of God Heritage* 18 (summer 1998): 23–24, 34.

Elbert, Paul, ed. *Faces of Renewal: Studies in Honor of Stanley M. Horton on His 70th Birthday.* Peabody, Mass.: Hendrickson Publishers, 1988.

Gell, Alan and Ryan Beaty. "The Legacy of Royal Rangers: Mentoring Future Men." *Assemblies of God Heritage* 30 (2010): 6–15.

Gohr, Glenn. "J. Bashford Bishop." Parts 1 and 2. *Assemblies of God Heritage* 13 (spring 1993): 10–13; 13 (summer 1993): 27–29, 35.

Hammar, Richard R. *Pastor, Church & Law.* Matthews, N.C.: Christian Ministry Resources, 2000.

Horton, Stanley M. *What the Bible Says About the Holy Spirit.* Springfield, Mo.: Gospel Publishing House, 1976.

_____. ed. *Systematic Theology.* Rev. ed. Springfield, Mo.: Gospel Publishing House, 1995.

Lee, Sylvia. "Billie Davis: Voice for Education and Appreciation." *Assemblies of God Heritage* 19 (summer 1999): 4–8.

McGee, Gary B. "The Indispensable Calling of the Pentecostal Scholar." *Assemblies of God Educator* 35 (July–September 1990): 1, 3–5, 16.

Miranda, Jesse. "Realizing the Hispanic Dream." *Pentecostal Evangel* (22 October 1989): 21–23.

Murray, Ferne H. "The Santa Cruz Cheerbringers: Today's Missionettes Has Its Roots in This Club." *Assemblies of God Heritage* 12 (summer 1992): 7–8, 14, 32.

Olena, Lois E. and Raymond L. Gannon. *Stanley M. Horton: Shaper of Pentecostal Theology.* Springfield, MO: Gospel Publishing House, 2009.

Sellers, Jeff M. "You Can Take the Boy Out of the Barrio . . . " *Christianity Today* (9 September 2002): 56–58, 60.

Shultz, Lee. "A Tribute to Gwen Jones." *Onward* (June 1990): 1–2.

Smolchuck, Fred. *From Azusa Street to the U.S.S.R.: A Brief History of Pentecost Among Slavic Immigrants 1900–1991.* Springfield, Mo.: By the author, 1992.

Spittler, Russell P. "The Cooley Inauguration: A Celebration of Sovereignty." *Agora* 5, no. 1: 14.

Villafañe, Eldin. *The Liberating Spirit: Toward an Hispanic American Pentecostal Social Ethic.* Grand Rapids: William B. Eerdmans Publishing Co., 1993.

UNIT SIX
1993-2003

TIME LINE 1993-2003

1993—G. Raymond Carlson and Joseph Flower retire. New executive officers elected: Thomas E. Trask, superintendent; Charles T. Crabtree, assistant superintendent; George O. Wood, secretary; James K. Bridges, treasurer.

1994—"Memphis Miracle"—racial reconciliation begins among white and black Pentecostals. Pentecostal Fellowship of North America (PFNA) dissolves; replaced with more inclusive Pentecostal/Charismatic Churches of North America (PCCNA). Mehdi Dibaj and Haik Hovsepian Mehr, Iranian national AG leaders martyred. First World AG Congress held in Seoul, Korea, with over one million in attendance.

1995—Senior Adult Ministries established; *Revivaltime* radio broadcast ends after forty-five years of ministry (succeeded by the short-lived *MasterPlan* with Jeff Brawner). Council joins new PCCNA.

1997—Dedication of new facilities for the Assemblies of God Theological Seminary in Springfield; AGTS begins Doctor of Ministry program. Loren Triplett retires as executive director of foreign missions, succeeded by L. John Bueno.

1999—Dedication of new Flower Pentecostal Heritage Center at headquarters in Springfield.

2000—AG 2000 Celebration convenes in Indianapolis.

2001—"9/11" attack stuns America. "War on Terrorism" reflects the growing world challenge of Islamic Fundamentalism.

2003—America invades Iraq. Vision for Transformation accepted by General Council meeting in Washington, D.C.

CHAPTER 25

LEADING THE CHURCH IN MISSION

W e are a people of the Spirit," declared the "Vision Statement" prepared for the 2000 Celebration of the Assemblies of God in Indianapolis. "We are a people of vision. Birthed in the fire of renewal, still less than one hundred years ago, we have now become a worldwide influence for worship, discipleship, and evangelism in the twenty-first century. What God has done, and is doing, should fill us with gratitude and awe, and should move us to deep prayer and faith in understanding God's vision for us in this new century. Who can predict what the Holy Spirit may yet do before the return of the Lord? His vision is that the glory of Christ be revealed among every people and culture. Our church must proclaim Christ to this world in the twenty-first century with first century fervor."[1]

By all accounts, the Pentecostal vision had already born fruit. The statistics for 2002 sharply contrasted with the humble number of persons and congregations that affiliated with the fledgling organization at Hot Springs nine decades earlier. It had grown to encompass a church constituency in the United States of 2,687,366 with 12,133 churches and 32,556 ministers. It also supported 1,880 missionaries serving overseas, working with fraternally related constituencies whose members and adherents numbered more than 40 million people. Giving by the American churches totaled more than $338 million.[2] With the addition of the Brazilian district (U.S.A.) in 2003, the Council now had 59 districts.

And yet, never did the challenges seem greater. In the family photo album of the Assemblies of God, one now finds snapshots of exciting new mission endeavors, multicultural congregations, and new church plants—all treasured hopes. But along beside them, one also finds photos of an aging clergy, sluggish growth, misgivings about traditional church structures, and fears about the continued Pentecostal identity of the denomination.[3] Most surprisingly, the family picture shows that the earlier cultural and social homogeneity of the membership has been replaced by a striking diversity.

Learning that only an estimated 50 percent of Assemblies of God church members had been baptized in the Holy Spirit, General Superintendent Thomas Trask remarked in 1993, "This means we might be Pentecostal in doctrine, but we're not Pentecostal in experience."[4] He called the General Council to pray for a new outpouring of the Spirit. Confronting the issue of identity head-on, he stated, "Church history has taught us that whenever an organization departs from its original mission, it ends up becoming a byword. The Assemblies of God was raised up to be a Pentecostal voice. I have great respect and love for the evangelical churches, but we are more than evangelical; we are Pentecostal!

"I look back to the years of our growth when this Fellowship was such a viable force in the world and when we allowed the Holy Spirit to guide us, empower us, and compel us. If you call that a throwback to the old, then that's exactly where I'm at because I'm coming back to what has to be the driving force. . . . We must minister through the person and work of the Holy Spirit, because that's why God raised us up!"[5]

Sociologist Margaret M. Poloma has also noted this tension. Like Trask, she says that returning to the charismatic dimension of ministry must be more than verbal.

Forward in Faith

"The Vision for Transformation process was launched to study what changes the Assemblies of God can make to better serve the local church and facilitate the work of the kingdom of God," declared General Superintendent Thomas Trask in anticipation of the August 2003 General Council in Washington, D.C. Concerned about finding more effective ways to evangelize in a rapidly changing culture, the Executive Presbytery inaugurated a study process in 2002 to gain grass roots input into "where the Holy Spirit is leading this Fellowship." The self-study included sponsoring open forums across the nation where church executives listened to thousands of ministers and church leaders, as well as the preparation of key resolutions to bring about change.

The challenge at hand was to detect and remove barriers within the Council's organizational structures that hinder church planting and evangelism. "The Holy Spirit is still calling men, women, and young people to Christian service and giving them a vision for ministry. As a church, it's our responsibility to provide opportunities for them to carry out their God-given assignments," he added.

The self-study centered on church practice, not church doctrine—considered "off-limits" for the project. Three core themes emerged:

1. The Assemblies of God should be a network of fully empowered Pentecostal churches that multiply themselves through church planting.
2. The Fellowship should give emphasis and priority to the call of God and effective ministry in the credentialing process.
3. The Fellowship's organizational structure should be aligned around mission and ministry to serve our ministers and empower the local church.

Among other resolutions passed in Washington, D.C., the Council approved the creation of a local church-level ministerial credential; restored the "Cooperative Assembly" status for independent congregations wishing to work with the Council, but not seeking official membership; authorized the establishment of a national placement service to assist ministers in finding opportunities for ministry; gave licensed ministers the right to vote at General Council meetings; and passed a bylaw resolution that prioritized the importance of church planting.

Through the years, Pentecostal spirituality has been threatened by the "growing alignment with the successful evangelical denominations, many of which [still] deny the validity of Pentecostal experiences, and [refuse] to cooperate with mainstream charismatics who share a Pentecostal ideology."[6]

While admittedly Pentecostals have changed through the years, so have many evangelicals, including those not on the roster of the National Association of Evangelicals. "Largely through the itinerant ministry of David du Plessis, the roving global ambassador of Pentecostal understandings of the Holy Spirit," wrote Russell P. Spittler, "Pentecostal beliefs and practices were increasingly absorbed into mainstream churches, and not merely by their charismatics." Significantly, "much of the mainstream evangelical tradition surrendered the cessationist viewpoint that insisted that spiritual gifts disappeared from the life of the church following the death of the apostles in the first century."[7] The growing popularity of charismatic worship music and Pentecostal modes of expression (e.g., clapping hands, raising arms in prayer) in the historic churches represents two other areas of influence. Protestant mission leaders have discovered that Pentecostal spirituality has become commonplace among many third world Christians.

A restorationist zeal to imitate the ministry and church life of the Early Church has distinguished Pentecostals. Among other things, they are less aware of the Christian tradition, less involved in politics, and more focused on personal charismatic experiences. Furthermore, they exhibit a more generous attitude toward other believers and generally avoid the contentious spirit of their fundamentalist relatives.[8] Even so, church leaders decry the decline in the number of believers having the charismatic experience of speaking in tongues, seeing this as a threat to Pentecostal vigor.

Trask's anxiety, therefore, reflects that of other leaders across the denomination. What is at stake centers on the spiritual dynamic that has propelled the Movement: the "first century fervor." In their estimation, expansion must come from the fires of revival. Leadership, therefore, has become a paramount concern as the Assemblies of God faces the future. This chapter explores the offices and leaders of the denomination in place at the beginning of the twenty-first century.

THOMAS E. TRASK
(1936-)

"I am not geared for the status quo," said Thomas Trask, after taking office. "I'm just not programmed that way."[9] Whether pastoring a local church, making changes in the headquarters operation, or calling clergy and laity to personal repentance and prayer for a worldwide spiritual awakening, Trask has already left his imprint.

He was born into the family of Waldo and Beatrice Trask of Brainerd, Minnesota. When Waldo, a nonpracticing Presbyterian, married Beatrice Stith, a nonpracticing Roman Catholic, the differences in their faiths hardly mattered. After training and working as a bartender in Brainerd, they moved to Fargo, North Dakota, where he worked as a meat cutter. The first person concerned about their spiritual welfare was their landlady, "Mrs. Jacobson," who attended the Assembly of God in the city. She witnessed to them every time they needed to use the telephone in her apartment.

Moving back to Brainerd, Waldo became part owner of a local bar, the Dutch Room, and was on his way to becoming an alcoholic. "I would often think about that," he recalled, "my boys would grow up as children of the town drunk."[10]

Difficulty in the birth of their second son, Thomas, changed Beatrice's spiritual outlook. "God, if You will spare my life so that I can raise my children," she promised,

"I'll serve You." A successful birth followed. Two years later in 1938, she remembered the vow, a memory that soon led to her conversion. Without Waldo's knowledge, she attended a service at the Brainerd Gospel Tabernacle led by evangelist Guy Shields. Receiving Christ as Savior and testifying to immediate deliverance from chain smoking, she returned home only to be confronted with the anger of her unsympathetic husband. Ready to leave home without her and the children, she stopped him at the door and pleaded with him: "Waldo, please stay for the sake of the boys. Please stay. The boys need a father."[11] Consequently, he decided to remain and then went to bed.

Thomas E. Trask

At breakfast, he cursed preachers and the church while blowing smoke in Beatrice's face. More than her disinterest in cigarettes, he noticed a significant change in her behavior. That evening, he returned home from work angry and confused. Kneeling down, he began to pray the Lord's Prayer that he remembered from his Presbyterian Sunday School class: "Our Father who art in heaven, Hallowed be Thy name."

"About halfway through the Lord's Prayer," young Thomas remembered, "all heaven broke upon him, and he was gloriously saved."[12] Before long, he entered the ministry and began pastoring Assemblies of God congregations in Minnesota.

His sons, Ray and Thomas, enrolled at North Central Bible College in Minneapolis and then became pastors themselves after graduation. A revival during their freshman year led Thomas to recommit his life to Christ. "What happened was that a revival broke out, and classes were dismissed," he remembered. "God sovereignly moved across the student body, and for days I watched young people and professors wait before God. Hour after hour we were in the presence of God, and courses were set for people's lives. Even though I was saved as a boy in the local church and received the infilling of the Holy Spirit at youth camp, it was that revival in Bible college and the refilling with the Holy Spirit that changed my life." Looking back at the campus revival, he muses, "That's why I believe it is so important that people who have an initial experience in their youth need to have a 'reexperience,' a rebaptism in the Spirit, as they grow up and mature. Our experience needs to remain up-to-date and fresh in our hearts and spirits."[13]

World Assemblies of God Fellowship (WAGF)

General superintendents from forty nations met in Springfield, Missouri, in July 1988 to discuss the possibility of cooperating in world evangelism in the final decade of the twentieth century. Resulting from this meeting came the concept of the "Decade of Harvest" and a decision to form a worldwide Assemblies of God fellowship.

The newly formed International Decade of Harvest Conference convened in Indianapolis in August 1989 where the proposed WAGF adopted a constitution. It was named the "World Pentecostal Assemblies of God Fellowship" and J. Philip Hogan, retired executive director of foreign missions, USA, became the first chairperson. David Yonggi Cho of Seoul, Korea, succeeded him in 1992; the current chairperson is Thomas E. Trask, general superintendent of the USA Assemblies of God. The name was shortened in 1993 to "World Assemblies of God Fellowship."

The purpose centers on evangelizing the world in the shortest possible time by providing everyone the opportunity to hear and respond to the gospel. Under the leadership of the Holy Spirit, member bodies have pledged to assist and encourage one another in partnership in mission. While representatives meet tri-annually, an executive committee of fourteen meets every year for the transaction of business. The quarterly magazine *WorldLink* functions as the official voice and is available through e-mail.

A WAGF World Congress convenes every three years.

Concern for humanitarian needs led to the formation of a relief agency in 1994—the "Assemblies of God Relief and Development Agency" (WAGRA).

In less than nine years, nearly $2 million has been sent overseas to provide basic necessities and financial assistance to AG constituents in times of disaster.

—Warren Newberry

At North Central, he met Shirley Burkhart, who hailed from Toledo, Ohio, and they were married. After graduation, they spent twenty-five years in pastoral ministry in Minnesota and Michigan. Whether it was in Vicksburg, Saginaw, or Detroit, Michigan, each of the churches he pastored experienced revival. Arriving in Saginaw after a church split, he faced the discouraged remaining parishioners. "Look, we're not going to worry about where some people have gone," he told them. "We're going to believe God for a move of the Spirit." When revival came, he observed, "It was so effortless to see people saved, healed, and filled with the Holy Ghost week after week after week. This went on for years."[14]

After three years as Michigan district superintendent, he returned to the pastorate: that of Brightmoor Tabernacle in Detroit, a church rich in Pentecostal history. In 1988, the Trask family moved to Springfield, where he took over as general treasurer when Raymond H. Hudson resigned midterm. At the 1989 Council, Trask was officially elected to this position. Five years after arriving at headquarters, Trask was elected general superintendent. He entered office with more years in the pastorate than any of his predecessors. "I promise not to rest content with any numerical growth," Trask said at his installation, "until the Spirit of God has touched every church in this great Fellowship and brought them a new Pentecostal revival."[15]

GENERAL OFFICERS AND EXECUTIVE DIRECTORS

The election of leaders at the General Council in Minneapolis in 1993 signaled that the third generation of Assemblies of God leaders had come to the fore. The members of the headquarters Board of Administration (general superintendent, assistant general superintendent, general secretary, and general treasurer), as well as the two executive directors for world and home missions, came to their positions with significant practical ministry experience. While previous national leaders had often moved to the top through the church bureaucracy, most of the new officers had more immediately been pastors of large congregations.

GENERAL SUPERINTENDENT
–THOMAS E. TRASK

The office of general superintendent carries the commission to "emphasize and implement the threefold mission of the church: the evangelization of the world, the worship of God, and the building of a body of saints being perfected in the image of His Son; and promote and coordinate efforts directed toward the fulfilling of that mission."[16] With this comes the responsibility of president of the corporation, presiding at sessions of the Executive Presbytery, General Presbytery, General Council, General Council Credentials Committee, and Board of Administration, among other functions.

Trask has also represented the Assemblies of God to larger evangelical audiences, such as the National Association of Evangelicals, charismatic Christians, and more recently World Assemblies of God Fellowship (as the president).

ASSISTANT GENERAL SUPERINTENDENT
–CHARLES T. CRABTREE (1937-)

As the vice president of the corporation, the assistant superintendent assists the general superintendent in various capacities and chairs meetings of the Executive Presbytery and the Board of Administration in the latter's absence. Charles Crabtree moved to this post after many years as a successful pastor and popular preacher in the denomination.

Son of New England Pentecostal pioneers Clifford and Helen Crabtree, he grew up in a parsonage with a strict holiness code. "I didn't attend one ball game in my life until I came to Central Bible (College [CBC])," he remembered with a chuckle. "No comics . . . no socializing. I was never in anyone's home overnight growing up. No school activities except the chess club, and they [his parents] would play chess and checkers with us."[17]

Since worldly activities were frowned upon, the life of the family centered on the church. Like many Pentecostals who loved

Charles T. Crabtree

music and found abundant opportunities to share their gifts in worship services, the Crabtree children all played musical instruments: Charles played the piano, trumpet, and marimba; David, the trombone; and Hazel, the piano. Family devotions at 7 a.m. before they went to school rounded out their spiritual formation. With a strong belief in God's ability to answer prayer, the parents believed "the Word was supreme. They would talk to us about trouble, problems with kids, and we'd pray over these situations."[18]

The Bible college experience led the younger Crabtree away from the independent Pentecostal fellowship of his home church to join the Assemblies of God. Ministry for him and his wife Ramona began in Paramount, California, in 1958. (Crabtree met Ramona Hudgins, an Evangel student and a gifted gospel pianist, while he was enrolled at CBC.) Accepting an invitation from A. M. Alber to hold a two-week revival to be focused on the youth at First Assembly in Des Moines, Iowa, Crabtree discovered— much to his surprise—that most of the youth were children, in fact, sixty of them. This meant changing their plans and providing the children with different activities each evening as they shared the gospel with them. His preaching on the two Sundays remained in the memory of the congregation.

Shortly thereafter, when Alber announced his retirement, the Crabtrees moved to Des Moines to pastor the congregation and lead it in a new building program. A larger pastorate followed in San Jose, California, before his selection as director of the U.S. Decade of Harvest. Initially resisting the invitation, he credits his willingness to heed a divine summons, which came to him in prayer. After accepting the position, he received a long-distance telephone call from a woman who abruptly asked, "What's going on?" Not recognizing the voice or knowing the person, Crabtree heard that she had been praying and fasting for him for three weeks at the direction of the Lord, but didn't know the reason why. Satisfied that he had obeyed God and the prayers had been answered, the woman hung up.[19] Election as assistant general superintendent came several years later in 1993.

With a keen interest in seeing revival sweep across the denomination, but avoiding the problems that have plagued some renewal movements, he wrote in the *Pentecostal Evangel*, "Many times people are wanting a revival of 1960 or 1920. But what we should want is a renewal and a revival of spiritual life and effectiveness. Instead of seeking for demonstrations, we should seek first of all for the reality of spiritual life in Jesus Christ and a new love and new dimension of spiritual effectiveness." Then focusing on physical manifestations that sometimes receive criticism in Pentecostal and charismatic circles, he notes: "In this day and time we need to have discernment between what is supernatural and divine and what is simply carnal. We must know what is of God and be able to administrate with such love that these gifts can be free and that we can have a supernatural display of God's Spirit. Then out of the church will go perfected people."[20]

In looking at the prospects for the Assemblies of God, he says with the rhetoric of a preacher, "If we have a historical Pentecost instead of a contemporary Pentecost, then we will have a historical Jesus rather a contemporary Jesus. The Holy Spirit has come to reveal Jesus as he is and what he does in this moment."[21]

GENERAL SECRETARY
—GEORGE O. WOOD (1941-)

Serving as the chief record keeper for the General Council, the general secretary maintains accurate minutes of the biennial General Council meetings, as well as sessions of the Executive Presbytery, General Council Credentials Committee, and the General Presbytery. With this comes the responsibility to update the ministerial lists, the signing of all official and legal documents, the issuance of credentials, and

George O. Wood

oversight of the Flower Pentecostal Heritage Center at the headquarters complex in Springfield. Not a secretary in the traditional sense, the general secretary serves as an executive in the top policy-making bodies of the Assemblies of God.

A missionary kid, campus pastor, senior pastor with two doctorates, author, and member of the California Bar Association, George O. Wood brought an unusual combination of gifts to the office. His parents, George and Elizabeth Wood, returned with their three children to China in 1947, hoping to spend many more years in ministry there. Young George was six years old when they made the journey across the Pacific Ocean on the *Marine Lynx* with other Assemblies of God missionaries, including the rookie missionaries J. Philip and Virginia Hogan and the veterans Howard and Edith Osgood.

Political upheaval and the Communist Revolution, however, forced them to return to America two years later. "I really believe that in a lot of ways their life ended in 1949, even though Mom did not die till 1979, and Dad died in 1984," he concludes. "They always felt God had called them to China and Tibet, and when that door closed, they floundered. Dad's ministry floundered. He never quite found himself. He'd stay in a place a year or two and then move on, struggling with small works. They had only one or two decent-sized churches in their whole life. But they had felt called, and they would have gone back at the drop of a hat had the door been open. They would be thrilled with what's happened in the local church they left in Xining, China, which now has 14,000 adult baptized believers."[22]

While his father pastored the Assembly of God in Bristow, Oklahoma, the younger Wood heard the call to ministry at age ten. The example of his parents strongly shaped his outlook. "I would not be in the ministry today without my folks' influence, especially my mother's," he notes. "I admired the way my dad worked hard. I admired my mother's gentleness and her prayer life. She prayed . . . probably prayed 2 hours daily. . . . Got up at 4–5 o'clock in the morning and spent the first couple of hours of the day in prayer and reading her Bible. She made a practice of reading her Bible through every year."[23]

Wood enrolled at Evangel University in Springfield for his undergraduate work. While there he met Jewel Waite, a student from Greenville, Alabama, who was an education major. Further study took him to Fuller Theological Seminary in Pasadena, California. He then returned to Evangel as campus minister and director of student life. "My first Sunday back at Central Assembly [in Springfield], I saw her in the choir and she saw me in the back of the congregation. We met each other after the service and began to talk with each other. We had long talks every Sunday for about a month—but I was afraid to ask her out because I knew she was too pretty and attractive to go out with a dud like me. Finally, I got the courage to ask her out. Our first date was October 16, 1965. I asked her to marry me on October 30, 1965. It took her about a week to think it over, and we were married December 27, 1965."[24]

Returning to the West Coast, Wood served for many years as senior pastor of Newport-Mesa Christian Center in Costa Mesa, California, and as assistant superintendent of the Southern California district. He also completed a doctorate in pastoral theology from Fuller and a law degree (Juris Doctor) from Western State University College of Law. With his election as general secretary in 1993, Wood became the third officer in this position to have legal training (J. Roswell Flower had read law) and the second to have a degree in law (after Bartlett Peterson).

He became well known in the General Council not only for his preaching, but also for his articles in the *Evangel*. Eventually, one series of his columns was published in the two-volume book *A Psalm in Your Heart*. "You will value the Psalms most when you experience a season of pain, misunderstanding, or deep need," he tells the reader, "for the greater part of the Psalms reverberate with cries for God to help in desperate times." Wood then shares what brought the book about: "I found myself in such a

The Saints Declare

" Pentecost! What does it mean? . . . To be filled with the Spirit is to be filled with Christ, and so to live that our constant experience and testimony will be 'I live, yet not I, but Christ liveth in me.'"

—*Marie Burgess Brown*

"It is fundamental with us to preach the Gospel . . . . We all understand that what one cannot do alone, others co-operating, can do. It becomes therefore almost indispensable that we realize we have come to the Kingdom for such an hour as this; that we put our hearts together, that we put our hands together, that we co-operate largely for the Kingdom of our Christ to spread the Gospel to the uttermost parts of the earth, and that we do it quickly."

—*E. N. Bell*

"We can talk about plans and programs. We can cite statistics and quote reports. We can laud past accomplishments, but any efforts on our part are destined to fall far short unless the Holy Spirit anoints and directs."

—*G. Raymond Carlson*

"How long will this revival last? It doesn't have to stop if we just keep being changed—from glory to glory."

—*Thomas E. Trask*

place several years ago. In those moments of hope abandoned the Lord met me in the Psalms. . . . I felt impressed to take the time early each morning to journal through Psalms. . . . By allowing the psalms to help me gain perspective on my most personal needs, I was permitting the Holy Spirit to speak God's truth into my life. I would have drowned in the depression of my own feelings—I needed truth from outside my unreliable and wildly oscillating emotions to provide stability, balance, and hope. . . . So, what began as a psalm in David's heart and the hearts of the other Psalmists became a psalm in my own heart."[25]

GENERAL TREASURER
—JAMES K. BRIDGES (1935-2010)

The general treasurer serves as the custodian of all funds by keeping an accurate record of revenue and disbursements and reporting periodically to the General Council and the Executive Presbytery of which he or she is a member. In this capacity, the treasurer also administers the Benevolences ministry of the denomination that includes Highlands Child Placement Services and Maternity Home in Kansas City, Missouri; Hillcrest Children's Home in Hot Springs, Arkansas; Disaster Relief; and the Aged Minister Assistance program.

James K. Bridges

James Bridges and Joyce Sterling met in their home city of Houston, Texas, at a church pastored by her parents. Both sets of parents—their fathers and mothers—uniquely held ministerial credentials with the Assemblies of God. James's father, Forrest Bridges, came from a Methodist background in the eastern part of Texas. His mother, Estelline (nee Clifton), came from rural Bokchito, Oklahoma; her parents had been converted in a Pentecostal brush arbor service. Forrest and Estelline met while picking cotton in a field near Lubbock, Texas, where their families had gone to find work.[26]

After they were married, they moved to Houston. Involvement in the activities at Airline Assembly of God, pastored by James Sterling, eventually led them to enter full-time ministry. "It developed while [Forrest] was an active deacon," his son James recalls. "Out of [his] ministry experiences [in jails, hospitals, and street meetings], he felt the Lord nudging him toward the ministry. He had a powerful experience at the altar one Sunday evening in which God just clearly impressed him. He said it was like Paul's heavenly vision that he felt the call into the ministry."[27] Several years later, when they pastored in Conroe, Texas, his mother received the call for ministry and acquired credentials.

By age fourteen, the younger Bridges had been strongly influenced by the spiritual tenor of the Sunday evening "Pentecostal rallies" at Airline Assembly. When his Sunday School teacher invited him to seek the baptism in the Holy Spirit at one of these services, she stayed with him until he received. This experience helped confirm a growing interest in pursuing the ministry.

Beyond Her Wildest Dreams

Dressed in yellow and black uniforms, an enthusiastic group of girls entered the nursing home. After talking to each resident about God's love, the young visitors strummed ukuleles and sang Christmas carols to the delight of the elderly audience.

When Goldie Olson awoke from her dream, she realized God had provided the solution for reaching girls in the often overlooked "crack" between children's church and youth programs. In 1949, with this dream as her guide, Goldie worked with her pastor to organize the Cheerbringers club for girls. The program combined spiritual training (Bible reading and prayer) with more practical ministry to others (visiting local nursing homes and making handicrafts for distribution by missionaries to children in other countries).

The "Santa Cruz Cheerbringers" tripled in attendance after only two years. The activities of the club expanded into a four-part training course based on Luke 2:52: Christian growth in wisdom (intellect), in stature (physical), with God (spiritual) and with man (social).

After presenting the Cheerbringers' idea at the 1953 General Council in Milwaukee, enthusiasm and demand for a systematic plan for older women to train younger women increased. Based on the original Cheerbringers model, the Missionettes club for girls ages twelve through seventeen received official approval in 1955. From that beginning, the Missionettes program ultimately expanded to include six grade-appropriate training and achievement programs: Rainbows (preschool children 3 and up), Daisies (kindergarten girls), Prims (first and second grade girls), Stars (third through fifth grade girls), Friends (sixth through eighth grade girls), and Girls Only Club (ninth through twelve grade girls).

"Grandma" Goldie's original dream of a few girls dressed in yellow and black has mushroomed into a multitude of girls and young women dressed in multicolored outfits all over the world. While much has changed, the ultimate purpose remains the same—winning girls to Jesus Christ and teaching them to live victoriously while serving God and humankind.

—Annette Newberry

He began preaching while still a teenager and at a time when money was scarce: "I would spend summers preaching revivals between the school terms. For instance, I held a revival over [in Magnolia Hill] in East Texas, and they paid me in potatoes, sweet potatoes, and banty chickens. And on the way home, I had a flat; and while I was trying to get the tire out, some of my chickens got loose. I had to chase them down."[28]

Educational preparation took him to the University of Houston and then to Southwestern Assemblies of God University in Waxahachie, Texas. The Bridgeses began their ministry in 1955 in Texas and, apart from pastoring for a short time in Wichita, Kansas, they spent most of their time in Texas. He also studied at the Wichita State University and then at Southern Methodist University in Dallas.

While pastoring University Assembly of God in Waxahachie, he served for a short time as vice president for academic affairs at Southwestern, his alma mater. From there, he moved to the office of assistant superintendent of the North Texas district. He then succeeded E. R. Anderson as district superintendent. Twelve years later in 1993, he became general treasurer.

Like the other general officers, Bridges remains committed to Pentecostal spirituality and sees this as the means for the future growth of the denomination. In an article in the *Pentecostal Evangel* entitled "Contending for the Truth," he writes: "This latter-day outpouring of the Holy Spirit is restoring to the Church the truth concerning the baptism in the Holy Spirit with the initial physical evidence of speaking in other tongues which the Early Church experienced (Acts 2:4). . . . God has allowed us to live in this remarkable period of history when God's truth is being restored in Pentecostal power to all who will allow the truth to set them free, to set them apart to live holy unto the Lord, and to set them ablaze to witness the truth 'as it is in Jesus' (Ephesians 4:21) to this lost generation."[29]

EXECUTIVE DIRECTOR OF ASSEMBLIES OF GOD WORLD MISSIONS —L. JOHN BUENO (1938-)

In an important development in 2001, the General Council renamed the Divisions of Home Missions and Foreign Missions to Assemblies of God Home Missions and Assemblies of God World Missions, respectively. In 2003, the former became Assemblies of God U.S. Missions. Both executive directors serve on the Executive Presbytery.

As the chief administrator of an international missions agency with. personnel around the world, the executive director of world missions represents the General Council in "all relationships with governments or authorities where our world missions work is involved."[30] This portfolio also involves supervising the distribution of funds, serving as chair of both the World Missions Committee and World Missions Board, and keeping the official records of these bodies.

"Staying true to our comprehensive, integrated mission of reaching, planting, training and touching—evangelism, church planting, training of national believers and compassion ministries—have paid multiplied Kingdom dividends," according to John Bueno. "Natural disasters and wars afford us the opportunity to reach out to the poor and suffering in obedience to God's commands. Yet what separates us from secular and government humanitarian organizations, as well as parachurch ministries, is that we make every attempt to proclaim the gospel as we minister to people's physical needs."[31] This unapologetic affirmation of holistic ministry not only depicts how the approach to missions has evolved in the last fifty years in the Assemblies of God, but also describes the course of Bueno's own labors in El Salvador as a missionary.

L. John Bueno

The son of missionaries Theodore and Kathryn Bueno, who served variously in Cuba, Venezuela, and Chile, he grew up in the latter country, familiar with the culture and fluent in Spanish. When the family returned to the United States, the elder Bueno became director of Latin American Bible Institute in La Puente, California.

After graduation from high school in La Puente, John enrolled at Bethany College of the Assemblies of God in Santa Cruz. While there, he met and married Lois Lebeck, whose parents were pastors. In 1961, the young couple was assigned to pastor the Evangelistic Center in San Salvador, the capital of El Salvador in Central America. The church had been struggling with indebtedness, and the attendance had plummeted to about two hundred people.

The church would never be the same. Bueno began preaching on stewardship to put it on a sound financial basis and inaugurated a pastoral visitation program to evangelize. In a strategic decision based on his study of the Book of Acts, he started the "Filial Church" plan in 1970.[32] "Filiales"—branch congregations—were established throughout the city, "mothered, staffed, and financed" for the first year by the Evangelistic Center. "After the site was selected, a lay pastor was named to oversee the spiritual and material progress of the new work," according to Bueno. "He must be a man of maturity, worthy of respect, and willing to work under the guidance of the Evangelistic Center pastor and board. Once each month he met with the board to discuss the progress of the work, to make plans, and to set goals."

After the first year, the branch church became self-supporting and was expected to contribute to the development of other filial churches under the guidance of the mother church. "Each church was encouraged to maintain a passion for souls in its vicinity and to let nothing interfere with the stated purpose: making disciples for the kingdom of God."[33] The program proved to be spectacularly successful. In ten years, the Evangelistic Center grew to have a Sunday School attendance of eighteen thousand and had sponsored twenty satellite churches, of which eight had become sovereign churches.[34]

The thousands of children in the city growing up in dehumanizing poverty and despair, however, could not be ignored. After prayer and discussion, the Buenos opened a Christian school at the church, and eighty-one children enrolled in the first year. From this venture emerged Latin America ChildCare, an Assemblies of God agency that in 2003 ministered to the spiritual, educational, and physical needs of over eighty thousand children through three hundred schools in twenty countries.[35]

While in San Salvador, he also worked as the area director for Central America for Assemblies of God World Missions. When Loren Triplett became executive director in 1989, Bueno succeeded him as field director for Latin America and the Caribbean. In

1997, he became the sixth person to direct the international enterprise. "So we follow the chart of God's Word, propelled by the wind of the Spirit, and stay the course in our worldwide mission."[36]

Assemblies of God World Missions embraces a myriad of programs from the five transnational ministries (Center for Ministry to Muslims, Global University, Health-Care Ministries, International Media Ministries, and Life Publishers) to Mission Abroad Placement Service to regional efforts. The latter include, among many others, Africa Tabernacle Evangelism, Asia's Little Ones, Continental Theological Seminary in Belgium, Latin America Theological Seminary, Project Rescue!, and Royal Rangers.[37]

EXECUTIVE DIRECTOR OF ASSEMBLIES OF GOD U. S. MISSIONS —CHARLES E. HACKETT (1934-)

The responsibilities of the executive director of U.S. missions include oversight of the following departments: Chaplaincy, Chi Alpha Campus Ministries, Church Planting, Intercultural Ministries, Mission America Placement Service, and Teen Challenge. These activities are administered from Springfield "insofar as such activities are not already directed within and by the respective district councils."[38]

Coming from a pastorate in Indiana, the General Council elected Charles E. Hackett to head the denomination's many homeland endeavors in 1991. A graduate of Southwestern Assemblies of God University, Hackett traveled as an evangelist for two years before becoming the Indiana district youth director. While still an evangelist, he met Dixie Cowgill, daughter of Assemblies of God church members, at the district campground in Hartford City on Memorial Day in May 1957. This began their courtship—at times conducted long distance due to his traveling schedule—and they were married in November. He later became a pastor and spent time as assistant district superintendent.

Charles E. Hackett

"In the summer of 1975," he recalls, " I was pastoring First Assembly of God in Lafayette, Indiana. The congregation was holding its own, but the church was not growing. Nothing spectacular was happening in the a.m., p.m., or midweek services. That is, until one Sunday evening while we were conducting the song service and two drunken hippies came in. Wearing large white cowboy hats and muddied boots, they climbed over the last row of seats and stood on the seats talking to each other in loud voices. Their actions and noise naturally drew the attention of the entire congregation." Hackett then sent his youth pastor back to ask them to be seated and remain quiet. "That evening, I preached and gave the altar call as I usually did, and, to my surprise, these two hippies came to the altar and gave their hearts to the Lord. They were genuinely saved and became a key factor to the beginning of revival in our church and a catalyst in bringing many families to the Lord. They were delivered from drugs and were influential in helping others with life-controlling problems.

Rodeo chaplain Paul Scholtz baptizing a new believer in a stock tank

"This explosion of power was the beginning of a 5-year revival that added over 1,000 people to the Sunday morning attendance." Reflecting on the nature of revival, he added, "The point is, when revival comes, God will give you people you don't like. He won't do it like you are expecting. People who come won't be perfect. And some of your 'Christians' will leave the church."[39]

Hackett's growing church and burden for evangelism drew the attention of Council leaders. "Among the various boards on which he has served effectively is the national Home Missions Board," announced G. Raymond Carlson at Hackett's appointment as national director. "His leadership in building a great congregation in Lafayette and his service to our Fellowship make him well qualified to serve."[40]

After taking office, he boldly announced, "The Division of Home Missions will serve any person, church, district, or college. God has called us to serve, and we will do our best to fulfill that call. . . . The Assemblies of God began among the poor and downtrodden. Let us return to our roots. We must keep the middle-class God has given us, but we can no longer ignore the sea of humanity in America who need the gospel."[41]

The "Mission America" agenda of Assemblies of God U.S. Missions received a major boost in 1993 when the General Council elevated the office of national director to that of executive director with membership on the Executive Presbytery.

Like Bueno, Hackett oversees a dizzying array of programs. The Chaplaincy department includes institutional and occupational chaplains working in jails and prisons, hospitals, nursing homes, industries, rescue missions, and airports. It also serves "Rodeo/Cutting Horse Chaplains," "Motorcycle Chaplains," "Trucker Chaplains," and "Political Chaplains." Chaplains minister in all branches of the U.S. military and at veteran's hospitals. To these personnel can be added Teen Challenge workers, Deaf Culture missionaries, and ministers to persons with disabilities. U.S. missionaries also work among Native Americans, African Americans, Alaskan natives, Gypsies, Hispanics, other ethnic peoples, university students, and persons with AIDS.

The membership of the Executive Presbytery includes the general officers and the two executive directors mentioned above—resident executives—as well as nonresident executive presbyters. The latter represent eight geographical areas: Northwest, Southwest, North Central, South Central, Great Lakes, Gulf, Northeast, and Southeast. Nonresident presbyters also come from the language districts: one for the eight Hispanic districts including Puerto Rico, and one from either the German, Korean, Brazilian (U.S.A.), or Portuguese districts. Finally, a duly recognized leader of an "ethnic fellowship" also serves as a nonresident presbyter.[42]

RECOMMENDED READING

Bridges, James K., ed. *The Bible: The Word of God*. Springfield, Mo: Gospel Publishing House, 2003.

Crabtree, Charles T. *The Pentecostal Priority*. Springfield, Mo.: National Decade of Harvest, 1993.

Lewis, Paul W., ed. *All the Gospel to All the World: 100 Years of Assemblies of God Missiology*. Springfield, MO: Assemblies of God Theological Seminary, 2014.

Malcolm, Sarah. "Chi Alpha: Reconciling Students to Christ." In *U.S. Missions: Celebrating 75 Years of Ministry*. Springfield, MO: Gospel Publishing House, 2012.

McGee, Gary B. "Assemblies of God Missions: Strategy on the Run." In *Working Together with God to Shape the New Millennium*, ed. by Gary Corwin and Kenneth B. Mulholland, 189–196. Pasadena: William Carey Library, 2000.

Molenaar, William. "The World Assemblies of God Fellowship: United in the Missionary Spirit." *Assemblies of God Heritage* 31 (2011): 40–47.

Trask, Thomas E., and David A. Womack. *Back to the Altar: A Call to Spiritual Awakening*. Springfield, Mo.: Gospel Publishing House, 1994.

Trask, Thomas E., and Wayde I. Goodall. *The Blessing: Experiencing the Power of the Holy Spirit Today*. Grand Rapids: Zondervan Publishing House, 1998.

Warner, Wayne. "A Powerful Witness in New England: The Pentecostal Legacy of Clifford and Helen Crabtree." *Assemblies of God Heritage* 14 (summer 1994): 10–13, 27–29.

———. "Reflecting on a Godly Heritage: The Important Roles Parents, Grandparents, and In-Laws Played on the Life of James K. Bridges." *Assemblies of God Heritage* 14 (fall 1994): 5–8, 27–29.

———. "Waldo and Beatrice Trask: General Superintendent's Parents Lead by Word and Example." *Assemblies of God Heritage* 14 (spring 1994): 6–9, 31.

———. "Workers for the Lord: General Secretary George O. Wood Reflects on the Life of His Parents, George R. and Elizabeth Weidman Wood." *Assemblies of God Heritage* 14 (winter 1994–95): 18–22, 33.

Wood, George O. A *Psalm in Your Heart*. Vol. 1: Psalms 1–75. Springfield, Mo.: Gospel Publishing House, 1997.

———. A *Psalm in Your Heart*. Vol. 2: Psalms 76–150. Springfield, Mo.: Gospel Publishing House, 1999.

ENDNOTES

[1] "Vision Statement," General Council of the Assemblies of God, 2000, 1.

[2] Statistics for 2002 provided by the Assemblies of God Office of Public Relations.

[3] "Clergy Watch," *Enrichment* (spring 2003): 9.

[4] "New AG Leader Calls for Revival," *Ministries Today* (November/December 1993): 70.

[5] Thomas E. Trask and David A. Womack, *Back to the Altar: A Call to Spiritual Awakening* (Springfield, Mo.: Gospel Publishing House, 1994), 25.

[6] Margaret M. Poloma, *The Assemblies of God at the Crossroads: Charisma and Institutional Dilemmas* (Knoxville: University of Tennessee Press, 1989), 241.

[7] Russell P. Spittler, "Are Pentecostals and Charismatics Fundamentalists? A Review of American Uses of These Categories," in *Charismatic Christianity as a Global Culture*, ed. Karla Poewe (Columbia: University of South Carolina Press, 1994), 112–113.

[8] Ibid., 113–114.

[9] Thomas E. Trask cited in Trask and Womack, *Back to the Altar*, 41.

[10] Waldo Trask cited in Wayne Warner, "Waldo and Beatrice Trask: General Superintendent's Parents Lead by Word and Example," *Assemblies of God Heritage* 14 (spring 1994): 7.

[11] Beatrice Trask cited in Ibid., 8.

[12] Thomas Trask cited in Ibid.

[13] Trask cited in Trask and Womack, *Back to the Altar*, 22.

[14] Ibid., 41.

[15] "New Assemblies of God Executive Officers Installed," *Pentecostal Evangel* (2 January 1994): 14.

[16] General Council Minutes, 2001, 107.

[17] Wayne Warner, "A Powerful Witness in New England: The Pentecostal Legacy of Clifford and Helen Crabtree," *Assemblies of God Heritage* 14 (summer 1994): 28.

[18] Ibid., 29.

[19] Charles T. Crabtree, interview by the author, Springfield, Mo., 13 February 2003.

[20] Charles Crabtree with Ken Horn, "Charles Crabtree Discusses the Work of the Holy Spirit," *Pentecostal Evangel* (18 May 1997): 7.

[21] Interview with Crabtree.

[22] Wayne Warner, "Workers for the Lord: General Secretary George O. Wood Reflects on the Life of His Parents, George R. and Elizabeth Weidman Wood," *Assemblies of God Heritage* 14 (winter 1994–95): 22.

[23] Ibid., 33.

[24] George O. Wood, interview by the author, Springfield, Mo., 17 February 2003.

[25] George O. Wood, *A Psalm in Your Heart*, vol. 1: Psalms 1–75 (Springfield, Mo.: Gospel Publishing House, 1997), 3–4.

[26] Wayne Warner, "Reflecting on a Godly Heritage: The Important Roles Parents, Grandparents, and In-Laws Played in the Life of James K. Bridges," *Assemblies of God Heritage* 14 (fall 1994): 6.

[27]Ibid., 8

[28]Ibid., 27.

[29]James K. Bridges, "Contending for the Truth," *Pentecostal Evangel* (24 January 1999): 15.

[30]General Council Minutes, 2001, 109.

[31]L. John Bueno, "Staying the Course," *Pentecostal Evangel* (2 June 2002): 19.

[32]John Bueno, "We Recognize the Lordship of Christ," *Pentecostal Evangel* (22 August 1976): 20–21.

[33]John Bueno, "Saturating San Salvadore," *Mountain Movers* (September 1973): 14.

[34]John Bueno, "Year of Jubilee in El Salvador," *Pentecostal Evangel* (6 July 1980): 9.

[35]Janet Walker, "Latin America ChildCare: Offering Hope for 40 Years," *Pentecostal Evangel* (2 March 2003): 28.

[36]Bueno, "Staying the Course," 19.

[37]Gary B. McGee, "Assemblies of God Missions: Strategy on the Run," in *Working Together with God to Shape the New Millennium*, ed. Gary Corwin and Kenneth B. Mulholland (Pasadena: William Carey Library, 2000), 192.

[38]General Council Minutes, 2001, 109.

[39]Charles E. Hackett, interview by the author, Springfield, Mo., n.d.

[40]"Hackett Appointed to Head Division of Home Missions," *Pentecostal Evangel* (24 March 1991): 25.

[41]Charles E. Hackett, "Harvest in America," *Pentecostal Evangel* (20 October 1991): 20.

[42]General Council Minutes, 2001, 104–105.

CHAPTER 26

CHANGING THE WORLD

Our rule is simple. We will not close a church," said Saturnino Gonzalez in 1999, then district superintendent of Puerto Rico. "A church could be down to two members; it could be in financial difficulty, but we will not close it. We place that church into the hands of a layperson who has been a leader in a local church and has been gifted by the Holy Spirit. That person is placed under the supervision of a pastor. He'll preach and teach, and the church remains open." Furthermore, "there are hundreds of laypersons who already have the passion and vision to minister; they only need an opportunity."

This dogged determination reveals the dynamic that has made the Assemblies of God what it is today. "The church must move under the power of the Holy Spirit," added Gonzalez, "just like our Pentecostal fathers did at the beginning of the [twentieth] century. We need to model for our young people and our children what God is doing—not only in words but in actions."[1]

Handing on the Pentecostal heritage with its entrepreneurial boldness to the next generation weighs heavily on the minds of church leaders at virtually all levels. Despite the problems of an aging denomination just a few years shy of its centenary, signs of vitality readily appear, sometimes in unusual and surprising forms.

People driving south from Springfield, Missouri, on U.S. Highway 65 easily noticed the twenty-foot billboard image of Jay Risner with the words, "I'm 'up in the air for kids' for ten days. Help me raise $100,000 for BGMC/Kids Charities." Below the picture, but forty feet above the ground on the platform stood

Jay Risner on the billboard platform raising money for BGMC/Kids Charities

Risner himself, a former missionary to Kenya and children's pastor at nearby James River Assembly of God. He lived on the platform for ten days—complete with a tent, portable toilet, shower, camping and table chairs, exercise bike, and even a refrigerator. At the conclusion of the ten days in November 2001, people had donated $142,000 in cash and pledged $30,000 more. Channeled through the Boys and Girls Missionary Crusade (BGMC) of the Assemblies of God, the funds went to assist needy children in Kenya (for example, wheelchairs, crutches, and even a water well).[2]

On a broader scale, Convoy of Hope—a transdenominational ministry to the needy that works closely with the Assemblies of God—has been described as "part grocery giveaway, part carnival, part revival."[3] The creative combination of food distribution and fun for the kids, along with the preaching of the gospel, works through a coordinated effort with local pastors and church leaders.

Convoy began through the efforts of three brothers: Hal, Steve, and Dave Donaldson in Northern California. The family had suffered trauma when a drunk driver struck their parents' car head-on and killed their father, Harold Donaldson, an Assemblies of God pastor. Their injured mother, Betty, was unable to work or cook for some time. Fortunately, people in the community came to the aid of Betty and her four children.[4]

In 1994, the three brothers started a nonprofit organization to help others that eventually became known as Convoy of Hope. When hurricanes devastated the Caribbean and Central America in 1998, the organization sent more than a half-mil-

The Dream Center, formerly Queen of Angels hospital, in Los Angeles, California

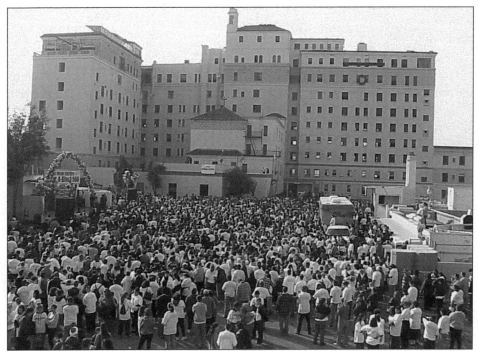

lion pounds of food and supplies. Equipped with a fleet of eighteen-wheelers, and working with partners in government, business, and the church, it annually sponsors outreaches in cities across the country and overseas as well. Thousands have responded to the gospel call through this holistic ministry.

At the Dream Center—the former Queen of Angels hospital campus in Los Angeles—thousands of people participate in its sundry activities each week. A $10 million annual operation in 2003, led by a large pastoral staff and assisted by hundreds of volunteers, it supports a feeding program, after-school sports, sidewalk Sunday Schools, youth outreaches, a clothing store, a program for rescuing runaways, care for the homeless, rehabilitation for drug addicts, bus ministry, and multiple congregations (e.g., services for Cambodians, Samoans, Filipinos, Russians, and others), among many other endeavors.

The vision for the Dream Center, a ministry of the Assemblies of God, originated with Tommy Barnett, pastor of the large First Assembly of God in Phoenix, Arizona, and his son Matthew. "When I was a young man," the elder Barnett said, "the Lord impressed on me that someday I would pastor a church in this area." When the opportunity came to pastor the historic Bethel Temple in Los Angeles in 1994, he felt directed of the Lord to install his son as the pastor, whom he discovered also felt called to Los Angeles. Despite the church's location in a high crime area, Matthew began to minister to the people of the neighborhood—even moving his office out to the sidewalk so he could meet passers-by. At the end of the year, the attendance had outgrown the facilities.

Matthew Barnett

The availability of the hospital, less than two miles away from the church, grabbed the attention of the father and son. "Right there, God showed me the picture of what He wanted to do on this campus, all 15 floors," said the younger Barnett. "A home for unwed pregnant mothers. A floor for rehab and discipleship. A floor for young men in wheelchairs who have been shot in gang warfare. I could see volunteers from all over the world coming, working one year. I saw an army of thousands of people going out all week long serving their communities. I saw a 24-hour, seven-day-a-week church." With contributions pouring in from across the nation to purchase the building and scores of construction teams from churches to remodel it, the vision soon became a reality, a place where "people could dream."[5]

Since the Dream Center lacks a large sanctuary for church services, Matthew Barnett became pastor of nearby Angelus Temple, the mother church of the International Church of the Foursquare Gospel, founded by Aimee Semple McPherson. This church, noted historically for its own outreach to the poor, provides the Center even more opportunities for worship and evangelism.

The creativity of these ministries—ranging from a billboard to an eighteen-wheeler to a fifteen-story multiplex of ministries, each undergirded by a strong sense of the leading of the Holy Spirit—explains why historian William Menzies remarked, "The story of the modern Pentecostal revival is a story worth telling."[6] This chapter traces key events in the progress of the Assemblies of God since 1993: the new hope for racial reconciliation, influential and controversial revival movements, renewed emphasis on evangelism, and key individuals whose activities reflect the kaleidoscope of ministry in a denomination determined to change the world.

THE "MEMPHIS MIRACLE"

If the early Pentecostals asked questions about how they could win the world for Christ in the last days, later generations added questions of their own. Among them, What is the role of the Christian in society? How should Christians respond to poverty, hunger, abortion, injustice, and other social problems? With its witness to the reconciling power of the Holy Spirit, the memory of the interracial Azusa Street revival took on new meaning for the younger generations.

When white pastor Donald Evans knelt down and washed the feet of Bishop Ithiel Clemmons of the Church of God in Christ, the largest African-American Pentecostal denomination in the United States, people started to weep and embrace each other. The Spirit was breaking down walls of prejudice and misunderstanding. While this was happening, Bishop Charles E. Blake went to General Superintendent Thomas E. Trask and began washing his feet. "I can readily testify," said Foursquare pastor Jack Hayford, "that what has been described as 'the Memphis miracle' was a miracle indeed, with all the elements of a Red Sea crossing."[7] Such demonstrations of humility and penitence were without precedent among American Pentecostal leaders.

It was a historic moment for the Pentecostal movement. The Pentecostal Fellowship of North America (PFNA) had been founded in 1948 as a network among white Trinitarian Pentecostal bodies: Assemblies of God, Church of God (Cleveland, Tennessee), International Church of the Foursquare Gospel, Open Bible Standard Churches, Pentecostal Assemblies of Canada, and the Pentecostal Holiness Church. Convening in October 1994 for its annual conference, it met with African-American leaders. At the opening service, Bishop Gilbert Patterson of the Church of God in Christ enthusiastically announced, "Reconciliation is possible!"[8] The long trail of racism and mistrust had finally intersected in Memphis, Tennessee, with the road to repentance.

Bishop Charles E. Blake of the West Angeles Cathedral Church of God in Christ in Los Angeles, California, has spoken at several conferences of the Assemblies of God.

Racial separation between Pentecostals had begun at least by 1906, within months of the beginning of the Azusa Street revival. Eighty-eight years later in Memphis, African-American and white leaders had come to chart a new course. The PFNA was dissolved and replaced by the much more inclusive Pentecostal/Charismatic Churches of North America (PCCNA) with an interracial general executive committee.[9]

All agreed that the way ahead would not be easy—long-standing cultural, racial, and political differences would severely test the commitment of church officials. Both communities have profound differences in outlook: For example, while white Pentecostals have experienced social and economic lift since World War II, the majority of African-American Pentecostals still live just above or below the poverty line. White Pente-

Assemblies of God Pastor Donald J. Evans preparing to wash the feet of Bishop Ithiel Clemmons of the Church of God in Christ during a reconciliation service in Memphis, Tennessee, an event that has been called the "Miracle in Memphis"

costals have increasingly identified with the religious right and joined the Republican party. Not surprisingly, they don't understand or readily sympathize with the cries among African-Americans over the recent dismantling of Affirmative Action programs, initiatives designed to help minorities share in the "lift."

Speaking for the Assemblies of God, Trask said, "We cannot undo the racism that is past, but we can with the Lord's help write a new and better chapter."[10] Testifying to the sincerity of his remark, General Council leaders began inviting bishops of the Church of God in Christ to speak at its conventions. To highlight reconciliation as indispensable to the mission of the Church and to honor William J. Seymour's contributions to the Pentecostal movement and burden for reconciliation, Assemblies of God Theological Seminary dedicated its new chapel to his memory.

Addressing the heart of the problem, Bishop Barbara Amos of the Faith Deliverance Christian Center said, "Racial reconciliation in the Pentecostal movement will occur when diversity of gifts, talents and ministry style caused by cultural or ethnic differences are accepted as complementary to the body and not divisive."[11] Social ethicist Leonard Lovett of the Church of God in Christ declared that real unity requires more than token acceptance of African-American Pentecostals. "I am ill-prepared to make a call for racial reconciliation between black and white Pentecostals until such a call is preceded by repentance, a call for remedial and distributive justice, and authentic reconciliation between people of color all over the globe. The journey must begin in a radical way within each of us, and, hopefully, this will be the beginning of a new future for all of us."[12]

At the close of this historic gathering, delegates enthusiastically endorsed "The Memphis Manifesto." Its conclusion states: "At the beginning of the 20th century, the Azusa Street Mission was a model of preaching and living the gospel message to the world. We desire to drink deeply from the well of Pentecost as it was embodied in that mission. We, therefore, pledge our commitment to embrace the essential commitments of that mission in evangelism and missions, in justice and holiness, in spiritual renewal and empowerment, and in the reconciliation of all Christians regardless of race or gender as we move into the new millennium."[13]

"REVIVE US AGAIN"

Prayers for a new outpouring of the Spirit, coming from a wide spectrum of Pentecostals, charismatics, and evangelicals, steadily rose as the year 2000 approached.[14] In many ways, the scenario resembled that of a century before when believers also sought for the fulfillment of Joel's prophecy. The lyrics of a popular nineteenth-century gospel song still resonated with the faithful at the turn of the third millennium:

"Revive us again,
fill each heart with Thy love;
May each soul be rekindled with fire from above.
Hallelujah! Thine the glory,
Hallelujah! Amen;
Hallelujah! Thine the glory;
Revive us again."[15]

Despite the shared hope of being "revived again," Christians have differed widely in their expectations about what forms it would take. During the Northern Ireland revival in 1859, observers were scandalized when people fell to the ground under the power of God's Spirit. Years later, in 1905 and 1906, Western missionaries in India flinched when normal patterns of worship gave way to "prayer storms"—loud and emotional times of prayer and praise that extended for hours. Finally, many holiness Christians, accustomed to their own noisy and emotional meetings, stood back in horror when some of their own spoke in tongues—the "Pentecostals."[16]

Revival phenomena have varied as a result of cultural, social, and doctrinal factors. Thus, neither the Great Awakening (c. 1740), the Welsh revival (1904–1905), or even the Azusa Street revival can claim to be exclusive models for what all revivals should be like.[17] In regard to their different features, historian Peter Hocken says: "The irruption of the Spirit in the Pentecostal and charismatic movements has given rise to many practices, experiences, and phenomena that have a quality of newness. This does not mean that they have no historical precedents, which is evidently untrue. However, they do represent a distinctive form of making present and operative specific gifts and graces previously known in different patterns. They also reach us as things outside our previous horizons of experience and expectation." Furthermore, "knowledge of historical precedents never equips anyone to predict contemporary manifestations of the Spirit."[18]

Recent awakenings in North America include the Toronto Blessing, an event that began at Airport Vineyard Fellowship in Toronto, Canada, in 1994. Despite the subsequent growth of the church to about two thousand people and the testimonies

Pastor John Kilpatrick and others praying on the platform at Brownsville Assembly of God, Pensacola, Florida. Evangelist Steve Hill is standing third from left. Photo by Cathy Wood

of many to the positive influences of the revival, controversy ensued. The physical manifestations that sometimes occurred—deep belly-laughing, screaming and shouting, intense weeping, jerking and shaking, staggering from being "drunk in the Spirit" (Acts 2:13), persons being "slain in the Spirit," and especially "animal sounds"—generated mounting criticism. Though such phenomena had characterized other revivals, most notably the famous Cane Ridge revival in Kentucky (1801) and early Pentecostal revivals, they led to the congregation's being ousted from the Association of Vineyard Churches.[19] For some observers, these happenings undermined the credibility of the revival.

The Pensacola Outpouring—also called the Brownsville revival—centered at Brownsville Assembly of God in Pensacola, Florida, and began on Father's Day, June 18, 1995.

News of the Toronto revival and prayer for revival had preceded the events there. After evangelist Steve Hill called people forward to pray after his Sunday morning sermon, about one thousand responded. When Pastor John Kilpatrick and Hill laid hands on a man's head to pray for him, he fell to the ground; others started to weep and dance and shake.

"Suddenly," remembers Kilpatrick, "I felt a wind blow through my legs, just like in the second chapter of Acts. A strong breeze went through my legs and suddenly both my ankles flipped over so that I could hardly stand. I thought, 'That's weird! O God,' I prayed, 'What in the world is happening?'" Finally, taking the microphone, he announced to the congregation, "'Folks, this is it. The Lord is here. Get in, get in!' I realized God had indeed come, that He had answered our prayers for revival."[20]

Before long, the church sponsored services seven days a week, and the crowds grew. By 1998, more than 2.5 million visitors had attended the meetings, with thousands professing conversion or the rededication of their lives to Christ.[21] Like Toronto, criticism followed, particularly over people being slain in the Spirit and persons shaking. To provide assistance and encouragement, the Executive Presbytery appointed an oversight committee to provide counsel for Kilpatrick and his staff when needed. Because the revival took place in an Assemblies of God church and had the denomination's endorsement, it had a far greater influence on pastors and churches than the revival in Toronto.[22]

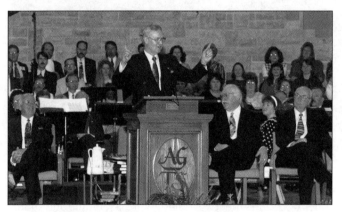

Del Tarr preaching at the Signs and Wonders conference sponsored by the Assemblies of God Theological Seminary

Just as Azusa Street sparked other revivals, so Toronto and Pensacola were catalysts for similar revivals across North America and overseas. When people who had visited these sites returned home with new zeal, however, they occasionally encountered a mixture of responses. The exuberant worship and physical manifestations that marked the worship at Brownsville did not suit everyone. As a result, polarization in local Assemblies of God churches, between pastors, and within districts sometimes occurred. At the same time, new teachings were circulating in some quarters of the denomination that stirred concern; for example, the restoration of apostles and prophets, imparting personal leadings to others by means of the gifts of utterance (tongues and interpretation, prophecy), and the need for deliverance from "generational curses." Some credited these beliefs to the lingering influence of the New Order of the Latter Rain movement that originated in the late 1940s, whose teachings the Council had officially condemned in 1949.

In reaction to the new revival movements and the disputed teachings, several pastors presented a resolution at the General Council meeting in Orlando in 1999 to reaffirm the Council's condemnation of the Latter Rain on its fiftieth anniversary.[23] After its reading, the resolution was postponed when the delegates adopted the recommendation of the General Presbytery that the issues involved be examined by the Commission on Doctrinal Purity. This resulted in an official statement of response by the General Presbytery in August 2000 entitled "Endtime Revival—Spirit-Led and Spirit-Controlled." The document addressed the contested teachings and predictably cautioned pastors about potential "excesses and abuses," while calling for genuine spiritual renewal: "We reaffirm our desire not to hinder any move of the Spirit. If it is of God, we cannot and do not wish to stop it. If it is of man, it will in time fail, but we are advised by Scripture to discern with the help of the Holy Spirit who seeks to bless the church with lasting spiritual growth."[24]

Council leaders acknowledged a widespread hunger for revival by convening Sacred Assemblies in Springfield in 1994 and 1997 for ministers, college students, college and seminary faculty members, and headquarters personnel to fast and pray for revival.[25] The Assemblies of God Theological Seminary in Springfield hosted the March 1995 "Signs & Wonders" conference. Then president Del Tarr declared in his keynote sermon: "Many Pentecostals have become satisfied with retelling stories of yesterday's revivals and spiritual victories; they are blind to the new outpourings of the Spirit. When this happens, the old wineskins can no longer contain the new wine of the Spirit."[26] Those attending the conference agreed. Afterwards, Tarr reported, "The Spirit of God moved mightily, with church officials, pastors, faculty members, and students experiencing a signal visitation of God's power as they worshiped and prayed."[27] This and the seminary's "Revival Now!" conference a year later, as well as the Sacred Assemblies, sparked more revivals as pastors went home spiritually refreshed.

The dissension over physical manifestations revealed much more than differing attitudes about what constitutes acceptable behavior in revival settings. It showed the increasing diversity of opinion in the denomination over many things, including worship patterns, approaches to ministry, and new teachings thought to further restore the dynamics of the New Testament church. More than ever before, governance in the denomination challenged leaders to help various constituencies appreciate one another and work together.

To address such tensions, Richard Dresselhaus, pastor of First Assembly in San Diego, California, and an executive presbyter, wrote in *Enrichment*: "The church has never been so threatened by imbalance as today. Sadly, some churches are being torn to pieces over peripheral issues. For example, a pastor visits a conference where he is introduced to new methods, teachings, and experiences. To the dismay of some and the delight of others, those things are introduced at home. The result is division. The body of Christ is fractured."[28]

Richard Dresselhaus

To explain "how people can serve the Lord with joy in the midst of diversity," he appealed to the balance of the Early Church displayed in the pages of the Book of Acts. "Spare me from a church without diversity," he declared, "where the pendulum is allowed no room to swing, where intolerance is absolute. This setting will stymie personal creativity, destroy initiative, and quench the Spirit of the Lord."[29] Whether over issues of "law and grace," "emotionalism and intellectualism," "winning the lost and caring for the needy," or "old ways and the new," a commitment to balance will enable Assemblies of God churches "to fulfill their God-given mission."[30]

RETOOLING FOR THE HARVEST

Although the Assemblies of God had strongly promoted the Decade of Harvest as a nationwide endeavor to multiply itself in the 1990s, the failure to meet several important goals quickly became apparent. Many districts had been ill prepared to mount major church planting projects within their jurisdictions. Though Decade of Harvest activities found success in countries overseas and one million people attended the first World Assemblies of God Congress in Seoul, Korea, in 1994 to pray and step up activities for world evangelism,[31] some observers pointed to the stagnation of the American Assemblies.[32]

Acknowledging the mixed results, Council leaders called for "Retooling for the Harvest" in 1994. This proposal focused on spiritual renewal, training, church planting, and more evangelistic efforts, without setting statistical goals. Too much attention had been placed on numbers, according to Thomas E. Trask: "If we want the numbers without the work of the Spirit, what are we going to do at the end of the decade with 5,000 new churches without the Holy Ghost in them? So if we have the work of the Spirit, God will propel us into the twenty-first century, and the church will live in the victory and accomplishments God has wrought."[33]

Efraim Espinoza, the new U.S. Decade of Harvest coordinator, added, "We have moved away from emphasizing numerical goals to reaching spiritual goals—from a goal-oriented to a soul-oriented approach. When we pushed numbers, we lost sight of assimilating and incorporating converts into the body of Christ. We not only need to win souls, but to nurture them to become part of the Body."[34]

Several new initiatives came about as a result. The National Prayer Center in Springfield was established to minister to persons in need of prayer and spiritual counsel. Whether through telephone calls to the Center or faxed prayer requests, volunteers began logging thousands of hours answering phones and praying with callers.[35] Sunday Schools adopted the values-driven "We Build People" model for discipleship training in local churches. Ministry to men evolved into the "HonorBound: Men of Promise" program.

Council leaders established the Office of Enrichment with its *Enrichment* magazine to speak to the needs of ministers. Dan Betzer, former *Revivaltime* speaker and pastor of First Assembly in Fort Myers, Florida, continued to represent the Assemblies of God on the airwaves with the new program *ByLine*.[36]

Raising the visibility of women in professional ministry gained momentum with supportive articles in *Enrichment* and the *Pentecostal Evangel*, as well as the first-ever national Women in Ministry Conference in March 2001.[37] "In the Assemblies of God, we have always believed God is an equal opportunity employer," declared General Secretary George O. Wood at the gathering. "We want to do everything we can to encourage the development of women in ministry, and encourage young women who are in training for ministry in our schools."[38] The memories of the contributions of women like Maria B. Woodworth-Etter, Marie Brown, Alice Luce, Chonita Howard, Cornelia

Jones Robertson, Hattie Hammond, Anna B. Lock, Zelma Argue, and Helen Wannenmacher to the building of the Assemblies of God had too easily been forgotten.

Schools for training ministers specifically for urban areas arose in New Orleans; New York City; Oakland, California; and elsewhere. George Neau founded the New Orleans School of Urban Missions as a two-year institution to prepare African Americans, whites, Hispanics, and Asian Americans for the challenge of ministry in New Orleans and other cities. After his father committed suicide, Neau searched for answers, but became a hardened youth far from religious faith. Healed from a stomach disorder while working as a traveling rock 'n' roll musician, he later heard the Lord call him to start an inner-city school for young people. "I was in the church parking lot one night, and I sensed God was saying that He wanted me to start a college. I literally pulled my pockets inside out and showed God that I didn't have a dime," he remembered. "He spoke to my heart that He would open the doors if I would walk through them. And God did.

"God is saying that this is the hour to raise up a generation of radicals for Jesus Christ," he told his students. "We let them know that no matter whether they are black, white, pink, or blue, they can do something for God. It is contingent upon Him, not them." When a graduate of the school received an invitation to work in a Seattle church-planting project, he hesitated and asked, "Brother George, don't they realize that I'm just a kid out of the projects in Norfolk, Virginia?" With the pluck of other Pentecostal pioneers, Neau responded, "What does that have to do with anything? You are a man called of God. That's all that counts."[39]

Pentecostal Women in Ministry

In the past few years, Pentecostals have been looking at the history of women in their tradition and becoming discouraged by trends that seem to indicate that women are losing their distinctive place in Pentecostalism. They see the intrusion of Reformed theology into Pentecostal thinking about women and blame the Charismatic Renewal or the increasing acceptance of Evangelical theology for the decline of women's ministry in Pentecostal churches. Others suggest that the anti-cultural stance of Pentecostalism, which saw the change in women's roles in this century as anti-biblical, is responsible for this change. It can be seen in the backlash among Pentecostals against denominational statements which affirm women's ministries. It is also possible to blame the waning of revival for this trend. In revival, spiritual power reigns and social patterns are disrupted, so women who have spiritual power can operate autonomously. But when revival wanes, the original social and religious patterns are restored. . . .

But there is also reason for Pentecostals to have confidence in their tradition and the way that it has empowered and continues to empower women in ministry. Pentecostals should not forget that over half of all women ever ordained come from their tradition or closely related traditions.

—*Janet Everts Powers, "Your Daughters Shall Prophesy," in* The Globalization of Pentecostalism: A Religion Made to Travel *(1999), 332.*

To further facilitate the study of the Pentecostal heritage, the Assemblies of God Archives became the Flower Pentecostal Heritage Center with enlarged facilities at the headquarters complex in Springfield. It publishes the quarterly *Assemblies of God Heritage*, edited by Director Wayne Warner. Biblical scholars made vital contributions to the study of Pentecostal doctrine and spirituality. Important publications included *Systematic Theology: A Pentecostal Perspective*, edited by Stanley M. Horton (1994); *The Prophethood of Believers: A Study in Luke's Charismatic Theology* by Roger Stronstad, a theologian of the Pentecostal Assemblies of Canada (1999); *Spirit and Power: Foundations of Pentecostal Experience* by William W. and Robert P. Menzies (2000); and *The Holy Spirit: A Pentecostal Perspective* by Anthony D. Palma (2001). To these should be added numerous published articles by systematic theologian Frank D. Macchia.[40]

In line with the concern to improve skills and study effective practices of ministry, the Assemblies of God Theological Seminary launched its doctor of ministry program in Pentecostal leadership in 1997, the first doctoral program inaugurated in Assemblies of God higher education. "We rejoice in the accomplishment," said General Superintendent Trask at the first graduation of doctoral students in 2001, "but our anticipation is even greater that the grass roots research represented in the work of the graduates will energize and enrich our Fellowship's ministry around the world. As we move into the third millenium, vital and growing churches are demanding Spirit-anointed and effective leadership."[41]

Kansas City's Joyful Church

Located near an industrial sector of the city's sprawling metropolis, Sheffield is the church home to more than [5,000] blacks, whites, Hispanics and Asians [in 2003]. Blacks and whites equally comprise some 80 percent of the congregation; Hispanics and Asians make up the rest. A vibrant, joyful atmosphere is contagious from the moment we walk through the door. . . .

Sheffield's nonexclusive, multicultural mix has attracted many from the inner city. People from all backgrounds and walks of life are welcome. Former homosexuals, lesbians, prostitutes, gang members and drug dealers worship and serve alongside educators, doctors, lawyers and business professionals.

Why is the multiracial mix working so well at Sheffield? "I wish I had the answer to that," [Pastor George] Westlake admits, noting that some church growth experts say it shouldn't work. "They say that in order for a church to survive it must be made up of homogenous groups. My response to that is we are all God's children. You can't get anymore homogenous than that!"

"I asked God to give us a church that represents the Kingdom," Westlake continues. "If you travel around the world you will see that the majority of the world's population is non-white. So why should the church be all white? Why should it be all black? I think we have a pretty good picture of the Kingdom at Sheffield Family Life Center."
—John T. Maempa, "Experiencing the Way God Loves Us: Sheffield Family Life Center," Pentecostal Evangel *(February 21, 1999): 27–8.*

The first class of Doctor of Ministry graduates at the Assemblies of God Theological Seminary in 2001: First row (l to r): Gary Allen, Steven Lim (D. Min. project coordinator), President Byron Klaus, Earl Creps (D. Min. Director), Sol Codillo; Second row: Robert Rose, Steven Allen, Gary Denbow, Jim McCorkle, Douglass Norwood, and Jay Taylor (not pictured: James L. Davis)

Standing behind various church-related endeavors, including funding for the building of new churches, has been Assemblies of God Financial Services Group. This agency serves as an umbrella for several financial ministries: Ministers Benefit Association, Assemblies of God Foundation, AG Loan Services, Ministers Insurance, and MasterPlan Stewardship Services.

MINISTRY IN THE CROSSROADS

By the year 2000, the world had become a global village. The long-cherished distinction between U.S. and foreign missions had blurred. Mission to the peoples of Colombia, Haiti, Nigeria, India, China, and the Pacific Islands could be done in the cities of North America as well.

Neither could the mission of the Church be neatly separated from the physical needs of people any longer. As had so frequently happened in Assemblies of God history, ministries of Word and deed naturally worked together, as in the case of Rocky White Mountain, pastor on the Rock Sioux Reservation in South Dakota. Delivered from alcohol, drugs, and crime, his ministry then gravitated "to those afflicted by drugs and alcohol and showing them they can overcome their circumstances."[42] In Washington, D.C., Marvin Calderon planted a Hispanic church with the partnership of Assemblies of God U.S. Missions, Convoy of Hope, and the Spanish Eastern district.[43] After the 2000 Celebration in Indianapolis, Thomas Trask reminded the Fellowship in an editorial in the *Pentecostal Evangel* that it needed to evangelize through preaching "under the anointing of the Holy Spirit," and "we must reach people outside the church by loving them through caring, compassion ministries."[44]

The individuals who are introduced below have all engaged in ministries that show how mission works today in the crossroads of the world. Though operating out of Springfield, their ministries intersect with widely differing populations. While training to be a pharmacist, Efraim Espinoza heard the call to pastor and minister in both the Hispanic and Anglo worlds. Dennis Gaylor found that when secular college and university students were converted and discipled, they would evangelize in the far corners of the earth.

A former gang member, Patrick Donadio went on to pioneer churches in Alaska and work with retired "RVers" in ministry projects across the nation. Finally, in a long line of ordained women who have made notable contributions to the Church's worldwide mission, JoAnn Butrin added directing HealthCare Ministries to her calling as a missionary nurse.

EFRAIM ESPINOZA
(1947-)

Born a fourth-generation member of an Assemblies of God family, young Efraim Espinoza grew up in poverty as an army brat. Determined to make something of his life, he earned an associate's degree in science and then enrolled in the College of Pharmacy of the University of Houston. A scholarship and an offer of a career from a pharmaceutical company seemed to guarantee a bright future. "All this time," he recalled, "I had been pushing aside a calling on my life. While I thought I had my

future under control, I was unhappy, because life without a personal, nurturing relationship with God is harsh."

Visiting his fiancé, Elois Patton, in San Antonio, he attended Sunday service at Highlands Assembly of God where he had a transforming spiritual experience: "This was the first and only time I have danced in the Spirit, but after a prolonged experience in the presence of God, I knew that I had made peace with God and my life was going to be different." Feeling called to the ministry and to study at the Latin American Bible Institute in Texas (then located in El Paso), he applied to the school, though he had lost his fluency in Spanish. After his freshman year, Efraim and Elois were married.

Efraim Espinoza

After graduation three years later, he felt prepared for ministry. In those years, the superintendent of the Gulf Latin district decided the candidates who could be considered to pastor local churches. After he informed the superintendent of his interest in pastoring, Espinoza was then surprised to discover that Templo Emanuel in Crystal City, Texas, had voted him in as pastor and that he was expected to report for duty after graduation in May 1971.

With a large Hispanic majority, Crystal City seethed with racial and political discontent in the 1960s and 1970s. The "Brown Power" movement with its demand, "Anglos get out of town!" heightened tensions among the eight thousand residents. The awkwardness of Elois's being an Anglo and not knowing Spanish did not help matters for them as a couple. Furthermore, Templo Emanuel had never had a pastor last more than two years in its forty years of existence. The superintendent told the Espinozas that if they survived six months at the church, he would arrange for them to minister at a healthier congregation in the Dallas area.

With the firm belief that "God will not lead us where He cannot keep us," they stayed for fourteen years.[45] During this time the church grew to 225 in attendance, went through two building programs, and sponsored a day-care program. As a personal initiative, the Espinozas started a Christian bookstore that supplied over a hundred Hispanic churches with Sunday School curricular materials in Spanish and English. He also worked as the Gulf Latin district's Sunday School director in addition to his pastoral responsibilities.

Tapped by Council leaders to work in the national Sunday School Department, they moved to Springfield in 1985. For eight years, he traveled throughout the country and the Caribbean conducting Sunday School seminars and conventions. Further assignments involved work as national coordinator for the U.S. Decade of Harvest and in the We Build People office, as well as editorial coordination of the quarterly magazine *Evangelio Pentecostal Hoy.* He also pastored the growing El Faro Assembly of God in Springfield in addition to his other responsibilities. Espinoza continues to minister in two worlds.

DENNIS GAYLOR
(1949-)

At an international students' conference in Branson, Missouri, several years ago, someone asked a freshman Chinese student if she found it lonely being so far away

Barbara and Dennis Gaylor receiving a financial gift from Chi Alpha ministers for 25 years of service.

from home. She immediately responded, "Yes, but I love Chi Alpha." Not only had she found Christ, but a family of warm friends as well. Already the crossroads of global culture, universities have offered unique opportunities for ministry.

The work of Chi Alpha, which began in 1953, continued to flourish under the administration of Dennis Gaylor, who succeeded C. David Gable in 1979 and has remained at the post. Familiar with the university context, Gaylor had graduated from North Texas State University and completed an MA degree at the University of Houston. While serving as youth pastor at Lindale Assembly of God in Houston, a campus minister, Herschel Rosser, invited him to a Chi Alpha conference. This opened the eyes of Gaylor and his wife, Barbara, to the potential fruitfulness of such ministry. Following his own experience in campus ministry, he served as South Texas district's Chi Alpha director in 1974, before moving to Springfield to help at the national office.

Gaylor attended a strategic meeting of Chi Alpha leaders led by Gable in San Antonio, Texas, in 1977 to reflect on the operating principles for the development of the program and prepare a handbook for campus ministers. The others who attended included Rosser, David Argue, Jim Hall, Harvey Herman, and Brady Bobbink. Together they became affectionately known within Chi Alpha circles as the "San Antonio Seven."

A year later, Gable invited Gaylor to move to Springfield and work as the national campus ministries training coordinator. He then became the director of the program in 1979. This entailed more responsibilities including the ongoing training programs, planning national conferences, and overseeing the production of Chi Alpha literature and training materials.

In 1986, under Gaylor's leadership, Chi Alpha made a strategic move from the national Youth Department to Assemblies of God U.S. Missions, a repositioning that gave it greater visibility and opportunities. In his estimation, "God may have raised up the modern university as we know it today as a decisive and strategic answer for

Chi Alpha Ministry

Chi Alpha Campus Ministries dates back to the vision of long-time Christian educator J. Robert Ashcroft. "Many of the servicemen came to our Assemblies of God colleges [after World War II] but the vast majority of them settled into state universities under the financing of the GI Bill," he remembered. "I became quite concerned about this. My concern was that the values of the young people who were in these colleges and universities had started to change. There was a secularization—a kind of infidelity, almost an atheism—that came in. There was a turning away from historical, theological, and biblical values. . . . How are we going to reach these young people coming back from the war without the habits of . . . church values [and] family values, dumped into the university and infected by the secular views?" At a National Sunday School Convention, he challenged the Assemblies of God to develop a ministry to students attending schools outside the denomination.

The ministry began with the publication The College Fellowship Bulletin, which later evolved into *Campus Ambassador Magazine*. During the 1953–1954 school year at Southwest Missouri State University in Springfield, J. Calvin Holsinger organized the first on-campus group of students as a pilot project for a program that would soon be called Chi Alpha (XA). As the program grew across the United States, it moved from centering on Assemblies of God students to recognizing the university as a strategic place for evangelism and discipleship. When C. David Gable became the national director of Chi Alpha in 1971, the endeavor blossomed in new ways through the addition of SALT (Student Activist Leadership Training) conferences, Institute of Campus Missions (after 2000 known as Reach the University Institute), District Chi Alpha Directors Conference, and Campus Ministers Conference. Under his leadership, the fivefold Chi Alpha mission statement began to evolve that grounds the purpose of the organization in providing a campus community for worship, fellowship, discipleship, witness, and prayer. Overseas activities were launched when Jerry and Pat Sandidge pioneered University Action at the University of Leuven in Belgium in 1971.

fulfilling the Great Commission in our day. We can reach students if we bring the gospel into the university environment where students live, study, and congregate. College students are more open to considering the claims of Jesus Christ while on the university campus than at any other time in their lives." [46]

Chi Alpha Bible study

With 221 Chi Alpha personnel having appointment as national U.S. missionaries in 2003, they could be found across the country on secular campuses. Along with its campus chapters, intensive discipleship-training program, and national conferences, the organization has begun to equip international students with skills for evangelism when they return to their home countries. In reflecting on both American and international students who have gone through the Chi Alpha program, veteran campus minister Joe Zickafoose stated: "Students I've seen who come through the fire of a secular campus and stand firm are the people who go overseas, who become activists in the church. They tend to carry a broad vision of the kingdom of God that they apply in all areas of their lives."[47]

PATRICK DONADIO
(1940-2012)

At Lake Williamson Christian Center in Carlinville, Illinois, 557 RVers gathered for an annual convention in 1999. The campground became a motor home city, housing 190 motor homes, trailers and campers, and fifth-wheelers. The volunteers, mostly in their retirement years, heard ministers and ministry leaders from California to Rhode Island ask for carpenters, painters, electricians, and other skilled workers, along with those who would share the gospel in evangelism outreaches.

A "contagious camaraderie and unity" reigned among the volunteers as they swapped stories about the projects they had worked on and the places they had been. Among those in attendance, Forrest Matthews, a retired civil engineer, and his wife, Jesserene, of Austin, Texas, had visited Alaska twice to help on church projects. Lloyd Luithle, a retired railroad conductor, and his wife, Florice, a former banker, from Chardon, Ohio, had worked on Teen Challenge projects.

George and Janet Rhoads of Delaware, members of another denomination, grew excited about the RVers program when they picked up a copy of the *Pentecostal Evangel*. A local Assemblies of God pastor encouraged them, and they attended the first such national convention in 1987. For six winters, they had helped in construction at Latin American Bible Institute in La Puente, California.[48] By the year 2003, RVers like the Matthews, Luithles, and Rhoads had saved more than $250 million in construction costs on a considerable variety of ministry projects and had fun and fellowship doing it. An important component of Mission America Placement Service, the RVers program has proven to be successful beyond expectations.

To develop the program, General Superintendent G. Raymond Carlson invited Alaska pastor Patrick Donadio to Springfield to head up the office. Donadio's story, however, does not start with his successful church planting work in the forty-ninth state, but on the unpromising streets of Schenectady, New York, among the gangs. Although his Italian-American parents and brother and sister were eventually converted and joined an Assemblies of God church, he resisted the gospel message, the authority of his parents, and the correction of school officials.

Patrick Donadio (r) at an RVers' construction site

In his book *Touch Me If You Dare!*, Donadio retraces his downward spiral from rebellion into crime and the increasing sorrow it brought to his family. Finally, while burglarizing a house in a resort area with other gang members, he was shot in the leg four times, but managed to escape. Although doctors informed him and his parents that they would need to amputate the leg, the circulation returned just before the scheduled surgery. "This is a miracle," said the doctor. "His circulation is restored."[49]

Donadio's life dramatically changed after that, and he enrolled at Pinecrest Bible Institute in Salisbury Center, New York, directed by N. J. Tavani. While there he bunked with Ed Spuler from New Jersey. He later married Spuler's sister Ruth. Further study took the couple to Northeast Bible Institute in Green Lane, Pennsylvania (later Valley Forge Christian College in Phoenixville), and finally to Central Bible College in Springfield, Missouri.

When Donadio heard missionary Arvin Glandon speak at Pinecrest on the need for more workers in Alaska, his heart was touched. "It's one of the most primitive places in the entire world," Glandon told the students. "You go to these places and there is nothing there. There are igloos made of sod, and conditions as primitive as in the prehistoric age."[50] At the "top of the world," one could find isolated villages of Eskimos where the gospel had never been preached—communities of one, two, or three hundred people.

"I felt a heaviness in my heart that I could not explain," said Donadio, "and I could not make it go away as the missionary continued to speak." Glandon used the story of Philip the evangelist to illustrate the value of someone leaving a large population area, in this case the city of Samaria, to witness to the Ethiopian eunuch—a single individual—on the desert road from Jerusalem to Gaza (Acts 8:26–40). "I left the chapel service, unable to get past that picture: a man on fire for God, forsaking the masses to meet a single need," recalled Donadio. "Back in my room, the veil of the Alaskans' need descended on me, and I could not stop thinking and praying about a land I had only known as a . . . good place for hunting and fishing. It was preposterous, yet so clear, so decisive, as the Holy Spirit prompted me to answer the call. I answered, still filled with awe by the strangeness of it. "Yes, I will go," my heart said to the Lord."[51]

Years later, he could not escape the humor about the call: "It was only right, I suppose, that God should take an Italian New Yorker and his Italian wife from Jersey, both of whom grew up in Italian neighborhoods, knowing nothing but Italian thinking and Italian culture and Italian food, and fling them as far from anything Italian as they could possibly be."[52]

JOANN BUTRIN
(1950-)

You Can Be Healthy is an easy-to-read book on hygiene and nutrition being used in schools across Latin America and other parts of the world. It was written by JoAnn Butrin, director of HealthCare Ministries (HCM), the medical arm of Assemblies of God World Missions. Not only providing information on health education like *You Can Be Healthy*, HCM offers medical professionals and other volunteers opportunities to work on short-term medical evangelism teams, promotes children's health programs, and works to help local pastors plant churches.[53]

Inaugurated by Paul Williams, M.D., in 1983, HCM has grown extensively in the scope of its operation. Doctors, dentists, nurses, and many other skilled volunteers donate their free time and pay their expenses. The linkage of medicine and prayer has met a vital need. When a team set up a weeklong clinic in El Bosque, Chile, they saw over 1,835 patients and more than 400 "prayed the sinner's prayer." Physical healings also occurred. On the final night, an evangelistic crusade began in a small storefront building. Fourteen months later, the congregation had grown to over four hundred members and was meeting in a new building.[54]

"I was called to be a missionary at the age of five," said Butrin. "Most of my life has been spent in preparation—first as a nurse, then for the ministry, and later for international health and disaster relief. Everything has contributed to becoming as prepared as possible for the task God has called me to do."[55] The training has been extensive: an RN diploma from Geisinger Medical Center School of Nursing in Pennsylvania, a BS in nursing from Evangel University, an MS in community health from Pennsylvania State University, and a PhD in nursing from the University of Minnesota.

Butrin began her missionary career in 1971 in the isolated bush region of the northern sector of the Democratic Republic of the Congo in Central Africa. Despite the primitive living conditions, she wrote home in a Christmas letter: "Many good

JoAnn Butrin with Latin American schoolchildren

things have been happening here. We've just concluded a series of special meetings with a Holy Spirit emphasis. I was thrilled at the number of people who received the Spirit." Later, when she and her coworker Peggy Johnson were given a mobile clinic to reach a broader area, she wrote, "We've been moving out into many new places. While meeting the physical needs of these people, we've seen quite a few souls come to the Lord. . . . A number of times when we have done all we could medically, God has supernaturally healed very sick bodies. What a thrill to see Him work!"[56]

The ultimate goal of HCM remains the conversion of the spiritually lost. Even *You Can Be Healthy* explains how a person can become a Christian. Since her appointment as director of international operations in 1994, Butrin has supervised a ministry of global proportions that changes the world one patient at a time.

The stories in *People of the Spirit* represent but a few of the countless others that could be told from the historical records and oral tradition of the Assemblies of God. In fact, the story of one Pentecostal usually overlaps that of another or many others. These grassroots connections help explain why insiders have referred to the Assemblies of God as "the Fellowship." In their interlocking stories one finds common people with an intense desire for a deeper life in Christ as empowered by Holy Spirit baptism. Many heard the call to ministry and courageously and sacrificially obeyed God in Christian service in the U.S. and abroad. Certainly some failed, but the overall

What the Gospel Is All About

Before entering the ministry and later working with HealthCare Ministries, Physician Assistant Rick Salvato played soccer with the New York Cosmos. The following are excerpts from an interview with the *Pentecostal Evangel*:

PE: Describe your responsibilities with HealthCare Ministries.

Salvato: I'm in charge of our Emergency Response program, responding to natural disasters, wars, famine, or any kind of emergency situation overseas. I'm also very involved with our HIV/AIDS program as well as doing our regular short-term medical teams.

PE: Do any specific trips or people's needs stand out?

Salvato: Somalia was one of the most atrocious situations I've been in. People were starving to death in the midst of a war and no one was doing anything.

Rick Salvato treating a patient on a HealthCare Ministries assignment

PE: What difference does Christ make in those situations?

Salvato: When you deal with people who have been kicked out of society and told all their lives that they don't matter, and you see them encounter the reality of God, you see them realize for the first time that they have dignity and value. It is such a transformation. Regardless of their material circumstances they now have something that means so much more than anything else we could give them. To me, that's what the gospel is all about.

—Interview with Rick Salvato by Scott Harrup, "Meeting Medical and Spiritual Needs Around the World," Pentecostal Evangel *(November 24, 2002): 13.*

picture depicts commitment and determination to serve the Lord in every available avenue of ministry to change the world.

In my opinion, the irrepressible advance of these Pentecostal men and women in proclaiming the gospel suggests that only the inattentive will underestimate the fortitude of the Assemblies of God constituency in facing the challenges ahead.

Indeed, "May each soul be rekindled with fire from above!"

RECOMMENDED READING

Arnott, John. *The Father's Blessing.* Orlando: Creation House, 1995.

Blumhofer, Edith L., Russell P. Spittler, and Grant A. Wacker, eds. *Pentecostal Currents in American Protestantism.* Urbana: University of Illinois Press, 1999.

Chevreau, Guy. *Catch the Fire: The Toronto Blessing.* Toronto: HarperCollins, 1995.

Cox, Harvey. *Fire From Heaven: The Rise of Pentecostal Spirituality and the Reshaping of Religion in the Twenty-First Century.* Reading, Mass.: Addison-Wesley Publishing Co., 1995.

Dempster, Murray W., Byron D. Klaus, and Douglas Petersen, eds. *The Globalization of Pentecostalism: A Religion Made to Travel.* Irvine, Calif.: Regnum Books International, 1999.

Donadio, Patrick J., with Doug Brendel. *Touch Me If You Dare!* Springfield, Mo.: Maranatha Publishers, 1983.

Donaldson, Hal, and Joel Kilpatrick. "Inside the Los Angeles Dream Center." *Pentecostal Evangel* (28 November 1999): 8–11.

Dresselhaus, Richard L. "The Crying Need for Balance." *Enrichment* (summer 2000): 76–80.

Gaylor, Dennis, ed. *Reach the U: A Handbook for Effective Campus Ministry.* Springfield, Mo.: Chi Alpha Campus Ministries, 2003.

Gonzalez, Nino. *Manteniendo Pentecostés Pentecostal: Hacia un Avivamiento Permanente.* Miami: Editorial Vida, 1998.

Grant, David and Beth Grant. *Beyond the Soiled Curtain: Project Rescue's Flight for the Victims of the Sex-Slave Industry.* Springfield, MO: Onward Books, 2009.

Hill, Stephen. *White Cane Religion, and Other Messages from the Brownsville Revival.* Shippensburg, Pa.: Revival Press, 1997.

Kilpatrick, Joel. *The Miracle of Hope.* Springfield, Mo.: Gospel Publishing House, 1999.

Kilpatrick, John. *Feast of Fire: The Father's Day Outpouring.* Pensacola, Fla.: Brownsville Assembly of God, 1995.

Knutti, Peggy Johnson. *Healing Hands: Touching the Suffering through Medical Missions.* Springfield, MO: The Access Group, 2010.

Roever, Dave. *The Dave Roever Story: Miracle in Vietnam.* Springfield, Mo.: Evangelism Literature for America, 1982.

Synan, Vinson, ed. *The Century of the Holy Spirit: 100 Years of Pentecostal and Charismatic Renewal.* Nashville: Thomas Nelson Publishers, 2001.

ENDNOTES

[1] Saturnino Gonzalez, "Revival in Puerto Rico," *Pentecostal Evangel* (17 October 1999): 6.

[2] John Cockroft, "Pastor Breaks Giving Record After 10 Days Atop Billboard," *Pentecostal Evangel* (13 January 2002): 23.

[3] Efraim Espinoza, "Convoy of Hope: Part Grocery Giveaway, Part Carnival," *Pentecostal Evangel* (20 July 1997): 28.

[4] Joel Kilpatrick, *The Miracle of Hope* (Springfield, Mo.: Gospel Publishing House, 1999), 9–22.

[5] Hal Donaldson and Joel Kilpatrick, "Inside the Los Angeles Dream Center," *Pentecostal Evangel* (28 November 1999): 10.

[6] William W. Menzies, *Anointed to Serve: The Story of the Assemblies of God* (Springfield, Mo.: Gospel Publishing House, 1971), 10.

[7] Jack Hayford, "The 'Memphis Miracle' Is Real!" *Ministries Today* (January/ February 1995): 37.

[8] Ibid., 36.

[9] J. Lee Grady, "Pentecostals Renounce Racism," *Christianity Today* (12 December 1994): 58.

[10] Thomas Trask, "We Repent!" *Ministries Today* (January/February 1995): 68.

[11] Barbara Amos, "Diversity within Unity," *Ministries Today* (January/February 1995): 71.

[12] Leonard Lovett, "Confronting the Underlying Problem," *Ministries Today* (January/February 1995): 42.

[13] "The Memphis Manifesto," *Ministries Today* (January/February 1995): 38. Cracks in the racial harmony at Azusa Street appeared within six months of the revival's beginning; see Frank Bartleman, *How Pentecost Came to Los Angeles* (Los Angeles: By the author, 1925), 83–84.

[14] Frank D. Macchia, "The 'Toronto Blessing': No Laughing Matter," *Journal of Pentecostal Theology* 8 (April 1996): 3–6.

[15] William P. Mackay and John J. Husband, "Revive Us Again," in *Worship and Service Hymnal* (Carol Stream, Ill.: Hope Publishing Co., 1984), 346.

[16] See Grant A. Wacker, "Travail of a Broken Family: Radical Evangelical Responses to the Emergence of Pentecostalism in America, 1906–16," in *Pentecostal Currents in American Protestantism*, ed. Edith L. Blumhofer, et al., 23–49 (Urbana: University of Illinois Press, 1999).

[17] Colin C. Whittaker, *Great Revivals* (Springfield, Mo.: Gospel Publishing House, 1984), 13.

[18] Peter Hocken, *The Glory and the Shame: Reflections on the 20th Century Outpouring of the Holy Spirit* (Guildford, Surrey, U.K.: Eagle, 1994), 101.

[19] James A. Beverley, "Vineyard Severs Ties with 'Toronto Blessing' Church," *Christianity Today* (8 January 1996): 66.

[20] John Kilpatrick, *Feast of Fire: The Father's Day Outpouring* (Pensacola, Fla.: Brownsville Assembly of God, 1995), 76.

[21] Hal Donaldson, "Brownsville: Three Years Later," *Pentecostal Evangel* (19 July 1998): 8–9.

[22] Alice Crann, "Revival Stirs Florida Panhandle Church," *Charisma and Christian Life* (October 1995): 20–21; Randy Hurst, "Pensacola," *Pentecostal Evangel* (10 November 1996): 11, 13–14.

[23] General Council Minutes, 1999, 80–81.

[24] General Presbytery of the Assemblies of God, "Endtime Revival: Spirit-Led and Spirit-Controlled: A Response to Resolution 16," (11 August 2000), 2.

[25] "Sacred Assembly Calls Fellowship to Seek Revival," *Pentecostal Evangel* (1 May 1994): 14–15; Joel Kilpatrick, "Revival Report: Sacred Assembly II," *Pentecostal Evangel* (27 April 1997): 23.

[26] Del Tarr, "The Church and the Spirit's Power," in *Sign and Wonders in Ministry Today*, ed. Benny C. Aker and Gary B. McGee (Springfield, Mo.: Gospel Publishing House, 1996), 15.

[27] Ibid., 13.

[28] Richard L. Dresselhaus, "The Crying Need for Balance," *Enrichment* (summer 2000): 77.

[29] Ibid., 78.

[30] Ibid., 80.

[31] J. Philip Hogan, "Fulfillment of a Dream," *Pentecostal Evangel* (18 December 1994): 3.

[32] Edith L. Blumhofer, *Restoring the Faith: The Assemblies of God, Pentecostalism, and American Culture* (Urbana: University of Illinois Press, 1993), 264–274.

[33] Juleen Turnage, "Retooling for the Harvest," *Pentecostal Evangel* (10 July 1994): 18.

[34] John Maempa, "Conversation with Efraim Espinoza," *Pentecostal Evangel* (30 July 1995): 7.

[35] "National Prayer Center Marks First Anniversary," *Pentecostal Evangel* (17 December 1995): 23.

[36] See Dan Betzer, "*Revivaltime*: A 40-Year Legacy," *Pentecostal Evangel* (26 December 1993): 22–23.

[37] Barbara Liddle Cavaness, "Factors Influencing the Decrease in the Number of Single Women in Assemblies of God World Missions" (PhD diss., Fuller Theological Seminary, 2001), 253.

[38] George Wood cited in Katy Attanasi, "Fellowship Convenes Conference for Women," *Pentecostal Evangel* (29 April 2001): 24.

[39] Hal Donaldson, "George Neau: Ministering in 'Dark' Places," *Pentecostal Evangel* (24 August 1997): 17.

[40] For example, Frank D. Macchia, "Sighs Too Deep for Words: Toward a Theology of Glossolalia," *Journal of Pentecostal Theology* 1 (October 1992): 47–73.

[41] Thomas Trask cited in "AGTS Awards First Doctorate Degrees in Assemblies of God History," AGTS *Rapport* (winter 2002): 5.

[42] Rocky White Mountain, "Standing Rock Sioux Finds Solid Rock," *Pentecostal Evangel* (17 December 1995): 20.

[43] "Reaching Ethnic Groups," *Pentecostal Evangel* (8 February 1998): 17.

[44] Thomas E. Trask, "What Happened in Indianapolis?" *Pentecostal Evangel* (8 October 2000): 4.

[45] Efraim Espinoza, "Lessons from the School of Life," email to author (2003), 1–4.

[46] Dennis Gaylor, "Why University Ministry," in *Reach the U: A Handbook for Effective Campus Ministries*, ed. Dennis Gaylor (Springfield, Mo.: Chi Alpha Campus Minstries, 2003), 12.

[47] Joe Zickafoose cited in Dennis Gaylor, "Thriving—Not Just Surviving—On Campus," *Pentecostal Evangel* (17 September 1995): 22.

[48] John T. Maempa, "RVers Meet for Camp, Fellowship," *Pentecostal Evangel* (16 January 2000): 23, 25.

[49] Patrick J. Donadio with Doug Brendel, *Touch Me If You Dare!* (Springfield, Mo.: Maranatha Publishers, 1983), 104.

[50] Arvin Glandon cited in Ibid., 131–132.

[51] Ibid., 133.

[52] Ibid., 131.

[53] "HealthCare Ministries—Ministry to the Hurting," *Pentecostal Evangel* (20 November 1994): 17.

[54] Peggy Johnson and Evelyn Knutti, "HealthCare Ministries: Short-Term Tips with Long-Term Results," *Mountain Movers* (April 1997): 6.

[55] Cynthia Norman, "JoAnn Butrin: The Touch of Compassion," *Leader's Touch* (July/August 2000): L2.

[56] JoAnn Butrin cited in John V. Ohlin, "Help a Dream Come True," *Advance* (August 1974): 10.

TOWARD THE CENTENNIAL: TIMES OF TRANSFORMATION

CHARLES E. SELF

INTRODUCTION AND REMEMBRANCE

People of the Spirit by the late Dr. Gary B. McGee is an appreciative and critical look at the Assemblies of God (USA) history through a biographical lens. His respect for the women and men that have led and served is evident. He is also forthcoming on some of the failures and shortcomings that are part of the narrative. In between the biographical profiles, Dr. McGee highlights important trends, connecting the Assemblies of God with global Pentecostal and charismatic movements and well as larger Christian missions trends and world events.

This brief afterword helps to bring the story current as the Assemblies of God celebrates its centennial. It highlights key events between 2002 and 2014, with several biographical profiles.

A DECADE OF GROWTH AND TRANSFORMATION

The last ten years have seen unprecedented global growth for Pentecostal/charismatic Christianity. Spirit baptism, manifestation gifts, healings, and miracles are normative as Christians in developing nations multiply in number and influence. The number of Christians identifying with Pentecostal/charismatic movements overall is somewhere between six hundred and seven hundred million. An amazing story for a movement not even acknowledged by leaders at the 1910 World Missionary Conference in Edinburgh!

In the last decade, the Assemblies of God has experienced growth in many of its diverse districts. Renewed passion for prayer, strategic planting, and revitalization are making an impact. Between 2010 and 2013, there has been a net gain of 335 churches. As of this writing, the Fellowship is planting one church a day in the United States and rapidly moving toward its goal of four thousand new churches by 2020.

The demographics of the United States continue to change as increasing immigration from around the world bring new populations to cities and counties, and new possibilities for evangelization and discipleship. Space does not permit an exhaustive review of all the changes; however, the rapid increase in the percentage of

Hispanics is notable. In 2000, Hispanics were 13 percent of the total population; in 2010, they were 17 percent and the trajectories are for nearly 25 percent by 2020, with large concentrations in various states, especially Florida and states in the Southwest. As a result, the Assemblies of God has added several new Spanish ethnic/language districts, and the total number of Hispanic adherents has increased 50 percent from 2002 to 2012.

Here are some of the broad areas of Assemblies of God change and growth in recent decades:

- The U.S. Assemblies of God (USA) is part of the World AG Fellowship that has grown from 44,000,000 worldwide adherents in 2002 to 66,000,000 believers in 252 countries, territories, and provinces in 2012.
- The U.S. Assemblies of God has grown from 2.7 million adherents in 2002 to 3.1 million in 2012.
- The number of credentialed ministers has increased from 32,732 to 36,434 in 2013.
- The number of AG churches has grown from 12,222 in 2003 to 12,792 in 2013.
- Hispanic church members in the various Spanish ethnic/language districts have increased from 193,917 in 2002 to 261,447 in 2012.
- In addition to Spanish ethnic/language districts and churches, the U.S. Assemblies of God has added Brazilian, Korean, Samoan, and Slavic districts as well as recognizing twenty ethnic fellowships. Churches begun as outreaches to immigrants are rapidly becoming multilingual in their outreach.

NATIONAL LEADERSHIP DEVELOPMENTS

EXECUTIVE LEADERSHIP TEAM TO 2008

THOMAS E. TRASK

General Superintendent Thomas E. Trask tirelessly called the Fellowship "back to altar" with a hunger for revival, passionate prayer, and total surrender to the will of God. Trask led the Convoy of Hope Prayer Initiative, reminding all participants that supernatural power is the foundation for all outreach, from preaching to feeding the poor and the victims of tragedies.

He currently leads the Global Prayer Initiative and the "12-12" Movement, calling upon God's people to dedicate December 12 of each year to praying for the poor.

CHARLES T. CRABTREE

Charles Crabtree served as assistant general superintendent until accepting a call as president of Zion Bible College in 2007. Zion (now Northpoint Bible College) is one of the oldest Pentecostal Bible colleges and is a critical center of equipping in a challenging geography for the gospel. Under his leadership and with the generous financial contributions of the Green family, Zion Bible College relocated from

Barrington, Rhode Island, to Haverhill, Massachusetts, occupying and renovating the facilities of the recently closed Bradford College. Crabtree's inspirational and strategic leadership brought growth in both programs and number of students. When he resigned in 2013, the campus was not only renovated, but expanding its mission.

JAMES K. BRIDGES

Rev. James K. Bridges stepped down as general treasurer in 2008 and was actively engaged in the work of the growing Southwestern University of the Assemblies of God, as well as preaching and promoting Pentecostal doctrine and experience. On May 31, 2010, he died, leaving a legacy of fidelity, passion, and principled leadership. Superintendent George O. Wood, reflecting on Bridge's lifetime of service, offered these words: "James Bridges has lived his life with the greatest of integrity and commitment to God's Word. He served and deeply loved his family, his church, his community, and his God. He was a true Pentecostal statesman whom we will greatly miss."

EXECUTIVE LEADERSHIP TEAM SINCE 2007

GEORGE O. WOOD

Dr. George O. Wood assumed the general superintendent position in 2007 (and was elected in 2009 and reelected in 2013). He was the first general superintendent with an earned doctorate (in fact, he has two: one in pastoral theology and the other a juris doctor degree). He is a member of the State Bar of California and the Bar of the Supreme Court of the United States.

L. ALTON GARRISON

Rev. Alton Garrison was elected assistant general superintendent in 2007. He is the executive leader of the Division of Church Ministries of the growing Discipleship Ministries, with responsibilities for resourcing every age and stage of equipping the saints. He came to this office with over forty years of ministry. From 1968–1985, he was a full-time evangelist traveling thousands of miles each year across the country and around the world. For fifteen years (1986–2001), he was the senior pastor of First Assembly of God in North Little Rock, Arkansas, where the church experienced exponential growth and gave millions to AGWM and AGUSM ministries.

He was superintendent of the Arkansas District from 2001–2005, where, ahead of his time, he implemented coaching and mentoring initiatives for pastors in his district. From 2005–2007, Garrison was executive director of U.S. Missions.

As part of his current portfolio, Rev. Garrison is also a member of the Global Council of the Empowered 21 movement, a global Pentecostal/charismatic network of leaders and movements dedicated to evangelization and discipleship. This group is cochaired by George O. Wood and Billy Wilson (president of Oral Roberts University) and now has eleven regional networks.

Garrison is the author of several works, including the recent *Acts 2 Church* and *The 360° Disciple* (Gospel Publishing House). Both of these books focus on the biblical and practical fruit of true discipleship and offer practical insights for equipping congregations for their missional calling.

JAMES T. BRADFORD

Another leader with advanced education, James T. Bradford, assumed the office of general secretary in 2008 after John Palmer resigned (Bradford was elected in 2009 and reelected in 2013).

Bradford is a scientist with a PhD in aerospace engineering from the University of Minnesota. After finishing his degree, God called him to pastoral ministry, with great fruitfulness. In 1988, he accepted the call as senior pastor of Newport Mesa Christian Center in California. His early Canadian roots were re-established when he accepted the pastorate of Broadway Church in Vancouver, British Columbia, in 2000. In 2003, he became the senior pastor of Central Assembly in Springfield, Missouri.

He is the author of two recent books, *Preaching: Maybe It Is Rocket Science* (GPH) and *Second Chronicles Seven:Fourteen: A 28-Day Journey in Prayer* (My Healthy Church).

Bradford's office is also engaged in a variety of educational and empowering initiatives. This includes cosponsoring with Evangel University the 2011 and 2014 Faith and Science Conferences in coordination with the AG Alliance for Higher Education. These conferences invited AG school faculty and outside speakers to participate in wide-ranging learning that integrates empirical scientific research with biblical authority and revelation. His office also was engaged in the follow-through of the consolidation of the Springfield schools and new ideas for strengthening the process and benefits of ordination for credentialed ministers.

DOUG CLAY

In 2008, Rev. Doug Clay was appointed to fill the unexpired term of James Bridges. His 2009 election and 2013 re-election represents expanded diversity in age and experience. Clay came to the Executive Leadership Team (ELT) with fruitful leadership in youth/student ministries, including director of National Youth Ministries (1995–1997). He was a successful pastor of a turnaround church (Calvary Assembly of God in Toledo, Ohio, from 1997–2004), and district superintendent in Ohio (2004–2008). As superintendent, he led a transformation of district offices, resources, and structures, improving financial stability, resourcing more church planting, and offering exemplary relational and strategic leadership.

He is the author of *Dreaming in 3D* (Influence Resources) and multiple practical guides for growing in discernment and wisdom as a leader. He is particularly focused on seeing more young adults find the insights and resources they need to fulfill their callings.

When asked by seminary students in 2013 why he loved the Assemblies of God, Clay responded, "Missions! I love the fact that we were founded with the purpose of world evangelization. May we never lose that focus!"

The Executive Leadership Team (left to right)
Zollie L. Smith, Jr., executive director, AGUSM; Doug Clay, General Treasurer;
George O. Wood, general superintendent; L. Alton Garrison, assistant general superintendent;
James T. Bradford, general secretary; and Greg Mundis, executive director, AGWM

GREG MUNDIS

Greg Mundis was elected the executive director of Assemblies of God World Missions (AGWM) in 2011 at the 54th General Council. He came to this position with more than thirty years of foreign missionary experience in church planting, leadership development, and field and regional administration. Under the leadership of Greg Mundis, AGWM continues to transform its methods and structures to respond to opportunities and complete the Great Commission.

A native of Youngstown, Ohio, Mundis became a born-again believer at age thirteen through the ministry of Billy Graham, and was baptized in the Holy Spirit at the age of sixteen. While a student at Youngstown State University, he heard the call to ministry. He is a graduate of Central Bible College, the Assemblies of God Theological Seminary (AGTS), and he earned his doctor of ministry from Gordon-Conwell Theological Seminary. This deep commitment to being a "scholar on fire" made Mundis an effective leader in the challenging missions fields of Europe.

Mundis and his wife, Sandie, served in Austria for seventeen years. Their duties included outreach and equipping—through Global University—a variety of evangelistic outreaches to all ages, Christian radio and television, leadership empowerment, and church planting efforts. One of their most notable achievements is the planting and growth of Vienna Christian Center. Today this church numbers over two thousand members, a rare megachurch in post-Christian Europe. In 1991, they were appointed area directors for Central Europe and, in 1998, regional directors for the entire European field.

ZOLLIE L. SMITH, JR.

Zollie Smith, director of AGUSM, is the first African-American to hold an executive leadership position and a key voice in transforming some of the structures for unleashing even more workers into the domestic harvest. He was elected in 2009 and reelected in 2013. He previously served as the leader of the AG National Black Fellowship and in leadership roles in the New Jersey district office.

Zollie Smith's unique educational and occupational background equips him well for the diverse ministries he oversees. His bachelor's degree is in criminal justice and his master's degree is in business management. Like Bradford, God called him from these fields to pastoral ministry. He earned a diploma in ministerial studies from Berean College.

He has been a pioneer pastor (Plainfield AG in New Jersey) and a senior pastor of a growing local church (Eternal Life Christian Center in New Jersey). In addition to these fruitful efforts, his adult journey has included times as a United States postal inspector and as a police officer and detective. He was also decorated with a Bronze Star and Purple Heart for his service in Vietnam as an Airborne Infantryman.

Smith shares the mission in a compassionate, direct, and personal style, calling on every believer to evangelize and disciple.

CHANGES IN THE EXECUTIVE PRESBYTERY

ORDAINED MINISTER UNDER 40

The 2007 General Council in session approved new executive presbyter positions, reflecting the growing diversity of the Assemblies of God. One was the addition

R. Bryan Jarrett

of an "ordained minister under 40." The aging of ministerial leadership and the desire for listening to younger voices had been growing for two decades. R. Bryan Jarrett, a senior pastor from the Dallas-Fort Worth area, was the first under-40 minister elected to this office at the 2009 General Council. He expressed gratitude for the "forward thinking" of the leadership. This position is a mission-critical one, as the median age of ordained ministers has increased from fifty in 1979 to fifty-nine in 2013.

Jarrett has accomplished much as a young leader. In his own words, he testifies to God's grace:

I grew up in a small farm town on the Arkansas side of the Mississippi River. My mom and I spent most of my formative years in the home of my conservative Pentecostal grandparents. As a teen, I rebelled against the legalism that accompanied the Holiness tradition and threw myself into the party scene of our little town. In the fall of 1990, while in a drunken stupor, I had an encounter with God that altered my life and eternity. My life had been so marked by God that others compared my dramatic transformation to that of Paul's on the Damascus Road. There was an immediate passion to reproduce in others what God had started in me. On November 25, 1990, my first sermon was delivered to a group of seventy-five students ninety minutes before I was to be baptized. Four of them gave their lives to Christ and the five of us were baptized together. I was hooked!

Jarrett graduated from Central Bible College and completed his graduate studies at Oral Roberts University—all while married and preaching full time. "God has graciously expanded the reach of our ministry from the little room of seventy-five students to opportunities around the world. But the most rewarding part of our ministry and the greatest honor of our lives is being called "Pastor" at Northplace Church in Sachse, Texas."

ORDAINED FEMALE

Another new position was an ordained female executive presbyter. The growing number of credentialed women reflects the missional and theological commitment of the Movement to recognize God's calling on "all flesh." Beth Grant was the first ordained female to be elected to this position. At the 2007 Council, she was one of the top three candidates in the balloting for assistant general superintendent, the first time in General Council history that a female candidate received such affirmation. Grant has teamed with her husband, David, in missionary ministry since 1976. A Central Bible College and AGTS graduate with a PhD in intercultural studies from Biola University, she has taught cross-cultural understanding and missions for more than twenty years. She is part of the regular faculty at AGTS and with her husband coordinates the efforts of Project Rescue (more about this below).

Beth Grant

Grant brings a voice of insight, reason, and missionary focus to the various strategic groups she is part of. For more than a decade, she served as the chair of the Network for Women in Ministry of the Assemblies of God. This growing group encourages and resources credentialed female leaders.

ADDITIONAL LANGUAGE EXECUTIVE PRESBYTER

The 2009 Council also saw a third new Executive Presbytery position established for the Language Area—East Spanish region. Saturnino (Nino) Gonzalez was chosen as the first representative in this office.

SHIFTS IN PHILOSOPHY OF THE U.S. ASSEMBLIES OF GOD

FIVE CORE VALUES

In 2008, General Superintendent Wood published a strategic book called *Core Values*. He and the ELT affirmed that these values would guide their leadership within the fourfold mission of the Fellowship. These core values are:

- Passionately proclaim, at home and abroad, by word and deed, Jesus as Savior, Baptizer in the Holy Spirit, Healer, and Soon-Coming King
- Strategically invest in the next generation
- Vigorously plant new churches
- Skillfully resource our constituency
- Fervently pray for God's favor and help as we serve Him with pure hearts and noble purpose

The first and last values are the essential foundations for the middle three. Without the passion for "the whole Church taking the whole gospel to the whole world," the very reason for the Fellowship ceases to exist. And the fuel for this fearless proclamation is prayer—fervent, Spirit-inspired, sustaining intercession and petition that God uses to transform lives.

The AG Trust is one key resource emerging from the integration of these five values. Established under Wood's leadership in 2008 and administrated under Assistant General Superintendent Alton Garrison, the Trust represents stewardship maturation of the Fellowship as long-term endowments are invested in

- Planting new churches: In partnership with Church Multiplication Network and AG Trust, in the past nine years, 443 churches have received $13.03 million as matching funds for the launch of new churches. Over 1.06 million people have received a clear presentation of the gospel and twenty-eight thousand decisions for Christ have been made. These new plants have an average attendance of eighty-five in weekly worship.
- Helping existing churches become healthier: Healthy Church Network is resourcing churches ready to improve their effectiveness.
- Providing scholarships for the training of young ministers at AG schools: Already $1.4 million dollars in scholarships and debt relief have been given to young ministers.
- Creating new church resources: Digital resources for children and youth, and a variety of products have been designed to resource the local church, reaching thousands of AG churches and blessing other Pentecostal fellowships.

The decentralized and entrepreneurial nature of the Fellowship—an important part of the DNA of a "voluntary cooperative fellowship"—makes the progress of the AG Trust truly historic as churches and individuals give strategically and for the long-term.

COMPASSION: A FOURTH REASON FOR BEING

General Council 2009 was an important moment as the Fellowship added a fourth reason for being. The three historic reasons for being are evangelism, worship, and discipleship. The fourth, compassion, represents the expansion of the evangelistic and missionary vision, and the anointed success of ministries such as Convoy of Hope and HealthCare Ministries led by Joanne Butrin. Adopting this fourth reason for being reflected the growth and maturity of the Movement without any dilution of missionary urgency. Historic ministries such as Mission of Mercy in Calcutta founded by Mark and Huldah Buntain integrated Pentecostal evangelism, discipleship, and leadership training with excellent feeding and medical programs. Recent efforts such as Project Rescue for victims of sex trafficking, led by David and Beth Grant, and Convoy of Hope, which works with Assemblies of God churches and other churches to feed the poor and provide relief efforts across the United States and on the foreign missions fields, are evidence of this whole-life evangelism and discipleship approach.

The vote was close and took two business sessions to pass. The global missions to the unreached continue to expand and often integrate compassion expressions and even economic development in order to reach closed nations.

HEADQUARTERS TO NATIONAL LEADERSHIP AND RESOURCE CENTER

When re-elected general superintendent in August 2009, Dr. George O. Wood felt impressed by the Holy Spirit to get hold of the business operations of the General Council. Gospel Publishing House revenues were declining, national ministry departments were siloed, and the welter of publications emanating from the national office provided adherents with redundant and sometimes contradictory information. If the Assemblies of God Fellowship wanted to respond to the cultural challenges of the twenty-first century—challenges such as the information revolution, the flattening of leadership hierarchies, multiculturalism, and globalization—the national office needed to be restructured for greater effectiveness and efficiency.

The reorganization began in early 2010 with a name change. For years, the national office had been affectionately referred to as "Headquarters." But as Wood humorously observed, "We are the 'head' of no one and do not 'quarter' anyone either!" So the name was changed to the National Leadership and Resource Center (NLRC). This change was not cosmetic, however. Instead, it embodied Wood's vision to align everything the national office does by way of leadership and resources with the goal of equipping the local church for health. Toward that end, the NLRC would produce Spirit-empowered resources for ministries to children, youth, adults, and families, as well as resources for church development and leadership. By doing so, the NLRC would become the premier ministry resource provider not only for its own churches, but also for the broader Pentecostal, charismatic, and evangelical communities.

In August 2012, the General Presbytery approved the structural change, adding five new executive management positions that report to the COO: chief financial officer; chief information officer; vice president of Ministries; vice president of Integrated Communications, Marketing and Sales; and vice president of Publishing, Production, and Fulfillment. After the 2015 General Council, the Executive Management Team was restructured and renamed; however, the chief financial officer, chief information officer, director of publications, and director of marketing still directly report to the COO. These positions lead and manage integrated work teams across the organization to fulfill the mission and vision of the NLRC.

AG PUBLISHING TRANSFORMED

If the Assemblies of God Fellowship was to become the premier ministry resource provider for local churches, its publishing arm needed to be transformed. Gospel Publishing House has served Assemblies of God churches well for over one hundred years, but as a denominational publishing house and distributor, its reach was limited. The need for a new publishing and distribution model that would deliver Spirit-empowered resources to AG churches, as well as to churches in the broader Pentecostal, charismatic, and evangelical communities was noted. And through time spent seeking the Holy Spirit's guidance, the vision for two new publishing initiatives was born: My Healthy Church and Influence Resources.

While Gospel Publishing House (GospelPublishing.com) still services the Assemblies of God churches, My Healthy Church (MyHealthyChurch.com) serves as the distribution arm for getting AG resources—and those of select other publishers and content providers—to a growing network of churches and bookstores. Since its launch in 2011, My Healthy Church has become the official resource provider for an increasing number of like-minded denominations and associations of churches, enabling the Assemblies of God to expand its reach and impact from its own 12,792 churches to nearly triple that number in just three years.

Mi Iglesia Saludable (MiIglesiaSaludable.com) is the Spanish-language side of My Healthy Church. Today, nearly one hundred distributors provide training and education, marketing, and sales support to Hispanic churches, bookstores, and libraries in the United States, Latin America, and throughout the world.

The inspiration behind My Healthy Church is Acts 2:42–47, which describes five characteristics of a healthy church: pursuing and obeying God passionately (Worship), engaging and maintaining loving relationships (Connect), developing and mobilizing people (Grow), acting with clear direction and outward focus (Serve), and reproducing and multiplying His mission in other people and places (Go). Alton Garrison outlined these characteristics in his 2009 book, The Acts 2 Church.

Influences Resources is the imprint for resources designed for the broader evangelical market. It provides a way to take what is happening in the Assemblies of God and present it to those outside the Fellowship. General Superintendent Wood explains it this way: "Some of the most creative and effective evangelism, church growth, and discipleship endeavors are being done by the Assemblies of God pastors and leaders. Often their story has not even been told within our Fellowship, let alone the broader Christian world. I believe what these pastors and authors are experiencing has the potential to enrich ministers and laity all across the Christian community."

These resources range in style and format for all ages, including books and Bible studies for leaders and laypeople, comic books and graphic novels, ebooks, and apps. Recognizing the role that music plays in culture, Influence Music launched in 2013, giving Influence Resources yet another media format to reach the world for Christ. Its first praise and worship CD debuted at number 1 on the Nielsen Soundscan music chart for its category.

CHURCH TRANSFORMATION INITIATIVE

The Church Transformation Initiative, also introduced at the 2011 General Council (initially known as the Healthy Church Network), offers consultation and resources for churches ready to move forward. Based on the Acts 2 model, the Church Transformation Initiative offers an array of services for churches of all cultures and sizes, with a focus on clarity in mission and prayerful planning for growth. Its goal is to help churches fulfill their God-given vision. A transformative process led by an experienced team helps strengthen churches spiritually, numerically, and relationally.

NETWORK OF WOMEN MINISTERS

Another ministry established in the last decade is the Network of Women Ministers, dedicated to "developing, mentoring, and resourcing vocational women ministers and women preparing for ministry." It is helping the Fellowship live up to its core commitment to recognize and release anointed servants for the harvest. Leaders such as Beth Grant, Jodi Detrick, and current director, Judy Rachels, are responding to the unique needs of women called to evangelistic, missionary, and pastoral ministries. Between 2000 and 2013, the percentage of female credential holders has increased from 16.3 percent to 22.3 percent of all credentialed ministers. By 2020, women are projected to number more than one-quarter of all credentialed ministers in the Assemblies of God and exercise increasing influence in the Fellowship.

TRANSFORMING HIGHER EDUCATION: TWENTY-FIRST CENTURY CHALLENGES
COLLEGES AND UNIVERSITIES

Movement affirmation, networking, and resourcing of the sixteen colleges and universities, as well as the Assemblies of God Theological Seminary comes through the Assemblies of God Alliance for Higher Education. Like all ministries located at the NLRC, the Alliance is a resource, a servant to the unique missions of the different schools. It sponsors significant educator and student conferences, allowing peers to connect, share insights and improve their work.

Robert Cook was appointed president of the Alliance (formerly the Commission on Christian Higher Education) in 2007 and capably led an expansion of its promotional, networking, and resourcing efforts until 2012. This included expanded faculty, staff, and student leader conferences, improved promotion, and even a biennial Seminarians Conference, where Assemblies of God men and women who attend other seminaries come to Springfield for their History and Polity of the Assemblies of God course and interact with the ELT, tour the national office, and learn from key ministry leaders.

Since 2012 (first as interim, and now as president), Marilyn Abplanalp continues the stewardship of enrichment, inspiration, and networking for the endorsed schools.

TRANSFORMATION OF AG SCHOOLS IN SPRINGFIELD

For over fifty years there have been a variety of attempts to consolidate or merge the AG schools in Springfield—Central Bible College and Evangel University. Central Bible College (CBC) has focused for ninety years on undergraduate preparation for full-time ministry, while Evangel provides Christ-centered Pentecostal education for liberal arts and professional vocations. In the 1960s, J. Robert Ashcroft was president of both schools and commuted between campuses for five years. He desired both missions to continue on one campus. Robert Cooley and other leaders initiated multiple attempts to unite these schools, along with AGTS into one consolidated university with an embedded seminary.

In October 2010, the ELT received two reports from concerned faculty urging consolidation with the continuation of all three missions. This prompted a meeting with educators, Alliance leadership, and General Superintendent Wood. After discussion and prayer, the participants agreed that consolidation was a good plan, but further prayer and work, along with financial provision, would be needed.

The next day, completely separate from this meeting, Wood received a call from the Green family, owners of Hobby Lobby, offering a gift of five million dollars to help toward the consolidation of the Springfield schools. This was the sign needed to start a rapid process that included General Council approval of the consolidation—pending approval from the accrediting agencies—in August 2011. The Higher Learning Commission and the Association of Theological Schools granted full approval on April 15, 2013.

As a result of much of hard work before and after final approval by the accrediting associations, there is now one consolidated Evangel University, with the undergraduate ministry majors of CBC continuing and AGTS as an embedded seminary. The missions of all three institutions will continue with greater efficiencies, integration of learning, and continued focus on Pentecostal empowerment for service in all vocations. Although CBC no longer exists as an independent school, its endowments and scholarships for ministry continue and the General Council commitment to undergraduate ministry training is stronger than ever.

Robert Spence has completed forty years of distinguished leadership at Evangel University. The new president and CEO of Evangel is Carol Taylor, an alumna of Evangel and AGTS fresh from a significant turnaround season as president of Vanguard University.

Taylor is the first graduate and the first female president of Evangel. She attended classes at CBC and graduated with a BA in elementary education from Evangel University. She earned her MA in cross-cultural communication from AGTS, appreciating the biblical-theological depth and missiological focus of the program. She earned her PhD in multilingual and multicultural education from Florida State University.

Carol Taylor

Her service includes several years of teaching at all levels, twelve years in executive management at Educational Testing Services (ETS) in Princeton, New Jersey, and seven years as vice provost for undergraduate education at Biola University. She served as provost/vice president of academics at Vanguard University before being chosen to lead the school as its ninth president.

From 2009–2013, Taylor was president of Vanguard University, an AG comprehensive university in Costa Mesa, California. She led a dramatic turnaround effort, with the school going from the brink of lost accreditation and serious questions about its future to a stable university with much less debt, a growing endowment, and a waiting list for admissions. She was awarded Evangel University's Alumna of the Year award in 2012.

The Assemblies of God Theological Seminary, now part of Evangel University, continues as one of the leading voices in global Pentecostal/charismatic education and empowerment of spiritual and theological leaders. In addition to its innovative and growing doctor of ministry program, AGTS has added three new doctoral programs. The doctor of missiology and the PhD in intercultural studies are already making an impact around the world as AGWM leaders and other Pentecostal missionary personnel learn and contribute to the advance of the gospel. In 2010, AGTS launched the first fully accredited PhD in Bible and theology (now named biblical interpretation and theology) from an Assemblies of God institution.

GLOBAL UNIVERSITY AND NEW INTERNET RESOURCES

Global University—the marriage of Berean School of the Bible (domestic training from new converts to credentialing classes) and International Correspondence Institute (ICI, AGWM's educational outreach to the nations, offering certificates to doctoral degrees)—continues to see growth in all of its programs. The last decade has seen the acceleration of online learning modalities as well as the continuation of some traditional correspondence methods. In the past four years, Global University has received regional accreditation in the United States. It has also added MDiv and DMin programs to its offerings as a missionary outreach of the Fellowship.

One of the pioneers of ICI, George M. Flattery, established a new educational outreach in 1998 called Global Colleagues. The goal is evangelism and discipleship through the Internet to 230 nations. Now called Network 211, he and his team are in the midst of a drive to see ten million people come to Christ before 2020. Already more than seven hundred thousand decisions for Christ have been made. Leveraging new technology for the Great Commission is yielding fruitful impact.

BETHANY UNIVERSITY CLOSES

On August 8, 2011, Bethany University, the oldest educational institution in the Assemblies of God, officially closed its doors. Founded in 1919 by Robert and Mary Craig as Glad Tidings Bible Institute, Bethany was a mission that launched thousands of pastoral, missionary, and educational leaders into fruitful service. The Craigs prayed in 1919 that God would give them one hundred thousand souls through their local church and her outreaches, including the Bible Institute. That prayer has been answered many times over through the graduates of this school. Hal Donaldson, cofounder of Convoy of Hope, and Byron Klaus, current vice president at Evangel University and president of AGTS, are graduates. A great heritage and dedicated leaders could not stem declining enrollment and increased indebtedness.

PROSPECTS FOR THE TWENTY-FIRST CENTURY

Several Alliance schools have experienced significant changes and growth in the past decade, each demonstrating integration of Pentecostal passion and academic excellence. Northwest University has added programs in nursing and graduate degrees in leadership. Southeastern University added several new building and programs, and more than three thousand total students by 2006. Southwestern University is another growing school, with new masters and doctoral programs. Zion Bible College moved to Haverhill, Massachusetts, and changed its name to Northpoint Bible College. It has also added a new masters degree program.

TRANSFORMING ETHNIC RELATIONS IN THE UNITED STATES
A WINDOW OF CHANGE IN THE USA: HISPANIC LEADERS

There has been a transformation of the ethnic diversity in the U.S. Assemblies of God. By 2014, one-third of all local churches and more than 40 percent of adherents were ethnic minorities and immigrants, a significant increase. The Spanish ethnic/language districts in particular have seen remarkable growth.

This change in demographics and outreach is personified in the honor bestowed on the senior pastor of New Life Covenant Church in Chicago, Rev. Wilfredo De Jesús, known to his flock as Pastor Choco. *Time* magazine, in its April 18, 2013, edition named Pastor Choco one of the one hundred most influential people in the United States. His church is ranked as the largest in the Assemblies of God. He is currently vice president of the National Hispanic Christian Leadership Conference and the author of *Amazing Faith* and *In the Gap* (Influence Resources).

Wilfredo De Jesús

In 1997, while still an associate pastor, De Jesús insisted that his church respond to the city's request that they help the homeless and needy. River of Life Shelter was established with modest financial help from the city and the generous giving of time and treasure of the church, which at the time numbered about one hundred members. Today the church has more than fourteen thousand attendees on four campuses. There are 130 ministries, including a farm, a Dream Center, and a Teen Center, all serving vulnerable people, including former addicts and prostitutes, single mothers, hurting teens and women liberated from sex trafficking. Their annual Hope Fest provides more than six thousand elementary and secondary students with haircuts, immunizations, and book bags and uniforms so they begin the school year well. When asked about financial and volunteer resources to accomplish these large tasks, Pastor Choco declares that one can begin with just a handful of willing people and watch the Lord multiply the compassion.

Two other Hispanic churches, Iglesia El Calvario in Orlando, Florida, (Nino Gonzalez, pastor) and Templo Calvario in Santa Ana, California, (Pastor Daniel de León, Sr.), are also among the top churches in the Movement.

INCREASE OF NATIONAL BLACK FELLOWSHIP CHURCHES

The National Black Fellowship has enjoyed a season of increase during the last decade. In 2001, there were 226 churches with 164,071 people in attendance. By 2012, the number of churches had increased to 409 churches, reflecting a 81 percent increase, and the adherents had increased to 308,520, an 88 percent increase. In 2011, Herbert Cooper, pastor of the over 4,500 member People's Church in Oklahoma City, was noted by *Outreach* magazine as one of thirty emerging influencers in Christian ministry today.

The National Black Fellowship has also become a platform for black pastors and ministers to become more involved in the leadership of the districts where their churches are. They are serving as district executive presbyters, on district committees, and in other district leadership positions. Notable examples of the many black ministers emerging as leaders in the Assemblies of God are Michael Nelson, Peninsular Florida district, president of the National Black Fellowship and General Council general presbyter; Sam Huddleston, assistant superintendent of the Northern California-Nevada district and General Council general presbyter; Louis Walton, Inner Urban Section presbyter of the Minnesota district; and John Cummings, district executive presbyter for Metro Region West in the New York district.

THE MEMPHIS MIRACLE BEARS NEW FRUIT: RECONCILIATION AND PARTNERSHIP IN MISSION
HEALING A SCHISM

In 2010, the Rev. Thomas Barclay, international presiding elder of the United Pentecostal Council of the Assemblies of God (UPCAG), reached out to the Assemblies of God with a desire to heal a schism dating back to 1917. In 1917, an African-American minister named Alexander Howard requested AG appointment as a missionary to Liberia. Sadly, he was refused due to his race. By 1919, a group of churches in the northeast United States was formed out of this rejection and have remained a small but vibrant Pentecostal witness. Rev. Barclay reached °ut and was warmly received at the 2011 General Council as he shared his historic journey and deep desire for cooperation.

Rev. Barclay's courage and the humility of Assemblies of God leaders culminated in a historic agreement for "cooperative affiliation" signed on February 11, 2014. UPCAG churches are now welcomed into local districts and national ministries, and maintain their own credentialing. This was truly a moment of divine redemption.

FRIENDSHIP GROWS WITH CHURCH OF GOD IN CHRIST

In a spirit of humility and faith, the Assemblies of God continues to forge strong bonds of fellowship with African-American Pentecostal fellowships such as the Church of God in Christ (COGIC). On November 27, 2013, the full executive leadership of the U.S. Assemblies of God and the COGIC met in Springfield, Missouri, to dialogue together. General Superintendent Wood shared that both denominations were children of the Azusa Street Revival. Bishop Charles Mason, the founder of the COGIC, addressed the first General Council in 1914 in a spirit of love and unity. The later division on racial lines, while never formal, reflected a nation divided instead of a church united.

Wood and COGIC Presiding Bishop Charles E. Blake, Sr., agreed it was a new day. Bishop Blake addressed the national office personnel in their weekly chapel, exhorting them from Paul's example in the Book of Acts to thank God before, during, and after the storms of life and ministry.

This meeting was preceded by a delightful and profound moment of fraternal joy and trust on September 17 and 18, 2012, as "Mother" Mary P. Patterson, widow of the late Bishop J. O. Patterson, presiding bishop of the COGIC fellowship, presented her husband's papers to the Flower Pentecostal Heritage Center archive for organization and safekeeping. Such respect for the Assemblies of God spoke volumes of the progress made in relationships over the past two decades.

TRANSFORMATION IN GLOBAL MISSIONS: DEVELOPMENTS IN AGWM

The Great Commission is the heartbeat of the Assemblies of God. From 1914 to the present, the call to "all nations" has produced—in partnership with other evangelical and Pentecostal churches—the greatest missionary expansion of the church in history. In 1910, the global population was about 1.9 billion souls. The percentage of people confessing Christian faith was about 33 percent, almost all located in the Western nations. But the last century has witnessed unprecedented church growth in developing nations. Today, the percentage of Christians is about the same, but with a world population of more than seven billion people. Real progress has been made, yet much work remains until all hear the good news. In spite of domestic economic challenges, political upheavals, and global persecution of believers, the mission is going forward, with thousands of anointed servant-leaders being sent, supported, and sustained by the Spirit of God and the prayers and gifts of His people.

NEW INITIATIVES IN THE TWENTY-FIRST CENTURY

Three new initiatives highlight some of the transformation of global missions in the last decade. The first is the maturation of the Center for Muslim Ministry into the Global Initiative: Ministry to Muslim Peoples. Under the current leadership of Mark Hausfeld, an appointed AGWM missionary and associate professor at AGTS, this expanding Center is offering undergraduate and graduate training in ministry to Muslims and well as resources for local churches and missions agencies around the world. Women and men with decades of experience are mobilizing to reach the more than one billion Muslims without an effective witness of the gospel.

The second initiative also focuses on reaching the unreached, Entitled "Live|Dead," this mission aims to mobilize a generation of missionary teams ready to give their lives for the salvation of the 2.8 billion people in more than three hundred unreached people groups around the world. The Cairo Initiative facet of this mission is challenging a generation of young women and men to give their lives for the salvation of the unreached, calling forth a Cross-shaped life of service, prayer, abiding in Christ, and insightful evangelism. Young adults are longing for a cause to live for that is more than self-gratification or business as usual. The Live|Dead Journal, published by Influence Resources, is touching thousands of young hearts with its timeless message of sacrificial service rooted in deep love for Christ.

The third new mission highlighted here is Project Rescue, founded by Eurasian missionaries David and Beth Grant. This is a mission devoted to victims of sexual slavery and trafficking around the world. The Grants began this new ministry with local Assemblies of God leaders in India and have watched it expand to other nations, including the United States. Their goals are rescue, restoration, and prevention. In 2013, it was estimated that there are between twenty-five and thirty-five million victims being trafficked. But the challenge is more than awareness. Thousands of believers in thousands of churches must be equipped with hearts of compassion and minds filled with wisdom to befriend and disciples the ones being rescued.

U.S. MISSIONS: GLOBALIZATION COMES TO THE USA

Assemblies of God U.S. Missions (AGUSM) under the leadership of Zollie L. Smith, Jr., exists so "that none perish." The goal today is to reach the more than 117 million unevangelized people in the United States. The motto of AGUSM is "We are there"—among the homeless, the lonely, the hurting, and the unbelieving.

SEVEN WINDOWS OF OUTREACH AND DISCIPLESHIP

- Chaplaincy—from cowboys to hospital, from military to hospice, prisons to sporting events, these rugged servants minister to often hidden populations.

In 2015, the number of chaplains was 621, including 275 military chaplains, 108 correctional leaders, and 159 in healthcare fields.

- **Chi Alpha Campus Ministries, U.S.A.**—As of 2015, this ministry numbers 313 campus groups with 1,162 staff. Of this, 422 are female Chi Alpha leaders. Of the more than 28,000 U.S. student adherents, 2,500 are international students. In 2015 alone, there were more than five thousand salvations through campus groups.
- **Intercultural Ministries**—This ministry exists to resource evangelism and discipleship to diverse populations and foster cultural understanding through the unity of Christ. There are over three hundred U.S. missionaries serving diverse fields and populations as the United States itself is a global missions field.
- **Missionary Church Planters and Developers**—In conjunction with the Church Multiplication Network, the ministry aim is to establish four thousand new churches from 2011 to 2020. Between 2009 and 2013, there was a net gain of 421 AG churches, many of these new plants and strategic revitalizations. There are currently more than 150 church developers and planters, and their numbers are growing as the many resources of AGUSM coordinate their efforts.
- **Teen Challenge USA**—This ministry is celebrating over fifty years of delivering, healing, and restoring work in addicts through the power of the gospel. There are 196 centers with more than 1,800 staff leading 16,500 students with deliverance, healing, and training.
- **U.S. MAPS (Mission America Placement Service)**—U.S. MAPS coordinates thousands of women and men who volunteer their skills in serving other ministries. There are currently more than 900 RV volunteers and 140 missionary associates, plus thousands of volunteers. From church construction and repair to a variety of local facility and outreach needs, U.S. MAPS continues to make an impact.
- **Youth Alive**—This outreach to public secondary school campuses has twenty-eight U.S. missionaries catalyzing the creation of new groups and equipping leaders for evangelization and discipleship in conjunction with local churches.

The Assemblies of God continues its passion for global evangelization and resourcing foreign missionaries and national leaders. The Movement is also awakening to the missions field of a globalized United States and the reality of a generation with no Christian background in need of hearing the gospel for the first time.

GLOBAL PARTNERSHIPS STRENGTHENED

The U.S. Assemblies of God is part of the World Assemblies of God Fellowship, representing the sixty-six million adherents mentioned at the beginning of this chapter. Though influential, the United States church does not dictate or dominate the national fellowships. Even a cursory examination of doctrine and polity around the world unveils great variety, within a biblical unity. All AG fellowships share a deep commitment to Spirit baptism with the evidence of tongues as vital for the empowerment of all disciples. As the twenty-first century dawned, the influence of other national fellowships grew as the sons and daughters of AGWM are now leaders of missionary movements and multiplying churches.

The U.S. Assemblies of God is also part of an even broader Pentecostal World Fellowship, representing fifty-nine member organizations uniting Spirit-empowered believers to fulfill the Great Commission. The sparks of Azusa Street and the Bible Women in India, the flames of Methodist revival in Chile and the hunger for Pentecost in Sweden—are now a family of churches in the hundreds of millions cooperating in mission.

Another example of growing global partnerships is in Malawi, West Africa. The modest Bible Institute nurtured by Warren and Annette Newberry in the 1960s is now the Malawi Assemblies of God University offering undergraduate and graduate programs, in ministry, commerce and humanitarian fields, with both AGWM leaders and African professors. Under the current leadership of John Easter, there are more than two hundred centers of learning for African leadership development, with U.S. and African pastors and professors serving together.

THE NEXT CENTURY

CURRENTS OF CONCERN AND OPPORTUNITY

From the 1940s to the present, Assemblies of God leaders have called for a "return to the original fires of Pentecost" and expressed concern that success might bring laxity in doctrine, morality, and mission. The Assemblies of God has weathered many storms of spiritual controversy, from the Oneness divide in the 1910s to the Latter Rain movement of the 1940s and 1950s, and the extreme elements of diverse renewals since the 1980s. "Cautious embrace" of fresh experiences and ideas has been the hallmark of a Fellowship that respects its distinctive ideas while working in fraternal partnership with evangelical and Pentecostal believers across the nation and around the world. Assemblies of God leaders such as Cecil M. "Mel" Robeck, Frank Macchia, and the late Gary B. McGee have engaged in dialogue with Roman Catholic, Eastern Orthodox, and Protestant groups, with salutary reductions in misunderstanding and increased cooperation where possible.

The Assemblies of God was part of the 1943 founding of the National Association of Evangelicals as well as an active leader in the Lausanne Movement. Some Pentecostals see this as compromise and long for greater separation of Pentecostal and evangelical. What the separatists forget is that the global evangelical families of faith are almost all touched by the fires of Pentecost! There are, of course, diverse opinions on the universality of tongues and stewardship of expressions, But in the words of Byron Klaus, "We won. The battle for legitimacy is over." There are even a million

Reformed believers in the United States embracing all the gifts of the Spirit. At the 2011 General Council, Rick Warren, a Southern Baptist pastor, urged the AG ministers to be *more* Pentecostal—and explain it better to their hearers!

CHALLENGES AND OPPORTUNITIES

Global Pentecostal/charismatic growth is heartening and an affirmation that the Assemblies of God is part of an amazing latter days move of the Spirit. There is a phenomenon, however, that is a legitimate cause for concern within the Fellowship. For nearly two decades, the percentage of adherents baptized in the Spirit with the initial physical evidence of speaking with tongues has remained about 50 percent. According to many researchers and scholars, the number of AG churches experiencing manifestation gifts in weekly worship had declined since the 1970s. Some attribute this to the influence of evangelical identity and the seeker-sensitive movements that aim for inoffensive public meetings. These are factors, along with movements that embrace deliverance, gifts, and healing without the universality of Spirit baptism and tongues. There is a real danger, in the words of Earl Creps, of a generation of Assemblies of God "post-Pentecostal Pentecostals" that affirm the Statement of Fundamental Truths and enjoy relationships, but do not seek to practice or promote Spirit baptism and speaking in tongues.

Charisma magazine

General Superintendent Wood disputes this pessimistic picture in a 2014 centennial interview in *Charisma* magazine. His observations, interviews with leaders, and wide travel affirm that Spirit baptism with the initial physical evidence of tongues is alive and growing. He affirmed that the statistics are imperfect, not reflecting practices in thousands of churches in recent years.

A 2013 Pew Research study, evaluating both American and global Christianity, noted a significant rise in Pentecostal practices, even among those not traditionally labeled Pentecostal or charismatic. For much the evangelical world in particular, praying for healing and miracles, exercising spiritual gifts, trusting the Lord for deliverance, and speaking in tongues are all valid biblical practices. This is a significant change within one generation.

Cessationism (the belief that the manifestations of the Spirit in 1 Corinthians 12–14 ceased with the death of the original apostles or the close of the New Testament canon in the fourth century) is a declining movement as believers of all denominations and theological persuasions affirm the contemporary work of the Spirit. Though many of these groups do not share the "classical" Pentecostal distinctive of tongues as the initial physical evident of Spirit baptism, the affirmation that the Spirit works in and through all the gifts is a heartening change.

There are some signs across the United States that cause concern among thoughtful persons. The number of people that answered "none" when asked for religious affiliation has grown from a minuscule percentage in the 1980s to 16.1 percent in a 2007 poll by Pew Research. And 28 percent have left the faith they were raised in or affiliate with no religion at all.[1] This reflects two trends: (1) the loss of denominational loyalty among some that might still (vaguely) identify themselves as Christians; and (2) an increasing number of the U.S. population (both immigrant and native-born) with no religious affiliation.

"Post-Christian" and "postmodern" are labels tossed about with great frequency in popular analysis. The United States remains much more religious than most of Western Europe; however, "being spiritual and not religious" is gaining as a category of a generation without significant exposure to the gospel.

The new challenge for Assemblies of God leaders is evangelization of people with no Christian memory. This is a new phenomenon for many U.S. leaders (though not for the appointed missionaries of AGWM).

Another concern among thoughtful adherents is moral compromise with the subversion of traditional marriage and sexuality in the last half-century. The public consensus in the West and the United States of lifelong heterosexual marriage and celibacy for singles is no longer the prevailing opinion of popular culture or even a majority of people. While strong elements within American society advocate or support gay marriage, the Assemblies of God stands firmly committed to scriptural teaching that marriage is between a man and a woman.

When confronted by actual or potential compromise in other evangelical or Pentecostal fellowships and organizations, steadfast adherence to biblical marriage is quickly affirmed. The Assemblies of God leadership has been uncompromising it its standards of sexual conduct while affirming love for all people broken by sin.

OPPORTUNITIES AHEAD!

The evangelical revivals of the eighteenth and nineteenth centuries fueled the birth of global missions. The Pentecostal awakenings have accelerated the spread of the gospel in the twentieth century. We are now witnesses the re-evangelizing of Europe and the United States by missional believers from developing nations. The gospel is now going from everywhere to everywhere as former missions fields become missions-sending agencies.

When Melvin Hodges penned *The Indigenous Church* in 1953, the aim of missions was a self-sustaining local church and, in the long-term, a self-sustaining national fellowship. These remain important goals; however, a more complete goal is emerging in the twenty-first century: establishing churches and fellowships of churches that become not only self-sustaining, but missionary sending. Fresh voices such as Ivan Satyavrata, Wonsuk and Julie Ma, DeLonn Rance, and others are helping AG adherents around the world answer the Great Commission call and become "360 Churches." Missionary-scholars such as Alan Johnson in Thailand are now articulating an integration of apostolic pioneering and church planting united with holistic care for communities.

In the post-Christian West, Pentecostal spirituality and theology are the answer for generations that are hungry for experience and meaning rooted in love and truth. Apologetics and careful explanations of truth must be united with the proclamation of the Cross and power of the Spirit to deliver, heal, forgive, redeem, and transform. Now is not the time to lessen Pentecostal emphases. The exact opposite is true. The signs and wonders demonstrated in Scripture are alive and well on the frontiers of evangelization and missions today. The Assemblies of God has a bright future as we recognize those frontiers across the street and around the world.

Gary McGee's final work, *Miracles, Missions and American Pentecostalism* (2010), details the supernatural confirmation of the missionary pioneers. As a new Spirit-empowered generation hears the call to evangelism, worship, discipleship, and compassion, they can expect the Lord of the harvest to again confirm the message of grace.

ENDNOTE

[1] "Religious Landscape Survey, Report 1: Religious Affiliation," Pew Research Center's Religion & Public Life Project, 2013, http://religions.pewforum.org/reports.

STATEMENT OF FUNDAMENTAL TRUTHS

The Bible is our all–sufficient rule for faith and practice. This Statement of Fundamental Truths is intended simply as a basis of fellowship among us (i.e., that we all speak the same thing, 1 Corinthians 1:10; Acts 2:42). The phraseology employed in this statement is not inspired or contended for, but the truth set forth is held to be essential to a full–gospel ministry. No claim is made that it contains all biblical truth, only that it covers our need as to these fundamental doctrines.

1. THE SCRIPTURES INSPIRED

The Scriptures, both the Old and New Testaments, are verbally inspired of God and are the revelation of God to man, the infallible, authoritative rule of faith and conduct (2 Timothy 3:15–17; 1 Thessalonians 2:13; 2 Peter 1:21).

2. THE ONE TRUE GOD

The one true God has revealed himself as the eternally self–existent "I AM," the Creator of heaven and earth and the Redeemer of mankind. He has further revealed himself as embodying the principles of relationship and association as Father, Son, and Holy Spirit (Deuteronomy 6:4; Isaiah 43:10,11; Matthew 28:19; Luke 3:22).

THE ADORABLE GODHEAD

(a) Terms Defined

The terms *trinity* and *persons*, as related to the godhead, while not found in the Scriptures, are words in harmony with Scripture, whereby we may convey to others our immediate understanding of the doctrine of Christ respecting the Being of God, as distinguished from "gods many and lords many." We therefore may speak with propriety of the Lord our God, who is One Lord, as a Trinity or as one Being of three persons, and still be absolutely scriptural (examples, Matthew 28:19; 2 Corinthians 13:14; John 14:16,17).

(b) Distinction and Relationship in the Godhead

Christ taught a distinction of persons in the godhead which He expressed in specific terms of relationship, as Father, Son, and Holy Spirit, but that this distinction and relationship, as to its mode is inscrutable and incomprehensible, because unexplained (Luke 1:35; 1 Corinthians 1:24; Matthew 11:25–27; 28:19; 2 Corinthians 13:14; 1 John 1:3,4).

(c) Unity of the One Being of Father, Son, and Holy Spirit

Accordingly, therefore, there is that in the Father which constitutes Him **the Father** and not the Son; there is **that** in the Son which constitutes Him **the Son** and not the Father; and there is **that** in the Holy Spirit which constitutes Him **the Holy Spirit** and not either the Father or the Son. Wherefore, the Father is the Begetter; the Son is the Begotten; and the Holy Spirit is the One proceeding from the Father and the Son. Therefore, because these three persons in the godhead are in a state of unity, there is but one Lord God Almighty and His name one (John 1:18; 15:26; 17:11,21; Zechariah 14:9).

(d) Identity and Cooperation in the Godhead

The Father, the Son, and the Holy Spirit are never **identical** as to **person**; nor **confused** as to **relation**; nor **divided** in respect to the godhead; nor **opposed** as to **cooperation**. The Son is **in** the Father and the Father is **in** the Son as to relationship. The Son is **with** the Father and the Father is **with** the Son, as to fellowship. The Father is not **from** the Son, but the Son is **from** the Father, as to authority. The Holy Spirit is from the Father and the Son proceeding, as to nature, relationship, cooperation, and authority. Hence, no person in the godhead either exists or works separately or independently of the others (John 5:17–30,32,37; 8:17,18).

(e) The Title, Lord Jesus Christ

The appellation **Lord Jesus Christ**, is a proper name. It is never applied in the New Testament either to the Father or to the Holy Spirit. It therefore belongs exclusively to the **Son of God** (Romans 1:1–3,7; 2 John 3).

(f) The Lord Jesus Christ, God With Us

The Lord Jesus Christ, as to His divine and eternal nature, is the proper and only Begotten of the Father, but as to His human nature, He is the proper Son of Man. He is, therefore, acknowledged to be both God and man; who because He is God and man, is "Immanuel," God with us (Matthew 1:23; 1 John 4:2,10,14; Revelation 1:13,17).

(g) The Title, Son of God

Since the name **Immanuel** embraces both God and man, in the one person, our Lord Jesus Christ, it follows that the title **Son of God** describes His proper deity, and the title **Son of Man**, His proper humanity. Therefore, the title **Son of God** belongs to the order of eternity, and the title **Son of Man** to the **order of time** (Matthew 1:21–23; 2 John 3; 1 John 3:8; Hebrews 7:3; 1:1–13).

(h) Transgression of the Doctrine of Christ

Wherefore, it is a transgression of the doctrine of Christ to say that Jesus Christ derived the title **Son of God** solely from the fact of the Incarnation, or because of His relation to the economy of redemption. Therefore, to deny that the Father is a real and eternal Father, and that the Son is a real and eternal Son, is a denial of the distinction and relationship in the Being of God; a denial of the Father and the Son; and a displacement of the truth that Jesus Christ is come in the flesh (2 John 9; John 1:1,2,14,18,29,49; 1 John 2:22,23; 4:1–5; Hebrews 12:2).

(i) Exaltation of Jesus Christ as Lord

The Son of God, our Lord Jesus Christ, having by himself purged our sins, sat down on the right hand of the Majesty on high, angels and principalities and powers having been made subject unto Him. And having been made both Lord and Christ, He sent the Holy Spirit that we, in the name of Jesus, might bow our knees and confess that Jesus Christ is Lord to the glory of God the Father until the end, when the Son shall become subject to the Father that God may be all in all (Hebrews 1:3; 1 Peter 3:22; Acts 2:32–36; Romans 14:11; 1 Corinthians 15:24–28)

(j) Equal Honor to the Father and to the Son

Wherefore, since the Father has delivered all judgment unto the Son, it is not only the **express duty** of all in heaven and on earth to bow the knee, but it is an **unspeakable** joy in the Holy Spirit to ascribe unto the Son all the attributes of deity, and to give Him all the honor and the glory contained in all the names and titles of the godhead except those which express relationship (see paragraphs b, c, and d), and thus honor the Son even as we honor the Father (John 5:22,23; 1 Peter 1:8; Revelation 5:6–14; Philippians 2:8,9; Revelation 7:9,10; 4:8–11).

3. THE DEITY OF THE LORD JESUS CHRIST

The Lord Jesus Christ is the eternal Son of God. The Scriptures declare:
a. His virgin birth (Matthew 1:23; Luke 1:31,35).
b. His sinless life (Hebrews 7:26; 1 Peter 2:22).
c. His miracles (Acts 2:22; 10:38).
d. His substitutionary work on the cross (1 Corinthians 15:3; 2 Corinthians 5:21).
e. His bodily resurrection from the dead (Matthew 28:6; Luke 24:39; 1 Corinthians 15:4).
f. His exaltation to the right hand of God (Acts 1:9,11; 2:33; Philippians 2:9–11; Hebrews 1:3).

4. THE FALL OF MAN

Man was created good and upright; for God said, "Let us make man in our image, after our likeness." However, man by voluntary transgression fell and thereby incurred not only physical death but also spiritual death, which is separation from God (Genesis 1:26,27; 2:17; 3:6; Romans 5:12–19).

5. THE SALVATION OF MAN

Man's only hope of redemption is through the shed blood of Jesus Christ the Son of God.

a. Conditions to Salvation

Salvation is received through repentance toward God and faith toward the Lord Jesus Christ. By the washing of regeneration and renewing of the Holy Spirit, being justified by grace through faith, man becomes an heir of God according to the hope of eternal life (Luke 24:47; John 3:3; Romans 10:13–15; Ephesians 2:8; Titus 2:11; 3:5–7).

b. The Evidences of Salvation

The inward evidence of salvation is the direct witness of the Spirit (Romans 8:16). The outward evidence to all men is a life of righteousness and true holiness (Ephesians 4:24; Titus 2:12).

6. THE ORDINANCES OF THE CHURCH

a. Baptism in Water

The ordinance of baptism by immersion is commanded in the Scriptures. All who repent and believe on Christ as Savior and Lord are to be baptized. Thus they declare to the world that they have died with Christ and that they also have been raised with Him to walk in newness of life (Matthew 28:19; Mark 16:16; Acts 10:47,48; Romans 6:4).

b. Holy Communion

The Lord's Supper, consisting of the elements—bread and the fruit of the vine—is the symbol expressing our sharing the divine nature of our Lord Jesus Christ (2 Peter 1:4); a memorial of His suffering and death (1 Corinthians 11:26); and a prophecy of His second coming (1 Corinthians 11:26); and is enjoined on all believers "till He come!"

7. THE BAPTISM IN THE HOLY SPIRIT

All believers are entitled to and should ardently expect and earnestly seek the promise of the Father, the baptism in the Holy Spirit and fire, according to the command of our Lord Jesus Christ. This was the normal experience of all in the early Christian church. With it comes the enduement of power for life and service, the bestowment of the gifts and their uses in the work of the ministry (Luke 24:49; Acts 1:4,8; 1 Corinthians 12:1–31). This experience is distinct from and subsequent to the experience of the new birth (Acts 8:12–17; 10:44–46; 11:14–16; 15:7–9). With the baptism in the Holy Spirit come such experiences as an overflowing fullness of the Spirit (John 7:37–39; Acts 4:8), a deepened reverence for God (Acts 2:43; Hebrews 12:28), an intensified consecration to God and dedication to His work (Acts 2:42), and a more active love for Christ, for His Word, and for the lost (Mark 16:20).

8. THE INITIAL PHYSICAL EVIDENCE OF THE BAPTISM IN THE HOLY SPIRIT

The baptism of believers in the Holy Spirit is witnessed by the initial physical sign of speaking with other tongues as the Spirit of God gives them utterance (Acts 2:4). The speaking in tongues in this instance is the same in essence as the gift of tongues (1 Corinthians 12:4–10,28), but different in purpose and use.

9. SANCTIFICATION

Sanctification is an act of separation from that which is evil, and of dedication unto God (Romans 12:1,2; 1 Thessalonians 5:23; Hebrews 13:12). Scriptures teach a life of "holiness without which no man shall see the Lord" (Hebrews 12:14). By the power of the Holy Spirit we are able to obey the command: "Be ye holy, for I am holy" (1 Peter 1:15,16).

Sanctification is realized in the believer by recognizing his identification with Christ in His death and resurrection, and by faith reckoning daily upon the fact of that union, and by offering every faculty continually to the dominion of the Holy Spirit (Romans 6:1–11,13; 8:1,2,13; Galatians 2:20; Philippians 2:12,13; 1 Peter 1:5).

10. THE CHURCH AND ITS MISSION

The Church is the body of Christ, the habitation of God through the Spirit, with divine appointments for the fulfillment of her Great Commission. Each believer, born of the Spirit, is an integral part of the general assembly and church of the firstborn, which are written in heaven (Ephesians 1:22,23; 2:22; Hebrews 12:23).

Since God's purpose concerning man is to seek and to save that which is lost, to be worshiped by man, to build a body of believers in the image of His Son, and to demonstrate His love and compassion for all the world, the priority reason for being of the Assemblies of God as part of the Church is:

a. To be an agency of God for evangelizing the world (Acts 1:8; Matthew 28:19,20; Mark 16:15,16).
b. To be a corporate body in which man may worship God (1 Corinthians 12:13).
c. To be a channel of God's purpose to build a body of saints being perfected in the image of His Son (Ephesians 4:11–16; 1 Corinthians 12:28; 14:12).
d. To be a people who demonstrate God's love and compassion for all the world (Psalm 112:9; Galatians 2:10; 6:10; James 1:27).

The Assemblies of God exists expressly to give continuing emphasis to this reason for being in the New Testament apostolic pattern by teaching and encouraging believers to be baptized in the Holy Spirit. This experience:

a. Enables them to evangelize in the power of the Spirit with accompanying supernatural signs (Mark 16:15–20; Acts 4:29–31; Hebrews 2:3,4).
b. Adds a necessary dimension to a worshipful relationship with God (1 Corinthians 2:10–16; 1 Corinthians 12–14).
c. Enables them to respond to the full working of the Holy Spirit in expression of fruit and gifts and ministries as in New Testament times for the edifying of the body of Christ and care for the poor and needy of the world (Galatians 5:22–26; Matthew 25:37–40; Galatians 6:10; 1 Corinthians 14:12; Ephesians 4:11,12; 1 Corinthians 12:28; Colossians 1:29).

11. THE MINISTRY

A divinely called and scripturally ordained ministry has been provided by our Lord for the fourfold purpose of leading the Church in: (1) evangelization of the world (Mark 16:15–20), (2) worship of God (John 4:23,24), (3) building a Body of saints being perfected in the image of His Son (Ephesians 4:11,16), and (4) meeting human need with ministries of love and compassion (Psalm 112:9; Galatians 2:10; 6:10; James 1:27).

12. DIVINE HEALING

Divine healing is an integral part of the gospel. Deliverance from sickness is provided for in the Atonement, and is the privilege of all believers (Isaiah 53:4,5; Matthew 8:16,17; James 5:14–16).

13. THE BLESSED HOPE

The resurrection of those who have fallen asleep in Christ and their translation together with those who are alive and remain unto the coming of the Lord is the imminent and blessed hope of the Church (1 Thessalonians 4:16,17; Romans 8:23; Titus 2:13; 1 Corinthians 15:51,52).

14. THE MILLENNIAL REIGN OF CHRIST

The second coming of Christ includes the rapture of the saints, which is our blessed hope, followed by the visible return of Christ with His saints to reign on the earth for one thousand years (Zechariah 14:5; Matthew 24:27,30; Revelation 1:7; 19:11–14; 20:1–6). This millennial reign will bring the salvation of national Israel (Ezekiel 37:21,22; Zephaniah 3:19,20; Romans 11:26,27) and the establishment of universal peace (Isaiah 11:6–9; Psalm 72:3–8; Micah 4:3,4).

15. THE FINAL JUDGMENT

There will be a final judgment in which the wicked dead will be raised and judged according to their works. Whosoever is not found written in the Book of Life, together with the devil and his angels, the beast and the false prophet, will be consigned to everlasting punishment in the lake which burneth with fire and brimstone, which is the second death (Matthew 25:46; Mark 9:43–48; Revelation 19:20; 20:11–15; 21:8).

16. THE NEW HEAVENS AND THE NEW EARTH

"We, according to His promise, look for new heavens and a new earth, wherein dwelleth righteousness" (2 Peter 3:13; Revelation 21,22).

Scripture quotations are from the King James Version of the Holy Bible.

OFFICERS OF THE GENERAL COUNCIL 1914-2013

1. HOT SPRINGS, ARKANSAS
APRIL 2-12, 1914

Chairman: E. N. Bell
Secretary: J. Roswell Flower

2. CHICAGO, ILLINOIS
NOVEMBER 15-29, 1914

Chairman: Arch P. Collins
Assistant Chairman: Daniel C. O.
    Opperman
Secretary: J. Roswell Flower
Assistant Secretary: Bennett F. Lawrence

3. ST. LOUIS, MISSOURI
OCTOBER 1-10, 1915

Chairman: John W. Welch
Secretary: J. Roswell Flower

4. ST. LOUIS, MISSOURI
OCTOBER 1-7, 1916

Chairman: John W. Welch
Secretary: Stanley H. Frodsham

5. ST. LOUIS, MISSOURI
SEPTEMBER 9-14, 1917

Chairman: John W. Welch
Secretary: Stanley H. Frodsham

6. SPRINGFIELD, MISSOURI
SEPTEMBER 4-11, 1918

Chairman: John W. Welch
Secretary: Stanley H. Frodsham

7. CHICAGO, ILLINOIS
SEPTEMBER 25-30, 1919

Chairman: John W. Welch
Secretary and Editor: E. N. Bell
Foreign Missions Secretary:
    J. Roswell Flower

8. SPRINGFIELD, MISSOURI
SEPTEMBER 21-27, 1920

Chairman: E. N. Bell
Secretary: John W. Welch
Foreign Missions Secretary:
    J. Roswell Flower
Editor: John T. Boddy

9. ST. LOUIS, MISSOURI
SEPTEMBER 21-28, 1921

Chairman: E. N. Bell
Secretary: John W. Welch
Foreign Missions Secretary:
    J. Roswell Flower
Editor: Stanley H. Frodsham

(E. N. Bell died in office, June 15, 1923. His office was not filled until the 1923 General Council. In 1921, it was decided the Councils would meet every two years.)

10. ST. LOUIS, MISSOURI
SEPTEMBER 13-18, 1923

Chairman: John W. Welch
Assistant Chairman: David H. McDowell
Secretary: J. R. Evans
Foreign Missions Secretary: William Faux
Foreign Missions Treasurer:
   J. Roswell Flower
Editor: Stanley H. Frodsham

11. EUREKA SPRINGS, ARKANSAS
SEPTEMBER 17-24, 1925

Chairman: W. T. Gaston
Assistant Chairman: David H. McDowell
Secretary: J. R. Evans
Foreign Missions Secretary–Treasurer:
   William Faux
Editor: Stanley H. Frodsham

12. SPRINGFIELD, MISSOURI
SEPTEMBER 16-22, 1927

General Superintendent: W. T. Gaston
Assistant Superintendent: David H.
   McDowell
General Secretary: J. R. Evans
Foreign Missions Secretary: Noel Perkin
Editor: Stanley H. Frodsham

13. WICHITA, KANSAS
SEPTEMBER 20-26, 1929

General Superintendent: E. S. Williams
Assistant Superintendent: (Vacant)
General Secretary: J. R. Evans
Foreign Missions Secretary: Noel Perkin
Editor: Stanley H. Frodsham

14. SAN FRANCISCO, CALIFORNIA
SEPTEMBER 8-13, 1931

General Superintendent: E. S. Williams
Assistant Superintendent: J. Roswell Flower
General Secretary: J. R. Evans
Foreign Missions Secretary: Noel Perkin
Editor: Stanley H. Frodsham

15. PHILADELPHIA, PENNSYLVANIA
SEPTEMBER 14-20, 1933

All officers reelected.

16. DALLAS, TEXAS
SEPTEMBER 12-19, 1935

General Superintendent: E. S. Williams
Assistant Superintendent: J. Roswell Flower
General Secretary: J. Roswell Flower
Foreign Missions Secretary: Noel Perkin
Editor: Stanley H. Frodsham

17. MEMPHIS, TENNESSEE
SEPTEMBER 2-9, 1937

General Superintendent: E. S. Williams
Assistant Superintendent: Fred Vogler
General Secretary: J. Roswell Flower
Foreign Missions Secretary: Noel Perkin
Editor: Stanley H. Frodsham

18. SPRINGFIELD, MISSOURI
SEPTEMBER 7-12, 1939

All officers reelected.

19. MINNEAPOLIS, MINNESOTA
SEPTEMBER 5-11, 1941

All officers reelected.

20. SPRINGFIELD, MISSOURI
SEPTEMBER 1-9, 1943

General Superintendent: E. S. Williams
Assistant General Superintendent:
    Ralph M. Riggs
General Secretary: J. Roswell Flower
Foreign Missions Secretary: Noel Perkin
Editor: Stanley H. Frodsham

21. SPRINGFIELD, MISSOURI
SEPTEMBER 13-18, 1945

General Superintendent: E. S. Williams
Assistant General Superintendents:
    Ralph M. Riggs, Gayle F. Lewis,
    Fred Vogler, Wesley R. Steelberg
General Secretary: J. Roswell Flower
Foreign Missions Secretary: Noel Perkin
Editor: Stanley H. Frodsham

22. GRAND RAPIDS, MICHIGAN
SEPTEMBER 4-11, 1947

General Superintendent: E. S. Williams
Assistant General Superintendents:
    Ralph M. Riggs, Gayle F. Lewis,
    Fred Vogler, Wesley R. Steelberg
General Secretary: J. Roswell Flower
General Treasurer: Wilfred A. Brown
Foreign Missions Secretary: Noel Perkin
Editor: Stanley H. Frodsham

23. SEATTLE, WASHINGTON
SEPTEMBER 8-14, 1949

General Superintendent:
    Wesley R. Steelberg
Assistant General Superintendents:
    Ralph M. Riggs, Gayle F. Lewis,
    Fred Vogler, Bert Webb
General Secretary: J. Roswell Flower
General Treasurer: Wilfred A. Brown
Foreign Missions Secretary: Noel Perkin

Editor: Robert C. Cunningham
(Cunningham served as editor of the
Pentecostal Evangel, an appointive position,
until 1984. Richard Champion served from
1984–1994. Hal Donaldson assumed the
position in November 1994, and Ken Horn
in 2008.)

24. ATLANTA, GEORGIA
AUGUST 16-23, 1951

All officers reelected.
(Wesley R. Steelberg died in Cardiff,
Wales, July 8, 1952. Gayle F. Lewis was
chosen to fill the unexpired term of
general superintendent by the General
Presbytery on September 2, 1952. James O.
Savell was selected as assistant general
superintendent to fill the vacancy created
by Lewis's election.)

25. MILWAUKEE, WISCONSIN
AUGUST 26 TO SEPTEMBER 2, 1953

General Superintendent: Ralph M. Riggs
Assistant General Superintendents:
    Gayle F. Lewis, Bert Webb, J. O. Savell,
    Thomas F. Zimmerman
General Secretary: J. Roswell Flower
General Treasurer: Wilfred A. Brown
Foreign Missions Secretary: Noel Perkin

26. OKLAHOMA CITY, OKLAHOMA
SEPTEMBER 1-6, 1955

All officers reelected.
(Wilfred A. Brown died on September 19,
1955. Atwood Foster was appointed by the
General Presbytery to fill the unexpired
term.)

27. CLEVELAND, OHIO
AUGUST 28 TO SEPTEMBER 3, 1957

General Superintendent: Ralph M. Riggs
Assistant General Superintendents:
Gayle F. Lewis, Bert Webb,
C. W. H. Scott, Thomas. F. Zimmerman
General Secretary: J. Roswell Flower
General Treasurer: Martin B. Netzel
Foreign Missions Secretary: Noel Perkin

28. SAN ANTONIO, TEXAS
AUGUST 26 TO SEPTEMBER 1, 1959

General Superintendent:
Thomas F. Zimmerman
Assistant General Superintendents:
Gayle F. Lewis, Bert Webb,
C. W. H. Scott, Howard S. Bush
General Secretary: Bartlett Peterson
General Treasurer: Martin B. Netzel
Foreign Missions Secretary:
* J. Philip Hogan
(*The director of Foreign Missions was given the title of assistant general superintendent, carrying the portfolio of Foreign Missions. J. Philip Hogan was elected to this position, filling the position vacated by Noel Perkin, who retired in 1959.)

29. PORTLAND, OREGON
AUGUST 23-29, 1961

All officers reelected.

30. MEMPHIS, TENNESSEE
AUGUST 21-26, 1963

All officers reelected.

31. DES MOINES, IOWA
AUGUST 25-30, 1965

General Superintendent:
Thomas F. Zimmerman
Assistant General Superintendents:
Howard S. Bush, Theodore E. Gannon,
C. W. H. Scott, Bert Webb,
J. Philip Hogan
General Secretary: Bartlett Peterson
General Treasurer: Martin B. Netzel

32. LONG BEACH, CALIFORNIA
AUGUST 24-29, 1967

All officers reelected.
(In 1965, the office of general superintendent was made a four-year term, so that office was not voted upon in 1967. Howard S. Bush died on March 26, 1969. His office was left vacant until the August 1969 General Council.)

33. DALLAS, TEXAS
AUGUST 21-26, 1969

General Superintendent:
Thomas F. Zimmerman
Assistant General Superintendents:
G. Raymond Carlson, T. E. Gannon,
Kermit Reneau, C. W. H. Scott,
J. Philip Hogan
General Secretary: Bartlett Peterson
General Treasurer: Martin B. Netzel

34. KANSAS CITY, MISSOURI
AUGUST 19-24, 1971

General Superintendent:
Thomas F. Zimmerman
Assistant General Superintendent:
G. Raymond Carlson
General Secretary: Bartlett Peterson
General Treasurer: Martin B. Netzel

(Martin B. Netzel died on May 20, 1973. His office was left vacant until the August 1973 General Council.)

35. MIAMI BEACH, FLORIDA
AUGUST 16-21, 1973

General Superintendent:
Thomas F. Zimmerman
Assistant General Superintendent:
G. Raymond Carlson
General Secretary: Bartlett Peterson
General Treasurer: Raymond H. Hudson

36. DENVER, COLORADO
AUGUST 14-19, 1975

General Superintendent:
Thomas F. Zimmerman
Assistant General Superintendent:
G. Raymond Carlson
General Secretary: Joseph R. Flower
General Treasurer: Raymond H. Hudson

37. OKLAHOMA CITY, OKLAHOMA
AUGUST 18-23, 1977

All officers reelected.

38. BALTIMORE, MARYLAND
AUGUST 16-21, 1979

All officers reelected.

39. ST. LOUIS, MISSOURI
AUGUST 20-25, 1981

All officers reelected.

40. ANAHEIM, CALIFORNIA
AUGUST 11-16, 1983

All officers reelected.

41. SAN ANTONIO, TEXAS
AUGUST 8-13, 1985

General Superintendent:
G. Raymond Carlson
Assistant General Superintendent:
Everett R. Stenhouse
All others reelected.

42. OKLAHOMA CITY, OKLAHOMA
AUGUST 6-11, 1987

All officers reelected.
(Raymond H. Hudson resigned the general treasurer position midterm. Thomas E. Trask finished the term.)

43. INDIANAPOLIS, INDIANA
AUGUST 8-13, 1989

J. Philip Hogan retired from his position as Foreign Missions director. Loren Triplett was elected to that position.
General Treasurer: Thomas E. Trask
All others reelected.

44. PORTLAND, OREGON
AUGUST 6-11, 1991

All officers reelected.

45. MINNEAPOLIS, MINNESOTA
AUGUST 10-14, 1993

General Superintendent: Thomas E. Trask
Assistant General Superintendent:
Charles T. Crabtree
General Secretary: George O. Wood
General Treasurer: James K. Bridges

46. ST. LOUIS, MISSOURI
AUGUST 8-13, 1995

All officers reelected.

47. INDIANAPOLIS, INDIANA
AUGUST 5-10, 1997

General Superintendent: Thomas E. Trask
Assistant General Superintendent:
Charles T. Crabtree
General Secretary: George O. Wood
General Treasurer: James K. Bridges
(Loren Triplett retired from his position as
Foreign Missions director. L. John Bueno
was elected to this position.)

48. ORLANDO, FLORIDA
AUGUST 10-13, 1999

Officers reelected.
The General Council approved the transition to 4-year terms from 2-year terms
for the assistant general superintendent,
general secretary, and executive director
of DFM in the 1999 General Council, and
for the general treasurer and the executive
director of Home Missions beginning in
2001 General Council.

49. KANSAS CITY, MISSOURI
AUGUST 7-10, 2001

The general superintendent, general treasurer, and the executive director of AGUSM
were reelected.

50. WASHINGTON, D.C.
JULY 31-AUGUST 3, 2003

The assistant general superintendent,
general secretary, and executive director of
AGWM were reelected.

51. DENVER, COLORADO
AUGUST 2-5, 2005

The general superintendent, general treasurer, and the executive director of AGUSM
were reelected.

52. INDIANAPOLIS, INDIANA
AUGUST 8-11, 2007

General Superintendent: George O. Wood
(elected to fill unexpired term).
Assistant General Superintendent:
L. Alton Garrison
General Secretary: John M. Palmer
Executive Director of AGWM:
L. John Bueno
Executive Director of AGUSM:
Zollie L. Smith, Jr. (elected to fill
unexpired term).

53. ORLANDO, FLORIDA
AUGUST 4-7, 2009

General Superintendent: George O. Wood
General Treasurer: Doug Clay
Executive Director of AGUSM:
Zollie L. Smith, Jr.
General Secretary: James Bradford (elected
to fill unexpired term.)

54. PHOENIX, ARIZONA
AUGUST 1-5, 2011

The assistant general superintendent,
general secretary, and executive director of
AGWM were reelected.

55. ORLANDO, FLORIDA
AUGUST 5-9, 2013

The general superintendent, general treasurer, and the executive director of AGUSM
were reelected.

54. ORLANDO, FLORIDA
AUGUST 3-7, 2015

The assistant general superintendent,
general secretary, and executive director of
AGWM were reelected.

INDEX

NOTE: Boldface page numbers indicate photograph or illustration.